# INDIAN ECONOMY

*For Civil Services Examination*

# INDIAN ECONOMY

*For Civil Services Examination*

DR. BIRENDRA PRASAD, IAS

PRABHAT EXAMS

Publisher

**PRABHAT EXAMS**

**Imprint of Prabhat Prakashan Pvt. Ltd.**

4/19 Asaf Ali Road, New Delhi–110 002

Ph. 23289555 • 23289666 • 23289777 • Helpline/ 7827007777

e-mail: prabhatbooks@gmail.com • Website: www.prabhatexam.com





*Price*

One Thousand Twenty five Rupees

ISBN 978-93-90906-43-7

*Printed at*

Sita Fine Arts Pvt. Ltd., New Delhi

**INDIAN ECONOMY**

For Civil Services Examination

*by* Dr. Birendra Prasad, IAS

ISBN 978-93-90906-43-7

₹ 1025.00

# Preface

The Indian economic structure is changing dramatically with unpredictable and predictable circumstances. The book is designed to explain the impact of these circumstances on each sector of the Indian economy in a systematized manner.

Written in a lucid style, the book caters to the needs of both the students preparing for their examinations as well as all readers. The book suffices the requirements of the aspirants of UPSC and State Civil Services Examinations.

Beginning from learning about the Development Strategy and Economic Reforms, the book steers through various sectors, such as Banking, Finance, Industries, Agriculture, Service, Infrastructure and External. In addition, concepts on Inflation, National Income, Public Finance, Economic Planning, Black Money, Social sector, Climate Change, and GST are covered comprehensively.

The Economic Survey (2021–22) and the Union Budget (2022–23) have been presented elaborately. The book has been thoroughly updated in relation to the present scenario and Glossary has been incorporated at the end to assist in learning and memorizing of the complex terminology.

Constructive suggestions from the readers are welcomed and would be incorporated in the future edition.

# Contents

# 1 CHAPTER Introduction

## ECONOMICS AND ECONOMY

### ❖ Economics

Economics is concerned with the efficient use or management of limited productive resources to achieve maximum satisfaction of human material wants.

J. S. Mill defined economics as "the practical science of the production and distribution of wealth." Alfred Marshall said that, "economics is a study of mankind in the ordinary business of life." In the words of Marshall, "Economics is on the one side a study of wealth, and on the other and more important side, a part of the study of man."

Lionel Robbins said, "Economics is the science which studies human behaviour as a relationship between ends, and scarce means which have alternative uses."

Basic assumptions of Robbins contains that the ends are various. The term 'ends' mean wants. Human wants are unlimited. Means are limited. Means like time, money and resources are limited. We can put time and money to alternative uses. For example, though time is limited, we can use it for different purposes. We can use time for earning money, or we may enjoy it as leisure. All wants are not of equal importance.

In fact, economics is a social science that deals with the creation of wealth from scarce resources: the production and distribution of goods and services for consumption; the behaviour, interaction and well-being of the groups involved in the above activities; there is a trade-off involved in production and in consumption.

The economics as a subject has been divided into two main parts: (i) Microeconomics and (ii) Macroeconomics. Microeconomics is the study of the choices that individuals and businesses make, the way these choices interact in markets and the influence of governments. Macroeconomics is the study of the performance of the national economy and the global economy.

### ❖ Economy

The economy is, according to the Oxford Learner's Dictionary, "the relationship between production, trade and the supply of money in a particular country or region." It is effective management of the resources of a community or system. The economy covers all activities related to production, consumption and trade of goods and services in an area performed by economic agents. Economic agents can be individuals, businesses, organizations or governments. A given economy is the result of a set of processes that involves its culture, values, education, technological evolution, history, social organization, political structure and legal systems, geography, natural resource endowment, ecology, etc. That is why no two economies are the same. The scientific study of the economy and the factors affecting the economy are called economics.

## TYPES OF ECONOMY

Based on the criterion of degree of individual freedom and profit motive, economies are classified as:

(i) Capitalist or free enterprise economy
(ii) Socialist or centrally planned economy
(iii) Mixed economy

### ❖ Capitalist Economy

A capitalist economy is an economic system in which the production and distribution of commodities take place through the mechanism of free markets. Hence, it is also called as market economy or free-trade economy. Each individual be it a producer, consumer or resource owner has considerable economic freedom.

The right to private property is an important feature of capitalism. Individuals have the right to buy and own property. There is no limit, and they can own any amount of property. They also have legal rights to use their property in any way they like. Profit is the only motive for the functioning of capitalism. There is freedom of choice to both producers and consumers. Market forces like demand, supply and price are the signals to direct the system. As most of the basic economic problems are expected to be solved by market forces, the government has minimal role in the economy.

In a capitalist economy, every farmer, trader or industrialist can increase the productivity to meet his own self-interest. This in turn leads to increase in income, saving and investment.

However, capitalism may create extreme inequalities in income and wealth. The inequality may lead to monopoly. Mega corporate units replace smaller units of production. They ultimately emerge as multinational corporations (MNCs) or transnational corporations (TNCs).They often hike prices against the welfare of consumer. Capitalism encourages mechanization and automation. This results in unemployment particularly in labour surplus economies. Stringent labour laws are enacted for the exclusive profit-motive of capitalists. Fire and hire policy becomes the order of the day. As the profit margin in basic social sectors, like literacy, public health, poverty, drinking water, etc., is low, capitalists do not want to invest in them.

### ❖ Socialist Economy

In a socialist economy, the means of production are owned and operated by the State. All decisions regarding production and distribution are taken by the central planning authority. Hence, the socialist economy is also called as planned economy or command economy. The government plays an active role. Social welfare is given importance, and equal opportunity is given to all.

The right to private property is limited. All properties of the country are owned by the State. Most of the economic policy decisions are taken by a centralized planning authority. There is stability in the system because the production and consumption of goods and services are well regulated. The State provides free education, cheap and congenial housing, public health amenities and social security for the people. There is a state monopoly, but it produces quality goods at reasonable price. There is no concentration of wealth.

However, people in socialist economic system work out of fear of higher authorities. The system does not give any initiative for the people to work hard. There is no freedom of occupation. The consumer's choice is very limited. Everything is rigid and technological changes are limited. Gradually in the absence of competition the system may become inefficient.

### ❖ Mixed Economy

In a mixed economy, both public and private institutions exercise economic control. The public sector functions as a socialistic economy and the private sector as a free enterprise economy.

A mixed economy possesses the freedom to hold private property, to earn profit, to consume, produce and distribute and to have any occupation. However, if these freedoms affect public welfare adversely, they are regulated and controlled by the State.

Mixed economy is expected to retain only the merits of the two systems. For instance, the government is expected to allow private investment, but the government also controls monopolies. Planning of government directs the relative roles of public and private sectors and their respective jurisdictions.

However, it has been seen that the coordination between the public and private sectors remains poor in a mixed economy. This lack of policy coordination results in economic fluctuations. Again, there is every chance that the public sector works inefficiently. There is too much of red-tapism and corruption leading to delays in decision-making and project implementation.

## ECONOMIC GROWTH VS ECONOMIC DEVELOPMENT

Economic growth refers to an increase over time in a country's real output of goods and services (GNP) or real output per capita income. It is a quantitative measure that shows the increase in the number of commercial transactions in an economy. Growth relates to a gradual increase in one of the components of gross domestic product (GDP): consumption, government spending, investment and net exports. Economic growth is a more relevant metric for progress in developed countries. But it's widely used in all countries, because growth is a necessary condition for development.

Economic development is a normative concept, i.e., it applies in the context of people's sense of morality. The definition of economic development given by Michael Todaro is an increase in living standards, improvement in self-esteem needs and freedom from oppression as well as a greater choice. According to Professor Todaro, economic development is a multi-dimensional process involving major changes in social structures, popular attitudes and national institutions, as well as the acceleration of economic growth, the reduction of inequality and the eradication of absolute poverty.

Economic development implies an upward movement of the entire social system in terms of income, savings and investment along with progressive changes in socioeconomic structure of country (institutional and technological changes). Development relates to growth of human capital indexes, a decrease in inequality figures and structural changes that improve the general population's quality of life. Economic development is more relevant to measure progress and quality of life in developing nations. Development must be conceived for as a multi-dimensional process involving major change in social structures, popular attitudes and national institutions as well as the acceleration of eco-growth, the eradication of poverty and reduction of inequality of wealth.

It is also worth pointing out that between economic growth and economic development there are similarities and differences. The similarities between them are: (i) growth and development are continuous processes, with stimulating effects in economy (ii) both processes involve the allotment and utilization of resources and the increase of efficiency (iii) the aim of growth and development is the improvement of the standard and quality of life and (iv) growth and development are cause and result of the general trend, influencing its rhythm and ensuring passages from one level to the other level.

Economic growth is a narrower concept than economic development. The fundamental differences between economic growth and development are: (i) economic growth is the positive change in the real output of the country in a particular financial year. Economic development involves a rise in the level of production in an economy along with the advancement of technology, improvement in living standards and so on (ii) economic growth is one of the features of economic development (iii) economic growth is an automatic process. Unlike economic development, which is the outcome of planned and result-oriented activities (iv) economic growth enables an increase in the indicators like GDP, per capita income, etc. On the other hand, economic development enables improvement in the life expectancy rate, infant mortality rate, literacy rate and poverty rates (v) economic growth can be measured when there is a positive change in the national income, whereas economic development can be seen when there is an increase in real national income (vi) economic growth is a short-term process which takes into account yearly growth of the economy. But if we talk about economic development it is a long-term process (vii) economic growth applies to developed economies to gauge the quality of life, but as it is an essential condition for the development, it applies to developing countries also. In contrast, economic development applies to developing countries to measure progress and (viii) economic growth results in quantitative changes, but economic development brings both quantitative and qualitative changes.

Growth of an economy can be measured through the increase in its size in the current year in comparison to previous years, but economic development includes not only physical but also non-physical aspects that can only be experienced like improvement in the lifestyle of the inhabitants, increase in individual income, improvement in technology and infrastructure, etc.

Human Development Index (HDI) is the appropriate tool to gauge the development in the economy. Based on the development, the HDI statistics rank countries. It considers the overall development in an economy regarding the standard of living, GDP, living conditions, technological advancement, improvement in self-esteem needs, the creation of opportunities, per capita income, infrastructural and industrial development and much more.

## MEASURES OF ECONOMIC DEVELOPMENT

The term economic development is a multifaceted concept, embodying not just national income and its growth, but also achievements on other fronts such as reductions in infant mortality, higher life expectancy, advances in literacy rates, widespread access to medical and health services and so on. Per capita income is sometimes used as an (incomplete) indicator for overall economic development, but should not be identified conceptually with development in the broader sense.

Apart from GDP and per capita income, there are several different measures of economic development, such as:

1. Human Development Index (HDI)
2. Physical Quality of Life Index (PQLI)
3. Quality of Life Index (QLI)/Where-to-be-born Index
4. Gross National Happiness (GNH)
5. World Happiness Report (WHR)
6. Human Poverty Index (HPI)
7. Inequality-adjusted Human Development Index (IHDI)
8. Gender Development Index (GDI)
9. Gender Inequality Index (GII)
10. Good Country Index (GCI)

1. **Human Development Index (HDI):** Human development focuses on improving the lives people lead rather than assuming that economic growth will lead, automatically, to greater well-being for all. Income growth is seen as a means to development, rather than an end in itself.

   Human development is about giving people more freedom to live lives they value. In effect, this means developing people's abilities and giving them a chance to use them. For example, educating a girl would build her skills, but it is of little use if she is denied access to jobs, or does not have the right skills for the local labour market. Three foundations for human development are to live a long, healthy and creative life, to be knowledgeable and to have access to resources needed for a decent standard of living. Many other things are important too, especially in helping to create the right conditions for human development. Once the basics of human development are achieved, they open up opportunities for progress in other aspects of life.

Human development is, fundamentally, about more choice. It is about providing people with opportunities, not insisting that they make use of them. No one can guarantee human happiness, and the choices people make are their own concern. The process of development –human development–should at least create an environment for people, individually and collectively, to develop to their full potential and to have a reasonable chance of leading productive and creative lives that they value.

As the international community seeks to define a new development agenda post-2015, the human development approach remains useful to articulating the objectives of development and improving people's well-being by ensuring an equitable, sustainable and stable planet.

The HDI is defined as the composite statistics used to rank countries by levels of human development. The first HDI was published in 1990 by the United Nations Development Programme (UNDP). The HDI is a composite statistic of life expectancy, education and income per capita. These indicators are used to rank countries into four tiers of human development. A country scores higher HDI when the life expectancy at birth is longer, the education period is longer and the income per capita is higher. The HDI was developed by the Pakistani economist Mahbub- ul-Haq working alongside Indian economist Amartya Sen, often framed in terms of whether people are able to 'be' and 'do' desirable things in their life, and was published by the UNDP. The HDI embodies Amartya Sen's 'capabilities' approach to understanding human well-being, which emphasizes the importance of ends (like a decent standard of living) over means (like income per capita). Presently, it ranks 188 countries of the world.

**Three Dimensions of HDI**

(i) **Long and healthy life:** The long and healthy life dimension uses life expectancy at birth as its indicator, defined as 'the number of years a new-born infant could expect to live, if prevailing patterns of age-specific mortality rates at the time of birth were to stay the same throughout the child's life'. The life expectancy index is calculated using a minimum value of 20 years and a maximum value of 85 years. These maximum and minimum values are fixed goalposts adopted in the 2014 HDI.

(ii) **Knowledge:** The education component of the HDI is measured by two indicators: (i) mean years of schooling for adults aged 25 years and older and (ii) the expected years of schooling for children of school entering age. Estimates for mean years of schooling are based on the duration of schooling at each level of education. Expected years of schooling estimates are based on two factors: (i) enrolment by age at all levels of education and (ii) the number of children of school age in the population for each level of education. It is important to note that the duration of each level of education may differ from country to country, and this is taken into account when calculating mean and expected years of schooling. The two indicators are first normalized using a minimum value of 0 and maximum value of 15 for mean years of schooling and aged 18 for expected years of schooling. As societies can exist without formal education, the minimum value of 0 years is used for both education variables.

(iii) **Decent standard of living:** The decent standard of living component is measured using an income based measure. Income is, of course, not an outcome measure reflecting a person's capability or human development directly. Yet income is an important means and can proxy aspects of living standard that are provided by markets. The income component is measured using the natural logarithm of gross national income (GNI) per capita adjusted by PPP. For this component, the minimum value is PPP $100, this low value is justified by the considerable amount of unmeasured subsistence and nonmarket production in economies close to the minimum, which is not captured in the official data. The maximum value is set at PPP $75,000.

Kahneman and Deaton (2010) have shown that there is a virtually no gain in human development and well-being from annual income above $75,000. Assuming an annual growth rate of 5 per cent, only three countries are projected to exceed the $75,000 ceiling in the next 5 years, at which point the income index will be capped at 1.

The HDI takes the natural logarithm of income to reflect the diminishing importance of income among richer countries (an extra dollar of income is worth much more to a poor person than a rich one – that is, the ability to transform additional income into equivalently valuable functioning declines as incomes rise). Thus, the index is computed by normalizing the natural logarithm of GNI with respect to the natural logarithm of the minimum and maximum values.

**Aggregation and weights–** After calculating the indices for the three dimensions, the scores are aggregated into a composite index using a geometric mean, which is the cube root of the product of the three dimension indices. The global HDI assigns equal weight to all three dimension indices, as it has since 1990. The two education 'sub-indices' (the indices for each indicator) are also weighted equally. The choice of equal weights is based on the normative judgement that all three dimensions are equally important.

The 2010 Human Development Report introduced an IHDI. While the simple HDI remains useful, it stated that the IHDI is the actual level of human development (accounting for inequality), and the HDI can be viewed as an index of 'potential' human development (or the maximum IHDI that could be achieved, if there were no inequality).

2. **Physical Quality of Life Index (PQLI):** In 1979, D. Morris constructed a composite PQLI. He found that most of the indicators were inputs to development process rather than result of the development process. These indicators reflected that economically less developed countries are simply underdeveloped versions of industrialized countries.

   He, therefore, combines three component indicators of infant mortality, life expectancy and basic literacy to measure performance in meeting the basic needs of the people. All components are equally weighted on a 1–100 scale, where 1 represents the worst performance by any country and 100 is the best performance. For life expectancy, the PQLI is relatively neutral. It measures results, not inputs.

   The choice of indicators are: (i) Life Expectancy Indicator (LEI); (ii) Infant Mortality Indicator (IMI) and (iii) Basic Literacy Indicator (BLI).

   Physical Quality of Life = (LEI + IMI + BLI)/3

   These three indicators can be improved in a variety of ways. However, Professor Morris used Life Expectancy (LE) at birth as the indicator. Infant mortality implies deaths before age one instead of life expectancy at birth.

3. **Quality of Life Index (QLI)/Where-to-be-born index:** It has long been accepted that material well-being, as measured by GDP per person, cannot alone explain the broader quality of life in a country.

   The Economist Intelligence Unit's (an independent business) where-to-be-born index (previously called the QLI) attempts to measure which country will provide the best opportunities for a healthy, safe and prosperous life in the years ahead. It is based on a method that links the results of subjective life-satisfaction surveys to the objective determinants of quality of life across countries along with a forward-looking element.

   **Determinants of Quality of Life**

   The nine quality-of-life factors and the indicators used to represent these factors are as follows:

   (i) **Material well-being:** GDP per person, at ppp in $.

   (ii) **Health:** Life expectancy at birth in years.

   (iii) **Political stability and security:** Political stability and security ratings.

   (iv) **Family life:** Divorce rate (per 1,000 population), converted into index of 1 (lowest divorce rates) to 5 (highest).

   (v) **Community life:** Dummy variable taking value 1, if country has either high rate of church attendance or trade-union membership; zero otherwise.

   (vi) **Climate and geography:** Latitude, to distinguish between warmer and colder climes.

   (vii) **Job security:** Unemployment rate in percentage.

   (viii) **Political freedom:** Average of indices of political and civil liberties. Scale of 1 (completely free) to 7 (unfree).

   (ix) Gender equality Ratio of average male and female earnings, latest available data.

4. **Gross National Happiness:** The phrase Gross National Happiness (GNH) was coined in 1972 by Bhutan's fourth Dragon King, Jigme Singye Wangchuck. Originally, the phrase represented a commitment to building an economy

that would serve Bhutan's culture based on Buddhist spiritual values, instead of western material development gauged by GDP.

GNH is a much richer objective than GDP or economic growth. In GNH, material well-being is important, but it is also important to enjoy sufficient well-being in things like community, culture, governance, knowledge and wisdom, health, spirituality, and psychological welfare, a balanced use of time and harmony with the environment. The GNH is to achieve a balanced development in all the facets of life that are essential for our happiness.

Thus, the GNH is a holistic and sustainable approach to development, which balances material and non-material values with the conviction that humans want to search for happiness.

From an economic perspective, critics state that because GNH depends on a series of subjective judgments about well-being, governments may be able to define GNH in a way that suits their interests. Economics professor Deirdre McCloskey criticizes such measurements as unscientific.

5. **World Happiness Report:** The **World Happiness Report** (WHR) is a measure of happiness published by the United Nations Sustainable Development Solutions Network. The WHR is edited by John F. Helliwell, Richard Layard and Jeffrey Sachs.

In July 2011, the UN General Assembly passed a resolution inviting member countries to measure the happiness of their people and to use this to help guide their public policies.

On 2 April 2012, the first UN High Level Meeting called 'Happiness and Well-Being: Defining a New Economic Paradigm', chaired by Prime Minister Jigme Thinley of Bhutan decided to launch the WHR.

Each variable measured reveals a populated-weighted average score on a scale running from 0 to 10 that is tracked over time and compared against other countries. These variables currently include: real GDP per capita, social support, healthy life expectancy, freedom to make life choices, generosity, and perceptions of corruption.

It is to be noted that Bhutan is the first and so far only country to have officially adopted GNH instead of GDP as their main development indicator.

The Sustainable Development Solutions Network (SDSN) was commissioned by UN Secretary-General Ban Ki-moon in 2012 to mobilize scientific and technical expertise from academia, civil society, and the private sector to support practical problem solving for sustainable development at local, national, and global scales.

6. **Human Poverty Index (HPI)/Multi-dimensional Poverty Index:** The Human Poverty Index (HPI) was an indication of the standard of living in a country, developed by the United Nations (UN) to complement the HDI and was first reported as part of the Human Development Report in 1997. It was considered to better reflect the extent of deprivation in developed countries compared to the HDI. In 2010, it was supplanted by the UN's Multidimensional Poverty Index.

The HPI concentrates on the deprivation in the three essential elements of human life already reflected in the HDI: longevity, knowledge and a decent standard of living. The HPI is derived separately for developing countries (HPI-1) and a group of select high-income OECD countries (HPI-2) to better reflect socio-economic differences and also the widely different measures of deprivation in the two groups.

**HPI-1**

The Human Development Reports website summarizes this as 'A composite index measuring deprivations in the three basic dimensions captured in the HDI – a long and healthy life, knowledge and a decent standard of living'.

**HPI-2**

The Human Development Reports website summarizes this as 'A composite index measuring deprivations in the four basic dimensions captured in the HDI – a long and healthy life, knowledge and a decent standard of living – and also capturing social exclusion'.

The MPI can help the effective allocation of resources by making possible the targeting of those with the greatest intensity of poverty. It can help address MDGs strategically and monitor impacts of policy intervention. The MPI can be adapted to the national level using indicators and weights that make sense for the region or the country, it can also be adopted for national poverty eradication programs, and it can be used to study changes over time.

7. **Inequality-adjusted Human Development Index (IHDI):** According to the 2010 HDR Report, 'the IHDI is the actual level of human development (accounting for inequality)' and the unadjusted calculations for the HDI 'can be viewed as an index of potential human development (or the maximum IHDI that could be achieved if there were no inequality)'.

The IHDI combines a country's average achievements in health, education and income with how those achievements are distributed among country's population by 'discounting' each dimension's average value according to its level of inequality. Thus, the IHDI is distribution-sensitive average level of HD. Two countries with different distributions of achievements can have the same average HDI value. Under perfect equality, the IHDI is equal to the HDI, but falls below the HDI when inequality rises.

The difference between the IHDI and HDI is the human development cost of inequality, also termed – the loss to human development due to inequality. The IHDI allows a direct link to inequalities in dimensions; it can inform policies towards inequality reduction and lead to better understanding of inequalities across population and their contribution to the overall human development cost. A recent measure of inequality in the HDI, the Coefficient of human inequality, is calculated as an average inequality across three dimensions.

While the IIDI can be viewed as an index of average achievements in human development dimensions, the IHDI measures the level of human development when the distribution of achievements across people in the society is accounted for. The IHDI will be equal to the HDI when there is no inequality, but falls below the HDI as inequality rises. The difference between the HDI and IHDI, expressed as a percentage of the HDI, indicates the loss in human development due to inequality.

8. **Gender Development Index (GDI) – UNDP:** The Gender Development Index (GDI) is an index designed to measure the gender equality.

GDI together with the Gender Empowerment Measure (GEM) was introduced in 1995 in the Human

Development Report written by the United Nations Development Program. The aim of these measurements was to add a gender-sensitive dimension to the HDI.

The GDI measures differences between male and female achievements in three basic dimensions of human development: health, measured by female and male life expectancy at birth; education, measured by female and male expected years of schooling for children and female and male mean years of schooling for adults ages 25 and older and equitable command over economic resources, measured by female- and male-estimated earned income.

To calculate the GDI, the HDI is calculated separately for females and for males using the same methodology as in the HDI. The same goalposts as in the HDI are used for transforming the indicators into a scale between zero and one. The only exception is life expectancy at birth where calculations are adjusted for the average of 5 years biological advantage that women have over men.

The GDI provides insights into gender disparities in achievements in three basic capabilities: health, education and command over economic resources. It helps further understanding of the real gender gap in human development achievements and is useful for navigating policies to close the gap.

9. **Gender Inequality Index (GII):** The **Gender Inequality Index (GII)** is an index for measurement of gender disparity that was introduced in the 2010 Human Development Report 20th anniversary edition by the UNDP.

Gender inequality remains a major barrier to human development. Girls and women have made major strides since 1990, but they have not yet gained gender equity. The disadvantages facing women and girls are a major source of inequality. All too often, women and girls are discriminated against in health, education, political representation, labour market, etc. with negative repercussions for development of their capabilities and their freedom of choice.

The GII is an inequality index. It measures gender inequalities in three important aspects of human development – reproductive health, measured by maternal mortality ratio and adolescent birth rates; empowerment, measured by proportion of parliamentary seats occupied by females and proportion of adult females and males aged 25 years and older with at least some secondary education and economic status, expressed as labour market participation and measured by labour force participation rate of female and male populations aged 15 years and older. The GII is built on the same framework as the IHDI – to better expose differences in the distribution of achievements between women and men. It measures the human development costs of gender inequality, thus the higher the GII value the more disparities between females and males and the more loss to human development.

There is no country with perfect gender equality–hence all countries suffer some loss in achievements in key aspects of human development when gender inequality is taken into account. The GII is similar in method to the IHDI. It can be interpreted as a combined loss to achievements in reproductive health, empowerment and labour market participation due to gender inequalities. Since the GII includes different dimensions than the HDI, it cannot be interpreted as a loss in HDI itself. The GII ranges between 0 and 1, and higher GII values indicate higher levels of inequalities.

10. **Good Country Index:** For the first time in history, this is an index that measures what each country contributes to the common good of humanity and to the planet.

    The idea of the Good Country Index (GCI) is pretty simple: to measure what each country on earth contributes to the common good of humanity, and what it takes away, relative to its size.

    Using a wide range of data from the U.N. and other international organizations, GCI gives each country a balance sheet to show at a glance whether it's a net creditor to mankind, a burden on the planet or something in between.

    GCI do not make any moral judgments about countries. What it means by a Good Country is something much simpler: it's a country that contributes to the greater good of humanity. A country that serves the interests of its own people, but without harming – and preferably by advancing – the interests of people in other countries too.

    The GCI is one of a series of projects that Simon Anholt and his friends are launching to start a global debate about what countries are really for. Do they exist purely to serve the interests of their own politicians, businesses and citizens, or are they actively working for all of humanity and the whole planet?

## SUSTAINABLE DEVELOPMENT

### ❖ Definition

More than one hundred definitions of sustainable development exist, but the most widely used one is from the World Commission on Environment and Development (WCED), presented in 1987. It states that sustainable development is 'Development that meets the needs of the present without compromising the ability of future generations to meet their own needs'. Sustainable development promotes the idea that social, environmental and economic progress are all attainable within the limits of our earth's natural resources.

It contains two key concepts:

1. the concept of needs, in particular the essential needs of the world's poor, to which overriding priority should be given and
2. the idea of limitations imposed by the state of technology and social organization on the environment's ability to meet present and future needs.

The sustainable development requires that there is need to see the world as a system – a system that connects space and a system that connects time. When one thinks of the world as a system over space, one grows to understand that air pollution from North America affects air quality in Asia, and that pesticides sprayed in Argentina could harm fish stocks off the coast of Australia. On the flip side, clean air practices on one continent will positively impact air quality across the ocean.

The earth's connection to time is demonstrated in how we, today, are either benefitting or suffering from the choices of our grandparents and other ancestors. Their decisions about how to farm their land, for example, continue to impact the agricultural practices of today. Looking to the future, the economic choices we make and policies we endorse today will be the ones affecting our children and grandchildren as adults.

The concept of sustainable development is rooted in this sort of systems thinking. It helps us understand ourselves and our world. The problems we face are complex and serious—and we can't address them in the same way we created them. However, we can address them. Sustainable development approaches everything in the world as being connected through space, time and quality of life.

Sustainable development constantly seeks to achieve social and economic progress in ways that will not exhaust the earth's finite natural resources. The needs of the world today are real and immediate, yet it's necessary to develop ways to meet these needs that do not disregard the future. The capacity of our ecosystem is not limitless, meaning that future generations may not be able to meet their needs the way we are able to now.

## ❖ Three Pillars of Sustainable Development

At the core of sustainable development is the need to consider 'three pillars' together: **the society, the economy and the environment.** No matter the context, the basic idea remains the same – people, habitats and economic systems are interrelated. We may be able to ignore that interdependence for a few years or decades, but history has shown that before long we are reminded of it by some type of alarm or crisis.

The fact of the matter is that we depend on ecosystems and the services they provide in order to do what we do: run businesses, build communities, feed our populations and much more. Whether we consider the more obvious, immediately vital examples – the need for soil that can grow food or for clean water to drink – or the less obvious but equally significant things like oxygen production during photosynthesis or waste processing by bacterial decomposers, we cannot avoid the conclusion that we depend on the environment for our existence. If we damage or destroy the capacity of the environment to provide these services, we may face consequences for which we are completely unprepared.

In the same way, the long-term stability and success of societies rely on a healthy and productive population. A society (or communities within a larger society) that faces unrest, poverty and disease will not develop in the long term: social well-being and economic well-being feed off each other, and the whole game depends on a healthy biosphere in which to exist.

Understanding the complex connections and interdependence of the three pillars requires some effort, and the effort has to be constant. Whether we're talking about the duration of political cycles or the length of time the media focuses on a particular issue, the question of our collective attention span is an important one for sustainable development.

## ❖ Some of the Common Sustainable Development Practices

1. **Solar and wind energy:** Energy from these resources is limitless, meaning we have the ability to eliminate dependence on non-renewable power sources by harnessing power from renewable resources.
2. **Sustainable construction:** Homes, offices and other structures that incorporate recycled and renewable resources will be more energy efficient and stand the test of time.
3. **Crop rotation:** Many farmers and gardeners are using this method as a chemical free way to reduce diseases in the soil and increase growth potential of their crops.
4. **Water fixtures:** Water conservation is critical to sustainable development, and more and more products are available that use less water in the home, such as showers, toilets, dishwashers and laundry systems.

## ❖ Twelfth 5-Year Plan on Sustainable Development

The Twelfth Plan strategy suggests that there are significant 'co-benefits' for climate action with inclusive and sustainable growth. India, as a large responsible player with very low income, has also to ensure that these efforts are matched by equitable and fair burden sharing among countries, taking into account the historical responsibilities for emissions.

India's approach to a lower-carbon growth strategy explicitly recognizes that policies have to be inclusive and differentiated across sectors according to national priorities, so as to lower the transaction costs of implementing the policy, and conform with a nationally fair burden-sharing mechanism.

An Expert Group on Low Carbon Strategies appointed by the Planning Commission has outlined the lower carbon strategies for major potential carbon mitigation sectors:

1. **Power:** On the supply side, adopt super-critical technologies in coal-based thermal power plants; use gas in combined heat and power systems; invest in renewable technologies and develop hydropower in a sustainable manner. On the demand side, accelerate adoption of super-efficient electrical appliances through market and regulatory mechanisms; enhance efficiency of agricultural pump sets and industrial equipment with better technology; modernize transmission and distribution to bring technical and commercial losses down to world average levels; universalize access to electricity and accelerate power-sector reforms.
2. **Transport:** Increase the share of rail in overall freight transport; improve the efficiency of rail freight transport; make it price competitive by bringing down the levels of cross-subsidization between freight and passenger transport; complete dedicated rail corridor; improve share and efficiency of public transport system and improve fuel efficiency of vehicles through both market-based and regulatory mechanisms.
3. **Industry:** Greenfield plants in the iron and steel and cement sectors adopt best available technology; existing plants, particularly small and medium ones, modernize and adopt green technology at an accelerated pace, with transparent financing mechanisms.
4. **Buildings:** Evolve and institutionalize green building codes at all levels of government.
5. **Forestry:** 'Green India Mission' to regenerate at least 4 million hectares of degraded forest; increase density of forest cover on 2 million hectares of moderately dense forest; overall increase the density of forest and tree cover on 10 million hectares of forest, waste and community lands.

## ❖ United Nations Sustainable Development Goals (SDGs) – Post-2015 Agenda

**Seventeen Sustainable Development Goals (SDGs) are:**

1. **End poverty in all its forms everywhere:** End extreme poverty in all forms by 2030. Yes, it's an ambitious goal – but we believe it can be done. In 2000, the world committed to cutting the number of people living in extreme poverty by half in 15 years and we met this goal. However, more than 800 million people around the world still live on less than $1.25 a day – that's about the equivalent of the entire population of Europe living in extreme poverty.
2. **End hunger achieve food security and improved nutrition, and promote sustainable agriculture:** In the past 20 years, hunger has dropped by almost half. Many countries that used to suffer from famine and hunger can now meet the nutritional needs of their most vulnerable people. It's an incredible accomplishment. Now we can go further and end hunger and malnutrition once and for all. That means doing things such as promoting sustainable agriculture and supporting small farmers. It's a tall order. However, for the sake of the nearly 1 out of every 9 people on earth who go

to bed hungry every night, we've got to try. Imagine a world where everyone has accessed to sufficient and nutritious food all year round. Together, we can make that a reality by 2030.

3. **Ensure healthy lives and promote well-being for all at all ages:** Since 1990, we've made big strides – preventable child deaths are down by more than half, and maternal mortality is down by almost as much. And yet some other numbers remain tragically high, like the fact that every year 6 million children die before their fifth birthday, or that AIDS is the leading cause of death for adolescents in sub-Saharan Africa. We have the means to turn that around and make good health more than just a wish.
4. **Ensure inclusive and equitable quality education and promote life-long learning opportunities for all:** First, the bad news on education. Poverty, armed conflict and other emergencies keep many, many kids around the world out of school. In fact, in developing regions, kids from the poorest households are four times more likely to be out of school than those of the richest households. Now for some good news. Since 2000, there has been enormous progress on the goal to provide primary education to all children worldwide. The primary school enrolment rate in developing regions reached 91 per cent. By measures in any school, that's a good grade. Now, let's get an even better grade for all kids and achieve the goal of universal primary and secondary education, affordable vocational training, access to higher education and more.
5. **Achieve gender equality and empower all women and girls:** The great progress the world has made in becoming more prosperous and fair is worth celebrating. And yet, in just about every way, women and girls lag behind. There are still gross inequalities in work and wages, lots of unpaid 'women's work' such as childcare and domestic work and discrimination in public decision-making. But, there are grounds for hope. More girls are in school now compared to in 2000. Most regions have reached gender parity in primary education. The percentage of women getting paid for their work is on the rise. The Sustainable Development Goals aim to build on these achievements to ensure that there is an end to discrimination against women and girls everywhere. It's a basic human right.
6. **Ensure availability and sustainable management of water and sanitation for all:** Everyone on earth should have access to safe and affordable drinking water. That's the goal for 2030. While many people around the world take clean drinking water and sanitation for granted, many others don't. Water scarcity affects more than 40 per cent of people around the world, and that number is projected to go even higher as a result of climate change. If we continue the path we're on, by 2050 at least one in four people are likely to be affected by recurring water shortages. But we can take a new path–more international cooperation, protecting wetlands and rivers, sharing water-treatment technologies and more – that leads to accomplishing this Goal.
7. **Ensure access to affordable, reliable, sustainable and modern energy for all:** Between 1990 and 2010 – the number of people with access to electricity increased by 1.7 billion. That's progress to be proud of. And yet, as the world's population continues to rise, still more people will need cheap energy to light their homes and streets, use phones and computers and do their everyday business. The way we get that energy is at issue; fossil fuels and greenhouse gas emissions are making drastic changes in

the climate, leading to big problems on every continent. Instead, we can become more energy-efficient and invest in clean energy sources such as solar and wind. That way we'll meet electricity needs and protect the environment.

8. **Promote sustained, inclusive and sustainable economic growth, full and productive employment and decent work for all:** An important part of economic growth is that people have jobs that pay enough to support themselves and their families. The good news is that the middle class is growing worldwide, almost tripling in size in developing countries in the last 25 years, to more than a third of the population. But in 2015, we also have widening inequalities, and job growth is not keeping pace with the growing labour force – over 200 million people don't have jobs. That's the equivalent of the entire population of Brazil. Things don't have to be that way. We can promote policies that encourage entrepreneurship and job creation. We can eradicate forced labour, slavery and human trafficking. And in the end we can achieve the goal of decent work for all women and men by 2030.
9. **Build resilient infrastructure, promote inclusive and sustainable industrialization and foster innovation:** Technological progress helps us address big global challenges such as creating jobs and becoming more energy efficient. The world is becoming ever more interconnected and prosperous thanks to the Internet. The more connected we are, the more we can all benefit from the wisdom and contributions of people everywhere on the earth. And yet, four billion people have no way of getting online, the vast majority of them in developing countries. The more we invest in innovation and infrastructure, the better of we'll all be. Bridging the digital divide, promoting sustainable industries, and investing in scientific research and innovation are all important ways to facilitate sustainable development.
10. **Reduce inequality within and among countries:** We can and must adopt policies that create opportunity for everyone, regardless of who they are or where they come from. Income inequality is a global problem that requires global solutions. That means improving the regulation of financial markets and institutions, sending development aid where it is most needed and helping people migrate safely so they can pursue opportunities.
11. **Make cities and human settlements inclusive, safe, resilient and sustainable:** More than half the world's population now lives in cities, and that figure will go to about two-thirds of humanity by the year 2050. Cities are getting bigger. In 1990, there were ten 'mega-cities' with 10 million inhabitants or more. In 2014, there were 28 mega-cities, home to 453 million people. Incredible, huh? A lot of people love cities; they're centres of culture and business and life. The thing is, they're also often centres of extreme poverty. To make cities sustainable for all, we can create good, affordable public housing. We can upgrade slum settlements. We can invest in public transport, create green spaces and get a broader range of people involved in urban planning decisions.
12. **Ensure sustainable consumption and production patterns:** Some people use a lot of stuff, and some people use very little – in fact, a big share of the world population is consuming too little to meet even their basic needs. It doesn't have to be this way. We can have a world where everybody gets what they need to survive and thrive. And, we can consume in a way that preserves our natural resources so that our children can enjoy them, and

their children and their children after that. The hard part is how to achieve that goal. We can manage our natural resources more efficiently and dispose of toxic waste better. Cut per capita food waste in half globally. Get businesses and consumers to reduce and recycle waste, and help countries that have typically not consumed a lot to move towards more responsible consumption patterns.

13. **Take urgent action to combat climate change and its impacts:** Every country in the world is seeing the drastic effects of climate change, some more than others. On average, the annual losses just from earthquakes, tsunamis, tropical cyclones and flooding count in the hundreds of billions of dollars. We can reduce the loss of life and property by helping more vulnerable regions – such as land-locked countries and island states – become more resilient. The impact of global warming is getting worse. We're seeing more storms, more droughts and more extremes than ever before. It is still possible, with political will and technological measures, to limit the increase in global mean temperature to two degrees Celsius above pre-industrial levels – and thus avoid the worst effects of climate change. The Sustainable Development Goals lay out a way for countries to work together to meet this urgent challenge.
14. **Conserve and sustainably use the oceans, seas and marine resources for sustainable development:** The oceans make human life possible. Their temperature, their chemistry, their currents, their life forms. For one thing, more than 3 billion people depend on marine and coastal diversity for their livelihoods. But today, we are seeing nearly a third of the world's fish stocks overexploited. That's not a sustainable way of life. Even people who live nowhere near the ocean can't live without it. Oceans absorb about 30 per cent of the carbon dioxide that humans produce; but we're producing more carbon dioxide than ever before and that makes the oceans more acidic – 26 per cent more, since the start of the industrial revolution. Our trash doesn't help either – 13,000 pieces of plastic litter on every square kilometre of ocean. The Sustainable Development Goals indicate targets for managing and protecting life below water.
15. **Protect, restore and promote sustainable use of terrestrial ecosystems, sustainably manage forests, combat desertification and halt and reverse land degradation and halt biodiversity loss:** Humans and other animals rely on other forms of life on land for food, clean air, clean water and as a means of combatting climate change. Plant life makes up 80 per cent of the human diet. Forests, which cover 30 per cent of the Earth's surface, help keep the air and water clean and the Earth's climate in balance. That's not to mention they're home to millions of animal species. But, the land and life on it are in trouble. Arable land is disappearing 30 to 35 times faster than it has historically. Deserts are spreading. Animal breeds are going extinct. We can turn these trends around. Fortunately, the Sustainable Development Goals aim to conserve and restore the use of terrestrial ecosystems such as forests, wetlands, drylands and mountains by 2020.
16. **Promote peaceful and inclusive societies for sustainable development, provide access to justice for all and build effective, accountable and inclusive institutions at all levels:** Some regions of the world enjoy relative peace and justice, and may come to take it for granted. Other regions seem to be plagued by armed conflict, crime, torture and exploitation, all of which hinders their development.

The goal of peace and justice is one for all countries to strive towards. The Sustainable Development Goals aim to reduce all forms of violence and propose that governments and communities find lasting solutions to conflict and insecurity. That means strengthening the rule of law, reducing the flow of illicit arms and bringing developing countries more into the centre of institutions of global governance.

17. **Strengthen the means of implementation and revitalize the global partnership for sustainable development:** The world is more interconnected today than ever before, thanks to the internet, travel and global institutions. There is a growing consensus about the need to work together to stop climate change. And the Sustainable Development Goals are no small matter either. One hundred ninety three countries agreed on these Goals.

## ❖ Challenges for India in Attaining SDGs

There are broadly four main areas of concern:

1. **Defining Indicators:** Past record indicates that we have been not very successful in setting relevant indicators to measure outcomes. Quality education has not successfully been defined. India's myopic definition of 'safe' drinking water (with hand pumps and tube wells considered as safe as piped water supply) means that official data suggests 86 per cent of Indians have access to safe drinking water and, as a result, we are 'on track' for the MDG goal on drinking water.
   However, the number of waterborne diseases and deaths due to diarrhoea clearly indicate, this is not the case.
2. **Financing SDGs:** A new study estimates that implementing SDGs in India by 2030 will cost around US$14.4 billion. Given the recent cut in social sector schemes by the Union government, unless states devote a significant portion of their resources on the social sector, there is likely to be a significant funding gap. High growth and redistribution itself are also not enough. According to the United Nations MDG 2014 report, despite high economic growth, in 2010, one-third of the world's 1.2 billion extreme poor lived in India alone. Given these constraints, it is likely that domestic revenues aside, private finance could be a crucial source for financing the SDGs.
3. **Monitoring and Ownership:** A significant challenge is going to be with respect to ownership. Reports suggest that National Institution for Transforming India (NITI) Aayog will play a significant role in tracking progress. However, members at the Aayog have expressed reservations on being able to take on this mammoth task. Moreover, if states are expected to play a pivotal role (giving the devolution post 14th Finance Commission), it will require ownership not just nationally, but also at the state and local level.
4. **Measuring Progress:** Lastly but most importantly is the question of measuring progress or achievement. By the government's own admission, non-availability of data (particularly in respect to sub-national levels), periodicity issues and incomplete coverage of administrative data, made accurate measuring progress of even MDGs virtually impossible.

These four challenges aside, it is important to remember that while SDGs provide broad goals and targets, it will be up to the national and state governments to identify priorities, decide appropriate locally relevant policies, harness innovation and ensure that an implementation and monitoring plan is in place. Only then we will have any chance in ensuring that the 'S' in SDGs, also stand for successful.

## INCLUSIVE GROWTH

According to Organization for Economic Co-operation and Development (OECD), 'Inclusive Growth' is an economic growth that creates opportunity for all segments of the population and distributes the dividends of increased prosperity, both in monetary and non-monetary terms, fairly across society. It is often used interchangeably with a suite of other terms, including 'broad-based growth', 'shared growth' and 'pro-poor growth'.

As per the World Bank rapid and sustained poverty reduction requires inclusive growth that allows people to contribute to and benefit from economic growth. Rapid pace of growth is unquestionably necessary for substantial poverty reduction, but for this growth to be sustainable in the long run, it should be broad-based across sectors, and inclusive of the large part of the country's labour force. This definition of inclusive growth implies a direct link between the macro and micro determinants of growth. The micro dimension captures the importance of structural transformation for economic diversification and competition, including creative destruction of jobs and firms.

Inclusive growth refers both to the pace and pattern of growth, which is considered interlinked, and therefore in need to be addressed together.

The inclusive growth approach takes a longer term perspective as the focus is on productive employment rather than on direct income redistribution, as a means of increasing incomes for excluded groups.

Policies for inclusive growth are an important component of most government strategies for sustainable growth.

The main instrument for a sustainable and inclusive growth is assumed to be productive employment. The ability of individuals to be productively employed depends on the opportunities to make full use of available resources as the economy evolves over time.

### ❖ Inclusive Growth and India

According to former Prime Minister Manmohan Singh, the key components of the inclusive growth strategy included a sharp increase in investment in rural areas, rural infrastructure and agriculture spurt in credit for farmers, increase in rural employment through a unique social safety net and a sharp increase in public spending on education and health care.

Some elements of inclusive growth are: (i) poverty reduction (ii) employment generation and Increase in quantity and quality of employment (iii) agriculture development (iv) industrial development (v) social sector development (vi) reduction in regional disparities (vii) protecting the environment and (viii) equal distribution of income.

India's government has made 'inclusive growth' a key element of their policy platform, stating as a goal: 'Achieving a growth process in which people in different walks in life... feel that they too benefit significantly from the process'. (Ahluwalia, 2007).

The policy for inclusive growth includes: (i) to subsidise only the lowest income people and not special groups of people; (ii) helping people invest in their own skills and future incomes; (iii) keeping government in the economy as light as possible; (iv) making tax rates low and broad based; (v) keeping the ratio of public debt to GDP under control by limiting liabilities; (vi) applying rigorous social cost benefit tests to all spending and regulation decisions; (vii) aligning responsibilities and resources among levels of government namely, the states and finally and (viii) tolerating a measure of inequality during a phase of rapid economic development.

The Union Finance Minister Arun Jaitley said in 2015 that the inclusive growth is high on the priorities of the present Government and the Government will take adequate measures to ensure social security for the children, women and senior citizens of the country.

The development agenda of the Government is focused on triggering a development process which will meet the objective of not just faster economic growth but also inclusive growth, that is, a growth process which yields broad-based benefits and ensures equality of opportunity for all.

In this regard the government has initiated various measures to ameliorate the standard of living of the people and to benefit the people at the lower end of the income distribution through direct intervention by implementing specific poverty reduction and mitigation programmes. Also, all the policy initiatives of the government which leads to higher GDP growth in the country are likely to contribute, individually and collectively, in raising the living standard of the common man across the country.

## SECTORS OF ECONOMY

An economy is best understood when we study its components or sectors. On the basis of economic activities, the economy of any country can be divided into three sectors namely Primary Sector, Secondary Sector and Tertiary Sector.

1. **Primary Sector:** When we produce a good by exploiting natural resources, it is an activity of the primary sector. Agriculture and allied activities like mining, fishery, forestry, dairy and poultry are included in this sector. It is also known as agriculture and related sector. It is called primary sector because it forms the base for all other products that we subsequently make.
2. **Secondary Sector:** The secondary sector covers activities in which natural products are changed into other forms through ways of manufacturing that we associate with industrial activity. It is the next step after primary. The product is not produced by nature but has to be made and therefore some process of manufacturing is essential. This could be in a factory, a workshop or at home. For example, using cotton fibre from the plant, we spin yarn and weave cloth. Since this sector gradually became associated with the different kinds of industries that came up, it is also called as industrial sector.
3. **Tertiary Sector:** These are activities that help in the development of the primary and secondary sectors. These activities, by themselves, do not produce a good but they are an aid or a support for the production process. For example, goods that are produced in the primary or secondary sector would need to be transported by trucks or trains and then sold in wholesale and retail shops. Transport, storage, communication, banking, trade, etc. are some examples of tertiary activities. Since these activities generate services rather than goods, the tertiary sector is also called the service sector.
   - (i) **Economic agents:** They are persons, companies, or organizations that have an influence on the economy by producing, buying, selling, or investing.
   - (ii) **Market Economy:** The market economy gives people strong financial incentives for producing goods that other people want. They tend to be more efficient than traditional or command economies and give people more economic freedom. Major features

are: (a) private ownership of property/resources; (b) business decisions are driven by the desire to earn a profit; (c) a great deal of competition and (d) consumers have many choices.

(iii) **Transnational Corporation (TNC):** A transnational or multinational corporation has its headquarters in one country and operates wholly or partially owned subsidiaries in one or more other countries.

(iv) **Social welfare:** A social welfare system provides assistance to needy individuals and families. Assistance is provided through programmes for health care, food security, nutrition, employment, housing, insurance, etc.

(v) **United Nations Development Programme (UNDP):** UNDP is the UN's global development network, advocating for change and connecting countries to knowledge, experience and resources to help people build a better life. Created in 1949, the UNDP has its headquarters in New York City, but works primarily through its offices in about 170 member countries and territories.

UNDP's work is concentrated on three main focus areas: (i) Sustainable development; (ii) democratic governance and peace-building and (iii) climate and disaster resilience. Moreover, its support for the Sustainable Development Goals (SDGs) putting partnership at the centre of all aspects of its work. It helps countries attract and use aid effectively. It promotes gender equality and also protects of human rights.

(vi) **Mahbub ul Haq:** He revolutionalized the entire development thinking by introducing and promoting people-centred development paradigm. In his capacity as the Special Adviser to the UNDP Administrator, Dr. Mahbub ul Haq conceived and launched annual Human Development Reports in 1990.

(vii) **Amartya Sen:** Amartya Sen (born on 3 November 1933, Santiniketan, India), Indian economist, who was awarded the 1998 Nobel Prize in Economic Sciences for his contributions to welfare economics and social choice theory and for his interest in the problems of society's poorest members. Sen was best known for his work on the causes of famine, which led to the development of practical solutions for preventing or limiting the effects of real or perceived shortages of food. In 18 January 1999 Amartya Sen became the third Nobel laureate and the first social scientist of any description to receive the India's highest civilian honour, the Bharat Ratna.

Welfare economics seeks to evaluate economic policies in terms of their effects on the well-being of the community. Sen devised methods of measuring poverty that yielded useful information for improving economic conditions for the poor. For instance, his theoretical work on inequality provided an explanation for why there are fewer women than men in some poor countries in spite of the fact that more women than men are born and infant mortality is higher among males. Sen claimed that this skewed ratio results from the better health treatment and childhood opportunities afforded to boys in those countries.

The theory of social choice considers the problem of aggregating the preferences of the members of a given society in order to derive a social preference that represents this society or community. Social choice blends elements of welfare economics and voting theory.

(viii) **World Commission on Environment and Development (WCED):** In response to mounting concern surrounding ozone depletion, global warming and other environmental problems associated with raising the standard of living of the world's population, the UN General Assembly convened the WCED, an international group of environmental experts, politicians and civil servants, in 1983. The WCED (also called the Brundtland Commission) was charged with proposing long-term solutions for bringing about sustainable development and continuing it into the 21st century. The Brundtland Commission was officially dissolved in December 1987 after releasing 'Our Common Future', also known as the 'Brundtland Report' in October 1987, a document which coined and defined the meaning of the term 'Sustainable Development'.

(ix) **Organization for Economic Co-operation and Development (OECD):** The Organization for European Economic Cooperation (OEEC) was established in 1948 to run the US-financed Marshall Plan for reconstruction of a continent ravaged by war. Encouraged by its success and the prospect of carrying its work forward on a global stage, Canada and the US joined OEEC members in signing the new OECD Convention on 14 December 1960. The OECD was officially born on 30 September 1961, when the Convention entered into force. Other countries joined in, starting with Japan in 1964. Today, 35 OECD member countries worldwide regularly turn to one another to identify problems, discuss and analyse them, and promote policies to solve them.

❑❑❑

# 2 CHAPTER

# Development Strategy and Economic Reform

## ECONOMY DURING THE PRE-BRITISH PERIOD

During the pre-British period, the village community was composed of different groups based on simple division of labour. There were farmers who cultivated land and tended cattle. Other groups of people were weavers, goldsmith, potters, washermen, carpenters, cobblers, oil pressers, barber, surgeons, etc. All the occupations were hereditary. These **Indian villages were functioning independently** as most of food articles and raw materials produced within the villages were either consumed or purchased by the village communities itself.

Agricultural and handicraft industries were interdependent and thus the village republics were able to function independently. Indian villages were almost **self-sufficient in respect of daily necessities** excepting commodities like salt, spices, fine cloth, luxury and semi-luxury goods.

## INDUSTRIES AND URBAN HANDICRAFTS

Although agriculture had dominated the Indian economy during the pre-British period, yet some Indian industries, producing certain special products, enjoyed worldwide reputation. During those days, many of the handicrafts produced in the urban areas of India were quite famous. Among all those various famous urban handicrafts, textile handicrafts earned a special status and were also spread over the whole country. During those days, the muslin of Dacca, silk sarees of Benaras, shawls and carpets of Kashmir and Amritsar, the calicos of Bengal, dhoti and dopattas of Ahmedabad, silk and bordered cloth of Nagpur and Murshidabad, etc. were very famous and received much recognition in international markets.

## ECONOMIC IMPACT OF BRITISH RULE IN INDIA

British rule in India caused a transformation of India's economy into a colonial economy, i.e., the structure and operation of Indian economy were determined by the interests of the British economy.

1. **Deindustrialization:** Cheap and machine-made imports flooded the Indian market after the Charter Act of 1813, allowing one-way free trade for the British citizens. On the other hand, Indian products found it more and more difficult to penetrate the European markets.

   After 1820, European markets were virtually closed to Indian exports. The newly introduced rail network helped the

European products to reach the remotest corners of the country.

The loss of traditional livelihood was not accompanied by a process of industrialization in India, as had happened in other rapidly industrializing countries of the time. This resulted in deindustrialization of India at a time when Europe was witnessing a re-intensified Industrial Revolution.

Another feature of deindustrialization was the decline of many cities and a process of ruralization of India. This resulted in increased pressure on land. An overburdened agriculture sector was a major cause of poverty during British rule and this upset the village economic set-up. From being a net exporter, India became a net importer.

2. **Impoverishment of Peasantry:** The Government, only interested in maximization of rents and in securing its share of revenue, had enforced the Permanent Settlement system in large parts. Transferability of land was one feature of the new settlement which caused great insecurity to the tenants who lost all their traditional rights in land.

   There was little spending by Government on improvement of land productivity The overburdened peasants had to approach the money-lenders to be able to pay their dues to the Zamindars.

   The peasant turned out to be the ultimate sufferer under the triple burden of the Government, zamindar and money-lender. His hardship increased at the time of famine and scarcity.

3. **Emergence of New Land Relations:** By 1815, half the total land in Bengal had passed into new hands. The new Zamindars, with increased powers but with little or no avenues for new investments, resorted to land grabbing and sub-infeudation. Increase in number of intermediaries to be paid gave rise to absentee landlordism and increased the burden on the peasant.

4. **Stagnation and Deterioration of Agriculture:** The cultivator had neither the means nor any incentive to invest in agriculture. The zamindar had no roots in the villages, while the Government spent little on agricultural, technical or mass education. All this, together with fragmentation of land due to sub-infeudation, made it difficult to introduce modern technology which caused a perpetually low level of productivity.

5. **Commercialization of Indian Agriculture:** Till latter half of the nineteenth century, agriculture had been a way of life rather than a business enterprise.

   Now agriculture began to be influenced by commercial considerations. Certain specialized crops began to be grown not for consumption in the village but for sale in the national and even international markets.

   Commercial crops like cotton, jute, groundnut, oilseeds, sugarcane, tobacco, etc. were more remunerative than food grains. Again, the cultivation of crops like condiments, spices, fruits and vegetables could cater to a wider market.

   Perhaps, the commercialization trend reached the highest level of development in the plantation sector, i.e., in tea, coffee, rubber, indigo, etc., which was mostly owned by Europeans and the produce was for sale in a wider market.

   The new market trend of commercialization and specialization was encouraged by many factors – spread of money economy, replacement of custom and tradition by competition and contract, emergence of a unified national market, growth of internal trade, improvement in communications through rail and roads, boost to international trade given by entry of British finance capital, etc. For the Indian peasant, commercialization seemed a forced process. There was hardly any surplus for him to invest in commercial crops, given the subsistence level at which he lived, while commercialization linked Indian agriculture with international market trends and their fluctuations.

6. **Development of Modern Industry:** It was only in the second half of the nineteenth century that modern machine-based industries started coming up in India. The first cotton textile mill was set up in 1853 in Bombay by Cowasjee Nanabhoy, and the first jute mill came up in 1855 in Rishra (Bengal). But most of the modern industries were foreign-owned and controlled by British managing agencies.

   There was a rush of foreign capital in India at this time due to prospects of high profits, availability of cheap labour, cheap and readily available raw material, ready market in India and the neighbours, diminishing avenues for investments at home, willingness of the administration to provide all help, and ready markets abroad for some Indian exports such as tea, jute and manganese.

   Indian-owned industries came up in cotton textiles and jute in the nineteenth century and in sugar, cement, etc. in the twentieth century. Indian-owned industries suffered from many handicaps – credit problems, no tariff protection by Government, unequal competition from foreign companies and stiff opposition from British capitalist interests who were backed by sound financial and technical infrastructure at home.

7. **Rise of Indian Bourgeoisie:** Indian traders, money-lenders and bankers had amassed some wealth as junior partners of English merchant capitalists in India. Their role fitted in the British scheme of colonial exploitation. The Indian money-lender provided loans to hard-pressed agriculturists and thus facilitated the state collection of revenue.

8. **Economic Drain:** The drain theory was put forward by Dadabhai Naoroji in his book Poverty and Un-British Rule in India. The major components of this drain were salaries and pensions of civil and military officials, interests on loans taken by the Indian Government from abroad, profits on foreign investment in India, stores purchased in Britain for civil and military departments, payments to be made for shipping, banking and insurance services which stunted the growth of Indian enterprise in these services. The drain of wealth checked and retarded capital formation in India while the same portion of wealth accelerated the growth of British economy.

9. **Famine and Poverty:** Regular recurrence of famines became a common feature of daily existence in India. These famines were not just foodgrain scarcity-based phenomena, but were a direct result of poverty unleashed by colonial forces in India. Between 1850 and 1900, about 2.8 crore people died in famines.

## POST-INDEPENDENCE DEVELOPMENT STRATEGY

After independence, the broad objectives that guided India's development strategy were:

1. Achievement of a high rate of economic growth, which would lead to a sustained improvement in the standard of living of the population.
2. Reduction in inequalities and more especially an accelerated effort to remove poverty at a pace faster than would be achieved solely through the normal growth process.
3. Development of a mixed economy with a strong public sector, especially in key areas of the economy.
4. Achievement of a high order of self-reliance.

5. Promotion of balanced regional development, with a narrowing of economic difference across regions.
6. The social and economic objectives were to be pursued in the framework of a constitutional democracy.

Various strategies adopted were as follows:

1. **Mixed Economy:** Mixed economy means an economy that contains both privately owned and state-owned enterprises or that combines elements of capitalism and socialism, or a mix of market economy and planned economy characteristics. This system overcomes the disadvantages of both the market and planned economic systems.

   Under mixed economy strategy, government of India directed economic activities in some socially important areas of the economy, and the rest was left to the price mechanism to operate. The public and private sectors cooperated each other to achieve the social objectives. The private sector was considered to be an important instrument of economic growth.

   The public sector was allotted activities like coal, mining, steel, power, roads, etc. Private sector was allotted to establish industries, mainly in consumer goods, subject to control and regulations in the form of law.
2. **Modernization through Industrialization:** The focus of India's development strategy was modernization through industrialization. Emphasis was given on state-led industrialization, with all industries and sectors like steel, mining, machine tools, chemicals, telecommunications, power plants, etc. as well as trade and finance were reserved for the public sector. The second Five-Year Plan adopted the strategy of 'machine-for-producing machine' and strongly emphasized on technology and capital-intensive heavy industries to achieve rapid industrial growth, which in turn is the pre-condition for overall economic development.
3. **Restrictive Policy towards International Trade and Finance:** The policymakers favoured a restrictive policy regime, with strong restrictions on international trade and finance. This is mainly due to the negative perceptions towards international openness, which were after India's experience during the colonial rule.
4. **Agriculture Sector:** The strategy of the Green Revolution was initiated in 1965. Emphasis was given in building institutional and physical infrastructure, such as irrigation and dams, rural roads and markets, cooperative credits, price support and extension programmes for education and training of farmers, etc. to improve agricultural productivity. Similarly, land reform was also initiated for improving productivity as well as achieving distributional equity.
5. **Social Justice:** As per the Directive Principles of State Policy laid down in the Constitution, achievement of justice–social, economic and political were proclaimed as a national commitment. The Five-Year Plans were an inherent part of state policy where social justice figured as the most important objective.
6. **Import Substitution:** Import substitution is generally referred to policy that eliminates the import and allows for the production in the domestic market. The objective of this policy is to bring about structural changes in the economy by substituting the articles imported by domestic production.

   In India, in the first seven plans, trade was characterized by an inward-looking trade strategy.

Technically, this strategy was called import substitution. This policy was aimed at replacing or substituting imports with domestic production.

The policy of protection was based on the notion that industries of developing countries were not in a position to compete against the goods produced by more developed economies.

## FOREIGN INVESTMENT POLICY INSTRUMENTS

After independence, new foreign investment has been rigidly controlled in line with established development thinking. Investment was mostly restricted to industries where it was felt that the acquisition of foreign technology was important, or where the promise of exports was convincing.

Thus, India has followed an inward-looking, controlled development strategy after independence, where the state has played the dominant role. It has emphasized on state-led industrialization, substitution, a large public sector and import control on private sector. The entire system involved a set of restrictive policies like industrial licensing, exchange control, import licensing, capital control, price controls, etc.

## ECONOMIC REFORM

Economic reform is an action taken by the government targeting economic policy instruments designed to effect changes in the behaviours of public and/or private economic agents with a view towards either boosting their sustainable and non-inflationary demand addressed to the national economy or increasing their productive investments to achieve national economic growth and employment creation targets. The essence of economic reform is dismantling state control over economy. It refers to the state yielding to the market (privatization), opening trade and investment, tax reform and inflation control (neo-liberalism). The goal of economic reform is greater benefits to all sections of society.

In India, the first attempt of economic reform was made in 1966 which was reversed in 1967, and a stronger version of socialism was adopted. The second major attempt was made in 1985 by Prime Minister Rajiv Gandhi which came to a halt in 1987. Finally, in 1991, PM Narsimha Rao was forced to adopt the reform.

The 1991 economic reform was crisis driven:

1. Balance of payment (BoP) crisis – Forex reserve came down to 1.1 b $, while Current Account Deficit (CAD) increased to 5.5 b $ (2.2 per cent of GDP)
2. External debt increased to as high as 22.8 per cent of GDP (62.3 b $)
3. Internal debt amounted to 53 per cent of GDP
4. Massive NRI deposit outflow (1.3 b $) took place leading to loss of investor confidence.

The root cause of the crisis was the large and growing fiscal imbalance due to mounting government expenditures in form of subsidies and unbridled consumption expenditure under policy of populism causing high inflation (more than 10 per cent). The gross fiscal deficit of the government (centre and states) rose to 12.7 per cent in 1990–91 due to fall in resource mobilization (revenue expenditure outpacing revenue receipts). Subsidies grew at faster rate. Meanwhile, the Gulf war in 1990 hampered the petro-product import from Iraq which forced government to buy petroleum from other countries at higher cost. At the same time India witnessed political instability due to implementation of Mandal Commission Report giving reservation to OBCs in government jobs.

## MEASURES UNDERTAKEN

The post-crisis adjustment programme featured macroeconomic stabilization and structural reforms.

1. **Macroeconomic Stabilization:** India pledged 20 tonnes of gold to Union Bank of Switzerland and 47 tonnes to Bank of England; taken loans from multilateral financial institutions and donor countries reduction in fertilizer and sugar subsidy.

   Policy adopted for macroeconomic stabilization:

   (i) Reduction in Fiscal deficit
   (ii) Reduction in non-plan expenditure
   (iii) Revenue generation by broadening tax base, rationalizing tax rates and non-tax sources
   (iv) Resource mobilization from public services
   (v) Low and stable inflation by controlled money supply, faster growth, freezing fuel prices, etc.
   (vi) Balance of Payment adjustment by improved invisible account and more export earnings.

2. **Structural Reforms:** Objectives of the structural reform were:

   (i) Shift resources from non-traded goods to traded goods sectors and from government sector to private sector.
   (ii) Improve resource utilization by opening economy and reducing government intervention.
   (iii) Rely more on price mechanism instead of governmental control.
   (iv) Wind down Public Sector Units (PSUs).

The policy adopted was called liberalization, privatization and globalization (LPG).

## LIBERALIZATION

Liberalization means elimination of state control over economic activities. It implies greater autonomy to the business enterprises in decision-making and removal of government interference in economy.

The major aspects of liberalization in India are:

1. Providing more opportunity to private enterprises and capital
2. Removal of restrictions on movements of goods and services
3. Tax rates have been reduced and rationalized
4. Pricing of goods to be done by producers
5. Liberalization of capital and money market
6. **Abolition of licensing:** NIP 1991 abolished licensing for most industries except 5 industries of strategic significance.
7. **Liberalization of Foreign Investment:** While earlier prior approval was required by foreign companies, now automatic approvals were given for Foreign Direct Investment (FDI) to flow into the country.
8. **Relaxation of Locational Restrictions:** No requirement anymore for obtaining approval from the Central Government for setting up industries anywhere in the country except those specified under compulsory licensing or in cities with population exceeding one million.
9. **Liberalization of Foreign Technology imports:** In projects where imported capital goods are required, automatic licence would be given for foreign technology imports up to 2 million US dollars.
10. **Phased Manufacturing Programmes:** Under PMP any enterprise had to progressively substitute imported inputs,

components with domestically produced inputs under local content policy.

11. **Public Sector Reforms:** Greater autonomy was given to the PSUs through the MOUs.
12. **MRTP Act:** Monopolies and Restrictive Trade Practises Act has been abolished.
13. Foreign Exchange Regulation Act (FERA) was liberalized in 1993 and later Foreign Exchange Management Act (FEMA) 1999 was passed to enable foreign currency transactions.

## PRIVATIZATION

Privatization is the transfer of control of ownership of economic resources from the public sector to the private sector. Thus, it refers to the private purchase of all or part of a public company.

The main aspects of privatization in India are as follows:

1. **Denationalization:** Complete transfer of ownership of a public enterprise.
2. **Joint Venture:** Partial introduction of private ownership.
3. **Disinvestment Policies:** Sale of a part of equity of a public company.
4. Restriction on further expansion of PSUs.
5. **Dereservation of Public Sector:** Out of 17 reserved industries, only 3 are reserved – (i) Atomic Energy, (ii) Atomic Energy Minerals and (iii) Railways (many processes have been privatized). Reserved products for SSI has been gradually reduced to Zero
6. **Autonomy to Public Sector:** Greater autonomy was granted to nine PSUs referred to as 'navaratnas' to take their own decisions.
7. Transfer of management and control, i.e., franchise, contract, lease, etc.

### ❖ Advantages of Privatization

1. Benefits to taxpayers as lower subsidy may lower tax rates.
2. May lead to better quality and lower price as a result of competitions.
3. No massive subsidy to loss-making units.
4. Privatization can provide the necessary impetus to the underperforming PSUs.
5. May brings about radical structural changes in economy providing momentum in the competitive sectors.
6. May lead to adoption of the global best practices along with management and motivation of the best human talent to foster sustainable competitive advantage and improvised management of resources.

### ❖ Disadvantages of Privatization

1. Private sector focuses more on profit maximization and less on social objectives unlike public sector that initiates socially viable adjustments in case of emergencies and criticalities.
2. There is lack of transparency in private sector, and stakeholders do not get the complete information.
3. Privatization has provided the unnecessary support to the corruption and illegitimate ways of accomplishments of licences.
4. Privatization escalates inflation in general.
5. International agencies may find difficult to finance private sectors.
6. There is no guarantee that privatization would improve the productivity of PSUs.

## GLOBALIZATION

Globalization essentially means integration of the national economy with the world economy.

It implies a free flow of information, ideas, technology, goods and services, finance and even people across different countries and societies. It increases connectivity between different markets in the form of trade, investments and cultural exchanges.

The concept of globalization has been explained by the IMF (International Monetary Fund) as 'the growing economic interdependence of countries worldwide through increasing volume and variety of cross border transactions in goods and services and of international capital flows and also through the more rapid and widespread diffusion of technology'.

The main elements of globalization are:

1. To open the domestic markets for inflow of foreign goods, India reduced customs duties on imports.
2. The FDI policy of the GOI encouraged the inflow of fresh foreign capital by allowing 100 per cent foreign equity in certain projects under the automatic route.
3. Outsourcing (PBO, KPO, LPO) is one of the important outcomes of the globalization process.

### ❖ Advantages of Globalization

**A. For Developing Countries**

1. **Trade:** They have potential to increase their share in world trade.
2. Free flow of capital and technology enables developing countries to speed up the process of industrialization and lay the path for faster economic progress.
3. Labour may move towards developed countries.
4. Spread of technology may benefit developing countries.
5. There may be decline in the number of people living below the poverty line.

**B. For Developed Countries**

1. They get new market for their products.
2. They find better investment opportunity.

### ❖ Disadvantages of Globalization

1. Domestic companies are unable to withstand competition from efficient MNCs.
2. Development of indigenous technology may take a backseat.
3. It increases the disparities in the incomes of the rich and poor.
4. It leads to overcrowding of cities and puts pressure on the amenities and facilities available in urban areas.
5. Globalization poses certain risks for any country in the form of business cycles, fluctuations in international prices, etc.

## SECOND-GENERATION REFORM

### ❖ Background

First-generation reform were

1. Crisis driven.
2. Focused on industry first strategy, but inter-relation between industry and agriculture was forgotten. Thus, strategy failed to create enough job opportunity and bring equality in society.
3. Advocated for agro-export, but much of it depended on external factors, i.e., developed country's protective tariff and non-tariff barriers. India continued to struggle at the World Trade Organization to reduce these barriers.

**Philosophy of Second-generation Reform:** 'Growth is not an end in itself but a vehicle to increase employment and raise living standard'.

For this, a sustainable, equitable and job-creating growth path was targeted.

### ❖ Development Strategy

1. A higher rate of growth of GDP.
2. Enlarge the employment potential.
3. Decrease BPL population.
4. Provide social services (education, health, sanitation, etc.) specially to poor.
5. Reduce regional disparities.
6. While the first-generation reform was based on executive and administrative measures, the second-generation reform required legislative actions.

### ❖ Important Features

1. It is development driven.
2. Enlarge the base of reform to agriculture and SSIs.
3. Shift emphasis from corporate sector to agriculture, agro-based industries, SSIs and on improving infrastructure and social sectors like health education, food security, poverty, etc.
4. Central and state governments to work in harmony.

### ❖ Fiscal Strategy Adopted

1. Reduce fiscal deficit to a limit of 3 per cent for the Centre and 2 per cent for states.
2. Reduce revenue deficit to zero.
3. Raise capital expenditure in rural infrastructure and stimulate growth in agriculture.
4. Reduce subsidy on non-merit goods and hidden subsidy benefitting more to well-to-do people.
5. Create environment of better cost recoveries on social services, i.e., irrigation, power, roads, etc.

### ❖ Major Reforms Undertaken

1. Fiscal Responsibility and Budget Management (FRBM) Act, 2003, was passed.
2. Reduction in corporate tax rate from the existing levels of 36.75 per cent to 30 per cent for domestic companies and to 35 per cent for foreign companies.
3. Competition Act 2002 was passed.
4. Commercial banks were allowed to raise capital from the market to meet capital adequacy norms by diluting the government's stake up to 52 per cent.
5. RBI released guidelines and invited applications for setting up payment banks and local area banks.
6. Promulgation of Insurances Laws (Amendment) Ordinance 2014.
7. Ujwal DISCOM Assurance Yojana or UDAY provides for the financial turnaround and revival of Power Distribution companies (DISCOMs).

### ❖ Challenges to Overcome

1. Slow infrastructure development.
2. Failure in increasing labour-intensive manufacturing.
3. Not taking advantage of demographic dividend.
4. Slow social sector development.
5. Governance failures.
6. Lack of labour reform.
7. The combined deficit at the centre and states exceeds 10 per cent of GDP. Given an already high debt-to-GDP ratio of nearly 60 per cent, this deficit is unsustainable. It is also crowding out private investment.
8. Fertilizer and food subsidies pose yet another challenge.
9. Economic reforms of the last decade have virtually bypassed agriculture.
10. Financial sector reforms, particularly the reform of banking, remain a distant goal.

## THIRD-GENERATION ECONOMIC REFORM

Started with 10th Five-Year Plan in 2002, it is aimed at devaluation of the benefits of Economic Reforms. Under the reform, inclusive growth has been emphasized.

After 2014, the reform intensified by focusing on creation, promotion rearing of entrepreneurship. Micro Units Development & Refinancing Agency (Mudra) Bank has been established for availability of capital to start-ups and small entrepreneurs. The Goods and Service Tax (GST) came into existence on 1 July 2017.

## FOURTH-GENERATION ECONOMIC REFORM

It is a non-official concept. It envisaged economic development fully based on Information Technology.

Reforms of all the above four generations are being implemented simultaneously, and they indicate directions and depths of the reform.

## TWENTY-FIVE YEARS OF ECONOMIC REFORM

### ❖ GDP

India in 2015 had the third-largest GDP ($7.98 trillion) in the world in purchasing power parity terms after China (19.52 $) and the United States (17.95 $).

### ❖ GDP Growth

India's annual GDP growth rose from 3.5 per cent in 1950–80 and 5.5 per cent in 1980–92 to an average of 8 per cent from 2003 to 2015, with a peak exceeding 9 per cent in the three years (2005–08).

In a depressed global economy, the IMF sees the United States and India as the two bright spots, as the two major economies holding up an otherwise slowing world.

Per capita income is up from $375 per year in 1991 to $1,700 in 2015. India has long ceased to be a low-income country as defined by the World Bank, which uses a threshold of $1,045, and has become a middle-income country.

In 1991, India was a member of the G77 group of developing countries. In 2016, India is a proud member of the G20, the most-powerful countries in the world.

## COMMERCIAL FINANCE

Its commercial finance has been spurred by economic reforms that have attracted inflows of foreign exchange other than foreign aid. Total foreign investment (equity plus portfolio inflows) came to $51.2 billion in 2014–15.

Foreign commercial borrowing in the same year came to $68.2 billion gross and $10.4 billion net, whereas remittances from Indians overseas exceeded $70 billion. The remittance boom was a consequence of globalization, of Indians going abroad.

## INDIA HAS BECOME A DONOR COUNTRY

In 1991, India was infamous as the world's biggest beggar, a bottomless pit for foreign aid. It soaked up 40 per cent of the funds of the International Development Association (IDA), the soft-loan window of the World Bank. Today, India is as much a donor as a recipient. It is still a substantial aid recipient in gross terms. But the inflow is barely half-a-billion dollars net of debt service. Meanwhile, India itself has become a substantial donor, including a line of credit of $10 billion to Africa, $2 billion to Bangladesh.

## INDIAN COMPANIES BECAME MULTINATIONAL

In 1991, Indian politicians and industrialists feared that economic liberalization would mean the collapse of Indian industry or its conversion into subsidiaries of multinational companies. Twenty-five years later, Indian companies not only have held their own but also have become multinationals in their own right. Through acquisitions, Arcelor Mittal became the biggest steel company in the world. The Tata Group acquired Corus Steel and Jaguar Land Rover and in the process became the largest private-sector employer in the United Kingdom.

## IMPORTS AND EXPORTS

Imports and exports, of both goods and services, have soared as a proportion of GDP because of India's opening up and consequent globalization.

## FOREIGN EXCHANGE RESERVES

In June 1991, at the height of the Balance of Payments crisis, India's foreign exchange reserves had dipped to a mere $1 billion just sufficient for two weeks of import requirements. Presently (August 2016), India's foreign exchange reserves have touched $ 366.776 billion – one of the highest in the world. Remittances into the country from abroad and software exports – two major benefits of globalization – contributed substantially to the accretion in foreign exchange reserves.

## FDI

Liberalization of FDI led to sustained increase in FDI. In 2015–16, India emerged as the largest recipient of FDI among emerging nations with FDI inflows of $55.56 billion. FDI inflows along with Foreign Portfolio Investment (FPI) enabled India to finance her current account deficit.

## SPURT IN SOCIAL SECTOR

A major benefit of the high growth was the spurt in tax: GDP ratio from 8 per cent in 1991 to 11.5 per cent by 2008. This tax buoyancy enabled the government to undertake ambitious social sector projects like MGNREGS, Bharath Nirman, etc. The annual outlay for MGNREGS is higher than the total tax revenue of the central government in 1990–91. The ambitious food security programme being implemented now entails huge expenditure. The insurance programmes targeted at the poor and the MUDRA initiatives are laudable inclusive programmes. For sustaining such ambitious social sector programmes, it is very important that India should sustain a high growth rate for a long time.

## POVERTY DECLINE (TENDULKAR COMMITTEE METHODOLOGY)

| Years | Percentage of Poor |
|---|---|
| 1993–94 | 45.3 |
| 2004–5 | 37.2 |
| 2011–12 | 21.9 |

India has become a global hub for computer software development.

India is now a low-cost commercial satellite launcher. By October 2015, it had launched 51 satellites for foreign countries, with payloads of less than 1,600 kilograms.

India's economic success after 1991 has spurred the creation of thousands of private engineering colleges, with estimated admissions of 1.5 million students per year.

## CHALLENGES AHEAD

India's spectacular economic performance since liberalization is, indeed, a great achievement. India was one of the few large economies of the world, which did not experience recession or sharp economic slow-down during the Great Recession of 2009. However, it is important that some deficiencies of this growth be recognized and addressed. A major deficiency of India's spectacular growth is that the growth has not been adequately 'inclusive'. Large number of poor, marginalized, vulnerable sections of the society has been left out of the growth process. This deficiency has to be addressed, and growth has to be made more inclusive.

Another major deficiency is the infrastructure deficit, which is becoming a major constraint on sustainable high growth. Land acquisition, environmental clearances and speedy execution of infrastructure projects brook no delay. Hence, we can say India's achievements of 25 years of reforms are laudable. The deficiencies, too, are glaring and need to be addressed seriously. Though India has a long way to go in achieving stable, sustainable and inclusive growth, the economy is on the right path.

❑❑❑

# 3 CHAPTER

# Banking Sector

## RESERVE BANK OF INDIA (RBI)

### ❖ Introduction

The genesis of the Reserve Bank of India (RBI) can be traced back to 1926 when the Hilton Young Commission or the Royal Commission on Indian Currency and Finance made recommendations to the British Government of India for creation of a central bank. The chief recommendations were twofold: (i) to separate the control of currency and credit from the government; (ii) to augment banking facilities throughout the country.

The RBI as a central bank of India (CBI) was established as a shareholder's bank on 1 April 1935 via the Reserve Bank of India Act, 1934. Its share capital was ₹ 5 crore.

The Bank began its operations by taking over from the Government the functions so far being performed by the Controller of Currency and from the Imperial Bank of India, the management of Government accounts and public debt. The existing currency offices at Calcutta, Bombay, Madras, Rangoon, Karachi, Lahore and Cawnpore (Kanpur) became branches of the Issue Department. Offices of the Banking Department were established in Calcutta, Bombay, Madras, Delhi and Rangoon.

Burma (Myanmar) seceded from the Indian Union in 1937, but the Reserve Bank continued to act as the Central Bank for Burma till Japanese Occupation of Burma and later up to April 1947. After the partition of India, the Reserve Bank served as the central bank of Pakistan up to June 1948 when the State Bank of Pakistan commenced operations.

After independence, the government passed Reserve Bank (Transfer to Public Ownership) Act, 1948, and took over the RBI from private shareholders after paying appropriate compensation. Thus, nationalization of RBI took place in 1949 and from 1 January 1949, the RBI started working as a government-owned CBI. Its headquarters is at Mumbai.

An interesting feature of the RBI was that at its very inception, the Bank was seen as playing a special role in the context of development, especially Agriculture.

## FUNCTIONS OF RBI

The RBI performs many functions; some of them are as follows:

1. **Issue of Currency Notes:** Under Section 22 of the RBI Act, the bank has the sole right to issue currency notes of all denominations except one-rupee coins and notes. The one-rupee notes and coins and small coins are issued by Central Government, Ministry of Finance and their distribution is undertaken by the

RBI as the agent of the government.

The Currency Department in RBI attends to the core statutory function of note and coin issue and currency management. This involves forecasting the demand for fresh notes and coins, placing the indent with four printing presses and mints, receiving supplies against those indents and distributing them through the 18 offices of the Bank, a wide network of currency chests, repositories and small coin depots. At present, there is a network of 4,281 Currency Chests and 4,044 Small Coin Deposits.

The distribution of Coins is undertaken by the RBI as an agent of the Government (coins are minted by the Government and not by RBI). Coins up to 50 paisa are called 'small coins', and coins of Rupee one and above are called 'Rupee coins'.

*Minimum Reserve System*: Originally, the assets of the Issue Department were to consist of not less than 2/5th of the Gold or sterling securities, provided Gold was not less than ₹ 40 crores in value. Remaining 3/5th of the assets might be rupee coins. This was called 'Proportional Reserve System'. In 1956, this system was changed. Now, the RBI is required to maintain a Gold and Foreign Exchange Reserves of ₹ 200 Crore of which at least ₹ 115 crore should be in Gold. This is called Minimum Reserve System. This system continues till date.

*Note Printing Presses*: The Security Printing and Minting Corporation of India Limited (SPMCIL) prints the notes. It is a wholly owned company of the Government of India. Its printing presses are located at Nasik (Maharashtra) and Dewas (Madhya Pradesh). Apart from that, the Bharatiya Reserve Bank Note Mudran Pvt. Ltd. (BRBNMPL), a wholly owned subsidiary of the Reserve Bank, also has set up printing presses. The presses of BRBNMPL are located at Mysore in Karnataka and Salboni in West Bengal. The SPMCIL also has 4 mints for coin production located at Mumbai, Noida, Kolkata and Hyderabad.

2. **Banker to the Governments:** The RBI acts as a banker, agent and adviser to the governments. It has obligation to transact the banking business of the Central Government as well as State Governments.

   Under the administrative arrangements, the Central Government is required to maintain a minimum cash balance with the Reserve Bank. Currently, this amount is ₹ 10 crore on a daily basis and ₹100 crore on Fridays.

   As banker to the Central Government, the RBI works out the overall fund position and sends daily advice showing the balances in its books, *Ways and Means Advances* granted to the government and investments made from the surplus fund. The daily advices are followed up with monthly statements.

   All the State Governments are required to maintain a minimum balance with the Reserve Bank, which varies from state to state depending on the relative size of the state budget and economic activity. To tide over temporary mismatches in the cash flow of receipts and payments, the Reserve Bank provides Ways and Means Advances/Overdraft to the State Governments.

3. **Management of Public Debt:** The Reserve Bank manages public debt on behalf of the Central and the State Governments. It involves issue of new rupee loans, payment of interest and repayment of these loans and other operational matters such as debt certificates and their registration.

4. **Banker's bank And Lender Of Last Resort:** The RBI acts as a banker to the

commercial banks. The RBI continuously monitors operations of the accounts of commercial banks to ensure that defaults do not take place. Among other provisions, the Reserve Bank stipulates minimum balances to be maintained by banks in these accounts.

Since banks need to settle transactions with each other occurring at various places in India, they are allowed to open accounts with different regional offices of the Reserve Bank.

The RBI facilitates remittance of funds from a bank's surplus account at one location to its deficit account at another. Such transfers are electronically routed through a computerized system called e-Kuber.

In addition, the RBI has also introduced the Centralized Funds Management System (CFMS) to facilitate centralized funds enquiry and transfer of funds across Deposit Accounts Departments (DADs). This helps banks in their fund management as they can access information on their balances maintained across different DADs from a single location.

As a banker to banks, the RBI provides short-term loans and advances to select banks, when necessary, to facilitate lending to specific sectors and for specific purposes. These loans are provided against promissory notes and other collateral given by the banks.

As a banker to banks, the RBI also acts as the 'lender of the last resort'. It can come to the rescue of a bank that faces temporary liquidity problems by supplying it with much needed liquidity when no one else is willing to extend credit to that bank. The Reserve Bank extends this facility to protect the interest of the depositors of the bank and to prevent possible failure of the bank, which in turn may also affect other banks and institutions and can have an adverse impact on financial stability and thus on the economy.

5. **Controller of Credit:** The RBI has power to control the volume of credit created by banks. The RBI through its various quantitative and qualitative techniques regulates total supply of money and bank credit in the interest of economy. This becomes all the more important as India is following the managed paper currency system which has inherent inflationary tendency. The RBI pumps in money during busy season and withdraws money during slack season.

   The basic needs of credit control in the economy are: to encourage the overall growth of the 'priority sector'; to keep a check over the channelization of credit so that credit is not delivered for undesirable purposes; to achieve the objective of controlling 'inflation' as well as 'deflation'; and to boost the economy by facilitating the flow of adequate volume of bank credit to different sectors.

6. **Exchange Rate Policy and Custodian of Foreign Reserve:** The RBI's exchange rate policy focuses on ensuring orderly conditions in the foreign exchange market. For the purpose, it closely monitors the developments in the financial markets at home and abroad. When necessary, it intervenes in the market by buying or selling foreign currencies. The market operations are undertaken either directly or through public sector banks (PSBs).

   In addition to the traditional instruments like forward and swap contracts, the RBI has facilitated increased availability of derivative instruments in the foreign exchange market.

   The RBI is the custodian of the country's foreign exchange reserves and is vested with the responsibility of managing their investment.

The Reserve Bank's reserves management function has in recent years grown both in terms of importance and sophistication for two main reasons. First, the share of foreign currency assets in the balance sheet of the RBI has substantially increased. Second, with the increased volatility in exchange and interest rates in the global market, the task of preserving the value of reserves and obtaining a reasonable return on them has become challenging. The basic parameters of the RBI's policies for foreign exchange reserves management are safety, liquidity and returns.

7. **Collection and Publication of Data:** The RBI is the main source of monetary data and also of the data relating to banking. The data are very important for framing the economic policies and banking policies. The bank collects and publishes the data regularly through weekly statements, monthly bulletins, annual report, report on trend and progress of banking in India, etc.

8. **Regulatory and Supervisory Functions:** The RBI has wide powers of **supervision and control** over commercial and co-operative banks, relating to licensing, establishment, branch expansion, liquidity of Assets, management and methods of working, amalgamation, re-construction and liquidation.

   The Banking Regulation Act, 1949, empowers the RBI to inspect and supervise commercial banks. These powers are exercised through on-site inspection and off-site surveillance.

   The aims of regulation and supervision are: (i) to maintain capital standards to overcome risks; (ii) to assure transparency in banking operations; (iii) to sustain the health of the banking system; (iv) to guard against moral hazards; (v) to maintain stability and soundness of banking system; (vi) to guard against speculative activities and market destabilization; (vii) to ensure price stability; (viii) to lead economic growth; (ix) to pave way for market discipline and (x) to ensure safety of depositor's funds.

9. **Clearing House Functions:** The RBI acts as a clearing house for all member banks. This avoids unnecessary transfer of funds between the various banks.

   Clearing house is a central office where banks exchange cheques and other financial documents. It is a voluntary association of banks under the management of a bank where the settlement accounts are maintained. Wherever the RBI has its office, the clearing house is managed by it. In the absence of an office of the RBI, the clearing house is managed by the State Bank of India (SBI) and in a few cases by PSBs.

   There are 860 Bankers clearing houses in India, of which 840 are managed by the SBI, 14 by the RBI and the rest 6 by nationalized banks.

10. **Development and Promotional Functions:** The RBI has helped in setting up Industrial Finance Corporations of India (IFCI), State Financial Corporations (SFCs), Deposit Insurance Corporation, Agricultural Refinance and Development Corporation (ARDC), units Trust of India (UTI), etc. These institutions were set up to mobilize savings, promote saving habits and to provide industrial and agricultural finance.

11. **Regulation of Financial Market:** Major market segments under the regulatory ambit of the RBI are interest rate markets, including the government securities market and money markets; foreign exchange markets; derivatives on interest rates/prices, repo, foreign exchange rates as well as credit derivatives.

    The RBI derives statutory powers to regulate market segments from specific provisions of the Reserve Bank of India Act, 1934.

12. **Priority Sector Lending:** Priority sector refers to those sectors of the economy, which may not get timely and adequate credit in the absence of this special dispensation.

According to the priority sector norms set by the RBI, the scheduled commercial banks have to give 40 per cent of their loans (measured in terms of Adjusted Net Bank Credit or ANBC) to the identified priority sectors in accordance with the RBI regulations. ANBC denotes the outstanding Bank Credit in India minus bills rediscounted with RBI and other approved Financial Institutions plus permitted non-SLR bonds/debentures under Held to Maturity (HTM) category plus other investments eligible to be treated as part of priority sector lending (e.g., investments in securitized assets).

The RBI has modified Priority Sector Lending norms after the recommendations of the Internal Working Group in 2015.

Categories under priority sector are: (i) Agriculture 18 per cent: within it a target of 8 per cent is prescribed for Small and Marginal Farmers; (ii) Micro, Small and Medium Enterprises 7.5 per cent; (iii) Export Credit: Incremental export credit up to 2 per cent for domestic banks and foreign banks with 20 branches and above; (iv) Education: Loans to individuals for educational purposes including vocational courses up to ₹ 10 lakh; (v) Housing: Loans to individuals up to ₹ 28 lakh in metropolitan centres and loans up to ₹ 20 lakh in other centres; (vi) Social Infrastructure: Bank loans up to a limit of ₹ 5 crore per borrower for building social infrastructure for activities namely schools, health care facilities, drinking water facilities and sanitation facilities; (vii) Renewable Energy: Bank loans up to a limit of ₹ 15 crore to borrowers including for public utilities viz. street lighting systems, and remote village electrification and (viii) Others: Self-Help Groups (SHGs), Joint Liability Groups (JLGs), etc.

## CREDIT CONTROL BY RBI

RBI has power to control the volume of credit created by banks. The RBI through its various quantitative and qualitative techniques regulates total supply of money and bank credit in the interest of economy. The RBI pumps in money during busy season and withdraws money during slack season.

1. **Quantitative Credit Control:** The Monetary Policy of the RBI is not merely one of credit restriction, but it has also the duty to see that legitimate credit requirements are met, and at the same time, credit is not used for unproductive and speculative purposes.

   ***Quantitative Credit Control Tools:*** In India, the legal framework of RBI's control over the credit structure has been provided. Under the Reserve Bank of India Act, 1934, and the Banking Regulation Act, 1949, quantitative credit controls are used to maintain proper quantity of credit of money supply in market.

   Some of the important general credit control methods are as follows:

   (i) **Bank Rate Policy:** Bank rate is the rate at which the Central bank lends money to the commercial banks for their liquidity requirements. Bank rate is also called discount rate. In other words, bank rate is the rate at which the Central Bank rediscounts eligible papers (like approved securities, bills of exchange, commercial papers, etc.) held by commercial banks.

   (ii) **Cash Reserve Ratio (CRR):** The CRR is an effective instrument of credit control. Under the RBl Act, 1934, every commercial bank has to keep certain minimum cash reserves with RBI.

A high CRR reduces the cash for lending, and a low CRR increases the cash for lending.

(iii) **Statutory Liquidity Ratio (SLR):** Under the SLR, the government has imposed an obligation on the banks to maintain a certain ratio to its total deposits with RBI in the form of liquid assets like cash, gold and other securities.

(iv) **Open Market Operations:** It refers to the buying and selling of government securities in open market in order to expand or contract the amount of money in the banking system. This technique is superior to the bank rate policy.

Purchases inject money into the banking system while sale of securities do the opposite. This policy aims at preventing unrestricted increase in liquidity.

(v) **Repo and Reverse Repo Rates:** In determining interest rate trends, the repo and reverse repo rates are becoming important. Repo means Sale and Repurchase Agreement. Repo is a swap deal involving the immediate Sale of Securities and simultaneous purchase of those securities at a future date, at a predetermined price. Repo rate helps commercial banks to acquire funds from the RBI by selling securities and also agreeing to repurchase at a later date.

A reverse repo is the mirror image of a repo. In a reverse repo, securities are acquired with a simultaneous commitment to resell.

Hence, whether a transaction is a repo or a reverse repo is determined only in terms of who initiated the first leg of the transaction.

When the reverse repurchase transaction matures, the counterparty returns the security to the entity concerned and receives its cash along with a profit spread.

(vi) **Long Term RePO:** It aimed at promoting enhanced lending and cutting the cost of short-term funds for the banks. In February 2020, the RBI announced to offer Long Term Repo Operation (LTRO) of ₹ 1.50 lakh crores at a fixed rate (i.e. at the Repo rate). The tenure of the LTRO will be from one to three years. This was aimed at ensuring permanent and deeper liquidity in the financial system together with enhancing lending by cutting cost of funds for the banks.

2. **Qualitative Credit Control:** Under the selective or qualitative credit control, credit is provided to selected borrowers for selected purpose, depending upon the use to which the control try to regulate the quality of credit – the direction towards the credit flows.

The selective controls are as follows:

(i) **Ceiling on Credit:** The ceiling on level of credit restricts the lending capacity of a bank to grant advances against certain controlled securities.

(ii) **Margin Requirements:** A loan is sanctioned against the Collateral Security. Margin means that proportion of the value of security against which loan is not given. Margin against a particular security is reduced or increased in order to encourage or to discourage the flow of credit to a particular sector. It varies from 20 to 80 per cent. For agricultural commodities, it is as high as 75 per cent. Higher the margin lesser will be the loan sanctioned.

(iii) **Discriminatory Interest Rate (DIR):** Through DIR, the RBI makes credit flow to certain priority or weaker sectors by charging concessional rates of interest. RBI issues supplementary instructions regarding granting of additional credit against sensitive commodities, issue of guarantees, making advances, etc..

(iv) **Directives:** The RBI issues directives to banks regarding advances. Directives are regarding the purpose for which loans may or may not be given.

(v) **Direct Action:** It is too severe and is therefore rarely followed. It may involve refusal by the RBI to rediscount bills or cancellation of license, if the bank has failed to comply with the directives of RBI.

(vi) **Moral Suasion:** Under the moral suasion, the RBI issues periodical letters to the bank to exercise control over credit in general or advances against particular commodities. Periodic discussions are held with authorities of commercial banks in this respect.

## RBI'S MONETARY POLICY

The main objective of monetary policy in India is 'growth with stability'. Monetary Management regulates availability, cost and use of money and credit. It also brings institutional changes in the financial sector of the economy.

The main objectives of monetary policy are: growth with stability; regulation, supervision and development of financial stability; promoting priority sector; generation of employment; external stability; encouraging savings and investments; redistribution of income and wealth and regulation of NBFIs.

Report of the Urjit R. Patel Committee to revise and strengthen the Monetary Policy Framework.

Policy Framework headed by **Urjit R. Patel**, Deputy Governor of the Reserve Bank of India, was appointed to recommend what needs to be done to revise and strengthen the current monetary policy framework with a view to, inter alia, making it transparent and predictable. The committee presented its report in January 2014.

The recommendations of the Committee are as follows:

- Inflation should be the nominal anchor for the monetary policy framework.
- The RBI should adopt the new CPI (combined) as the measure of the nominal anchor for policy communication. The nominal anchor or the target for inflation should be set at 4 per cent with a band of (+/− 2) per cent around it (a) in view of the vulnerability of the Indian economy to supply/external shocks and the relatively large weight of food in the CPI and (b) the need to avoid a deflation bias in the conduct of monetary policy.
- Consistent with the Fiscal Responsibility and Budget Management (Amendment) Rules, 2013, the Central Government needs to ensure that its fiscal deficit as a ratio to GDP is brought down to 3 per cent by 2016–17.
- Monetary policy decision-making should be vested in a Monetary Policy Committee (MPC). The Governor of the RBI will be the Chairman of the MPC.
- The MPC will be accountable for failure to establish and achieve the nominal anchor.
- Provision of liquidity by the RBI at the overnight repo rate will, however, be restricted to a specified ratio of bank-wise net demand and time liabilities (NDTL), that is consistent with the objective of price stability.
- To support the operating framework, some new instruments be added to the

toolkit of monetary policy. Firstly, a (low) remunerated standing deposit facility may be introduced.

Secondly, term repos of longer tenor may also be conducted. Thirdly, dependence on market stabilization scheme (MSS) and cash management bills (CMBs) may be phased out, consistent with Government debt and cash management being taken over by the Government's Debt Management Office (DMO).

- SLR should be reduced to a level in consonance with the requirements of liquidity coverage ratio (LCR) prescribed under the Basel III framework.
- OMOs have to be detached from fiscal operations and instead linked solely to liquidity management. OMOs should not be used for managing yields on government securities.

## MONETARY POLICY FRAMEWORK AGREEMENT

Accepting the Urjit R. Patel committee recommendation, the Government of India and the RBI signed a Monetary Policy Framework Agreement on 20 February 2015. The objective of monetary policy framework is to primarily maintain price stability, while keeping in mind the objective of growth. As per the Agreement, RBI would set the policy interest rates and would aim to bring inflation below 6 per cent by January 2016 and within 4 per cent with a band of (+/−) 2 per cent for 2016–17 and all subsequent years.

## COMMERCIAL BANKS IN INDIA

### ❖ Historical Background

The East India Company established the Bank of Bengal/Calcutta (1809), Bank of Bombay (1840) and Bank of Madras (1843). The next bank was Bank of Hindustan, which was established in 1870. Allahabad Bank, which was established in 1865, was for the first time completely run by Indians. Punjab National Bank Ltd. was set up in 1894 with headquarters at Lahore. Between 1906 and 1913, Bank of India, CBI, Bank of Baroda, Canara Bank, Indian Bank and Bank of Mysore were set up. In 1921, all presidency banks were amalgamated to form the Imperial Bank of India which was run by European Shareholders.

## NATIONALIZATION OF BANKS IN INDIA

Nationalization of banks in India was done in two phases. The first phase of nationalization started in 1955 when the erstwhile Imperial Bank of India became the SBI with an Act of parliament. During 1959, seven subsidiaries were nationalized and associated with the SBI one by one. However, all the seven subsidiaries have gradually been merged to the SBI by 1 April 2017.

The second phase of nationalization started in 1969 with the nationalization of 14 major commercial banks with deposits of over ₹ 50 crore. The Lead Bank Scheme was introduced with a view to mobilize deposits on a massive scale throughout the country and also for stepping up lending to weaker sections.

Six more commercial banks with demand and time liabilities greater than ₹ 200 crore were nationalized on 15 April 1980 and became PSBs.

The nationalized banks in India were compelled to focus on rural and agricultural sectors as a part of their social responsibility. Their resources were utilized to empower farmers and agricultural labourers in order to free them from the clutches of moneylenders.

## CLASSIFICATION OF COMMERCIAL BANKS

Commercial Banks refer to both scheduled and non-scheduled commercial banks which are regulated under the Banking Regulation Act, 1949.

1. **Scheduled Commercial Banks** are grouped under following categories:
   (i) SBI and its Associates
   (ii) Nationalized Banks
   (iii) Foreign Banks like ABN Amro Bank, Abu Dhabi Commercial Bank, American Express Banking Corporation, Citibank and Standard Chartered Bank.
   (iv) Regional Rural Banks (RRBs)
   (v) Other Scheduled Commercial Banks like IDBI and Bhartiya Mahila Bank, ING Vysya Bank, Lakshmi Vilas Bank, Dhanlaxmi Bank, City Union Bank and Catholic Syrian Bank.
2. **Non-Scheduled Commercial Banks:** The SBI and its associates and the nationalized banks are known as PSBs, whereas others are known as private sector banks.

## FOREIGN BANKS

**Foreign banks** like Citibank, HSBC, Standard Chartered Bank, etc. are the branches of those banks which are incorporated in foreign countries. Most of them perform essentially the same range of services as local banks, except that their focus in terms of product and customers may be different due to their limited branch network.

They bring in new technology and facilitate in the introduction as well as assimilation of international products into the domestic markets.

They help the local banking industry keep pace with developments in the financial centres abroad.

They also help provide Indian corporations access to foreign capital markets.

In keeping with the general trend towards liberalization, the Government has introduced several measures for widening the scope for foreign banks to enter and operate in India.

## NON-SCHEDULED BANKS

These are those banks of which the total capital is less than ₹ 5 lakhs. These are not included in the second schedule of the Reserve Bank. Reserve Bank has no specific control upon these banks. However, they have to send details of their business to the Reserve Bank every month.

## FUNCTIONS OF COMMERCIAL BANKS

A commercial bank is an institution that operates for profit. The traditional functions of a commercial bank relate the acceptance of deposits from the public and provision of credit to different sectors of the economy.

The various functions of commercial banks are as follows:

1. Accepting or attracting deposits
   (i) Savings deposits
   (ii) Demand deposits
   (iii) Fixed deposits
2. Advancing of loans
   (i) Cash credit
   (ii) Provision of overdraft facilities
   (iii) Discounting bills of exchange
3. **Creation of money or credit:** Credit creation refers to the unique power of the banks to multiply loans and advances. With a little cash in hand, the banks can create additional purchasing power to a considerable degree.
4. Other functions

(i) Transfer of funds
(ii) Agency functions
(iii) General utility services

## CO-OPERATIVE BANKS

Cooperative banks are an important constituent of the Indian financial system. They are the primary financiers of agricultural activities, some small-scale industries and self-employed workers.

## STRUCTURE OF COOPERATIVE BANKING IN INDIA

The structure of cooperative network in India can be divided into two broad segments:

1. Urban Cooperative Banks
2. Rural Cooperatives

## URBAN COOPERATIVES

Urban Cooperatives can be further divided into scheduled and non-scheduled. Both the categories are further divided into multiple states and single state. Majority of these banks fall in the non-scheduled and single-state category. Banking activities of Urban Cooperative Banks are monitored by the RBI. Registration and management activities are managed by the Registrar of Cooperative Societies (RCS). These RCS operate in single state, and Central RCS (CRCS) operate in multiple states.

## RURAL COOPERATIVES

The rural cooperatives are further divided into short-term and long-term structures. The short-term cooperative banks are three-tiered operating in different states. These are as follows:

1. **State Cooperative Banks:** They operate at the apex level in states.
2. **District Central Cooperative Banks:** They operate at the district levels.
3. **Primary Agricultural Credit Societies:** They operate at the village or grass-root level.

Likewise, the long-term structures are further divided:

1. **State Cooperative Agriculture and Rural Development Banks (SCARDBs):** These operate at state level.
2. **Primary Cooperative Agriculture and Rural Development Banks (PCARDBs):** They operate at district/block level.

## LOCAL AREA BANK (LAB)

The establishment of local banks in the private sector was allowed on 1996. These banks were expected to bridge the gaps in credit availability and enhance the institutional credit framework in the rural and semi-urban areas and provide efficient and competitive financial intermediation services in their area of operation. Around 5 LABs were licensed by 2002 under the Banking Regulation Act, 1949, i.e., Krishna Bhima Samrudhi Local Area Bank.

The minimum start-up capital of a LAB was fixed at ₹ 5 crore. The promoters of these banks were required to bring in the entire minimum share capital up front. It was also decided that a family among the promoter group could hold equity not exceeding 40 per cent of the capital.

The area of operation of an LAB was restricted to a maximum of three geographically contiguous districts. The activities of an LAB were to be focused on local customers predominantly in the rural and semi-urban areas so as to bridge the credit gap in these areas.

LABs are required to finance agriculture and allied activities, SSI, agro-industrial activities, trading activities and non-farm sector. Their lending to priority sector is to be at least 40 per cent of the net bank credit.

## REGIONAL RURAL BANK (RRB)

RRBs came into existence on 2 October 1975 on the recommendations of the Narasimham

Working Group. The rural banks had the legislative backing of the RRBs Act, 1976. This act allowed the government to set up banks from time to time wherever it considered necessary.

The RRBs are required to function within a limited area for which they are established. Usually, the functional area of each RRB is confined to a few districts of the state in which they are set up.

The objective is to provide credit to small and marginal farmers, agricultural labourers, artisans and small entrepreneurs so as to develop productive activities in the rural areas. They have been conceived as institutions that combine the features of both the co-operatives and commercial banks.

### ❖ Functions of the RRB

1. Granting of loans and advances to small and marginal farmers and agricultural labourers, whether individually or in groups, and to co-operative societies, agricultural processing societies, co-operative farming societies, primarily for agricultural purposes or for agricultural operations and other related purposes.
2. Granting of loans and advances to artisans, small entrepreneurs and persons of small means engaged in trade, commerce and industry or other productive activities within its area of co-operation.
3. Accepting deposits.

## PAYMENT BANKS

The RBI in August 2015 granted 'in principle' approval for payment bank to six entities.

(i) Airtel Payment Bank
(ii) India Post Payment Bank
(iii) Fino Payment Bank
(iv) Jio Payment Bank
(v) Paytm Payment Bank
(vi) NSDL Payment Bank

Payment banks are new stripped-down type of banks, which are expected to reach customers mainly through their mobile phones rather than traditional bank branches.

### ❖ Objectives

The primary objective of setting up of payments banks is to further financial inclusion by providing (i) small savings accounts and (ii) payments/remittance services to migrant labour workforce, low-income households, small businesses, other unorganised sector entities and other users.

### ❖ Activities

1. Acceptance of demand deposits
2. Issuance of ATM/Debit Cards
3. Payments and remittance services
4. Internet banking
5. Functioning as Business Correspondent (BC) of another

## BANDHAN BANK

Bandhan, the largest micro-finance company in India, from August 2015 began operations as a full-fledged bank (Universal Bank). Bandhan, a Kolkata-headquartered bank will offer complete retail financial solutions, including a variety of savings and loan products. It is the first instance in India of a microfinance entity transforming into a universal bank.

Currently, Bandhan Bank offers seven types of savings account including an account for the differently abled. Unlike major private- and state-run banks, there is no charge for non-maintenance of a minimum average balance.

## IDFC BANK

IDFC Bank in October 2015 went live with a 'soft launch' at 23 locations becoming the 91st scheduled commercial bank in the country.

The bank, which is aiming to be a 'hatke bank' with a stress on technology, has started operations in corporate and wholesale banking, rural banking and treasury verticals as part of the launch.

The biggest advantage of IDFC Bank will be that after demerger of IDFC (holding company, IDFC, FHCL) and IDFC Bank, all assets and liabilities related to banking operations have been transferred to IDFC Bank.

The personal and business banking unit of the bank, focusing on retail, small and medium enterprises (SMEs) and self-employed professionals, started operations in January 2016.

## POST BANK OF INDIA

Indian postal department has started to work as a payment bank called the India Post Payments Bank (IPPB). It was launched on 30 January 2017 in Ranchi and Raipur. With a network of over 1.55 lakh post offices, the department already provides various financial services including a post office savings bank (POSB), postal life insurance, pension payments and money transfer services.

The IPPB aims to give every Indian access to efficient banking services.

It has been incorporated as a Public Sector Bank under the Department of Posts with 100 per cent Government of India equity.

For now, IPPB is offering Savings Account up to a balance of ₹ 1 Lakh, along with digitally enabled payments and remittance services of all kinds between individuals. In due course, IPPB will also provide current accounts and access to third-party financial services like insurance, mutual funds, pension, credit products, FOREX and more.

The three features central to IPPB's operating philosophy are as follows:

1. **Convenience at your fingertips:** It promises to make banking a simple, affordable and convenient experience for Indians across the nation.
2. **Pioneer in inclusive banking**: The IPPB encourages smart saving and investment habits with its easily accessible banking services. Its vision is to extend banking facilities to the remotest corner of the nation. Its services transcend geographical borders. That's how it aims to simplify banking and bring prosperity to every doorstep.
3. **Efficiency of banking network**: IPPB provides the most effective, accessible and readily available banking network across the nation. IPPB will soon offer banking services through digital channels, like mobile, UPI, debit cards, which can be used at automated teller machines (ATMs), PoS and mobile-PoS.

## SMALL BANKS

The RBI in July 2014 paved the way for niche banking by issuing draft guidelines for setting up payment banks and small banks (niche banks) in the private sector.

Resident individuals/professionals with 10 years of experience in banking and finance, companies and societies are eligible as promoters to set up small banks. Existing Non-Banking Finance Companies (NBFCs), Micro Finance Institutions (MFIs) and LABs can also opt for conversion into small banks after complying with all legal and regulatory requirements from various authorities if they conform to these guidelines.

Small banks has been allowed taking into account that small local banks can play an important role in the supply of credit to micro and small enterprises, agriculture and banking services in unbanked and under-banked regions in the country. The minimum paid up voting equity capital for small banks is ₹ 100 crore.

The small banks are being registered as a public limited company under the Companies Act, 2013. It has been licensed under the Banking Regulation Act, 1949, and governed by the provisions of the Banking Regulation Act, 1949, Reserve Bank of India Act, 1934, Foreign Exchange Management Act, 1999, Payment and Settlement Systems Act, 2007, Credit

Information Companies (Regulation) Act, 2005 and other relevant statutes.

The objectives of setting up of small banks will be for furthering financial inclusion by (i) provision of savings vehicles to underserved and unserved sections of the population and (ii) supply of credit to small business units, small farmers, micro and small industries, and other unorganized sector entities, in their limited areas of operations, through high technology low-cost operations.

The area of operations of the small bank will normally be restricted to contiguous districts in a homogenous cluster of States/ Union Territories so that the bank has the local feel and culture.

In the initial five years, the small bank shall further the objectives for which it is set up. Therefore, the small bank shall primarily undertake basic banking activities of acceptance of deposits and lending to small farmers, small businesses, micro and small industries and unorganized sector entities. It can also undertake other simple financial services activities with the prior approval of the RBI. It cannot set up subsidiaries to undertake non-banking financial services activities.

## MOBILE BANKING

Mobile banking is a service provided by a bank or other financial institution that allows its customers to conduct a range of financial transactions remotely using a mobile device such as a mobile phone or tablet, and using software, usually called an app, provided by the financial institution for the purpose. Mobile banking is usually available on a 24-hour basis. Some financial institutions have restrictions on which accounts may be accessed through mobile banking, as well as a limit on the amount that can be transacted.

Mobile banking gives you the privilege of anytime and anywhere banking.

The service provided by bank is free of charge, there is no limit for number of times you can access your account. Various banking services provided include account balance inquiry, credit/debit alerts, bill payment alerts, transaction history, fund transfer facilities, minimum balance alerts, etc. can be accessed from mobile.

The app comes with advanced encryption technologies making it safe and secure as internet banking.

However, to make maximum benefit of mobile banking one should have smart phone. As phishing exist for internet banking users, there is 'smishing' for mobile banking users.

## MICRO-ATMS

Micro-ATMs are biometric authentication enabled hand-held device. In order to make the ATMs viable at rural/semi-urban centres, low-cost Micro-ATMs would be deployed at each of the Bank Mitra location. This enables a person for instantly deposit or withdraw funds regardless of the bank associated with a particular Bank Mitra/Business Correspondent.

This device will be based on a mobile phone connection and would be made available to every Bank Mitra/Business Correspondent. Customers would have to get their identity authenticated and withdraw or put money into their bank accounts. The basic transaction types to be supported by micro ATM are deposit, withdrawal, fund transfer and balance enquiry. Micro-ATM offers one of the most promising options for providing financial services to the unbanked population.

Micro-ATMs would have various options of authentication like biometric, PIN based and so on. In addition, it would also be used as mobile ATMs tenable transactions near the door step of the customers. The Micro-ATMs offer an online interoperable, low-cost payments platform to everyone in the country.

## HYBRID CARDS

Hybrid cards which are also known as the smart cards can also be utilized as a technique for last mile payments. They can be used with ATMs as well as with the point of transaction terminals (POT). This assists the rural people to conveniently upgrade to normal banking services when they move to the urban areas. Resultantly the banks get the chance to retain these customers even in the extremely competitive markets.

## MOBILE VANS

Banks can also look up for utilizing mobile vans to reinforce their brands in the rural areas. The vans could be fitted with a personal computer and Very Small Aperture Terminal (VSAT) connectivity to the core server, attached to a base branch. These mobile vans are a good option as they can effectively act as mini mobile bank branches, might also prove to be of great help in implementing the bank's marketing, promotional and corporate social responsibility strategies.

## WHITE LABEL ATMS

In its attempt to hasten financial inclusion across the country, the RBI in 2011 declared to allow all non-banking entities to set up and operate their own ATMs known as White Label ATMs. White label ATMs are those ATMs that are being set up by non-bank entities. However, any non-bank entity intending to set up WLAs should have a minimum net worth of 100 crore rupees. In White Label ATM (WLA) scenario, logo displayed on ATM machine and in ATM premises pertain to WLA Operator instead of a bank.

Main objective is extending the financial inclusion principal even to the Tier III to VI cities.

The extended reach of ATMs will allow beneficiaries of the Pradhan Mantri Jan Dhan Yojana to avail a wide variety of banking services like accessing their accounts for dispensing cash and non-financial services without the need for actually visiting their bank branch.

WLAs may offer many other services to bank customers, such as account information; mini/short statement; PIN change and request for cheque book. But, cash deposit is not permitted. Regular Bills Payment is not permitted, and purchase of reload vouchers for mobiles is not permitted at WLAs.

## NON-BANKING FINANCIAL COMPANY (NBFC)

A Non-Banking Financial Company (NBFC) is a company registered under the Companies Act, 1956, engaged in the business of loans and advances, acquisition of shares/stocks/bonds/debentures/securities issued by the Government or local authority or other marketable securities of a like nature, leasing, hire-purchase, insurance business, chit business but does not include any institution whose principal business is that of agriculture activity, industrial activity, purchase or sale of any goods (other than securities) or providing any services and sale/purchase/construction of immovable property.

A non-banking institution which is a company and has principal business of receiving deposits under any scheme or arrangement in one lump sum or in instalments by way of contributions, or in any other manner, it is also a non-banking financial company (Residuary Non-banking Company).

NBFCs may get itself rated by any of the six rating agencies namely, CRISIL, CARE, ICRA, FITCH Ratings India Pvt. Ltd, Brickwork Ratings India Pvt. Ltd. and SMERA. 263 NBFCs were registered with the RBI in March, 2019.

### ❖ Difference Between Banks and NBFCs

NBFCs lend and make investments, and hence, their activities are akin to that of banks; however, there are a few differences as given below:

1. NBFC cannot accept demand deposits;
2. NBFCs do not form part of the payment and settlement system and cannot issue cheques drawn on itself;
3. Deposit insurance facility of Deposit Insurance and Credit Guarantee Corporation is not available to depositors of NBFCs, unlike in case of banks.

## ❖ Different Types/Categories of NBFCs

The different types of NBFCs are as follows:

1. **Asset Finance Company (AFC):** An AFC is a company which is a financial institution carrying on as its principal business the financing of physical assets supporting productive/economic activity, such as automobiles, tractors, lathe machines, generator sets, earth moving and material handling equipments, moving on own power and general purpose industrial machines.
2. **Investment Company (IC):** An IC means any company which is a financial institution carrying on as its principal business the acquisition of securities.
3. **Loan Company (LC):** LC means any company which is a financial institution carrying on as its principal business the providing of finance whether by making loans or advances or otherwise for any activity other than its own but does not include an Asset Finance Company.
4. Infrastructure Finance Company (IFC)
5. **Systemically Important Core Investment Company (CIC-ND-SI):** CIC-ND-SI is an NBFC carrying on the business of acquisition of shares and securities.
6. **Infrastructure Debt Fund-Non- Banking Financial Company (IDF-NBFC):** IDF-NBFC is a company registered as NBFC to facilitate the flow of long term debt into infrastructure projects. IDF-NBFC raise resources through issue of Rupee or Dollar denominated bonds of minimum 5-year maturity.
7. Non-Banking Financial Company-Micro Finance Institution (NBFC-MFI)
8. Non-Banking Financial Company-Factors (NBFC-Factors)
9. Mortgage Guarantee Companies (MGC)
10. NBFC-Non-Operative Financial Holding Company (NOFHC)

# DEVELOPMENT BANKS AND FINANCIAL INSTITUTIONS IN INDIA

Apart from commercial banks, the financial institutions in India include development banks, LIC, General Insurance Corporation of India (GIC), SFCs, SIDCs and specialized financial institutions like IFCI Venture Capital Funds Ltd. and IL&FS.

Development bank is essentially a multi-purpose financial institution with a broad development outlook. A development bank may, thus, be defined as a financial institution concerned with providing all types of financial assistance (medium as well as long term) to business units, in the form of loans, underwriting, investment and guarantee operations and promotional activities—economic development in general, industrial development, in particular.

In India, the first development bank called the Industrial Finance Corporation of India (IFCI) was established on 1 July 1948 under the Industrial Finance Corporation Act, 1948.

**As per the RBI, presently (March 2016) there are following Financial Institutions:**

1. Industrial Investment Bank of India Ltd. (IIBIL)
2. National Bank for Agriculture and Rural Development (NABARD)
3. Export-Import Bank of India (Exim Bank)

4. Small Industries Development Bank of India (SIDBI)
5. North Eastern Development Finance Corporation (NEDFC)

Major industrial development banks in India (many of them has been converted into universal banks) are as follows:

(i) **IFCI:** The IFCI was set up to provide term finance to large industries in India.

The main objective of IFCI is too provide medium- and long-term financial assistance to large scale industrial undertakings, particularly when ordinary bank accommodation does not suit the undertaking or finance cannot be profitably raised by the concerned by the issue of shares.

By the early 1990s, it was recognized that there was need for greater flexibility to respond to the changing financial system. It was also felt that IFCI should directly access the capital markets for its funding needs. It is with this objective that the constitution of IFCI was changed in 1993 from a statutory corporation to a company under the Indian Companies Act, 1956. Subsequently, the name of the company was also changed to IFCI Limited with effect from October 1999.

(ii) **Industrial Development Bank of India (IDBI):** The IDBI was established on 1 July 1964 under an Act of Parliament as a wholly owned subsidiary of the RBI. The main objective was to promote and finance the development of industries. In 16 February 1976, the ownership of IDBI was transferred to the Government of India, and it was made the principal financial institution for coordinating the activities of institutions engaged in financing, promoting and developing industry in the country. Although the Government shareholding in the Bank came down below 100 per cent following IDBI's public issue in July 1995, the former continues to be the major shareholder.

IDBI continued to serve as a DFI for 40 years till the year 2004 when it was transformed into a Bank.

(iii) **SIDBI:** SIDBI is an independent financial institution aimed to aid the growth and development of micro-, small- and medium-scale enterprises in India. Set up on 2 April 1990 through an Act of parliament, it was incorporated initially as a wholly owned subsidiary of IDBI.

SIDBI has taken the initiative to promote several institutions viz., Credit Guarantee Fund Trust for Micro and Small Enterprises, SIDBI Venture Capital, SME Rating Agency of India Ltd. and India SME Technology Services Ltd., for the benefit of the MSME sector.

Micro Units Development and Refinance Agency (MUDRA) Bank, a new initiative by Government of India to support non-corporate small business, is proposed to initiate it as a unit of SIDBI to benefit from SIDBI's initiatives and expertise.

## ❖ IIBI

The IIBI was a fully government of India-owned financial investment institution. It was established in 1971 by resolution of the Parliament of India. The bank was headquartered at Kolkata.

In 2005, a merger of IIBI, IDBI and IFCI was considered, but IDBI refused and it was decided in 2006–2007 to close the bank. Deloitte Touche was appointed to dispose of IIBI's Non-Performing Assets (NPAs).

However, in a move towards winding up of the IIBI, its board in January 2008 decided to sell the entire loan book at one go.

## LIFE INSURANCE CORPORATION (LIC)

In 1956, 245 Indian and foreign insurers and provident societies are taken over by the central government and nationalized. Life Insurance Corporation (LIC) was formed by an Act of Parliament, viz., LIC Act, 1956, with a capital contribution of ₹ 5 crore from the Government of India.

**Mission**: Ensure and enhance the quality of life of people through financial security by providing products and services of aspired attributes with competitive returns, and by rendering resources for economic development.

**Vision:** A transnationally competitive financial conglomerate of significance to societies and Pride of India.

**Objectives of LIC are as follows:**

1. Spread message and products of life insurance widely and in particular to the rural areas and to the socially and economically backward classes with a view to reaching all insurable persons in the country and providing them adequate financial cover against death at a reasonable cost.
2. Maximize mobilization of people's savings by making insurance-linked savings adequately attractive.
3. Bear in mind, in the investment of funds, the primary obligation to its policyholders, whose money it holds in trust, without losing sight of the interest of the community as a whole; the funds to be deployed to the best advantage of the investors as well as the community as a whole, keeping in view national priorities and obligations of attractive return.
4. Conduct business with utmost economy and with the full realization that the moneys belong to the policyholders.
5. Act as trustees of the insured public in their individual and collective capacities.
6. Meet the various life insurance needs of the community that would arise in the changing social and economic environment.

### ❖ General Insurance Corporation (GIC)

In 1972, the General Insurance Business (Nationalization) Act, 1972, (GIBNA) nationalized the general insurance business in India with effect from 1 January 1973.

The Government of India (GOI), through nationalization, took over the shares of 55 Indian insurance companies and the undertakings of 52 insurers carrying on general insurance business.

GIC was formed for the purpose of superintending, controlling and carrying on the business of general insurance.

**Vision:** To be a leading global reinsurance and risk solution provider.

**Mission**

- To achieve our vision by building long-term mutually beneficial relationship with business partners.
- Practicing fair business ethics and values.
- Applying 'state-of-art' technology, processes including enterprise risk management and innovative solutions.
- Developing and retaining highly motivated professional team of employees.
- Enhancing profitability and financial strength befitting the global position.

After a process of mergers among Indian insurance companies, four companies were left as fully owned subsidiary companies of GIC.

1. National Insurance Company Limited
2. The New India Assurance Company Limited
3. The Oriental Insurance Company Limited
4. United India Insurance Company Limited

1. **National Insurance Company Limited:** The National Insurance Company Ltd. was established during 1906, and its

registered office is in Kolkata. After GIBNA was passed in 1972, 11 Indian insurers and 21 international companies were merged into it. The insurer consequently became a part of the GIC, which was wholly owned by the Indian government. National Insurance Company Limited is one of the top general insurers in the public sector of India.

2. **New India Assurance Company Limited:** New India Assurance Co Ltd., today, is a fully government owned multinational general insurance company operating in 28 countries and headquartered at Mumbai, India. Founded by Sir Dorabji Tata in 1919, we have been market leaders in India in non-life business for more than 40 years.

   **Vision:** To be the most respected, trusted and preferred non-life Insurer in the Global markets we operate.

   **Mission**

   - To develop General Insurance Business in the best interest of the community.
   - To provide financial security to individuals, trade, commerce and all other segments of the society by offering insurance products and services of high quality at affordable cost.

3. **Oriental Insurance Company Limited:** The headquarter of the company is located in New Delhi with 30 regional offices and more than 1800 active branches across the country. The company also has branches in Nepal, Kuwait and Dubai.

4. **United India Insurance Company Limited:** United India Insurance Company Limited was incorporated as a Company on 18 February 1938. After nationalization, United India has grown by leaps and bounds. The Company has variety of insurance products to provide insurance cover from bullock carts to satellites.

## GIC Re

As a sole reinsurer in the domestic reinsurance market, GIC Re provides reinsurance to the direct general insurance companies in the Indian market. GIC Re is a wholly owned company of the Government of India.

As GIC Re is spreading its wings to emerge as an effective reinsurance solutions partner for the Afro-Asian region. It has started leading the reinsurance programmes of several insurance companies in SAARC countries, South East Asia, Middle East and Africa.

## SOME SPECIALIZED FINANCIAL INSTITUTIONS

1. **IFCI Venture Capital Funds Ltd:** IFCI Venture Capital Funds Ltd. (IFCI Venture) was established as a Risk Capital Foundation (RCF) in 1975 by the IFCI Ltd., a society to provide financial assistance to first generation professionals and technocrat entrepreneurs for setting up own ventures through soft loans, under the Risk Capital Scheme.
2. **Technology Development and Information Company of India (TDICI):** TDICI Ltd. is the country's largest and oldest venture capital fund in India and co-promoted by Industrial Credit and Investment Corporation of India (ICICI) and Unit Trust of India.
3. **Infrastructure Leasing & Financial Services Limited (IL & FS):** It is one of the India's leading infrastructure development and finance companies. IL&FS was promoted by the CBI, Housing Development Finance Corporation Limited (HDFC) and Unit Trust of India (UTI).

IL&FS has a distinct mandate–catalysing the development of infrastructure in the country. The organization has focused on the commercialization and development of infrastructure projects and creation of value added financial services.

IL & FS Financial Service Limited (IFIN) is one of India's leading Non-Banking Finance Company providing a wide range of financial and advisory solutions under one umbrella. IFIN is a 100 per cent subsidiary of IL & FS.

4. **HDFC:** HDFC is India›s premier housing finance company and enjoys an impeccable track record in India as well as in international markets. Since its inception in 1977, the Corporation has maintained a consistent and healthy growth in its operations to remain the market leader in mortgages.

   Its outstanding loan portfolio covers well over a million dwelling units. HDFC has developed significant expertise in retail mortgage loans to different market segments and also has a large corporate client base for its housing related credit facilities. With its experience in the financial markets, strong market reputation, large shareholder base and unique consumer franchise, HDFC was ideally positioned to promote a bank in the Indian environment.

## STATE LEVEL INDUSTRIAL FINANCIAL INSTITUTIONS

1. **State Finance Corporations (SFCs):** The SFCs promote small and medium industries of the states. Besides, SFCs are helpful in ensuring balanced regional development, higher investment, more employment generation and broad ownership of industries.

**Functions:**

(i) The SFCs grant loans mainly for acquisition of fixed assets like land, building, plant and machinery.

(ii) The SFCs provide financial assistance to industrial units whose paid-up capital and reserves do not exceed ₹ 3 crore (or such higher limit up to ₹ 30 crore as may be specified by the central government).

(iii) The SFCs underwrite new stocks, shares, debentures, etc. of industrial concerns.

(iv) The SFCs provide guarantee loans raised in the capital market by scheduled banks, industrial concerns and state cooperative banks to be repayable within 20 years.

At present, there are 19 state finance corporations (out of which 17 SFCs were established under SFC Act, 1951).

2. **State Industrial Development Corporations (SIDCs):** The SIDCs/SIICs came on the scene much after the SFCs. The State Industrial Development Corporations have been set up by the State Governments as companies wholly owned by them. At present, 22 such SIDCs are functioning in India.

   SIDCs are not merely financing agencies, but are intended to act as instruments for accelerating the pace of industrialization in the respective states.

   SIDCs also undertake the development of industrial areas, construction of sheds and provision of infrastructural facilities and also the development of new growth centres. They also administer various State Government Incentive Schemes.

The IDBI grants refinance to SIDCs also against the term loans provided by them. SIDCs also borrow by way of bonds and from the Government and accept deposits to augment their resources.

## NORTH EASTERN DEVELOPMENT FINANCE CORPORATION (NEDFC)

The NEDFC is a Public Limited Company registered under the Companies Act, 1956, on 9 August 1995. It is notified as a Public Financial Institution under Section 4A of the said Act and was registered as an NBFC in 2002 with the RBI. The shareholders of the Corporation are IDBI, SBI, LICI, SIDBI, ICICI, IFCI, SUUTI, GIC and its subsidiaries.

NEDFC provides financial assistance to micro, small, medium and large enterprises for setting up industrial, infrastructure and agri-allied projects in the North Eastern Region of India and also microfinance through MFI/NGOs.

## BANKING REFORM

Banking is now a global issue. Reform in the financial sector is a major catalyst in strengthening the fundamentals of the Indian economy. The broad objective of the financial sector reform has thus been to create a viable and efficient banking system. The major banking sector reforms comprises of modifying the policy framework; improving the financial soundness and credibility of banks; creating a competitive environment and strengthening of the institutional framework.

The banking sector reform measures to enhance efficiency and productivity through competition were initiated and sequenced to create an enabling environment for banks to overcome the external constraints which were related to administered structure of interest rates, high levels of pre-emption in the form of reserve requirements and credit allocation to certain sectors.

To match the liberalization, privatization and globalization needs, the Indian banking sector is being reformed since the 1990s.

## NARASIMHAM-I COMMITTEE REPORT (1991)

1. The committee recommended the reduction of the higher proportion of the 'SLR' and the 'CRR'. Both of these ratios were very high at that time.

   SLR was recommended to reduce from 38.5 to 25 per cent and CRR from 15 to 3 to 5 per cent.
2. Phasing out Directed Credit Programme.
3. The determination of the interest rate should be on the grounds of market forces such as the demand for and the supply of fund.
4. Structural reorganizations of the Banking sector:
   - (a) Three to four big banks including SBI should be developed as international banks.
   - (b) Eight to ten banks having nationwide presence should concentrate on the national and universal banking services.
   - (c) Local banks should concentrate on region specific banking.
   - (d) Regarding the RRBs should focus on agriculture and rural financing.
5. The committee recommended the establishment of an Asset Reconstruction Fund (ARF). This fund will take over the proportion of the bad and doubtful debts from the banks and financial institutes. It would help banks to get rid of bad debts.
6. Those days banks were under the dual control of the Reserve Bank of India (RBI) and the Government of India. The committee recommended that the RBI should be the only main agency to regulate banking in India.
7. The PSBs should be free and autonomous.

## NARASIMHAM-II COMMITTEE REPORT (1998)

The Narasimham-II Committee was tasked with the progress review of the implementation of the banking reforms since 1992 with the aim of further strengthening the financial institutions of India.

It focused on issues like size of banks and capital adequacy ratio among other things. The report of the Committee was submitted to the Finance Minister in April 1998.

### ❖ Major Recommendations of the 1998 Report

1. **Autonomy in Banking:** Greater autonomy was proposed for the PSBs in order for them to function with equivalent professionalism as their international counterparts. For this the panel recommended that recruitment procedures, training and remuneration policies of PSBs be brought in line with the best-market-practices of professional bank management.

   The Government of India equity in nationalized banks be reduced to 33 per cent for increased autonomy.
2. Reform in the role of RBI
3. **Stronger banking structure:** The Committee recommended for merger of large Indian banks to make them strong enough for supporting international trade. It recommended a 3-tier banking structure in India through establishment of 3 large banks with international presence, 8 to 10 national banks and a large number of regional and local banks.
4. **NPAs:** The Committee recommended creation of ARFs or asset reconstruction companies to take over the bad debts of banks, allowing them to start on a clean slate.

   The committee's recommendations led to introduction of a new legislation called Securitization and Reconstruction of Financial Assets and Enforcement of Security Interest Act (SARFAESI), 2002.
5. **Capital adequacy and tightening of provisioning norms:** The committee targeted raising the capital adequacy ratio to 9 per cent by 2000 and 10 per cent by 2002 and have penal provisions for banks that fail to meet these requirements. For asset classification, the Committee recommended a mandatory 1 per cent in case of standard assets and for the accrual of interest income to be done every 90 days instead of 180 days.
6. **Entry of Foreign Banks:** The foreign banks seeking to set up business in India should have a minimum start-up capital of $25 million as against the existing requirement of $10 million.

## NAYAK COMMITTEE REPORT (2014)

The report of an RBI appointed committee under the Chairmanship of P. J. Nayak that reviewed issues of governance in banks was released on 12 May 2014.

It made the following main recommendations:

1. There is a need to upgrade the quality of board deliberation in PSBs to provide greater strategic focus.
2. The Government needs to move rapidly towards establishing fully empowered boards in PSBs, solely entrusted with the governance and oversight of the management of the banks.
3. The Government should set up a Bank Investment Company (BIC) to hold equity stakes in banks which are presently held by the Government.
4. The RBI should designate a specific category of investors in banks as Authorised Bank Investors (ABIs), defined to include all funds with diversified investors, which are discretionally

managed by fund managers and are deemed to be fit and proper.

## INDRADHANUSH

Considering all the above issues alongside recommendation of multiple committees, important being Narsimhan II (1998) and Nayak (2014) Committees, measures have been taken by the government including the launch of Indradhanush in August 2015 by the Ministry of Finance for revamp of Public Sector Banks (PSBs).

'Indradhanush' stands for seven areas (A to G) mainly, Appointment, Bank Board Bureau, Capitalization, De-stressing PSB, Empowerment, Framework of Accountability and Governance Reforms.

1. **Appointments:** The government decided to separate the post of Chairman and Managing Director by prescribing that in the subsequent vacancies to be filled up the CEO will get the designation of MD & CEO, and there would be another person who would be appointed as a Non-Executive Chairman of PSBs.
2. **Bank Board Bureau:** The announcement of the Bank Board Bureau (BBB) was made in Budget 2015–16. The BBB will be a body of eminent professionals and officials, which will replace the Appointments Board for appointment of Whole-time Directors as well as Non-Executive Chairman of PSBs.

   The Government has set up an autonomous BBB to recommend for selection of heads. The BBB has started functioning from 1 April 2016. The Bureau will have three ex-officio members and three expert members in addition to Chairman. Former Comptroller and Auditor General (CAG) Vinod Rai has been appointed as the first Chairman of Banks Board Bureau (BBB).
3. **Capitalization:** The Government of India wants to adequately capitalize all the banks to keep a safe buffer over and above the minimum norms of Basel III.
4. **(i) De-stressing PSBs:** The infrastructure sector and core sector have been the major recipient of PSBs' funding during the past decades. But due to several factors, projects are increasingly stalled/stressed thus leading to NPA burden on banks.

   **(ii) Strengthening Risk Control measures and NPA Disclosures:** Besides the recovery efforts under the DRT & SARFASI mechanism, the following additional steps have been taken to address the issue of NPAs:

   (a) Creation of a Central Repository of Information on Large Credits (CRILC) by the RBI to collect, store and disseminate credit data to banks on credit exposures of ₹ 5 crore and above.

   (b) Formation of Joint Lenders Forum (JLF), Corrective Action Plan (CAP) and sale of assets.

   (c) Flexible Structuring of Loan Term Project Loans to Infrastructure and Core Industries.

   (d) Wilful Default/Non-Cooperative Borrowers.

   (e) Asset Reconstruction Companies.

   (f) **Establishment of six New DRTs:** Government has decided to establish six new Debt Recovery Tribunals (DRT) (at Chandigarh, Bengaluru, Ernakulum, Dehradun, Siliguri, Hyderabad) to speed up the recovery of bad loans of the banking sector.
5. **Empowerment:** There will be no interference from the Government and Banks are encouraged to take their

decision independently keeping the commercial interest of the organization in mind. A cleaner distinction between interference and intervention has been made.

6. **Framework of Accountability:** A new framework of Key Performance Indicators (KPIs) to be measured for performance of PSBs is being announced.
7. **Governance Reforms:** The process of governance reforms started with 'Gyan Sangam' – a conclave of PSBs and FIs organized at the beginning of 2015 in Pune. The decision to set up a Bank Board Bureau that was subsequently announced in the Budget Speech.

## INDRADHANUSH 2.0

Government of India has come out with 'Indradhanush 2.0', a comprehensive plan for recapitalization of public sector lenders, with a view to make sure they remain solvent and fully comply with the global capital adequacy norms, Basel III.

'Indradhanush 2.0' has been finalized after completion of the Asset Quality Review (AQR) by the Reserve Bank.

Under Indradhanush roadmap announced in 2015, the government had announced to infuse ₹ 70,000 crore in state-run banks over four years while they will have to raise a further ₹ 1.1 lakh crore from the markets to meet their capital requirement in line with global risk norms, known as Basel III.

In line with the plan, public sector banks were given ₹ 25,000 crore in 2015–16, and similar amount has been earmarked for the current fiscal. Besides, ₹ 10,000 crore each would be infused in 2017–19.

## BASEL BANKING NORMS

Basel is a city in Switzerland which is also the headquarter of Bureau of International Settlement (BIS). BIS fosters co-operation among central banks with a common goal of financial stability and common standards of banking regulations. Currently, there are 27 member nations in the committee. Basel guidelines refer to broad supervisory standards formulated by this group of central banks, called the Basel Committee on Banking Supervision (BCBS). Three sets of guidelines have been issued called Basel I, Basel II and Basel III.

### ❖ Basel I

In 1988, BCBS introduced capital measurement system Basel I. It focused almost entirely on credit risk. It defined capital and structure of risk weights for banks. The minimum capital requirement was fixed at 8 per cent of the Risk-Weighted Assets (RWA). The RWA means amount of funds that a bank must hold on hand. This amount of capital is determined by taking a percentage of the assets held at that institution and then weighting it by risk.

### ❖ Basel II

In 2004, Basel II guidelines were published by BCBS, which were considered to be the refined and reformed versions of Basel I accord.

The guidelines were based on three parameters. Banks should maintain a minimum capital adequacy requirement of 8 per cent of risk assets, banks were needed to develop and use better risk management techniques in monitoring and managing all the three types of risks that is credit and increased disclosure requirements.

Banks need to mandatorily disclose their risk exposure, etc. to the central bank. Basel II norms in India and overseas are yet to be fully implemented.

Its goal is to better align the required regulatory capital with actual bank risk.

Basel II has three pillars: minimum capital, supervisor review and market discipline.

Minimum capital is the technical, quantitative heart of the accord. Banks must hold capital against 8 per cent of their assets, after adjusting their assets for risk.

Supervisor review is the process whereby national regulators ensure their home country banks are following the rules. If minimum capital is the rulebook, the second pillar is the referee system.

The accord recognizes three big risk buckets: credit risk, market risk and operational risk. In other words, a bank must hold capital against all three types of risks. A charge for market risk was introduced in 1998.

## ❖ Basel III

In 2010, Basel III guidelines were released. These guidelines were introduced in response to the financial crisis of 2008.

The guidelines aim to promote a more resilient banking system by focusing on four vital banking parameters viz., capital, leverage, funding and liquidity.

Basel III is the global regulatory standard on bank capital adequacy, stress testing and market liquidity risk. (Basel I and Basel II are the earlier versions of the same, but were less stringent.)

The basic structure of Basel III remains unchanged with three mutually reinforcing pillars.

1. **Minimum Regulatory Capital Requirements based on the RWAs:** Maintaining capital calculated through credit, market and operational risk areas.
2. **Supervisory Review Process:** Regulating tools and frameworks for dealing with peripheral risks that banks face.
3. **Market Discipline:** Increasing the disclosures that banks must provide to increase the transparency of banks.

### Features of Basel III

1. Better Capital Quality
2. **Capital Conservation Buffer:** Banks will be required to hold a capital conservation buffer of 2.5 per cent.
3. **Countercyclical Buffer:** It has been introduced with the objective to increase capital requirements in good times and decrease the same in bad times. The buffer will range from 0 per cent to 2.5 per cent, consisting of common equity or other fully loss-absorbing capital.
4. **Minimum Common Equity and Tier 1 Capital Requirements:** The minimum requirement for common equity, the highest form of loss-absorbing capital, has been raised under Basel III from 2 per cent to 4.5 per cent of total RWAs.

   The overall Tier 1 capital requirement, consisting of not only common equity but also other qualifying financial instruments, will also increase from the current minimum of 4 to 6 per cent. Although the minimum total capital requirement will remain at the current 8 per cent level, yet the required total capital will increase to 10.5 per cent when combined with the conservation buffer.
5. **Leverage Ratio:** A leverage ratio is the relative amount of capital to total assets (not risk-weighted). This aims to put a cap on swelling of leverage in the banking sector on a global basis. Three per cent leverage ratio of Tier 1 will be tested before a mandatory leverage ratio is introduced in January 2018.

## FINANCIAL SECTOR LEGISLATIVE REFORMS COMMISSION

The Financial Sector Legislative Reforms Commission (FSLRC) was constituted by the Government of India on 11 March 2011 headed by B. N. Srikrishna to rewrite and harmonize financial sector legislations, rules and regulations. The FSLRC gave its recommendations on 22 March 2013.

## ❖ Draft Indian Financial Code

The draft Code addresses nine components, which the FSLRC believes any financial legal framework should address:

1. **Consumer Protection:** Regulators should ensure that financial firms are doing enough for consumer protection. The draft Code establishes certain basic rights for all financial consumers and creates a single unified Financial Redressal Agency (FRA) to serve any aggrieved consumer across sectors. In addition, the FSLRC considers competition an important aspect of consumer protection and envisages a detailed mechanism for cooperation between regulators and the Competition Commission.
2. **Micro-prudential Regulation:** Regulators should monitor and reduce the failure probability of a financial firm. The draft Code specifies five powers for micro-prudential regulation: regulation of entry, regulation of risk-taking, regulation of loss absorption, regulation of governance and management and monitoring/supervision.
3. **Resolution:** In cases of financial failure, firms should be swiftly and sufficiently wound up with the interests of small customers. A unified resolution corporation (RC), dealing with various financial firms, should be created to intervene when a firm is close to failure. The RC would charge a fee to all firms based on the probability of failure.
4. **Capital Controls:** While the FSLRC does not hold a view on the sequencing and timing of capital account liberalization, any capital controls should be implemented on sound footing with regards to public administration and law. The FSLRC sees the Ministry of Finance creating the 'rules' for inbound capital flows, and the RBI creating the 'regulations' for outbound capital flows. All capital controls would be implemented by the RBI.
5. **Systemic Risk:** Regulators should undertake interventions to reduce the systemic risk for the entire financial system. The FSLRC envisages establishing the Financial Stability and Development Council (FSDC) as a statutory agency taking a leadership role in minimizing systemic risk.
6. **Development and Redistribution:** Developing market infrastructure and process would be the responsibility of the regulator while redistribution policies would be under the purview of the Ministry of Finance.
7. **Monetary policy:** The law should establish accountability mechanisms for monetary policy. The Ministry of Finance would define a quantitative target that can be monitored, while the RBI will be empowered with various tools to pursue this target. An executive MPC would be established to decide on how to exercise the RBI's powers.
8. **Public debt management:** The draft Code establishes a specialised framework for public debt management with a strategy for long-run low-cost financing. The FSLRC proposes a single agency to manage government debt.
9. **Contracts, trading and market abuse:** The draft Code establishes the legal foundations for contracts, property and securities markets.

The FSLRC recommended a seven agency structure for the financial sector: the RBI, Unified Financial Agency (UFA), Financial Sector Appellate Tribunal (FSAT), RC, FRA, FSDC and PDMA.

## SARFAESI ACT, 2002

The SARFAESI Act, 2002, allows banks and financial institutions to auction properties (residential and commercial) when borrowers fail to repay their loans. It enables banks to reduce their NPAs by adopting measures for recovery or reconstruction.

The Act gives powers of 'seize' to banks. Banks can give a notice in writing to the defaulting borrower requiring it to discharge its liabilities within 60 days. If the borrower fails to comply with the notice, the Bank may take recourse to one or more of the following measures:

(i) Take possession of the security for the loan;

(ii) Sale or lease or assign the right over the security and

(iii) Manage the same or appoint any person to manage the same.

The SARFAESI Act also provides for the establishment of asset reconstruction companies regulated by the RBI to acquire assets from banks and financial institutions.

The Act provides for sale of financial assets by banks and financial institutions to asset reconstruction companies. The RBI has issued guidelines to banks on the process to be followed for sales of financial assets to asset reconstruction companies.

## ARBITRATION AND CONCILIATION (AMENDMENT) ACT, 2015

The Arbitration and Conciliation (Amendment) Act, 2015, (Amendment Act) was notified in the Official Gazette on 1 January 2016 for making arbitration a preferred mode for settlement of commercial disputes by making it more user-friendly and cost effective and leading to expeditious disposal of cases.

The Act facilitates quick enforcement of contracts, easy recovery of monetary claims, reduce the pendency of cases in courts and hasten the process of dispute resolution through arbitration so as to encourage foreign investment by projecting India as an investor-friendly country having a sound legal framework and ease doing business in India.

## INSOLVENCY AND BANKRUPTCY CODE, 2016

The Insolvency and Bankruptcy Code (IBC), 2016, was passed by the Parliament on 11 May 2016, received Presidential assent on 28 May 2016 and was notified in the official gazette on the same day. The code seeks to ensure time-bound settlement of insolvency, faster turnaround of businesses and create a unified database of serial defaulters.

The Code creates time-bound processes for insolvency resolution of companies and individuals. These processes will be completed within 180 days. If insolvency cannot be resolved, the assets of the borrowers may be sold to repay creditors.

The resolution processes will be conducted by licensed insolvency professionals (IPs). These IPs will be members of insolvency professional agencies (IPAs). IPAs will also furnish performance bonds equal to the assets of a company under insolvency resolution.

Information utilities (IUs) will be established to collect, collate and disseminate financial information to facilitate insolvency resolution.

The National Company Law Tribunal (NCLT) will adjudicate insolvency resolution for companies. The DRT will adjudicate insolvency resolution for individuals.

The Insolvency and Bankruptcy Board of India will be set up to regulate functioning of IPs, IPAs and IUs.

## THE INSOLVENCY AND BANKRUPTCY CODE (AMENDMENT) BILL, 2021

- The Insolvency and Bankruptcy Code (Amendment) Bill, 2021 was introduced in Lok Sabha on July 26, 2021. It amends the Insolvency and Bankruptcy Code, 2016. Insolvency is a situation where individuals or companies are unable to repay their outstanding debt. The Bill replaces the Insolvency and Bankruptcy Code (Amendment) Ordinance, 2021, which was promulgated on April 4, 2021.
- The Code provides a time-bound process for resolving the insolvency of corporate debtors (within 330 days) called the corporate insolvency resolution process (CIRP). The debtor himself or its creditors may apply for initiation of CIRP in the event of a default of at least one lakh rupees. Under CIRP, a committee of creditors is constituted to decide on the insolvency resolution. The committee may consider a resolution plan which typically provides for the payoff of debt by merger, acquisition, or restructuring of the company. If a resolution plan is not approved by the committee of creditors within the specified time, the company is liquidated. During CIRP, the affairs of the company are managed by the resolution professional (RP), who is appointed to conduct CIRP.

### ❖ Provisions of the Bill

- It specifies a minimum threshold of not more than Rs 1 crore for initiating the pre-packaged insolvency resolution process
- It provides for disposal of simultaneous applications for initiation of the insolvency resolution process and pre-packaged insolvency resolution process, pending against the same corporate debtor.
- Penalty for fraudulent or malicious initiation of pre-packaged insolvency resolution process or with intent to defraud persons, and for fraudulent management of the corporate debtor during the process.
- **Pre-packaged insolvency resolution:** The Bill introduces an alternate insolvency resolution process for micro, small, and medium enterprises (MSMEs), called the pre-packaged insolvency resolution process (PIRP). Unlike CIRP, PIRP may be initiated only by debtors. The debtor should have a base resolution plan in place. During PIRP, the management of the company will remain with the debtor.
- Minimum default amount: Application for initiating PIRP may be filed in the event of a default of at least one lakh rupees. The central government may increase the threshold of minimum default up to one crore rupees through a notification.
- Debtors eligible for PIRP: PIRP may be initiated in the event of a default by a corporate debtor classified as an MSME under the MSME Development Act, 2006. Currently, under the 2006 Act, an enterprise with an annual turnover of up to Rs 250 crore, and investment in plant and machinery or equipment up to Rs 50 crore, is classified as an MSME. For initiating PIRP, the corporate debtor himself must apply to the National Company Law Tribunal (NCLT). The authority must approve or reject the application for PIRP within 14 days of its receipt.
- **Approval of financial creditors:** For applying for PIRP, the debtor must obtain approval of at least 66% of its financial creditors (in value of debt due to creditors) who are not related parties of the debtor. Before seeking such approval, the debtor must provide creditors with a base resolution plan. The debtor must also propose the name of RP along with the application for PIRP. The proposed RP must be approved by at least 66% of the financial creditors.

- **Proceedings under PIRP:** The debtor will submit the base resolution plan to the RP within two days of the commencement of the PIRP. A committee of creditors will be constituted within seven days of the PIRP commencement date, which will consider the base resolution plan. The committee may provide the debtor with an opportunity to revise the plan. The RP may also invite resolution plans from other persons. Alternative resolution plans may be invited if the base plan: (i) is not approved by the committee, or (ii) is unable to pay the debt of operational creditors (claims related to the provision of goods and services).
- A resolution plan must be approved by the committee (with at least 66% of the voting shares) within 90 days from the commencement date of PIRP. The resolution plan approved by the committee will be examined by the NCLT. If no resolution plan is approved by the committee, the RP may apply for the termination of PIRP. The authority must either approve the plan or order termination of PIRP within 30 days of receipt. Termination of PIRP will result in the liquidation of the corporate debtor.
- **Moratorium:** During PIRP, the debtor will be provided with a moratorium under which certain actions against the debtor will be prohibited. These include filing or continuation of suits, execution of court orders, or recovery of property.
- **Management of debtor during PIRP:** During PIRP, the board of directors or partners of the debtor will continue to manage the affairs of the debtor. However, the management of the debtor may be vested with the RP if there has been fraudulent conduct or gross mismanagement.
- **Initiation of CIRP:** At any time from the PIRP commencement date but before the approval of the resolution plan, the committee of creditors may decide (with at least 66% of the voting shares) to terminate PIRP and instead initiate CIRP.

### What are 'pre-packs?

- A pre-pack is an agreement for the resolution of the debt of a distressed company. It is an agreement between secured creditors and investors instead of a public bidding process.
- The scheme allows only the debtor to trigger its own bankruptcy process with the approval of financial creditors.
- In general bankruptcy provisions, the proprietors or major shareholders of a small business lose operational control of the enterprise to lenders.
- In a pre-pack insolvency scheme, the shareholders or proprietors do not lose control over the enterprise.
- The creditors will agree to terms with the promoters or a potential investor, and seek approval of the resolution plan from the NCLT.
- The approval of at least 66 per cent of financial creditors that are unrelated to the corporate debtor would be required before a resolution plan is submitted to the NCLT.
- The NCLTs either accept or reject the application for a pre-pack insolvency proceeding before considering a petition for a CIRP.
- According to analysts, this scheme would yield resolution faster than the corporate insolvency resolution process (CIRP).

## BANKING REGULATION (AMENDMENT) BILL, 2017

- The Banking Regulation (Amendment) Bill, 2020 was introduced in Lok Sabha by the Minister of Finance, Ms. Nirmala Sitharaman, on March 3, 2021. The Bill seeks to amend the Banking Regulation Act, 1949, with regard to cooperative banks. The Act regulates the functioning of banks and provided details on various aspects such as licensing, mangement, and operations of banks.

- **Exclusion:** The Act does not apply to certain cooperative societies. These are: (i) primary agricultural credit societies, (ii) cooperative land mortgag banks, and (iii) any other cooperative societies (except those specified in the Act.)
- The Bill amends this provision to state that the Act will not apply to: (i) primary agricultural credit societies, and (ii) cooperative societies whose principal business is long term financing for agricultural development. Further, these societies must not: (i) use the words 'bank', 'banker' or 'banking' in their name or in connection with their business, and (ii) act as an entity that clears cheques.
- **Issuance of shares and securities by cooperative banks:** The bill provides that a cooperative bank may issue equity shares, preference shares, or special shares on face value or at a premium to its members or to its members or to any other person residing within its area of operation. Further, it may issue unsecure debentures or bonds or similar securities with maturity of ten or more years to such persons. Such issuance will be subject to the prior approval of the Reserve Bank of India (RBI), and any other conditions as may be specified by RBI.
- The Bill states that no person will be entitled to demand payment towards surrender of shares issued to him by a co-operative bank. Futher a co-operative bank cannot withdraw or reduce its share capital, except as specified by the RBI.
- **Supersession of Board of Directors:** The Act states that RBI may supersede that Board of Directors of a multi-state cooperative bank for up to five years under certain conditions. These conditions include cases where it is in the public interest for RBI to supersede the Board, and to protect depositors.
- The bill adds that in case of a co-operative bank registered with the Registrar of Co-operative Societies of a state, the RBI will Superseds the Board, of Directors after consultation with the concerned state government, and withing such period as specified by it.
- **Power to exempt cooperative banks:** The Bill states that RBI may exempt a cooperative bank or a class of cooperative banks from certain provisions of the Act through notification. These provisions relate to restrictions of certain types of employment, qualifications of the Board of Directors and, appointment of a chairman. The time period and conditions for the exemption will also be specified by the RBI.
- **Certain provisions omitted:** The Bill seeks to omit certain provisions from the Act. Some of these provisions are listed below:
- The Act restricts cooperative banks from making loans or advances on the security of its own shares. Further, it prohibits the grant of unsecured loans or advances to its directors, and to private companies where the bank's directors or chairman is an interested party. The Act also specifies conditions when unsecured loans or advances may be granted and specifies the manner in which the loans may be reported to RBI. The Bill omits this provision from the Act.
- The Act states that cooperative banks cannot open a new place of business or change the location of the bank outside of the city, town or village in which it is currently located without permission from RBI. The Bill omits this provision.
- The Act requires a scheduled cooperative bank to maintain assets with a value not exceeding 40% of the its total demand and time liabilities, within India. The Bill omits this provision.

author(s). PRS makes every effort to use reliable and comprehensive information, but PRS does not represent that the contents of the report are accurate or complete. PRS is an independent, not-for-profit group. This document has been prepared without regard to the objectives or opinions of those who may receive it.

The Union Finance Minister in July 2017 introduced the Banking Regulation (Amendment) Bill, 2017, in the Lok Sabha. It seeks to amend the Banking Regulation Act, 1949, and replace the Banking Regulation (Amendment) Ordinance, 2017.

It empowers the RBI to resolve the problem of stressed assets. It allows the RBI to initiate insolvency resolution process on specific stressed assets. The RBI will also be empowered to issue directives for resolution and appoint authorities or committees to advise the banking companies on stressed asset resolution. The recovery proceedings will be carried out under the Insolvency and Bankruptcy Code, 2016, that provides for a time-bound process to resolve defaults.

## MARGINAL COST OF FUNDS-BASED LENDING RATE (MCLR)

In April 2016, all banks moved to a new lending rate regime called the MCLR. The new rate regime is likely to improve transmission of rates to the end consumers.

It is the new benchmark lending rate at which banks will now lend to new borrowers. Till 31 March 2016, banks used base rate as the benchmark rate to lend. While the MCLR will be the benchmark rate for new borrowers, for existing borrowers, the base rate regime will continue. The MCLR is closely linked to the actual deposit rates. Banks have to publish at least five MCLR rates (overnight, one-month, three-month, six-month and one-year). Banks are also free to set rates for longer durations, such as two and three years.

The RBI expects the new formula to make floating lending rates more responsive to its policy rate cuts. Ratings agency ICRA believes that the norms will improve policy transmission for new borrowings.

## NON-PERFORMING ASSET (NPA)

According to the RBI, an asset, including a leased asset, becomes non-performing when it ceases to generate income for the bank. An NPA was defined as a credit facility in respect of which the interest and/or instalment of principal has remained 'past due' for a specified period of time.

With a view to moving towards international best practices and to ensure greater transparency, it has been decided to adopt the '90 days' overdue' norm for identification of NPAs, from the year ending 31 March 2004. Accordingly, with effect from 31 March 2004, an NPA shall be a loan or an advance where interest and/or instalment of principal remain overdue for a period of more than 90 days in respect of a term loan; the account remains 'out of order' for a period of more than 90 days, in respect of an Overdraft/Cash Credit (OD/CC); the bill remains overdue for a period of more than 90 days in the case of bills purchased and discounted; interest and/or instalment of principal remains overdue for two harvest seasons but for a period not exceeding two half years in the case of an advance granted for agricultural purposes; and any amount to be received remains overdue for a period of more than 90 days in respect of other accounts.

NPAs assets are further classified into substandard asset, doubtful asset, and loss assets depending upon how long a loan remains as an NPA.

Stressed accounts are the ones that show incipient signs of becoming NPA like bounced cheques, not submitting financial data, stock shortages, request for frequent overdrawal of account, etc. Overall net stressed loans defined as net NPAs plus outstanding standard restructured loans.

Restructured asset or loan are that assets which got an extended repayment period, reduced interest rate, converting a part of the loan into equity, providing additional financing or some combination of these measures. Hence, under restructuring a bad loan is modified as a new loan. But, the real problem is that it was actually an NPA.

Hence, the restructured loan is also a weak loan. NPAs and restructured loans together show the low asset quality of banks. These together are hence called stressed assets.

## ❖ Causes for NPAs

The following factors were identified by the RBI which contribute to creation of NPAs:

1. Internal Factors
   - (i) Lack of coordination among lending institutions
   - (ii) Slackness in credit management and its monitoring
   - (iii) Inappropriate technology/technical problems
   - (iv) Management inefficiency
   - (v) Business failure
   - (vi) Cost overrun
   - (vii) Diversion of funds
2. External Factors
   - (i) Economic recession
   - (ii) Changes in government policies
   - (iii) Natural calamities
   - (iv) Volatility in exchange rates
   - (v) Input price escalation
   - (vi) Power shortage

Other factors are as follows:

1. Wilful defaulters diverting the funds for other than the declared purpose
2. High interest rates/cost of funds
3. Utilization of short term loans for acquisition of fixed assets (long-term transactions)
4. Highly geared borrowers failure to meet adverse economic developments
5. Over-optimistic Promoters losing interest when their expectations fail
6. Lack of post sanction follow-up and monitoring and failure to recognize early warning signals
7. Liberalization of economy, easing of restrictions, lowering of tariff, etc.

## ❖ Legal Measures

The following legal and regulatory measures are initiated by the Banks for recovery of its NPAs.

1. **DRTs (1992):** These Tribunals are empowered to entertain cases for recovery of debts on fast track basis.
2. The Lok Adalats (1987) help to resolve disputes between Parties (Financial Institutions and Borrowers) by conciliation, mediation, compromise and amicable settlement.
3. **SARFAESI Act:** This Act empowers the secured creditors to take over the possession of secured assets of the borrower including right to transfer by way of lease, assignment of sale, etc. This act have removed the real legal hurdles and helped the Banks in resolving large number of NPAs expeditiously.
4. Compromise Settlement Scheme

## ❖ Present Mechanism

Banks have preferred to address the problem of stressed loans through restructuring of debt under the aegis of Corporate Debt Restructuring (CDR). While the CDR mechanism was used extensively, the objective seems to have been to provide temporary relief to the borrower rather than make active efforts to revive businesses. CDRs have met with limited success in reviving stressed loans owing to poor evaluation of business viability and lack of effective monitoring.

## ❖ Recommended Measures

1. **Bad Bank:** A bank may be set up to buy the bad loans of a bank with significant NPAs at market price. By transferring the bad assets of an institution to the bad bank, the banks clear their balance sheet of toxic assets but would be forced to take write downs. Shareholders and bondholders stand to lose money from this solution (but not depositors). Banks that become insolvent as a result of the process can be recapitalized, nationalized or liquidated.
2. **Fund for Stressed Assets:** The government is looking to set up a special fund to tackle the issue of stressed assets. This is expected to be part of the National Investment and Infrastructure Fund (NIIF), which would be like India's sovereign wealth fund. Although banks are seeing a slowdown in growth of fresh NPAs, they are grappling with a huge pile of bad debt due to problems in certain companies and some sectors such as metals and inability of several infrastructure projects to take off.

# FINANCIAL INCLUSION IN INDIA

In the Indian context, the term 'financial inclusion' was used for the first time in April 2005 in the Annual Policy Statement presented by Y. Venugopal Reddy, the then Governor of the RBI.

Financial inclusion denotes delivery of financial services at an affordable cost to the vast sections of the disadvantaged and low-income groups.

The kinds of services provided include banking, easy credit, investment opportunity and insurance.

On 25 June 2013, CRISIL, India's leading credit rating and research company launched an index to measure the status of financial inclusion in India. CRISIL Inclusix index is a one-of-its-kind tool to measure the extent of inclusion in India, right down to each of the 632 districts. The all-India CRISIL Inclusix score of 58.0 at the end of fiscal 2016, though there is clear signs of progress from 40.1 from 2011.

Measures taken by the RBI to promote financial inclusion are: opening of no-frills accounts; relaxation on know-your-customer (KYC) norms; engaging business correspondents (BCs); use of technology (use of payment gateways, i.e., VISA, RuPay, etc.); adoption of Electronic Benefit Transfer (EBT); revised General Credit Card (GCC) intended to cover all entrepreneurial credit, e.g., Artisan Credit Card, Laghu Udyami Card, Swarojgar Credit Card, and Weaver's Card, etc.; simplified branch authorization; opening of branches in unbanked rural centres; tapping technology platforms like mobile banking, and Adhaar Enabled Payment Systems (AEPS) and allowing opening of payments banks and small banks like Bandhan bank and IDFC bank.

Measures taken by the government to promote financial inclusion are: nationalization of banks; opening Cooperatives banks, and RRBs, Post Office Bank; introduction of mandated priority sector lending targets; formation of self-help groups; running lead bank scheme, and National Mission on Financial Inclusion or Sampoorn Vittiya Samaveshan; Jan Dhan Yojana; Pahal, Pradhan Mantri Jeevan Jyoti Bima Yojana (PMJJBY), Pradhan Mantri Suraksha Bima Yojana (PMSBY), Atal Pension

Yojana (APY), Kisan Credit Card and Financial Inclusion Funds

Corporate sector efforts for financial inclusion include working of NBFCs and opening of White ATMs.

### ❖ Advantages of Financial Inclusion

1. It helps making the Direct Benefit Transfer.
2. Access to finance by the poor and vulnerable groups is a prerequisite for poverty reduction and social cohesion.
3. Financial inclusion has become an integral part of the efforts to promote inclusive growth.
4. Providing access to finance is a form of empowerment of the vulnerable groups.
5. It promotes women empowerment.

## DEMONETIZATION

Demonetization is the act of stripping a currency unit of its status as legal tender. The opposite of demonetization is remonetization, in which a form of payment is restored as legal tender.

The reasons why a nation demonetizes its local units of currency may be: combating inflation; combating corruption and crime (counterfeiting, tax evasion); discouraging a cash-dependent economy and facilitating trade.

On 8 November 2016, the Government of India announced the demonetization of all 500 and 1,000 banknotes of the Mahatma Gandhi Series. The government has stated objective behind the demonetization policy are: first, it is an attempt to make India corruption free. Second, it is done to curb black money and counterfeit currency, third to control escalating price rise, fourth to stop funds flow to illegal activity and terrorism, fifth to make people accountable for every rupee they possess and pay income tax return. Finally, it is an attempt to make a cashless society and create a Digital India.

### ❖ Merits of Demonetization

1. It will help India to become corruption-free. Those indulging in taking bribe will refrain from corrupt practices as it will be hard for them to keep their unaccounted cash.
2. It will help the government to track the black money. Those individuals who have unaccounted cash are now required to show income and submit PAN for any valid financial transactions. The government can get income tax return for the income on which tax has not been paid.
3. It will stop funding to the unlawful activities that are thriving due to unaccounted cash flow. Banning high-value currency will rein in criminal activities like naxalism and terrorism.
4. It will also curb the menace of money laundering. Now such activity can easily be tracked and income tax department can catch such people who are in the business of money laundering.
5. It will stop the circulation of fake currency. Most of the fake currency put in circulation is of the high-value notes.
6. This move has generated interest among those people who had opened Jan Dhan accounts under the Prime Minister's Jan Dhan Yojana. They can now deposit their cash under this scheme, and this money can be used for the developmental activity of the country.
7. It will force people to pay income tax returns. Most of the people who have been hiding their income are now forced to come forward to declare their income and pay tax on the same.
8. It will make India a cashless society. All the monetary transaction has to be through the banking methods and

individuals have to be accountable for each penny they possess.

9. It will encourage digitalization of currency.

## ❖ Demerits of Demonetization

1. It has caused huge inconvenience to the people.
2. It has deeply affected business. Due to the cash crunch, the entire economy has been made to come to a standstill.
3. Many poor daily wage workers were left with no jobs and their daily income was stopped because employers are unable to pay their daily wage.
4. The government fought hard to implement this policy. It had to bear the cost of printing of the new currency notes. It is also found it difficult to put new currency into circulation. The 2000 rupees note became a burden on the people as no one liked to do transaction with such high value currency. Some critics think it will only help people to use black money more easily in future.
5. India's economic growth faced slow down.

Earlier, on 16 January 1978, ₹ 1,000, ₹ 5,000 and ₹ 10,000 currency notes were scrapped through an ordinance, impacting 0.6 per cent of the total currency in circulation at the time. Before that, India had experienced demonetization of high-value currency in January 1946. On both occasions, it impacted only a minuscule segment of the society and economy.

# CASHLESS ECONOMY

A cashless economy is a situation in which the flow of cash within an economy doesn't actually exist, and all the transactions take place digitally through internet banking, debit and credit cards and apps like paytm, freecharge, etc.

## ❖ Advantages

Following advantages are expected to accrue:

1. Carrying high amount of cash is always a security hazard. For other modes like credit/debit cards, in the event of loss or robbery, one can block the card. It may also reduce pickpocketing and highway robbery.
2. It is not necessary to be physically present to conduct cashless transaction. There is also no limitation on timing of transaction as it can be done at any time and from anywhere.
3. The electronic payment will help the entrepreneur to increase their customer base and breach the geographical limitations.
4. Increasing share of cashless will improve government revenue as online transaction lead a trail of events that can be traced to find out tax evasion if any.
5. Since the cashless transactions are more visible, it will help in curbing the black money.
6. If subsidy or wages for the welfare schemes like MGNREGA are paid online through bank transfer instead of cash, it would also help in plugging the leakages and help in ensuring that subsidies are better targeted.
7. As the people increasingly started using cashless transactions, it will help in increasing the tax base. It will be easy for the public as well to explain the tax authorities their past expenditure.
8. Being cashless also inculcates budget discipline.
9. It will also be easy to ward off the borrowers if you are cashless.
10. Cashless transactions do away with the need of change. One can pay in exact amount even in fraction of rupee or paisa through card payment or online transaction.

11. Problem of counterfeit currency will also be reduced in online transactions.
12. One can also trace the funding of terror activities as online transactions leave a trail.
13. There is high cost of printing currency notes. Switching to cashless transactions will decrease this cost.

## ❖ Disadvantages

1. The biggest fear is the risk of identity theft. One can also become a victim of phishing trap.
2. Since mobile phone had become an important element of cashless economy, loss of phone may become a double whammy as many financial details can be retrieved from it.
3. If we take into account the proportion of non-tech-savvy population, the practical implementation of cashless economy will take enormous efforts.
4. With a literacy level of 74.04 per cent, India is likely to face the obvious hurdles on its way to achieve a total digitalization of its transactions.
5. With the recent hack of 32 lakh Rupay and Visa debit cards, there is a doubt in cyber security of Indian Banking. Before going for completely cashless economy, India needs to strengthen its cyber security first.
6. Network connectivity issues must be resolved before dreaming about a cashless society.
7. The Internet cost in India is still substantially high.
8. There are additional charges that are levied by the vendors when they offer an online payment facility.
9. A cashless society needs a proper infrastructure. The banks need to be fully equipped to handle the surge in e-transactions. Infrastructure is also needed in terms of opening more accounts in the banks.

Despite its drawbacks, the cashless system is indeed an improvement over the traditional cash based system. However, none of the advanced economy has fully replaced the cash as it is practically not possible but reducing the amount of cash and increasing the cashless transactions will definitely improve the transparency in business transactions and therefore is good for the country and economy. In fact, a cashless society is a welcome idea but not without preparation.

❑❑❑

# CHAPTER 4

# Financial Markets in India

## FINANCIAL MARKET

Financial market is a broad term used for a marketplace where trading of securities including equities, bonds, currencies and derivatives is done.

The financial market can broadly be divided into money market and capital market. Money market is a market for debt securities that pay off in the short term usually less than one year, for example, the market for 91-day treasury bills. This market encompasses the trading and issuance of short-term non-equity debt instruments including treasury bills, commercial papers, banker's acceptance, certificates of deposits, etc.

Capital market is a market for long-term debt and equity shares. In this market, the capital funds comprising of both equity and debt are issued and traded. This also includes private placement sources of debt and equity as well as organized markets like stock exchanges.

### ❖ Capital Market in India

Capital market can be divided into primary and secondary markets.

**Primary Market:** The Primary Market, also known as a New Issue Market, is where new securities are issued – it is part of the capital market. Corporations, national and local governments, and other public sector institutions can get financing through the sale of new stock or bond issues through the primary market. Put simply, the primary market creates new securities and offers them for sale to the public. These securities may be issued at face value, at premium or at discount. Face value is the original cost of the security as shown in the certificate/instrument. Most equity shares have a face value of ₹ 1, ₹ 5, ₹ 10 or ₹ 100 and do not have much bearing on the actual market price of the stock. When issuing securities, they may be offered at a discount or at a premium. When the security is offered at a price higher than the face value, it is called a premium. When the security is offered at a price lower than the face value, it is called a discount.

Following are the features of primary markets:

1. This is the market for new long-term equity capital.
2. The securities are issued by the company directly to investors.
3. Primary issues are used by companies for the purpose of modernizing the existing business, opening new business, etc.
4. The primary market performs the crucial function of facilitating capital formation in the economy.
5. The new issue market doesn't include certain other sources of new long-term external finance, such as loans from financial institutions.

6. Borrowers in the new issue market may be raising capital for converting private capital into public capital. This is known as 'going public'.
7. The financial assets sold can only be redeemed by the original holder.

**Secondary Market:** It refers to a market where securities are traded after being initially offered to the public in the primary market and/or listed on the Stock Exchange. Majority of the trading is done in the secondary market. Secondary market comprises of equity markets and the debt markets. Equity is the stock capital/share capital (shares of ownership of a public corporation that are sold to investors) of a company. Debt consists of all the loans taken by the business.

For the general investor, the secondary market provides an efficient platform for trading of his securities. For the management of the company, secondary equity markets serve as a monitoring and control conduit – by facilitating value-enhancing control activities, enabling implementation of incentive-based management contracts and aggregating information (via price discovery) that guides management decisions.

### ❖ Difference Between Primary Market and Secondary Market

In the primary market, securities are offered to public for subscription for the purpose of raising capital or fund. Secondary market is an equity-trading avenue in which already existing/preissued securities are traded among investors. Secondary market could be either auction or dealer market. While stock exchange is the part of an auction market, over-the-counter (OTC) is a part of the dealer market.

## STOCK EXCHANGE

Stock exchanges are organized and regulated financial market where securities are bought and sold at prices governed by the forces of demand and supply. In other words, an exchange is an institution, organization or association which hosts a market where stocks, bonds, options and futures, and commodities are traded.

Stock exchanges basically serve as:

1. primary markets where corporations, governments, municipalities and other incorporated bodies can raise capital by channelling savings of the investors into productive ventures; and
2. secondary markets where investors can sell their securities to other investors for cash, thus reducing the risk of investment and maintaining liquidity in the system.

Stock exchanges impose stringent rules, listing requirements and statutory requirements that are binding on all listed and trading parties.

Earlier the trades in exchanges were conducted on the floor (called the 'trading floor') of the exchange itself, by shouting orders and instructions (called open outcry system). Now at exchanges, trades are conducted over telephone or online. Almost all exchanges are 'auction exchanges' where buyers enter competitive bids and sellers enter competitive orders through a trading day.

### ❖ Functions of Stock Exchange

Stock exchanges serve as an economic barometer of a country. They perform several economic functions and render invaluable services to the investors, companies and to the economy as a whole. They play an important role in the economic development of a nation.

Major functions are as follows:

1. **Marketability of securities:** Stock exchange provides a market for the purchase and sale of securities. As a result, any person holding securities can get back his money invested in the securities (share, debentures, government bonds, etc.) by selling them through the brokers of a stock exchange at the market price. Similarly, a person willing to

make investment in securities or conduct speculation in securities can do so with the help of these stock markets.

2. **Liquidity to investment:** People readily invest in the industrial securities as the money blocked in these securities can be released by selling them in stock exchange. In the absence of these stock exchanges, the public would not have freely invested in the industrial and government securities. As a result, the industry and government would have starved for the capital. Thus, stock exchanges provide liquidity for the industrial securities and help the industrial development of a country.
3. **Supply of long-term funds:** The securities traded in stock market are negotiable. They can be transferred with minimum formalities from one person to another. As a result of this facility, people readily invest in the industrial securities and companies receive a good response for their public issue of shares and debentures whenever they need funds. Thus, they are assured a long-term availability of funds due to the existence of stock markets.
4. **Evaluation of securities:** Stock exchange keeps a record and makes a public declaration of prices at which securities are traded. On the basis of these prices for the securities quoted in the markets, the investors and speculators can evaluate the values of securities held by them.
5. **Motivation for the companies for improvement in performance:** The performance of a company is reflected through the prices quoted for their securities in the stock markets. With the improvement in the performance of a company, the prices of its shares in the market increase, enhancing the goodwill of the company. Thus, stock markets indirectly motivate the companies to improve their financial performance through continual increase in productivity and profitability.
6. **Assistance of capital formation:** Stock market ensures liquidity of industrial securities; it also ensures the appreciation of funds invested in the securities with the improvement in the performance of companies and increase in the demand for their securities. Thus, they motivate the public to invest their savings in the capital of companies. These savings are channelized in the productive activities of the companies, resulting in the capital formation which is essential for the economic development of a nation.
7. **Protection of investors:** Stock markets conduct the trade in securities subject to certain rules and regulation. These rules prevent overtrading, illegitimate speculations and charging of excess commission on trading by the brokers in order to protect the interest of common investors. Thus, stock exchanges safeguard the innocent investors from the malpractices of clever brokers dealing in securities. This strengthens the investors' confidence and promotes large investments.
8. **Encouragement of savings:** Stock exchanges provide an attractive avenue for investors wherein they can invest their small savings in industrial securities and obtain a regular return on investment as well as capital appreciation. Thus, they encourage savings' habits among the public.
9. **Listing of securities:** Stock exchanges do the listing of securities of various companies. Only listed securities are traded on stock exchanges. Listing of a security means permission to the security to quote officially on trading floor of the stock exchange. Shares or debentures of a particular company can be listed and traded at stock exchange only if the company fulfils certain standard norms fixed by the exchange.

10. **Maintaining business information:** Companies whose securities are listed on stock exchange are required to furnish the financial statements and other reports and statements. The stock exchange maintains a detailed record of the various companies whose securities are traded on its floor.
11. **Raising capital for businesses:** Stock exchanges help joint stock companies to capitalize by selling shares to the investing public.

## ❖ Advantages of Listing Securities in Stock Exchange

1. **Facilitates marketing of securities:** If a company does the listing of its shares on recognized stock exchanges, its shareholders will be able to release their investment in the shares at market price whenever they want by selling these shares on stock exchanges. Similarly, an investor who wants to purchase the shares of that company may buy those shares at market price in those stock exchanges. Thus, constant marketing facilities are availed to the securities that are listed on stock exchange.
2. **Assures finance to the companies:** Whenever a company offers its shares to the public, it receives proper response from the investors only if such shares are listed on recognized stock exchanges. This is for the reason that listing enables the investor to release his money in the shares by selling those on stock exchange. Thus, listing enables the companies to raise the necessary finance by the issue of its securities to the public.
3. **Ensures liquidity:** The prices of listed securities are quoted daily in the share markets. Hence, the listed securities can be readily converted into cash at the quoted price. Thus, listing ensures liquidity of securities.
4. **Enables the investors to borrow the funds:** Banks and other financial institutions accepted the listed securities as collateral securities against their loans and advances because these listed securities have a ready market. Thus, the people holding the listed securities can raise loan against such securities without any difficulty.
5. **Protects investors:** The companies that have listed their securities on stock markets have to follow the rules and regulations of stock markets and Securities and Exchange Board of India (SEBI). They have to maintain transparency in their working and have to disclose their financial information and policies. All these rules, regulations and transparency aim at protection of interest of small investors who should not be deceived or put to loss.
6. **Offers wide publicity:** Names of companies whose securities are listed on stock exchanges are mentioned regularly in stock market reports, TV, newspapers, radios, etc. Thus, listed securities offer wide advertising and publicity to the companies concerned.
7. The companies whose securities have been listed on a stock exchange enjoy a better goodwill and credit-standing than other companies because they are supposed to be financially sound. As a result of enhanced goodwill and higher demand, the value of their securities increases and their bargaining power in collective ventures, mergers, etc. is enhanced.
8. The companies have the convenience to decide upon the size, price and timing of the issue.
9. The investors enjoy the ready availability of facility and convenience of buying and selling the securities at will and at an opportune time. Availability of regular

information on prices of securities traded at the stock exchanges helps them in deciding on the timing of their purchase and sale. It becomes easier for them to raise loans from banks against their holdings in securities traded at the stock exchange because banks prefer them as collateral on account of their liquidity and convenient valuation.

10. The availability of lucrative avenues of investment and the liquidity thereof induces people to save and invest in long-term securities. This leads to increased capital formation in the country.
11. Since government securities are also traded at the stock exchanges, the government borrowing is highly facilitated. The bonds issued by governments, electricity boards, municipal corporations and public sector undertakings (PSUs) are found to be on offer quite frequently and are generally successful.
12. The volume of activity at the stock exchanges and the movement of share prices reflect the changing economic health.

### ❖ Limitations of Stock Exchanges

One of the common evils associated with stock exchange operations is the excessive speculation. Speculation implies buying or selling securities to take advantage of price differential at different times. The speculators generally do not take or give delivery and pay or receive full payment. They settle their transactions just by paying the difference in prices. Normally, speculation is considered a healthy practice and is necessary for successful operation of stock exchange activity. But, when it becomes excessive, it leads to wide fluctuations in prices and various malpractices by the vested interests. In the process, genuine investors suffer and are driven out of the market.

Security prices may fluctuate due to unpredictable political, social and economic factors as well as on account of rumours spread by interested parties. This makes it difficult to assess the movement of prices in future and build appropriate strategies for investment in securities. However, these days good amount of vigilance is exercised by stock exchange authorities and SEBI to control activities at the stock exchange and ensure their healthy functioning.

## PRODUCTS DEALT IN THE SECONDARY MARKETS

Following are the main financial products/instruments dealt in the secondary market:

1. **Rights Issue/Rights Shares:** The issue of new securities to existing shareholders at a ratio to those already held.
2. **Bonus Shares:** Shares issued by the companies to their shareholders free of cost by capitalization of accumulated reserves from the profits earned in the earlier years.
3. **Preferred Stock/Preference Shares:** Owners of these kinds of shares are entitled to a fixed dividend or dividend calculated at a fixed rate to be paid regularly before dividend can be paid in respect of equity share. They also enjoy priority over the equity shareholders in payment of surplus. But in the event of liquidation, their claims rank below the claims of the company's creditors and bondholders/debenture holders.
4. **Cumulative Preference Shares:** A type of preference shares on which dividend accumulates if remains unpaid. All arrears of preference dividend have to be paid out before paying dividend on equity shares.
5. **Cumulative Convertible Preference Shares:** A type of preference shares

where the dividend payable on the same accumulates, if not paid. After a specified date, these shares will be converted into equity capital of the company.

6. **Participating Preference Share:** The right of certain preference shareholders to participate in profits after a specified fixed dividend contracted for is paid. Participation right is linked with the quantum of dividend paid on the equity shares over and above a particular specified level.
7. **Security Receipts:** Security receipt means a receipt or other security, issued by a securitization company or reconstruction company to any qualified institutional buyer pursuant to a scheme, evidencing the purchase or acquisition by the holder thereof, of an undivided right, title or interest in the financial asset involved in securitization.
8. **Government securities (G-Secs):** These are sovereign (credit risk-free) coupon bearing instruments which are issued by the Reserve Bank of India (RBI) on behalf of Government of India, in lieu of the Central Government's market borrowing programme. These securities have a fixed coupon that is paid on specific dates on half-yearly basis. These securities are available in wide range of maturity dates, from short dated (less than 1 year) to long dated (up to 20 years).
9. **Debentures:** Bonds issued by a company bearing a fixed rate of interest usually payable half yearly on specific dates and principal amount repayable on particular date on redemption of the debentures. Debentures are normally secured/charged against the asset of the company in favour of debenture holder.
10. **Bond:** A negotiable certificate evidencing indebtedness. It is normally unsecured. A debt security is generally issued by a company, municipality or government agency. A bond investor lends money to the issuer, and in exchange, the issuer promises to repay the loan amount on a specified maturity date. The issuer usually pays the bondholder periodic interest payments over the life of the loan. The various types of bonds are as follows:
    (a) **Zero-Coupon Bond:** Bond issued at a discount and repaid at a face value. No periodic interest is paid. The difference between the issue price and redemption price represents the return to the holder. The buyer of these bonds receives only one payment, at the maturity of the bond.
    (b) **Convertible Bond:** A bond giving the investor the option to convert the bond into equity at a fixed conversion price.
11. **Commercial Paper:** A short-term promise to repay a fixed amount that is placed on the market either directly or through a specialized intermediary. It is usually issued by companies with a high credit standing in the form of a promissory note redeemable at par to the holder on maturity; therefore, it doesn't require any guarantee. Commercial paper is a money market instrument issued normally for tenure of 90 days.
12. **Treasury Bills:** Short-term (up to 91 days) bearer discount security issued by the Government as a means of financing its cash requirements.

**Major Stock Exchanges in the World**

1. **New York Stock Exchange:** It is located in New York City, USA. In 1817, New York brokers established formal organizations named as the New York Stock and Exchange Board. In 1863, the New York Stock and Exchange Board were renamed as New York Stock Exchange.
2. **NASDAQ:** It stands for the 'National Association of Securities Dealers Automated Quotation'. This electronic stock exchange is located in New York City, USA. It is the world's first electronic stock market incorporated in 1971. As the world's largest stock market, it has 4,000 listed companies.
3. **London Stock Exchange:** Located in London, England.
4. **Tokyo Stock Exchange:** Formally known as the Japan Exchange Group, located in Tokyo.
5. **Shanghai Stock Exchange:** Located in Shanghai, China.
6. **Hong Kong Stock Exchange:** Located in Hong Kong.
7. **Euronext:** Located throughout Europe (France, Portugal, the Netherlands, and Belgium).
8. **Shenzhen Stock Exchange:** Located in Shenzhen, China.
9. **TMX Group:** The Canadian stock exchange is located in Toronto, Canada.

**Deutsche Börse:** The German stock exchange, located in Frankfurt, Germany.
**Bombay Stock Exchange:** Located in Mumbai, India.
**National Stock Exchange of India:** Located in Mumbai, India.
**SIX Swiss Exchange:** The Zurich stock exchange, located in Zurich, Switzerland.
**Australian Securities Exchange:** Located in Sydney, Australia.
**Korea Exchange:** The South Korean stock exchange located in Seoul, South Korea.

## STOCK EXCHANGES IN INDIA

The Bombay Stock Exchange (BSE) and National Stock Exchange (NSE) are the largest Indian exchanges, satisfying the needs of nearly all foreign investors. They together accounted for more than 98 per cent of the total turnover for all markets.

**BSE:** The BSE, Asia's first stock exchange, was established in 1875. It is located on Dalal Street, Mumbai. The BSE is one of the world's fastest stock exchanges, with a median trade speed of 6 microseconds. In 1986, the BSE developed its Index named as SENSEX to measure the performance of the exchange. Initially, there was an open outcry floor trading system which in 1995 switched to electronic trading system. The exchange made the whole transition in just 50 days. The BSE Online Trading, known as BOLT, is an automated, screen-based trading platform with a capacity of 8 million orders per day. The BSE provides a transparent and efficient market for trading in equities, debentures, bonds, derivatives, mutual funds, etc. It also provides opportunity to trade in the equities of small- and medium-term enterprises. It is the first exchange across India and second across world to get an ISO 9000:2000 certification. It is the world's 9th largest stock exchange with an overall market capitalization of $3.16 trillion as of March 2021. More than 5,000 companies are publicly listed on the BSE.

**NSE:** The NSE is located in Mumbai. It was incorporated in 1992 and became a stock exchange in 1993. The basic purpose of this exchange was to bring the transparency in the stock markets. It started its operations in the wholesale debt market in June 1994. The equity market segment of the NSE commenced its operations in November 1994, whereas in the derivatives segment, it started it operations in June 2000. It was the first exchange in the country to provide a modern, fully automated screen-based electronic trading system which offered easy trading facility to the investors spread across the length and breadth of the country.

The NSE offers trading and investment in the following segments:

(i) **Equities:** Equities, indices, mutual funds, exchange traded funds, initial public offerings and security lending and borrowing scheme, etc.

(ii) **Derivatives:** Equity derivatives (including Global Indices like CNX 500, Dow Jones and FTSE), currency derivatives and interest rate futures.

(iii) **Debt:** Corporate Bonds.

A total of 1,920 companies are listed in the NSE. The NSE has a total market capitalization of more than US$1.41 trillion, making it the world's 10th-largest stock exchange as of March 2021.

Both exchanges – BSE and NSE – follow the same trading mechanism, trading hours, settlement process, etc.

## OVER-THE-COUNTER EXCHANGE OF INDIA (OTCEI)

The over-the-counter exchange of India (OTCEI) is an electronic stock exchange based in India. It comprises of small- and medium-sized firms to get access to the capital markets.

The OTCEI was incorporated in 1990 as a company under the Companies Act, 1956, and is recognized as a stock exchange under the Securities Contracts Regulation Act, 1956. The Exchange was set up to aid enterprising promoters in raising finance for new projects in a cost-effective manner and to provide investors with a transparent and efficient mode of trading.

Modelled along the lines of the NASDAQ market of the USA, the OTCEI introduced many novel concepts to the Indian capital markets such as screen-based nationwide trading, sponsorship of companies, market making and scripless trading.

The OTCEI is a floorless exchange where all the activities are fully computerized. Its promoters have been designated as sponsor members, and they alone are entitled to sponsor a company for listing there. Trading on the OTCEI takes place through a network of computers or OTC dealers located at different places within the same city and even across the cities. These computers allow dealers to quote, query and transact through a central OTC computer using the telecommunication links. A company which is listed on any other recognized stock exchange in India is not permitted simultaneously for listing on the OTCEI. The OTCEI deals in equity shares, preference shares, bonds, debentures and warrants.

## SENSEX

An Index is a statistical aggregate that measures change. Remember this throughout this post – 'statistical aggregate'. All indexes are not same – they can be differentiated based on countries, the market cap of stocks they cover or even how any stock will become part of Index. The first stock index in the Indian stock market is Sensex. Sensex means Sensitive Index. It is the stock market index of the BSE – it is also called BSE Sensex. It is the market weighted stock index of 30 companies that are selected on the basis of financial soundness and performance. Usually, large and well-established companies that are representatives of the various industrial sectors are chosen. It was first published in 1986. It is the first benchmark in India which reflects the 'Free-Float Market Cap' methodology. It provides time data over a fairly long period, making it suitable for research purposes. Various core sectors of the economy are represented in the SENSEX. The base value of Sensex is 100, and the base year is 1978–79. As of 15 March 2017, the Full Market capitalization of Sensex is 4,986,299 crores, and the free float market capitalization is ₹ 2,687,777 crores.

Presently, the companies under Sensex include Reliance Industries, ICICI Bank, Larsen & Toubro, Infosys, HDFC Ltd., Bharti, ITC Ltd., State Bank of India, ONGC, HDFC Bank, Reliance Communications, Tata Steel, BHEL, Satyam Hindustan Unilever, NTPC Ltd., Reliance Energy, TCS, Grasim Industries, DLF Ltd., Jaiprakash Associates, Tata Motors, Hindalco, Mahindra & Mahindra, Wipro Ltd., Maruti, Ranbaxy, Cipla, Ambuja Cements and ACC.

**Stock Exchanges in India**

There are 23 stock exchanges in India. Among them two are national-level stock exchanges namely BSE and NSE. The rest 21 are Regional Stock Exchanges (RSE).

**Regional Stock Exchanges in India**

1. Ahmedabad
2. Bangalore
3. Bhubaneswar
4. Calcutta
5. Cochin
6. Coimbatore
7. Delhi
8. Guwahati
9. Hyderabad
10. Jaipur
11. Ludhiana
12. Madhya Pradesh
13. Madras
14. Magadh
15. Mangalore
16. Meerut
17. OTC Exchange Of India
18. Pune
19. Saurashtra Kutch
20. Uttar Pradesh
21. Vadodara

(All stock exchanges except BSE, NSE, Calcutta and Magadh Stock Exchange have been granted exit by SEBI by April 2018.)

## SECURITIES AND EXCHANGE BOARD OF INDIA (SEBI)

The SEBI was established in 1988 but was given regulatory powers on 12 April 1992, through the SEBI Act, 1992. Its headquarters is located in Mumbai. It also has northern, eastern, southern and western regional offices.

SEBI's management team consists of a chairman nominated by the Union Government of India, two members who are officers from the Union Finance Ministry, one member from the RBI and five other members who are also nominated by the Union Government of India.

### ❖ Objectives of SEBI

The objectives of SEBI are as follows:

1. To regulate the activities of stock exchange.
2. To protect the rights of investors and ensuring safety to their investment.
3. To prevent fraudulent and malpractices by having balance between self-regulation of business and its statutory regulations.
4. To regulate and develop a code of conduct for intermediaries such as brokers, underwriters, etc.

## ❖ Functions of SEBI

The SEBI has three broad functions:

1. Protective functions
2. Developmental functions
3. Regulatory functions.

## ❖ Protective Functions of SEBI

As clear from the name, SEBI's protective function is to protect investors' interest and provide them security by taking following actions:

1. Manipulation of security prices to inflate or depress the market prices (price rigging) and thereby cheating investors is prohibited by SEBI.
2. The SEBI keeps check on insiders who buy securities of the company and then takes strict action on insider trading, i.e., trading by insiders by using such information that is not available to general public.
3. The SEBI also prohibits fraudulent unfair trade practices by not letting the companies make misleading statements which might induce the investors.
4. The SEBI also undertakes steps in educating investors so that they can evaluate and make correct decisions.
5. The SEBI promotes code of conduct and fair practices in the security market.

## ❖ Developmental Functions

These are implemented by the SEBI to promote and develop stock exchange activities or dealings. It promotes training of intermediaries, allows internet trading and also made underwriting optional so as to reduce issue cost.

## ❖ Regulatory Functions

These are implemented by the SEBI for regulating stock exchange. It registers and regulates mutual funds and working of those connected with stock exchange in any manner, e.g., brokers, merchant bankers, etc. The SEBI also regulates the takeover of companies and conducts the inquiries.

## ❖ Other Functions or Powers Given to SEBI

1. The SEBI has been empowered to seek records and information from any board or statutory authority or corporation established by the Central, state or local governments.
2. If there are reasonable grounds of believing that a particular company might be indulging in unfair trade practices, then the SEBI may conduct inspection of registers, books or of documents and records of listed company or any public company that intends to get the securities listed.
3. It shall have similar powers as given to a civil court in certain matters like summoning, oath examination, issuing of commissions and also in matters of inspection or production of books of account, records or documents of a company or of any person specified in section 12 of the SEBI Act, 1992.
4. It has been empowered to levy fees for carrying out various functions.
5. The SEBI may take any of these measures during the investigation or inquiry or on completion of such an investigation or inquiry:
   (i) Suspending any security's trading in a recognized stock exchange.
   (ii) Prohibiting a person to deal in securities or restraining the person from gaining access to the securities market.
   (iii) Suspending office bearers of stock exchanges or of self-regulatory organizations from holding of such positions.
   (iv) Retaining the proceeds of securities of a transaction under investigation.

(v) Attach after passing of the order.

(vi) Directing intermediary or person associated with securities market not to alienate or dispose of an asset that forms part of transaction under investigation.

(vii) Regulating or prohibiting the issue of prospectus or advertisements, or offer document or advertisement for issue of securities.

6. The SEBI may make enquiries to protect interest of investors, to prevent activities from being conducted in an unfair manner and to ensure proper management of the intermediaries.
7. The SEBI is empowered to conduct search and seizure if there exist reasonable grounds in believing that operations are being carried on in a way that affects badly the interests of those associated with securities market.
8. The SEBI is empowered to issue desist and cease order if after the inquiry board finds that the person has violated or may violate provisions of the SEBI Act or rules made there under.
9. Under Securities Contracts Regulations Act of 1956, following powers have been given to SEBI:

(i) Granting of recognition to stock exchange.

(ii) Withdrawing such recognition in the interest of the trade.

(iii) Requiring stock exchange to provide periodical returns.

(iv) Approving stock exchange for making bye-laws.

(v) Suspending for a limited period the business of recognized stock exchange.

(vi) Compelling listing of securities by the public companies.

## NATIONAL FINANCIAL REPORTING AUTHORITY SETUP

Under the provisions of the Companies Act 2013, the National Financial Reporting Authority (NFRA) was set up in August 2013, which replaced the National Advisory Committee on Accounting Standards (NACAS).

The NFRA is a quasi-judicial body overseeing the overall quality of financial reporting. And like NACAS, it will also advise the government on accounting policies and standards for companies or class of companies.

The other functions performed by the NFRA are:

1. To make recommendations to the Government on formulation of accounting and auditing policies and standards for auditors.
2. To monitor and enforce compliance with accounting and auditing standards.
3. To oversee the service quality of the professions involved in ensuring compliance with standards, and suggest improvements.
4. To perform other prescribed functions.

## STEPS TAKEN BY SEBI TO IMPROVE CAPITAL MARKET IN INDIA

The important steps taken by the SEBI to improve the functioning of capital market in India are as follows:

1. Periodic inspection of stock exchanges.
2. An advertisement code has been laid down to ensure that the advertisements are fair and do not contain misleading statements.
3. Appointment of SEBI representative to supervise the allotment process in the event of oversubscription.
4. Stock brokers and sub-brokers are required to register under the SEBI Act.
5. Merchant banking has been brought under the supervisory role of the SEBI and hence pricing and premium fixation is regulated by the SEBI.
6. 'Insider trading' has been prohibited in November 1992.
7. Free pricing is permitted subject to consistent track record for three years, and credit rating is compulsory for

debentures and bonds of more than 18 months.

8. The SEBI (Mutual Fund) Regulations provide for an approval of the offer documents of schemes by the SEBI. The regulations prescribe minimum amount to be raised by each scheme. A close-ended scheme with a fixed size of mutual fund must raise a minimum of ₹ 20 crores and open-ended scheme of ₹ 50 crores. The entire subscription amount must be refunded within six weeks of the closure of the scheme in case the amount collected by the scheme falls short of the prescribed amount.
9. Brokers are mandatorily required to maintain separate accounts for their clients and for themselves. They must disclose the transaction prices and brokerages separately in the contract notes issued to their clients and file their audited reports with the SEBI. Brokers are required to issue contract notes to the clients within 24 hours of the execution of the contract. In order to ensure execution of the deals and to give protection to the investors, capital adequacy norms for brokers have been introduced.
10. Infrastructure firms have been exempted from requirements such as making a minimum public offer of 25 per cent of equity, five shareholders per ₹ 1 lakh of offer and minimum subscription of 90 per cent while floating a public issue.
11. A company can finance buyback out of its free reserves, the securities premium account or proceeds of an earlier issue other than fresh issue of shrews made specifically for buyback purposes.
12. Companies have been given the freedom to fix the par value of shares issued by them. Companies who have issued shares at ₹ 10 and ₹ 100 can fix the par value of their shares either by consolidating or by splitting their existing shares.
13. Floating of public issues through the Book Building mechanism.
14. Collective Investment Schemes needs to be registered with the SEBI. In case of failure of registration, the scheme will have to be wound up.
15. In January 2000, compulsory rolling settlement in ten select scrips was introduced and since then more scrips have come under the system. In June 2000, the SEBI introduced derivatives trading.
16. An ordinance promulgated on 28 October 2002 gave SEBI the power to search an entity's premises, seize documents, impound cash proceeds and securities connected to any transaction it is investigating and freeze bank accounts. In case of market manipulation or insider trading violations, the SEBI can impose a fine of ₹ 25 crore or three times the profits made by the entity concerned whichever is higher, and for other violations like non-disclosures, ₹ 1 crore fine can be imposed.
17. In November 2002, the SEBI approved the establishment of a Central Listing Authority.
18. In May 2006, listed companies were permitted to raise funds in the form of Qualified Institutional Placement.
19. Permanent Account Number (PAN) was made the sole identification number for all participants in the securities market from July 2007.
20. From January 2008, entry load by mutual funds was waived from investors making applications for investment in mutual fund schemes directly.

The SEBI has introduced numerous measures to improve the efficiency of the capital market in India. By improving market efficiency, increasing transparency and preventing unfair trade practices, the SEBI has succeeded in raising the standard of Indian capital market to the international level.

## TERMS RELATED TO CAPITAL MARKET

### ❖ Corporate Bonds

The term Corporate Bonds referred includes all debt securities issued by institutions such as banks, PSUs, municipal corporations, bodies corporate and companies having a tenure of more than 365 days. Such an issue of bonds, if offered to the public, shall require to comply with the SEBI (Disclosure and Investor Protection Guidelines), 2000.

### ❖ Broker

A broker is a member of a recognized stock exchange, who is permitted to do trades on the screen-based trading system of different stock exchanges. He is enrolled as a member with the concerned exchange and is registered with the SEBI.

### ❖ Sub-broker

A sub-broker is a person who is registered with the SEBI as such and is affiliated to a member of a recognized stock exchange.

### ❖ Risk Disclosure Document

In order to acquaint the investors in the markets of the various risks involved in trading in the stock market, the members of the exchange have been required to sign a risk disclosure document with their clients, informing them of the various risks like risk of volatility, risks of lower liquidity, risks of higher spreads, risks of new announcements, risks of rumours, etc.

### ❖ Securities Transaction Tax

Securities Transaction Tax (STT) is a tax being levied on all transactions done on the stock exchanges at rates prescribed by the Central Government from time to time. Pursuant to the enactment of the Finance (No. 2) Act, 2004, the Government of India notified the Securities Transaction Tax Rules, 2004, and STT came into effect from 1 October 2004.

### ❖ Account Period Settlement

An account period settlement is a settlement where the trades pertaining to a period stretching over more than one day are settled. For example, trades for the period Monday to Friday are settled together. The obligations for the account period are settled on a net basis. Account period settlement has been discontinued since 1 January 2002, pursuant to SEBI directives.

### ❖ Rolling Settlement

In a Rolling Settlement, trades executed during the day are settled based on the net obligations for the day.

Presently, the trades pertaining to the rolling settlement are settled on a T+2 day basis where T stands for the trade day. Hence, trades executed on a Monday are typically settled on the following Wednesday (considering 2 working days from the trade day). The funds and securities pay-in and pay-out are carried out on T+2 day.

### ❖ Pay-in Day and Pay-out Day

Pay-in day is the day when the brokers shall make payment or delivery of securities to the exchange. Pay-out day is the day when the exchange makes payment or delivery of securities to the broker. Settlement cycle is on the T+2 rolling settlement basis with effect from 1 April 2003. The exchanges have to ensure that the pay-out of funds and securities to the clients is done by the broker within 24 hours of the pay-out. The exchanges will have to issue press release immediately after pay out.

### ❖ Auction

The exchange purchases the requisite quantity in the auction market and gives them to the buying trading member. The shortages are met through auction process, and the difference in price indicated in contract note and price received through auction is paid by member to the exchange, which is then liable to be recovered from the client.

### ❖ Margin Trading Facility

Margin Trading is trading with borrowed funds/securities. It is essentially a leveraging mechanism which enables investors to take exposure in the market over and above what is possible with their own resources. The SEBI has been prescribing eligibility conditions and procedural details for allowing the Margin Trading Facility from time to time.

Corporate brokers with net worth of at least ₹ 3 crore are eligible for providing margin trading facility to their clients subject to their entering into an agreement to that effect. Before providing margin trading facility to a client, the member and the client have been mandated to sign an agreement for this purpose in the format specified by the SEBI. It has also been specified that the client shall not avail the facility from more than one broker at any time.

The facility of margin trading is available for Group 1 securities and those securities which are offered in the initial public offers and meet the conditions for inclusion in the derivatives segment of the stock exchanges.

For providing the margin trading facility, a broker may use his own funds or borrow from scheduled commercial banks or NBFCs regulated by the RBI. A broker is not allowed to borrow funds from any other source.

### ❖ SEBI Risk Management System

The primary focus of risk management by the SEBI has been to address the market risks, operational risks and systemic risks. To this effect, the SEBI has been continuously reviewing its policies and drafting risk management policies to mitigate these risks, thereby enhancing the level of investor protection and catalysing market development.

### ❖ Short Selling

Short Selling means selling of a stock that the seller does not own at the time of trade. Short selling can be done by borrowing the stock through Clearing Corporation/ Clearing House of a stock exchange which is registered as Approved Intermediaries (AIs). Short selling can be done by retail as well as institutional investors. Naked short sale is not permitted in India, all short sales must result in delivery and information on short sale has to be disclosed to the exchange by end of day by retail investors, and at the time of trade for institutional investors. The Securities Lending and Borrowing mechanism allows short sellers to borrow securities for making delivery. Securities in the F&O segment are eligible for short selling.

### ❖ Arbitration

Arbitration is an alternative dispute resolution mechanism provided by a stock exchange for resolving disputes between the trading members and their clients in respect of trades done on the exchange.

### ❖ BSE Indo*Next*

RSEs have registered negligible business during the last few years and thus small- and medium-sized companies (SMEs) listed there find it difficult to raise fresh resources in the absence of price discovery of their securities in the secondary market. As a result, investors also do not find exit opportunity in case of such companies.

BSE Indo*Next* has been formed to benefit such SMEs, the investors in these companies and capital markets at large. It has been set up as a separate trading platform under the present BSE Online Trading (BOLT) system of the BSE. It is a joint initiative of BSE and the Federation of Indian Stock Exchanges (FISE).

### ❖ Corporatization of Stock Exchanges

Corporatization is the process of converting the organizational structure of the stock exchange from a non-corporate structure to a corporate structure.

Traditionally, some of the stock exchanges in India were established as 'Association of persons', e.g., BSE, Ahmedabad Stock Exchange (ASE) and Madhya Pradesh Stock Exchange (MPSE). Corporatization of such exchanges is the process of converting them into incorporated companies.

### ❖ Demutualization of Stock Exchanges

Demutualization refers to the transition process of an exchange from a 'mutually-owned' association to a company 'owned by shareholders'. In other words, transforming the legal structure of an exchange from a mutual form to a business corporation form is referred to as demutualization. The above, in effect, means that after demutualization, the ownership, the management and the trading rights at the exchange are segregated from one another.

### ❖ Day Trading

Day trading refers to buying and selling of securities within the same trading day such that all positions will be closed before the market close of the trading day. In the Indian securities market, only retail investors are allowed to day trade.

### ❖ Direct Market Access

Direct Market Access (DMA) is a facility which allows brokers to offer clients direct access to the exchange trading system through the broker's infrastructure without manual intervention by the broker. Some of the advantages offered by the DMA are direct control of clients over orders, faster execution of client orders, reduced risk of errors associated with manual order entry, greater transparency, increased liquidity, lower impact costs for large orders, better audit trails and better use of hedging and arbitrage opportunities through the use of decision support tools/algorithms for trading. Presently, the DMA facility is available for institutional investors.

## CAPITAL MARKET REFORMS

Capital market reforms initiated by government after 1991 are as follows:

### ❖ Introduction of Dematerialization

Share certificates were printed on paper resulting in operational cost and risk. Theft and counterfeiting of share certificates gave rise to criminal activities. In order to solve this problem, the National Securities Depository Services (India) Limited was set up in November 1996. The depository maintains a computer record of ownership of securities and dispenses with physical share certificates. This form of trading is known as 'Demat'.

### ❖ Derivatives Trading

Derivatives are contracts whose value is derived from the underlying asset. The underlying asset can be equity/foreign exchange/any other financial asset. Derivatives help in transferring the price risks either partially or fully by locking-in asset prices. By doing so, derivatives minimize the impact of asset price fluctuations on profitability and cash fallow status of investors who are averse to risk. Derivative trading in equities began in India in June 2000. There are four equity derivative products in India. They are stock options, stock futures, index options and index futures. Derivatives trading take place only in the NSE and the BSE.

## TRADING IN CENTRAL GOVERNMENT SECURITIES

Trading in government securities was introduced in January, 2003. It can be carried out through a nationwide, anonymous, orderdriver, screen-based trading system of stock exchanges. Retail investors are allowed to buy and sell government securities in stock exchanges. Individuals, firms, companies, corporate bodies, institutions, trusts and other entities approved by the RBI are allowed to participate in the retail market.

## ROLLING SETTLEMENT

Rolling settlement improves the efficiency and integrity of the securities market. Under rolling settlement, all trades executed on a trading day (T) are settled after certain days (N). This is called T + N rolling settlement. Since 1 April 2002, trades are settled under T + 3 rolling settlement. The NSE has introduced T + 2 rolling settlement from 1 April 2003. Under it, each order has a unique settlement date specified at the time of order entry. It is mandatory for trades to be settled on the predetermined settlement date.

## ESTABLISHMENT OF CREDITORS RATING AGENCIES

Mainly there are three credit rating agencies. The Investment Information & Credit Rating Agency of India Limited (ICRA, 1991), The Credit Rating Information Services of India Limited (CRISIL, 1988) and Credit Analysis and Research Limited (CARE) were set up in order to assess the financial health of different financial institutions and agencies related to the stock market activities. It is helpful for the investors also in evaluating the risk of their investments.

## INVESTOR'S PROTECTION

The SEBI was established by the Central Government of India for the purpose of Investors Education and Protection Fund (IEPF) in 2001. It works in educating and guiding investors. It tries to protect the interest of the small investors from frauds and malpractices in the capital market.

## GROWTH OF DERIVATIVE TRANSACTIONS

Since June 2000, the NSE has introduced the derivatives trading in the equities. In November 2001, it also introduced the future and options transactions. These innovative products have given variety for the investment leading to the increase of the capital market.

## COMMODITY TRADING

Along with the trading of ordinary securities, the trading in commodities is also recently encouraged.

In 2002, the Government of India allowed the reintroduction of commodity futures in India. The MCX (Multi Commodity Exchange) is set up. The volume of such transactions is growing at a splendid rate. As of now, apart from numerous regional exchanges, India has six national commodity exchanges namely, MCX started on 10 November 2003, National Commodity and Derivatives Exchange (NCDEX), National Multi-Commodity Exchange (NMCE), Indian Commodity Exchange (ICEX), the ACE Derivatives exchange (ACE) and the Universal Commodity Exchange (UCX).

The regulatory body is Forward Markets Commission (FMC) which was set up in 1953. As of September 2015, the FMC was merged with the SEBI.

## MANDATORY PAN REQUIREMENT

In order to maintain a good audit trail of the transactions in the securities market and to strengthen the 'know your client' concept, PAN has been made compulsory with effect from 01 January 2007.

## STOCK EXCHANGES PERMITTED TO SET TRADING HOURS

In 2009–10, the stock exchanges were permitted to set their trading hours in the cash and derivative segments subject to the condition that the trading hours are between 9 a.m. and 5 p.m., and the stock exchange has a risk management system and infrastructure commensurate with the trading hours.

## REITS/INVITS

Real Estate Investment Trust (REIT) or Infrastructure Investment Trust (InvIT) is a form of alternative investment vehicle conceptualized in 2008. The working mechanism of an REIT involves purchase of commercial properties and then providing them on rent to tenants. The funding is done through issuance of units to public which are tradable on stock exchanges. The main advantage of an REIT structure is grounded on the tax exemptions that it receives.

REITs are modelled after mutual funds and provide their investors with all types of income streams – as well as the benefits of long-term capital appreciation. An REIT also trades on major stock exchanges and provides investors with a highly liquid stake in real assets typically offering high yields.

InvITs, on the other hand, are a globally popular financial instrument. Scoring points due to its tax-efficient nature (not liable to pay Dividend Distribution Tax (DDT) and corporate tax) and higher yields compared to global market. InvITs are instruments that work like mutual funds. InvITs are designed to pool small sums of money from a number of investors to invest in assets that give cash flow over a period of time. Part of this cash flow would be distributed as dividend back to investors. Often, infrastructure projects such as roads or highways take some time to generate steady cash flows. Meanwhile, the infrastructure company has to pay interest to banks for the loans taken by it. An InvIT essentially gives the company the leeway to fulfil its debt obligations quickly.

## DERIVATIVE MARKET

A derivative is a contract between two parties which derives its value/price from an underlying asset. Originally, underlying corpus is first created which can consist of one security or a combination of different securities. The value of the underlying asset is bound to change as the value of the underlying assets keeps changing continuously. Generally, stocks, bonds, currency, commodities and interest rates form the underlying asset.

As derivatives are merely contracts between two or more parties, anything like weather data or amount of rain can be used as underlying assets.

The derivatives can be classified as future contracts, forward contracts, options, swaps and credit derivatives.

### ❖ Financial Derivatives in India

At present, the Indian stock markets are not having any risk-hedged instruments that would allow the investors to manage and minimize the risk. In industrialized countries apart from money market and capital market securities, a variety of other securities known as 'derivatives' have now become available for investment and trading.

A derivative is a financial product which has been derived from another financial product or commodity.

### ❖ Characteristics

Accounting standard SFAS133 defines 'a derivative instrument is a financial derivative or other contract' which will comprise of all three of the following characteristics:

1. It has one or more underlying asset, and one or more notional amount or payments provisions or both. Those terms determine the amount of the settlement or settlements.
2. It requires no initial net investment or an initial net investment that is smaller than would be required for other types of contract that would be expected to have a similar response to changes in market factors.

3. Its terms require or permit net settlement. It can be readily settled net by a means outside the contract or it provides for delivery of an asset that puts the recipients in a position not substantially different from net settlement.

From the aforementioned, derivatives refer to securities or to contracts that derive from another whose value depends on another contract or assets. As such the financial derivatives are financial instrument whose prices or values are derived from the prices of other underlying financial instruments or financial assets.

The underlying instruments may be an equity share, stock, bond, debenture, treasury bill, foreign currency or even another derivative asset. Hence, financial derivatives are financial instruments whose prices are derived from the prices of other financial instruments. As defined above, its value is entirely derived from the value of the underlying asset.

## ❖ Uses of Financial Derivatives

Some of the uses and applications of financial derivatives can be enumerated as following:

1. **Management of risk:** One of the most important services provided by the derivatives is to control, avoid, shift and manage efficiently different types of risk through various strategies like hedging, arbitraging, spreading, etc. Derivative assists the holders to shift or modify suitably the risk characteristics of the portfolios. These are specifically useful in highly volatile financial conditions like erratic trading, highly flexible interest rates, volatile exchange rates and monetary chaos.
2. **Price discovery:** The important application of financial derivatives is the price discovery which means revealing information about future cash market prices through the future market. Derivative markets provide a mechanism by which diverse and scattered opinions of future are collected into one readily discernible number which provides a consensus of knowledgeable thinking.
3. **Liquidity and reduced transaction cost:** As we see that in derivative trading, no immediate full amount of the transaction is required since most of them are based on margin trading. As a result, large number of traders, speculators and arbitrageurs operate in such markets. So, derivative trading enhances liquidity and reduces transaction cost in the markets of underlying assets.
4. **Measurement of market:** Derivatives serve as the barometers of the future trends in price which result in the discovery of new prices both on the spot and future markets. They help in disseminating different information regarding the future market trading of various commodities and securities to the society which enables to discover or form suitable or correct or true equilibrium price in the markets. As a result, the assets will be in an appropriate and superior allocation of resources in the society.
5. **Efficiency in trading:** Financial derivatives allow for free trading of risk components and that leads to improving market efficiency. Traders can use a position in one or more financial derivatives as a substitute for a position in underlying instruments. In many instances, traders find financial derivatives to be a more attractive instrument than the underlying security. This is mainly because of the greater amount of liquidity in the market offered by derivatives as well as the lower transaction costs associated with trading a financial derivative as compared to the costs of trading the underlying instruments in cash market.
6. **Speculation and arbitrage:** Derivatives can be used to acquire risk, rather than to hedge against risk. Thus, some individuals and institutions will enter

into a derivative contract to speculate on the value of the underlying asset, betting that the party seeking insurance will be wrong about the future value of the underlying asset. Speculators look to buy an asset in the future at a low price according to a derivative contract when the future market price is high, or to sell an asset in the future at a high price according to derivative contract when the future market price is low. Individual and institutions may also look for arbitrage opportunities, as when the current buying price of an asset falls below the price specified in a futures contract to sell the asset.

7. **Hedging:** Hedge or mitigate risk in the underlying, by entering into a derivative contract whose value moves in the opposite direction to their underlying position and cancels part or all of it out. Hedging also occurs when an individual or institution buys an asset and sells it using a future contract. They have access to the asset for a specified amount of time and can then sell it in the future at a specified price according to the futures contract of course; this allows them the benefit of holding the asset.
8. **Price stabilization function:** Derivative market helps to keep a stabilizing influence on spot prices by reducing the short-term fluctuations. In other words, derivatives reduce both peak and depths and lends to price stabilization effect in the cash market for underlying asset.
9. **Gearing of value:** Special care and attention about financial derivatives provide leverage (or gearing) such that a small movement in the underlying value can cause a large difference in the value of the derivative.
10. **Develop the complete markets:** It is observed that derivative trading develops the market towards 'complete markets'. Complete market concept refers to that situation where no particular investors be better off than others, or patterns of returns of all additional securities are spanned by the already existing securities in it, or there is no further scope of additional security.
11. **Encourage competition:** The derivative trading encourages the competitive trading in the market by different risk-taking preferences at market operators like speculators, hedgers, traders, arbitrageurs, etc., resulting in increase in trading volume in the country. They also attract young investors, professionals and other experts who will act as catalysts to the growth of financial market.
12. **Other uses:** The other uses of derivatives are observed from the derivative trading in the market that the derivatives have smoothen out price fluctuations, squeezed the price spread, integrated price structure at different points of time and removes gluts and shortage in the markets. The derivatives also assist the investors, traders and managers of large pools of funds to device such strategies so that they may make proper asset allocation to increase their yields and achieve other investment goals.

## ❖ Major Derivatives

1. **Forward Contract:** A forward contract is a customized contract between the buyer and the seller where settlement takes place on a specific date in future at a price agreed today. In case of a forward contract, the price which is paid/received by the parties is decided at the time of entering into contract. It is simplest form of derivative contract mostly entered by individual in day-to-day life.

   The holder of a long (short) forward contract has an agreement to buy (sell) an asset at a certain time in the future for a certain price, which is agreed upon today. The buyer (or seller) in a forward contract:

(i) Acquires a legal obligation to buy (or sell) an asset (known as the underlying asset)

(ii) At some specific future date (the expiration date)

(iii) At a price (the forward price) which is fixed today

2. **Futures Contract:** Futures contract is an agreement between two parties to buy or sell a specified quantity of an asset at a specified price and at a specified time and place. Future contracts are normally traded on an exchange which sets the certain standardized norms for trading in futures contracts. The features of a futures contract may be specified as follows:

(i) Futures are traded only in organized exchanges.

(ii) Futures contract required to have standard contract terms.

(iii) Futures exchange is associated with clearing house.

(iv) Futures trading required margin payment and daily settlement.

(v) Futures positions can be closed easily.

(vi) Futures markets are regulated by regulatory authorities like the SEBI.

(vii) The futures contracts are executed on expiry date.

(viii) The futures prices are expressed in currency units, with a minimum price movement called a tick size.

3. **Options Contracts:** Options are derivative contract that gives the right, but not the obligation, to either buy or sell a specific underlying security for a specified price on or before a specific date. In theory, option can be written on almost any type of underlying security. Equity (stock) is the most common, but there are also several types of non-equity options, based on securities such as bonds, foreign currency, indices or commodities such as gold or oil. The person who buys an option is normally called the buyer or holder. Conversely, the seller is known as the seller or writer. Again, we can say 'An option is a particular type of a contract between two parties where one person gives the other person the right to buy or sell a specific asset at a specified price within a specified time period'. Today, options are traded on a variety of instruments like commodities, financial assets as diverse as foreign exchange, bank time deposits, treasury securities, stock, stock indexes, petroleum products, food grains, metals, etc. The main characteristics of options are following:

(i) Options holders do not receive any dividend or interest.

(ii) Option yields only capital gains.

(iii) Options holder can enjoy a tax advantage.

(iv) Options are traded on OTC and in all recognized stock exchanges.

(v) Option holders can control their rights on the underlying assets.

(vi) Options create the possibility of gaining a windfall profit.

(vii) Option holder can enjoy a much wider risk–return combinations.

(viii) Options can reduce the total portfolio transaction costs.

(ix) Options enable the investors to gain a better returns with a limited amount of investment.

4. **Swap Contract:** A swap is an agreement between two or more people or parties to exchange sets of cash flows over a period in future. Swaps are agreements between two parties to exchange assets at predetermined intervals. Swaps are generally customized transactions. The swaps are innovative financing which reduces borrowing costs and increases control over interest rate risk and FOREX exposure. The swap includes both spot

and forward transactions in a single agreement. Swaps are at the centre of the global financial revolution. Swaps are useful in avoiding the problems of unfavourable fluctuation in FOREX market. The parties that agree to the swap are known as counter parties. The two commonly used swaps are interest rate swaps and currency swaps. Interest rate swaps entail swapping only the interest-related cash flows between the parties in the same currency. Currency swaps entail swapping both principal and interest between the parties, with the cash flows in one direction being in a different currency than the cash flows in the opposite direction.

## COMMODITIES MARKET/ COMMODITIES FUTURES

The commodities market is a physical or a virtual space, where one can buy, sell or trade various commodities at current or future date.

One can also do commodity trading using futures contracts. A futures contract is an agreement between the buyer and the seller, wherein the buyer promises to pay the agreed-upon sum at the moment of the transaction when the seller delivers the commodity at a predecided date in the future.

A farmer can thus buy wheat futures to fix a price at which he would want to sell a certain amount in future. Similarly, a trader might buy or sell wheat futures for delivery on a future date at a price decided now.

Like a stock, one can invest in a commodity through the commodity bourses. India has six commodity exchanges such as MCX, NCDEX, NMCE, ICEX, ACE and the UCX.

## SCHEMES RELATED TO CAPITAL MARKET IN INDIA

### ❖ Rajiv Gandhi Equity Savings Scheme (RGESS)

The Rajiv Gandhi Equity Savings Scheme (RGESS) is a new equity tax advantage savings scheme for equity investors in India, with the stated objective of 'encouraging the savings of the small investors in the domestic capital markets'. It was approved by The Union Finance Minister, Shri. P. Chidambaram on 21 September 2012. It is exclusively for the first time retail investors in securities market.

### Salient Features of the Scheme

1. The scheme is open to new retail investors identified on the basis of their PAN.
2. The tax deduction allowed will be over and above the ₹ 1 lakh limit permitted allowed under Section 80C of the Income Tax Act.
3. In addition to the 50 per cent tax deduction for investments, dividend income is also tax free.
4. For investments up to ₹ 50,000 in the sole RGESS demat account, if the investor opts for a basic service demat account, annual maintenance charges for the demat account are zero and for investments up to ₹ 2 lakh, ₹ 100.
5. Stocks listed under BSE 100 or CNX 100, or stocks of PSUs that are Navratnas, Maharatnas and Miniratnas will be eligible under the scheme. Follow-on public offers (FPOs) of these companies will also be eligible.
6. IPOs of PSUs, which are scheduled to get listed in the relevant financial year and whose annual turnover is not less than ₹ 4,000 crores for each of the immediate past 3 years, will also be eligible.
7. Exchange-traded funds (ETFs) and MFs that have RGESS-eligible securities as their underlying and are listed and traded in the stock exchanges and settled through a depository mechanism have also been brought under the RGESS to provide the advantage of diversification and consequent risk minimization.
8. To benefit the small investors, investments are allowed in instalments in the year in which tax claims are made.

9. The total lock-in period for investments will be 3 years including an initial blanket lock-in of 1 year.
10. After the first year, investors will be allowed to trade in the securities. Investors are free to trade/churn their portfolios for around 90 days in each of the years following the first year of investment.
11. Investors would, however, be required to maintain their level of investment during these 2 years at the amount for which they have claimed income tax benefit or at the value of the portfolio before initiating a sale transaction, whichever is less, for at least 270 days in a year.
12. The general principle under which trading is allowed is that whatever is the value of stocks/units sold by the investor from the RGESS portfolio, RGESS-compliant securities of at least the same value are credited back into the account subsequently. However, the investor is allowed to take benefit of the appreciation of his RGESS portfolio, provided its value remains above the investment for which he has claimed income tax benefit.
13. In case the investor fails to meet the conditions stipulated, the tax benefit will be withdrawn.

## GOLD-RELATED SCHEMES

On 5 November 2015, the Union government launched three gold-related schemes, viz., Gold Monetization Scheme, Sovereign Gold Bond Scheme and Gold Coin/Bullion Scheme.

1. **Gold Monetization Scheme (GMS), 2015:** The GMS replaced the earlier Gold Deposit Scheme, 1999. However, the deposits outstanding under the Gold Deposit Scheme were allowed to run till maturity unless the depositors prematurely withdraw them.

**Objective**

The objective of introducing the modifications in the schemes is to make the existing schemes more effective and to broaden the ambit of the existing schemes from merely mobilizing gold held by households and institutions in the country to putting this gold into productive use.

The long-term objective which is sought through this arrangement is to reduce the country's reliance on the import of gold to meet domestic demand.

GMS would benefit the Indian gems and jewellery.

The mobilized gold will also supplement RBI's gold reserves and will help in reducing the government's borrowing cost.

2. **Sovereign Gold Bond (SGB):** The SGBs are government securities denominated in grams of gold. They are substitutes for holding physical gold. Investors have to pay the issue price in cash, and the bonds will be redeemed in cash on maturity. The bond is issued by the Reserve Bank on behalf of the Government of India.

The SGB offers a superior alternative to holding gold in physical form. The risks and costs of storage are eliminated.

The main idea is to reduce the demand for physical gold and shift part of the estimated 300 tons of physical bars and coins purchased every year for investment into 'demat' gold bonds.

3. **Gold Coin/Bullion Scheme:** The Indian gold coin and bullion is a part of the Gold Monetization Programme. The coin is the first-ever national gold coin minted in India and has the National Emblem of Ashok Chakra engraved on the one side and Mahatma Gandhi on the other side.

Initially, they are available in denominations of 5 and 10 grams. A 20-gram bullion will also be available.

The Indian gold coin and bullion are of 24 karat purity and 999 fineness. All coins and bullions are hallmarked as per the BIS standards.

## MONEY MARKET IN INDIA

Money market is a short-term credit market for short-term funds. Money market deals in financial securities whose period of maturity is in the range of one day to one year. Money market financial securities or assets are near substitutes of money. In the money market, the commercial banks are the major lenders of money. The central bank is the controlling authority of the money market.

### ❖ Components of Indian Money Market

The Indian money market is divided into two parts, namely, the organized and the unorganized money markets. Interest rates are different in both the markets, and there is no relationship whatsoever between the two markets.

The unorganized sector consists of indigenous bankers, money lenders and unregulated non-bank financial intermediaries such as finance companies, chit funds and nidhis. Farmers, artisans and other small-time producers and traders borrow money from the unorganized money market.

The organized money market is the formal market for money regulated by the central bank with commercial banks being the main players. Foreign banks, co-operative banks, Discount and Finance House of India, finance companies, provident funds, Securities Trading Corporation of India, PSUs and mutual funds are the other institutions which operate in the formal Indian money market. The RBI is the monetary authority controlling the formal money market.

The formal Indian money market is well organized and integrated. Mumbai, Kolkata, Delhi, Chennai, Ahmedabad and Bangalore are the main centres of the organized sector. Out of these, the Mumbai money market is the largest.

### ❖ The Organized Sector of the Indian Money Market

The components of the organized Indian Money Market are as follows:

1. The Call Money Market
2. The Treasury Bill Market
3. The Repo Market
4. The Commercial Bill Market
5. The Certificate of Deposit Market
6. The Commercial Paper Market
7. Money Market Mutual Funds

These components are explained below:

1. **The Call Money Market:** In this market, borrowing and lending transactions are carried out for one day. These loans are called Call Loans. They may not be renewed on the following day.

   It is also known as the Inter-bank Call Money Market. Scheduled commercial banks, co-operative banks and DFHI operate in it. The Unit Trust of India, the Life Insurance Corporation of India, the General Insurance Corporation of India, the Industrial Development Bank of India and the National Bank of Agriculture and Rural Development also operate in the Indian money market as lenders.

   The Call Money Market is a mechanism whereby temporary surplus of some banks is made available to others who have a temporary deficit. It is a very sensitive market and hence reflects the liquidity condition of the money market. The RBI monitors the call money market to make day-to-day adjustment in its monetary policy.

2. **The Treasury Bill Market:** In India, treasury bills have maturity periods ranging from 14 days to 364 days. They are short-term liabilities of the Central

Government. The different maturity periods are 14 days, 91 days, 182 days and 364 days. Out of these, the auction of 14 days and 182 days treasury bills was discontinued from May 2001.

Treasury bills are issued for meeting temporary deficits which a government faces due to its excess of expenditure over revenue. Treasury bills are issued at a minimum amount of ₹ 25,000 and in multiples of ₹ 25,000. They are issued at a discount to face value and are redeemed at par.

From 01 April 1997, ad hoc treasury bills have been replaced by ways and means advances for financing the central government's temporary deficits. The Treasury Bill market in India is in a state of underdevelopment. The RBI is a captive holder of the bills issued by the Central Government. The RBI rediscounts treasury bills presented by other banks. This has resulted in monetization of public debt and has become a cause of expansion of money supply and price rise.

3. **The Repo Market:** Repo is a repurchase agreement in which the seller sells a security under an agreement to repurchase at a predetermined date and rate. It is a money market instrument which enables short-term borrowing and lending through sale and purchase operations. The Repo was introduced in the year 1992. The Reverse Repo was introduced in the year 1994 by the RBI.

   Repos help to manage liquidity conditions. They are used to provide banks an opportunity to invest funds generated by capital inflows. During times of foreign exchange volatility, repos have been used to prevent speculative activity as the funds tend to flow from the money market to the foreign exchange market.

4. **The Commercial Bill Market:** The commercial bill market is the market for short-term bills of 3-month duration. It provides short-term finance to trade and industry. The commercial bills are used to finance the transactions of goods taking place between different companies. When goods are sold on credit, companies which receive the goods become liable to make payment on a specific date in future. The companies who sell the goods can wait till the specified date or can make use of commercial bill of exchange. The seller of the goods draws the bill, and the buyer accepts it. Once the bill is accepted, it becomes a marketable instrument. The drawer or the seller of goods can approach a commercial bank and get the bill discounted.

5. **The Certificate of Deposit Market:** The certificate of deposit is a short-term money market instrument introduced in the year 1989. Certificate of Deposits are issued by banks against the deposits kept by individuals, companies and institutions. Certificate of Deposits are issued at a discounted rate, and the discount rate is market determined. They are freely transferable by endorsement and delivery. CDs are a marketable and negotiable instrument. The CDs were issued by scheduled commercial banks in multiples of ₹ 25 lakh subject to the minimum size of an issue being ₹ 1 crore and the maturity ranged between 3 months and 1 year.

6. **The Commercial Paper Market:** The Commercial paper (CP) was introduced by the RBI in March 1989 and was made effective in January 1990. The CPs were introduced to provide companies with good credit rating a source of short-term borrowing. The CPs are issued in the form of unsecured usance promissory notes by the companies with good credit rating at a discount, and the discount rate

is market determined. They are freely transferable and negotiable.

The company wanting to issue CP is required to obtain every 6 months a specified rating from an agency approved by the RBI. According to the RBI's guidelines, a company will have to obtain P2 rating from Credit Rating Information Services of India Limited or A2 rating from Investment Information and Credit Rating Agency of India Limited. Maturity period of CP issued by various companies ranged from 3 months to 6 months, and the effective interest rates were in the range of 9.35 to 20.9 per cent per annum.

7. **Money Market Mutual Funds:** A scheme of money market mutual funds was introduced by the RBI in April 1992. The objective of the scheme was to provide one more short-term avenue to the individual investors. Banks, public and private financial institutions were allowed to set up MMMFs in 1995.

   Resources mobilized by MMMFs are required to be invested in call money, CDs, CPs, commercial bills arising out of genuine trade transactions, treasury bills and government dated securities having an unexpired maturity up to one year.

   Banks are now allowed to set up MMMFs only as a separate entity in the form of a trust.

## ❖ Unorganized Sector of the Indian Money Market

The constituents of the unorganized sector of the Indian Money Market are as follows:

1. **Non-Banking Financial Companies (NBFCs):** These companies assume various forms. Some of the prominent forms of NBFCs are loan/finance companies, chit funds and nidhis.

   These companies offer loans to retailers, wholesale traders, artisans and self-employed persons. They charge very high rates of interest ranging from 36 to 48 per cent.

   The Chit funds are saving institutions. A Chit fund has regular members who make periodic subscriptions to the fund. The periodic collection is given to some member of the chit fund selected on the basis of agreed criterion. Each member of the fund is assured of his/her turn before the second round starts and any member becomes entitled to get periodic collection again. The chit fund business is conducted all over the country, but Tamil Nadu and Kerala account for the largest share of the business. The RBI has no control over the activities of chit funds.

   The RBI has started regulating NBFCs engaged in equipment leasing, hire purchase finance, loan and investment, residuary non-banking companies and the deposit receiving activity of miscellaneous non-banking financial companies. According to the amendment to the RBI Act in 1997, the NBFCs are obliged to apply for a certificate of registration.

2. **Indigenous Bankers:** Individual Bankers are individuals or private firms that receive deposits and give loans. These bankers have been engaged in the banking business from ancient times.

   There are four main sub-groups of indigenous bankers: Gujarati shroffs, Multani or Shikarpuri Shroffs, Chettiars and Marwari Kayas. The Gujarati shroffs are the most prosperous bankers.

3. **Money Lenders:** They are three types of money lenders: professional money lenders, itinerant money lenders like pathans and Kabulis, and non-professional money lenders. These money lenders charge exploitative rates of interest, indulge in manipulation of loan records and extract free labour from the poor borrowers. They are not regulated or supervised by the government.

The unorganized money market survives and flourishes in India because of two important factors. They are as follows:

1. A large amount of unaccounted wealth and income floats in the country, and the creamy section of the black economy both on the lenders and the depositors side operate in this market, and
2. The poor who cannot access the organized market for want of securities look at the unorganized market as the lender of last resort.

## TERMS RELATED TO FINANCIAL MARKET

- **Arbitrageurs:** Arbitrageurs are traders who simultaneously buy and sell the same (or different, but related) assets in an effort to profit from unrealistic price differentials. They attempt to make profits by locking in a riskless trading by simultaneously entering into transaction in two or more markets. They try to earn riskless profit from discrepancies between futures and spot prices and among different futures prices.
- **Arbitration:** Arbitration is an alternative dispute resolution mechanism provided by a stock exchange for resolving disputes between the trading members and their clients in respect of trades done on the exchange.
- **Auction:** The Exchange purchases the requisite quantity in the Auction Market and gives them to the buying trading member. The shortages are met through auction process, and the difference in price indicated in contract note and price received through auction is paid by member to the Exchange, which is then liable to be recovered from the client.
- **Averaging:** The process of gradually buying more and more securities in a declining market (or selling in a rising market) in order to level out the purchase (or sale) price.
- **Backwardation/Ulta Badla/Undha Badla:** The payment of money charges made by a seller of shares which he borrows to deliver against his sale. These charges become payable only when there are more sellers who are not in a position to deliver against their sale. These charges become payable to the buyer, when the seller is not in a position to deliver the documents to the buyers who demand delivery.
- **Badla:** Carrying forward of transactions from one settlement period to another without effective delivery. This is permitted only in specified securities and is done at the making up price which is usually the closing price of the last day of settlement.
- **Basis:** In a futures market, basis is defined as the cash price (or spot price) of whatever is being traded minus its futures price for the contract in question. It is important because changes in the relationship between cash and futures prices affect the values of using futures as a hedge. A hedge, however, will always reduce risk as long as the volatility of the basis is less than the volatility of the price of whatever is being hedged.
- **Bear Market:** A weak or falling market characterized by the dominance of sellers.
- **Bear Trap:** A false signal indicating that the rising trend of a stock or index has reversed when in fact it has not. This can occur during a bear market reversal when short sellers believe the markets will sink back to its declining ways. If the market continues to rise, the shorters get trapped and are forced to cover their position at higher prices.
- **Blue Chip:** The best rated shares with the highest status as investment based on return, yield, safety, marketability and liquidity.
- **Bond:** A negotiable certificate evidencing indebtedness – a debt security or IOU, issued by a company, municipality or government agency. A bond investor lends money to the issuer and, in exchange, the issuer promises to repay the loan amount

on a specified maturity date. The issuer usually pays the bondholder periodic interest payments over the life of the loan.

- **Bonus Shares:** Shares issued by companies to their shareholders free of cost by capitalization of accumulated reserves from the profits earned in the earlier years.
- **Boom:** A condition of the market denoting increased activity with rising prices and higher volume of business resulting from greater demand of securities. It is a state where enlarged business, both investment and speculative, has been taking place for a sufficiently reasonable period of time.
- **Broker:** A member of a Stock Exchange who acts as an agent for clients and buys and sells shares on their behalf in the market. He is enrolled as a member with the concerned exchange and is registered with the SEBI. Though strictly a stock broker is an agent, yet for the performance of his part of the contract both in the market and with the client, he is deemed as a principal, a peculiar position of dual responsibility.
- **BSE Indo*Next*:** Regional stock exchanges (RSEs) have registered negligible business during the last few years and thus small and medium-sized companies (SMEs) listed there find it difficult to raise fresh resources in the absence of price discovery of their securities in the secondary market. As a result, investors also do not find exit opportunity in case of such companies. BSE Indo*Next* has been formed to benefit such small and medium size companies (SMEs), the investors in these companies and capital markets at large. It has been set up as a separate trading platform under the present BSE Online Trading (BOLT) system of the BSE. It is a joint initiative of BSE and the Federation of Indian Stock Exchanges (FISE).
- **Bubble:** A speculative sharp rise in share prices which like the bubble is expected to suddenly burst.
- **Bull Market:** A rising market with abundance of buyers and relatively few sellers.
- **Bull:** A market player who believes prices will rise and would, therefore, purchase a financial instrument with a view to selling it at a higher price. Opposite of a bear.
- **Buy back:** The repurchase by a company of its own stock or bonds.
- **Call option:** An agreement that gives an investor the right, but not the obligation, to buy an instrument at a known price by a specified date. For this privilege, the investor pays a premium, usually a fraction of the price of the underlying security.
- **Chinese walls:** Artificial barriers to the flow of information set up in large firms to prevent the movement of sensitive information between departments.
- **Close-ended Fund:** A type of investment company that has a fixed number of shares which are publicly traded. The price of a closed-end share fluctuates based on investor supply and demand. Closed-ended funds are not required to redeem shares and have managed portfolios.
- **Corporate Bonds:** The term Corporate Bonds referred includes all debt securities issued by institutions such as banks, PSUs, municipal corporations, bodies corporate and companies having a tenure of more than 365 days. Such an issue of bonds, if offered to the public, shall be required to comply with the SEBI (Disclosure and Investor Protection Guidelines), 2000.
- **Corporatization of Stock Exchanges:** Corporatization is the process of converting the organizational structure of the stock exchange from a non-corporate structure to a corporate structure.

  Traditionally, some of the stock exchanges in India were established as 'Association of persons', e.g., the Stock Exchange, Mumbai (BSE), Ahmedabad Stock Exchange (ASE) and Madhya Pradesh Stock Exchange (MPSE). Corporatization of such exchanges is the process of converting them into incorporated Companies.

- **Coupon:** The interest paid on a bond expressed as a percentage of the face value. If a bond carries a fixed coupon, the interest is paid on an annual or semi-annual basis. The term also describes the detachable certificate entitling the bearer to payment of the interest. The interest rate stated on the face of coupon is called coupon rate.
- **Credit rating:** Credit ratings measure a borrower's creditworthiness and provide an international framework for comparing the credit quality of issuers and rated debt securities. Rating agencies allocate three kinds of ratings: issuer credit ratings, long-term debt and short-term debt
- **Dabba trading:** Trading of securities outside the stock exchanges. The broker instead of routing the trade of his clients in the system of stock exchanges matches or executes the trades of its clients in a system provided by him outside the stock exchange.
- **Day Trading:** Day trading refers to buying and selling of securities within the same trading day such that all positions will be closed before the market close of the trading day. In the Indian securities market, only retail investors are allowed to day trade.
- **Demutualization of Stock Exchanges:** Demutualization refers to the transition process of an exchange from a 'mutually-owned' association to a company 'owned by shareholders'. In other words, transforming the legal structure of an exchange from a mutual form to a business corporation form is referred to as demutualization. The above, in effect, means that after demutualization, the ownership, the management and the trading rights at the exchange are segregated from one another.
- **Depository:** A system of organization, which keeps records of securities, deposited by its depositors. The records may be physical or simply electronic records. Depository participant (DP) is an agent of the depository through which it interfaces with the investor. A DP can offer depository services only after it gets proper registration from the SEBI.
- **Derivative:** (1) A security derived from a debt instrument, share, loan whether secured or unsecured, risk instrument or contract for differences or any other form of security; (2) A contract which derives its value from the prices, or index or prices, of underlying securities. Derivative Markets are markets such as futures and option markets that are developed to satisfy specific needs arising in traditional markets. These markets provide the same basic functions as forward markets, but trading usually takes place on standardized contracts.
- **DMA:** DMA is a facility which allows brokers to offer clients direct access to the exchange trading system through the broker's infrastructure without manual intervention by the broker. Some of the advantages offered by DMA are direct control of clients over orders, faster execution of client orders, reduced risk of errors associated with manual order entry, greater transparency, increased liquidity, lower impact costs for large orders, better audit trails and better use of hedging and arbitrage opportunities through the use of decision support tools/algorithms for trading. Presently, DMA facility is available for institutional investors.
- **Discount:** When a security is quoted at a price below its nominal or face value, it is said to be at a discount.
- **Dividend:** Payment made to shareholders, usually once or twice a year out of a company's profit after tax. Dividend payments do not distribute the entire net profit of a company, a part or substantial part of which is held back as reserves for the company's expansion. Dividend is declared on the face value or par value of a share, and not on its market price.

- **Exchange traded derivative:** Those derivative instruments that are traded via specialized derivative exchange of other exchange. A derivative exchange is a market where individual trade standardized contracts that have been defined by the exchange. Derivative exchange acts as an intermediary to all related transactions and takes initial margin from both sides of the trade to act as a guarantee.
- **Haircut:** (1) The margin or, more frequently, the capital tied up when a financial intermediary takes a position. (2) A commission or fee for execution of a transaction (uncommon).
- **Hedge:** An asset, liability or financial commitment that protects against adverse changes in the value of or cash flows from another investment or liability. An unhedged investment or liability is called an 'exposure'. A perfectly matched hedge will gain in value what the underlying exposure loses or what the underlying exposure gains.
- **Hedgers**: Hedgers are traders who use derivatives to reduce the risk that they face from potential movements in a market variable, and they want to avoid exposure to adverse movements in the price of an asset. Majority of the participants in derivatives market belongs to this category.
- **Insider trading:** Practice of corporate agents buying or selling their corporation's securities without disclosing to the public significant information which is known to them but which has not yet affected the price. Institutional Investors Organizations those invest, including insurance companies, depository institutions, pension funds, investment companies and endowment funds. Insider is any person who is or was connected with the company or is deemed to have been connected with the company, and who is reasonably expected to have access, connection, to unpublished price sensitive information in respect of securities of a company, or who has received or has had access to such unpublished price sensitive information.
- **Intangible Assets:** An item of value whose true worth is hard or almost impossible to determine such as goodwill reputation, patents and so on.
- **Jobber:** Member brokers of a stock exchange who specialize, by giving two way quotations, in buying and selling of securities from and to fellow members. Jobbers do not have any direct contact with the public but they serve the useful function of imparting liquidity to the market.
- **Kiting:** The act of misrepresenting the value of a financial instrument for the purpose of extending credit obligations or increasing financial leverage. Kiting generally occurs when securities firms fail to deliver securities involved in buy and sell transactions in a timely manner (before the three-day settlement period). When this occurs, the firm failing to receive the securities is required to purchase the shortage on the open market and charge the delinquent firm any associated fees.
- **Long Position:** A position showing a purchase or a greater number of purchases than sales in anticipation of a rise in prices. A long position can be closed out through the sale of an equivalent amount.
- **Margin Trading**: Margin Trading is trading with borrowed funds/securities. It is essentially a leveraging mechanism which enables investors to take exposure in the market over and above what is possible with their own resources. SEBI has been prescribing eligibility conditions and procedural details for allowing the Margin Trading Facility from time to time.

  Corporate brokers with net worth of at least ₹ 3 crore are eligible for providing Margin trading facility to their clients subject to their entering into an agreement to that effect. Before providing margin trading facility to a client, the member and the client have been mandated to sign an agreement for this purpose in the format specified by SEBI. It has also been specified that the client shall not avail the facility from more than one broker at any time.

The facility of margin trading is available for Group 1 securities and those securities which are offered in the initial public offers and meet the conditions for inclusion in the derivatives segment of the stock exchanges.

For providing the margin trading facility, a broker may use his own funds or borrow from scheduled commercial banks or NBFCs regulated by the RBI. A broker is not allowed to borrow funds from any other source.

- **Naked Option:** An option that is written without corresponding security or option position as protection in seller's account.
- **Net Asset Value (NAV):** The current market worth of a mutual fund's share. A fund's net asset value is calculated by taking the fund's total assets, securities, cash and any accrued earnings, deducting liabilities, and dividing the remainder by the number of units outstanding.
- **Pay-in Day and Pay-out Day:** Pay in day is the day when the brokers shall make payment or delivery of securities to the exchange. Pay out day is the day when the exchange makes payment or delivery of securities to the broker. Settlement cycle is on T+2 rolling settlement basis w.e.f. April 01, 2003. The exchanges have to ensure that the pay out of funds and securities to the clients is done by the broker within 24 hours of the payout. The Exchanges will have to issue press release immediately after pay out.
- **Ponzi Scheme:** A classic contrick that has been repeated many times both before and since Charles( Carlo) Ponzi gave it its name in the 1920s. The scheme begins with a crook setting up as a deposit taking institution. The crook invites the public to place deposits with the institution, and offers them a generous rate of interest. The interest is then paid out of new depositors' money, and the crook lives well off the old deposits. The whole scheme collapses when there are not enough new deposits coming in to cover the interest payment due on the old ones. By that time the modern day Ponzi hopes to be living under an alias in a hot country with few extradition laws.
- **Portfolio:** A collection of securities owned by an individual or an institution (such as a mutual fund) that may include stocks, bonds and money market securities.
- **Preferred Stock / Preference Shares:** Owners of this kind of stock are entitled to a fixed dividend to be paid regularly before dividend can be paid on common stock. They also exercise claims to assets, in the event of liquidation, senior to holders of common stock but junior to bondholders. Holders of preferred stock normally do not have a voice management.
- **Premium:** If an investor buys a security for a price above its eventual value at maturity he has paid a premium for it.
- **Price discovery:** A general term for the process by which financial markets attain an equilibrium price, especially in the primary market. Usually refers to the incorporation of information into the price
- **Prospectus:** Any document described or issued as a prospectus and includes any notice, circular, advertisement or other document inviting deposits from the public or inviting offers from the public for the subscription or purchase of any shares in, or debentures of, a body corporate.
- **Public Issue:** An invitation by a company to public to subscribe to the securities offered through a prospectus.
- **Put Option:** An option that gives the right to sell a fixed number of securities at a specified price (the strike price) within a specified period of time.

- **Redemption Price:** The price at which a bond is redeemed (cashed in).
- **Reverse book building:** Reverse book building is similar to the process of book building, which is aimed at securing the optimum price for a company's share. In reverse book building the investors' aim is to sell the shares to exit the company.
- **Securities Transaction Tax:** Securities Transaction Tax (STT) is a tax being levied on all transactions done on the stock exchanges at rates prescribed by the Central Government from time to time. Pursuant to the enactment of the Finance Act, 2004, the Government of India notified the Securities Transaction Tax Rules, 2004 and STT came into effect from October 1, 2004.
- **Securitization:** The process of homogenizing and packaging financial instruments into a new fungible one. Acquisition, classification, collateralization, composition, pooling and distribution are functions within this process.
- **Selling Short:** A manner in which an investor sells securities he does not possess in the hope of buying them back later at a lower price.
- **Share transfer agent:** Any person who on behalf of anybody corporate maintains the record of holders of securities issued by such body corporate and deals with all matters connected with the transfer and redemption of its 66 securities. It can also be a department or division (by whatever name called) of a body corporate performing the above activities if, at any time the total number of the holders of securities issued exceed one lakh.
- **Short Covering:** Buying of stocks by a seller to complete his previous commitments.
- **Short position:** In futures, the short has sold the commodity or security for future delivery; in options, the short has sold the call or the put and is obligated to take a futures position if he or she is assigned for exercise.
- **Short Selling:** Short Selling means selling of a stock that the seller does not own at the time of trade. Short selling can be done by borrowing the stock through Clearing Corporation/Clearing House of a stock exchange which is registered as Approved Intermediaries (AIs). Short selling can be done by retail as well as institutional investors. Naked short sale is not permitted in India, all short sales must result in delivery, and information on short sale has to be disclosed to the exchange by end of day by retail investors, and at the time of trade for institutional investors. The Securities Lending and Borrowing mechanism allows short sellers to borrow securities for making delivery. Securities in the F&O segment are eligible for short selling.
- **Speculators:** Speculators are traders who buy/sell the assets only to sell/buy them back profitably at a later point in time. They want to assume risk. They use derivatives to bet on the future direction of the price of an asset and take a position in order to make a quick profit. They can increase both the potential gains and potential losses by usage of derivatives in a speculative venture.
- **Sub-broker:** A sub broker is a person who is registered with SEBI as such and is affiliated to a member of a recognized stock exchange.
- **Underwriter:** One who does underwriting. A financial organization that handles sales of new securities which a company or municipality wishes to sell in order to raise money. Typically, the underwriters will guarantee subscription to securities say, an issue of equity from the company at a stated price, and are under an obligation to purchase securities up to the amount they have underwritten, should the public not subscribe for the issue.

  Underwriting is an agreement with or without conditions to subscribe to the securities of a body corporate when the existing shareholders of such body corporate or the public do not subscribe to the securities offered to them.

- **Venture Capital:** Professional moneys co-invested with the entrepreneur usually to fund an early stage, more risky venture. Offsetting the high risk is the promise of higher return that the investor takes. A venture capitalist not only brings in moneys as 'equity capital' (i.e. without security/charge on assets) but also brings on to the table extremely valuable domain knowledge, business contacts, brand equity, strategic advice, etc. He is a fixed interval investor, whom the entrepreneurs approach without the risk of 'takeover'.
- **Volatility:** Volatility equates to the variability of returns from an investment. It is an acceptable substitute for risk; the greater the volatility, the greater is the risk that an investment will not turn out as hoped because its market price happens to be on the downswing of a bounce at the time that it needs to be cashed in. The problem is that future volatility is hard to predict and measures of past volatility can, themselves, be variable, depending on how frequently returns are measured (weekly or monthly, for example) and for how long. Therefore, putting expectations of future volatility into predictive models is of limited use, but resorting to using past levels of volatility is equally limited.
- **Volume of Trading:** The total number of shares which changes hands in a particular company's securities. This information is useful in explaining and interpreting fluctuation in share prices.
- **Warrant:** An options contract often sold with another security. For instance, corporate bonds may be sold with warrants to buy common stock of that corporation. Warrants are generally detachable.
- **Wolf:** Speculators who make a kill in the market.
- **Writer:** A person who issues an option. The individual who at the end of the day has to buy or sell the asset on which the option is written, should the person who holds the option wish to exercise his rights.
- **X-Dividend:** A term meaning 'without dividend'. A stock bought on or after the X-dividend day will not pay the purchaser the dividend already declared.

❑❑❑

CHAPTER 5

# Industrial Sector in India

The industrial sector in India, including construction, is an important contributor to the growth with the sector accounting for 31.1 per cent of the total Gross Value Added (GVA) in 2016–17. A strong and a robust industrial and manufacturing sector helps in promoting domestic production, exports and employment, all of which can be catalysts for higher growth in the economy.

## INDUSTRIAL POLICIES IN INDIA

Policies are framed to provide direction to obtain an end. The Industrial Policies of India were also framed to meet the challenges as an end and to give direction to obtain economic development and growth through industrialization after independence.

## INDUSTRIAL POLICY RESOLUTION, 1948

The first important industrial policy statement was made in the Industrial policy Resolution (IPR), 1948. The main thrust of the IPR was to lay down the foundation of mixed economy whereby the private and public sector was accepted as important components in the development of industrial economy of India.

The policy divided the industries into four broad categories:

1. **Industries with Exclusive State Monopoly:** It included industries engaged in the activity of atomic energy, railways and arms and ammunition.
2. **Industries with Government Control:** It included the industries of national importance and so needs to be registered. Eighteen such industries were put under this category, e.g., fertilizers, heavy chemical, heavy machinery, etc.
3. **Industries in the Mixed Sector:** It included the industries where private and public sector were allowed to operate. The Government was allowed to review the situation to acquire any existing private undertaking.
4. **Industries under Private Sector:** Industries not covered by above categories fell in this category.

In order to regulate the industry and to promote planned industrial development according to the IPR, 1948, the Industrial (Development and Regulation) Act in 1951 was passed to arm the Government with sufficient power.

## INDUSTRIAL POLICY RESOLUTION, 1956

The IPR of 1956 was meant to give a concrete shape to the mixed economy model and the ideology of socialist pattern of society.

The important provisions were as follows:

1. The IPR, 1956, divided the industries into the following three categories:
   (i) **Schedule A industries:** The industries that were the monopoly of state or Government. It included 17 industries. The private sector was allowed to operate in these industries if national interest so required.

   The reserved industries were: Arms and ammunition and allied items of defence equipment; Atomic energy; Iron and Steel; Heavy castings and forgoing of iron and steel; Heavy plant and machinery required for iron and steel production for mining, for machine tool manufacture and for such other basic industries as may be specified by the Central Government; Heavy electric plant including large hydraulic and steam turbines; Coal and lignite, gypsum, Sulphur, gold and diamond; Mining and processing of copper, lead, zinc, tin, molybdenum and wolfarm; Minerals specified in the schedule to the atomic energy (control of production and use) order 1953; Aircraft; Air transport; Railway transport; Ship-buildings; Telephones; Telephone cables; Telegraph and Wireless apparatus (excluding radio receiving sets) and Generation and distribution of electricity.

   (ii) **Schedule B industries:** In this category of industries, state was allowed to establish new units, but the private sector was not denied to set up or expand existing units. In this category, 12 industries were included, e.g., chemical industries, fertilizer, synthetic, rubber, aluminium, etc.

   (iii) **Schedule C industries:** The industries not mentioned in the above two categories formed part of Schedule C. Thus, the IPR, 1956, emphasized the mutual existence of public and private sector industries.

2. **Encouragement to Small-scale and Cottage Industries:** In order to strengthen the small-scale sector supportive measures were suggested in terms of cheap credit, subsidies, reservation, etc.

3. **Emphasized on Reduction of Regional Disparities:** Fiscal concessions were granted to open industries in backward regions. Public sector enterprises (PSEs) were given greater role to develop these areas.

## INDUSTRIAL POLICY OF 1977

The Industrial Policy of 1977 classified the small sector into three categories:

(a) Cottage and household industries, (b) Tiny sector and (c) Small-scale industries.

The purpose of the classification was to design policy measures for each category.

The Industrial Policy of 1977 attempted to define the role of large-scale sector by declaring them: (a) Basic industries for providing infrastructural items like cement, non-ferrous, steel, oil, etc. to small industries and others; (b) Capital goods industries required by small-scale industries; (c) High technology industries widely required by small scale and agriculture sector and (d) Other industries.

The Industrial Policy of 1977 specified that the public sector would not only be the producer of important and strategic goods of basic nature, but it would also be used effectively as a stabilizing force for maintaining essential supplies for the consumer.

The strategy of Industrial Policy of 1977 depended on the enforcement of Foreign Exchange Regulations Act (FERA).

## INDUSTRIAL POLICY OF 1980

The Industrial Policy Statement of July 1980 spells out the following socio-economic objectives: (i) Optimum utilization of installed capacity; (ii) Maximum production and achieving higher productivity; (iii) Higher employment generation; (iv) Correction of regional imbalances; (v) Strengthening of the agricultural base through agro-based industries and promotion of optimum inter-sectoral relationship; (vi) Promotion of export-oriented industries; (vii) Promotion of economic federalism through equitable spread of investment and dispersal of returns and (viii) Consumer protection against high prices and bad quality.

## INDUSTRIAL POLICY OF 1991

On 24 July 1991, the government announced a new industrial policy with an aim to correct the distortion and weakness of the industrial structure of the country that had developed in last four decades, raise industrial efficiency to the international level and accelerate industrial growth.

### ❖ Major Objectives

1. Development and utilization of indigenous capabilities in technology and manufacturing as well as its up gradation to world standard.
2. Dismantling of the regulatory system, development of the capital market and increasing competitiveness for the benefit of the common man.
3. Running of the public sector on business lines and
4. Promoting workers participation in management, enhancing their welfare and equipping them to deal with inevitability of technological change.

To fulfil the above objectives, the government introduced a series of initiatives in the new industrial policy in the following areas:

1. **Industrial Licensing Policy:** Industrial licensing has been abolished for all projects except for a short list of industries related to security and strategic concerns, social reasons hazardous chemicals and overriding environmental reason, and items of elitist consumption.

   Now, licensing is compulsory for only five Industries, (i.e., alcohol, cigarettes, hazardous chemical, electronic aero scope, defence equipment and industrial explosive).
2. **Foreign Investment**
   - (i) Automatic approval will be given for direct foreign investment up to 51 per cent equity in high priority industries.
   - (ii) The Foreign Investment Promotion Board has been constituted to negotiate with a number of large international firms and approve direct foreign investment.
   - (iii) Automatic permission will be given for foreign technology agreements in high priority industries.
3. **Public Sector Policy**
   - (i) The policy reduced the number of industries reserved for the public sector to three industries, i.e., atomic energy, minerals and rail transport.
   - (ii) Public enterprises, which are chronically sick and which are unlikely to be turned to normal health, will be referred to the Board for Industrial and Financial Reconstruction (BIFR) for advice about rehabilitation and reconstruction.
   - (iii) In order to raise resources and encourage wider public participation, a part of the government's shareholding in the public sector would be offered to mutual funds, financial

institutions, general public and workers.

(iv) Board of public sector companies would be made more professional and given greater powers.

4. **MRTP Act:** The Monopolies and Restrictive Trade Practices (MRTP) Act has been abolished. Emphasis was placed on controlling and regulating monopolistic, restrictive and unfair trade practices.
5. Abolition of Phased Manufacturing Programmes and removal of mandatory convertibility clause and liberalization of location policy, etc. are some other provisions of this policy.

## NATIONAL MANUFACTURING POLICY, 2011

The need to raise the global competitiveness of the Indian manufacturing sector is imperative for the country's long-term growth. The National Manufacturing Policy is by far the most comprehensive and significant policy initiative taken by the Government. The policy is the first of its kind for the manufacturing sector as it addresses areas of regulation, infrastructure, skill development, technology, availability of finance, exit mechanism and other pertinent factors related to the growth of the sector.

### ❖ Vision of the Policy

1. An increase in manufacturing sector growth to 12–14 per cent per annum over the medium term.
2. An increase in the share of manufacturing in the country's Gross Domestic Product from 16 to 25 per cent by 2022.
3. To create 100 million additional jobs by 2022 in manufacturing sector
4. Creation of appropriate skill sets among rural migrants and the urban poor for inclusive growth.
5. An increase in domestic value addition and technological depth in manufacturing.
6. Enhancing the global competitiveness of the Indian manufacturing sector.
7. Ensuring sustainability of growth, particularly with regard to environment.

The Policy focuses following sectors:

1. Employment-intensive industries like textiles and garments, leather and footwear, gems and jewellery and food processing industries.
2. Capital goods industries like machine tools, heavy electrical equipment, heavy transport, earthmoving and mining equipment.
3. Industries with strategic significance like aerospace, shipping, IT hardware and electronics, telecommunication equipment, defence equipment and solar energy.
4. Industries where India enjoys a competitive advantage such as automobiles, pharmaceuticals and medical equipment.
5. Small and medium enterprises.
6. Public sector enterprises.

## NATIONAL INVESTMENT AND MANUFACTURING ZONES (NIMZ)

The National Investment and Manufacturing Zones have been conceived as giant industrial Greenfield townships to promote world-class manufacturing activities. The minimum size is 5,000 hectares wherein the processing area has to be at least 30 per cent.

The central government will be responsible for bearing the cost of master planning, improving/providing external physical infrastructure linkages including rail, road, ports, airports and telecom, providing institutional infrastructure for productivity, skill development and the promotion of domestic and global investments.

The identification of land will be undertaken by state governments. State governments will be responsible for water requirement, power connectivity, physical infrastructure, utility linkages, environmental impact studies and bearing the cost of resettlement and rehabilitation packages for the owners of acquired land. The state government will also play a role in its acquisition if necessary.

In government, purchase preferences will be given to units in the national investment and manufacturing zones.

The Central and State governments are to provide exemptions from rules and regulations related to labour, environment, etc. A single window clearance would be provided for units in NIMZ.

## ❖ Incentives

**Transfer of Assets:** In case a unit is declared sick, the transfer of assets will be facilitated by the company managing the affairs of NIMZ.

**Green Technology and Practices:** 5 per cent interest in reimbursement and 10 per cent capital subsidy for the production of equipment/machines/devices for controlling pollution, reducing energy consumption and water conservation.

**Technology Development:** Incentives for the production of equipment/machines/ devices for controlling pollution, reducing energy consumption and water conservation. Small and Medium Enterprises (SMEs) will be given access to the patent pool and/or part of reimbursement of technology acquisition costs up to a maximum of ₹ 20,00,000 for the purpose of acquiring appropriate technologies up to a maximum of 5 years.

**Special benefits to SMEs:** Rollover relief from long-term capital gains tax to individuals on sale of residential property in case of reinvestment of sale consideration. A tax pass-through status for venture capital funds with a focus on SMEs in the manufacturing sector.

The NIMZs identified under DMIC are: (i) Ahmedabad-Dholera Investment region, Gujarat; (ii) Shendra-Bidkin Industrial Park City near Aurangabad, Maharashtra; (iii) Manesar-Bawal investment Region, Haryana; (iv) Khushkhera-Bhiwadi-Neemrana Investment Region, Rajasthan; (v) Pithampur-Dhar-Mhow Investment Region, Madhya Pradesh; (vi) Dadri-Noida-Ghaziabad Investment Region, Uttar Pradesh; (vii) Dighi-Port Industrial Area, Maharashtra and (viii) Jodhpur-Pali-Marwar region, Rajasthan.

National Investment and Manufacturing Zones identified outside DMIC are: Kuhi and Umred Taluka, Maharashtra; Tumkur, Karnataka; Chittoor, Andhra Pradesh; Medak, Telangana; Prakasam, Andhra Pradesh; Gulbarga, Karnataka; Kolar, Karnataka; Bidar, Karnataka and Kalinganagar, Odisha.

# NATIONAL MANUFACTURING COMPETITIVENESS PROGRAMME (NMCP)

On 8 December 2014, the Government of India has announced formulation of a NMCP with an aim to support the Micro, Small and Medium Enterprises (MSMEs) in their endeavour to become competitive.

The objective of NMCP is to develop global competitiveness among Indian MSMEs.

This programme targets at enhancing the entire value chain of the MSME sector through its nine components, i.e., (i) Lean Manufacturing Competitiveness Scheme for MSMEs; (ii) Promotion of Information and Communication Tools (ICT) in MSME sector; (iii)Technology and Quality Upgradation Support to MSMEs; (iv) Design Clinics scheme for MSMEs; (v) Enabling Manufacturing Sector to be Competitive through Quality Management Standards and Quality Technology Tools; (vi) Marketing

Assistance and Technology Up gradation Scheme for MSMEs; (vii) National campaign for building awareness on Intellectual Property Rights (IPR); (viii) Support for Entrepreneurial and Managerial Development of SMEs through Incubators and (ix) Bar Code under Market Development Assistance (MDA) scheme.

## MAKE IN INDIA

The Make in India initiative was launched by the Prime Minister in September 2014 as part of a wider set of nation-building initiatives. Devised to transform India into a global design and manufacturing hub.

The initiative aims at promoting India as an important investment destination and a global hub for manufacturing, design and innovation. The 'Make in India' initiative does not target manufacturing sector alone, but also aims at promoting entrepreneurship in the country. The initiative is further aimed at creating a conducive environment for investment, modern and efficient infrastructure, opening up new sectors for foreign investment and forging a partnership between government and industry through positive mindset.

The initiative is based on four pillars, which have been identified to give boost to entrepreneurship in India, not only in manufacturing but also in other sectors. The four pillars are:

1. **New Processes:** 'Make in India' recognizes 'ease of doing business' as the single most important factor to promote entrepreneurship. A number of initiatives have already been undertaken to ease business environment.
2. **New Infrastructure:** The Government intends to develop industrial corridors and smart cities, create world-class infrastructure with state-of-the-art technology and high-speed communication. Innovation and research activities are supported through a fast-paced registration system and improved infrastructure for IPR registration. The requirement of skills for industry are to be identified and accordingly development of workforce to be taken up.
3. **New Sectors:** Foreign Direct Investment (FDI) has been opened up in defence production, insurance, medical devices, construction and railway infrastructure in a big way.
4. **New Mindset:** In order to partner with industry in economic development of the country, Government shall act as a facilitator and not a regulator.

Components of the initiative are equally available to all regions of the country. In all, 25 sectors have been included in the programme.

The most striking indicator of the progress of the initiative is the unprecedented opening up of key sectors – including railways, defence, insurance and medical Devices – to FDI.

## PRADHAN MANTRI KAUSHAL VIKAS YOJANA (PMKVY)

On the occasion of the first ever World Youth Skills Day on 15 July 2015, the Ministry of Skill Development and Entrepreneurship (MSDE) launches the Skill India Campaign that aims to train over 40 crore people in India in different skills by 2022. It includes various initiatives of the government like 'National Skill Development Mission (NSDM)', 'National Policy for Skill Development and Entrepreneurship, 2015', 'Pradhan Mantri Kaushal Vikas Yojana' and 'Skill Loan Scheme'.

The Union Cabinet on 20 March 2015 gave its approval for the PMKVY with an outlay of ₹ 1,500 crore for skill training of youth through the National Skill Development Corporation (NSDC). It is a flagship scheme of the MSDE.

The objective of this Skill Certification Scheme is to enable a large number of Indian youth to take up industry-relevant skill training that will help them in securing a better livelihood. Individuals with prior learning experience or skills will also be assessed and certified under Recognition of Prior Learning (RPL).

Under this Scheme, training and assessment fees are completely paid by the Government.

Key Components of the Scheme are:

1. Short-term training
2. RPL
3. Special projects
4. Kaushal and Rozgar Mela
5. Placement guidelines
6. Monitoring guidelines

## PRADHAN MANTRI KAUSHAL KENDRAS (PMKK)

Vocational training needs to be made aspirational to transform India into the skill capital of the world. In line with the same, MSDE intends to establish visible and aspirational model training centres in every district of the country. NSDC is the implementation agency for the project.

These training centres will be state-of-the-art Model Training Centres (MTCs), called as Pradhan Mantri Kaushal Kendra (PMKK).

These centres would offer advanced training and also courses in foreign languages. This will help those of our youth who seek job opportunities outside the country.

The model training centres envisage to:

1. create benchmark institutions that demonstrate aspirational value for competency based skill development training.
2. focus on elements of quality, sustainability and connect with stakeholders in skills delivery process.
3. transform from a mandate driven footloose model to a sustainable institutional model.

## NATIONAL POLICY FOR SKILL DEVELOPMENT AND ENTREPRENEURSHIP, 2015

The Union Government on 1 July 2015 gave its approval for the India's first integrated National Policy for Skill Development and Entrepreneurship 2015. The Policy acknowledges the need for an effective roadmap for promotion of entrepreneurship as the key to a successful skills strategy.

### ❖ Vision

To create an ecosystem of empowerment by skilling on a large scale at speed with high standards and to promote a culture of innovation-based entrepreneurship which can generate wealth and employment so as to ensure sustainable livelihoods for all citizens in the country.

### ❖ Mission

The mission is to create a demand for skilling across the country; correct and align skilling with required competencies; connect the supply of skilled human resources with sectoral demands; certify and assess in alignment with global and national standards and catalyse an ecosystem wherein productive and innovative entrepreneurship germinates, sustains and grows leading to creation of a more dynamic entrepreneurial economy and more formal wage employment.

### ❖ Objectives

The core objective of the Policy is to empower the individual, by enabling her/him to realize their full potential through a process of lifelong learning where competencies are accumulated via instruments such as credible certifications, credit accumulation and transfer, etc. As individuals grow, the society and nation also benefit from their productivity and growth.

This will involve:

1. Make quality vocational training aspirational for both youth and employers whereby youth sees it as a matter of choice and employer acknowledges the productivity linked to skilled workforce by paying the requisite premium.
2. Ensure both vertical and horizontal pathways to skilled workforce for further growth by providing seamless integration of skill training with formal education.
3. Focus on an outcome-based approach towards quality skilling that on one hand results in increased employability and better livelihoods for individuals, and on the other hand translates into improved productivity across primary, secondary and tertiary sectors.
4. Increase the capacity and quality of training infrastructure and trainers to ensure equitable and easy access to every citizen.
5. Address human resource needs by aligning supply of skilled workers with sectoral requirements of industry and the country's strategic priorities including flagship programmes like Make in India.
6. Establish an IT-based information system for aggregating demand and supply of skilled workforce which can help in matching and connecting supply with demand.
7. Promote national standards in the skilling space through active involvement of employers in setting occupational standards, helping develop curriculum, providing apprenticeship opportunities, participating in assessments, and providing gainful employment to skilled workforce with adequate compensation.
8. Operationalize a well-defined quality assurance framework aligned with global standards to facilitate mobility of labour.
9. Leverage modern technology to ensure scale, access and outreach, in addition to ease of delivering content and monitoring results.
10. Recognize the value of on-the-job training, by making apprenticeships in actual work environments an integral part of all skill development efforts.
11. Ensure that the skilling needs of the socially and geographically disadvantaged and marginalized groups (like the SCs, STs, OBCs, minorities, differently abled persons, etc.) are appropriately taken care of.
12. Promote increased participation of women in the workforce through appropriate skilling and gender mainstreaming of training.
13. Promote commitment and ownership of all stakeholders towards skill development and create an effective coordination mechanism.

## NATIONAL SKILL DEVELOPMENT MISSION (NSDM)

The NSDM was approved by the Union Cabinet on 1 July 2015, and officially launched by the Prime Minister on 15 July 2015 on the occasion of World Youth Skills Day.

The Mission has been developed to create convergence across sectors and states in terms of skill training activities.

To achieve the vision of 'Skilled India', the NSDM would not only consolidate and coordinate skilling efforts, but also expedite decision-making across sectors to achieve skilling at scale with speed and standards.

It will be implemented through a streamlined institutional mechanism driven by MSDE.

Key institutional mechanisms for achieving the objectives of the Mission have been divided into three tiers: (i) a Governing Council for policy guidance at apex level; (ii) a Steering

Committee and (iii) a Mission Directorate as the executive arm of the Mission.

Mission Directorate will be supported by three other institutions: (i) National Skill Development Agency (NSDA); (ii) NSDC and (iii) Directorate General of Training (DGT).

Seven sub-missions have been proposed initially to act as building blocks for achieving overall objectives of the Mission. They are: (i) Institutional Training; (ii) Infrastructure; (iii) Convergence; (iv) Trainers; (v) Overseas Employment; (vi) Sustainable Livelihoods and (vii) Leveraging Public Infrastructure.

## ❖ Mission Objectives

1. Create an end-to-end implementation framework for skill development, which provides opportunities for life-long learning. This includes: incorporation of skilling in the school curriculum, providing opportunities for quality long- and short-term skill training, by providing gainful employment and ensuring career progression that meets the aspirations of trainees.
2. Align employer/industry demand and workforce productivity with trainees' aspirations for sustainable livelihoods, by creating a framework for outcome focused training.
3. Establish and enforce cross-sectoral, nationally and internationally acceptable standards for skill training in the country by creating a sound quality assurance framework for skilling, applicable to all Ministries, States and private training providers.
4. Build capacity for skill development in critical unorganized sectors (such as the construction sector, where there few opportunities for skill training) and provide pathways for re-skilling and up-skilling workers in these identified sectors, to enable them to transition into formal sector employment.
5. Ensure sufficient, high quality options for long-term skilling, benchmarked to internationally acceptable qualification standards, which will ultimately contribute to the creation of a highly skilled workforce.
6. Develop a network of quality instructors/trainers in the skill development ecosystem by establishing high quality teacher training institutions.
7. Leverage existing public infrastructure and industry facilities for scaling up skill training and capacity building efforts.
8. Offer a passage for overseas employment through specific programmes mapped to global job requirements and benchmarked to international standards.
9. Enable pathways for transitioning between the vocational training system and the formal education system, through a credit transfer system.
10. Promote convergence and co-ordination between skill development efforts of all Central Ministries/Departments/States/implementing agencies.
11. Support weaker and disadvantaged sections of society through focused outreach programmes and targeted skill development activities.
12. Propagate aspirational value of skilling among youth, by creating social awareness on value of skill training.
13. Maintain a national database, known as the Labour Market Information System (LMIS), which will act as a portal for matching the demand and supply of skilled workforce in the country.

## NATIONAL SKILL DEVELOPMENT CORPORATION

The NSDC of India was setup as a one of its kind, Public Private Partnership Company with the primary mandate of catalysing the skills landscape in India.

NSDC's philosophy is based on the following pillars:

1. **Create:** Proactively catalyse creation of large, quality vocational training institutions.
2. **Fund:** Reduce risk by providing patient capital including grants and equity.
3. **Enable:** The creation and sustainability of support systems required for skill development. This includes the Industry led Sector Skill Councils (SSCs).

The main objectives of the NSDC are to:

(i) Upgrade skills to international standards through significant industry involvement and develop necessary frameworks for standards, curriculum and quality assurance

(ii) Enhance, support and coordinate private sector initiatives for skill development through appropriate Public-Private Partnership (PPP) models; strive for significant operational and financial involvement from the private sector

(iii) Play the role of a 'market-maker' by bringing financing, particularly in sectors where market mechanisms are ineffective or missing

(iv) Prioritise initiatives that can have a multiplier or catalytic effect as opposed to one-off impact.

## SKILL LOAN SCHEME

Skill Loan Scheme was launched by the union government on 15th July, 2015 to provide loan facility to aspirants wanting to do skill development courses aligned to National Skill Qualification Framework (NSQF).

The important features of the Scheme are as follows:

1. Any Indian National who has secured admission in a course run by Industrial Training Institutes (ITIs), Polytechnics or in a school recognised by the Central or State education Boards or in a college affiliated to recognised university, training partners affiliated to NSDC SSCs, State Skill Mission and State Skill Corporation can avail loan for the purpose.
2. No processing fee is charged by banks.
3. Amount of loan ranges from ₹ 5,000 to ₹ 1,50, 000 depending on the course having a repayment period of 3 to 7 years.
4. Simple rate of interest @ 11 per cent and 12 per cent per annum is charged during the period of study.
5. No minimum course duration.
6. No specific restriction with regard to age.
7. Risk of banks covered through Credit Guarantee Fund Scheme for Skill Development (CGFSSD).
8. The loan is sanctioned without any collateral security or third party guarantee.

## SKILL ACQUISITION AND KNOWLEDGE AWARENESS FOR LIVELIHOOD PROMOTION PROGRAMME (SANKALP)

The Union Finance Minister announced that in the Financial Year 2017–18, a programme SANKALP (Skill Acquisition and Knowledge Awareness for Livelihood Promotion Programme) will be launched at a cost of ₹ 4,000 crore. SANKALP will provide market relevant training to 3.5 crore youth.

The objective is to enhance the employability potential of the youth to the maximum extent possible. It is indeed a good answer to the situation of unemployment among youths prevailing in our country that is preventing the economic and social development.

There are two phases to this Scheme: the first is the initial ₹ 4,000 crore, and the second phase starts with ₹ 2,200 crore. The second stage is termed as Skill Strengthening for Industrial Value Enhancement ( STRIVE).

## UDAAN

UDAAN is a Special Industry Initiative for Jammu & Kashmir in the nature of partnership between the corporates of India and Ministry of Home Affairs and implemented by NSDC.

The scheme was initially up to the 2015–16 which has been extended to 2019–20.

The programme aims to provide skills training and enhance the employability of unemployed youth of J & K.

The Scheme covers graduates, post-graduates and three year engineering diploma holders.

It has two objectives:

(i) To provide an exposure to the unemployed graduates to the best of Corporate India and

(ii) To provide Corporate India, an exposure to the rich talent pool available in the State.

The Scheme aims to cover 40,000 youth of J&K over a period of 5 years, and ₹ 750 crore has been earmarked for implementation of the scheme over a period of 5 years to cover other incidental expenses such as travel cost, boarding and lodging, stipend and travel and medical insurance cost for the trainees and administration cost. Further corporates are eligible for partial reimbursement of training expense incurred for the candidates who have been offered jobs.

## VOCATIONALIZATION OF EDUCATION

### ❖ School Education

The Centrally Sponsored Scheme of Vocationalization of Secondary Education of Ministry of HRD lists out a crucial role for NSDC and its SSCs in implementation of NSQF. The trainings conducted in the scheme are based on the National Occupational Standards set by NSDC through its SSCs. The scheme also mandates the SSCs to conduct assessments and certification jointly with the State Board.

Stakeholders in the Implementation are: State Government; NSDC; SSCs and NSDC Training Partner.

### ❖ Higher Education

In order to bridge the industry academia gap – NSDC has developed a unique model to integrate skill-based trainings into the academic cycle of the Universities. These are based on National Occupational Standards set by industry through SSCs.

NSDC is working with 21 Universities, UGC and AICTE catering to more than 1,200 colleges and 400 community colleges across the country.

## INVEST INDIA

Invest India is the official Investment Promotion and Facilitation Agency of the Department of Industrial Policy and Promotion (DIPP), mandated to facilitate investments into India. It is envisaged to be the first point of reference for potential investors.

The team of domain and functional experts of the agency provide sector-and state-specific inputs, and handholding support to investors through the entire investment cycle, from preinvestment decision-making to aftercare.

The agency assist with location identification; expediting regulatory approvals; facilitating meetings with relevant government and corporate officials and also provide aftercare services that include initiating remedial action on problems faced by investors.

All facilitation and handholding support to investors under the 'Make in India' programme is being provided by Invest India.

## eBiz PROJECT

eBiz is one of the integrated services projects and part of the 31 Mission Mode Projects (MMPs) under the National E-Governance Plan (NEGP) of the Government of India.

eBiz is being implemented by Infosys Technologies Limited (Infosys) under the guidance and aegis of Department of Industrial Policy and Promotion (DIPP).

The focus of eBiz is to improve the business environment in the country by enabling fast and efficient access to Government-to-Business (G2B) services through an online portal. This will help in reducing unnecessary delays in various regulatory processes required to start and run businesses.

This project aims at creating an investor-friendly business environment in India by making all regulatory information starting from the establishment of a business, through its ongoing operations, and even its possible closure – easily available to the various stakeholders concerned. In effect, it aims to develop a transparent, efficient and convenient interface, through which the government and businesses can interact in a timely and cost effective manner, in the future.

### ❖ Vision

The vision of eBiz is to be the entry point for all individuals, businesses and organizations (local and international) which would like to do business or have any existing business in India by creating a one-stop-shop of convenient and efficient online G2B services to the business community, by reducing the complexity in obtaining information and services related to starting businesses in India, and dealing with licenses and permits across the business life cycle.

## SPECIAL ECONOMIC ZONES (SEZs)

The SEZs Policy was announced in April 2000 with a view to overcome the shortcomings experienced on account of the multiplicity of controls and clearances; absence of world-class infrastructure and an unstable fiscal regime and with a view to attract larger foreign investments in India. The Policy was announced with the objective of making the SEZ an engine for economic growth, supported by quality infrastructure and an attractive fiscal package both at the Central and State level with a single window clearance.

SEZ is a specifically delineated duty-free enclave and shall be deemed to be foreign territory for the purposes of trade operations and duties and tariffs. In order words, SEZ is a geographical region that has economic laws different from a country's typical economic laws. Usually, the goal is to increase foreign investments.

The SEZ concept recognizes the issues related to economic development and provides for developing self-sustaining Industrial Townships so that the increased economic activity does not create pressure on the existing infrastructure.

India was one of the first in Asia to recognize the effectiveness of the Export Processing Zone (EPZ) model in promoting exports, with Asia's first EPZ set up in Kandla in 1965.

Today, there are approximately 3,000 SEZs operating in 120 countries, which account for over US$ 600 billion in exports and about 50 million jobs.

### ❖ Objectives of SEZ in India

1. Generation of additional economic activity
2. Promotion of exports of goods and services
3. Promotion of investment from domestic and foreign sources
4. Creation of employment

5. Development of infrastructure facilities
6. Simplified procedures for development, operation, and maintenance of the SEZ and for setting up units and conducting business
7. Single window clearance for setting up of a SEZ and a unit in SEZ.
8. Single window clearance on matters relating to Central as well as State Governments
9. Easy and simplified compliance procedures and documentations

## ❖ SEZ Act, 2005, and SEZ Rules, 2006

To instil confidence in investors and signal the Government's commitment to a stable SEZ policy regime and with a view to impart stability to the SEZ regime thereby generating greater economic activity and employment through the establishment of SEZs, a comprehensive Special Economic Zones Act, 2005, which received Presidential assent on the 23 June 2005.

The SEZ Act supported by SEZ Rules, came into effect on 10 February 2006, providing for drastic simplification of procedures and for single window clearance on matters relating to central as well as State governments.

As a result of this Act and Rules coming into force, it was envisaged that the SEZs would attract a large flow of foreign and domestic investment in infrastructure and productive capacity leading to generation of additional economic activity and creation of employment opportunities.

The main objectives of the SEZ Act are: generation of additional economic activity; promotion of exports of goods and services; promotion of investment from domestic and foreign sources; creation of employment opportunities and development of infrastructure facilities.

However, the SEZ Act does not require 'Environmental Impact Assessment' as part of the application for new units. This is because SEZs are only permitted to contain 'non-polluting' industries and facilities.

The SEZ Rules, 2006, provide for:

1. Simplified procedures for development, operation, and maintenance of the Special Economic Zones and for setting up units and conducting business in SEZs;
2. Single window clearance for setting up of an SEZ;
3. Single window clearance for setting up a unit in a Special Economic Zone;
4. Single Window clearance on matters relating to Central as well as State Governments;
5. Simplified compliance procedures and documentation with an emphasis on self-certification.

## ❖ Approval Mechanism of SEZs

The developer submits the proposal for establishment of SEZ to the concerned State Government. The State Government has to forward the proposal with its recommendation within 45 days from the date of receipt of such proposal to the Board of Approval. The applicant also has the option to submit the proposal directly to the Board of Approval.

The Board of Approval has been constituted by the Central Government in exercise of the powers conferred under the SEZ Act. All the decisions are taken in the Board of Approval by consensus. The Board of Approval has 19 Members.

## ❖ Administrative Setup

The functioning of the SEZs is governed by a three-tier administrative set up. The Board of Approval is the apex body and is headed by the Secretary, Department of Commerce. The Approval Committee at the Zone level deals with approval of units in the SEZs and other-related issues. Each Zone is headed by a Development Commissioner, who is ex officio chairperson of the Approval Committee.

### ❖ Incentives and Facilities Offered to the SEZs

The incentives and facilities offered to the units in SEZs for attracting investments into the SEZs, including foreign investment, include:

1. Duty free import/domestic procurement of goods for development, operation and maintenance of SEZ units.
2. Hundred per cent Income Tax exemption on export income for SEZ units under Section 10AA of the Income Tax Act for first 5 years, 50 per cent for next 5 years thereafter and 50 per cent of the ploughed back export profit for next 5 years.
3. Exemption from minimum alternate tax under section 115JB of the Income Tax Act.
4. External commercial borrowing by SEZ units up to US $500 million in a year without any maturity restriction through recognized banking channels.
5. Exemption from Central Sales Tax.
6. Exemption from Service Tax.
7. Single window clearance for Central and State level approvals.
8. Exemption from State sales tax and other levies as extended by the respective State Governments.

In September 2016, the number of formal approvals was 408 (204 operationalized) and the number of notified SEZs was 328+ (7 Central + 11 State SEZs).

Total Investment in SEZs on 31 March 2016 was ₹ 3,76,494 crore.

Seven Central Government SEZs are located at Santa Cruz (Maharashtra), Cochin (Kerala), Kandla and Surat (Gujarat), Chennai (Tamil Nadu), Visakhapatnam (Andhra Pradesh), Falta (West Bengal) and Noida (Uttar Pradesh) in India.

### ❖ Argument Against SEZs

1. Loss in revenue of government due to special incentives offered
2. May result in land scams
3. Too many small SEZs, even China has few and large SEZs
4. May force non-SEZs units to shift to SEZs.
5. Create powerful and regional private monopolies
6. Shift focus on exports from serving the local markets.

## INDUSTRIAL PARK IN INDIA

An 'Industrial Park' means a project in which plots of developed space or built up space or a combination with common facilities and quality infrastructure facilities is developed and made available to the units for the purposes of industrial activities or commercial activities.

Objectives to be fulfilled by an industrial park are:

1. An 'Industrial Model Town' for the development of industrial infrastructure for carrying out integrated manufacturing activities, including research and development, by providing plots or sheds and common facilities within its precincts.
2. An industrial park for development of infrastructural facilities or built-up space with common facilities in any area allotted or earmarked for the purposes of industrial use.
3. A 'Growth Centre' under the Growth Centre Scheme of the Government of India provided that the scheme referred in this clause is implemented by an undertaking and the 'Growth Centre' is distinctly developed as a separate profit centre.

   The criteria for automatic approval for an industrial park as stated by DIPP include:

4. Minimum area required to be 1,000 acres (4.047 km$^2$) with minimum 50 units in case of 'Industrial Model Town' and varied area requirement with a minimum of 30 units in case of Industrial Park and 'Growth Centre';
5. Allocated area for industrial use to be not less than 60 per cent of total allocable area;
6. Area for commercial use to be not more than 10 per cent of total allocable area;
7. Investment on infrastructure to be not less than 50 per cent of the total project cost, in the case of an Industrial Model Town Industrial Park, or Growth Centre and 60 per cent of the total project cost in the case of an Industrial Park or Growth Centre and
8. No single unit shall occupy more than 50 per cent of the allocable industrial area.

The industrial estates are meant to curb the scattered growth of industrial activity and encourage industrial growth within geographical locations centrally linked by transport communication water power supply etc. Industrial estates support the confinement of industrial activities to defined areas in order to delimit any social and environmental damage caused by the industries.

## MODIFIED INDUSTRIAL INFRASTRUCTURE UPGRADATION SCHEME (MIIUS)

Industrial Infrastructure Upgradation Scheme (IIUS) was launched in 2003 with the objective of enhancing industrial competitiveness of domestic industry by providing quality infrastructure through public private partnership in selected functional clusters/ locations which have potential to become globally competitive. The Scheme was recast in February, 2009 on the basis of an independent evaluation to strengthen the implementation process. A modified version of IIUS viz. 'Modified Industrial Infrastructure Upgradation Scheme (MIIUS)' was notified in July 2013. Under MIIUS, projects have been undertaken to upgrade infrastructure in existing Industrial Parks/ Estates/ Areas. Greenfield Projects have also been undertaken in backward areas and North Eastern Region (NER). Projects are being implemented by the State Implementing Agency (SIA) of the State Government. Central Grant upto 50% of the project cost with a ceiling of Rs.50.00 crore is provided under MIIUS with at least 25% contributions of State Implementing Agency and in case of North Eastern States, the central grant and minimum contribution of the SIA are up to 80% and 10% respectively. A two stage approval mechanism has been retained in the Scheme.

Under MIIUS scheme, 21 projects have been sanctioned, out of which 14 projects have been completed and remaining 7 are under implementation. These projects have been provided central assistance of Rs. 371.616 crore (up to 31.08.2021), out of sanctioned central grant of Rs. 390.376 crore. Further, the scheme has not been continued beyond 31.03.2017 for taking up new projects.

## INDIA'S FIRST DEFENCE INDUSTRIAL PARK

The Union government's DIPP in July 2015 approved a proposal from the Kerala Industrial Infrastructure Development Corporation (KINFRA) to set up the country's first defence industrial park at Ottappalam.

The proposed park, which will be established as part of the Make in India, Make in Kerala project, will have modern common infrastructure facilities aimed at attracting component manufacturers in the defence industry. The Union government has agreed to bring it under the MIIUS.

The total expenditure for the defence park is estimated at ₹ 231.25 crore. KINFRA will invest ₹ 181.35 crore, while the rest of the amount is being expected as grant from the Union government.

The project is in line with the declaration of self-sufficiency in production in the defence sector. In addition to domestic production, exports are also on the rise. The central assistance is Rs.50 crore. Priority will be given to defence manufacturing, defence navigation products, aviation and naval systems, computer hardware and electronics, tactical communications systems, personal equipment and safety clothing.

Industrial land, building complex, warehouse and common facility centre are available for entrepreneurs. Infrastructure such as water, electricity, road and training room. are ready. The lease period is 30 years. Land and other facilities in the park will be allotted to those who qualify through KINFRA.

## WOMEN INDUSTRIAL PARK

India's first fully owned by women industrial park opened its doors in Hyderbad. The park, that is promoted by the FICCI Ladies Organization – FLO in collaboration with the State government, consists of 25 units which represent 16 different sectors of green category, and all of them are owned and controlled completely by women.

This FLO industrial park exemplifies the power and self-reliance of women in the business, from electronics to packaging, medical devices, wellness, engineering, and food processing. The FLO members has contributed a substantial amount of money for the construction of the park, while the government has provided the roads, electricity, water, sewerage, and sub-station.

### ❖ Significance

'It is estimated that the defence components manufacturing sector has demand estimated at $700 million a year from India and other countries having friendly relationship with it. In India, there is a 15 per cent gap between demand and supply. The defence park can bridge the gap apart from providing the country an opportunity in defence-related export of products from small- and medium-sized enterprises'.

Ottappalam was selected for the defence park keeping in view its strategic location as far as connectivity was concerned. Apart from common facilities such as dedicated power and water supply, the park will have a research and development centre.

## INDUSTRIAL SICKNESS

Industrial sickness is defined in India as an industrial company (being a company registered for not less than 5 years) which has, at the end of any financial year, accumulated losses equal to, or exceeding, its entire net worth and has also suffered cash losses in such financial year and the financial year immediately preceding such financial year.

According to Companies (Second Amendment) Act, 2002, Sick Industrial Company means an industrial company which has:

1. The Accumulated losses in any financial year equal to 50 per cent or more of its average net worth during 4 years immediately preceding such financial year or
2. Failed to repay its debts within any three consecutive quarters on demand made in writing for its repayment by a creditor or creditors of such company.

## REASONS FOR SICKNESS IN COMPANIES

There are different factors as a reason for industrial sickness.

**Internal Causes:**

- Entrepreneurial Incompetence
- Financial Problems
- Management Problems
- Gestation Period

- Defective Plant & Machinery
- Demand Forecasting: The company production schedule is completely based on demand forecasting.
- Labour Problems

**External Causes:**

- Demand and Credit Restrains
- Erratic Supply of Inputs/Power Cuts
- Government Policy
- Revival and Rehabilitation Measures

In the wake of sickness in the country's industrial climate prevailing in the eighties, the Government of India set up in 1981, a Committee of Experts under the Chairmanship of T. Tiwari to examine the matter and recommend suitable remedies therefore. Based on the recommendations of the Committee, the Government of India enacted a special legislation namely, the Sick Industrial Companies (Special Provisions) Act (SICA), 1985. The SICA received presidential assent on 8 January 1986.

The main objective of SICA was to determine sickness and expedite the revival of potentially viable units or closure of unviable units (unit here in refers to a Sick Industrial Company). It was expected that by revival, idle investments in sick units will become productive and by closure, the locked up investments in unviable units would get released for productive use elsewhere.

The Board of experts named the BIFR was set up in January 1987 and functional with effect from 15 May 1987. The Appellate Authority for Industrial and Financial Reconstruction (AAIFR) was constituted in April 1987. Government companies were brought under the purview of SICA in 1991 when extensive changes were made in the Act including, inter alia, changes in the criteria for determining industrial sickness.

SICA applies to companies both in public and private sectors owning industrial undertakings.

The criteria to determine sickness in an industrial company were given below:

1. The accumulated losses of the company to be equal to or more than its net worth, i.e., its paid up capital plus its free reserves.
2. The company should have completed 5 years after incorporation under the Companies Act, 1956.
3. It should have 50 or more workers on any day of the 12 months preceding the end of the financial year with reference to which sickness is claimed.
4. It should have a factory license.

## ❖ SICA Repealed

In an event that took more than a decade to fructify, the Ministry of Finance vide a notification dated 25th November 2016, has repealed the Sick Industrial Companies (Special Provisions) Act, 1985 (SICA) with effect from 1 December 2016. The Ministry also dissolved the BIFR and AIFR.

The Companies (Second Amendment) Act, 2002, inserted sections 424A to 424L that deal with sick companies to be administered by the Tribunal, in the Companies Act, 1956. The Repeal Act also was passed in 2004. However, neither of the amendments was notified or became operative.

The Companies Act, 2013, also included sections dealing with sick companies, but were not notified or made operative.

The Insolvency and Bankruptcy Code, 2016, (Insolvency Act) received the President's assent on 28 May 2016, and is to become operative from the notified date. The administrative provisions under the Insolvency Act were notified on different dates from August to November. Relevant operative provisions were notified on 30 November 2016. The Insolvency Act amended the Companies Act, 2013, to delete the provisions relating to sick companies. It also amended the Repeal Act to allow companies having pending proceedings under the SICA to approach the National Company Law Tribunal (NCLT) under the provisions of the Insolvency Act (preamendment applicable provisions were under the Companies Act, 1956) within the specified time without payment of fees.

The Repeal Act (as amended by the Insolvency Act) inter alia provides for the following:

- Repeal of the SICA and providing that such repeal shall not affect the orders passed under the SICA.
- Dissolution of the BIFR and the AIFR.
- Abatement of references/inquiries/appeals and all other proceedings that were pending before the BIFR/AIFR immediately before the appointed date.
- Such terminated appeals or references may be referred to the NCLT, constituted under the Companies Act, 2013, under the provisions of the Insolvency Act within 180 days from the commencement of the Insolvency Act.
- No fees would be charged on abated appeals/references referred to the NCLT within the prescribed time.
- Provides power to the central government to make rules for the implementation of the Repeal Act.

These notifications settle the long-term uncertainties prevailing around existence of the SICA, and provisions regulating sick companies. The Insolvency Act is expected to provide faster resolution, and is in line with efforts to promote the ease of doing business in India.

## INSOLVENCY AND BANKRUPTCY CODE, 2016

The objective of the new law is to promote entrepreneurship, availability of credit, and balance the interests of all stakeholders by consolidating and amending the laws relating to reorganization and insolvency resolution of corporate persons, partnership firms and individuals in a time bound manner and for maximization of value of assets of such persons and matters connected therewith or incidental thereto.

The law aims to consolidate the laws relating to insolvency of companies and limited liability entities (including limited liability partnerships and other entities with limited liability), unlimited liability partnerships and individuals, presently contained in a number of legislations, into a single legislation. Such consolidation will provide for a greater clarity in law and facilitate the application of consistent and coherent provisions to different stakeholders affected by business failure or inability to pay debt.

The salient features of the law are as follows:

(i) Clear, coherent and speedy process for early identification of financial distress and resolution of companies and limited liability entities if the underlying business is found to be viable.

(ii) Two distinct processes for resolution of individuals, namely- 'Fresh Start' and 'Insolvency Resolution'.

(iii) Debt Recovery Tribunal and NCLT to act as Adjudicating Authority and deal with the cases related to insolvency, liquidation and bankruptcy process in respect of individuals and unlimited partnership firms and in respect of companies and limited liabilities entities respectively.

(iv) Establishment of an Insolvency and Bankruptcy Board of India to exercise regulatory oversight over insolvency professionals, insolvency professional agencies and information utilities.

(v) Insolvency professionals would handle the commercial aspects of insolvency resolution process. Insolvency professional agencies will develop professional standards, code of ethics and be first level regulator for insolvency professionals members leading to development of a competitive industry for such professionals.

(vi) Information utilities would collect, collate, authenticate and disseminate financial information to be used in insolvency, liquidation and bankruptcy proceedings.

(vii) Enabling provisions to deal with cross border insolvency.

## DISINVESTMENT IN INDIA

Investment refers to the conversion of money or cash into securities, debentures, bonds or any other claims on money. As follows, disinvestment involves the conversion of money claims or securities into money or cash. Disinvestment can also be defined as the action of an organisation selling or liquidating an asset or subsidiary.

In Indian context, disinvestment typically refers to sale from the government, partly or fully, of a government-owned enterprise.

Privatization implies a change in ownership resulting in a change in management. However, disinvestment need not always imply change in management. Disinvestment is actually dilution of the stake of the government in a public enterprise. If the dilution is less than 50 per cent the government retains management even though disinvestment takes place. It is not privatized. But, if the dilution is more than 50 per cent, there is transfer of ownership and management. It will be called privatization.

### ❖ Reasons for Disinvestment

It is believed that the private ownership leads to better use of resources and their more efficient allocation.

The proliferation of market-based economy resulted in the fact that state could no longer meet the growing demands of the economy.

Globalization and WTO commitments need quick restructuring of the Public Sector Undertakings. If they are not able to adapt to this, they would not be able to survive.

There were two major reasons offered by the government for disinvestment. One was to provide fiscal support, and the other was to improve the efficiency of the enterprise.

### ❖ Objectives of Disinvestment

The following are the main objectives of disinvestment policy of the government.

1. To reduce the financial burden on government.
2. To improve public finances.
3. To introduce, competition and market discipline.
4. To find growth.
5. To encourage wider share of ownership.
6. To de-politicise essential services.
7. To diversify the ownership of PSU for enhancing efficiency of individual enterprise.
8. To introduce, competition and market discipline.

## THE DISINVESTMENT PROCESS IN INDIA

The following are the three methods adopted by the Government of India for disinvesting the Public Sector Undertakings.

1. **Minority Disinvestment:** A minority disinvestment is one such that, at the end of it, the government retains a majority stake in the company, typically greater than 51 per cent, thus ensuring management control.

   Examples of minority sales via auctioning to institutions go back into the early and mid-1990s. Some of them were Andrew Yule & Co. Ltd., CMC Ltd. etc. Examples of minority sales via Offer for Sale include recent issues of Power Grid Corp. of India Ltd., Rural Electrification Corp. Ltd., NTPC Ltd., NHPC Ltd., etc.
2. **Majority Disinvestment:** A majority disinvestment is one in which the government, post disinvestment, retains a minority stake in the company, i.e., it sells off a majority stake.

Majority disinvestments took place in the sale of Modern Foods to Hindustan Lever, BALCO to Sterlite, CMC to TCS, etc.

3. **Complete Privatisation:** Complete privatisation is a form of majority disinvestment wherein 100 per cent control of the company is passed on to a buyer. Examples of this include 18 hotel properties of ITDC and 3 hotel properties of HCI. Disinvestment and Privatisation are often loosely used interchangeably.

### ❖ Methods of Disinvestment of Central Public Sector Enterprises (CPSEs)

1. **Initial Public Offering (IPO):** Offer of shares by an unlisted CPSE or the Government out of its shareholding or a combination of both to the public for subscription for the first time.
2. **Further Public Offering (FPO):** Offer of shares by a listed CPSE or the Government out of its shareholding or a combination of both to the public for subscription.
3. **Offer for Sale (OFS) of shares by Promoters through Stock Exchange mechanism:** Method allows auction of shares on the platform provided by the Stock Exchange; extensively used by the Government since 2012.
4. **Strategic sale:** Sale of substantial portion of the Government shareholding of a CPSE of up to 50 per cent, or higher percentage, along with transfer of management control.
5. **Institutional Placement Program (IPP):** Only Institutions can participate in the offering.
6. **CPSE Exchange Traded Fund (ETF):** Disinvestment through ETF route allows simultaneous sale of Government's stake in various CPSEs across diverse sectors through single offering. It provides a mechanism for the government to monetize its shareholding in those CPSEs which form part of the ETF basket.

## RANGARAJAN COMMITTEE, 1993

The Rangarajan Committee of 1993 was constituted by the government for making recommendations in context with the disinvestment. The committee said that,

1. The units to be disinvested should be identified and disinvestment could be made up to any level, except in defence and atomic energy where the government should retain the majority holding in equity.
2. Disinvestment should be a transparent process duly protecting the right of the workers.
3. An autonomous body for the smooth functioning and monitoring of the disinvestment programme should be established. This recommendation led to the Disinvestment Commission in 1996 as an advisory body having a full time chairman and four part-time members. The Commission was required to advise the government on the extent, made, timing and pricing of disinvestment.
4. It suggested four modes of disinvestment viz. Trade sale, Strategic Sale, Offer of shares and Closure or sale of Assets.
5. It suggests 49 per cent disinvestment in PSUs reserved for public sector, and 74 per cent disinvestment in all other PSUs, but government did not implement them.

Vajpayee government classifies PSUs into two parts:

1. **Strategic:** PSUs related to arms and ammunition, railway, nuclear energy, etc. Here no disinvestment was to be done.
2. **Non-strategic:** Disinvestment was to be done in a phased manner. Disinvestment was taken up in Hindustan Zinc, BALCO and Maruti Udyog Limited.

To implement above policy, the Department of Disinvestment was set up under the Ministry of Finance.

The UPA-2 government announced that all PSUs can be disinvested, but upper limit would be 49 per cent and the disinvestment method would be only public offer. Disinvestment of Indian Oil, BHEL, NHPC, Neyveli Lignite, etc. was allowed.

Narendra Modi cabinet approved disinvestment in NHPC, Coal India and ONGC. Other identified names include insurance companies and three railway PSUs – IRTCTC, IRFC and IRCON.

## RATNA STATUS OF PUBLIC SECTOR ENTERPRISES

The CPSEs have played a key and vital role in developing the nation on the global map. In 1996–1997, it was decided by Government of India that public sector companies having comparative advantages should be supported in terms of grant of autonomy in their drive to become global giants by giving the Navaratna status. Seeing the performance of Navaratna companies, government decided to introduce Maharatna scheme to empower mega CPSEs to expand their operations as global giants on 4 February 2010. Seven CPSEs have been given Maharatna status.In October 1997, a concept of Miniratna was introduced.

1. **Maharatna Scheme:** The Government had introduced the 'Navratna' scheme, in 1997, to identify CPSEs that had comparative advantages and to support them comparative advantages and to support them in their drive to become global giants.

   The CPSEs which are at the higher end of the 'Navratna' category and have higher end of the 'Navratna' category and have potential to become Indian Multinational Companies (MNCs), are recognized as a separate class, i.e., 'Maharatna'.

   The new objective of the 'Maharatna' scheme is to empower mega CPSEs to expand their operations and emerge as global giants. The 'Maharatna' Scheme will empower big sized CPSEs to expand their operations and emerge as global giants.

   The CPSEs fulfilling the following criteria are eligible to be considered for grant of Maharatna status:

   (i) Having Navratna status.

   (ii) Listed on Indian stock exchange with minimum prescribed public shareholding under SEBI regulations.

   (iii) Average annual turnover of more than ₹ 25,000 crore, during the last 3 years.

   (iv) 4. Average annual net worth of more than ₹ 15,000 crore, during the last 3 years.

   (v) Average annual net profit after tax of more than ₹ 5,000 crore, during the last 3 years.

   (vi) Should have significant global presence/international operations.

2. **Navratna Scheme:** Navratna was the title given originally to nine PSEs, identified by the Government of India in 1997 as its most prestigious, which allowed them greater autonomy to compete in the global market.

   The Navratna status is offered to PSEs, which gives a company enhanced financial and operational autonomy and empowers it to invest up to ₹ 1,000 crore or 15 per cent of their net worth on a single project without seeking government approval. In a year, these companies can spend up to 30 per cent of their net worth not exceeding ₹ 1,000 crore. They will also have the freedom to enter joint ventures, form alliances and float subsidiaries abroad.

**Criteria for grant of Navratna status**

The Miniratna Category – I CPSEs which have obtained 'excellent' or 'very good' rating, and have composite score of 60 or above in the six-selected performance parameters, namely,

(i) net profit to net worth,
(ii) manpower cost to total cost of production/services,
(iii) profit before depreciation, interest and taxes to capital employed,
(iv) profit before interest and taxes to turnover,
(v) earning per share and
(vi) inter-sectoral performance.

3. **Miniratna Scheme:** In October 1997, the Government had also decided to grant enhanced autonomy and delegation of financial powers to some other profit-making companies subject to certain eligibility conditions and guidelines to make them efficient and competitive. These companies, called 'Miniratnas', are in two categories.

The eligibility conditions and criteria are as follows:

(i) **Category-I:** CPSEs should have made profit in the last 3 years continuously, the pre-tax profit should have been ₹ 30 crore or more in at least one of the 3 years and should have a positive net worth.
(ii) **Category-II:** CPSEs should have made profit for the last 3 years continuously and should have a positive net worth.
(iii) These CPSEs shall be eligible for the enhanced delegated powers provided they have not defaulted in the repayment of loans/interest payment on any loans due to the Government.
(iv) These public sector enterprises shall not depend upon budgetary support or Government guarantees.
(v) The Boards of these CPSEs should be restructured by inducting at least three non-official Directors as the first step before the exercise of enhanced delegation of authority.
(vi) The administrative Ministry concerned shall decide whether a Public Sector Enterprise fulfilled the requirements of a Category-I/Category-II company before the exercise of enhanced powers.

## ❖ List of Maharatna and Navratna Companies in India 2022

As of January 2022, India has 10 Maharatna companies, 14 Navratna companies in India, and 73 Miniratna companies divided into Category 1 and Category 2.

### List of Maharatna Companies in India 2022

1. Bharat Heavy Electricals Limited
2. Bharat Petroleum Corporation Limited
3. Coal India Limited
4. GAIL (India) Limited
5. Hindustan Petroleum Corporation Limited
6. Indian Oil Corporation Limited
7. NTPC Limited
8. Oil & Natural Gas Corporation Limited
9. Power Grid Corporation of India Limited
10. Steel Authority of India Limited

### List of Navratna Companies in India 2022

1. Bharat Electronics Limited
2. Container Corporation of India Limited
3. Engineers India Limited

4. Hindustan Aeronautics Limited
5. Mahanagar Telephone Nigam Limited
6. National Aluminium Company Limited
7. NBCC (India) Limited
8. NMDC Limited
9. NLC India Limited
10. Oil India Limited
11. Power Finance Corporation Limited
12. Rashtriya Ispat Nigam Limited
13. Rural Electrification Corporation Limited
14. Shipping Corporation of India Limited

## MICRO, SMALL AND MEDIUM ENTERPRISES (MSMEs)

Indian Small and Medium Enterprises (SME) sector has emerged as a highly vibrant and dynamic sector of the Indian economy over the last five decades. SMEs not only play crucial role in providing large employment opportunities at comparatively lower capital cost than large industries but also help in industrialization of rural areas. SMEs are complementary to large industries as ancillary units and this sector contributes enormously to the socio-economic development of the country.

MSMEs account for about 45 per cent of India's manufacturing output. MSMEs account for about 40 per cent of India's total exports. The sector is projected to employ about 73 million people in more than 31 million units spread across the country. MSMEs manufacture more than 6,000 products ranging from traditional to high tech items.

Despite their high enthusiasm and inherent capabilities to grow, SMEs in India are also facing a number of problems like sub-optimal scale of operation, technological obsolescence, supply chain inefficiencies, increasing domestic and global competition, working capital shortages, not getting trade receivables from large and multinational companies on time, insufficient skilled manpower, change in manufacturing strategies and turbulent and uncertain market scenario.

### ❖ Definition of MSMEs

MSME stands for Micro, Small, and Medium Enterprises. In accordance with the Micro, Small, and Medium Enterprises Development (MSMED) Act in 2006, the enterprises are classified into two divisions.

1. Manufacturing enterprises – engaged in the manufacturing or production of goods in any industry
2. Service enterprises – engaged in providing or rendering services

| Updated MSME Definition | | |
|---|---|---|
| Type of enterprise | Investment | Turnover |
| Micro | Rs 1 crore | Rs 5 crore |
| Small | Rs 10 crore | Rs 50 crore |
| Medium | Rs 50 crore | Rs 250 c |

| Composite criteria: Investment and annual turnover | | | |
|---|---|---|---|
| Classification | Micro | Small | Medium |
| Manufacturing & services | Investment < Rs 1 crore and turnover < Rs 5 crore | Investment < Rs 10 crore and turnover < Rs 50 crore | Investment < Rs 20 crore and turnover < Rs 100 crore |

### ❖ Key Challenges

Key Challenges in MSME sector are as follows:

1. Lack of availability of adequate and timely credit
2. High cost of credit
3. Collateral requirements
4. Limited access to equity capital
5. Procurement of raw material at a competitive cost
6. Problems of storage, designing, packaging and product display
7. Lack of access to global markets
8. Inadequate infrastructure facilities, including power, water, roads, etc.

9. Low technology levels and lack of access to modern technology
10. Lack of skilled manpower for manufacturing, services, marketing, etc.
11. Multiplicity of labour laws and complicated procedures associated with compliance of such laws.

## ❖ MSMEs – Opportunity Areas

Growth of the new wave MSME led by entrepreneurship focused on innovation and technologies, creating opportunities for women entrepreneurs and developing skilled resources across the following opportunity areas:

1. **Make in India:** Promote an ecosystem for 'Make in India' for foreign companies to invest in manufacturing, service and agricultural and agro-processing-related segments for meeting the domestic as well as global demand.
2. **Digital India:** Promote MSMEs' manufacturing and service capabilities in the ICT sector in line with the government vision.
3. **Export contribution:** Promote export contribution by supporting and developing MSME segment to be globally competitive and adopt research and development, innovation and global technologies. Provide MSME with global market access by entering into bilateral trade agreements and set off arrangements.
4. **Public procurement policy:** Promote an ecosystem for supplies to defence and public sector enterprises so as to achieve at least 25 per cent portion of total procurement by defence and public sector enterprises from MSME.
5. **Procurement by large Indian and foreign corporate across industry sectors from MSMEs:** Promote an ecosystem, provide incentives for investments and support efforts by large corporate in vendor development for MSME segment particularly adapting to research and development, innovation and global technologies.
6. **Indigenisation:** Incentivise any investments and outputs by large players and their MSME vendors to indigenise and/or enable import substitution particularly adapting to research and development, innovation and global technologies.
7. **Traditional and heritage industries:** Incentivise and support any stakeholder that invests in development, growth and opening global markets for India's traditional and heritage industries for goods, services and agricultural and natural medicines and therapy-related products and services.
8. **Infrastructure:** National, regional and sector specific clusters and business centres for MSME in PPP model for state of the art infrastructure comprising physical infra, knowledge infra, e-platforms, B2B access and technology and innovation support for MSME.
9. **Skill India:** Rewarding MSME for initiatives towards skill development and employment generation, particularly for women and special classes, by way of direct incentives, weighted deductions and reliefs in indirect taxes combined with low-cost funding and credit access for stakeholders.

## FRAMEWORK FOR REVIVAL AND REHABILITATION OF MSMEs

On 29 May 2015, the Ministry of Micro, Small and Medium Enterprises has notified a framework for Revival and Rehabilitation of MSMEs, in exercise of the powers conferred under the Micro, Small and Medium Enterprises Development Act, 2006.

## ❖ Salient Features

The main features of the framework which complements to the features of the existing RBI notification of 2012 and 2014 are as below:

1. **Identification of Incipient Stress:** Before a loan account of a MSME turns into a non-performing asset (NPA), banks/ creditors are required to identify incipient stress in the account.
2. **Committees for Distressed MSMEs:** All banks shall constitute one or more committees at such locations as may be considered necessary by the board of directors of such bank to provide reasonable access to all eligible MSMEs, which have availed credit facilities from such bank.
3. **Corrective Action Plan (CAP) by the Committee:** The Committee may explore various options to resolve the stress in the account.
4. **Options under Corrective Action Plan (CAP):** The options under the CAP by the Committee may include: (i) rectification – regularize the account so that the account does not slip into the NPA category, (ii) restructuring the account if it is prima facie viable and the borrower is not a wilful defaulter and (iii) recovery – once the first two options at (i) and (ii) above are seen as not feasible, due recovery process may be resorted to.
5. **Restructuring Process:** If the Committee decides restructuring of the account as CAP, it will have the option of either referring the account to Enterprise Debt Restructuring (EDR) Cell after a decision to restructure is taken or restructure the same independent of the EDR mechanism.
6. **Prudential Norms on Asset Classification and Provisioning:** While a restructuring proposal is under consideration by the Committee/EDR, the usual asset classification norm would continue to apply.
7. **Wilful Defaulters and non-cooperative borrowers:** Banks are required to strictly adhere to the guidelines issued by the RBI from time to time regarding treatment of wilful defaulters.

It is expected that above Framework helps the lenders and debtors in revival and rehabilitation of enterprises and shall unlock the potential of MSMEs.

## ❖ Related Programmes

1. **Deen Dayal Upadhyaya Antyodaya Yojana (DAY):** Government of India Ministry of Housing and Urban Poverty Alleviation on 25 September 2014 announced 'Deen Dayal Upadhyaya Antyodaya Yojana' (DAY ) for uplift of urban and rural poor through enhancement of livelihood opportunities through skill development and other means keeping in view the objective of Make in India, Skill Development is essential for socio-economic betterment.

   The scheme is integration of the National Urban Livelihoods Mission (NULM) and National Rural Livelihoods Mission (NRLM).

   National Urban Livelihoods Mission (NULM) is renamed as Deen Dayal Antyodaya Yojana-National Urban Livelihoods Mission (DAY-NULM) and in Hindi as – Rashtriya Shahri Aajeevika Mission.

   **Components of DAY-NULM**

   The scheme has two components, one for the urban India and other for the rural India.

(i) The Urban component named as DAY will be implemented by the Ministry of Housing and Urban Poverty Alleviation.

(ii) The rural component named as Deen Dayal Upadhyaya Grameen Kaushalya Yojana will be implemented by the Ministry of Rural Development.

**Highlights of the Scheme**

(i) **Employment through Skill Training and Placement:** An expenditure of ₹ 15,000 per person is allowed on training of the urban poor which is ₹ 18,000 in North-East and J&K.

(ii) Training urban poor to meet the enormous demand from urban citizens by imparting market-oriented skills through City Livelihood Centres.

(iii) **Social Mobilization and Institution Development:** It will be done through formation of self-help groups (SHG) for training members and hand holding, an initial support of 10,000 is given for each group. Assistance of ₹ 50,000 is provided to the Registered Area Level Federations.

(iv) **Subsidy to urban poor:** An interest subsidy of 5–7 per cent for setting up individual micro-enterprises with a loan of up to 2 lakh and for group enterprises with a loan limit of up to ₹ 10 lakhs.

(v) **Shelters for urban homeless:** Cost of construction of shelters for urban homeless is fully funded under the Scheme.

(vi) **Other means:** Development of vendor markets and also the promotion of skills for the vendors through setting up infrastructure and special projects for the rag picker and differently abled, etc.

2. **Prime Minister's Employment Generation Programme (PMEGP):** Prime Minister's Employment Generation Programme (PMEGP) scheme announced on 15 August 2008. This is a credit-linked Scheme of the Government of India by merging erstwhile REGP and PMRY Scheme.

**Objectives**

(i) To generate continuous and sustainable employment opportunities in Rural and Urban areas of the country.

(ii) To provide continuous and sustainable employment to a large segment of traditional and prospective artisans, rural and urban unemployed youth in the country through setting up of micro-enterprises.

(iii) To facilitate participation of financial institutions for higher credit flow to micro sector.

3. **Pradhan Mantri MUDRA Yojana:** Micro Units Development and Refinance Agency Ltd. (MUDRA) is a new institution set up by Government of India to provide funding to the non-corporate, non-farm sector income generating activities of micro and small enterprises whose credit needs are below 10 Lakh.

Under the aegis of Pradhan Mantri MUDRA Yojana (PMMY), MUDRA has created three products, i.e., 'Shishu', 'Kishore' and 'Tarun' as per the stage of growth and funding needs of the beneficiary micro unit. These schemes cover loan amounts as below:

(i) **Shishu:** covering loans up to ₹ 50,000.

(ii) **Kishore:** covering loans above ₹ 50,000 and up to ₹ 5,00,000.

(iii) **Tarun:** covering loans above ₹ 5,00,000 and up to ₹ 10,00,000.

All Non-Corporate Small Business Segment (NCSBS) comprising of proprietorship or partnership firms running as small manufacturing units, service sector units, shopkeepers, fruits/vegetable vendors, truck operators, food service units, repair shops, machine operators, small industries, food processors and others in rural and urban areas, are eligible for assistance under MUDRA.

Bank branches would facilitate loans under MUDRA scheme as per customer requirements. Loans under this Scheme are collateral free loans.

**Kinds of MUDRA Loans**

(i) **Vehicle loan:** Commercial vehicle loan, car loan and two-wheeler loan.

(ii) **Business Instalment Loan (BIL):** Loan for working capital requirement, buying plant and machinery, renovating offices, etc.

(iii) **Business Loans Group (BLG) and Rural Business Credit (RBC):** It offers drop line overdraft/overdraft facility/working capital loans.

4. **Scheme of Fund for Regeneration of Traditional Industries (SFURTI):** SFURTI Scheme was launched in 2005–06 for making traditional industries more productive and competitive.

The objectives of SFURTI is to organize the traditional industries and artisans into clusters to make them competitive and provide support for their long-term sustainability by way of enhancing the marketability of products, improving the skills of artisans, making provision for common facilities and strengthening the cluster governance systems.

The Scheme guidelines of SFURTI have been revamped in 2015 and the Scheme has taken giant strides in 2015. Funds to the tune of ₹ 62 Crore have been sanctioned under the Scheme in 2015 as against Nil in 2014.

The objectives of the Scheme are as follows:

(i) To organize the traditional industries and artisans into clusters to make them competitive and provide support for their long-term sustainability and economy of scale.

(ii) To provide sustained employment for traditional industry artisans and rural entrepreneurs.

(iii) To enhance marketability of products of such clusters by providing support for new products, design intervention and improved packaging and also the improvement of marketing infrastructure.

(iv) To equip traditional artisans of the associated clusters with the improved skills and capabilities through training and exposure visits.

(v) To make provision for common facilities and improved tools and equipment for artisans to promote optimum utilization of infrastructure facilities.

(vi) To tap the e-commerce as a major marketing channel given the outreach and the growing market penetration of e-commerce.

5. **Start-up India, Stand up India Campaign:** The Prime Minister of India on 15 August 2015 launched a new campaign **Start-up India, Stand up India** to promote bank financing for start-ups and offer incentives to boost entrepreneurship and job creation. The initiative is aimed at encouraging entrepreneurship and job creation among the youth of India.

**Start-up – As Defined by Government of India**

A start-up has been defined as an entity, incorporated or registered in India not prior to five years, with annual turnover not exceeding ₹ 25 crore in any preceding financial year, working towards innovation, development, deployment or commercialisation of new products, processes or services driven by technology or intellectual property.

The entity should not be formed by splitting up, or reconstruction, of a business already in existence. Further, entity will cease to be a start-up if its turnover for the previous financial year has exceeded ₹ 25 crore, or it has completed 5 years from the date of incorporation/registration.

The start-up will be eligible for tax benefits only after it has obtained certificate of an eligible business from the Inter-Ministerial Board of Certification consisting of various bodies, set up by DIPP to validate the innovative nature of the business for granting tax-related benefits.

6. **Start-up India Movement Launched:** PM Narendra Modi on 16 January 2016 launched the 'Start-Up India' movement by unveiling the action plan aimed at boosting entrepreneurship and jobs at the grassroots level.

Features are as under:

(i) A separate fund will be created with ₹ 10,000 crore corpus for development and growth of innovation driven enterprises. It will be ₹ 2,500 crore a year for 4 years.

(ii) No inspection for 3 years of start-up businesses in respect of labour, environment law compliance post self-certification.

(iii) Start-ups will be exempted from paying income tax on their income for the first 3 years.

(iv) Government to start the Atal Innovation Mission to give an impetus to innovation and encourage the talent among our people.

(v) Under the mission, 35 new incubators, 7 new research parks and 31 innovation centres will be set up at the premier technology institutes under the public private partnership mode.

7. **Stand up India Scheme:** Prime Minister Narendra Modi launched the 'Stand up India Scheme' and a Web portal for the scheme on 5 April 2016 to promote entrepreneurship among Scheduled Caste/Schedule Tribe and Women for loans in the range of ₹ 10 Lakhs to ₹ 100 Lakhs.

The broad features of the scheme are as under:

(i) Composite loan between ₹ 10 lakh and up to ₹ 100 lakh, inclusive of working capital component for setting up any new enterprise.

(ii) Debit Card (RuPay) for drawal of working capital.

(iii) Credit history of borrower to be developed.

(iv) Refinance window through Small Industries Development Bank of India (SIDBI) with an initial amount of ₹ 10,000 crore.

(v) Creation of a corpus of ₹ 5,000 crore for credit guarantee through NCGTC.

(vi) Handholding support for borrowers with comprehensive support for pre loan training needs, facilitating loan, factoring, marketing, etc.

(vii) Web portal for online registration and support services. The overall intent of the proposal is to leverage the institutional credit structure to reach out to these underserved sectors of the population by facilitating bank loans in the non-farm sector set up by such SC, ST and women borrowers. The initiative will also develop synergies with ongoing schemes of other departments.

The process would be led by SIDBI. The offices of SIDBI and National Bank for Agriculture and Rural Development (NABARD) shall be designated Stand-Up Connect Centres (SUCC).

8. **Udyog Aadhaar Memorandum (UAM):** The Union Minister for Micro, Small and Medium Enterprises in September 2015 under the MSME Development Act, 2006, has notified that every MSME unit shall file Udyog Aadhaar Memorandum (UAM).

This is a path-breaking step to promote ease-of-doing-business for MSMEs in India as the UAM replaces the filing of Entrepreneurs' Memorandum (EM) with the respective States/UTs.

While some of the States/UTs had made the process online, either by themselves or through the portal created by this. The cumbersome filing of EM has now been dispensed with and the entrepreneurs in the MSME sector just need to file online, a simple one-page UAM to instantly get a unique Udyog Aadhaar Number (UAN). The information sought is on self-certification basis and no supporting documents are required at the time of online filing of UAM.

9. **Atal Innovation Mission:** The Union Cabinet on 24 February 2016 has given its approval for establishment of Atal Innovation Mission (AIM) and Self Employment and Talent Utilization (SETU) in NITI Aayog with appropriate manpower.

The AIM and AIM Directorate would be responsible in implementation of Mission activities in a focussed manner. This would be a focal point for innovation and entrepreneurship in the country. The NITI Aayog will hire Mission Director and other appropriate manpower. The headquarter of the mission will be New Delhi.

## ❖ Objective

The AIM including SETU is an endeavour to promote a culture of innovation and entrepreneurship. Its objective is to serve as a platform for promotion of world-class

Innovation Hubs, Grand Challenges, Start-up businesses and other self-employment activities, particularly in technology driven areas.

The Atal Innovation Mission shall have two core functions:

(i) **Entrepreneurship promotion:** Through SETU, innovators would be supported and mentored to become successful entrepreneurs.

(ii) **Innovation promotion:** To provide a platform where innovative ideas are generated.

## CORPORATE SOCIAL RESPONSIBILITY (CSR)

The term 'Corporate Social Responsibility (CSR)' can be referred as corporate initiative to assess and take responsibility for the company's effects on the environment and impact on social welfare. The term generally applies to companies efforts that go beyond what may be required by regulators or environmental protection groups.

According to the United Nations Industrial Development Organization (UNIDO), 'Corporate social responsibility is a management concept whereby companies integrate social and environmental concerns in their business operations and interactions with their stakeholders. CSR is generally understood as being the way through which a company achieves a balance of economic, environmental and social imperatives (Triple-Bottom-Line Approach), while at the same time addressing the expectations of shareholders and stakeholders. In this sense it is important to draw a distinction between CSR, which can be a strategic business management concept, and charity, sponsorships or philanthropy. Even though the latter can also make a valuable contribution to poverty reduction, will directly enhance the reputation of a company and strengthen its brand, the concept of CSR clearly goes beyond that.'

From the above definitions, it is clear that:

- The CSR approach is holistic and integrated with the core business strategy for addressing social and environmental impacts of businesses.
- CSR needs to address the well-being of all stakeholders and not just the company's shareholders.
- Philanthropic activities are only a part of CSR, which otherwise constitutes a much larger set of activities entailing strategic business benefits.

### ❖ CSR in India

The Companies Act, 2013, has introduced the idea of CSR to the forefront and through its disclose-or-explain mandate, is promoting greater transparency and disclosure. Schedule VII of the Act, which lists out the CSR activities, suggests communities to be the focal point. On the other hand, by discussing a company's relationship to its stakeholders and integrating CSR into its core operations, the draft rules suggest that CSR needs to go beyond communities and beyond the concept of philanthropy. It will be interesting to observe the ways in which this will translate into action at the ground level, and how the understanding of CSR is set to undergo a change.

### ❖ CSR Rules under Companies Act, 2013

CSR, also called corporate conscience, corporate citizenship or responsible business, is a form of corporate self-regulation integrated into a business model.

CSR policy functions as a self-regulatory mechanism whereby a business monitors and ensures its active compliance with the spirit of the law, ethical standards and national or international norms.

With effect from 1 April 2014, every company, private limited or public limited, which either has a net worth of ₹ 500 crore or a turnover of ₹ 1,000 crore or net profit of ₹ 5 crore, needs to spend at least 2 per cent of its average net profit for the immediately preceding three financial years on CSR activities.

The CSR activities should not be undertaken in the normal course of business and must be with respect to any of the activities mentioned in Schedule VII of the 2013 Act.

Contribution to any political party is not considered to be a CSR activity and only activities in India would be considered for computing CSR expenditure.

## COMPETITION ACT, 2002

Competition Law for India was triggered by Articles 38 and 39 of the Constitution of India. These Articles are a part of the Directive Principles of State Policy. Pegging on the Directive Principles, the first Indian competition law was enacted in 1969 and was christened the MRTP, 1969 (MRTP Act).

The Competition Act, 2002, got presidential assent in January 2003 which replaced MRTP Act, 1969. It was subsequently amended by the Competition (Amendment) Act, 2007.

In accordance with the provisions of the Amendment Act, the Competition Commission of India (CCI) and the Competition Appellate Tribunal have been established.

The objectives of the Act are sought to be achieved through the CCI.

### ❖ Competition Commission of India (CCI)

The CCI was established on 1 March 2009 as an autonomous body comprising of a Chairperson and six members.

It is the duty of the CCI to eliminate practices having adverse effect on competition, promote and sustain competition, protect the interests of consumers and ensure freedom of trade in the markets of India.

The Commission is also required to give opinion on competition issues on a reference received from a statutory authority established under any law and to undertake competition advocacy, create public awareness and impart training on competition issues.

### ❖ Appellate Tribunal

Competition Appellate Tribunal (COMPAT) was set up by the Centre in May 2009. An appeal from a decision of the CCI is made to COMPAT. COMPAT can have one Chairperson and a maximum of two other members. Only a former SC Judge or Chief Justice of High Court can be appointed as Chairperson of COMPAT. The final appeal can be filed to the Supreme Court of India.

## DIFFERENCES BETWEEN MRTP ACT AND COMPETITION ACT

1. MRTP Act was based on the pre-liberalisation and globalisation era. Competition Act is based on the post-reforms scenario.
2. The objective of the MRTP Act is to prevent concentration of economic power to common detriment to control of monopolies, prevention of monopolistic and restrictive trade practices. The objective of the Competition Act is to prevent practices having adverse effect on competition and to promote as well as sustaining the competition to protect consumer interests at market place and ensuring freedom of trade.
3. MRTP lists out 14 offences, which are against the principle of natural justice. Competition Act recognizes only four

offences, which are deemed to be against the principle of natural justice.

4. MRTP Commission has the power to pass only 'Cease' and 'Desist' orders. The Competition Act can pass an order to prevent and punish such of those activities, which abuses competition.
5. The MRTP Act did not provide for the formation of fund for its activities. The Competition Act provides competition fund for promotion of competition advocacy and creation of awareness about competitive issues and training as may be prescribed in its rules.
6. Under MRTP entity having status of dominant position is itself considered as bad. Under Competition Act, entity having status of dominant position is not considered as bad, whereas abuse of dominant position affecting consumer interest is considered as immoral.
7. Under MRTP, in general, registration of agreement was mandatory. Competition Act does not lay down any such requirement for registration of agreements.
8. The size of the firm is the factor for determining dominance, etc. Competition Act focuses on the firm's structure not on the size factor.
9. MRTP Commission role was only advisory. Competition Commission can initiate the *suo motu* proceedings and levy penalties.
10. MRTP Commission dealt with the unfair trade practices. Under Competition Act, the cases relating to unfair trade practices will be transferred to consumer courts.
11. MRTP was focused on consumer interest at large. Competition Act is focuses on public at large.
12. The chairman of MRTP Commission was appointed by Central Government. The Chairman of the Competition Act is being appointed by a committee consisting of retired judiciary, person having professional expertise in various fields of trade commerce, industry, finance, etc.

## INDIAN COMPANIES ACT, 2013

The Companies Act, 2013, passed by the Parliament received the assent of the President of India on 29 August 2013 and came into force on April1 2014. The Act consolidates and amends the law relating to companies.

The new law is aimed at easing the process of doing business in India and improving corporate governance by making companies more accountable. The 2013 Act also introduces new concepts such as One - person company, small company, dormant company and CSR, etc. The Act introduces significant changes in the provisions related to governance, e-management, compliance and enforcement, disclosure norms, auditors, mergers and acquisitions, class action suits and registered valuers.

There are more than 450+ sections, 7 schedules and 29 chapters.

### ❖ One Person Company (OPC)

It's a Private Company having only one Member and at least One Director. This concept is already prevalent in the Europe, USA, China, Singapore and in several countries in the Gulf region. It was first recommended in India by an expert committee headed by Dr. J. J. Irani in 2005.

The one basic pre-requisite to incorporate an OPC is that the only natural-born citizens of India, including small businessmen, entrepreneurs, artisans, weavers or traders among others can take advantage of the OPC concept outlined in the new Companies Act. The OPC shall have minimum paid up capital of ₹ 1 Lakh and shall have no compulsion to hold Annual General meeting (AGM).

## ❖ Small Company

It means a company, other than a public company, paid-up share capital of which does not exceed ₹ 50 lakh or such higher amount as may be prescribed which shall not be more than ₹ 5 crore; or turnover of which as per its last profit and loss account does not exceed ₹ 2 crore or such higher amount as may be prescribed which shall not be more than ₹ 20 crore.

The 2013 Act provides exemptions to small companies primarily from certain requirements relating to board meeting, presentation of cash flow statement and certain merger process.

## ❖ Dormant Company

The 2013 Act states that a company can be classified as dormant when it is formed and registered under this 2013 Act for a future project or to hold an asset or intellectual property and has no significant accounting transaction. Such a company or an inactive one may apply to the ROC in such manner as may be prescribed for obtaining the status of a dormant company.

## ❖ Commencement of Business

For all the companies (public/private company) registered under the Companies Act, 2013, needs to file the following with the Registrar of Companies (ROC) in order to commence their business:

1. A declaration by the director in prescribed form stating that the subscribers/ promoters to the memorandum have paid the value of shares agreed to be taken by them.
2. A confirmation that the company has filed a verification of its registered office with the ROC.

In the case of a company requiring registration from any sectoral regulators such as RBI, SEBI, etc., approval from such regulator shall be required prior to starting the business.

## ❖ Independent Directors

The 2013 Act defines the term 'Independent Director'. In case of listed companies, one third of the board of directors should be independent directors. The 2013 Act also provides additional qualifications/restrictions for independent directors as compared to the 1956 Act.

## ❖ Resident Director

Every Company must have at least one director who has stayed in India for a total period of 182 days or more in previous calendar year. For existing companies, the compliance needs to be made before 31 March 2015.

## ❖ Board Meetings

At least 7 days of notice should be given to Board Meeting. The Board needs to meet at least 4 times within a year. There should not be a gap of more than 120 days between two consecutive meetings.

## ❖ Corporate Social Responsibility (CSR)

The company has to constitute a CSR committee of the Board and 2 per cent of the average net profits of the last three financial years are to be mandatorily spent on CSR activities by an Indian company if any of the following criteria is met:

1. Net worth of ₹ 500 crore or
2. Turnover of ₹ 1,000 crore or more or
3. Net profit of ₹ 5 crore or more.

Contributing to Incubators, which has been notified by the Government of India, is eligible for spending under CSR.

## ❖ Mergers and Acquisitions

The Act has streamlined as well as introduced concepts such as reverse mergers (merger of foreign companies with Indian companies) and squeeze-out provisions, which are significant. The Act has also introduced the requirement for valuations in several cases, including mergers and acquisitions, by registered valuers.

## ❖ Issuance of Securities

The 2013 Act has introduced a new section to explicitly provide the ways in which a public company or private company may issue securities.

This section explains that a public company may issue securities in any of the following manners: (i) To public through prospectus; (ii) Through private placement and (iii) Through rights issue or a bonus issue.

For private companies, this section provides that it may issue securities through private placement, by way of rights issue or bonus issue.

## ❖ Financial Statements

Financial Statements are now defined under the Act as comprising of the following. All companies (except one person Company, small company and dormant company) are now mandatorily required to maintain the following, which may not include the cash flow statement:

1. A balance sheet as at the end of the financial year
2. A profit and loss account/an income and expenditure account for the financial year, as the case may be
3. Cash flow statement for the financial year
4. A statement of changes in equity (if applicable)
5. Any explanatory note

Other important provisions of the Act are:

1. Private company to have a maximum of 200 members (earlier limit was up to 50).
2. E-Governance – maintenance and allowing inspection of documents by companies in electronic form.
3. Vigil mechanism (whistle blowing) introduced.
4. In prescribed class or classes of companies, there should be at least one woman director.
5. Restrictions on layers of subsidiaries.
6. The Financial Year of any Company can be only from April to March. Existing companies has to align within 2 years of the commencement of the Act.
7. Memorandum not to have 'other objects'.
8. A person cannot become director in more than 20 companies instead of 15 as provided in the Companies Act, 1956, and out of this 20, he cannot be director of more than 10 public companies.
9. Shareholders to have exit option if money raised has not been utilized.
10. A company can make buyback even if it had at any time defaulted in repayment of deposit or interest payable thereon, Concept of CSR introduced.

## ❖ National Company Law Tribunal (NCLT)

The Central Government has constituted NCLT under section 408 of the Companies Act, 2013, on 1 June 2016.

The NCLT is a quasi-judicial body, exercising equitable jurisdiction, which was earlier being exercised by the High Court or the Central Government. The Tribunal has powers to regulate its own procedures.

The NCLT has been empowered to exercise the following powers:

1. Most of the powers of the Company Law Board under the Companies Act, 1956;
2. All the powers of BIFR for revival and rehabilitation of sick industrial companies;
3. Power of High Court in the matters of mergers, demergers, amalgamations, winding up, etc.;

4. Power to order repayment of deposits accepted by Non-Banking Financial Companies;
5. Power to wind up companies;
6. Power to review its own orders.

### ❖ National Company Law Appellate Tribunal (NCLAT)

National Company Law Appellate Tribunal (NCLAT) was constituted under Companies Act, 2013, for hearing appeals against the orders of NCLT, with effect from 1 June 2016.

NCLAT is also the Appellate Tribunal for hearing appeals against the orders passed by Insolvency and Bankruptcy Board of India.

NCLAT is also the Appellate Tribunal to hear and dispose of appeals against any direction issued or decision made or order passed by the CCI with effect from 26 May 2017

## INTELLECTUAL PROPERTY RIGHTS (IPR)

Intellectual property refers to creations of the mind: inventions; literary and artistic works, symbols, names and images used in commerce.

Intellectual property is divided into two categories:

1. **Industrial Property:** It includes patents for inventions, trademarks, industrial designs and geographical indications.
2. **Copyright:** It covers literary works (such as novels, poems and plays), films, music, artistic works (e.g., drawings, paintings, photographs and sculptures) and architectural design. Rights related to copyright include those of performing artists in their performances, producers of phonograms in their recordings and broadcasters in their radio and television programs.

## NATIONAL INTELLECTUAL PROPERTY RIGHTS POLICY, 2016

The Union Cabinet has approved the National IPR Policy on 12 May 2016 to lay the future roadmap for IPRs in India. The National IPR Policy is a vision document that encompasses and brings to a single platform all IPRs.

Slogan of the policy is 'Creative India; Innovative India: रचनात्मक भारत; अभिनव भारत'

The Policy recognizes that India has a well-established TRIPS-compliant legislative, administrative and judicial framework to safeguard IPRs, which meet its international obligations while utilizing the flexibilities provided in the international regime to address its developmental concerns. It reiterates India's commitment to the Doha Development Agenda and the TRIPS agreement.

With this document, India aims to place before the world a vibrant and predictable IP regime, which stimulates creativity and innovation across sectors, as also facilitates a stable, transparent and service-oriented IPR administration in the country.

### ❖ Vision Statement

An India where creativity and innovation are stimulated by Intellectual Property for the benefit of all; an India where intellectual property promotes advancement in science and technology, arts and culture, traditional knowledge and biodiversity resources; an India where knowledge is the main driver of development, and knowledge owned is transformed into knowledge shared.

### ❖ Mission Statement

Stimulate a dynamic, vibrant and balanced IPR system in India to:

1. foster creativity and innovation and thereby, promote entrepreneurship and enhance socio-economic and cultural development and
2. focus on enhancing access to healthcare, food security and environmental protection, among other sectors of vital social, economic and technological importance.

## ❖ Objectives

The Policy lays down the following seven objectives:

1. **IPR Awareness:** Outreach and Promotion–To create public awareness about the economic, social and cultural benefits of IPRs among all sections of society.
2. **Generation of IPRs:** To stimulate the generation of IPRs.
3. **Legal and Legislative Framework:** To have strong and effective IPR laws, which balance the interests of rights owners with larger public interest.
4. **Administration and Management:** To modernize and strengthen service-oriented IPR administration.
5. **Commercialization of IPRs:** Get value for IPRs through commercialization.
6. **Enforcement and Adjudication:** To strengthen the enforcement and adjudicatory mechanisms for combating IPR infringements.
7. **Human Capital Development:** To strengthen and expand human resources, institutions and capacities for teaching, training, research and skill building in IPRs.

These objectives are sought to be achieved through detailed action points.

## ❖ Salient Features

1. **Cell for IPR Promotion and Management (CIPAM):** A Cell CIPAM shall be created as a professional body under aegis of DIPP to address the seven identified objectives of the Policy.
2. **Awareness Campaign:** To be launched in schools, institutions of higher education like engineering colleges and law schools, centres of skill development, industry clusters, etc., it aims to foster an IP culture in the country by creating awareness about the economic, social and cultural benefits of IPRs.
3. **IP Cells:** IP cells shall be created in key Ministries/Departments of the Govt. of India.
4. **Generation, registration and commercialization:** The Policy aims to encourage creativity and innovation, leading to generation of IPs and their protection through IPRs. Registration of Geographical Indications (GIs) shall be encouraged through support institutions.
5. **Traditional Knowledge Digital Library (TKDL):** TKDL's ambit is to be expanded to include other fields besides Ayurveda, Yoga, Unani and Siddha.

## ❖ Types of IPR in India

1. **Patent:** A patent is granted for an invention which is a new product or process involving an inventive step and capable of industrial application. 'New invention' means the subject matter has not fallen in public domain or that it does not form part of the state of the art; Inventive step is the feature(s) of the invention that involves technical advance as compared to the existing knowledge or having economic significance or both and that makes the invention not obvious to a person skilled in the art. Capable of Industrial application means that the invention is capable of being made or used in an industry. Concerned IP Act is the Patents Act, 1970 (as amended in 2005).
2. **Design:** A design refers only to the features of shape, configuration, pattern, ornamentation, composition of colour or line or a combination thereof, applied to any article, whether two or three dimensional or in both forms by any industrial process or means which, in the finished article, appeal to and are judged solely by the eye. Concerned IP Act is Designs Act, 2000.

3. **Trade Mark:** A trademark means a mark capable of being represented graphically and which is capable of distinguishing the goods or services of one undertaking from those of other undertakings.

   A trademark can be a sign, words, letters, numbers, drawings, pictures, emblem, colours or combination of colours, shape of goods, graphic representation or packaging or sound or any combination of the above as applied to goods or services. Concerned IP Act is Trade Marks Act, 1999 (as amended in 2010).

4. **Geographical Indications:** A geographical indication identifies agricultural or natural or manufactured goods as originating or manufactured in the territory of a country or region or locality in that territory, where a given quality, reputation or other characteristic of such goods is essentially attributable to its geographical origin and, in case where such goods are manufactured goods, one of the activities of either the production or processing or preparation of the goods concerned takes place in such territory, region, or locality, as the case may be. Concerned IP Act is the Geographical Indications of Goods (Registration and Protection) Act, 1999.

5. **Copyright:** Copyright is a right given by the law to creators of literary, dramatic, musical and artistic works and producers of cinematograph films and sound recordings. In fact, it is a bundle of rights including, *inter alia*, rights of reproduction, communication to the public, adaptation and translation of the work. Concerned IP Act is the Copyright Act, 1957 (as amended).

6. **Semiconductor Integrated Circuits Layout Design:** The aim of the Semiconductor Integrated Circuits Layout Design Act, 2000, is to provide protection of Intellectual Property Right in the area of Semiconductor Integrated Circuit Layout Designs and for matters connected therewith or incidental thereto.

7. **Plant Variety Protection:** Protection granted for plant varieties, the rights of farmers and plant breeders and to encourage the development of new varieties of plants. Concerned IP Act is the Protection of Plant Varieties and Farmers' Rights (PPV&FR) Act, 2001.

## INDEX OF EIGHT CORE INDUSTRIES

The Index of Eight Core Industries (ECI) is a monthly production index of industrial production (IIP), which is also considered as a lead indicator of the monthly industrial performance. The index is released by means of a press note prepared by the DIPP, Ministry of Commerce and Industry.

The objective of the ECI is to provide an advance indication on production performance of industries of 'core' nature before the release of Index of Industrial Production (IIP) by Central Statistics Office. These industries are likely to impact on general economic activities as well as industrial activities.

ECI measures collective and individual performance of production in selected eight core industries viz. Coal, Crude Oil, Natural Gas, Petroleum Refinery Products, Fertilizers, Steel, Cement and Electricity.

The Central Statistics Office (CSO) has revised the base year of the all India IIP from 2004–05 to 2011–12. The ECP has also been revised from 2011–12 to align with the IIP.

## EASE OF DOING BUSINESS

Ease of Doing Business Index (EDBI) is an index published by the World Bank. It is an aggregate figure that includes different parameters that define the ease of doing business in a country.

An EDBI is a composite measure of the various ways an economy facilitates production and a vital consideration that governs a country's ability to realize potential GDP.

Improved EDBI might result from many interactive changes in countries' business environments as they affect both domestic economies' activity and international trade. For example, an improved EDBI in a country might cause an increase in foreign direct investment, which in turn might increase competition in domestic markets. The latter lowers domestic prices, leads to an increase in local purchasing power, and thereby increases consumption. Ultimately, this dynamic scenario results in faster economic growth.

The ease of doing business index is a measure of the extent to which a country's regulatory environment is conducive to business operation.

A nation's ranking on the index is based on the average of 10 sub-indices. For each of the indicators that form a part of the statistic 'ease of doing business', a distance to frontier score is computed and all the scores are aggregated. The aggregated score becomes the ease of doing business index.

The sub-indices are as follows:

1. **Starting a business:** Procedures, time, cost and minimum capital to open a new business
2. **Dealing with construction permits:** Procedures, time and cost to build a warehouse
3. **Registering property:** Procedures, time and cost to register commercial real estate
4. **Getting credit:** Strength of legal rights index, depth of credit information index
5. **Protecting investors:** Indices on the extent of disclosure, extent of director liability and ease of shareholder suits
6. **Paying taxes:** Number of taxes paid, hours per year spent preparing tax returns and total tax payable as share of gross profit
7. **Trading across borders:** Number of documents, cost and time necessary to export and import
8. **Enforcing Contracts:** Procedures, time and cost to enforce a debt contract
9. **Resolving insolvency:** The time, cost and recovery rate (per cent) under bankruptcy proceeding
10. **Getting Electricity:** Procedures, time and cost required for a business to obtain a permanent electricity connection for a newly constructed warehouse

India has been placed at 63rd position among the 190 countries in the recently released World Bank's ease of doing business index for the year 2020.

## GLOBAL COMPETITIVENESS INDEX

The Global Competitiveness Report (GCR) is a yearly report published by the World Economic Forum. Since 2004, the GCR ranks countries based on the Global Competitiveness Index was developed by Xavier Sala-i-Martin and Elsa V. Artadi.

The Global Competitiveness Index integrates the macroeconomic and the micro/business aspects of competitiveness into a single index.

The Index assesses the competitiveness landscape of 138 economies, providing unique insight into the drivers of their productivity and prosperity.

The latest report, published in October 2019, placed India at 63rd in Doing Business, compared with 77th in 2018 and 100 in 2017. India, along with other top improvers, had implemented 59 regulatory reforms in 2018-19, accounting for a fifth of all reforms recorded worldwide.

The report assesses the ability of countries to provide high levels of prosperity to their citizens. This in turn depends on how productively a country uses available resources. Therefore, the Global Competitiveness Index measures the set of institutions, policies and factors that set the sustainable current and medium-term levels of economic prosperity.

The report has twelve pillars of competitiveness. These are:

1. institutions
2. appropriate infrastructure
3. a stable macroeconomic framework
4. good health and primary education
5. higher education and training
6. efficient goods markets
7. efficient labour markets
8. developed financial markets
9. the ability to harness the benefits of existing technologies
10. and its market size, both domestic and international
11. by producing new and different goods using the most sophisticated production processes
12. innovation

❑❑❑

# 6 CHAPTER Agriculture Sector

The agriculture sector is the backbone of the Indian economy which provides the basic ingredients to mankind and makes available raw material for rapid industrialization. Besides manufacturing sectors, agriculture sector provides great employment opportunities for rural people/youth on a large scale for their livelihood and also provides entrepreneurship. Though its contribution to the overall Gross Domestic Product (GDP) of the country has fallen from about 30 per cent in 1990–91 to 16.38 per cent in 2020–21, a trend that is expected in the development process of any economy, agriculture yet forms the backbone of development.

## AGRICULTURE POLICY

The Government of India has resorted to several measures under declared policies to meet the challenges of agricultural sector. Major challenges faced by Indian agriculture are: stagnation in production of major crops; high cost of farm inputs; soil exhaustion; depletion of fresh ground water; adverse impact of global climatic change; adverse impact of globalisation; hard to provide food security; farmers' suicides and lower yield of major commodities.

## NEW AGRICULTURE POLICY, 2000

The first ever the National Agriculture Policy was announced on 28 July, 2000. The policy seeks to realise the vast untapped growth potential of Indian agriculture, strengthen rural infrastructure to support faster agricultural development, promote value addition, accelerate the growth of agro business, create employment in rural areas, secure a fair standard of living for the farmers and agricultural workers and their families, discourage migration to urban areas and face the challenges arising out of economic liberalization and globalization.

The salient features of the policy are:

1. Over four per cent annual growth rate aimed over next two decades.
2. Greater private sector participation through contract farming.
3. Price protection for farmers.
4. National Agricultural Insurance Scheme (NAIS) to be launched.
5. Dismantling of restrictions on movement of agricultural commodities throughout the country.
6. Rational utilization of country's water resources for optimum use of irrigation potential.
7. High priority to development of animal husbandry, poultry, dairy and aquaculture.

8. Capital inflow and assured markets for crop production.
9. Exemption from payment of capital gains tax on compulsory acquisition of agricultural land.
10. Minimise fluctuations in commodity prices.
11. Continuous monitoring of international prices.
12. Plant varieties to be protected through legislation.
13. Adequate and timely supply of quality inputs to farmers.
14. High priority to rural electrification.
15. Setting up of agro-processing units and creation of off-farm employment in rural areas.

## NATIONAL POLICY FOR FARMERS, 2007

On the recommendations of the National Commission on Farmers under the chairmanship of Prof. M. S. Swaminathan, the Government of India approved the National Policy for Farmers, 2007, which aims to improve economic viability of farming and increase net income of farmers.

The primary focus of this policy is on 'farmer' defined holistically and not merely on agriculture. In that sense, it is much more comprehensive than an Agriculture Policy.

The major goals of the National Policy for Farmers are:

1. To improve economic viability of farming by substantially increasing the net income of farmers and to ensure that agricultural progress is measured by advances made in this income.
2. To protect and improve land, water, bio-diversity and genetic resources essential for sustained increase in the productivity, profitability and stability of major farming systems by creating an economic stake in conservation.
3. To develop support services including provision for seeds, irrigation, power, machinery and implements, fertilizers and credit at affordable prices in adequate quantity for farmers.
4. To strengthen the bio-security of crops, farm animals, fish and forest trees for safeguarding the livelihood and income security of farmer families and the health and trade security of the nation.
5. To provide appropriate price and trade policy mechanisms to enhance farmers' income.
6. To provide for suitable risk management measures for adequate and timely compensation to farmers.
7. To complete the unfinished agenda in land reforms and to initiate comprehensive asset and Aquarian reforms.
8. To mainstream the human and gender dimension in all farm policies and programmes.
9. To pay explicit attention to sustainable rural livelihoods.
10. To foster community-centred food, water and energy security systems in rural India and to ensure nutrition security at the level of every child, woman and man.
11. To introduce measures which can help attract and retain youths in farming and processing of farm products for higher value addition by making it intellectually stimulating and economically rewarding.
12. To make India a global outsourcing hub in the production and supply of the inputs needed for sustainable agriculture, products and processes developed through Biotechnology and Information and Communication Technology (ICT).
13. To restructure the agricultural curriculum and pedagogic methodologies for

enabling every farm and home science graduate to become an entrepreneur and to make agricultural education gender sensitive.

14. To develop and introduce a social security system for farmers.
15. To provide appropriate opportunities in adequate measure for non-farm employment for the farm households

## VISION-2050 – INDIAN COUNCIL OF AGRICULTURAL RESEARCH (ICAR)

The Indian Council of Agricultural Research (ICAR) to meet the future challenges has prepared a 'Vision-2050' in August 2015.

**Vision:** Lead India to attaining sustainable food, nutritional, environmental and livelihoods security through agricultural research and education.

**Mission:** Harness the power of science and innovation for food security, food safety, farmer prosperity and enhance natural resources base to promote inclusive growth and sustainable development.

**Focus Areas of Research:**

1. Genetic potential enhancement of agricultural commodities.
2. Agricultural productivity, efficiency and profitability improvement.
3. Resilience to climate change and abiotic and biotic stresses.
4. Improve nutritional food and health security.
5. Risk management against climate change and market stressors.
6. Agricultural value chains.
7. Sustainability of natural resources base of agriculture.
8. Valuation of ecosystem services.
9. Agricultural markets, policies and institutions.
10. Biosecurity, especially emerging from gene piracy and cross-border vector borne diseases.
11. New products and uses (e.g., bioenergy, new crops, synthetic foods, special foods).

The steps taken by ICAR for providing new technologies to the farmers across the country include setting up of 642 Krishi Vigyan Kendras (KVKs) and 652 Agricultural Technology Management Agencies (ATMAs) at district level. In addition, the farmers are provided information through Focused Publicity Campaigns, Kisan Call Centres (KCCs), Agri-Clinics and Agri-Business Centres (ACABC) of entrepreneurs, Agri Fairs and exhibitions, Kisan SMS Porta, DD Kisan TV Channel and Community Radio Stations.

The major projects run by ICAR are:

1. **Farmers FIRST:** The objectives of the 'Farmer FIRST' initiative is to move beyond the production and productivity and to privilege the complex, diverse and risk prone realities of the farmers through enhancing farmers-scientists contact with multi stakeholders participation for technology development and application.
2. **ARYA:** The ICAR has initiated a program on 'Attracting and Retaining Youth in Agriculture (ARYA) in selected districts through KVKs with an objective for entrepreneurial development of Youth in Rural Areas to take up various agriculture, allied and service sector enterprises for sustainable income and gainful employment. The identified youth are trained on entrepreneurship development skills by providing a basket of options to start agriculture ventures for self-employment.
3. **Mera Gaon Mera Gaurav:** The 'Mera Gaon Mera Gaurav' has been conceptualized in which scientists of ICAR and Agricultural Universities will identify villages in the vicinity of the Institutions for providing advisories and consultations to farmers

for increasing farm productivity and production.

## INTEGRATION OF SCHEMES

The Department of Agriculture and Cooperation in July 2014 integrated erstwhile 51 schemes for development of agriculture and welfare of farmers in the country into 5 Centrally Sponsored Missions, 5 Central Sector Schemes and 1 State Plan Scheme as given below:

### ❖ Centrally Sponsored Missions

1. National Food Security Mission (NFSM)
2. National Mission on Sustainable Agriculture (NMSA)
3. National Mission on Oilseeds and Oil Palm (NMOOP)
4. National Mission on Agricultural Extension and Technology (NMAET)
5. Mission of Integrated Development of Horticulture (MIDH)

### ❖ Central Sector Schemes

1. National Crop Insurance Programme (NCIP)
2. Integrated Scheme on Agriculture Cooperation (ISAC)
3. Integrated Scheme for Agriculture Marketing (ISAM)
4. Integrated Scheme on Agriculture Census, Economics and Statistics (ISACE & S)
5. Secretariat Economic Service (SES)

### ❖ State Plan Scheme

(i) Rashtriya Krishi Vikas Yojna (RKVY)

## AGRI EXPORT ZONES (AEZs)

The concept of AEZ was initiated by the Government of India in 2001 under Exim Policy.

The objective of AEZ was to focus on potential products from the export perspective and address critical issues in creation of exportable quantity and quality and to synergize the use of all available resources and logistics from central and state sector schemes in existence.

Earlier, the Agricultural and Processed Food Products Export Development Authority (APEDA) was established by the Government of India to develop and promote export of agricultural and processed food products from India. It links Indian exporters to global markets besides providing comprehensive export-oriented services.

The AEZ takes a comprehensive view of a particular produce/product located in a geographically contiguous area for the purpose of developing and sourcing raw materials, their processing/packaging and leading to final exports.

The major components of AEZ concept are:

1. Cluster approach of identifying the potential products and geographical region in which these products are grown.
2. Adopting an end-to-end approach of integrating the entire process, right from the stage of production till it reaches the consumption stage.
3. Integration of the activities of various agencies connected with the department of the product.

Sixty AEZs in 20 States were notified by the government till 2005. It was decided not to consider notification of any new AEZs unless there are strong compelling reasons.

Benefits of AEZ are: (i) strengthening of backward linkages with a market-oriented approach; (ii) product acceptability and its competitiveness abroad as well as in the domestic market; (iii) value addition to basic agricultural produce; (iv) bring down cost of production through economy of scale. (v) better price for agricultural produce. (vi) improvement in product quality and packaging; (vii) promote trade-related research and development and (viii) increase employment opportunities.

### ❖ Mode of Operation

The entire approach of promoting the Agri Export Zone has been taken on a project mode. The state governments identify potential export products that could be selected for development with a cluster approach. The state governments evolve projects which are feasible and are possible to be implemented immediately.

The states forward such project proposals to APEDA that will conduct the initial scrutiny of the proposals. If found feasible, APEDA may provide necessary guidance in preparing the detailed project report.

### ❖ Problems of AEZs

A number of problems related to AEZs have been identified such as increase in exploitation of farmers and farmers becoming landless. There has been decrease in agricultural production thereby an increase in the cost of food items. An increase in economic imbalance and disparity regarding the ownership rights has been observed. A number of negative externalities like increase in pollution, endangerment to wildlife due to pollution and related diseases observed.

## RASHTRIYA KRISHI VIKAS YOJANA (RKVY)

Rashtriya Krishi Vikas Yojana was launched by the Government of India during 2007–08 to incentives states to draw up plans for their agriculture sector more comprehensively, taking agro-climatic conditions, natural resource and technology into account and integrating livestock, poultry and fisheries fully.

The RKVY aims at achieving 4 per cent annual growth in the agriculture sector during the XI Plan period, by ensuring a holistic development of Agriculture and Allied Sectors.

RKVY is part of state plan and has two streams, Stream-I and Stream-II. Stream-I is project based and Stream-II is for strengthening of existing schemes and filling up of resource gap under the State Plan.

### ❖ Objectives

1. To incentivize the states that increase their investment in Agriculture and allied sectors.
2. To provide flexibility and autonomy to the states in planning and executing programmes for agriculture.
3. To ensure the preparation of Agriculture Plans for the districts and states
4. To achieve the goal of reducing the yield gaps in important crops.
5. To maximize returns to the farmers.
6. To address the agriculture and allied sectors in an integrated manner.

## KISAN CALL CENTRES

In order to harness the potential of ICT in Agriculture, Ministry of Agriculture launched the scheme KCCs on 21 January 2004. Main aim of the project is to answer farmers' queries on a telephone call in their own dialect. These call centres are working in 14 different locations covering all the states and UTs. A countrywide common 11-digit Toll Free number has been allotted for KCC. This number is accessible through mobile phones and landlines of all telecom networks including private service providers. Replies to the farmers' queries are given in 22 local languages.

## AGRICULTURE CREDIT

### ❖ National Bank for Agriculture and Rural Development (NABARD)

NABARD was established as an apex development bank for meeting the credit needs of all types of agricultural and rural development.

The bank came into existence on 12 July 1982 in accordance with NABARD Act, 1981, by transferring the agricultural credit functions of RBI and refinance functions of the then Agricultural Refinance and Development Corporation (ARDC).

Set up with an initial capital of ₹ 100 crore, its' paid up capital stood at ₹ 14,080 crore as on 31 March 2020.

**Mission:** Promote sustainable and equitable agriculture and rural prosperity through effective credit support, related services, institution development and other innovative initiatives.

#### Functions of NABARD

1. **Credit Functions:** NABARD provides refinance, loans and advances to state cooperative banks, central co-operative banks, regional rural banks, or to any financial institution approved by the RBI.

   Refinance facility is provided for following activities of the institutions:

   (i) agricultural operations or the marketing of crops;

   (ii) the marketing and distribution of inputs necessary for agriculture or rural development;

   (iii) any other activity for the promotion of or in the field of agriculture or rural development;

   (iv) commercial or trade transactions or

   (v) the production or marketing activities of artisans or of small-scale industries, industries in the tiny and decentralized sector, village and cottage industries or of those engaged in the field of handicrafts and other rural crafts.

   The bank makes loans and advances against the security of stocks, funds and securities other than immovable property and promissory notes.

2. Provides assistance to the RBI and other organizations related with the development of the rural sector.
3. Coordinates the functions of the rural loan providers
4. Aids the state governments in assisting the rural developmental institutions
5. Provides training facilities for the cooperatives, banks and other organizations.
6. It has the responsibility of inspecting co-operative banks and RRBs.
7. It maintains a research and development fund to promote research in agriculture and rural development.
8. It provides long-term assistance (not exceeding 20 years) to the state governments.

### ❖ National Bank for Agriculture and Rural Development (Amendment) Bill, 2017

The National Bank for Agriculture and Rural Development (Amendment) Bill, 2017, was Passed by Lok Sabha in August 2017 to amend the NABARD Act, 1981.

Main Features of the Bill are as follows:

1. The Bill allows the central government to increase this capital to ₹ 30,000 crore. The

capital may be increased to more than ₹ 30,000 crore by the central government in consultation with the RBI, if necessary.

2. The Bill transfers the share capital held by the RBI valued at ₹ 20 crore to the central government.
3. The Bill replaces the terms 'small-scale industry' and 'industry in the tiny and decentralized sector' with the terms 'micro enterprise', 'small enterprise' and 'medium enterprise' and will extend loans to the maximum limits identified under the MSME Development Act, 2006.
4. Consistency with the Companies Act, 2013: These include provisions that deal with: (i) definition of a government company and (ii) qualifications of auditors.

## ❖ Cooperative Banks

**(See Chapter 3 Banking)**

## ❖ REGIONAL RURAL BANKs

**(See Chapter 3 Banking)**

# RURAL INFRASTRUCTURE DEVELOPMENT FUND (RIDF)

Rural Infrastructure Development Fund (RIDF) was instituted under NABARD in 1995–96 with the sole objective of giving low cost fund support to state governments and state owned corporations for quick completion of ongoing rural infrastructure projects relating to medium and minor irrigation, soil conservation, watershed management and other forms of rural infrastructure.

NABARD's support for creation of Rural Infrastructure through RIDF has resulted in considerable benefits such as:

(i) Committed supply of funds under RIDF sanctioned projects has enabled the state Governments to take up the implementation more expeditiously.

(ii) Financing of incomplete projects has resulted in unlocking of sunken investments already made by the state governments, thus, realizing the full benefits of the projects.

(iii) Creation of additional irrigation potential, generation of non-recurring employment and creation of jobs has contributed to the economic prosperity in the rural areas.

(iv) Monitoring of the projects has resulted in timely implementation of majority of the projects and has reduced the time and cost overrun.

(v) Completion of projects through RIDF assistance from NABARD has helped in growth of real sectors in rural areas by spurring the demand for credit from Banks.

RIDF Tranche I, was placed with NABARD during 1995–96 with an allocation of ₹ 2,000 crore. The annual corpus has now reached to ₹ 29,763 crore under RIDF XXVI (2020–21).

Sector-wise cumulative RIDF loans sanctioned till 31 March 2017, accounted for: 43 per cent to agriculture, irrigation and allied sectors; 16 per cent to social sector and 41 per cent to rural roads and bridges.

## ❖ Broad Achievements under RIDF

RIDF Tranche I was placed with NABARD during 1995-96 with an allocation of Rs 2,000 crore. The annual corpus has now reached to Rs 29,763 crores under RIDF XXVI (2020-21).

Cumulative Sanctions & Disbursements as on March 31, 2021

| Particulars | No. of Projects Sanctioned | RIDF Amount Sanctioned | RIDF Loan Disbursed | Utilisation |
|---|---|---|---|---|
| RIDF | 709318 | 390563 | 305177 | 78% |
| Bharat Nirman | | 18500 | 18500 | 100% |
| **Total** | **709318** | **409063** | **323677** | **79%** |

**Sector-wise Share of Cumulative Sanctions:** Sector-wise cumulative RIDF loans sanctioned as on March 31, 2021 (Rs.3,90,563 crore), accounted for:

- Agriculture, irrigation and allied sectors (44%)
- Social sector (18%)
- Rural roads and bridges (38%)

## KISAN CREDIT CARDS (KCC)

The Kisan credit cards (KCC) Scheme introduced in 1998–99 aims at providing crop loans to farmers in a flexible and cost-effective manner.

The Scheme is being implemented by all commercial banks, RRBs, state co-operative banks, central co-operative banks and primary agricultural co-operative societies.

Beneficiaries covered under the KCC are issued with a credit card and a passbook or a credit card-cum-passbook incorporating the name, address and particulars of land, borrowing limit and the validity period.

### ❖ Objectives

The KCC Scheme aims at providing adequate and timely credit support from the banking system under a single window with flexible and simplified procedure to the farmers for their cultivation and other needs as follow:

(i) To meet the short-term credit requirements for cultivation of crops;

(ii) Post-harvest expenses;

(iii) Produce marketing loan;

(iv) Consumption requirements of farmer household;

(v) Working capital for maintenance of farm assets and activities allied to agriculture;

(vi) Investment credit requirement for agriculture and allied activities.

### ❖ Benefits of KCC

1. Flexible repayment options
2. Hassle-free disbursement procedure
3. Single credit facility/term loan for all agricultural requirements
4. Dependable and easily available credit which enables a decrease in the farmer's interest burden.
5. Assists in the purchase of fertilizers, seeds, etc.
6. Assists in availing cash discounts from merchants/dealers
7. Credit is available for a period of up to 3 years, without any seasonal appraisals.
8. Income from agricultural sources determines the maximum credit limit.
9. There is no restriction on the cash withdrawals that can be made by the Kisan Credit Card holder, as long as it is within the credit limit set by the bank.
10. Repayment can be made once the harvest season in over.
11. Lower interest rates.
12. Margin, security and documentation terms and conditions are similar to that applicable to agricultural advance.
13. Credit is made available for annual agricultural requirements and expenses.
14. Minimal documentation and maximum flexibility offered for withdrawal of the required funds from the Bank.
15. Funds can be withdrawn from any of the Bank's branches, as per the sole discretion of the bank.
16. All new KCC must be issued as smart card cum debit card.

The cumulative number of KCC cards issued since inception (1988–89) till March 2020 had reached to 18.7 crore. However, the number of operative KCC as in March 2015 stood at 7.41 crore.

In financial year 2021, over 11 million credit cards were issued under the Kisan Credit Card Scheme in the Indian state of Uttar Pradesh. It was followed by Maharashtra and Andhra Pradesh with 6.8 million and 6.6 million cards respectively. In total, 73 million cards were active that year, an increase compared to the previous year. The value of outstanding agricultural loans stood at 7.53 trillion Indian rupee.

## COMMERCIAL BANKS

The commercial banks provide finance directly to agriculturists for the marketing of their produce, for the modernization and mechanization of their farms, for providing irrigation facilities, for developing land, etc. They also provide financial assistance for animal husbandry, dairy farming, sheep breeding, poultry farming, pisciculture and horticulture. The small and marginal farmers and landless agricultural workers, artisans and petty shopkeepers in rural areas are provided financial assistance through the regional rural banks in India.

## MICRO-FINANCE

Banks offer concessional interest rates for the rural credit. However, small farmers are unable to access them because of borrower-unfriendly products and procedures, inflexibility and delay, and high transaction costs, both legitimate and illegal. Thus, non-government organisations (NGOs) are providing alternative means to enhance access to credit by the poor since the 1970s. After pioneering efforts by organizations like SEWA, MYRADA, PRADAN and CDF, in 1992, the RBI and NABARD encouraged commercial banks to link up with NGOs to establish and finance self-help groups (SHGs) of the poor. The RBI has included financing of SHGs under priority sector lending (PSL). At present, there are three groups of SHGs viz. SHGs formed and financed by the banks (20 per cent); SHGs formed by other formal agencies but financed by banks; SHGs financed by banks using NGOs and other agencies (8 per cent). These institutions provide small loans to the poor at low-interest rates without collateral.

Microfinance Institutions Network (MFIN) is a self-regulatory organization which regulates the microfinance institutions in consultation with the RBI.

## LAND DEVELOPMENT BANKS (LDB)

The special banks providing long-term loans are called Land Development Banks (LDB). The history of LDB's is quite old. The first LDB was started at Jhang in Punjab in 1920. But the real impetus to these banks was received after passing the Land Mortgage Banks Act in 1930's (LDBs were originally called Land Mortgage Banks). After passing this Act, LDBs were started in different states of India.

The LDBs in due course diversified their activities and at the instance of the NABARD in the year 1982, they started financing for agriculture and rural development activities including wastelands. However, late eighties and the beginning of nineties were the crucial period in which LDBs adopted financing long-term loans for more significant rural development activities like, village and cottage industries, rural artisans, etc. Besides financing for rural housing schemes, under NHB, refinance was introduced by the banks in selected. In view of broader role of LDBs they are now known as State Co-operative Agriculture and Rural Development Banks (SCARDBs).

The main objective of the LDB is to promote the development of agriculture and increase the agricultural production.

The LDBs have two-tier structure:

1. Primary Land Development Bank at district level with branches at taluka level.

2. **State Land Development Bank:** All primary LDB are federated into Central Land Development Bank at the state level. In some states, there is 'unitary structure', wherein there is only one State Land Development Bank at the state level operating through its branches and sub-branches at district and below levels.

The sources of funds of State LDBs are:

1. Share capital
2. Issue of debentures
3. Loans from NABARD
4. Reimbursements of subsidies from the governmentand
5. Other funds

## AGRICULTURAL MARKETING

The National Commission on Agriculture defined agricultural marketing as a process which starts with a decision to produce a saleable farm commodity, and it involves all aspects of market structure of system, both functional and institutional, based on technical and economic considerations and includes pre- and post-harvest operations, assembling, grading, storage, transportation and distribution.

In the case of agricultural marketing in India, it is not exactly the marketing in the literal sense and we can call it as 'distributive handling' of agricultural produce as there are number of intermediaries who are involved in marketing the agricultural produce. However, with the liberalization, privatization and globalization, the economic scenario in India has changed drastically and tremendously.

## AGRO-MARKETING REFORM

There are several challenges involved in marketing of agricultural produce. There is limited access to the market information, literacy level among the farmers is low, multiple channels of distribution that eats away the pockets of both farmers and consumers. The government funding of farmers is still at nascent stage and most of the small farmers still depend on the local moneylenders who are leeches and charge high rate of interest.

There are several loopholes in the present legislation, and there is no organized and regulated marketing system for marketing the agricultural produce. The farmers have to face so many hardships and have to overcome several hurdles to get fair and just price for their produce.

The agriculture sector needs well-functioning markets to drive growth, employment and economic prosperity in rural areas of India. In order to provide dynamism and efficiency into the marketing system, large investments are required for the development of post-harvest and cold-chain infrastructure nearer to the farmers field.

A major portion of this investment is expected from the private sector, for which an appropriate regulatory and policy environment is necessary.

Also, enabling policies need to be put in place to encourage the procurement of agricultural commodities directly from farmers' fields and to establish effective linkage between the farm production and the retail chain and food processing industries. Accordingly, the state governments are requested to suitably amend their respective APMC Acts for deregulation of the marketing system in India, to promote investment in marketing infrastructure, thereby motivating the corporate sector to undertake direct marketing and to facilitate a national integrated market.

The National Commission on Agriculture (1976) and National Commission on Farmers (2004) have recommended that the facility of regulated market should be available to the farmers within a radius of 5 km.

Ministry of Agriculture has identified following seven vital areas of market reforms to pursue with the states/union territories.

1. Direct wholesale purchase from farmers outside the market yards at farmgate by Processors/Exporters/Bulk Retailers/ End user, etc.;
2. Establishment of private market yards/ private markets managed by a person other than a Market Committee;
3. Establishment of farmer/consumer market by a person other than Market Committee (Direct Sale by the producer to the consumers);
4. Provision for Contract Farming;
5. Provision for unified single registration/ license for trade transaction in the mandis across the state;
6. Provision for e-trading and
7. Provision for single point levy of market fee at first transaction.

## AGRICULTURAL PRODUCE MARKET COMMITTEE (APMC)

APMC is a statutory market committee constituted by a state government in respect of trade in certain notified agricultural or horticultural or livestock products, under the Agricultural Produce Market Committee Act issued by that state government.

APMCs are responsible for ensuring transparency in pricing system and transactions taking place in market area; providing market-led extension services to farmers; ensuring payment for agricultural produce sold by farmers on the same day; promoting agricultural processing including activities for value addition in agricultural produce; publicizing data on arrivals and rates of agricultural produce brought into the market area for sale and set up and promote public private partnership in the management of agricultural markets.

Most of the state governments and Union Territories have since enacted legislations (Agriculture Produce Marketing Committee Act) to provide for development of agricultural produce markets and to achieve an efficient system of buying and selling of agricultural commodities. The purpose of these Acts is basically the same, i.e., regulation of trading practices, increased market efficiency through reduction in market charges, elimination of superfluous intermediaries and protecting the interest of producer-seller.

The whole geographical area in the state is divided, and each one is declared as a market area which is managed by the APMC constituted by the state government. states also constitute a Market Board which supervises these market committees. APMCs generally consist of representatives of farmers, traders, warehousing entities, registrar of cooperative societies, etc. Market Boards generally consists of chairmen of all APMCs, representatives from the relevant government departments, etc.

The APMC system was introduced to prevent distress sale by farmers to their creditors, to protect farmers from the exploitation of intermediaries and traders and to ensure better prices and timely payment for their produce through the auctions in the APMC area. However, APMC Acts restrict the farmer from entering into direct contract with any processor/manufacturer/bulk processor, as the produce is required to be routed through these regulated markets. Over a period of time, these markets have acquired the status of restrictive and monopolistic markets, harming the farmers rather than helping them to realise remunerative prices. The APMC Act treats APMC as an arm of the state and the market fee as the tax levied by the state, rather than as a fee charged for providing services, which acts as a major impediment in creating a national common market.

## MODEL APMC ACT, 2003

The Ministry of Agriculture formulated a model law on agricultural marketing – State Agricultural Produce Marketing (Development and Regulation) Act, 2003, and requested the state governments to suitably amend their respective APMC Acts for deregulation of the marketing system in India, to promote investment in marketing infrastructure, thereby motivating the corporate sector to undertake direct marketing and to facilitate a national market.

The Model APMC Act, 2003, provided for the freedom of farmers to sell their produce. The farmers could sell their produce directly to the contract-sponsors or in the market set up by private individuals, consumers or producers. The Model Act also increases the competitiveness of the market of agricultural produce by allowing common registration of market intermediaries.

Though the Model Act provides for setting up of markets by private sector, this is not adequate to create competition even within the state since the owner will have to collect fees/ taxes on behalf of the APMC in addition to their own charges.

Lok Sabha passes The Farmers' Product Trade and Commerce (Promotion and Facilitation) Bill, 2020 and The Farmers (Empowerment and Protection) Agreement of Price Assurance and Farm Services Bill, 2020.

## APMC BILL, 2020

Two bills aimed at transforming agriculture in the country and raising farmers' income were passed by Lok Sabha. The Farmers' Product Trade and Commerce (Promotion and Facilitation) Bill, 2020 and The Farmers (Empowerment and Protection) Agreement of Price Assurance and Farm Services Bill, 2020 were introduced in Lok Sabha on 14th September. Farmers will now be freed from the restrictions of having to sell their product at designated places only, the procurement at Minimum Support Price will continue and mandis established under State laws will also continue to operate. Legislations will bring about revolutionary transformation and transparency in the agriculture sectior, electronic trading will increase, there will be accelerated agricultural growth as private investment will be attracted in building supply chains and agricultural infrastructure, new employment opportunities will be created and rural economy will get a boost, which will in turn help to strengthen the national economy.

The Farmers' Produce Trade and Commerce (Promotion and Facilitation) Bill, 2020 seeks to provide for the creation of an ecosystem where the farmers and traders enjoy the freedom of choice relating to sale and purchase of farmers' product which facilitates remunerative prices throught competitive alternative trading channels to promote efficient, transparent and barrier-free inter-State and intra-State trade and commerce of farmers' produce outside physical premises of markets or deemed markets notified under virious State agricultural produce market legislations; to provide a facilitative framework for electronic trading and for matters connected therewith or incidental thereto.

### ❖ Background

Farmers in India suffered from various restrictions in marketing their produce. There were restrictions for farmers in selling agri-produce outside the notified APMC market yards. The farmers were also regtricted to sell the produce only to registered lice nseer of the state Governments. Further, barriers existed in free flow of agriculture produce between various states owing to the prevalence of various APMC legislations enacted by state Government.

### ❖ Benefits

The new legislation will create an ecosystem whese the farmers and traders will enjoy freedom of choice of sale and purchase of agri-produce. It will also promote barrier-free inter-state and intra-state trade and commerce outside the physical premises of markets notified under State Agricultural Produce Marketing legislations.

It will open more choices for the farmer, reduce marketing costs for the farmers and help them in getting better prices. It will also help farmers of regions with surplus produce to get better prices and consumers of regions with shortages, lower prices. The Bill also proposes and electronic trading in transaction platform for ensuring a seamless trade electronically.

The farmers will not be charged any cess or levy for sale of their produce under this Act. Further there will be a separate dispute resolution mechanism for the farmers.

### ❖ One India, One Agriculture Market

The Bill basically aims at creating additional trading opportunities outside the APMC market yerds to help farmers get remunerative prices due to additional competition. This will supplement the existing MSP procurement system which is providing stable income to farmers.

It will certainly pave the way for creating One India, One Agriculture Market and will lay the foundation for ensuring goldern harvests for out hard working farmers.

The Farmers (Empowerment and Protection) Agreement of Price Assurance and Farm Services Bill, 2020 seeks to provide for a national framework on farming agreements that protects and empowers farmers to engage with agri-business firms, processors, wholesalers, exporters or large retailers for farm services and sale of future farming produce at a mutually agreed remunerative price framework in a fair and transparent manner and for matters connected therewith or incidental thereto.

### ❖ Background

Indian Agriculture is characterized by fragmentation due to small holding sizes and has certain weaknesses such as weather dependence, production uncertainties and market unpredictability. This makes agriculture risky and inefficient in respect of both input & output management.

### ❖ Benefits

The new legislation will empower farmers for engaging with processors, wholesalers, aggregators, wholesalers, large retailers, exporters, etc., on a level playing field without any fear of exploitation. It will transfer the risk of market unpredictability from the farmer to the sponsor and also enable the farmer to access modern technology and better inputs. It will reduce cost of marketing and improve income of farmers.

The legislation will act as a catalyst to attract private sector investment for building supply chains for supply of Indian farm produce to national and global markets, and in agricultural infrastructure. Farmers will get access to technology and advice for high value agriculture and get ready market for such produce.

Farmers will engage in direct marketing thereby eliminating intermediaries resulting in full realization of price. Farmers have been provided adequate protection. Sale, lease or mortgage of farmers' land is totally prohibited and farmers' land is also protected against any recovery. Effective dispute resolution mechanism has been provided for with clear time lines for redressal.

## NATIONAL COMMON MARKET IN AGRICULTURAL COMMODITIES

The Economic Survey suggests three incremental steps as possible solutions for setting up a national market.

1. It may be possible to get all states to drop fruits and vegetables from APMC schedule of regulated commodities and followed by other commodities.

2. The state governments may be specifically persuaded to provide policy support for alternative or special markets in private sector.
3. In view of the difficulties in attracting domestic capital for the setting-up marketing infrastructure, liberalization in FDI in retail could create possibilities for filling in the massive investment and infrastructure deficit in supply chain inefficiencies.

Economic Survey reemphasize that India needs a national common market for agricultural commodities by making the Agricultural Produce Market Committee just one among many options available for the farmers to sell their produce.

## THE NATIONAL AGRICULTURAL MARKET (NAM)

NAM through Agri-Tech Infrastructure Fund (ATIF) also known as e-NAM scheme was launched on 14 April 2016 as a portal in order to create a unified national market for agricultural commodities by integrating the APMCs across India in the states *which desire to be part of this initiative.*

NAM provides single window service for all APMC related services and information, such as commodity arrivals and prices, provision for responding to the trade offers, buy and sell trade offers, among other services.

NAM creates a unified market through online trading platform, both at state and national level, and promotes uniformity, streamlining of procedures across the integrated markets, removes information asymmetry between buyers and sellers and promotes real time price discovery, based on the actual demand and supply, promotes transparency in auction process and access to a nationwide market for the farmer, with prices commensurate with quality of his produce and online payment and availability of better quality produce and at more reasonable prices to the consumer.

### ❖ Objectives of NAM

1. A national e-market platform for transparent sale transactions and price discovery initially in regulated markets.
2. Liberal licensing of traders/buyers and commission agents by state authorities without any pre-condition of physical presence or possession of shop/premises in the market yard.
3. One license for a trader valid across all markets in the state.
4. Harmonization of quality standards of agricultural produce and provision for quality testing infrastructure in every market to enable informed bidding by buyers. Common tradable parameters have so far been developed for 69 commodities.
5. Single point levy of market fees, i.e., on the first wholesale purchase from the farmer.
6. Provision of Soil Testing Laboratories (STLs) in or near the selected mandi to facilitate visiting farmers to access this facility in the mandi itself.

## COMMODITY FUTURES AND FORWARD MARKETS

Commodity Futures are contracts to buy/sell specific quantity of a particular commodity at a future date. It is similar to the Index futures and Stock futures but the underlying happens to be commodities instead of Stocks and indices.

A forward contract is a legally enforceable agreement for delivery of goods or the underlying asset on a specific date in future at a price agreed on the date of contract. Under Forward Contracts (Regulation) Act, 1952, all the contracts for delivery of goods, which are settled by payment of money difference or where delivery and payment is made after period of 11 days, are forward contracts.

Commodity futures trading in India had been revived during the last few years. With effect from 1 April 2003, futures trading in 54 agricultural commodities have been permitted.

Futures are traded through 24 recognized exchanges, of which three have been recognized as national commodity exchanges. These are NMCE, Ahmedabad; MCX, Mumbai and NCDEX, Mumbai. These three exchanges account for 94 per cent of the total commodities futures trade in India. After the promotion of national multi commodity exchanges, there has been a rapid growth in the value of futures trade.

Forward/Futures trading performs two important functions, namely, price discovery and price risk management with reference to the given commodity.

It is useful to all segments of the economy. It enables the 'Consumer' in getting an idea of the price at which the commodity would be available at a future point of time. He can do proper costing and also cover his purchases by making forward contracts.

It is very useful to the 'exporter' as it provides an advance indication of the price likely to prevail, and thereby helps him in quoting a realistic price and secure export contract in a competitive market.

It ensures balance in supply and demand position throughout the year and leads to integrated price structure throughout the country. It also helps in removing risk of price uncertainty, encourages competition and acts as a price barometer to farmers and other functionaries in the economy.

## CROP INSURANCE

Crop insurance is an arrangement aimed at mitigating the financial losses suffered by the farmers due to damage and destruction of their crops resulting from various production risks.

The objectives of crop insurance are: (i) to provide financial support to the farmers in the event of failure of any of the notified crop as a result of natural calamities, pests and diseases; (ii) to restore the credit worthiness of farmers arising out of crop losses leading to non-repayment of crop loans; (iii) to encourage the farmers to adopt progressive farming practices, high value in-puts and higher technology in Agriculture and (iv) to help stabilize farm incomes, particularly in disaster years.

Almost the entire of Crop Insurance business comes from 'Schemes' or 'Programme'. These Schemes operate on principles of 'Area Approach'. Coverage is compulsory for farmers taking crop loans from Rural Financial Institutions (RFIs) for cultivation of crops, i.e., loanee farmers. non-loanee farmers can also insure their crops under the same schemes.

The main Schemes available to farmers in respect of crop insurance are as under:

1. NAIS of Government of India
2. **Modified National Agricultural Insurance Scheme (MNAIS):** It was approved for implementation on pilot basis in 50 districts during the remaining period of 11th Plan from Rabi 2010–11.
3. **Weather Based Crop Insurance Scheme (WBCIS):** It aims to provide insurance protection to the farmers against adverse weather incidence, such as deficit and excess rainfall, high or low temperature, humidity etc. which are deemed to impact adversely the crop production.
4. **Coconut Palm Insurance Scheme (CPIS):** It was implemented on pilot basis from the year 2009-10 in the coconut growing areas of Andhra Pradesh, Goa, Karnataka, Kerala, Maharashtra, Orissa, Tamil Nadu and West Bengal.

## NATIONAL AGRICULTURAL INSURANCE SCHEME (NAIS)

NAIS was introduced in the year 1999–2000. The Scheme is practically an all-risk insurance cover based on 'Area Yield Index'.

The Scheme covers all food, oilseeds and annual commercial/horticultural crops for which historical yield data is available and crop cutting experiments are planned for the current year. The state governments issue notifications containing names of crops, areas eligible for insurance, rates of premium, etc. at the beginning of each cropping season.

## NATIONAL CROP INSURANCE PROGRAMME (NCIP)

The NCIP was introduced by merging MNAIS, WBCIS and CPIS throughout the country in 2013–14.

The NCIP was started to provide financial support to the farmers for losses in their crop yield, to help in maintaining flow of agricultural credit, to encourage farmers to adopt progressive farming practices and higher technology in Agriculture and thereby, to help in maintaining production, employment and economic growth.

## AGRICULTURE INSURANCE COMPANY OF INDIA LIMITED (AIC)

In 2002–03 Budget, the Government of India proposed to form a new corporation for agriculture insurance called AIC to sub-serve the needs of farmers better and to move towards a sustainable actuarial regime.

AIC has taken over the implementation of NAIS which, until 2002–03 was implemented by General Insurance Corporation of India.

Presently the insurance products offered by AIC are: Pradhan Mantri Fasal Bima Yojana; Restructured WBCIS; Unified Package Insurance Scheme; NAIS; Bio-Fuel Tree/Plant Insurance; Cardamom Plant and Yield Insurance; Potato Crop Insurance; Pulpwood Tree Insurance Policy; Rainfall Insurance Scheme for Coffee (RISC) – 2011; Rubber Plantation Insurance; Varsha Bima/RainFall Insurance; Weather Insurance (RABI) and CPIS.

## RASHTRIYA KRISHI BIMA YOJANA (RKBY)

On 23 June 1999, the Prime Minister launched a crop insurance scheme called Rashtriya Krishi Bima Yojana (RKBY) under the NAIS.

The scheme intends to provide insurance cover and financial support to the farmers in the event of failure of crops as a result of natural calamities like natural fire, lightening, storms, cyclone, flood, draught, pests and diseases.

It is available to all the farmers irrespective of their size of holding. The scheme will be compulsory for loanee farmers and optional farmers. All the crops will be covered, and in addition, three cash crops like sugarcane, potato and cotton are brought under the purview of the scheme. For small and marginal farmers, a subsidy of 50 per cent on the premium.

The Scheme is expected to be a critical instrument of development in the field of crop production. It not only provides financially support in the event of crop failure but also would stimulate farmers to adopt progressive farming practices, high-value inputs and higher technology in farming. This will not only support and stimulate productions of food crops and oil seeds but also would help in stabilizing farm incomes even during disaster-hit years. Also, it will help in maintaining smooth flow of agricultural credit. Needless to say that the entire community will benefit directly or indirectly through spill over and multiplier effects in terms of production, maintenance, employment generation, revenue collection, etc. and the net accretion to economic growth.

The new scheme is expected to inculcate a habit of saving amongst the farmers and a sense of confidence in them to protect themselves against natural calamities. This scheme will be the umbrella for the farmers of our country to cover all risks, which affect in them in one form or the other. Ultimately, it will cease to be a mere insurance scheme and would blossom into a protective cover to the farming community as a whole.

## VARSHA BIMA

The Varsha Bima or Rainfall Insurance is a very special type of weather insurance scheme for the farmers whose crops get affected mainly by the rain conditions. Since this is a natural phenomenon and the farmers have very less to do with it, the government has thought that farmers would be provided with some financial support in case their crops fail due to this condition. Whether it is due to lack of rainfall or due to excess of rainfall, the Varsha Bima would certainly help the farmers to get out of the suffering caused by the crop loss.

## PRADHAN MANTRI FASAL BIMA YOJANA (PMFBY)

The Union Cabinet on 13 January 2016 approved the 'Pradhan Mantri Fasal Bima Yojana'.

The PMFBY aims at supporting sustainable production in agriculture sector by way of – (a) providing financial support to farmers suffering crop loss/damage arising out of unforeseen events; (b) stabilizing the income of farmers to ensure their continuance in farming; (c) encouraging farmers to adopt innovative and modern agricultural practices; (d) ensuring flow of credit to the agriculture sector which will contribute to food security, crop diversification and enhancing growth and competitiveness of agriculture sector besides protecting farmers from production risks.

All farmers including sharecroppers and tenant farmers growing the notified crops in the notified areas are eligible for coverage.

Special efforts shall be made to ensure maximum coverage of SC/ST/Women farmers under the scheme.

Main features of the Yojana are:

1. There will be a uniform premium of only 2 per cent to be paid by farmers for all Kharif crops and 1.5 per cent for all Rabi crops. In case of annual commercial and horticultural crops, the premium to be paid will be only 5 per cent.
2. The premium rates to be paid by farmers are very low and balance premium will be paid by the Government to provide full-insured amount to the farmers against crop loss in any natural calamities.
3. There is no upper limit on Government subsidy. Even if balance premium is 90 per cent, it will be borne by the Government.
4. Earlier, there was a provision of capping the premium rate which is low claims being paid to farmers. Now, this is removed and farmers will get claim against full sum insured without any reduction.
5. The use of technology will be encouraged to a great extent. Smart phones, Remote sensing drone and GPS technologies will be used to capture and upload data of crop cutting to reduce the delays in the claim payment.
6. The insurance plan will be handled under a single insurance company, AIC.
7. The PMFBY is a replacement scheme of NAIS and MNAIS and hence exempted from the service tax.

## KISAN PROJECT AND HAILSTORM APP

The Union Government on 5 October 2015 unveiled KISAN Project (Crop Insurance using Space Technology And Geoinformatics) which envisages use of high resolution remote sensing data from satellite and drone-based imaging, sophisticated modelling activity and other geospatial technology for improving the accuracy of crop yield estimation through more efficient crop cutting experiments.

The project will be implemented by Mahalanobis National Crop Forecast Centre (MNCFC) in collaboration with ISRO Centres, India Meteorological Department (IMD), Climate Change, Agriculture and Food Security (CCAFS), State Agriculture Departments and State Remote Sensing Centres.

A pilot study is already underway in rice and cotton fields of the ongoing kharif season in four districts. These districts include Kurukshetra (Haryana), Shimoga (Karnataka), Yavatmal (Maharastra) and Seoni (Madhya Pradesh).

The Government also plans to carry out the study in eight districts of the same states for the Rabi season to assess the yields of rice wheat and sorghum.

The project will eventually cover the entire country once the pilot study results are assessed.

## ANDROID APP TO COLLECT HAILSTORM DATA

The Central Government, with the help of Indian Space Research Organization (ISRO), has developed an Android App to collect hailstorm data. The maximum amount of damage caused to standing crops is because of hailstorms.

This App will assess the situation of crop damage due to hailstorm in the following ways:

1. Photographs of the location of the hailstorm can be uploaded through this app to the ISRO's Bhuvan server.
2. The application will collect data about hailstorms in real time along with photographs and geographical coordinates.
3. The pictures of the subsequent damage can also be immediately sent.
4. The data can then be collected by state agricultural department officials using this application.
5. This will allow the Central Government to survey crop loss quickly and more objectively.
6. Speedy assessment will benefit the farmers with accelerated settlement of insurance claims.

**Benefits:** Crop Insurance is usually calculated on the basis of crop cutting experiments. Waiting for the crop cutting often leads to delay in settlements. The project will address this concern and speed up payment of crop insurance claims to farmers. The project will also provide an accurate assessment of crop damage.

## GREEN REVOLUTION

Green Revolution refers to the quantum jump in food grain production following the use of high yielding varieties, fertilizers and pesticides coupled with expansion of irrigation facility, multiple cropping and use of modern mechanized implements like tractors, threshers, harvesters, etc.

The term Green Revolution was coined in 1968 by Dr. William S. Gaud to describe the breakthrough in food grain production and rapid diffusion of the semi-dwarf wheat and rice varieties in India and other countries of the developing world. The dwarf varieties of wheat were produced by American born Mexican scientist Dr. Norman E. Borlaug at International Centre for Wheat and Maize Improvement (CIMMYT), Mexico. For this contribution, Borlaug was honoured with Nobel Prize for peace in 1970. He is also known as the 'Father of Green Revolution'. M. S. Swaminathan is known as 'Indian Father of Green Revolution' for his leadership and success in introducing and further developing high-yielding varieties of wheat in India.

The Green Revolution occurred in India as a result of adoption of new agriculture strategy during mid-1960s by the Government of India to achieve self-sufficiency in the food grains production.

The objectives of the Green Revolution were to: (1) make available the required inputs in sufficient quantities; (2) encourage investment in fertilizer factories and the manufacturing of agricultural equipment; (3) identify and coordinate agricultural research activities to raise productivity; (4) intensify agricultural extension service in selected areas; (5) provide adequate credit to the farmers who are willing to grow varieties of cereals and adopt the appropriate farm practices and (6) implement a production-oriented cereal price policy.

The core components of agriculture strategy were: (i) Use of High-Yielding Variety (HYV) seeds that matures in short span of time; (ii) Application of fertilizers, manures and chemicals; (iii) Multiple Cropping Patterns that allows farmers to grow two or more crops on the same land; (iv) Mechanization of farming with the use of machines like tractors, harvesters pump sets, etc.; (v) Better Infrastructure facilities in terms of better transportation, irrigation, warehousing, marketing facilities, rural electrification were developed; (vi) Price Incentives involving provision of the minimum support prices (MSPs) for various crops so as to allow reasonable price to farmers for their produce; (vii) Better financial assistance through spread of credit facilities with the development of wide network of commercial banks, cooperative banks and establishment of NABARD as an apex bank to coordinate the rural finance in India and (viii) Protecting plants by using pesticides and other such devices.

## ❖ Impact of the Green Revolution

The Green Revolution resulted quantitative and qualitative changes in the agriculture in India. The quantitative changes occurred as a result of steep increase in the production of agriculture output. The qualitative change resulted into adoption of modernized technology in the agriculture.

The impact of green revolution is both positive and negative.

### Positive Impacts

1. **Spectacular increase in agriculture production:** The first major direct effect of the green revolution has been the sharp increase in agricultural production. As a result of new agricultural strategy, food grains output increased substantially.

   So far as food grains are concerned, wheat seems to have made rapid strides with its production increasing from 11.1 million tons in the Third Plan (annual average) 63 million tons in 1995–96.
2. **Improvement in productivity:** The productivity of agriculture, as measured in terms of yield per hectare, has increased. The productivity was quite low in the pre-green revolution period. The substantial increase in the productivity occurred in wheat and rice in the earlier periods, but later on it spread to other crops also.
3. **Increase in Employment:** The revolution generated employment opportunities into diverse activities which were created as a result of multiple cropping and mechanization of farming. It helped to stimulate non-farm economy that generated newer employment in various services such as milling, marketing, warehousing, etc.
4. **Price Stability of Food Grains:** The adoption of new agricultural technology has led to the increased production and marketable surplus of crops especially food grains that have resulted into price stability of food items.

5. **Strengthening linkages with industry:** The increase in agriculture production has strengthened the forward linkage of agriculture sector with industry in the sense of supplying inputs to the industry. The backward linkage with the industry has also received a boost as agricultural modernization created larger demand for inputs produced by the industry.
6. **Impact on Landless Labour:** In the green revolution areas, there has been a marked increase in demand for wage-labour particularly at the peak period. As a result of increased demand for labour, the position of labour in the market improved.
7. **Indian Council for Agricultural Research:** It developed new strains of high-yield value (HYV) seeds, mainly wheat and rice but also millet and corn. The most noteworthy HYV seed was the K68 variety for wheat.

## Negative Impacts

The Green Revolution is a unique event in the agricultural history of Independent India. This has saved us from the disasters of hunger and starvation and made our peasants more confident than ever before. But it has its own inherent deficiencies such as:

1. **Inter-Crop Imbalances:** The effect of the Green Revolution is primarily felt on food-grains. Although all food-grains including wheat, rice, jowar, bajra and maize have gained from the Green Revolution, it is wheat which has benefited the most. It has wrested areas from coarse cereals, pulses and oilseeds. The HYV seeds in latter crops have either not been developed so far at all, or they are not good enough for farmers to risk their adoption.

   Major commercial crops like cotton, jute, tea and sugarcane are also almost untouched by the Green Revolution.
2. **Regional Disparities:** Green Revolution technology has given birth to growing disparities in economic development at interred and intra-regional levels. It has so far affected only 40 per cent of the total cropped area and 60 per cent is still untouched by it. The most affected areas are Punjab, Haryana and western Uttar Pradesh in the north and Andhra Pradesh and Tamil Nadu in the south.

   It has hardly touched the Eastern region, including Assam, Bihar, West Bengal and Orissa and arid and semi-arid areas of Western and Southern India.
3. **Increase in Inter-Personal Inequalities:** It has been observed that it is the big farmers having 10 hectares or more land, who are benefited the most from the Green Revolution, because they have the financial resources to purchase farm implements, better seeds, fertilizers and can arrange for regular supply of irrigation water to the crops. As against this, the small and marginal farmers do not have the financial resources to purchase these farm inputs and are deprived of the benefits of the Green Revolution Technology.
4. **Other Problems:** Agriculture under Green Revolution has not grown at a rate which was expected in the beginning. The differential rates of growth of different crops and their regional variations have already been discussed. Some scholars have expressed serious doubts about the capability of HYV seeds itself.

   Apart from above, the burgeoning problems of land degradation, deforestation, environmental pollution, depletion of biodiversity, increased incidence of mosquito borne diseases, pest resurgence, and lowering of ground water table are the results of Green revolution in India.

## SECOND GREEN REVOLUTION

Once again, India needs to re-orient ourselves to create another Green Revolution. While the first Green Revolution was to ensure food security as there was severe scarcity of food in the country, the second Green Revolution aims at creating sustainable livelihood security for the poor and eradication of poverty by generating gainful self-employment.

While the first Green Revolution was aimed at undertaking mass production, the Second Green Revolution aims to promote production by the masses. This is in line with the Gandhian philosophy of involving the poor in development for equitable distribution of our prosperity.

The second Green Revolution focuses on generation of employment for the small and marginal farmers and the landless, while enhancing agricultural production.

In the second Green Revolution emphasis areas are: (i) non-food grains; (ii) improving rural infrastructure; (iii) improving irrigation, rural roads and rural electrification; (iv) increasing agricultural productivity; (v) generating rural employment; (vi) improving global market opportunities and (vii) developing technology to conserve water and energy.

### ❖ Second Green Revolution Approach

The second Revolution is a change in agricultural production widely thought necessary to feed and sustain the growing population of the world. These calls have precipitated in part, as a response to rising food commodity prices, rising demand of food articles, and fears of peak oil among other factors.

In India, a second Green Revolution needs an entirely new approach and an entirely new set of technologies. Climate change is tightening its grip and threatening food supply, not just in India but worldwide. It has never been more important to protect the scarce natural resources that are essential to agriculture. A new approach, termed as 'precision agriculture', is the key.

The correct type of fertilizer is, in fact, as important as the correct quantity, which should be an important consideration in any plan for a second Green Revolution in India.

Testing of samples of soil from agricultural fields is vital for achieving nutrient stewardship.

Mobile-based applications for farmers will form an important part of the data-driven precision agriculture approach. But it is important to ensure this meets the needs of the farmer. This signals an important area where governments and NGOs can intervene and offer this kind of detailed advice on an ongoing basis. It will also be key to ensure that applications are affordable and accessible.

The M. S. Swaminathan Research Foundation is working is working with Digital Green, an international non-profit development organization, to spread the use of clean technologies among women farmers in the Wardha and Yavatmal districts of Gujarat.

### ❖ Aims and Objectives

Four hundred million tons of food grain production as opposed to about 214 million tons in 2006–07 is the target of the 'Second Green Revolution'. To achieve the forgoing amount of production a growth rate of 5–6 per cent in agricultural sector has to be maintained over next 20 years.

Objectives of the second green revolution are: (i) to raise agricultural productivity to promote food security; (ii) more emphasis on biotechnology; (iii) to promote sustainable agriculture; (iv) to become self-sufficient in staple food, pulses, oil seeds and industrial raw material; (v) to increase the per capita income of the farmers and (vi) a holistic framework, thus, must incorporate rural infrastructure such as irrigation, roads and power.

It will require:

1. Genetically modified (GM) seeds to double the per acreage production, i.e., technology.
2. Private sector to develop and market the usage of GM foods, i.e., efficient marketing of the ideas.
3. Linking of rivers as much as economically possible to bring surplus water of one area to others, i.e., linking of the rivers.

## ❖ Government's Efforts

The Government's efforts to make second Green Revolution implemented include:

1. National Horticulture Mission, 2005
2. Rashtriya Krishi Vikas Yojana, 2007
3. National Food Security Mission, 2007
4. Mission for Integrated Development of Horticulture (MIDH), 2014–15
5. Pradhan Mantri Krishi Sinchayee Yojana (PMKSY), 2015
6. Neeranchal- Watershed Development
7. National Adaptation for Climate Change
8. Soil Health Card (SHC) to Every Farmer, 2016

# LAND REFORM

Land reform usually refers to redistribution of land from the rich to the poor. More broadly, it includes regulation of ownership, operation, leasing, sales and inheritance of land. In an agrarian economy like India with great scarcity and an unequal distribution of land, coupled with a large mass of the rural population below the poverty line, there are compelling economic and political arguments for land reform.

The major objectives of land reforms in India are as follows:

1. Restructuring of agrarian relations to achieve egalitarian social structure.
2. Elimination of exploitation in land relations.
3. Actualization of the goal of 'land to the tille'.
4. Improving the socio-economic conditions of the rural poor by widening their land base.
5. Increasing agricultural production and productivity.
6. Infusion of a greater measure of equality in local institutions.

For the fulfilment of these objectives, the major steps adopted under the land reforms programme are as follows:

1. Abolition of intermediaries
2. Tenancy reforms
3. Reorganization of agriculture

## ❖ Progress of Land Reforms

1. **Abolition of the Zamindari System:** The Zamindari system led to the exploitation and moral degradation of the tiller. As a result, a high priority was given to the abolition of the Zamindari system. Accordingly, by 1952, necessary legislation had been enacted in all the states.

More than 2 crore cultivators have been brought under direct relationship with the state. A considerable area of cultivable wastelands and private forests belonging to the intermediaries has been vested in the state. This has facilitated the distribution of 57.7 lakh hectares to landless agriculturists.

2. **Tenancy Reforms:** Tenants can be classified into the following:
(a) occupancy tenants,
(b) tenants at will and
(c) sub-tenants.

Special laws had to be enacted and implemented to protect the tenants. These laws relate to (i) regulation of rent (ii) security of tenure and (iii) conferment of ownership rights on tenants.

(i) **Regulation of rent:** The rate of rent prevalent during British period was one-half of the produce which was considered excessive by any standard of social justice. Consequently, the first and second plans recommended that rents should not exceed one-fourth or one-fifth of the gross produce. Accordingly, various states have passed necessary legislation in this regard, but there were variations in the rates of rent fixed in different states.

(ii) **Security of tenure:** Legislations have been passed in most of the states to protect tenants from ejectment and grant them permanent rights in the land. The purpose of these legislations were to ensure that (a) ejectment are lawful (b) land resumed by an owner is only for personal cultivation and (c) the tenant is assured of a prescribed minimum area in case of resumption.

(iii) **Conferment of ownership rights:** Legislative provisions have been made in many states for conferment of ownership rights on tenants or allowing cultivating tenants to acquire ownership rights on payment of compensation.

3. **Reorganization of Agriculture:** It includes – (i) ceiling on agricultural holdings; (ii) consolidation of holdings and (iii) co-operative farming.

(i) **Ceiling on Agricultural Holdings:** By ceiling on land holdings, we mean the fixing of the maximum size of holdings that an individual cultivator or a household may possess. The basic aim of ceiling is to accomplish the elimination of excess ownership of land.

To bring uniformity in land ceiling policies a conference of Chief Ministers was held in 1972.

The main features of the new policy were as follows:
(a) Lowering of ceilings to 18 acres of irrigated land and 54 acres of unirrigated land.
(b) Making family and not the individual as the unit for determining land holding.
(c) Lowering ceiling for a family of 5.
(d) Declaring benami transaction null and void.
(e) Including the land reform laws in the Ninth Schedule of the constitution.

In the light of new policy, land ceiling legislations were enacted by all the states, except Goa and the North East Region. However, the success has been limited due to poor enforcement.

(ii) **Consolidation of Holdings:** Consolidation of fragmented agricultural land has been an integral part of the land reform policy. Consolidation of holdings means bringing together into one compact block scattered fragments of land of a cultivator. Initially, the programme of consolidation was started on a voluntary basis but was later made compulsory.

Recognizing the importance of consolidation, legislations have been passed in most of the states to prevent sub-division and fragmentation of land. However, progress under the programme has been very slow.

(iii) **Co-operative Farming:** Co-operative farming has been one of the major objectives of the land reforms programme in India. By developing co-operative farming, the smallholdings will be pooled and cultivated jointly to increase the size of the operational unit.

Four kinds of co-operative farming were identified by the Co-operative Planning Committee. These are – (i) co-operative collective farming, in which members have to give up their land forever but are paid wages and gain a share in the surplus produces; (ii) co-operative tenant farming, in which land owned by a society is divided into holdings and then distributed among them. Each farmer has to pay a rent for his portion of land. However, the produce of his holdings is entirely his own; (iii) co-operative better farming where farmer get together to perform agricultural activities with improved methods but on their own separate lands and (iv) co-operative joint farming where in small farmers pool their lands together for better cultivation without giving up the ownership of their lands.

Co-operative farming in India has not been a success.

4. **Land Records:** Correct and up-to-date land records are an essential condition for effective implementation of land reforms programme. It is also necessary to ensure smooth flow of credit and agricultural inputs to land holders. Land records are now being computerized throughout the country, although the progress is slow.

## ❖ Limitations of Land Reforms

1. There are still many small and marginal farmers in India who pray to the clutches of moneylenders and continue to remain indebted.
2. Rural poverty still exists.
3. Land ceiling varies from state to state.
4. Many plantations were exempt from land ceiling act.
5. Many people own huge tracts of land under 'benami' names.

## CONTRACT FARMING

Contract farming is defined as a system for the production and supply of agricultural or horticultural produce under forward contracts between producers or suppliers and buyers. The essence of such an arrangement is the commitment of the producer or seller to provide an agricultural commodity of a certain type, at a time and a price, and in the quantity required by a known and committed buyer.

Contract farming usually involves the basic elements of pre-agreed price, quality, quantity or acreage (minimum/maximum) and time.

According to the contract, the farmer is required to plant the contractor's crop on his land and to harvest and deliver to the contractor a quantum of produce, based upon anticipated yield and contracted acreage. This could be at a pre-agreed price. Towards these ends, the contractor supplies the farmer with selected inputs, including the required technical advice.

Thus, the contractor supplies all the inputs required for cultivation, while the farmer supplies land and labour. However, the terms and nature of the contract differ according to variations in the nature of crops to be grown, agencies, farmers and technologies and the context in which they are practised.

For example, contract farming in wheat is being practised in Madhya Pradesh by Hindustan Lever Ltd (HLL), Rallis, PepsiCo India and ICICI. Launching its agro-business in India with special focus on exports of value-added processed foods, Pepsi Foods Ltd. (PepsiCo) entered India in 1989 by installing a Rs 22 crore state-of-the-art tomato processing plant at Zahura in Punjab. The company intended to produce pastes and purees for the international market.

### ❖ Advantages

Contract farming is looking towards the benefits both for the farm-producers as well as to the agro-processing firms.

Producer or farmer is benefited in following ways:

1. Makes small scale farming competitive – small farmers can access technology, credit, marketing channels and information while lowering transaction costs.
2. Assured market for their produce at their doorsteps, reducing marketing and transaction costs.
3. It reduces the risk of production, price and marketing costs.
4. Contract farming can open up new markets which would otherwise be unavailable to small farmers.
5. It also ensures higher production of better quality, financial support in cash and/ or kind and technical guidance to the farmers.
6. In case of agro-processing level, it ensures consistent supply of agricultural produce with quality, at right time and lesser cost.

Agri-based firms are benefited in following ways:

1. Optimally utilize their installed capacity, infrastructure and manpower and respond to food safety and quality concerns of the consumers.
2. Make direct private investment in agricultural activities.
3. The price fixation is done by the negotiation between the producers and firms.
4. The farmers enter into contract production with an assured price under term and conditions.

## IRRIGATION

Irrigation projects in India are classified into three categories, viz., major, medium and minor irrigation.

Projects which have a Cultivable Command Area (CCA) of more than 10,000 hector are termed as Major Projects, those irrigation projects which have a CCA of less than 10,000 hector but more than 2,000 hector are termed as medium projects, and those irrigation projects which have a CCA of 2,000 hector or less are known as minor projects.

### ❖ Types of Irrigation Techniques

The various irrigation techniques are as under:

1. **Surface Irrigation:** In surface irrigation systems, water moves over and across the land by simple gravity flow in order to wet it and to infiltrate into the soil. Surface irrigation can be subdivided into furrow, border strip or basin irrigation.

It is often called flood irrigation when the irrigation results in flooding or near flooding of the cultivated land.

2. **Localized Irrigation:** Localized irrigation is a system where water is distributed under low pressure through a piped network, in a predetermined pattern, and applied as a small discharge to each plant or adjacent to it. Drip irrigation, spray or micro-sprinkler irrigation and bubbler irrigation belong to this category of irrigation methods.

   **Drip Irrigation:** Drip irrigation, also known as trickle irrigation, functions as its name suggests. Water is delivered at or near the root zone of plants, drop by drop. This method can be the most water efficient method of irrigation, if managed properly, since evaporation and runoff are minimized. In modern agriculture, drip irrigation is often combined with plastic mulch, further reducing evaporation, and is also the means of delivery of fertilizer.

   **Sprinkler Irrigation:** In sprinkler or overhead irrigation, water is piped to one or more central locations within the field and distributed by overhead high-pressure sprinklers or guns. Automatically moving wheeled systems known as traveling sprinklers may irrigate areas such as small farms, sports fields, parks, pastures and cemeteries unattended.

3. **Sub-irrigation:** Sub-irrigation also sometimes called seepage irrigation has been used for many years in field crops in areas with high water tables. It is a method of artificially raising the water table to allow the soil to be moistened from below the plants' root zone.

## PRADHAN MANTRI KRISHI SINCHAYEE YOJANA (PMKSY)

PMKSY has been operationalized from 1 July 2015 with the objective of enhancing irrigation coverage and improving the delivery system at farm level. The programme aims at end-to-end solutions in irrigation supply chain, viz., water sources, distribution network and farm level applications. It will enhance physical access of water on farm and expand cultivable area under assured irrigation, improve on farm water use efficiency, introduce sustainable water conservation practices, etc. All the states and UTs are covered under the programme.

It comprises of various components such as Accelerated Irrigation Benefits Programme (AIBP), Har Khet Ko Pani (HKKP), Per Drop More Crop (PDMC) and Watershed development (WD).

The scheme has four components:

1. **AIBP:** To focus on faster completion of ongoing Major and Medium Irrigation including National Projects.
2. **HKKP:** Creation of new water sources through minor irrigation (both surface and ground water); repair, restoration & renovation of traditional water bodies; command area development (CAD); strengthening and creation of distribution network from sources to the farm etc.
3. **PDMC:** Precision irrigation systems, efficient water conveyance and application, micro level storage structures, topping up of input cost beyond Mahatma Gandhi National Rural Employment Guarantee Scheme (MGNREGS) permissible limits, secondary storage, water lifting devices, extension activities, coordination and management, etc.
4. **WD:** Ridge area treatment, drainage line treatment, soil and moisture conservation, rainwater harvesting and other watershed interventions.

Major, medium and minor irrigation projects are covered under PMKSY to bring more areas under irrigation and increase agricultural production. Major and medium irrigation projects are incorporated under AIBP and minor irrigation along with CAD comes under HKKP component of PMKSY.

### ❖ Objectives

The major objectives of the PMKSY are to achieve convergence of investments in irrigation at the field level, expand cultivable area under assured irrigation (HKKP), improve on-farm water use efficiency to reduce wastage of water, enhance the adoption of precision irrigation and other water saving technologies (PDMC), enhance recharge of aquifers and introduce sustainable water conservation practices by exploring the feasibility of reusing treated municipal based water for peri-urban agriculture and attract greater private investment in precision irrigation system.

The scheme also aims at bringing concerned ministries/departments/agencies/research and financial Institutions engaged in creation/use/recycling/potential recycling of water, brought under a common platform, so that a comprehensive and holistic view of the entire 'water cycle' is taken into account and proper water budgeting is done for all sectors namely, household, agriculture and industries.

The programme architecture of PMKSY aims at a 'decentralized State level planning and execution' structure, in order to allow states to draw up a District Irrigation Plan (DIP) and a State Irrigation Plan (SIP). DIP will have holistic developmental perspective of the district outlining medium to long-term developmental plans integrating three components namely, water sources, distribution network and water use application of the district to be prepared at two levels – the block and the district.

All structures created under the schemes will be geotagged.

## SOIL HEALTH CARD (SHC) SCHEME

Soil Health Card (SHC) scheme was launched in February, 2015 to issue 'Soil card' to farmers which will carry crop-wise recommendations of nutrients and fertilizers required for the individual farms to improve quality of soil and ultimately for better nutrient values and higher yields. This is aimed to help farmers to improve productivity through judicious use of inputs. This initiative would create a golden opportunity for the farmers to improve the productivity of their crops and also go for diversification. This will certainly contribute significantly to ensuring food security of the country. The scheme will be implemented on 50:50 sharing pattern between the central government and state governments. Government of India assists the state governments for setting up/strengthening of STLs.

At present, general fertilizer recommendations are followed by farmers for primary nutrients (N, P & K). However, secondary and micro nutrients are often overlooked leading to deficiency of nutrients like Sulphur, Zinc and Boron. This has become a limiting factor in increasing food productivity. Keeping this in view, Government of India is promoting soil test-based balanced and judicious use of chemical fertilizers, along with bio-fertilizers and locally available organic manures.

Awareness of soil health position and the role of manures would help in higher production of food grains in eastern India too and this would help tackle the decline in production in central and peninsular India. The growth in food grains, rice and wheat, from eastern India, would provide an opportunity to procure and create food grain reserves locally. This would reduce the agricultural pressure on Punjab and Haryana as well.

## ❖ Objectives

1. To issue soil health cards every three years, to all farmers of the country, so as to provide a basis to include nutrient deficiencies in fertilization practices.
2. To strengthen functioning of STLs through capacity building, involvement of agriculture students and effective linkage with Indian Council of Agriculture Research(ICAR)/State Agriculture Universities (SAUs).
3. To diagnose soil fertility related constraints with standardized procedures for sampling uniformly across states and analysis and design taluqa/block level fertilizer recommendations in targeted districts.
4. To develop and promote soil test-based nutrient management in the districts for enhancing nutrient use efficiency.
5. To build capacities of district and state level staff and of progressive farmers for promotion of nutrient management practices.

SHC is a printed report that a farmer will be handed over for each of his holdings. It will contain the status of his soil with respect to 12 parameters, namely N, P, K (Macro-nutrients); S (Secondary- nutrient); Zn, Fe, Cu, Mn, Bo (Micro - nutrients); and pH, EC, OC (Physical parameters). Based on this, the SHC will also indicate fertilizer recommendations and soil amendment required for the farm.

The card will contain an advisory based on the soil nutrient status of a farmer's holding. It will show recommendations on dosage of different nutrients needed. Further, it will advise the farmer on the fertilizers and their quantities he should apply, and also the soil amendments that he should undertake, so as to realize optimal yields.

Soil samples will be drawn in a grid of 2.5 ha in irrigated area and 10 ha in rain-fed area with the help of GPS tools and revenue maps.

The state government will collect samples through the staff of their Department of Agriculture or through the staff of an outsourced agency. The state government may also involve the students of local Agriculture/ Science Colleges.

At present, general fertilizer recommendations are followed by farmers for primary nutrients (N, P & K). However, secondary and micro nutrients are often overlooked leading to deficiency of nutrients like Sulphur, Zinc and Boron. This has become a limiting factor in increasing food productivity. Keeping this in view, Government of India is promoting soil test-based balanced and judicious use of chemical fertilizers, along with biofertilizers and locally available organic manures.

Government of India provides assistance to the state governments for setting up/ strengthening of STLs.

In the first two-year (2015–17) of the Soil Health Card scheme, 2.53 million samples were collected and so far 93 per cent samples have been tested. About 14 crore Soil Health Cards are being created by the State Governments and till May 31 it has been distributed among 8 crore farmers.

## SOIL HEALTH CARD PORTAL

Union Agriculture Minister launched three web portals, viz., Soil Health Card portal, Fertilizer Quality Control System portal and Participatory Guarantee System – India portal on 15 July 2015.

Under the scheme, a Soil Health Card portal has been developed for registration of soil samples, recording test results of soil samples and generation of Soil Health Card (SHC) along with fertilizer recommendations. This is a single, generic, uniform, web-based software.

It is a workflow-based application with following major modules: (i) Soil Samples Registration (ii) Test Result Entry by Soil Testing Labs (iii) Fertilizer Recommendations based on STCR and GFR (iv) Soil Health Card generation along with Fertilizer Recommendation and micronutrient suggestions and (v) MIS module for monitoring progress.

The system has sample-tracking feature and will provide alerts to farmers about sample registration and generation of Soil Health Card through SMS and e-mail.

The system envisages building up a single national database on soil health for future use in research and planning.

## NATIONAL MISSION FOR SUSTAINABLE AGRICULTURE (NMSA)

NMSA has been formulated for enhancing agricultural productivity especially in rain-fed areas focusing on integrated farming, water use efficiency, soil health management (SHM) and synergizing resource conservation.

NMSA has following four major programme components or activities:

1. Rain-fed Area Development (RAD)
2. On Farm Water Management (OFWM)
3. Soil Health Management (SHM)
4. Climate Change and Sustainable Agriculture: Monitoring, Modelling and Networking (CCSAMMN)

### ❖ Objectives

1. To promote water use efficiency, soil health/nutrient management and livelihood diversification through integrated farming in rain-fed areas.
2. To make agriculture more productive, sustainable, remunerative and climate resilient by promoting location specific integrated/composite farming systems.
3. To conserve natural resources through appropriate soil and moisture conservation measures.
4. To adopt comprehensive soil health management (SHM) practices.
5. To optimize utilization of water resources through efficient water management, to expand coverage for achieving more crop per drop.
6. To develop capacity of farmers and stakeholders in conjunction with other ongoing Missions.
7. To pilot models in select blocks for improving productivity of rain-fed farming by mainstreaming rain-fed technologies.
8. To establish an effective inter and intra Department/Ministerial co-ordination for accomplishing key deliverables of NMSA under the aegis of National Action Plan on Climate Change (NAPCC).

### ❖ Salient Features

1. Promoting Integrated Farming Systems (IFS).
2. Popularizing Resource Conservation Technologies.
3. Promoting effective management of available water resources and enhancing water use efficiency.
4. Encouraging improved agronomic practices.
5. Creating database on soil resources.
6. Promoting location and crop specific integrated nutrient management practices.
7. Involving knowledge institutions and professionals in developing Climate

Change adaptation and mitigation strategies.

8. Promoting interventions in select blocks as pilots for ensuring integrated development through dissemination and adaptation of rain-fed technologies.
9. Establishing platform to liaison, review and coordinate implementation of interventions outlined in Mission Document of NMSA.

## NEW UREA POLICY, 2015

New Urea Policy, 2015 (NUP-2015) has been notified by Department of Fertilizers on 25 May 2015 with the objectives of maximizing indigenous urea production; promoting energy efficiency in urea production and rationalizing subsidy burden on the government.

It is expected that the domestic urea sector would become globally competitive in terms of energy efficiency over a period of three years.

On the basis of actual energy consumption and preset norms, the units have been divided into three groups and revised energy consumption norms have been fixed for next three financial years and target energy norm have been fixed for 2018–19. It will drive urea units to select better technology and different measure to reduce energy consumption.

The higher energy efficiency due to aforesaid measure will reduce subsidy bill. It is expected that there would be reduction in the subsidy burden of the government in two ways – reduction in specific energy consumption norms and import substitution on account of higher domestic production.

It is expected that the new urea policy will lead to additional production of 1.7 LMT annually in the next three years.

## NEEM-COATED UREA

The Government of India on 25 May 2016 made neem coating of urea 100 per cent mandatory to stop its divergence for industrial use. Urea, which is subsidized for farmers' use, was diverted for industrial use especially in paints and ply wood industry, as it is cheaper compared to the urea for industrial use.

According to industry estimates, there could be savings of about ₹ 10,000 crore on account of lower use of urea after neem coating and fall in divergence for industrial use.

The use of neem-coated urea has been found to improve the uptake of N, P and K significantly.

### ❖ Benefits

Research institute like ICAR has found that neem-coated urea also acts as organic pesticide and with slow release of nitrogen, there will be 10 per cent less requirement of the fertilizer while the yield could go up by 10 per cent. Apart from the increase in yield, neem-coated urea application has other useful effect in paddy and wheat crops.

At one of the locations in the state of UP, farmers have observed that the menace of Neel Gai has reduced significantly in paddy crop. At Panipat, farmers observed no incidence of leaf folder and stem borer in paddy crop.

In Punjab, farmers observed that the incidence of white ant was reduced with the use of neem-coated urea in wheat crop. This is because of fragrance of neem oil that on dissolution was released in the standing water in the standing water and insecticidal properties of neem.

## ORGANIC FARMING

Organic farming is a method of farming system which primarily aims at cultivating the land and raising crops in such a way, as to keep the soil alive and in good health by use of organic wastes (crop, animal and farm wastes, aquatic wastes) and other biological materials along with beneficial microbes (biofertilizers) to release nutrients to crops for increased sustainable production in an eco-friendly pollution free environment.

This concept of organic farming is based on the following principles:

1. Nature is the best role model for farming, since it does not use any inputs nor demand unreasonable quantities of water.
2. The entire system is based on the intimate understanding of nature's ways. The system does not believe in mining of the soil of its nutrients and do not degrade it in any way for today's needs.
3. The soil in this system is a living entity.
4. The soil's living population of microbes and other organisms are significant contributors to its fertility on a sustained basis and must be protected and nurtured at all cost.
5. The total environment of the soil, from soil structure to soil cover is more important.

Key characteristics are that organic agriculture:

1. relies primarily on local, renewable resources;
2. makes efficient use of solar energy and the production potential of biological systems;
3. maintains the fertility of the soil;
4. maximizes recycling of plant nutrients and organic matter;
5. does not use organisms or substances foreign to nature (e.g., GMOs, chemical fertilizers or pesticides);
6. maintains diversity in the production system as well as the agricultural landscape; and
7. gives farm animals life conditions that correspond to their ecological role and allow them a natural behaviour.

The Government of India is promoting organic farming across the country through the dedicated scheme of Paramparagat Krishi Vikas Yojana (PKVY) and Organic Value Chain Development for Northeast regions (OVCDNER) under NMSA.

## PARAMPARAGAT KRISHI VIKAS YOJANA

PKVY, an initiative to promote organic farming in the country, was launched by the NDA government in 2015. According to the scheme, farmers will be encouraged to form groups or clusters and take to organic farming methods over large areas in the country.

To avail the scheme, each cluster or group must have 50 farmers willing to take up organic farming under the PKVY and possess a total area of at least 50 acres.

Each farmer enrolling in the scheme will be provided ₹ 20,000 per acre by the government spread over 3 years time. This fund can be utilized for obtaining organic seed, harvesting of the crops and transporting the produce to the local markets.

Organic farming will be promoted by using traditional resources and the organic products will be linked with the market.

### ❖ Aims of the Scheme

1. Promotion of commercial organic production through certified organic farming.
2. The produce will be pesticide residue free and will contribute to improve the health of consumer.
3. It will raise farmer's income and create potential market for traders.
4. It will motivate the farmers for natural resource mobilization for input production.

## PARTICIPATORY GUARANTEE SYSTEM

Participatory Guarantee System is a process of certifying organic products that ensures agriculture production process in accordance with the standards laid down for organic products and that desired quality has been maintained. This is exhibited in the form of documented logo or a statement.

It is a quality assurance initiative that is locally relevant with active participation of stakeholders including producers/farmers, traders and consumers in certification system. This group certification system is supported by the PKVY Scheme.

For online operation of this certification system, a Web portal has been created. This Web portal has online facility for (i) registration (ii) approval (iii) documentation (iv) record of inspection and (v) certification.

It will promote transparency in certification process. It will lead to creation of a database of (i) Organic producers and (ii) area under PGS certification with due traceability.

## FOOD SECURITY

According to P. V. Srinivasan, food security implies access by all people at all times to sufficient quantities of food to lead an active and healthy life. Food security exists when all people at all times have physical and economic access to sufficient, safe and nutritive food to meet the dietary needs and food preference for active and healthy life (FAO, 1996).

As per the Planning Commission of India, the most significant contribution of food management in India is to encourage food production, increase per capita availability, keep real price of food grains low and contain food price variability.

### ❖ Food Security in India

The green revolution initiated in the late 1960s was a historic watershed that transformed the food security situation in India. It tripled food grain production over the next three or four decades and consequently reduced by over 50 per cent both the levels of food insecurity and poverty in the country, this was achieved in spite of the increase in population during the period, which almost doubled.

## PUBLIC DISTRIBUTION SYSTEM (PDS)

The most important component of the food security system is public distribution of food grains through a network of fair price shops. The basic objectives of the public distribution system is to protect the interest of the vulnerable sections of population against high prices. It operates through a network of fair price shops. The PDS in India is the largest distribution network of its kind in the world.

Its broad features are as follows:

1. Selected essential commodities are distributed through the fair price shops and co-operatives
2. The government maintains a buffer stock and replenishes the same through the system of procurement.
3. Prices charged are lower than the market prices.
4. Free market mechanism co-exists with the public distribution system.
5. It has been basically an urban-oriented system.

The important objectives of the PDS are:

1. To improve the distribution of basic goods, e.g., rice, wheat, edible oil, sugar, kerosene, etc.
2. To control prices of essential commodities;
3. To meet consumption needs of masses;
4. To maintain good quality at low cost;
5. To bring stability in prices;

6. To weave production and marketing system into a unified whole.

Public distribution system is being seen more as an anti-poverty programme with the onset of the structural adjustment programme.

In January 1992, the government introduced a scheme of revamped PDS in 1700 blocks located in most difficult areas of the country. Food grains are allocated to these blocks at ₹ 50 per quintal lower than normal issue price. The other programmes, under which food grains are distributed, are National Food for Work Programme, Antyodaya Anna Yojana, Midday Meals Scheme, etc.

Public distribution system has been widely criticized for its failure to serve the population below the poverty lines, its urban bias, limited coverage in the states with high concentration of the rural poor and lack of transparent and accountable arrangements for delivery.

In order to meet some of these objections, in June 1997, the Government of India launched the Targeted Public Distribution System (TPDS) with focus on the poor.

## TARGETED PUBLIC DISTRIBUTION SYSTEM (TPDS)

Under the TDPS, food grains are distributed to the BPL families at highly subsidized rate. States are required to formulate and implement foolproof arrangements for identification of the poor for delivery of food grains and for its distribution in a transparent and accountable manner at the fair price shop level.

Under the TPDS, the prices for the below poverty line families were 50 per cent of the economic cost of the Food Corporation of India (FCI), but the amount was only 10 kg per family per month. APL families are also eligible for 10 kg per family per month but at a higher price. Later the Government of India increased allocation to BPL families from 10 to 20 kg of food grains per family per month at 50 per cent of the economic cost with effect from 1 April 2004.

The introduction of the TPDS combined with large-scale anti-TPDS suffers from several other deficiencies such as urban bias in coverage, diversion of grains to the open market, etc.

## MINIMUM SUPPORT PRICE (MSP)

The MSP is a form of market intervention to fix price of agro- produced by the Government of India to insure farmers against any sharp fall in farm prices. The MSP is a guarantee price given by the government for their produce. The MSP is announced at the beginning of the sowing season for certain crops on the basis of the recommendations of the Commission for Agricultural Costs and Prices (CACP).

The major objectives are to support the farmers from distress sales and to procure food grains for public distribution. In case the market price for the commodity falls below the announced minimum price due to bumper production and glut in the market, the government agencies purchase the entire quantity offered by the farmers at the announced minimum price.

The minimum support price is aimed to:

1. assure remunerative and relatively stable price environment for the farmers by inducing them to increase production and thereby augment the availability of food grains;
2. improve economic access of food to people and
3. evolve a production pattern which is in line with overall needs of the economy.

MSPs are currently announced for 24 commodities including seven cereals (paddy, wheat, barley, jowar, bajra, maize and ragi); five pulses (gram, arhar/tur, moong, urad and lentil); eight oilseeds (groundnut, rapeseed/mustard, toria, soyabean, sunflower seed, sesamum, safflower seed and nigerseed); copra, raw cotton, raw jute and virginia flu-cured (VFC) tobacco.

## PROCUREMENT PRICE

Sometimes, the government procures at a higher price than the MSP called procurement price. The procurement price is announced soon after the harvest. Normally, the procurement price is higher than the MSP, but lower than the market price. The price at which the procured and buffer stock food grains are provided through the PDS is called as issue price.

## BUFFER STOCK

The importance of building up a buffer-stock of food grains – normally rice and wheat – is to provide food security to the country. The argument in favour of buffer-stocking is that where there is large variation in food grain output, either due to weather conditions or due to man-made factors, it becomes essential for the state to ensure food security for the large mass of people by building adequate buffer stocks from the surpluses in good production years and/or by arranging to import the requisite amounts of food grains in times of need. Various committees have suggested the optimal size of the buffer-stock, which varies from 15 to 25 million tonnes, depending on the season.

## FOOD CORPORATION OF INDIA (FCI)

The FCI was setup under the Food Corporation's Act, 1964.

### ❖ Vision

Ensuring food security for citizens of the country.

### ❖ Mission

1. Efficient procurement at MSP, storage and distribution of food grains;
2. Ensuring availability of food grains and sugar through appropriate policy instrument, including maintenance of buffer stocks of food grains;
3. Making food grains accessible at reasonable prices, especially to the weak errand vulnerable sections of the society under PDS;
4. To intervene in market for price stabilization.

Since its inception, FCI has played a significant role in India's success in transforming the crisis management-oriented food security into a stable security system.

## HORTICULTURE

Horticulture can be defined as the 'Science of growing and management of fruits, vegetables including tubers, ornamental, medicinal and aromatic crops, spices, plantation crops their processing, value addition and marketing'.

Traditionally, horticulture involves four areas of study namely, pomology (fruit culture), olericulture (vegetable culture), floriculture (culture of ornamental crops) and post-harvest technology (management of produce after harvest). However, over the years the scope of the above field has been expanded to include other crops like mushroom, bamboo, plantation crops like tea, coffee and rubber. Bee keeping, one of the tools to improve the productivity of horticultural crops through enhanced pollination, is also being taken care by the horticulture division at the centre.

Government of India laid major emphasis on horticulture from mid-1980s onwards as a mean of diversification for making agriculture more profitable through efficient land use, optimum utilization of natural resources (soil, water and environment) and creating skilled employment for rural masses especially women folk. The past efforts have been rewarding and India has now emerged as the largest producer of coconut, areca nut, cashew, ginger, turmeric, black pepper and the second largest producer of fruits, vegetables and tea. Among the new crops, kiwi, olive, gherkins, Kinnow and oil palm have been successfully introduced for commercial cultivation in the country.

National Horticulture Board (NHB) was set up by the Government of India in April 1984 as a society under the Societies Registration Act, 1860, with its headquarters at Gurgaon. The main objectives of the NHB are to improve integrated development of Horticulture industry and to help in coordinating, sustaining the production and processing of fruits and vegetables.

## MISSION FOR INTEGRATED DEVELOPMENT OF HORTICULTURE (MIDH)

The MIDH was restructured in 2014–15.

Objectives of the scheme are to –

1. stimulate holistic growth of horticulture sector through area-based regionally differentiated strategies involving technology promotion, extension, post-harvest management (PHM), processing and marketing in consonance with comparative advantage of each state/region and its diverse agro-climatic features;
2. leverage economies of scale and scope by aggregating demand and consolidating supply through farmer groups or producer companies or organizations;
3. Create production clusters and hubs to facilitate setting up of infrastructure facilities for processing, post-harvest management and exports;
4. improve productivity by way of quality germplasm, planting material and water use efficiency through micro irrigation;
5. support skill development and create employment generation opportunities for rural youth in horticulture and post-harvest management, especially in the cold chain sector and
6. enhance horticulture production, augment farmers income and strengthen nutritional security.

## PRICE STABILIZATION FUND (PSF)

The PSF was set up in 2014–15 under the department of agriculture to help regulate the price volatility of important agri horticultural commodities like onion, potatoes and pulses were also added subsequently.

The scheme provides for maintaining a strategic buffer of aforementioned commodities for subsequent calibrated release to moderate price volatility and discouraging hoarding and unscrupulous speculation. For building such stock, the scheme promotes direct purchase from farmers/farmers' association at farm gate/Mandi.

The PSF is utilized for granting interest free advance of working capital to central agencies, state/UT governments/agencies to undertake market intervention operations. Apart from domestic procurement from farmers/wholesale mandis, import may also be undertaken with support from the Fund.

## FOOD PROCESSING

The Indian food industry is poised for huge growth, increasing its contribution to world food trade every year. In India, the food sector has emerged as a high-growth and high-profit sector due to its immense potential for value addition, particularly within the food processing industry.

Accounting for about 32 per cent of the country's total food market, the food processing industry is one of the largest industries in India and is ranked fifth in terms of production, consumption, export and expected growth. The total food production in India is likely to double in the next 10 years with the country's domestic food market estimated to reach US$ 535 billion by 2026.

Indian food processing industry is widely recognized as a 'sunrise industry' having huge potential for uplifting agricultural economy, creation of large-scale processed food manufacturing and food chain facilities and the resultant generation of employment and export earnings.

Two nodal agencies, Agricultural and Processed food products Export Development Authority (APEDA) and Marine Products Export Development Authority (MPEDA), were formed for promoting exports from India. MPEDA is responsible for overseeing all fish and fishery product exports; APEDA, on the other hand, holds responsibility for the exports of other processed food products.

### ❖ Policy

Food processing is recognized as a priority sector in the new manufacturing policy in 2011. Government had announced setting up of special fund of ₹ 2,000 crore in the financial year 2014–15 in NABARD for extending affordable credit to designated food parks and the individual processing units in the designated food parks at concessional rates. The fund is being continued in 2015–16.

The RBI has classified loan to food & agro-based processing units and Cold Chain under Agriculture activities for PSL subject to aggregate sanctioned limit of ₹ 100 crore per borrower. It will ensure greater flow of credit to entrepreneurs for setting up of food processing units and attract investment in the sector.

## SCHEME OF MEGA FOOD PARK

The Scheme of Mega Food Park aims at providing a mechanism to link agricultural production to the market by bringing together farmers, processors and retailers so as to ensure maximizing value addition, minimizing wastages, increasing farmers' income and creating employment opportunities particularly in rural sector. The Mega Food Park Scheme is based on 'Cluster' approach and envisages a well-defined agri/horticultural-processing zone containing state-of-the art processing facilities with support infrastructure and well-established supply chain.

With a view to promote investment in Mega Food Park, Ministry of Finance has covered Food Park including Mega Food Park under Infrastructure category.

There are 37 Mega Food Parks in India.

## SCHEME OF COLD CHAIN

The objective of the Scheme of Cold Chain, Value Addition and Preservation Infrastructure is to provide integrated cold chain and preservation infrastructure facilities without any break from the farm gate to the consumer. It covers pre-cooling facilities at production sites, reefer vans, mobile cooling units as well as value addition centres which includes infrastructural facilities like processing/multi-line processing/collection centres, etc. for horticulture, organic produce, marine, dairy, meat, poultry, etc.

Individual, Groups of Entrepreneurs, Cooperative Societies, SHGs, Farmers Producer Organizations (FPOs), NGOs, Central or State PSUs, etc. with business interest in Cold Chain solutions are eligible to set up integrated cold chain and preservation infrastructure and avail grant under the Scheme.

## FARMERS SUICIDE CRISIS

According to M. S. Swaminathan Commission on Farmers (October 2006) agrarian distress has led farmers to commit suicide in recent years. The major causes of the agrarian crisis are: unfinished agenda in land reform, quantity and quality of water, technology fatigue, access, adequacy and timelines of institutional credit and opportunities for assured and remunerative marketing. Adverse meteorological factors add to these problems.

More than one lakh farmers have taken their lives since 1997. Worst affected areas are Punjab, Haryana, Rajasthan, Karnataka, Kerala, Madhya Pradesh and Maharashtra. Cotton farmers are hardest hit by global competition and poor yield.

### ❖ Reasons of Crisis

1. In order to compete, many farmers turned to high-cost seeds, fertilizers and pesticides, believing in easier returns. Modified seeds cost nearly twice as much as ordinary ones, necessitating larger loans. There has been minimal financial support from the government for small farmers.
2. A crop failure, an unexpected health expense or the marriage of a daughter are perilous to the livelihood of these farmers.
3. The weather in India, these days, has become erratic at best and rainfall does not happen at the right time.
4. One of the most crucial problems faced by farmers in India is regarding marketing. The laws in India are outdated and most often a farmer has no option but to sell his produce in regulated markets, where the middlemen are the ones making the maximum gains.
5. ASSOCHAM estimates that each year 30–40 per cent of the entire agricultural produce in India is damaged, because there are not enough cold storages.
6. Farmers in India have to often make do with poor quality seeds. The fertilizers and pesticides that they use are also of a poor quality. All these factors often lead to complete loss of crops.
7. Problems in maintaining farm livestock owing to increasing costs.
8. Problems in getting credit at good terms and conditions because of reluctance of commercial banks
9. Lack of proper irrigation
10. Absence of mechanization
11. Insufficient transport facilities

### ❖ Solutions to the Crisis

1. They need to be educated about various facets of farming.
2. Centres of excellence need to be set up to help them.
3. Agricultural universities need to discover new science-based practices and technologies.
4. Insurance is needed.
5. They need to be given better access to credit and at better terms and conditions.
6. Landholdings should be consolidated.
7. Organic manure should be used.
8. Mechanization is needed.
9. Markets should be regulated.
10. Direct provision of capital to farmers by government.
11. Encouraging integrated, contract, and cooperative farming.
12. Developing water sheds.

❑❑❑

# 7 CHAPTER

# Service Sector in India

Fisher (1935) and Colin Clark (1940) have divided the economy into the primary sector, secondary sector and tertiary sector. At present, the primary sector includes agriculture, forestry, animal and husbandry, fisheries, etc., the secondary sector activities incorporate mining, manufacturing, electricity, gas, water supply, construction etc. and the tertiary sector or service sector activities include trade, commerce, transport, communications, hotel and restaurant, banking and finance, health and education, tourism, share market, film industry, insurance, astrology industry, advertisement industry, sports, legal service, publishing industry, mass media, etc.

Service sector is expanding at a faster rate. Service sector is 'Soft' part of the economy which includes all activities which people offer their knowledge and time to improve productivity, performance, potential and sustainability and also known as advice, experience and discussion include the service sector. Service sector involves of activities beginning from the production of goods and service until it reaches to the consumer. For the last three decades, there has been a substantial shift from the primary and secondary sector to the service sector. Now, it has become a largest sector of the economy.

Further, the service sector activities can be grouped into:

1. Trade, hotel and restaurants.
2. **Transport, storage and communication:** Transport includes roads and railways, airways and inland and overseas and water transport.
3. Financial institutions, insurance, real estate and business services..
4. **Community, social and personal services:** Community services include government establishment and its departments and personal services such as health, education, NGOs, etc.

## IMPORTANCE OF THE SERVICES SECTOR

Trade as a service sector activity facilitates the exchange of the goods and services between producers and consumers. Business includes both domestic trade as well as foreign trade. Domestic trade refers to the exchange of goods and services with in the country which provides income and employment to the people who have engaged in these activities.

Foreign trade plays a major role in the development of the country. Imports of machinery and equipment, which cannot be produced in the initial stages at home, are essential. Such imports which either help to create new capacity in some lines of production or enlarge capacity in the other lines of production are called developmental imports. The imports which are made in order to make a full use of the productive capacity are called maintenance imports.

Finance as a service sector activity plays an important role in undertaking any economic activities. Finance refers to funds of monetary resources required by individual, business houses and the government. People need funds to meeting their current requirement or day to day of expenses for buying capital goods. A business house require funds for paying wages and salaries, for buying raw materials, for purchasing new machinery or replacing an old one, etc. The government needs funds to provide various services to its subject. Finance institutions provide funds to various groups of people for variety of activities. In this process, the service sector activities provide income and employment to the people of a country.

In the previous days, this sector was responsible for distributing the output of the primary and secondary sectors for the intermediate and final consumption and also for the providing a variety of services to producers as well as consumers. Trade, transport and storage activities ensure distribution of goods and services where and when needed by consumers. Business and financial services facilitate mobilization of resources and their development in the activities of different sector of the economy.

The service sector activities generally require relatively less capital investment than activities in other sectors. However, a majority of these activities also require relatively less space for operations service sector is a knowledge intensive sector and substantial Human Resource Development (HRD) inputs are necessary for developing most of the services sector activities.

## SERVICE SECTOR IN INDIA

The services sector is not only the dominant sector in India's GDP, but has also attracted significant foreign investment flows, contributed significantly to exports as well as provided large-scale employment.

The services sector is the largest sector of India. Gross Value Added (GVA) at current prices for the services sector is estimated at 96.54 lakh crore INR in 2020-21.

The service sector is the key driver of India's economic growth. The sector contributed around 55 per cent of its Gross Value Added in 2020–21 and employed 28.6 per cent of the total population. In 1950–51, the primary sector was contributing about 56.5 per cent, the secondary sector 13.6 per cent and tertiary sector 29.9 per cent.

- Gross FDI equity inflow rise 33 per cent in 2019 to reach US$ 17.58 billion, about two-third of total gross FDI equity

## GOVERNMENT INITIATIVES TO PROMOTE SERVICE SECTOR

The Government of India recognizes the importance of promoting growth in services sectors and provides several incentives in wide variety of sectors such as health care, tourism, education, engineering, communications, transportation, information technology, banking, finance, management, among others.

India's priority is to work towards Trade Facilitation Agreement (TFA) for services, which is expected to help in the smooth movement of professionals.

The Indian service sector is expected to facilitate a knowledge-based economy, and the manufacturing sector will be dominated by services as a result of servicification of manufacturing.

The Government of India has adopted a few initiatives in the recent past. Some of these are as follows:

1. Ministry of Civil Aviation, Government of India, launched 'DigiYatra', a digital platform for air travellers that aims to develop a digital ecosystem providing consistent service and a delightful experience at every touch point of the journey.
2. Minister of Road Transport and Highways and Shipping, Government of India, launched INAM-Pro's upgraded version, INAM-Pro+, an online platform to bring together buyers and sellers of construction materials, equipment/machinery and services.
3. The Ministry of Electronics and Information Technology has launched a services portal, which aims to provide seamless access to government services related to education, health, electricity, water and local services, justice and law, pensions and benefits, through a single window.

Services sector growth is governed by both domestic and global factors.

## INDIA'S SERVICES TRADE

Services exports have been a dynamic element of India's trade and globalization in recent years. India's services export grew from 17 billion US$ in 2001 to 205.11 billion US$ in 2018 which constitutes 7.5 per cent of the GDP making the country the 8th largest services exporter in the world.

In order to promote trade in services, the Government of India follows a multi-pronged strategy of negotiating meaningful market access through multilateral, plurilateral and bilateral trade agreements, trade promotion through participation in international fairs/ exhibitions, focused strategies for specific markets and sectors.

## WORLD TRADE ORGANIZATION (WTO) NEGOTIATIONS

- The Eleventh ministerial conference (MC11) took place from 10 to 13 December 2017 in Bueons Aires. Argentina. It was chaired by Argentina. The conference ended with a number of ministerial decision, including on fisheries subsidies and e-commerce duties, and cornmitment to continue negotiation in all ares.
- Twerfth ministerial conference scheduled to take palce in June 2020 In Kazakhstan's Capital, Nursultan but was postponed due to Covid-19 Pandemic.

## BILATERAL AGREEMENTS

India has signed comprehensive bilateral trade agreements, including trade in services, with the governments of Singapore, South Korea, Japan and Malaysia. An FTA in services and investment was signed with the Association of South East Asian Nations (ASEAN) in September 2014, which came into effect from 1 July 2015.

India has joined the Regional Comprehensive Economic Partnership (RCEP) plurilateral negotiations. The RCEP is a proposed FTA which includes the 10 ASEAN countries and its six FTA partners, viz., Australia, China, India, Japan, South Korea and New Zealand. The RCEP is the only mega-regional FTA of which India is a part.

India is also engaged in bilateral FTA negotiations including trade in services with Canada, Israel, Thailand, the EU, the European Free Trade Association (EFTA), Australia and New Zealand.

## ❖ Issues and Challenges

Despite tremendous potential of service sector in India, there are some issues and challenges which need to be addressed. These are—limit of FDI allowed, trade in services, issues related to taxation, foreign exchange, patents, skewed growth, requirement of skilled workforce, capacity building, employability in service sector vis-a-vis Agriculture, etc.

While service sector-led growth contributed greatly to soaring GDP levels in India, it still employs less than 30 per cent of the total population. The source of most employment for Indian people still lies in the agriculture sector (45 per cent). IT and financial services are drivers of service sector growth in last two decades however both of these sector are not employment intensive. Thus, contributing to jobless growth in India.

The World Trade Organization (WTO)'s 12th Ministerial Conference (MC12) is being convened in Geneva, Switzerland at the end of this month, a year-and-a-half after it was scheduled to be held in Kazakhstan.

The MC12 is being held at an important juncture when the global trade scenario is quite upbeat.

## ❖ About World Trade Organization (WTO)

1. The World Trade Organization (WTO) is the only global international organization dealing with the rules of trade between nations.
2. At its heart are the WTO agreements, negotiated and signed by the bulk of the world's trading nations and ratified in their parliaments.
3. The WTO's goal is to help producers of goods and services, exporters, and importers conduct their business.
4. The WTO Ministerial Conference is the highest decision-making body of the World Trade Organization.
5. This conference is attended by the Trade Ministers and other officials from the organization's 164 members. So far from 1996, there have been 11 ministerial conferences.
6. WTO is a consensus-based, members-driven organization. The main advantage of this approach is that the decision taken is acceptable to all members.
7. Under the Marrakesh Agreement Establishing the WTO, the Ministerial Conference is to meet at least once every two years.

## ❖ The Outlook

1. Recent WTO estimates show that global trade volumes could expand by almost 11% in 2021, and by nearly 5% in 2022, and could stabilise at a level higher than the pre-COVID-19 trend.
2. The buoyancy in trade volumes has played an important role in supporting growth in economies such as India where domestic demand has not yet picked up sufficiently.
3. Therefore, these favourable tidings provide an ideal setting for the Trade Ministers from the WTO member-states to revisit trade rules and to agree on a work programme for the organisation, which can help maintain the momentum in trade growth.
4. But above all, the MC12 needs to consider how in these good times for trade, the economically weaker countries "can secure a share in the growth in

international trade commensurate with the needs of their economic development', an objective that is mandated by the Marrakesh Agreement Establishing the World Trade Organization.

## ❖ Demands of Technologies Necessary: IPRs and Vaccine Issue

1. From the very outset of the COVID-19 pandemic it had become clear that IPRs protected using the provisions of the WTO Agreement on Trade-Related Aspects of Intellectual Property Rights (TRIPS) are formidable barriers to ensuring equitable access to vaccines.
2. Pharmaceutical companies controlling the global markets have used monopoly rights granted by their IPRs to deny developing countries access to technologies and know-how, thus undermining the possibility of production of vaccines in these countries.
3. The involvement of developing countries in vaccine production could have increased supplies of affordable vaccines to the low-income countries.
4. Availability of vaccines remains a critical problem in these countries even after a year since the first dose of COVID-19 vaccine was administered.
5. Recent statistics show that until now, a mere 4.1% of the population in low-income countries have received at least one dose of the vaccine.
6. To remedy this situation, India and South Africa had tabled a proposal in the WTO in October 2020, for waiving enforcement of several forms of IPRs on "health products and technologies including diagnostics, therapeutics, vaccines, medical devices and their methods and means of manufacture" useful for COVID-19 treatment.
7. By doing so, barriers created by IPRs to timely access to affordable medical products could be removed.
8. This proposal, supported by nearly two-thirds of the organisation's membership, was opposed by the developed countries batting for their corporates.

❑❑❑

# CHAPTER 8

# Infrastructure Sector in India

## INTRODUCTION

A sound infrastructural foundation is the key to the overall socioeconomic development of a state. This acts as a magnet for attracting additional investment into a state and thus provides a competitive edge to it over other states. Good infrastructure is the basic requirement for any production process to work efficiently. Infrastructure itself may not be the part of the production process, but is important for the services it provides. It is an important input to the production process and raises the productivity of other sectors. Infrastructure connects goods to the markets, workers to industry, people to services and the poor in rural areas to urban growth centres. Infrastructure lowers costs, enlarges markets and facilitates trade. Thus, infrastructure provides services that support economic growth by increasing the productivity of labour and capital thereby reducing the costs of production and raising profitability, production, income and employment.

The Millennium Development Goals also highlighted the role of infrastructure in reducing poverty. It sets increasing access to water supply and sanitation service as targets. Infrastructure services contribute to poverty reduction and improvements in living standards in several ways. Greater access of the poor to education and health services, water and sanitation, employment, credit and markets is needed. Lack of access to product and factor markets prevents the rural poor to be a part of growth process. Making markets work for poor is the key element in reducing poverty. Infrastructure development enables the markets to expand and fall within the reach of the poor, thus making them part of the growth process.

The World Bank treats power, water supply, sewerage, communication, roads and bridges, ports, airports, railways, housing, urban services, oil/gas production and mining sectors as infrastructure. There is no clear definition of infrastructure according to the current usage of the term in India. For policy formulation, setting of sectoral targets and monitoring projects, a clear understanding of 'infrastructure' is necessary.

Dr. Rakesh Mohan Committee (1996) in 'The India Infrastructure Report' included electricity, gas, water supply, telecom, roads, industrial parks, railways, ports, airports, urban infrastructure and storage as infrastructure.

The National Statistical Commission (2001) headed by Dr. C. Rangarajan indicated six characteristics of infrastructure sectors:

(a) natural monopoly, (b) high-sunk costs, (c) non-tradability of output (d) non-rivalness (up to congestion limits) in consumption, (e) possibility of price exclusion and (f) bestowing externalities on society.

## INFRASTRUCTURE SUB-SECTORS

1. Transport infrastructure
   - (i) Road Transport–Roads and bridges, tunnels and motor vehicles
   - (ii) Rail Transport–Railways, signalling, communication system, rail yards and stations
   - (iii) Waterways – Inland waterways, inland water vessels
   - (iv) Sea and Coastal Transport–Seaports Ships and other vessels
   - (v) Air Transport–Airports, aircrafts
2. Energy infrastructure
   - (i) Petroleum and Natural Gas – Oil and gas pipeline networks and distribution terminals, gas fields/ wells and refineries.
   - (ii) Electricity (Thermal, Hydro, Nuclear) – Generation plants, wind mills, transmission and distribution lines, electric sub-stations, coal reserves, coal fields/ mines, coal washeries.
3. Communication infrastructure
   - (i) Telecommunication – Telephone network (landlines, mobiles) internet servers, communication satellites, cable television network
   - (ii) Postal Communication – Postal network, courier mail service
4. Irrigation infrastructure
   - (i) Major and medium irrigation
   - (ii) Minor irrigation
   - (iii) Flood control
   - (iv) Command Area Development Activities in the country
   - (v) Irrigation canals, reservoirs, water shed development
5. Drinking Water Supply–Water supply pipelines, filtration and treatment plants:
6. Sanitation infrastructure – Sewage treatment plants, drainage pipelines, on site sanitation facilities, landfills, incinerators.
7. Storage infrastructure – Food grain storage, cold storage, warehouses.

### ❖ Transport Infrastructure

A modern transportation infrastructure network is necessary for our economy to function, and is a prerequisite for the future growth. Businesses depend on a well-functioning transport infrastructure system to obtain their supplies, manage their inventories and deliver their goods and services to markets. Furthermore, it also opens up rural areas for development and makes cities internationally competitive. Transport infrastructure facilitates the transportation of people and goods and provides them access to markets, employment and investment opportunities. An efficient transportation system can have a multiplier effect on the economy, whereas a deficient transportation system can result in economic loss. For efficient transport system, an adequate infrastructure is very important. With growing population, there is a need to provide matching transport infrastructure to avoid overcrowding, overloading and poor maintenance of the available infrastructure. Transportation can be provided by various modes depending on the surface over which one has to travel – land (road, rail and pipelines), water (shipping) and air.

## ROAD TRANSPORT

Road transport is vital to the economic development and social integration of the country. Easy accessibility, flexibility of operations, door-to-door service and reliability have earned road transport an increasingly higher share of both passenger and freight traffic vis-à-vis other transport modes.

The total road length has increased from 4 lakh km in 1951 to about 58.9 lakh km in 2017, an increase to more than 14 times. The road length per 1,000 population has increased from 3.70 km in 2007–08 to 4.87 km in 2020, registering a Compound Annual Growth Rate (CAGR) of 2.2 per cent.

Indian roads are classified into three types namely the National Highways, the State Highways and the District and the rural roads. In addition, there are express ways and freeways.

## ❖ National Highways

At present, National Highway network of about 76.8 thousand km in 2019 comprises only 1.7 per cent of the total length of roads, but carries over 40 per cent of the total traffic across the length and breadth of the country.

Out of total National Highways about 24 per cent length is of 4-lane and above standard, 52 per cent length is of 2-lane standard and 24 per cent length of single and intermediate standard.

## ❖ National Highways Development Programme (NHDP)

The largest highway project ever undertaken in the country is implemented by the National Highway Authority of India (NHAI) which was constituted under the National Highway Authority of India Act, 1988, and was made operational in February 1995. Initially, it was entrusted with the task of implementing five externally aided National Highways' improvement projects. Subsequently, it was asked to implement several other projects including some BOT projects on National Highways.

The NHAI has been mandated to implement NHDP which constitutes 4/6 laning of Golden Quadrilateral connecting Delhi–Mumbai–Chennai–Calcutta–Delhi and North South and East-West Corridors connecting Kashmir in the North to Kanyakumari in the South and Silchar in the East to Saurashtra in the West. The Golden Quadrilateral is over 5,800 km. Under the Port Connectivity Project – roads connecting 12 major parts (380 km) and other projects (962 km) will be improved.

## ❖ State Highways

The State Highways and District roads account for nearly 6,00,000 km or about 15 per cent of the goods and passenger traffic. The construction and maintenance of these roads is the responsibility of the States.

## ❖ District and the Rural Roads

There are rural roads constructed under the Minimum Needs Programme (MNP), Rural Landless Employment Guarantee Programme (RLEGP), National Rural Employment Programme (NREP) and Command Area Development (CAD). In all these cases, the objective of road construction is linking villages in the country.

## ❖ Pradhan Mantri Gram Sadak Yojana (PMGSY)

In order to give boost to rural connectivity, a rural road programme, PMGSY was launched in October 2000. The primary objective of PMGSY is to provide connectivity, by way of all-weather roads to the unconnected habitations in the rural areas, so that habitations with populations of 1,000 and above are covered in three years (2000–2003).

## ❖ Expressways

The expressway is meant to function as arterial road for the movement of fast moving traffic in the big metropolitan cities, like Bombay, Calcutta, Delhi, etc. Two to three such expressways are necessarily to be provided around big cities of modern days to face the tremendous growth of the traffic.

As of now the Yamuna Expressway formerly known as Taj Expressway is the longest six-lane access-controlled expressway highway in India.

Maharashtra is also making its one of the longest highway known as Nagpur–Aurangabad–Mumbai express highway with a length of 700 km.

## ❖ Proposed and Planned Road Projects

1. The Ganga Expressway is a eight-lane access-controlled express highway of 1,047 km runs along with the holy river Ganges.
2. The Pathankot–Ajmer Expressway will run through the Punjab and Rajasthan state and connect Pathankot with Ajmer via Jalandhar. It will be the second longest expressway in India after the Ganga Expressway.
3. The Delhi–Jaipur Expressway is proposed six-lane expressway, connects Delhi to Jaipur.
4. The Outer Ring Road Expressway or ORR of Hyderabad is an eight-lane controlled-access expressway who will provide connectivity to National Highways NH 9, NH 7, NH 4 with other state highways.
5. The Mumbai–Nashik Expressway is long express highway connecting the financial capital Mumbai to the holy city Nashik.
6. The Hindon Expressway is officially known as Upper Ganga Canal Expressway, connecting Noida to Haridwar through Muzaffarnagar.
7. The Kundli Manesar Palwal Expressway or KMP Expressway is bypass the traffic from south Delhi to NH
8. The Eastern Peripheral Expressway is a controlled-access express highway runs through the Uttar Pradesh and Haryana.
9. The Raipur–Bilaspur Expressway is a under construction express highway connecting two major city of Chhattisgarh state.
10. The Hungund–Hospet Expressway is a 99km long access-controlled toll expressway runs through the Karnataka state and will connect Hungund and Hospet.

## ❖ Freeways

These are the special routes meant to carry fast moving traffic and therefore designed with high standard of alignment, clear visibility, wide carriageway, easy gradient and smooth curves, etc. There is no access from adjacent properties as a result full width of freeway is made available for the fast moving vehicles without any obstruction. The freeways function as arterial roads passing around the city with controlled access. They also act as main entrances and exits as such they form a part of major road system.

## ❖ Bharatmala Pariyojana

Bharatmala Pariyojana is a new umbrella program for the highways sector that focuses on optimizing efficiency of freight and passenger movement across the country by bridging critical infrastructure gaps through effective interventions like development of Economic Corridors, Inter Corridors and Feeder Routes, National Corridor Efficiency Improvement, Border and International connectivity roads, Coastal and Port connectivity roads and Green-field expressways. A total of around 24,800 km are being considered in Phase I. In addition, Phase I also includes 10,000 km of balance road works under NHDP. Estimated outlay for Phase I is ₹ 5,35,000 crore spread over 5 years. The objective of the program is optimal resource allocation for a holistic highway development/improvement initiative.

Bharatmala focuses on enhanced effectiveness of already built infrastructure, multi-modal integration, bridging infrastructure gaps for seamless movement and integrating National and Economic Corridors. Identification of the project stretches under the components of the proposed program has been done based on detailed Origin Destination (OD) study, freight flow projections and verification of the identified infrastructure gaps through geo mapping, using data from Bhaskaracharya Institute for Space Applications and Geo-Informatics (BISAG) as well as from other sources. This OD study has also taken into account integration of economic corridors with the ongoing projects under NHDP and infrastructure asymmetry in major corridors.

Phase-I of Bharatmala shall be implemented over a period of five years, i.e., 2017–18 to 2021–22.

## Components of Bharatmala

1. **Economic Corridors:** Identified Highways Corridors of Economic importance are expected to carry 25 per cent of freight in the coming years. Once built, the National and Economic corridors along with their inter-corridor and feeder routes would be able to carry 80 per cent of our freight traffic. Around 26,200 km of economic corridors have been identified to be developed as economic corridors out of which 9,000 km are being taken up in Phase-I of Bharatmala.
2. **Inter-corridor and feeder roads to national and economic corridors:** Around 8,000 km of inter-corridor and around 7,500 km of feeder routes have been identified out of which 6,000 km are being taken up in Phase-I of Bharatmala.
3. **National corridors efficiency improvement:** The Golden-Quadrilateral and NS-EW corridors carry 35 per cent of India's freight and would be declared as National Corridors. The National Corridors have developed choke points impacting logistics efficiency. There is a requirement to build Ring Road and bypasses/elevated corridors in addition to lane expansion to decongest these National Corridors. Further, Logistics Parks would also be developed at strategic locations to enhance logistics efficiency. A list of such identified locations of Logistics Parks is attached. Around 5,000 km are being taken up under this category in Phase-I of Bharatmala.
4. **Border and international connectivity roads:** Around 3,300 km of border roads have been identified to be built along the international border for their strategic importance. Around 2,000 km of roads are required for connecting India's major highway corridor to international trade points so as to facilitate Export-Import (EXIM) trade with our neighbours: Nepal, Bhutan, Bangladesh and Myanmar. Around 2,000 km are being taken up under this category in Phase-I of Bharatmala.
5. **Coastal and Port connectivity roads:** Around 2,100 km of coastal roads have been identified to be built along the coast of India. These roads would boost both tourism and industrial development of the coastal region. Around 2,000 km of port connectivity roads have been identified to facilitate EXIM trade with an emphasis to improve connectivity to non-major ports. The roads identified have been synergized with the Sagarmala program. Around 2,000 km are being taken up under this category in Phase-I of Bharatmala.
6. **Green-field expressways:** Certain sections of National and economic corridors have traffic exceeding 50,000 PCUs and have also developed several choke points. About 1,900 km of these

stretches have been identified for development of green-field expressways. Around 800 km are being taken up under this category in Phase-I of Bharatmala.

## ❖ Setu Bharatam Project

The Setu Bharatam project, launched on 5 February 2017 by Narendra Modi, is expected to make all the national highways in India free from railway crossings. The deadline, as of now, for completing the project is 2019. For project estimate cost of ₹ 102 million is sanctioned.

This is being done to prevent the frequent accidents and loss of lives at level crossings. Two hundred railway over bridges/railway under bridges will be built at the level crossings at a cost of ₹ 20,800 crore as part of the programme.

Setu Bharatam project provides benefits to close to 19 states by constructing 208 bridges which will lead to development of states. Construction of bridges will tend to reduction of accidents.

## Objectives

1. Construction of maximum 208 Railway bridges across 19 states
2. 1500 old and worn down bridges will also be improved by replacement/widening/strengthening in a phased manner at a cost of about ₹ 30,000 crore.
3. Development of states through transport development
4. Reduction of accidents

## ❖ Issues Related to Roads

Some of the common problems and issues related to roads are:

higher construction cost; uneven surface and poor riding quality; higher fuel cost; delays and loss of time due to traffic congestion; environmental Pollution; inadequacy in timely maintenance of roads due to funds constrains; absence of smoothly running traffic; removal of road side encroachment; abnormal delays due to existence of railway level crossings, octroi posts, other tax barriers, toll plazas, etc and inadequacy of in-built safety measures in the Road Projects during designing, construction, operation and maintenance.

## ❖ Viability Gap Funding (VGF)

VGF Means a grant one-time or deferred, provided to support infrastructure projects that are economically justified but fall short of financial viability. The lack of financial viability usually arises from long gestation periods and the inability to increase user charges to commercial levels. There are many projects with high economic returns, but the financial returns may not be adequate for a profit-seeking investor. For instance, a rural road connecting several villages to the nearby town. This would yield huge economic benefits by integrating these villages with the market economy, but because of low incomes it may not be possible to charge user fee. In such a situation, the project is unlikely to get private investment. In such cases, the government can pitch in and meet a portion of the cost, making the project viable. This method is known as VGF.

# RAILWAYS

The Indian Railways have been a great integrating force for more than 150 years. It has helped the economic life of the country and helped in accelerating the development of industry and agriculture. Indian Railways is known to be the largest railway network in Asia. The Indian Railways network binds the social, cultural and economic fabric of the country and covers the whole of country ranging from north to south and east to west removing the distance barrier for its people. The railway network of India has brought together the whole of country hence creating a feeling of unity among Indians.

The first proposals for construction of railways in India were presented in 1844 to East India Company in London by, (a) East Indian Railway Company headed by R. McDonald Stephenson and (b) Great Indian Peninsula Railway Company. The railway started in India on 16 April 1853, when the first train ran from Bombay to Thana, a distance of 21 miles (33.81 km.) with 14 railway carriages and 400 guests. The first passenger train steamed out of Howrah station destined for Hooghly, a distance of 24 miles, on 15th August 1854. Ajmer Workshop manufactured the first steam locomotive of India in 1895.

Since then, there has been no looking back. Today, it covers 6,909 stations over a total route length of more than 63,028 km. The lengths of track in broad gauge (1,676 mm) are 86,526 km, in meter gauge (1,000 mm) are 18,529 km and in narrow gauge (762/610 mm) are 3,651 km. Of the total route of 63,028 km, 16,001 km are electrified. The railways have 8,000 locomotives, 50,000 coaching vehicles, 2,22,147 freight wagons, 6,853 stations, 300 yards, 2,300 good sheds, 700 repair shops and 1.54 million work force. Indian Railways runs around 11,000 trains everyday, of which 7,000 are passenger trains.

**List of Zones available**

| Railway Zone | Code | Zone Headquarters |
|---|---|---|
| Central Railway | CR | Mumbai CSMT |
| Konkan Railway | KR | Navi Mumbai |
| Metro Railway, Kolkata | MTP | Kolkata |
| Northern Railway | NR | Delhi |
| North Central Railway | NCR | Prayagraj |
| North Eastern Railway | NER | Gorakhpur |
| Northeast Frontier Railway | NFR | Maligaon, Guwahati |
| North Western Railway | NWR | Jaipur |
| Eastern Railway | ER | Fairlie Place, Kolkata |
| East Central Railway | ECR | Hajipur |
| East Coast Railway | ECoR | Bhubaneswar |
| Southern Railway | SR | Chennai Central |
| South Central Railway[45] | SCR | Secunderabad Junction |
| South Coast Railway[45] | SCoR | Visakhapatnam |
| South Eastern Railway | SER | Garden Reach, Kolkata |
| South East Central Railway | SECR | Bilaspur |
| South Western Railway | SWR | Hubballi |
| Western Railway | WR | Mumbai (Churchgate) |
| West Central Railway | WCR | Jabalpur |

Kolkata is the city with most Zonal Headquarters of Indian Railways having the headquarters of Eastern Zone, South Eastern zone and Metro Railway, Kolkata.

## ❖ Management of Indian Railways

Indian Railways is a department of Government and the Ministry of Railways functions under the guidelines of Minister for Railways assisted by Minister of State for Railways. The policy formation and management of Indian Railways Board comprises of Chairman and six functional members. Wide powers are vested in the Board to effectively supervise the running of 16 zonal railways, metro railway (Calcutta), production units, construction organisation and other rail establishments.

The Ministry of Railways has following ten undertakings: 1. Rail India Technical & Economic Services Limited (RITES); 2. Indian Railway Construction (IRCON) International Limited; 3. Indian Railway Finance Corporation Limited (IRFC); 4. Container Corporation of India Limited (CONCOR); 5. Konkan Railway Corporation Limited (KRCL); 6. Indian Railway

Catering & Tourism Corporation Ltd. (IRCTC); 7. Railtel Corporation of India Ltd. (Rail Tel); 8. Mumbai Rail Vikas Nigam Ltd. (MRVNL) and 9. Rail Vikas Nigam Ltd. (RVNL). 10. Indian Railway Welfare Organisation (IRWO)

**Coach factories in India are:** (i) Integral Coach Factory (ICF), Perambur, Chennai, Tamil Nadu; (ii) Rail Coach Factory (RCF), Kapurthala, Punjab and (iii) Modern Coach Factory (MCF), Raebareli, Uttar Pradesh.

## ❖ E-enabled Track Management System (TMS) in Indian Railways

E-enabled TMS and Mobile Application of TMS on Indian Railways and Track Inventory Management System on Northern Railway started on 11th January 2016.

TMS is an important milestone in promoting e-working in civil engineering department of Indian Railways. It is being implemented on all the 68 divisions of Indian Railways. With its implementation, various activities of Track Inspection, Monitoring and Maintenance have come on IT platform. This system is designed for decentralized data capturing, speedy information dissemination along with centralized data keeping and analysis. It provides alerts in the form of SMS and e-mails to all concerned, right from Jr. Engineer in field up to the Railway Board.

**TMS Mobile Application** has also been developed to use this system on mobiles and tablets to view certain important exception reports. This will prove to be useful for senior management and for officials on the move.

**Track Store Inventory Management** for such a mammoth widespread system is an important facet of Asset Management. This application covers all the track inventory-holding units in the country numbering more than three thousand. All of them have been linked on one platform. This will enable optimization and balancing of inventory and speedy disposal of scrap and thereby increasing earnings from this source.

## ❖ Indian Railways Catering and Tourism Corporation (IRCTC)

IRCTC has launched online ticketing facility with the aid of Centre for Railway Information System, which can be booked on www.irctc.co.in. For the convenience of customers queries related to accommodation availability, passenger status, train schedule, etc. are can all be addressed online. Computerized reservation facilities have made the life easy of commuters across India. National Train Enquiry system is another initiative of Indian Railways which offers train running position on a current basis through various output devices such as terminals in the station enquiries and Interactive Voice Response Systems (IVRS) at important railway stations. Indian Railways are committed to provide improved telecommunication system to its passengers. For this, optical fibre communication (OFC) system has been embraced, which involves laying optical fibre cable along the railway tracks. In recent years, Indian Railways have witnessed the marked rise of collaboration between private and public sectors. Few of the notable examples here are the broad gauge connectivity to Pipya Port where a joint venture company is formed with Pipava Port authority.

## ❖ High Speed Rail Corporation of India Limited (HSRC)

The HSRC has been formed on the directions of Ministry of Railways, Government of India, for development and implementation of high-speed rail projects. **Objectives:**

1. To undertake feasibility studies and techno-economic investigations and prepare Detailed Project Reports and Bankability Reports of selected corridors for introduction of High Speed trains in India.

2. To plan, design and freeze technical parameters for high-speed rail systems including fixed assets, rolling stock and operations.
3. To develop financing models, explore Public-Private Partnership (PPP) options, coordinate with stakeholders and funding agencies and obtain various government approvals.
4. Project development, project execution, construction, upgradation, manufacture, operation and maintenance of high-speed rail systems on existing as well as new rail corridors.
5. To enter into and carry on all businesses related to High Speed Rail Systems and other rail based traffic as may be approved by Government of India or RVNL or any other Authority created by the government for such activities.

## ❖ First Bullet Train in India

India in September 2017 launched work on India's first bullet train, which will run between Ahmedabad in Gujarat and Mumbai. The train, which is expected to begin operating in 2022, will run at a maximum speed of 350 km per hour and will cover the 508-km stretch in under three hours. The ambitious project will cost around ₹ 1.10 lakh crore. Japan is giving a loan of ₹ 88,000 crore for the project at a minimal interest of 0.1 per cent.

The bullet train will have 12 stops of 165 seconds each. It will take two hours and 58 minutes from Ahmedabad to Mumbai if it stops at all 12. If it stops at four stations – Ahmedabad, Vadodara, Surat and Mumbai – it will cover the distance in two hours and seven minutes.

The Railways will run 35 bullet trains when it starts operations, with about 70 trips per day. It plans to increase the number to 105 trains by 2050. The government says by 2050, around 1.6 lakh commuters will travel by the high-speed train on a day. An institute that will come up at Vadodara, where around 4,000 people will be trained for the bullet train project.

## ❖ Indian Railways Bottlenecks

Indian Railways require finance for modernization; however, the required budgetary support is absent. For example, the provision of automated signalling system to prevent the crashes is missing. The stiff competition between private airlines has brought serious threat on upper class passengers of the railways. Though Rajdhanai and Shatabadi trains are the fastest and luxurious trains of India their speed and food service is not competitive as compared to the air travel. The other key problem faced by the Indian Railways is the high accident rate, which includes derailment and collisions.

## ❖ National Rail Plan Vision – 2030

Indian Railways have prepared a National Rail Plan (NRP) for India – 2030. The Plan is to create a 'future ready' Railway system by 2030. The NRP is aimed to formulate strategies based on both operational capacities and commercial policy initiatives to increase modal share of the Railways in freight to 45%. The objective of the Plan is to create capacity ahead of demand, which in turn would also cater to future growth in demand right up to 2050 and also increase the modal share of Railways to 45% in freight traffic and to continue to sustain it.

The key objectives of the National Rail Plan are:-

- Formulate strategies based on both operational capacities and commercial policy initiatives to increase modal share of the Railways in freight to 45%.
- Reduce transit time of freight substantially by increasing average speed of freight trains to 50Kmph.
- As part of the National Rail Plan, Vision 2024 has been launched for accelerated implementation of certain critical projects by 2024 such as 100% electrification, multi-

tracking of congested routes, upgradation of speed to 160 kmph on Delhi-Howrah and Delhi-Mumbai routes, upgradation of speed to 130kmph on all other Golden Quadrilateral-Golden Diagonal (GQ/GD) routes and elimination of all Level Crossings on all GQ/GD route.

- Identify new Dedicated Freight Corridors.
- Identify new High Speed Rail Corridors.
- Assess rolling stock requirement for passenger traffic as well as wagon requirement for freight.
- Assess Locomotive requirement to meet twin objectives of 100% electrification (Green Energy) and increasing freight modal share.
- Assess the total investment in capital that would be required along with a periodical break up.
- Sustained involvement of the Private Sector in areas like operations and ownership of rolling stock, development of freight and passenger terminals, development/operations of track infrastructure etc.
- 58 Super critical Projects of a total length of 3750 kms costing ₹39,663 Crore and 68 Critical Projects of a total length of 6913 kms costing ₹75,736 Crore, have been identified for completion by 2024.

## CIVIL AVIATION

In an increasingly globalized economy, air transport is a vital element of the country's transport infrastructure. The civil aviation sector contributes significantly to the process of development by generating employment opportunities directly and indirectly besides facilitating enhancement of productivity and efficiency in the movement of goods and services. Civil aviation is a key infrastructure sector that facilitates the growth of business, trade and tourism, with significant multiplier effects across the economy.

The civil aviation industry has ushered in a new era of expansion driven by factors such as low-cost carriers (LCCs), modern airports, Foreign Direct Investment (FDI) in domestic airlines, advanced information technology (IT) interventions and growing emphasis on regional connectivity.

Some of the key developments during 2000s, which aided the growth of the Indian aviation, include the following: ( a) Domestic 'open-skies policy', which allowed several new carriers to enter the market; (b) arrival of low-cost carriers (LCC) in India with the launch of Air Deccan, and subsequently by Spicejet, IndiGo and Go Air; (c) Airport modernization plans combined with encouragement of greenfield airport development; (d) liberalization of the international sector with private players permitted to operate overseas; (e) Greater access of foreign carriers and opening up of international routes at regional airports and (f) Increased foreign direct investment limits for airlines and other sub-sectors of the industry like airports, Air Cargo, ground handling, etc.

Presently, India is the ninth largest civil aviation market in the world and presently has a market size of USD 16 billion. The industry is poised to become the third largest aviation market by 2020 and the largest by 2030. It is among the five fastest growing aviation markets globally, growing at over 20 per cent year over year.

### ❖ Problems Facing the Aviation Sector

Most of the civil air carriers of India are suffering from huge financial crunch. Although the government calls for an increase in the foreign investment of airlines in Indian carriers, the operating cost discourages many. India has one of the highest airline fuel costs in the world. This is due to an import of huge amount of Aviation Turbine Fuel (ATF) and monopolization of price setting by PSUs in exclusion of other private sources.

## ❖ History

The Air Corporation Act, on 28 May 1953, nationalized the airline industry in India. In accordance with this Act, two air corporations, viz., Air India International and Indian Airlines Corporation were established and the assets of all the existing air companies were transferred to these two organizations. The Act prohibited any person, other than the corporations or their associates to operate any scheduled air transport services from, to or across India. This in effect gave monopoly to Indian Airlines and Air India on air transport in India.

In 1986, private airlines were allowed to operate charter and non-scheduled services under the Air Taxi Scheme which meant, *inter alia*, that they could not publish time schedules or issue tickets to passengers. The Air Taxi Scheme was introduced in 1986 to boost tourism and augment domestic air services. A host of private players commenced operations as air taxi operators including Air Sahara, Damania Airways, East-West Airlines, Jet airways, ModiLuft and NEPC Airlines.

The Air Corporation Act was repealed on 1 March 1994 and the air transport sector in India was opened to private players subject to fulfilment of statutory requirements for operation of scheduled services.

Another major development in this sector in 1997–98 was that the government approved foreign equity up to 40 per cent and NRI/OCB investment up to 100 per cent. By 1997, only four operators that started operations following the deregulation continued to operate – Jet Airways, Air Sahara (now defunct), Jagson and ModiLuft. In August 2003, Air Deccan commenced operations. Air Deccan was the first low-cost carrier to enter the domestic aviation industry. The entry of low cost carriers changed the competitive landscape of the industry. In 2005, Kingfisher began operation. In the same year, low cost carriers like Go Air, Paramount and Spicejet also entered the market. Indigo Airlines, low cost airlines also entered the market in 2006. In 2011 Indian (formerly Indian Airlines) merged with Air India. After merger, Alliance Air was renamed as 'Air India Regional'.

**Major Airlines in India are:** (i) Air India (ii) Jet Airways; (iii) GoAir; (iv) SpiceJet; (v) Indigo; (vi) Air Costa; (vii) Air Asia India; (viii) Vistara; (ix)Fly Easy; (x) TruJet; and (xi) Air Pegasus.

In 2017, out of total 86 scheduled international operators, 6 operators accounted for 50 per cent of International Passenger traffic. They are Jet Airways, Emirates Airline, Air India Express, Etihad Airways, and Qatar Airways.

## ❖ FDI Policy

100 per cent FDI is allowed under automatic route for 'Greenfield Projects' and 'Existing Projects' in airports. 49 per cent FDI is permitted in scheduled airlines and regional air transport services through automatic route and beyond 49 per cent with Government approval. For NRIs 100 per cent, FDI is permitted under automatic route. Hundred per cent FDI permitted via the automatic route for non-scheduled air transport services, helicopter services/sea plane services requiring the Director General of Civil Aviation (DGCA) approval, Maintenance, Repair and Overhaul (MRO), flying training and technical training institutions, ground handling services subject to security clearance and sectoral regulations.

## ❖ Airports

Airports are being developed in Public Private Partnership mode with Government actively involving private sector participation. 160 airports in the country are being revived and operationalized in an attempt to boost regional and remote air connectivity.

New Greenfield airports that have been approved are: (1) Dholera, Gujarat (2)

Bhugapuram, Vizianagaram, AP (3) Dagadarthi, Nellor, AP (4) Oravakal, Kurnool, AP (5) Bhiwadi, Rajasthan (6) Kothagudem, Telangana

## ❖ Airports Authority of India (AAI)

AAI was constituted on 1 April 1995 with the responsibility of creating, upgrading, maintaining and managing civil aviation infrastructure both on the ground and air space in the country.

The main functions of AAI *inter alia* include construction, modification and management of passenger terminals, development and management of cargo terminals, development and maintenance of apron infrastructure including runways, parallel taxiways, apron, etc.

AAI manages 125 airports, which include 18 international airport, 07 customs airports, 78 domestic airports and 26 civil enclaves at defence airfields. AAI provides air navigation services over 2.8 million square nautical miles of air space.

## ❖ Main Concerns of Aviation Sector in India

Although foreign direct investment in civil aviation has been relaxed by the government in 2012, it is surrounded by huge uncertainties. It could not attract prompt investment due to competing bureaucracies and delay in approvals.

Other major issues are: (i) concerns on the safety measures;(ii) high service tax and other charges; (iii) shortage of maintenance facilities; (iv) high foreign exchange rate; (v) competition from foreign airlines; (vi)congestion at airports and (vii) lack of qualified pilots and technical manpower, etc.

## ❖ National Civil Aviation Policy, 2016

The Union Government on 15 June 2016 released the National Civil Aviation Policy, 2016, in New Delhi. This is the first time since independence that an integrated Civil Aviation Policy has been brought out by the government. The policy is very comprehensive, covering 22 areas of the civil aviation sector.

## ❖ Salient Features

1. **Regional Connectivity Scheme**

   This scheme will come into effect in the second quarter of 2016–17. Airfare of about ₹ 2,500 per passenger for a one-hour flight. This will be implemented by way of:

   (i) Revival of airstrips/airports as No-Frills Airports at an indicative cost of ₹ 50 crore to ₹ 100 crore.

   (ii) Demand driven selection of Airports/airstrips for revival in consultation with the state governments and airlines

   (iii) VGF to airline operators.

   (iv) RCS only in those states which reduce VAT on ATF to 1 per cent or less, provide other support services and 20 per cent of VGF.

   (v) Concessions by Stakeholders.

   (vi) There will be no airport charges.

   (vii) Reduced service tax on tickets (on 10 per cent of the taxable value) for 1 year initially.

   (viii) Reduced excise duty at 2 per cent on ATF picked at RCS airports.

   (ix) State government will provide police and fire services free of cost. Power, water and other utilities at concessional rates.

   (x) Creation of Regional Connectivity Fund for VGF through a small levy per departure on all domestic flights other than Cat II/Cat IIA routes, RCS routes and small aircraft below 80 seats at a rate as decided by the Ministry from time to time.

(xi) VGF to be shared between the Minister of Civil Aviation (MoCA) and the state governments in the ratio of 80:20. For the North Eastern States, the ratio is 90:10.

2. **Route Dispersal Guidelines**

(i) Category I to be rationalized based on a transparent criteria, i.e., flying distance of more than 700 km, average seat factor of 70 per cent and above and annual traffic of 5 lakh passengers.

(ii) The percentage of category I traffic to be deployed on category II and IIA will remain the same while for category III it will be 35 per cent. Routes to Uttarakhand and Himachal Pradesh included in category II.

(iii) Revised categorization to apply from winter schedule of 2017.

(iv) There view of routes will be done by MoCA once every 5 years.

(v) Withdrawal or revision of domestic operations to and within North-East Region, etc., subject to full compliance of RDG, can be done under prior intimation to MoCA at least three months before withdrawal or revision of the service.

3. **5/20 Requirement**

(i) Replaced with a scheme which provides a level playing field.

(ii) All airlines can now commence international operations provided that they deploy 20 aircraft or 20 per cent of total capacity (in term of average number of seats on all departures put together), whichever is higher for domestic operations.

4. **Bilateral Traffic Rights**

(i) The Government of India will enter into 'Open Sky' ASA on a reciprocal basis with SAARC countries and countries located beyond 5,000 km from Delhi.

(ii) For countries within 5,000 km radius, where the Indian carriers have not utilized 80 per cent of their capacity entitlements but foreign carriers/countries have utilized their bilateral rights, a method will be recommended by a Committee headed by Cabinet Secretary for the allotment of additional capacity entitlements.

(iii) Whenever designated carriers of India have utilized 80 per cent their capacity entitlements, the same will be renegotiated in the usual manner.

5. **Ground Handling Policy**

(i) The Ground Handling Policy/ Instructions/Regulations will be replaced by a new framework:

(ii) The airport operator will ensure that there will be three ground handling agencies (GHA) including Air India's subsidiary/ JV at all major airports as defined in AERA Act.

(iii) At non-major airports, the airport operator to decide on the number of GHA, based on the traffic output, airside and terminal building capacity.

(iv) All domestic scheduled airline operators including helicopter operators will be free to carry out self-handling at all airports through their regular employees.

(v) Hiring of employees through manpower supplier or contract workers will not be permitted for security reasons.

6. **Airport PPP/AAI**

(i) Encourage development of airports by AAI, State Governments, the private sector or in PPP mode.

(ii) Future tariffs at all airports will be calculated on a 'hybrid till' basis, unless specified otherwise in concession agreements. Thirty per cent of non-aeronautical revenue will be used to cross-subsidise aeronautical charges.

(iii) Increase non-aeronautical revenue by better utilization of commercial opportunities of city side land.

(iv) AAI to be compensated in case a new greenfield airport is approved in future within a 150 km radius of an existing unsaturated operational AAI airport (not applicable to civil enclaves).

7. **Aviation Security, Immigration and Customs**

(i) MoCA will develop 'service delivery modules' for aviation security, Immigration, Customs, quarantine officers, etc. in consultations with respective Ministries/Departments.

(ii) Allow Indian carriers to provide security services to other domestic airlines subject to approval of BCAS.

(iii) Encourage use of private security agencies at airports for non-core security functions to be decided in consultation with MHA.

(iv) Such agencies should be registered under the Private Security Agencies (Regulation) Act, 2005, and will also be separately accredited by BCAS.

(v) Subject to minimum benchmarks being met, security architecture at the different airports will be proportionate to the threat classification and traffic volume.

8. **Helicopters and Charters**

(i) Separate regulations for helicopters will be notified by DGCA after due stakeholder consultation.

(ii) MoCA to coordinate with government agencies and other helicopter operators to facilitate Helicopter Emergency Medical Services.

(iii) Helicopters will be free to fly from point to point without prior Air Traffic Control (ATC) clearance in airspace below 5,000 feet and areas other than controlled, prohibited or restricted airspace.

(iv) Airport charges for helicopter operations will be suitably rationalized.

(v) The existing policy of allowing Inclusive tour package charters will be further reviewed to include more categories of passenger charter flights recognized globally.

9. **Maintenance, Repair and Overhaul (MRO):** The MRO business of Indian carriers is around ₹ 5,000 crore, 90 per cent of which is currently spent outside India. In the budget for 2016–17, customs duty has been rationalized and the procedure for clearance of goods simplified. Further, incentives proposed in the policy to give a push to this sector:

(i) MoCA will persuade the state governments to make VAT zero-rated on MRO activities.

(ii) Provision for adequate land for MRO service providers will be made in all future airport/heliport projects where potential for such MRO services exists.

(iii) Airport royalty and additional charges will not be levied on MRO service providers for a period of five years from the date of approval of the policy.

10. **Aviation Education and Skill Building:** Estimated direct additional employment requirement of the civil aviation sector by 2025 is about 3.3 lakh. All training in non-licensed category will conform to National Skill Qualification Framework standards. MoCA will provide full support to the Aviation Sector Skill Council and other similar organizations/agencies for imparting skills for the growing aviation industry. There are nearly 8,000 pilots holding CPL but who have not found any regular employment. MoCA will develop a scheme with budgetary support for type- rating of pilots. The detailed scheme will be worked out separately.

### ❖ Ude Desh Ka Aam Nagrik (UDAN) Scheme/Regional Connectivity Scheme(RCS)

Launched in October 2016, the scheme is targeted at improving connectivity and developing the regional aviation market. It also aims to make air travel more affordable to the common man. The Scheme is expect to boost tourism and employment generation in the country. Airline operators, who have to offer travel at subsidized rates, would be supported through concessions by both the central and state governments.

The central Government will offer concessions such as reduced excise duty, service tax, permission to trade ASKMs for Non-RCS (UDAN) Seats and flexibility of code sharing at the RCS (UDAN) airports. The state governments are being encouraged to lower the VAT on ATF to 1 per cent or less, besides providing security and fire services free of cost and electricity, water and other utilities at substantially concessional rates.

Airline operators will also receive funding support through VGF to meet the gap, if any, between the cost of airline operations and expected revenues on such routes. A Regional Connectivity Fund has been created to meet the VGF requirements.

## WATERWAYS IN INDIA

Navigation in rivers, lakes and other water bodies has been around since centuries; this has been more in the form of smaller vessels, connecting places not too far from each other. In some cases, especially near ports and coastal areas, this has evolved to more large-scale, commercial shipping.

Several advantages are put forward for such waterways. The most important advantage is that it is fuel-efficient compared to the other modes of transport, rail and road. Inland water transport is recognized as fuel efficient, cost-effective and environment-friendly mode of transport, especially for bulk goods, hazardous goods and over dimensional cargos. It also reduces time, cost of transportation of goods and cargos, as well as congestion and accidents on highways. For example, the Integrated National Waterways (NW) Transportation Grid Study states that one litre of fuel will move 24 tons through 1 km on road, 85 km on rail and 105 km on inland water transport.

The waterways will 'help to create seamless interconnectivity connecting hinterlands along navigable river coasts and coastal routes' and that 'riverine routes' are likely to play a crucial role in connecting the north-eastern states to the mainland.

On 1 August 2016, there are six operational NW in India.

These are:

1. NW-1: Ganga–Bhagirathi–Hooghly river system (Allahabad–Haldia).
2. NW-2: River Brahmaputra.
3. NW-3: West Coast Canal (Kottapuram–Kollam) along with Udyogmandal and Champakara Canals.
4. NW-68: M andovi River.
5. NW-97: Sundarbans waterways.
6. NW-111: Zuari River.

The Shipping Ministry in Nov. 2016 decided to undertake development of 37 NWs in the next three years. The Parliament of India enacted the National Waterways Act, 2016, (NWA, 2016) which came into force from 12 April 2017. This act declared 111 rivers or river stretches, creeks, estuaries as NW (inland). The passage of this legislation enables the central government to regulate these waterways for development with regard to shipping, navigation and transport through mechanically propelled vessels. The details of all 111 NW, including the latitude-longitude coordinates of the start and end points, are given in the NWA, 2016. These waterways pass through 24 states and 2 UTs, with an approximate total length of 20,274 km. These waterways will pass through nearly 13,811 river systems, creeks, estuaries and related canal systems of India.

### Operational National Waterways in the Country

Out of the 111 National Waterways (NWs) declared under the National Waterways Act, 2016, 13 NWs ae operational for shipping and navigation and cargo/passenger vessels are moving on them. The details of operational NWs are as follows:

**Details of Operational National Waterways**

| Sl. No. | National Waterway (NW) No. | Length (km) | Location (S) |
|---|---|---|---|
| 1. | **NW-1:** Ganga-Bhagirathi-Hooghly River System (Haldia-Allahabad) | 1620 | Uttar Pradesh, Bihar, Jharkhand, West Bengal |
| 2. | **NW-2:** Brahmaputra River (Dhubri-Sadiya) | 891 | Assam |
| 3. | **NW-3:** West Coast Canal (Kottapuram-Kollam), Champakara and Udyogmandal Canals | 205 | Kerala |
| 4. | **NW-4:** Phase-1 development of the stretch Mukriyala to Vijyawada of river Krishna | 82 | Andhra Pradesh |
| | **Waterways in Maharashtra** | | **Maharashtra** |
| 5. | (i) **NW-10** (Amba River) | | |
| 6. | (ii) **NW-83** (Rijpuri Creek) | 45 | |
| 7. | (iii) **NW-85** (Revadanda Creek- Kundalika River System) | 31 | |
| 8. | (iv) **NW-91** (Shastri River-Jaigad creek system) | 52 | |
| | **National Waterways in Goa** | | |
| 9. | **NW-68 – Mandovi** – Usgaon Bridge to Arabian Sea (41 km) | 41 | |
| 10. | **NW-111 – Zuari** – Sanvordem Bridge to Marmugao Port (50 km). | 50 | Goa |

| | National Waterways in Gujarat | | |
|---|---|---|---|
| 11. | **NW-73-** Narmade river | 226 | Gujarat & Maharastra |
| 12. | **NW-100-** Tapi river | 436 | |
| 13. | Sunderbans Waterwasy (NW-97): Namkhana to Athara Banki Khal in West Bengal. | 172 | West Bengal (Through Indo- Bangladesh Protocol Route) |

There is a scheme called 'Integrated National Waterways Transportation Grid' to link many of the NW to each other, to roads and railways and to major ports.

## WATER TRANSPORT

There are 13 major and 200 minor/intermediate ports (non-major ports) along the 7,517 km long coastline of India. The total 200 non-major ports are in the following states: Gujarat (42); Maharashtra (48); Tamil Nadu (15); Karnataka (10); Kerala (17); Andhra Pradesh (12); Odisha (13); Goa (5); West Bengal (1); Daman and Diu (2); Lakshadweep (10); Pondicherry (2) and Andaman and Nicobar (23).

**Major ports in India**

1. Kandla Western Coast, Gujarat
2. Paradip Eastern Coast, Odisha
3. Jawaharlal Nehru Port Trust (JNPT) Western Coast, Maharashtra
4. Mumbai Western Coast, Maharashtra
5. Visakhapatnam Eastern Coast, Andhra Pradesh
6. Chennai Eastern Coast, Tamil Nadu
7. Kolkata Eastern Coast, West Bengal
8. Mangalore Western Coast, Karnataka
9. Tuticorin Eastern Coast, Tamil Nadu
10. Mormugao Western Coast, Goa
11. Kochi Western Coast, Kerala
12. Krishnapatnam Port Eastern Coast, Andhra Pradesh
13. Ennore Eastern Coast, Tamil Nadu

Inland Waterways Authority of India (IWAI) has put in place a structured management and monitoring system with competent and experienced professionals, to ensure that the projects on NWs are qualitatively executed in a time bound manner. In addition, the progress of execution of projects is regularly reviewed at various levels within IWAI and the Government.

Inland Water Transport (IWT) mode is widely recognized as environment friendly and cost effective mode of transport. As per RITES Report of 2014 on Integrated National Waterways Transportation Grid, some of the important benefits of IWT mode compared to rail and road transportation are fuel efficiency and cost savings as given below:

1. 1 Litre of fuel moves 24 tonne - km on road, 95 tonne-km on rail and 215 tonne-km on IWT.
2. Comparative cost for movement of freight.

| Mode | Railways | Highways | IWT |
|---|---|---|---|
| **Freight (Rs./T. km)** | 1.36 | 2.50 | 1.06 |

In addition to the economic and environmental benefits, IWT aims to create for the shippers and logistic players, an alternative to the two dominant modes of transport viz. road and rail.

### ❖ Project Green Port Initiative

The government of India on 19 January 2016 started 'Project Green Ports' which will help in making the major ports across India cleaner and greener.

'Project Green Ports' will have two verticals: one is 'Green Ports Initiatives' related to environmental issues and another is 'Swachh Bharat Abhiyaan'.

The Green Port Initiatives include 12 initiatives which will be implemented under strict time bound fashion in order to achieve the targets.

Some of these initiatives are preparation and monitoring plan, acquiring equipments required for monitoring environmental pollution, acquiring dust suppression system, setting up of sewage/waste water treatment plants/garbage disposal plant, setting up projects for energy generation from renewable energy sources, completion of shortfalls of Oil Spill Response (OSR) facilities (Tier-1), prohibition of disposal of almost all kind of garbage at sea, improving the quality of harbour wastes, etc.

Under Swachh Bharat Abhiyaan, the Ministry has identified 20 activities with certain timeline to promote cleanliness at the port premises. Some of the activities include cleaning the wharf, cleaning and repairing of sheds, cleaning and repairing of port roads, painting road signs, zebra crossing, pavement edges, modernizing and cleanliness of all the toilet complexes in the operational area, placement of dustbins at regular intervals, beautification and cleaning of parks, boards indicating cleanliness messages, cleaning and repairing of all drainages and storm water systems and tree plantation.

In order to achieve these objectives, regular training will be provided to the staff in order to generate awareness and inculcate a positive attitude towards keeping the environment clean and green. All the major ports have already initiated action on the above-mentioned activities and are making good progress.

## ❖ Sagarmala Project

The concept of Sagarmala was approved by the Union Cabinet in March 2015. As part of the programme, a National Perspective Plan (NPP) for the comprehensive development of India's coastline and maritime sector has been prepared which was released by the prime minister, on 14 April 2016, at the Maritime India Summit 2016.

## ❖ Vision

Vision of the Sagarmala Programme is to reduce logistics cost for EXIM and domestic trade with minimal infrastructure investment. This includes:

1. Reducing cost of transporting domestic cargo through optimizing modal mix.
2. Lowering logistics cost of bulk commodities by locating future industrial capacities near the coast.
3. Improving export competitiveness by developing port proximate discrete manufacturing clusters.
4. Optimizing time/cost of EXIM container movement.

## ❖ Components of Sagarmala Programme

1. **Port Modernization and New Port Development:** De-bottlenecking and capacity expansion of existing ports and development of new Greenfield ports.
2. **Port Connectivity Enhancement:** Enhancing the connectivity of the ports to the hinterland, optimizing cost and time of cargo movement through multi-modal logistics solutions including domestic waterways (inland water transport and coastal shipping).
3. **Port-linked Industrialization:** Developing port-proximate industrial clusters and Coastal Economic Zones to reduce logistics cost and time of EXIM and domestic cargo.
4. **Coastal Community Development:** Promoting sustainable development of coastal communities through skill development and livelihood generation activities, fisheries development, coastal tourism, etc.

## ENERGY

An effective energy infrastructure is the backbone of every modern economy. Economic development cannot go ahead if there is not sufficient energy to fuel it and no headway can be made with living conditions either. Growing economies like India need to have stable and sustainable sources of energy supply, as it is an important input in the production process. Indirectly, it also affects the health and education system of the country. Affordable energy directly contributes to reducing poverty, increasing productivity and improving quality of life. An efficient energy system provides better opportunities for industries and production processes. A number of energy sources are used in India. In rural India, the main source is biomass. Most electricity supplies are generated by fossil fuels.

Coal is the most important and abundant fossil fuel in India. Coal and lignite together account for about 53.65 per cent of the country's energy need. Considering the limited reserve potentiality of petroleum and natural gas, eco-conservation restriction on hydel project and geo-political perception of nuclear power, coal will continue to occupy centre stage of India's energy scenario. Natural gas is fast emerging as an alternative source of energy. For petroleum, India is mainly dependent on imports. For transportation of oil and petroleum products, cross-country pipeline networks play a key role to meet the country's demand of energy. These pipelines transport crude oil from import terminals as well as domestic sources to inland refineries and finished products from refineries to major consumption centres. The most visible form of energy, which is often identified with progress in modern civilization, is power, commonly called electricity.

### ❖ Power Sector

India's power sector is one of the most diversified in the world. Sources of power generation range from conventional sources such as coal, lignite, natural gas, oil, hydro and nuclear power to viable non-conventional sources such as wind, solar, agricultural and domestic waste.

Power sector in India is undergoing a significant change that has redefined the industry outlook. Sustained economic growth continues to drive electricity demand in India. The Government of India's focus on attaining 'Power for all' has accelerated capacity addition in the country. At the same time, the competitive intensity is increasing at both the market and supply sides (fuel, logistics, finances and manpower). Total installed capacity of power stations in India stood at 330,260.53 Megawatt (MW) as on May 2017.

As the growth of the economy in general and the manufacturing sector in particular is largely dependent on creation of suitable power/energy infrastructure, the policy focus in India has been on infrastructure and energy investment.

### ❖ Ultra Mega Power Projects (UMPP)

Ministry of Power launched a unique initiative in 2005–06 to facilitate the development of Ultra Mega Power Projects (UMPPs) each having a capacity of about 4,000 MW each, at both the coal pitheads and coastal locations aimed at delivering power at competitive cost to consumers by achieving economies of the scale. The central government has accordingly taken the initiative for facilitating the development of UMPPs under tariff based competitive bidding route using super critical technology on build, own and operate (BOO) basis. The Central Electricity Authority (CEA) is the technical partner, and the Power Finance Corporation (PFC) is the Nodal Agency. In order to enhance investors' confidence, reduce risk perception and get good response to competitive bidding, The PFC incorporates Special Purpose Vehicles (SPVs) for each UMPP to undertake the bidding process on behalf of the power procuring (beneficiary) states. The purpose of the SPVs is to carry out the bid process management and obtain various clearances/consents for the projects so that the same are transferred to the successful bidder along with the SPV, who is selected through the tariff-based International Competitive Bidding (ICB) in accordance with the 'Guidelines for determination of tariff by bidding process for procurement of power by distribution licensees', issued by the Ministry of Power, Government of India.

## ❖ Transmission

Development of transmission sector did not get due importance earlier which has led to some imbalances. Investments in the transmission sector have been, therefore, inadequate due to the heavy emphasis on generation capacity. In most states, the existing distribution network has been formed by expanding and interconnecting smaller and disjointed networks. Consequently, there are several deficiencies in the transmission system, such as high losses and low reliability.

## ❖ National Power Grid

Developments in power sector emphasize the need for accelerated implementation of National Power Grid on priority to enable scheduled/unscheduled exchange of power as well as for providing open access to encourage competition in power market. In view of above, nationwide synchronous power grid, interconnecting all the five regional grids of the country, has been established on 31 December 2013.

Power Grid Corporation, a central level undertaking is strengthening its transmission network to establish interstate and inter-regional links for enhancing the capacity of National Grid in a time bound manner to ensure optimal utilization of uneven distribution of energy resources. As on 31 December 2014, National Grid with inter-regional power transfer capacity of about 46,450 MW has been established. The inter-regional power transfer capacity is envisaged to be augmented to about 72,250 MW by the end of the XII Plan (2016–17).

## ❖ Indian Electricity Grid Code

The Indian Electricity Grid Code (IEGC), a regulation made by the Central Commission in exercise of powers conferred under the Electricity Act, 2003, lays down the rules, guidelines and standards to be followed by various persons and participants in the system to plan, develop, maintain and operate the power system, in the most secure, reliable, economic and efficient manner, while facilitating healthy competition in the generation and supply of electricity.

## ❖ National Smart Grid Mission (NSGM)

Government has approved the National Smart Grid Mission (NSGM) in May 2015. The mission is an institutional mechanism for planning, monitoring and implementation of policies and programs related to Smart Grid activities.

The major activities envisaged under NSGM are development of smart grid, development of micro grids, consumer engagements and training and capacity building, etc. NSGM entails implementation of a smart electrical grid based on state-of-the art technology in the fields of automation, communication and IT systems that can monitor and control power flows from points of generation to points of consumption.

NSGM has three-tier structure. At the apex level, NSGM has a Governing Council headed by the Minister of Power. At the second level, the NSGM has an Empowered Committee headed by Secretary (Power). In the third level a supportive role, NSGM has a Technical Committee headed by Chairperson. For day-to-day operations, NSGM has a NSGM Project Management Unit (NPMU) headed by the Director NPMU.

Grant up to 30 per cent of the project cost is available from NSGM budget. For selected components such as training and capacity building, consumer engagement, etc., 100 per cent grant is available.

## ❖ Smart Grid

A smart grid is an electricity network based on digital technology that is used to supply electricity to consumers via two-way digital communication. This system allows for monitoring, analysis, control and communication within the supply chain to help improve efficiency, reduce energy consumption and cost and maximize the transparency and reliability of the energy supply chain. The smart grid was introduced with the aim of overcoming the weaknesses of conventional electrical grids by using smart net meters.

Smart grid technology is an extended form of analogue technology that has also been introduced for controlling the use of appliances by employing two-way communication. However, the prevalence of Internet access in most homes has made the smart grid more practically reliable to implement. Smart grid devices transmit information in such a way that enables ordinary users, operators and automated devices to quickly respond to changes in smart grid condition systems.

Smart grid is equally advantageous for enterprises, retail stores, hospitals, universities and multinational corporations. The entire smart grid system is automated for tracking the electricity consumption at all the locations. Grid architecture is also combined with energy management software for estimating the energy consumption and its associated cost for a specific enterprise. Generally, electricity prices increase along with demand. By providing consumers with information about current consumption and energy prices, smart grid energy management services help to minimize the consumption during high cost, peak-demand times.

A modern smart grid system has the following capabilities:

- It can repair itself.
- It encourages consumer participation in grid operations.
- It ensures a consistent and premium-quality power supply that resists power leakages.
- It allows the electricity markets to grow and make business.
- It can be operated more efficiently.

A smart grid's key features include:

1. **Load Handling:** The sum/total of the power grid load is not stable, and it varies over time. In case of heavy load, a smart grid system can advise consumers to temporarily minimize energy consumption.
2. **Demand Response Support:** Provides users with an automated way to reduce their electricity bills by guiding them to use low-priority electronic devices when rates are lower. Decentralization of Power Generation: A distributed or decentralized grid system allows the individual user to generate onsite power by employing any appropriate method at his or her discretion.

## ❖ Ujwal DISCOM Assurance Yojana (UDAY)

The Union Cabinet on 5 November 2015 gave its approval to a new scheme moved by the Ministry of Power, UDAY. UDAY provides for the financial turnaround and revival of Power Distribution Companies (DISCOMs) and also ensures a sustainable permanent solution to the problem.

UDAY assures the rise of vibrant and efficient DISCOMs through a permanent resolution of past as well as potential future issues of the sector. It empowers DISCOMs with the opportunity to break even in the next 2–3 years. This is through four initiatives: (i) Improving operational efficiencies of DISCOMs; (ii) Reduction of cost of power; (iii) Reduction in interest cost of DISCOMs; and (iv) Enforcing financial discipline on DISCOMs through alignment with State finances.

## ❖ Salient Features of UDAY

- States shall take over 75 per cent of DISCOM debt as on 30 September 2015 over two years
- 50 per cent of DISCOM debt shall be taken over in 2015–16 and 25 per cent in 2016–17.
- Government of India will not include the debt taken over by the States as per the above scheme in the calculation of fiscal deficit of respective States in the financial years 2015–16 and 2016–17.
- States will issue non-SLR including SDL bonds in the market or directly to the respective banks/Financial Institutions (FIs) holding the DISCOM debt to the appropriate extent.
- DISCOM debt not taken over by the State shall be converted by the Banks/FIs into loans or bonds with interest rate not more than the bank's base rate plus 0.1 per cent. Alternately, this debt may be fully or partly issued by the DISCOM as a state guaranteed DISCOM bonds at the prevailing market rates which shall be equal to or less than bank base rate plus 0.1 per cent.
- States shall take over the future losses of DISCOMs in a graded manner.
- State DISCOMs will comply with the renewable purchase obligation (RPO) outstanding since 1 April 2012, within a period to be decided in consultation with Ministry of Power.
- States accepting UDAY and performing as per operational milestones will be given additional/priority funding through Deen Dayal Upadhyaya Gram Jyoti Yojana (DDUGJY), Integrated Power Development Scheme (IPDS), Power Sector Development Fund (PSDF) or other such schemes of the Ministry of Power and the Ministry of New and Renewable Energy (MNRE).
- Such States shall also be supported with additional coal at notified prices and, in case of availability through higher capacity utilization, low cost power from NTPC and other Central Public Sector Undertakings (CPSUs).
- States not meeting operational milestones will be liable to forfeit their claim on IPDS and DDUGJY grants.
- UDAY is optional for all States. However, States are encouraged to take the benefit at the earliest, as benefits are dependent on the performance.

## ❖ Integrated Power Development Scheme (IPDS)

The Scheme was approved in November 2014 by the Government of India.

The objectives of scheme are:

1. Strengthening of sub-transmission and distribution networks in the urban areas;
2. Metering of distribution transformers/feeders/consumers in the urban area.
3. IT enablement of distribution sector and strengthening of distribution network.

## ❖ Deendayal Upadhyaya Gram Jyoti Yojana (DDUGJY)

Scheme approved on 29 November 2014 with a total outlay of ₹ 44,033 crore which includes a budgetary support of ₹ 33,453 crore from Govt. of India.

The objectives of scheme are:

1. Separation of agriculture and non-agriculture feeders;
2. Strengthening of sub-transmission and distribution networks in the rural areas;
3. Metering of distribution transformers/feeders/consumers in the rural area.
4. Rural electrification.

### ❖ Pradhan Mantri Sahaj Bijli Har Ghar Yojana—"Saubhagya"

The Prime Minister in September 2017 launched Pradhan Mantri Sahaj Bijli Har Ghar Yojana –'Saubhagya' scheme to ensure electrification of all willing households in the country in rural as well as urban areas here today.

The total outlay of the project is ₹ 16, 320 crore while the Gross Budgetary Support (GBS) is ₹ 12,320 crore. The Government of India will provide largely funds for the Scheme to all States/UTs.

The states and UTs are required to complete the works of household electrification by the 31 December 2018.

The beneficiaries for free electricity connections would be identified using Socio Economic and Caste Census (SECC) 2011 data. However, un-electrified households not covered under the SECC data would also be provided electricity connections under the scheme on payment of ₹ 500, which shall be recovered by DISCOMs in 10 instalments through electricity bill.

The solar power packs of 200 to 300 WP with battery bank for un-electrified households located in remote and inaccessible areas, comprises of Five LED lights, One DC fan, One DC power plug. It also includes the Repair and Maintenance (R & M) for 5 years.

## SOLAR ENERGY

The Government of India has presently set an installed capacity target of 1,75,000 MW from renewable energy sources by 2022. This includes 1,00,000 MW from solar, 60,000 MW from wind, 10,000 MW from biomass and 5,000 MW from small hydro power. Within the target of 100,000 MW for solar energy, 40,000 MW would be from solar rooftops and the balance 60,000 MW would be from off the ground large- and medium-scale projects involving both the state governments and also other Institutes like CPSUs, Independent Power Producers (IPPs), Solar Energy Corporation of India (SECI), etc.

Solar energy is genesis for all forms of energy. This energy can be made use of in two ways – the Thermal Route, i.e., using heat for drying, heating, cooking or generation of electricity, or through the Photovoltaic Route, which converts solar energy in to electricity, that can be used for a myriad purposes such as lighting, pumping and generation of electricity.

### ❖ Characteristics of Solar Energy

1. Solar energy is available throughout the day, which is the peak load demand time.
2. Solar energy conversion equipments have longer life and need lesser maintenance and hence provide higher energy infrastructure security.
3. Low running costs and grid tie-up capital returns (net-metering).
4. Unlike conventional thermal power generation from coal, they do not cause pollution and generate clean power.
5. Abundance of free solar energy throughout India.

### ❖ Major Solar Power Plants in India

1. Bhadla Solar Park, Rajasthan
2. Kamuthi Solar Power Project, Tamil Nadu
3. Charanka Solar Park, Gujarat
4. Sakri Solar Plant, Maharashtra
5. Welspun Solar MP Project, Madhya Pradesh
6. Dhirubhai Ambani Solar Park, Rajasthan

### ❖ Solar Energy Programmes

India has set a target of 175GW of renewable energy capacity to be reached by 2022. Major programs/schemes to achieve the above target include: Solar Park, Solar Defence Scheme, Solar scheme for CPSUs, Solar Photovoltaic (SPV) power plants on Canal Bank and Canal Tops, Solar Pump, Solar Rooftop, etc.

1. **Solar Park and Ultra Mega Solar Power Projects:** The Scheme for 'Development of Solar Parks and Ultra Mega Solar Power Projects' has been rolled out in December 2014. The Scheme has been conceived on the lines of the Charanka Solar Park in Gujarat which is a first-of-its-kind large-scale solar park in India with contiguous developed land and transmission connectivity.

   This scheme envisages supporting the states in setting up solar parks at various locations in the country with a view to create required infrastructure for setting up of solar power projects. The solar parks will provide suitable developed land with all clearances, transmission system, water access, road connectivity, communication network, etc. This scheme will facilitate and speed up installation of grid connected solar power projects for electricity generation on a large scale.

   **Objectives**

   The scheme aims to provide a huge impetus to solar energy generation by acting as a flagship demonstration facility to encourage project developers and investors, prompting additional projects of similar nature, triggering economies of scale for cost-reductions, technical improvements and achieving large-scale reductions in GHG emissions. It would enable States to bring in significant investment from project developers, meet its Solar Renewable Purchase Obligation (RPO) mandate and provide employment opportunities to local population. The state will also reduce its carbon footprint by avoiding emissions equivalent to the solar park's installed capacity and generation. Further, the state will also avoid procuring expensive fossil fuels to power conventional power plants.

2. **Solar Defence Scheme:** The MNRE will implement a scheme for setting up 300-MW grid-connected and off-grid solar photovoltaic power projects by defence establishments as well as paramilitary forces with VGF support of ₹ 750 crore under the second and third phases of Jawaharlal Nehru National Solar Mission (JNNSM) during the period 2014–15 to 2018–19.

   The objectives of the scheme are to achieve energy security by utilizing the available land and rooftops of the defence sector and paramilitary forces for installation of solar power plants, and at the same time, encourage the use of domestically manufactured equipment to boost indigenous production of solar cells and modules.

3. **Project for Development of Grid-Connected Solar PV Power Plants on Canal Banks and Canal Tops:** The objective of this scheme is to achieve gainful utilization of the unutilized area on top of Canals and also the vacant Governmentlandalongthebanksof Canals wherever available, for setting up Solar PV power generation plants for feeding the generated power to Grid and to set up a total capacity of 100 MW solar PV power projects to achieve targets set under National Solar Mission (NSM) announced by the Government of India.

4. **Solar scheme for CPSUs:** On January 16, 2015 the MNRE launched the scheme that promised to grant ₹ 1 crore per MW as 'VGF' to CPSUs and 'government of India organisations' that would put up solar plants. The Ministry allocated ₹ 1,000 crore for that purpose.

**The 'salient features' of the scheme are:** '1,000 MW of solar PV power projects would be set up by the CPSUs' and Government of India organisations like NTPC, NHPC, CIL, IREDA, Indian Railways, etc.

5. **Solar Rooftop:** A target of 40 GW grid connected solar rooftops to be achieved by 2022 has been set. So far, about 500 MW have been installed and about 3,000 MW has been sanctioned which is under installation. All major sectors, i.e., Railways, Airports, Hospitals, Educational Institutions, Government Buildings of Central/State/PSUs are being targeted besides, the private sector.

   A massive Grid-Connected Solar Rooftop Programme launched with 40 GW target. State Electricity Regulatory Commissions of 30 states/UTs notified regulations for net-metering/feed-in-tariff mechanism. ₹ 5,000 crore approved for solar rooftops. About 500 MW solar rooftop capacities installed till September 2016.

   A total sanction of 1300 million dollars has been received from the World Bank.

6. **Solar Pump:** Saur Sujala Yojana is a new scheme launched by Prime Minister Narendra Modi for farmers. Under the Saur Sujala Yojana, the state government would provide solar powered irrigation pumps to farmers.

   The main objective of the Saur Sujala Yojana is to empower farmers by providing them solar irrigation pumps at subsidized rates. The scheme is also aimed at strengthen the agriculture and rural development.

7. **Green Energy Corridor:** The Government in 2013 announced a National Green Corridor Program (NGCP) to enable the flow of renewable energy into the National Grid Network. Specifically, the green energy corridor is grid-connected network for the transmission of renewable energy produced from various renewable energy projects. The project was envisaged by Power Grid Corporation of India Limited (PGCIL) in its innovative report titled 'Green Energy Corridors'. It was proposed as a dedicated transmission network for renewable energy across different renewable energy potential states.

   **Objectives:** Synchronising electricity produced from renewable sources, such as solar and wind, with conventional power stations in the grid.

   The whole project has been divided into two parts:

   (i) Inter State: To be developed by state utilities

   (ii) Intra-state: To be developed by PGCIL

## ❖ Grid-connected Solar PV Power Projects

The Cabinet Committee on Economic Affairs (CCEA) on 20 January 2016 gave its approval for setting up over 5,000 MW of Grid-Connected Solar PV Power Projects on build, own and operate (BOO) basis.

The work will be implemented by Solar Power Developers (SPDs) with VGF under Batch-IV of Phase-II of the JNNSM. The total investments expected under the scheme is about 30,000 crore rupees.

This would help in creating additional 5000 MW capacity of Grid-connected solar PV power generation projects in four trenches of each 1,250 MW. It will also help in employment generation of about 30,000 people in rural and urban areas with reduction of about 8.525 Million T of $CO_2$ emissions into environment every year.

MNRE will provide 100 percent VGF to SECI to disburse to SPDs immediately after commissioning, subject to availability of funds.

## ❖ International Solar Alliance (ISA)

ISA was established by the Paris Declaration as an alliance dedicated to promotion of solar energy among its member countries. The ISA Framework Agreement entered into force in December 2017 making ISA formally treaty based International Intergovernmental Organization with headquarters at Gurugram, India. As of now, the ISA Framework Agreement has been signed by 48 countries.

Vision of the Alliance is to provide a dedicated platform for cooperation among solar resource rich countries where the global community, including bilateral and multilateral organizations, corporates, industry and other stakeholders, can make a positive contribution to assist and help achieve the common goals of increasing the use of solar energy in meeting energy needs of prospective ISA member countries in a safe, convenient, affordable, equitable and sustainable manner.

Its major objectives include global deployment of over 1,000 GW of solar generation capacity and mobilization of investment of over US$1000 billion into solar energy by 2030. It also aims to bring together countries with rich solar potential to aggregate global demand, thereby reducing through bulk purchase, facilitating deployment of existing solar technologies at scale and promoting collaborative solar R&D and capacity building.

# TELECOM SECTOR

Telecom sector as an important component of the infrastructure eco system. The Indian telecom industry is the second largest in the world by number of subscribers and the third highest number of internet users in the world. The sector has witnessed exponential growth over the last few years primarily driven by affordable tariffs, wider availability, roll out of Mobile Number Portability (MNP), 3G and 4G, evolving consumption patterns of subscribers and a conducive to regulatory environment.

In 1975, the DoT was given separate authority for running the telephone services in the country. The Mahanagar Telephone Nigam Limited (MTNL) initiated its services in the year 1985 for carrying out the telephone operations in the metros of India, viz. Delhi and Mumbai. In October 2000, the Bharat Sanchar Nigam Limited (BSNL) was set up by the DoT. Thereafter several private companies as Reliance Communications, Tata Indicom, Airtel, etc. in the sector came up.

## ❖ Major Players

Lava International Ltd, established in 2009, is one of the fastest growing mobile handset companies in India. Aksh Optifibre Ltd is one of the leading providers of transmission solutions for the telecom industries globally. The company was founded in 1986 with major focus on manufacturing of optical fibre cables. The key players for Telecom Infrastructure providers have come together to form a representative industry body known as Towers and Infrastructure Providers Association (TAIPA). It forms a critical component of the wireless telecom ecosystem. Started in 2005, Matrix Cellular is the leading telecom solution provider for Indian travellers going abroad and needing to use voice telephony and internet connectivity solutions. Nettlinx is an Internet infrastructure initiative of the Nettlinx Group. The company started its ISP/NLD operations in the year 1999 and has been catering to the networking requirements of the domestic enterprise market since then. Tata Teleservices Ltd spearheads the Tata Group's presence in the telecom sector. The Tata Group includes over 100 companies. GTL Infrastructure Ltd (GTL Infra), a Global Group enterprise, is in the business of shared passive telecom infrastructure in India. The company has a portfolio of over 30,000 towers located across India that will help bringing in connectivity at affordable prices to the poorest of poor, creating a positive impact on Indian economy. Bharti Infratel is a provider of tower and related infrastructure and on a consolidated basis; they are one of the largest tower infrastructure providers in India. Reliance Jio Infocomm Ltd (RJIL) is a part of the well-known Reliance Group and is a wholly owned subsidiary of Reliance Industries Ltd (RIL). The company has recently gained fourth-generation (4G) licences for operating across India. It is the first telecom operator to hold pan-India unified license. On Mobile is a leader in the delivery of high-quality mobile services, which are used by many of the best-known mobile operators to provide information, entertainment and personalization services to their customers.

Aircel is one of India's fastest growing GSM mobile service providers with a subscriber base of 65.1 million.

Tata Docomo is Tata Teleservices Ltd's telecom service on the GSM platform, and it has arisen out of the Tata Group's strategic alliance with Japanese telecom major NTT DOCOMO in November 2008. Reliance Communications Limited was founded in FY 2002–03 by late Shri Dhirubhai H Ambani and is the flagship company of the Reliance Anil Dhirubhai Ambani Group. Reliance Communications is India's largest private sector information and communications company, with over 150 million subscribers. Idea Cellular, an Aditya Birla Group company, is a pan-India integrated GSM operator offering 2G and 3G services, has its own National Long Distance (NLD) and International Long Distance (ILD) operations and Internet Service Provider (ISP) license. Vodafone India Ltd, headquartered at Mumbai, is the second largest mobile network operator serving over 150 million customers in India with a presence in all telecom circles. Bharti Airtel Ltd, Headquartered at New Delhi, India, is a leading global telecommunications company with operations in 20 countries across Asia and Africa. The company ranks amongst the top four mobile service providers, globally, in terms of number of subscribers.

## ❖ Digital India Initiative of Government of India

Digital India initiative of the Government of India has transformed the digital profile of India significantly. By February 2017, some of the key indicators of this are:

1. **Phone Users:** From 95 crore phone users in June 2014, India today has 108 crore mobile phone users.
2. **Aadhaar Holders:** From 63 crore Aadhaar holders in 2014, India today has 111 crore Aadhaar holders.
3. **Investments in Electronic Manufacturing:** Investments in electronic manufacturing which was just ₹ 11,000 crore in June 2014, has increased to ₹ 1,27,880.
4. **Mobile Phone Manufacturing Hub:** From 6 crore mobile handsets in 2014–15, India's mobile manufacturing capacity has increased to 11 crore mobile handsets in 2015–16. With 72 new mobile handset and component-manufacturing units set up in last two years, India has emerged as a mobile manufacturing hub.

**Electronic Manufacturing 2015–16**

| Item | Production |
|---|---|
| LCD/LED TVs | : 1.2 crore units |
| Mobile handsets (Nos.) | : 11 crore units |
| Mobile handsets (Value terms) | : ₹ 54,000 crore |
| LED products | : ₹ 3,590 crore |

5. **Common Service Centres:** To provide digital services to common people in villages the Common Services Centres were created. In June 2014, only 83,000 such centres were active across the country, which has now increased to 2.05 lakh centres.

6. **Bharat Net:** Optical Fibre Network to connect villages of India has seen rapid growth. In June 2014, only 358 km of optical fibre was laid. In January 2017, 1.72 lakh km of optical fibre has been laid across more than 76, 000 gram panchayats.
7. **MyGov:** A new platform created for participative governance now has over 40 lakh registered users.
8. **Jeevan Pramaan Portal:** A new initiative to provide convenience to pension holders was created which now has 56 lakh registered pensioners.
9. **DigiLocker:** A new initiative to provide safe online document storage to citizen now has more 42 lakh users. More than 165 crore digital documents have been issued by the government in these lockers.
10. **Scholarship Portal:** Online scholarship was easily made available to the students. 1.4 crore students have registered under this.
11. **Online Hospital Appointment:** Online appointment services in 60 major hospitals have been started. Total 47 lakh appointments have been taken online.
12. **eNAM**: Online National Agriculture Market was created so that farmers can get the best price for their produce. Today, more than 8.5 lakh farmers have registered on this portal.
13. **Growth in Digital Transactions**: eTaal portal, which measures the digital transactions of various e-Governance services, has seen a rapid growth. In 2016, there took place 3 crore transactions per day.
14. **Computerization of Land Records:** Land records have been computerized in 31 states and UTs. Record of Rights (RORs) made online for 22 States/UTs. Bhu-Naksha/ Map digitization done for 15 States/UTs.
15. **Digi Dhan Abhiyaan:** To promote digital payments across the country, Digi Dhan Abhiyaan was launched in December 2016. Under this effort of the Ministry, more than 2 crore people and 7.18 lakh shopkeepers were trained in digital payments across 5,636 blocks of 640 districts.

## ❖ National Telecom Policy-2012 (NTP-2012)

The Government approved NTP-2012, which addresses the vision, strategic direction and the various medium- and long-term issues-related to the telecom sector on 31 May 2012. NTP-2012 is aimed at maximizing public good by making affordable, reliable and secure telecommunication and broadband services available across the country.

### Vision

To provide secure, reliable, affordable and high quality converged telecommunication services anytime, anywhere for an accelerated inclusive socio-economic development.

### Mission

1. To develop a robust and secure state-of-the-art telecommunication network providing seamless coverage with special focus on rural and remote areas for bridging the digital divide and thereby facilitate socio-economic development.
2. To create an inclusive knowledge society through proliferation of affordable and high quality broadband services across the nation.
3. To reposition the mobile device as an instrument of socio-economic empowerment of citizens.
4. To make India a global hub for telecom equipment manufacturing and a centre for converged communication services.

5. To promote Research and Development, Design in cutting edge ICTE technologies, products and services for meeting the infrastructure needs of domestic and global markets with focus on security and green technologies.
6. To promote development of new standards to meet national requirements, generation of IPRs and participation in international standardization bodies to contribute in formation of global standards, thereby making India a leading nation in the area of telecom standardization.
7. To attract investment, both domestic and foreign.
8. To promote creation of jobs through all of the above.

## Objectives

1. Provide secure, affordable and high quality telecommunication services to all citizens.
2. Increase rural teledensity from the current level of around 39 to 70 by the year 2017, and 100 by the year 2020.
3. Provide affordable and reliable broadband-on-demand by the year 2015 and to achieve 175 million broadband connections by the year 2017 and 600 million by the year 2020 at minimum 2 Mbps download speed and making available higher speeds of at least 100 Mbps on demand.
4. Enable citizens to participate in and contribute to e-governance in key sectors like health, education, skill development, employment, governance, banking, etc. to ensure equitable and inclusive growth.
5. Provide high speed and high quality broadband access to all village panchayats through a combination of technologies by the year 2014 and progressively to all villages and habitations by 2020.
6. Promote innovation, indigenous R&D and manufacturing to serve domestic and global markets, by increasing skills and competencies.
7. Create a corpus to promote indigenous R&D, IPR creation, entrepreneurship, manufacturing, commercialisation and deployment of state-of-the-art telecom products and services during the 12th five-year plan period.
8. Promote the ecosystem for design, Research and Development, IPR creation, testing, standardization and manufacturing i.e. complete value chain for domestic production of telecommunication equipment to meet Indian telecom sector demand to the extent of 60 per cent and 80 per cent with a minimum value addition of 45 per cent and 65 per cent by the year 2017 and 2020 respectively.
9. Provide preference to domestically manufactured telecommunication products, in procurement of those telecommunication products that have security implications for the country and in government procurement for its own use, consistent with our World Trade Organization (WTO) commitments.
10. Develop and establish standards to meet national requirements, generate IPRs, and participate in international standardization bodies to contribute in formulation of global standards, thereby making India a leading nation in the area of international telecom standardization. This will be supported by establishing appropriate linkages with industry, R&D institutions, academia, telecom service providers and users.
11. Simplify the licensing framework to further extend converged high quality services across the nation including rural and remote areas. This will not cover content regulation.

12. Strive to create One Nation – One License across services and service areas.
13. Achieve One Nation – Full MNP and work towards One Nation – Free Roaming.
14. Reposition the mobile phone from a mere communication device to an instrument of empowerment that combines communication with proof of identity, fully secure financial and other transaction capability, multi-lingual services and a whole range of other capabilities that ride on them and transcend the literacy barrier.
15. Encourage development of mobile phones based on open platform standards.
16. Deliver high quality seamless voice, data, multimedia and broadcasting services on converged networks for enhanced service delivery to provide superior experience to users.
17. Put in place a simplified Merger and Acquisition regime in telecom service sector while ensuring adequate competition.
18. Optimize delivery of services to consumers irrespective of their devices or locations by Fixed-mobile convergence thus making available valuable spectrum for other wireless services.
19. Promote an ecosystem for participants in Value Added Services (VAS) industry value chain to make India a global hub for VAS.
20. Ensure adequate availability of spectrum and its allocation in a transparent manner through market-related processes. Make available additional 300 MHz spectrum for IMT services by the year 2017 and another 200 MHz by 2020.
21. Promote efficient use of spectrum with provision of regular audit of spectrum usage.
22. De-licensing additional frequency bands for public use.
23. Recognize telecom as Infrastructure Sector to realize true potential of ICT for development.
24. Address the Right-of-Way (RoW) issues in setting up of telecom infrastructure.
25. Mandate an ecosystem to ensure setting up of a common platform for interconnection of various networks for providing non-exclusive and non-discriminatory access.
26. Strengthen the framework to address the environmental and health related concerns pertaining to the telecom sector.
27. Enhanced and continued adoption of green policy in telecom and incentivise use of renewable energy sources for sustainability.
28. Protect consumer interest by promoting informed consent, transparency and accountability in quality of service, tariff, usage, etc.
29. Strengthen the grievance redressal mechanisms to provide timely and effective resolution.
30. Strengthen the institutional framework to enhance the pace of human capital formation and capacity building by assessing and addressing educational and training needs of the sector.
31. Encourage recognition and creation of synergistic alliance of public sector and other organisations of DoT. This should be achieved through appropriate policy interventions and support for optimum utilization of their resources and strengths in building a robust and secure telecom and information infrastructure.

32. Evolve a policy framework for financing the sector consistent with long-term sustainability.
33. Put in place appropriate fiscal and financial incentives required for indigenous manufacturers of telecom products and R&D institutions.
34. Achieve substantial transition to new Internet Protocol (IPv 6) in the country in a phased and time bound manner by 2020 and encourage an ecosystem for provision of a significantly large bouquet of services on IP platform.
35. Strengthen the institutional, legal, and regulatory framework and re-engineer processes to bring in more efficiency, timely decision making and transparency.
36. Put in place a web based, real time e-governance solution to support online submission of applications including processing, issuance of licences and clearances from DoT.

## URBAN INFRASTRUCTURE

India's urban population went up from 25.86 million to 377.11 million during the period 1901 to 2011. Nearly 31 per cent of India's population (Census 2011) lives in urban areas contributing to 63 per cent of India's GDP and with increasing urbanisation, urban areas are expected to house 40 per cent of India's population and contribute to 75 per cent of India's GDP by 2030. India's urban growth is largely concentrated in large cities with a population of 100,000 or more, the number of cities with a population exceeding one million has increased from 35 in 2001 to 53 in 2011, accounting for 43 per cent of India's urban population, and is expected to be 87 per cent by 2030.

The key areas of intervention for the improvement of urban infrastructure are:

1. Improved planning at regional, city and area level
2. Transportation infrastructure for better mobility through public transport, improved walkability and most importantly a policy on parking.
3. **Urban services:** sewerage, drainage and water supply, power distribution.
4. Solid waste management.
5. Housing including affordable housing.
6. Social infrastructure such as parks, playgrounds and leisure spaces.
7. Preservation of heritage precincts

### ❖ Major Infrastructure Bottlenecks in India

There are various bottlenecks that act as impediments for growth of infrastructure. The major ones are summed up below:

**Financing:** Infrastructure projects are highly capital intensive, and funding is considered as a major impediment in achieving the infrastructure goals. The infrastructure broadly can be divided into two types, one which is very essential for the public at large and have no or very little revenue potential and other which has handsome revenue potential. The first kind of infrastructure must be totally government financed, whereas the later can be developed on PPP mode. Since resource constraints will continue to limit public investment in infrastructure, PPP-based development needs to be encouraged wherever feasible.

**Land Acquisition:** Another significant challenge is the way land acquisition is done for infrastructure projects. Compensation fixed in terms of registered value is always the bone of contention. There is always a substantial difference between the compensation offered and the actual value of the land. The land owners always feel aggrieved which results in dispute and litigation.

However, The Land Acquisition and Rehabilitation and Resettlement Bill would be able to tackle this issue of land acquisition favourably.

**Clearances from numerous agencies:** Most of the infrastructure projects in India suffer from delays in completion. This is mainly due to an inadequate regulatory framework and inefficiency in the approval process. Infrastructure projects require multiple sequential clearances at various levels of government. There are various approvals needed at every stage which definitely delay the infrastructure projects.

**Environmental Impact Assessment (EIA):** Environmental safeguards and guidelines have proven to be one of the major reasons for delay in infrastructure projects, especially in the power sector. While new projects need to comply with these regulations, even a project under construction may need to comply with revised standards midway through the execution stage.

**Poor pre-construction planning:** Due to the already adverse effect of various impediments like land acquisition, statutory approvals, delayed financial closure, etc. the pre-construction phase of infrastructure projects is pretty long. Therefore, there is delayed commissioning and completion of projects.

## ❖ Major Urban Infrastructure Development Programmes

1. **Smart Cities Mission:** The Smart Cities Mission is an innovative and new initiative by the Government of India to drive economic growth and improve the quality of life of people by enabling local development and harnessing technology as a means to create smart outcomes for citizens.

The Mission will cover 100 cities and its duration will be five years (FY2015-16 to FY2019-20). The Mission may be continued thereafter in the light of an evaluation to be done by the Ministry of Urban Development (MoUD) and incorporating the learnings into the Mission.

Smart Cities focus on their most pressing needs and on the greatest opportunities to improve lives. They tap a range of approaches - digital and information technologies, urban planning best practices, PPP, and policy change – to make a difference. They always put people first.

In the approach to the Smart Cities Mission, the objective is to promote cities that provide core infrastructure and give a decent quality of life to its citizens, a clean and sustainable environment and application of 'Smart' Solutions. The focus is on sustainable and inclusive development, and the idea is to look at compact areas, create a replicable model which will act like a lighthouse to other aspiring cities. The Smart Cities Mission is meant to set examples that can be replicated both within and outside the Smart City, catalysing the creation of similar Smart Cities in various regions and parts of the country.

- **Objectives of Smart City Mission:** In the approach to the Smart Cities Mission, the objective is to promote cities that provide core infrastructure and give a decent quality of life to its citizens, a clean and sustainable environment and application of 'Smart' Solutions. The focus is on sustainable and inclusive development and the idea is to look at compact areas, create a replicable model, which will act like a lighthouse to other aspiring cities. The Smart Cities Mission of the Government is a bold, new initiative. It is meant to set examples that can be replicated both within and outside the Smart City, catalysing the creation of similar Smart Cities in various regions and parts of the country.

- **Infrastructure Elements in a Smart City:** The core infrastructure elements in a Smart City would include: (i) adequate water supply; (ii) assured electricity supply; (iii) sanitation, including solid waste management; (iv) efficient urban mobility and public transport; (v) affordable housing, especially for the poor; (vi) robust IT connectivity and digitalization; (vii) good governance, especially e-Governance and citizen participation; (viii) sustainable environment; (ix) safety and security of citizens, particularly women, children and the elderly and (x) health and education.

### Smart City

There is no universally accepted definition of a Smart City. It means different things to different people. The conceptualization of Smart City, therefore, varies from city to city and country to country, depending on the level of development, willingness to change and reform, resources and aspirations of the city residents. A Smart City would have a different connotation in India than, say, Europe. Even in India, there is no one way of defining a Smart City.

### Smart City Features

Some typical features of comprehensive development in Smart Cities are described below.

1. Promoting mixed land use in area-based developments — planning for 'unplanned areas' containing a range of compatible activities and land uses close to one another in order to make land use more efficient. The States will enable some flexibility in land use and building bye-laws to adapt to change;
2. Housing and inclusiveness – expand housing opportunities for all;
3. Creating walkable localities – reduce congestion, air pollution and resource depletion, boost local economy, promote interactions and ensure security. The road network is created or refurbished not only for vehicles and public transport, but also for pedestrians and cyclists, and necessary administrative services are offered within walking or cycling distance;
4. Preserving and developing open spaces – parks, playgrounds, and recreational spaces in order to enhance the quality of life of citizens, reduce the urban heat effects in Areas and generally promote eco-balance;
5. Promoting a variety of transport options – Transit Oriented Development (TOD), public transport and last mile para-transport connectivity;
6. Making governance citizen-friendly and cost effective – increasingly rely on online services to bring about accountability and transparency, especially using mobiles to reduce cost of services and providing services without having to go to municipal offices; form e-groups to listen to people and obtain feedback and use online monitoring of programs and activities with the aid of cyber tour of worksites;
7. Giving an identity to the city – based on its main economic activity, such as local cuisine, health, education, arts and craft, culture, sports goods, furniture, hosiery, textile, dairy, etc.;
8. Applying Smart Solutions to infrastructure and services in area-based development in order to make them better. For example, making areas less vulnerable to disasters, using fewer resources and providing cheaper services.

- **Implementation by Special Purpose Vehicle (SPV)**

  The implementation of the Mission at the City level will be done by a SPV created for the purpose. The SPV will plan, appraise, approve, release funds, implement, manage, operate, monitor and evaluate the Smart City development projects. Each Smart City will have a SPV which will be headed by a full time CEO and have nominees of the central government, state government and Urban Local Bodies (ULB) on its Board. The states/ULBs shall ensure that, (a) a dedicated and substantial revenue stream is made available to the SPV so as to make it self-sustainable and could evolve its own credit worthiness for raising additional resources from the market and (b) Government contribution for Smart City is used only to create infrastructure that has public benefit outcomes. The execution of projects may be done through joint ventures, subsidiaries, PPP, turnkey contracts, etc. suitably dovetailed with revenue streams.

  The SPV will be a limited company incorporated under the Companies Act, 2013, at the city level, in which the state/UT and the ULB will be the promoters having 50:50 equity shareholding. The private sector or financial institutions could be considered for taking equity stake in the SPV, provided the shareholding pattern of 50:50 of the State/UT, and the ULB is maintained and the State/UT and the ULB together have majority shareholding and control of the SPV.

  Funds provided by the Government of India in the Smart Cities Mission to the SPV will be in the form of tied grant and kept in a separate Grant Fund. These funds will be utilized only for the purposes for which the grants have been given and subject to the conditions laid down by the MoUD.

- **Financing of Smart Cities**

  The Smart City Mission will be operated as a Centrally Sponsored Scheme (CSS), and the central government proposes to give financial support to the Mission to the extent of ₹ 48,000 crores over five years, i.e., on an average ₹ 100 crore per city per year. An equal amount, on a matching basis, will have to be contributed by the state/ULB; therefore, nearly ₹ 1 lakh crore of Government/ULB funds will be available for Smart Cities development.

- **Mission Monitoring**

  At national level, an Apex Committee (AC), headed by the Secretary, MoUD and comprising representatives of related Ministries and organizations will approve the Proposals for Smart Cities Mission, monitor their progress and release funds. This Committee will meet periodically, as considered necessary.

  **At state level:** there shall be a State level High Powered Steering Committee (HPSC) chaired by the Chief Secretary, which would steer the Mission Programme in its entirety.

  **At city level:** A Smart City Advisory Forum will be established at the city level for all 100 Smart Cities to advise and enable collaboration among various stakeholders and will include the District Collector, MP, MLA, Mayor, CEO of SPV, local youths, technical experts, etc.

2. **Atal Mission for Rejuvenation and Urban Transformation (AMRUT) Project:** The Government of India has launched the AMRUT project with the aim of providing basic civic amenities like water supply, sewerage, urban

transport, parks as to improve the quality of life for all especially the poor and the disadvantaged.

The focus of the Mission is on infrastructure creation that has a direct link to provision of better services to the citizens.

The purpose of 'AMRUT' mission is to (i) ensure that every household has access to a tap with assured supply of water and a sewerage connection, (ii) increase the amenity value of cities by developing greenery and well-maintained open spaces, e.g., parks and (iii) reduce pollution by switching to public transport or constructing facilities for non-motorized transport, e.g., walking and cycling.

The major project components are Water Supply System, Sewerage, Septage, Storm Water Drainage, Urban Transport, Green Space and Parks, Reforms management and support, Capacity building, etc. in that order of priority. The universal coverage of water supply and sewerage services have first charge in the Mission. There is maximum allocation of 2.5 per cent of project cost for development of parks with children and elderly friendly features.

The Mission covers 500 cities that include all cities and towns with a population of over 1 lakh with notified Municipalities.

Total outlay for AMRUT is ₹ 50,000 crore for five years from 2015–16 to 2019–20 and the mission and is being operated as Central Sponsored Scheme.

The project fund is divided among states/UTs in an equitable formula in which 50:50 weightage is being given to the urban population of each state/UT and number of statutory towns.

The Mission is encouraging and supporting the states in conducting reforms that will improve the financial health of the Urban Local Bodies, delivery of citizen services, transparency and cut the cost of services.

3. **Pradhan Mantri Awas Yojana (Urban) or Housing for All by 2022 Mission:** The 'Housing for All by 2022' under the scheme of 'Pradhan Mantri Awas Yojana – Housing for All (Urban)' launched by the central government aims to provide housing to all urban people by 2022.

Components/options to states/UTs and cities are:

(i) Slum rehabilitation of Slum Dwellers with participation of private developers using land as a resource;

(ii) Promotion of affordable housing for weaker section through credit linked subsidy;

(iii) Affordable housing in partnership with Public and Private sectors and

(iv) Subsidy for beneficiary-led individual house construction or enhancement.

Central grant of ₹ 1 lakh per house, on an average, will be available under the slum rehabilitation programme.

The scheme will be implemented as a Centrally Sponsored Scheme except the credit-linked subsidy component, which will be implemented as a Central Sector Scheme.

The scheme will cover the entire urban area consisting of 4,041 statutory towns with initial focus on 500 Class I cities and it will be implemented in three phases.

A Technology Sub-mission under the Mission would be set up to facilitate adoption of modern, innovative and green technologies and building material for faster and quality construction of houses. The Technology Sub-Mission will also facilitate preparation and adoption of layout designs and building plans suitable for various geo-climatic zones. It will also assist states/cities in deploying disaster resistant and environment friendly technologies.

4. **Heritage City Development and Augmentation Yojana (HRIDAY):** The Ministry of Housing and Urban Affairs, Government of India, launched the National HRIDAY scheme on 21 January 2015, with a focus on holistic development of heritage cities. The scheme aims to preserve and revitalize soul of the heritage city to reflect the city's unique character by encouraging aesthetically appealing, accessible, informative and secured environment.

   The Scheme is being implemented in 12 identified cities namely, Ajmer, Amaravati, Amritsar, Badami, Dwarka, Gaya, Kanchipuram, Mathura, Puri, Varanasi, Velankanni and Warangal. The Scheme is implemented in a mission mode.

   The Scheme supports development of core heritage infrastructure projects that include revitalization of urban infrastructure for areas around heritage assets identified/approved by the Ministry of Culture, Government of India and state governments. These initiatives include development of water supply, sanitation, drainage, waste management, approach roads, footpaths, streetlights, tourist conveniences, electricity wiring, landscaping and such citizen services.

5. **Jawaharlal Nehru National Urban Renewal Mission (JNNURM):** JNNURM was launched on 3 December 2005 and closed in 2014. This Scheme is now succeeded by Atal AMRUT Mission. The JNNURM was a flagship scheme for urban development. The programme had two components, viz., Basic Services for Urban poor (BSUP) and Integrated Housing and Slum Development Programme (IHSDP). Civic amenities were improved under the programme including urban transportation. The programme aimed at integrated development of slums through projects for providing shelter, basic services and other related civic amenities.

6. **Urban transportation:** The transportation system in India is being equipped with Intelligent Transport System (ITS) and Metro Rail Projects. Delhi, Mumbai, Kolkatta, Chennai, Bengaluru, Hyderabad and Kochi have metro rail system.

## ❖ Terms

**Logistics Performance Index:** The Logistics Performance Index (LPI) released by the World Bank is an interactive benchmarking tool created to help countries identify the challenges and opportunities they face in their performance on trade logistics and what they can do to improve their performance. The LPI allows for comparisons across 160 countries.

The LPI is based on a worldwide survey of operators on the ground (global freight forwarders and express carriers), providing feedback on the logistics 'friendliness' of the countries in which they operate and those with which they trade. They combine in-depth knowledge of the countries in which they operate with informed qualitative assessments of other countries where they trade and experience of global logistics environment.

Feedback from operators is supplemented with quantitative data on the performance of key components of the logistics chain in the country of work.

The LPI consists therefore of both qualitative and quantitative measures and helps build profiles of logistics friendliness for these countries. It measures performance along the logistics supply chain within a country and offers two different perspectives: international and domestic. On LPI India in 2018 ranked 44 amongst 160 countries compared.

**India Infrastructure Finance Company Limited (IIFCL):** IIFCL was incorporated by the Ministry of Finance in consultation with the Planning Commission for providing long-term loans for financing infrastructure projects that typically involve long gestation periods. IIFCL provides financial assistance up to 20 per cent of the project cost both through direct lending to project companies and by refinancing banks and financial institutions. IIFCL raises funds from both domestic and overseas markets on the strength of government guarantees, which are extended, if considered necessary.

## NATIONAL INFRASTRUCTURE PIPELINE FOR 2019-2025

To achieve the GDP of $5 trillion by 2024-25, India needs to spend about $1.4 trillion (Rs. 100 lakh crore) over these years on infrastructure. In the past decade (FY 2008-17), India invested about $1.1 trillion on infrastructure. The challenge is to step-up annual infrastructure investment so that lack of infrastructure does not become a binding constraint on the growth of the Indian economy. The Union Finance Minister Smt. Nirmala Sitharaman made a brief statement on the contents of the National Infrastructure Pipeline at a Press Conference here today. She indicated that Government will examine the recommendations of the Task Force and take action early.

Hon'ble Prime Minister in his Independence Day-2019 speech highlighted that Rs.100 lakh crore would be invested on infrastructure over the next five years including social and economic infrastructure projects.

To achieve this objective, a Task Force was constituted to draw up the National Infrastructure Pipeline (NIP) for each of the years from FY 2019-20 to FY 2024-25 with the approval of the Finance Minister. The Task Force is chaired by Secretary, DEA with CEO (NITI Aayog), Secretary (Expenditure), Secretary of the Administrative Ministries, and Additional Secretary (Investments), DEA as members and Joint Secretary (IPF), DEA as Member Secretary.

The first meeting of the Task Force was held in September 2019. Subsequently, several meetings were held with various Departments/ Ministries engaged in infrastructure development, Corporates engaged in infrastructure development & construction, Banks/Financial Institutions, Private Equity funds, and Industry Associations, including CII, FICCI & ASSOCHAM, to seek information as well as suggestions on reforms required in infrastructure sectors.

This exercise, the first of its kind, is expected to be followed up by a periodical review process. NIP will enable a forward outlook on infrastructure projects which will create jobs, improve ease of living, and provide equitable access to infrastructure for all, thereby making growth more inclusive. NIP includes economic and social infrastructure projects.

On the basis of the information compiled as on date, total project capital expenditure in infrastructure sectors in India during the fiscals 2020 to 2025 is projected at over Rs 102 lakh crore.

During the fiscals 2020 to 2025, sectors such as Energy (24%), Roads (19%), Urban (16%), and Railways (13%) amount to around 70% of the projected capital expenditure in infrastructure in India. The detailed sector wise break of the pipeline is as follows:

| Ministry/ Department | FY 20-25 |
|---|---|
| **Energy** | |
| *Power* | *1175995* |
| *Renewable Energy* | *929500* |
| *Atomic Energy* | *154088* |
| *Petroleum and Natural Gas* | *194666* |
| **Total Energy** | **2,454,249** |

| Roads | |
|---|---|
| *Roads* | *1,963,943* |
| **Total Roads** | **1,963,943** |
| **Railways** | |
| *Railways* | *1,368,523* |
| **Total Railways** | **1,368,523** |
| **Ports** | |
| *Ports* | *100,923* |
| **Total Ports** | **100,923** |
| **Airports** | |
| *Airports* | *143,398* |
| **Total Airports** | **143,398** |
| **Urban** | |
| *AMRUT, SMART Cities, MRTS, Affordable Housing, Jal Jeevan Mission* | *1,629,012* |
| **Total Urban** | **1,629,012** |
| **Telecommunication** | |
| *Telecommunication* | *320,498* |
| **Total Telecommunications** | **320,498** |
| **Irrigation** | |
| *Irrigation* | *772,678* |
| **Total Irrigation** | **772,678** |
| **Rural Infrastructure** | |
| *Rural Infrastructure* | *410,955* |
| *Water and Sanitation* | *361,810* |
| **Total Rural Infrastructure** | **772,765** |
| **Agriculture and Food Processing Infrastructure** | |
| *Agriculture Infrastructure* | *54,298* |
| *Food Processing Industries* | *1,255* |
| *Food and Public Distribution* | *5,000* |
| **Total Agriculture and Food Processing Infrastructure** | **60,553** |
| **Social Infrastructure** | |
| *Higher Education* | *118,348* |
| *School Education* | *37,791* |
| *Health and Family Welfare* | *168,622* |
| *Sports* | *7,618* |
| *Tourism* | *24,321* |
| **Total Social Infrastructure** | **356,701** |
| **Industrial Infrastructure** | |
| *Industries and Internal Trade* | *299,237* |
| *Steel* | *8,225* |
| **Total Industrial Infrastructure** | **307,462** |
| **TOTAL (Rs. Crore)** | **10,250,704** |

Out of the total expected capital expenditure of Rs. 102 lakh crore, projects worth Rs 42.7 lakh crore (42%) are under implementation, projects worth Rs 32.7 lakh crore (32%) are in conceptualization stage and rest are under development. It is expected that projects of certain states, who are yet to communicate their pipelines, would be added to the pipeline in due course.

## ❖ NITI Aayog's "Strategy for New India @75"

NITI Aayog recently released the document "Strategy for New India@75" to define clear objectives for 2022-23 in a diverse range of 41 different areas. This aspirational strategy aims to achieve a 'New India' by 2022 when the country celebrates its 75th year of Independence.

### Strategy for "New India@75"

- The document has identified 41 different areas that require either a sharper focus on implementing the flagship schemes already in place or a new design and initiative to achieve India's true potential.
- Each chapter summarizes the current status of the sector, takes full cognizance of the progress made.
- It then identifies the binding constraints and proposes measures to address these constraints.

- The approach is believed to provide an inventory of readily implementable measures for the government departments and agencies both in the central and state.
- The focus is to improve the policy environment so that the contribution of private investors and other stakeholders can be maximized to achieve the goals set out for New India.

## Other details

- In the chapter focusing on ecological and related livelihood concerns, there are positive directions vis-à-vis the environment, such as a major focus on renewable energy, organic farming (with the zero budget natural farming model developed by Maharashtrian farmer Subhash Palekar being singled out for national application), increasing forest cover, and reducing pollution.
- It has a chapter titled 'Sustainable environment' states: "The objective is to maintain a clean, green and healthy environment with peoples' participation to support higher and inclusive economic growth through sustainable utilization of available natural "
- Its focus is primarily on air pollution, solid waste management, water pollution.
- The strategy has many progressive It follows the UN Sustainable Development Goals of Inclusion, sustainability, participation, gender equality, etc.

## Issue

- There are serious doubts if the strategy envisaged in the document relating to ecological and livelihood concerns will be any different from the crisis-ridden society we live in
- The government have been promising for more than three decades that with environmental safeguards, growth can be made
- There seems no indication that this is anywhere near achievable. The Confederation of Indian Industry has already indicated in 2008 that India was already using twice what its natural resources could sustain and that more than half its biocapacity had already been eroded. Things are likely to become worse.
- No political party in power has done anything to suddenly make growth.
- India faces a large number of environmental concerns but air pollution, solid waste management, water pollution, and forestry are only given much attention.
- Some other issues such as arresting land degradation and soil erosion and water conservation are also mentioned
- But issues that need urgent attention such as the increasing presence of toxic chemicals around us, the need to conserve a range of non-forest ecosystems.
- There is a forest department but no dedicated entity for grassland, marine and coastal, wetland, mountain, and desert.
- There is an absence of an integrated, comprehensive view on how ecological issues can be integrated into all sectors indicating that these issues are still not a priority for the planners.

## Alarming Features

Examples of the internal contradictions in the document. Mining:

- Mining is one of the biggest ecological and social disasters in India, especially the large-scale open-cast
- To "limit environmental damage" the only concession it makes is the suggestion to bring in "cutting-edge" technology, which will most likely not solve the fundamental need to deforest areas.

## Tourism

- It is one such sector which will have a large scale impact on the environment, as witnessed by the hill stations and the ruin that areas like Ladakh, Kutch, and the island regions.
- Despite this, NITI Aayog recommended doubling the number of domestic tourist visits to over 3,200 million from 1,614 million.

## River Valley Projects

- It also urges completion of mega river valley projects that have ecological nightmares, including Pancheshwar in the fragile Himalaya, the Ken-Betwa link in Madhya Pradesh, and dozens in the Northeast which will choke up rivers.

## Agriculture

- For all the mention of organic farming, there is no clear direction to phase out chemical fertilizers.
- The document says "Phase out old varieties of seeds and replace them with hybrid and improved seeds". This is the kind of Green Revolution approach that has caused huge loss of agricultural biodiversity and resilience.
- No focus is given to dryland farming though most farmers are engaged in.
- It says organic farming models should be replicated but it is silent on the amazing work of dryland farmers (such as the Dalit women of the Deccan Development Society in Telangana) showing productive, sustainable, biodiverse agriculture with millets and women as the fulcrum.

## Infrastructure Projects

- The most alarming feature of the document is its stress on rapid, single-window clearance of infrastructure and other.
- It suggests 180 days limit for assessment of a project which is too less as any decent ecological assessment of a project needs a year of study (overall seasons).
- This means compromising on crucial processes of social assessment, public hearings, and participatory decision-making, as already seen in the last few
- Nothing is there on the need to seek consent from local communities, which is mandated under the Forest Rights Act, 2006, and the Panchayat (Extension to Scheduled Areas) Act, 1996.
- The track record of government in safeguarding the environment and the livelihoods of Adivasis and other communities as they have found ways to bypass constitutional and policy safeguards these vulnerable sections.

❑❑❑

# 9 CHAPTER External Sector

The external sector means the international transactions that both the private and public sector of an economy conduct with the other economies of the world. These transactions are systematically rwithin a framework that groups them into accounts, where each account represents a separate economic process or phenomenon of the external sector.

## BALANCE OF PAYMENTS (BOP)

The BoP records the transactions in goods, services and assets between residents of a country with the rest of the world for a specified time period typically a year. The Reserve Bank of India (RBI) is responsible for compilation and dissemination of BoP data under the guidelines of the International Monetary Fund (IMF).

**BOP: Summary of Entry**

1. **Current Account**
    - (i) Exports
    - (ii) Imports
    - (iii) Trade Balance
    - (iv) Invisibles (net)
        - (a) Services
        - (b) Transfers
        - (c) Income
    - (v) Current Account Balance
2. **Capital Account**
    - (i) External Assistance
    - (ii) ECBs
    - (iii) Short-term Debt
    - (iv) Banking capital of which: Non-Resident Deposits
    - (v) Foreign Investment
        - (a) FDI
        - (b) Portfolio Investment
    - (vi) Other Flows
    - (vii) Capital Account Balance
3. **Errors and Omissions:** Capital Account Balance (including errors and omissions)
4. **Overall Balance**
5. **Reserves Change**

    (–) indicates increase,

    (+) indicates decrease

The BoP comprises of current account, capital account, errors and omissions and changes in foreign exchange reserves. Under current account of the BoP, transactions are classified into merchandise (exports and imports) and invisibles.

Invisible transactions are further classified into three categories, namely:

(a) Services-travel, transportation, insurance, government not included elsewhere (GNIE) and miscellaneous (such as communication, construction, financial, software, news agency, royalties, management and business services);
(b) Income and
(c) Transfers (grants, gifts, remittances, etc.) which do not have any quid pro quo.

There are two main accounts in the BoP – the current account and the capital account.

### ❖ Current Account

The current account records exports and imports in goods and services and transfer payments. The third item gives the trade balance which is obtained by subtracting imports of goods from the exports of goods. When exports exceed imports, there is a trade surplus and when imports exceed exports, there is a trade deficit.

The data on merchandise trade are available from two sources namely; (a) from the Directorate General of Commercial Intelligence and Statistics (DGCI&S) on customs basis and (b) from RBI on payments (which includes both receipts and payments) basis.

Trade in services denoted as invisible trade (because they are not seen to cross national borders) includes both factor income (net income from compensation of employees and net investment income, the latter equals, the interest, profits and dividends on our assets abroad minus the income foreigners earn on assets they own in India) and net non-factor income (shipping, banking, insurance, tourism, software services, etc.).

Transfer payments are receipts that the residents of a country receive 'for free', without having to make any present or future payments in return. They consist of remittances, gifts and grants. They could be official or private. The balance of exports and imports of goods is referred to as the trade balance. Adding trade in services and net transfers to the trade balance, we get the current account balance. If this figure had been a positive number, there would have been a current account surplus.

### ❖ Capital Account

The capital account records all international purchases and sales of assets such as money, stocks, bonds, etc. We note that any transaction resulting in a payment to foreigners is entered as a debit and is given a negative sign. Any transaction resulting in a receipt from foreigners is entered as a credit and is given a positive sign.

Under the capital account, capital inflows can be classified by instrument (debt or equity) and maturity (short or long term). The main components of the capital account include foreign investment, loans and banking capital. Foreign investment, comprising foreign direct investment (FDI) and portfolio investment consisting of Foreign Institutional Investors (FIIs) investment, American Depository Receipts/Global Depository Receipts (ADRs/GDRs) represents non-debt liabilities, while loans (external assistance, external commercial borrowings and trade credit) and banking capital, including non-resident Indian (NRI) deposits are debt liabilities.

## BOP SURPLUS AND DEFICIT

The essence of international payments is that just like an individual who spends more than her income must finance the difference by selling assets or by borrowing, a country that has a deficit in its current account (spending more abroad than it receives from sales to the rest of the world) must finance it by selling assets or by borrowing abroad. Thus, any current account deficit is of necessity financed by a net capital inflow. Alternatively, the country could engage in official reserve transactions, running down its reserves of foreign exchange, in the case of a deficit by selling foreign currency in the foreign exchange market. The decrease (increase) in official reserves is called the overall BoP deficit (surplus). The basic premise is that the monetary authorities are the ultimate financiers of any deficit in the BoP (or the recipients of any surplus). The BoP deficit or surplus is obtained after adding the current and capital account balances.

A country is said to be in BoP equilibrium when the sum of its current account and its non-reserve capital account equals zero, so that the current account balance is financed entirely by international lending without reserve movements. We note that the official reserve transactions are more relevant under a regime of pegged exchange rates than when exchange rates are floating.

### ❖ Autonomous and Accommodating Transactions

International economic transactions are called autonomous when transactions are made independently of the state of the BoP (for instance due to profit motive). These items are called 'above the line' items in the BoP. The BoP is said to be in surplus (deficit) if autonomous receipts are greater (less) than autonomous payments. Accommodating transactions (termed 'below the line' items), on the other hand, are determined by the net consequences of the autonomous items, that is, whether the BoP is in surplus or deficit. The official reserve transactions are seen as the accommodating item in the BoP (all others being autonomous).

## ERRORS AND OMISSIONS

Errors and Omissions constitute the third element in the BoP (apart from the current and capital accounts) which is the 'balancing item' reflecting our inability to record all international transactions accurately.

## TRANSFERS OF PAYMENTS

It (official, private) represents receipts and payments without a *quid pro quo*.

## INVISIBLES

'Invisibles' is a convenient catchall term that includes transactions in services, transfers and income.

Services are the most familiar of these categories, including as they do the dominant items of software, management services, financial services, etc.

Transfers represent one-sided transactions, involving no *quid pro quo*, such as remittances by our compatriots abroad.

Another category known as 'income' is defined to include both payments and receipts – payments on account of non-residents employed in India, interest payments made to those who have deposited FCNR deposits and interest charges on loans made to India, besides dividends and profit share to investors in India. FCNR deposits stands for Foreign Currency Non-repatriable account deposits. This is a fixed deposit foreign currency account and not a savings account.

## CURRENT ACCOUNT DEFICIT (CAD)

Current account deficit is a measurement of a country's trade where the value of the goods and services it imports exceeds the value of the goods and services it exports. The current account also includes net income, such as interest and dividends, as well as transfers, such as foreign aid, though these components make up only a small percentage of the current account when compared to exports and imports. The current account is essentially a calculation of a country's foreign transactions and, along with the capital account, is a component of a country's balance of payment.

## ❖ Policies to Reduce CAD

1. **Devaluation:** This involves reducing the value of the currency against others (e.g., selling pounds would cause the value of the Pound to fall). If there is a devaluation in the currency, the price of importing goods increases, and therefore, the quantity demanded of imports falls. Exports will be become cheaper and there will be an increase in the quantity of exports.
2. **Deflationary policies:** These policies aim at reducing the growth of aggregate demand and reducing inflation. They can include a tightening of fiscal policy or monetary policy, this will reduce aggregate demand.
   (i) **Monetary policy:** Tight monetary policy involves increasing interest rates. Higher interest rates will increase the cost of debt and mortgage repayments and leave people with less money to spend. Therefore, this will reduce their consumption of imports, improving the current account.

   Also, higher interest rates will cause a fall in AD and, therefore, reduce economic growth. This will reduce inflation and help to make UK exports more competitive.

   Deflationary policies will also put pressure on manufacturers to reduce costs and this will lead to more competitive exports and so exports may increase in the long run because of this effect.

   (ii) **Deflationary fiscal policy:** An alternative to using monetary policy is to use fiscal policy. For example, the government could increase income tax. This would reduce consumer discretionary income and reduce spending on imports.

   The advantage of fiscal policy is that it would not have an adverse effect on the exchange rate. Higher income tax would also improve government finances.

   However, this policy will conflict with other macroeconomic objectives – with lower aggregate demand (AD), growth is likely to fall causing higher unemployment. A government is unlikely to want to risk higher unemployment just to reduce a current account deficit.
3. **Supply side policies:** Supply side policies can improve the competitiveness of the economy and help make exports more attractive. This can improve the current account position, but it may take considerable time to have effect.

   For example, if the government pursued a policy of privatization and deregulation it may help to increase the efficiency of the economy because of the profit motive in the private sector. This increased efficiency would translate into lower costs of production and more exports.
4. **Lower wages:** A policy used by many Eurozone economies facing a large current account deficit (but unable to devalue within single currency) is to reduce wages. Lower wages will reduce costs of production and improve competitiveness.

   However, lower wages will also lead to lower aggregate demand and could lead to deflation and low growth. If the government cut public sector wages, it may have limited impact on improving competitiveness of exports. Reducing wages is also known as internal devaluation.

5. **Protectionism:** The government could increase tariffs on imports or even impose quotas. Both these measures would have the impact of reducing imports and, therefore, improve the current account.

   However, protectionism may lead to retaliation – with other countries placing tariffs on our exports – so exports could decrease. Protected by tariffs – domestic industries may become uncompetitive, because there is less incentive to cut costs.

Policies to reduce a current account could also be classified into two types:

1. **Expenditure switching policies:** This involves changing the goods that people buy. For example, devaluation makes domestic goods relatively cheaper and foreign imports more expensive. Therefore, consumers will switch from buying foreign imports to domestic goods. Supply side policies make British goods relatively more attractive.
2. **Expenditure reducing policies:** Policies to reduce overall spending on imports. This can involve tight fiscal or tight monetary policy.

### ❖ Measures Taken

The measures taken to reduce the CAD include:

1. Compression in import of gold and silver
2. Compression in demand for oil
3. Compression in certain imports (non-essential nature)

We will also take measures to enhance the capital inflows into India and these will include:

1. Public sector financial institutions to raise *quasi*-sovereign bonds to finance long-term infrastructure
2. Liberalizing ECB guidelines
3. PSU oil companies to raise additional funds through ECBs and trade finance
4. Liberalizing NRE/FCNR deposit schemes

## WHY FOREIGN EXCHANGE (FOREX) IS HORDED?

Although almost all countries hold foreign exchange reserves, their reasons for doing so differ widely. Before setting a strategic policy for the reserves, the authorities need to establish precisely why they are holding the reserves that they have. Only then can a sensible debate be held on such issues as the optimum size of the reserves, their funding and their investment.

The followings are some of the main reasons for holding reserves:

1. **Formal Backing for The Domestic Currency:** Reserves are sometimes held as formal backing for the domestic currency. This is a very traditional use of reserves, especially gold reserves. This use of reserves was at its height under the gold standard, and survived after the Second World War under the Bretton Woods system. After the breakdown of the Bretton Woods system, it became less common, though the use of gold especially to back a currency has never completely disappeared, and the idea of using foreign exchange reserves (rather than gold specifically) to back and provide confidence in a domestic currency has recently been revived with the rediscovery of currency boards. Nevertheless, for most countries this is not, these days, the prime use of the reserves.

2. **Tool of Exchange Rate or Monetary Policy:** More common is the use of reserves as a tool of exchange rate or monetary policy. This is most obviously the case for those countries who are pursuing a fixed exchange rate policy, and who wish to be able to influence the market in their domestic currency so as to maintain a fixed rate. In addition, countries may choose to use the FX

markets to affect domestic monetary policy, by supplying domestic currency to the market or buying it in the market against foreign currencies. This will affect the domestic money market balance and so domestic interest rates, and is a useful tool for those countries whose domestic markets are not yet fully developed. But even countries whose domestic markets are fully adequate for the exercise of monetary policy and whose currency is floating may wish to intervene to 'manage the float' to affect the rate at which their currency trades. Only a very few countries have decided not to intervene on the exchange markets at all (a 'free float' of their currency) – and even for these countries, holding reserves preserves the option to intervene or move to a more managed float later if circumstances or policy change.

3. **Funds for Servicing Foreign Currency Liabilities and Debt Obligations:** A third use of reserves is to provide funds for servicing foreign currency liabilities and debt obligations. Clearly, foreign currency is needed at the point in time when debt servicing payments fall due to avoid a default. While it would be possible to meet this need for foreign currency by buying it in the market (i.e., by selling domestic currency) as and when the need arises, this is not a course that many countries pursue, for several reasons:
   (i) the foreign exchange market (FX) markets might be unfavourable at the time that foreign currency is needed;
   (ii) the transactions might be disruptive to the markets;
   (iii) the strategy entails large open currency risks on the liability portfolio;
   (iv) this approach reduces credit rating agencies' confidence in the country as an issuer, and as a result both reduces the attractiveness of the country to lenders and increases the cost of foreign currency borrowing.

   Instead, therefore, most countries that have borrowed in foreign currency will aim to use some of their reserves to provide a fund for servicing at least the part of their debt which is falling due in the near future.

4. **Source of Funds to Pay for Government Expenditure Overseas:** Reserves can also be held as a source of funds to pay for government expenditure overseas. For many countries, especially those with known import bills for the authorities to meet, it can be sensible to plan their financing using the reserves. This is particularly the case when either foreign exchange receipts or outflows are 'bumpy' or show a marked seasonal pattern. In these cases, the reserves can be used to smooth out the payment schedules.

5. **Defence against Emergencies or Disaster:** Reserves can provide a defence against emergencies or disaster, by acting as a fund to finance recovery and rebuilding. This is most likely to be appropriate for small countries that are not large enough to provide self-insurance; larger countries are more likely to fund recovery from a crisis in one part of their domestic economy from elsewhere in the economy. But a small country may possibly be completely overwhelmed by a disaster; for example, a natural disaster that wipes out the only export, or a collapse in their terms of trade, or even military disaster. For such events, reserves can provide a diversification of assets, a pool of readily usable funds and security and comfort for potential lenders.

6. **Investment Fund:** Finally, reserves may be held as an investment fund, primarily for financial gain. This will not be a sensible reason for holding reserves for the majority of countries; few countries will find that the monetary income on their reserves represents the best use of those assets in the wider context of their whole economy. But for some countries, an investment fund can be a logical policy, for example:
   (i) in cases where the local economy cannot absorb more spending without overheating;
   (ii) where windfall profits would otherwise disrupt the domestic economy;
   (iii) to prepare for a less certain future (perhaps as a natural resource runs out);
   (iv) to diversify a small country's asset base. For any country, the reason it holds reserves will play a very important part in planning how those reserves should be managed and in what way they should be invested.

## FOREIGN TRADE POLICY (FTP) FOR 2015-2020

The Foreign Trade Policy (FTP), the basic framework of policy and strategy for promoting trade from India has conventionally been formulated for five years at the time, and reviewed periodically. The FTP for 2015–20, announced in April 2015, provided a framework for increasing exports of goods and services as well as generation of employment and increasing value addition in the country in keeping with the "Make in India" vision of the country.

The FTP lays down a roadmap for India's global trade engagement in the coming years. It seeks to enable India to respond to the challenges of external environment, keeping in step with rapidly evolving international trading architecture and most importantly make trade a major contributor to the country's economic growth and development. It is aligned with the broader priorities of the central government such as implementation of Goods and Services Tax. Digital India, Skill India, Startup India, Ease of Doing Business and Trade Facilitation Initiatives. Due to the pandemic the FTP was extended upto September 30, 2021.

### ❖ Goals and Objectives

A vision is best achieved through measurable targets. The government aims to increase India's exports of merchandise and services from USD 465.9 billion in 2013–14 to approximately USD 900 billion by 2019–20 and to raise India's share in world exports from 2 per cent to 3.5 per cent.

The FTP for 2015–20 seeks to achieve the following objectives:

1. To provide a stable and sustainable policy environment for foreign trade in merchandise and services;
2. To link rules, procedures and incentives for exports and imports with other initiatives such as 'Make in India', 'Digital India' and 'Skills India' to create an 'Export Promotion Mission' for India;
3. To promote the diversification of India's export basket by helping various sectors of the Indian economy to gain global competitiveness with a view to promoting exports;
4. To create an architecture for India's global trade engagement with a view to expanding its markets and better integrating with major regions, thereby increasing the demand for India's products and contributing to the government's flagship 'Make in India' initiative and

5. To provide a mechanism for regular appraisal in order to rationalize imports and reduce the trade imbalance.

## HIGHLIGHTS OF THE POLICY

### ❖ Simplification and Merger of Reward Schemes

**Export from India Schemes:**

1. **MEIS**
   (a) Earlier there were five different schemes (Focus Product Scheme, Market Linked Focus Product Scheme, Focus Market Scheme, Agri Infrastructure Incentive Scrip, VKGUY) for rewarding merchandise exports with different kinds of duty scrips with varying conditions (sector specific or actual user only) attached to their use. Now all these schemes have been merged into a single scheme, namely Merchandise Export from India Scheme (MEIS), and there would be no conditionality attached to the scrips issued under the scheme.
   (b) Rewards for export of notified goods to notified markets under 'Merchandise Exports from India Scheme (MEIS)' shall be payable as percentage of realized FOB value (in free foreign exchange). The debits towards basic customs duty in the transferable reward duty credit scrips would also be allowed adjustment as duty drawback. At present, only the additional duty of customs/excise duty/service tax is allowed adjustment as CENVAT credit or drawback, as per Department of Revenue rules.

**Nature of Rewards**

The Duty Credit Scrips shall be granted as rewards under MEIS. The Duty Credit Scrips and goods imported/domestically procured against them shall be freely transferable. The Duty Credit Scrips can be used for the following requirements:

(i) Payment of Customs Duties for import of inputs or goods, except items listed in Appendix 3A.
(ii) Payment of excise duties on domestic procurement of inputs or goods, including capital goods as per DoR notification.
(iii) Payment of service tax on procurement of services as per DoR notification.
(iv) Payment of Customs Duty and fee as per paragraph 3.18 of this Policy.

Objective of MEIS as per Indian FTP 2015–20 is to offset infrastructural inefficiencies and associated costs involved in export of goods/products, which are produced/manufactured in India, especially those having high export intensity, employment potential and thereby enhancing India's export competitiveness.

2. **Service Exports from India Scheme (SEIS)**
   (i) Served From India Scheme (SFIS) has been replaced with Service Exports from India Scheme (SEIS). SEIS shall apply to 'Service Providers located in India' instead of 'Indian Service Providers'. Thus, SEIS provides for rewards to all Service providers of notified services, who are providing services from India, regardless of the constitution or profile of the service provider.
   (ii) The rate of reward under SEIS would be based on net foreign exchange earned. The reward issued as duty credit scrip, would no longer be with actual user condition and will no longer be restricted to usage for specified

types of goods but be freely transferable and usable for all types of goods and service tax 3 debits on procurement of services/ goods. Debits would be eligible for CENVAT credit or drawback.

3. **Incentives** (MEIS and SEIS) to be available for SEZs. It is now proposed to extend incentives (MEIS and SEIS) to units located in SEZs also.
4. **Duty credit scrips** to be freely transferable and usable for payment of custom duty, excise duty and service tax.
   (i) All scrips issued under MEIS and SEIS and the goods imported against these scrips would be fully transferable.
   (ii) Scrips issued under Exports from India Schemes can be used for the following:
      (a) Payment of customs duty for import of inputs/ goods including capital goods, except items listed in Appendix 3A.
      (b) Payment of excise duty on domestic procurement of inputs or goods, including capital goods as per DoR notification.
      (c) Payment of service tax on procurement of services as per DoR notification.
   (iii) Basic Customs Duty paid in cash or through debit under Duty Credit Scrip can be taken back as Duty Drawback as per DoR Rules, if inputs so imported are used for exports.
5. **Status Holders**
   (i) Business leaders who have excelled in international trade and have successfully contributed to country's foreign trade are proposed to be recognized as Status Holders and given special treatment and privileges to facilitate their trade transactions, in order to reduce their transaction costs and time.
   (ii) The nomenclature of Export House, Star Export House, Trading House, Star Trading House, Premier Trading House certificate has been changed to One, Two, Three, Four, Five Star Export House.
   (iii) The criteria for export performance for recognition of status holder have been changed from Rupees to US-dollar earnings.

   The new criteria are as under:

| Status category | Export Performance FOB/FOR (as converted) Value (in US$ million) during current and previous 2 years |
|---|---|
| One Star Export House | 3 |
| Two Star Export House | 25 |
| Three Star Export House | 100 |
| Four Star Export House | 500 |
| Five Star Export House | 2000 |

   (iv) **Approved Exporter Scheme:** Self certification by Status Holders Manufacturers, who are also Status Holders, will be enabled to self-certify their manufactured goods as originating from India with a view to qualify for preferential treatment under different Preferential Trading Agreements (PTAs), Free Trade Agreements (FTAs), Comprehensive Economic Cooperation Agreements (CECAs) and Comprehensive Economic Partnerships Agreements (CEPAs) which are in operation. They shall be permitted to self-certify the goods as manufactured as per six their Industrial Entrepreneur

Memorandum (IEM)/Industrial Licence (IL)/Letter of Intent (LOI).

## ❖ Boost To 'Make In India'

1. Reduced Export Obligation (EO) for domestic procurement under EPCG scheme: Specific Export Obligation under EPCG scheme, in case capital goods are procured from indigenous manufacturers, which is currently 90 per cent of the normal export obligation (6 times at the duty saved amount) has been reduced to 75 per cent, in order to promote domestic capital goods manufacturing industry.
2. Higher level of rewards under MEIS for export items with high domestic content and value addition.

   It is proposed to give higher level of rewards to products with high domestic content and value addition, as compared to products with high import content and less value addition.

## ❖ Trade Facilitation and Ease of Doing Business

1. To allow online filing of documents/ applications and Paperless trade in 24 ×7 environment.
2. To allow online inter-ministerial consultations.
3. Simplification of procedures/processes, digitization and e-governance.
4. E-governance initiatives to be taken.

## ❖ Other new Initiatives

1. New initiatives for EOUs, EHTPs and STPs
   - (i) EOUs, EHTPs, STPs have been allowed to share infrastructural facilities among themselves. This will enable units to utilize their infrastructural facilities in an optimum way and avoid duplication of efforts and cost to create separate infrastructural facilities in different units.
   - (ii) Inter unit transfer of goods and services have been allowed among EOUs, EHTPs, STPs, and BTPs. This will facilitate group of those units, which source inputs centrally in order to obtain bulk discount. This will reduce cost of transportation, other logistic costs and result in maintaining effective supply chain.
   - (iii) EOUs have been allowed facility to set up warehouses near the port of export. This will help in reducing lead time for delivery of goods and will also address the issue of unpredictability of supply orders.
   - (iv) STP units, EHTP units and software EOUs have been allowed the facility to use all duty free equipment/goods for training purposes. This will help these units in developing skills of their employees.
   - (v) Hundred per cent EOU units have been allowed facility of supply of spares/components up to 2 per cent of the value of the manufactured articles to a buyer in domestic market for the purpose of after sale services.
   - (vi) At present, in a period of 5 years, EOU units have to achieve Positive Net Foreign Exchange Earning (NFE) cumulatively. Because of adverse market condition or any ground of genuine hardship, then such period of 5 years for NFE completion can be extended by one year.

(vii) Time period for validity of Letter of Permission (LOP) for EOUs/EHTP/STPI/BTP Units has been revised for faster implementation and monitoring of projects.

2. Facilitating and Encouraging Export of dual use items (SCOMET).
3. Validity of SCOMET export authorization has been extended from the present 3 months to 24 months. It will help industry to plan their activity in an orderly manner and obviate the need to seek revalidation or relaxation from DGFT.
4. Facilitating and Encouraging Export of Defence Exports.
5. E-Commerce Exports.
6. Duty Exemption.
7. Additional Ports allowed for Export and import.

   Calicut Airport, Kerala and Arakonam ICD, Tamil Nadu have been notified as registered ports for import and export.
8. Duty Free Tariff Preference (DFTP) Scheme.

   India has already extended duty free tariff preference to 33 Least Developed Countries (LDCs) across the globe. This is being notified under FTP.
9. Quality complaints and Trade Disputes
10. Vishakhapatnam and Bhimavaram added as Towns of Export Excellence.

## ANALYSIS OF THE TRADE POLICY

The Business Line analyses that the exports from SEZs suffering from high MAT would now be eligible for incentives. Another notable positive is the introduction of transferability of duty free scrips and allowing them for payment of customs, excise duties and service tax without any conditionality. However, it would be worth examining how effective the new FTP would be in pushing India's merchandise exports.

It is very difficult to decode what forms the basis of categorising India's export destinations into three groupings as well as allocation of MEIS rates for different commodities. What could explain the exclusion of countries such as Brazil, Bangladesh and China for export promotion with respect to top textile products?

Again, increasing exports to China should have been top priority, but there is no real incentive for China in the new FTP even though it is a top export destination for cotton fibre and yarn.

From a strict reading of the FTP, only direct export to Japan and the United States should be eligible for MEIS. The problem is India mostly exports fabrics to Bangladesh, Indonesia, Myanmar and Vietnam for conversion into garments that are ultimately shipped to Japan and the United States.

It is worth mentioning that some of India's well intentioned trade policy actions (to help LDCs like Bangladesh), though outside the purview of the FTP, are hurting indigenous manufacturing.

For instance, allowing duty free, quota free import of garments from Bangladesh (or Myanmar) without imposing sourcing obligations promotes the backdoor entry of Chinese textile material into India, and hurts the whole textile value chain in the country from fibre to yarn, fabrics and apparel.

## SOURCING BLUES

The FTP needs to follow up with other actions like making the use of fibres, yarns and fabrics of Indian origin mandatory for allowing duty free imports of apparel from Bangladesh and other LDCs seeking preferential market access on non-reciprocal basis.

It's not that India would be the first country to impose sourcing restrictions for allowing duty free imports of apparels. The United States imposes sourcing restrictions in all its existing and proposed trade pacts. Why can't India?

Because of India's FTAs and other trade deals such as Information Technology Agreement (ITA), India's manufacturing sector has to suffer what is called inverted duty structure, that is, high import duties on inputs/ raw materials and lower duties on finished goods. Thus, one can import an apparel item duty free in India, but its basic raw materials are subject to 5 –10 per cent import duties. The Union Budget 2015–16 did attempt to address some of the cases of inverted duties, but only partially.

Again, increasing the use of FTAs would require addressing non-tariff barriers in partner countries. For instance, Japan, as per the terms of the India-Japan CEPA, allows duty free import of apparels from India only, if all the material used for the manufacture of apparels are either of Indian or Japanese origin.

Indian businesses should realize that the days of export subsidies are numbered because of WTO (World Trade Organization) obligations. To deal with slowing demand and rising cost on a long-term basis, businesses must develop suitable global strategies for sourcing, production and trade.

## TERMS RELATED TO FOREIGN TRADE POLICY (FTP)

India's FTP has, conventionally, been formulated for 5 years at a time and reviewed annually. The focus of the FTP has been to provide a framework of rules and procedures for exports and imports and a set of incentives for promoting exports.

The FTP is notified by Central Government, in exercise of powers conferred under the Foreign Trade (Development and Regulation) Act, 1992.

The FTP is primarily focused on accelerating exports. This is sought to be implemented through various schemes intended to exempt and remit indirect taxes on inputs physically incorporated in the export product, import capital goods at concessional duty, stimulate services exports and focus on specific markets and products. The Policy attempts to dovetail these schemes with the specific market access openings that India has achieved through negotiations with its trading partners for various bilateral and regional trading arrangements.

Foreign trade today plays a significant part in India's economy, so much so that FTP deserves a special focus and dedicated attention as a key constituent of India's economic policies. FTP can neither be formulated nor implemented by any one department in isolation. Going forward, a 'whole-of-government' approach will be required.

A major path breaking initiative taken by the Department of Commerce, which can have far-reaching benefits if properly executed, is to mainstream state and UT Governments and various Departments and Ministries of the Government of India in the process of international trade.

## EXPORT ORIENTED UNIT (EOU)

The Export Oriented Unit (EOU) Scheme was introduced in the year 1980 vide Ministry of Commerce resolution dated 31 December 1980. The purpose of the scheme was basically to boost exports by creating additional production capacity. The EOU scheme is complementary to the EPZ scheme, except that it is widely dispersed in location, unlike EPZs, which are set up at specific locations. The Scheme remains in the forefront of country's export production schemes.

## STP SCHEME

The Software Technology Park (STP) scheme is a 100 per cent export oriented scheme for the development and export of computer software, including export of professional services using communication links or physical media.

This scheme is unique in its nature as it focuses on one product/sector, i.e., computer software. The scheme integrates the government concept of 100 per cent EOUs and Export Processing Zones (EPZs) and the concept of Science Parks/Technology Parks, as operating elsewhere in the world. A unique feature of the STP scheme is the provisioning of single-point contact services for member units, enabling them to conduct exports operations at a pace commensurate with international practices.

### ❖ Highlights of the Scheme

1. Approvals are given under single window clearance scheme.
2. A company can set up STP unit anywhere in India.
3. Jurisdictional STPI authorities clear projects costing less than ₹ 100 million with Indian Investment.
4. Hundred per cent foreign equity is permitted.
5. All the imports of hardware and software in the STP units are completely duty free, import of second hand capital goods also permitted.
6. Re-Export of capital goods is also permitted.
7. Simplified Minimum Export Performance norms, i.e., 'Positive Net Foreign Exchange Earnings'.
8. Use of computer system for commercial training purposes is permissible subject to the condition that no computer terminals are installed outside the STP premises.
9. The sales in the Domestic Tariff Area (DTA) shall be permissible up to 50 per cent of the export in value terms.
10. STP units are exempted from payment of corporate income tax up to 2011.
11. The capital goods purchased from the DTA are entitled for benefits like exemption of excise Duty and reimbursement of Central Sales Tax (CST).
12. Capital invested by foreign entrepreneurs, Know-How Fees, Royalty, Dividend, etc. can be freely repatriated after payment of Income Taxes due on them, if any.
13. The items like computers and computers peripherals can be donated to recognized non-commercial educational institutions, registered charitable hospitals, public libraries, public funded research and development establishments, organizations of the government of India, or government of a State or Union Territory without payment of any duties after 2 years of their import.
14. 100 per cent Depreciation on Capital Goods over a period of 5 years.

## EHTP SCHEME

Units undertaking to export their entire production of goods and services may be set up under the **Electronic Hardware Technology Park (EHTP) Scheme.** Such units may be engaged in manufacture and services.

Commensurate with the policy to give a special thrust to export of electronic hardware, such units would be encouraged to be set up under the aforementioned export oriented scheme.

### ❖ Highlights of the Scheme

1. EHTP unit may import free of duty all types of goods, including capital goods as defined in the EXIM Policy, required by it for manufacture, services, production and processing or in connection therewith.

2. The units shall also be permitted to import goods, including capital goods, free of cost or on loan from clients required for the approved activity.
3. EHTP units may procure goods required by them for manufacture, services, production and processing or in connection therewith, duty free, from bonded warehouses in the DTA set up under the Exim Policy.
4. Positive Net Foreign Exchange Earnings against Export Earnings to be achieved over a period of 5 years.

## EXPORT PROMOTION CAPITAL GOODS (EPCG) SCHEME

The scheme allows import of capital goods under exemption from basic and additional duties of customs, as well as domestic sourcing of capital goods by an exporter, with corresponding export obligation. The old scheme is continued in the new Policy, with some variations.

The export obligation for domestic sourcing will be 25 per cent less than in the case of imports of capital goods.

Clubbing of EPCG authorizations will be allowed only if the export product endorsed thereon is same or similar and the authorizations are issued by the same Regional Authority of the DGFT.

The period of maintenance of records is reduced from three years to 2 years.

## RULES OF ORIGIN (ROO)

ROO are the criteria needed to determine the country of origin of a product for purposes of international trade. Their importance is derived from the fact that duties and restrictions in several cases depend upon the source of imports.

## ADVANCE AUTHORIZATION SCHEME

Advance Authorization Scheme (AAS) is one of the incentive schemes provided by Indian Government through its government agency called DGFT – Director General of Foreign Trade.

Under the AAS, exporter can import raw materials and related inputs under 100 per cent duty exemption schemes. The importer has to approach DGFT who is the licensing authority under this category. Government fixes value addition as per the standard input-output norms. Once you fulfils the export obligation with the licensing authority, you can sell the manufactured products in domestic market.

## DUTY FREE IMPORT AUTHORIZATION (DFIA) SCHEME

The DFIA is issued to allow duty free import of inputs, with a minimum value addition requirement of 20 per cent. DFIA shall be exempted only from the payment of basic customs duty. DFIA shall be issued on post export basis for products for which SION has been notified. Separate schemes exist for gems and jewellery sector for which FTP may be referred. Similarly, for items where a higher value addition has been prescribed under Advance Authorization Scheme, the same value addition for DFIA shall be applied.

### ❖ RoDTEP Scheme Guidelines and Rates (Remission of Duties and Taxes on Exported Products):

Centre has notified RoDTEP Scheme Guidelines and Rates (Remission of Duties and Taxes on Exported Products). The scheme for zero rating of exports will boost our exports & competitiveness in the global markets .The rates of RoDTEP will cover 8555 tariff lines.

It may be noted that Government is leaving no stone unturned to support domestic industry and make it more competitive in the international markets. Export centric industries are being reformed and introduced to better mechanisms so as to increase their competitiveness, boost exports, generate employment and contribute to the overall economy. This will go a long way in achieving our vision of building an Aatmanirbhar Bharat.

Remission of Duties and Taxes on Exported Products (RoDTEP) is one such reform, based on the globally accepted principle that taxes and duties should not be exported, and taxes and levies borne on the exported products should be either exempted or remitted to exporters.

Scheme's objective is to refund, currently un-refunded:

- Duties/taxes/levies, at the Central, State and local level, borne on the exported product, including prior stage cumulative indirect taxes on goods & services used in production of the exported product, and
- Such indirect Duties/taxes/levies in respect of distribution of exported products.

It may be noted that rebate under the Scheme shall not be available in respect of duties and taxes already exempted or remitted or credited. RoDTEP is going to give a boost to Indian exports by providing a level playing field to domestic industry abroad.

RoDTEP support will be available to eligible exporters at a notified rate as a percentage of Freight On Board (FOB) value. Rebate on certain export products will also be subject to value cap per unit of the exported product.

Scheme is to be implemented by Customs through a simplified IT System. Rebate will be issued in the form of a transferable duty credit/ electronic scrip (e-scrip) which will be maintained in an electronic ledger by the Central Board of Indirect Taxes & Customs (CBIC).

Identified export sectors and rates under RoDTEP cover 8555 tariff lines in addition to similar support being extended to apparel and made-ups exports under RoSCTL scheme of Ministry of Textiles.

Employment Oriented Sectors like Marine, Agriculture, Leather, Gems & Jewellery etc. are covered under the Scheme. Other sectors like Automobile, Plastics, Electrical / Electronics, Machinery etc. also get support. The entire valve chain of textiles also gets covered through RoDTEP & RoSCTL.

## AGRICULTURAL AND PROCESSED FOOD PRODUCTS EXPORT DEVELOPMENT AUTHORITY (APEDA)

The APEDA was established by the Government of India under the APEDA Act passed by the Parliament in December 1985. APEDA has marked its presence in almost all agro potential states of India and has been providing services to agri-export community through its head office in New Delhi, five Regional offices and 13 Virtual offices.

### ❖ Functions

- Development of industries relating to the scheduled products for export;
- Registration of persons as exporters of the scheduled products on payment of such fees as may be prescribed;
- Fixing of standards and specifications for the scheduled products for the purpose of exports;
- Carrying out inspection of meat and meat products in slaughter houses, processing plants, storage premises, conveyances or other places where such products are kept or handled for the purpose of ensuring the quality of such products;
- Improving of packaging of the scheduled products;

- Improving of marketing of the scheduled products outside India;
- Promotion of export oriented production and development of the scheduled products;
- Collection of statistics from the owners of factories or establishments engaged in the production, processing, packaging, marketing or export of the scheduled products or from such other persons as may be prescribed on any matter relating to the scheduled products and publication of the statistics so collected or of any portions thereof or extracts therefrom;
- Training in various aspects of the industries connected with the scheduled products.

## SANITARY AND PHYTOSANITARY MEASURES IN TRADE (SPS)

SPS measures is an acronym for 'sanitary and phytosanitary' measures and broadly includes measures for the protection of plant, animal and human health. These measures are governed by the WTO Agreement on the Application of Sanitary and Phytosanitary Measures, and its Committee of Sanitary and Phytosanitary Measures.

## TBT

TBT is an acronym for 'technical barriers to trade' and broadly includes standards, technical regulations and conformity assessment procedures as defined in WTO's TBT Agreement. Since SPS and TBT could be barriers to trade, many FTAs deal with them.

Some of the other non-tariff measures that figure in FTA chapters are:

- import licencing procedures
- trade documentation
- pre-shipment inspections

The stakeholders encountering NTMs (including SPS and TBT measures) can bring these to the notice of the territorial divisions of the Department of Commerce. A database of such NTMs is also available on the website of the department.

The tariff concessions in an FTA are implemented at the ground level through customs notifications. In the case of phased implementation of concessions, the notifications are issued on a yearly basis and are available on the website of the Central Board of Excise and Customs. Any such inputs from stakeholders would enable to update this database.

## TOWNS OF EXPORT EXCELLENCE (TEE)

Selected towns producing goods of ₹ 750 crore or more are notified as TEE on potential for growth in exports and provide financial assistance under MAI Scheme to recognized Associations.

## BALTIC DRY INDEX (BDI)

The BDI is an economic indicator issued daily by the London-based Baltic Exchange. Not restricted to Baltic Sea countries, the index provides 'an assessment of the price of moving the major raw materials by sea'. Taking in 23 shipping routes measured on a time charter basis, the index covers Handysize, Supramax, Panamax and Capesize dry bulk carriers carrying a range of commodities including coal, iron ore and grain. It is also known as the 'Dry Bulk Index'.

Changes in the BDI can give investors insight into global supply and demand trends. This change is often considered a leading indicator of future economic growth (if the index is rising) or contraction (index is falling) because the goods shipped are raw, pre-production material, which is typically an area with very low levels of speculation.

BDI Hits All Time Low of 310 in February 2016. It hits a temporary peak on 20 May 2008, when the index hits 11,793.

## WORLD TRADE ORGANIZATION (WTO)

WTO can be looked from many angles. It may be called as organization for trade opening or a forum for governments to negotiate trade agreements or a place for them to settle trade disputes or a body to operate a system of trade rules. Essentially, the WTO is a place where member governments try to sort out the trade problems they face from each other.

Located at Geneva, Switzerland the WTO was established on 1 January 1995. WTO was born out of negotiations among participating governments. The bulk of the WTO's current work comes from the 1986–94 negotiations called the Uruguay Round and earlier negotiations under the General Agreement on Tariffs and Trade (GATT).

The 'WTO agreements' are foundation stone, negotiated and signed by the bulk of the world's trading nations. These documents provide the legal ground rules for international commerce. They are essentially contracts, binding governments to keep their trade policies within agreed limits. Although negotiated and signed by governments, the goal is to help producers of goods and services, exporters and importers conduct their business, while allowing governments to meet social and environmental objectives.

The overriding purpose of WTO is to help trade flow as freely as possible – so long as there are no undesirable side effects – because this is important for economic development and well-being. The rules have to be 'transparent' and 'predictable'.

Trade relations often involve conflicting interests. Agreements, including those painstakingly negotiated in the WTO system, often need interpreting. The most harmonious way to settle these differences is through some neutral procedure based on an agreed legal foundation. That is the purpose behind the dispute settlement process written into the WTO agreements.

**WTO's Main Functions**

1. Negotiating the reduction or elimination of obstacles to trade (import tariffs, other barriers to trade) and agreeing on rules governing the conduct of international trade (e.g. antidumping, subsidies, product standards, etc.)
2. Administering and monitoring the application of the WTO's agreed rules for trade in goods, trade in services, and trade-related Intellectual Property Rights (IPR)
3. Monitoring and reviewing the trade policies of our members, as well as ensuring transparency of regional and bilateral trade agreements
4. Settling disputes among our members regarding the interpretation and application of the agreements
5. Building capacity of developing country government officials in international trade matters
6. Assisting the process of accession of countries who are not yet members of the organization
7. Conducting economic research and collecting and disseminating trade data in support of the WTO's other main activities
8. Explaining to and educating the public about the WTO, its mission and its activities
9. Cooperation with other international organizations

The WTO agreements cover goods, services and intellectual property. They spell out the principles of liberalization and the permitted exceptions. They include individual countries' commitments to lower customs tariffs and other trade barriers, and to open and keep open services markets. They set procedures for settling disputes.

WTO agreements require governments to make their trade policies transparent by notifying the WTO about laws in force and measures adopted. Various WTO councils and committees seek to ensure that these requirements are being followed and that WTO agreements are being properly implemented. All WTO members must undergo periodic scrutiny of their trade policies and practices, each review containing reports by the country concerned and the WTO Secretariat.

The WTO's procedure for resolving trade quarrels under the Dispute Settlement Understanding is vital for enforcing the rules and therefore for ensuring that trade flows smoothly. Countries bring disputes to the WTO, if they think their rights under the agreements are being infringed. Judgments by specially appointed independent experts are based on interpretations of the agreements and individual countries' commitments.

WTO agreements contain special provision for developing countries, including longer time periods to implement agreements and commitments, measures to increase their trading opportunities, and support to help them build their trade capacity, to handle disputes and to implement technical standards. The WTO organizes hundreds of technical cooperation missions to developing countries annually. It also holds numerous courses each year in Geneva for government officials. Aid for Trade aims to help developing countries develop the skills and infrastructure needed to expand their trade.

The WTO maintains regular dialogue with non-governmental organizations, parliamentarians, other international organizations, the media and the general public on various aspects of the WTO and the ongoing Doha negotiations, with the aim of enhancing cooperation and increasing awareness of WTO activities.

## PRINCIPLE FOLLOWED BY WTO

1. **Non-Discrimination:** Under the WTO agreements, countries cannot normally discriminate between their trading partners. This is being implemented through:
   - (i) Giving status of Most Favoured Nation
   - (ii) Giving National Treatment to other countries' product or services
   - (iii) **Free Trade:** Gradually through negotiation

     Lowering trade barriers is one of the most obvious means of encouraging trade. The barriers concerned include customs duties (or tariffs) and measures such as import bans or quotas that restrict quantities selectively. From time to time, other issues such as red tape and exchange rate policies have also been discussed.
   - (iv) **Predictability:** With stability and predictability, investment is encouraged, jobs are created and consumers can fully enjoy the benefits of competition – choice and lower prices.
   - (v) **Promoting fair competition:** Many of the other WTO agreements aim to support fair competition: in agriculture, intellectual property, services, for example.
   - (vi) Encouraging Development and Economic Reforms.

## MAJOR AGREEMENTS OF WTO

1. **Agreement on Agriculture (AOA)** aims to increase market orientation in agriculture trade. It provides for commitments in the area of market access, domestic support and export competition. The members have to transform their non-tariff barriers like quotas into equivalent tariff measures. The tariffs are to be reduced by 36 per cent within 6 years in case of developed countries and by 24 per cent within 10 years in case of developed countries. The least developed countries need not make any commitment for reduction.
2. **Agreement on Trade in Textiles and Clothing (Multi-Fiber Arrangement)** provides for phasing out the import quotas on textiles and clothing in force under the Multi-Fibre Arrangement since 1974, over a span of 10 years, i.e., by 1 January 2005. With this agreement, quota on textile and clothing has now been abolished.
3. **Agreement on Manufactured Goods** caused the developed countries agreed to reduce tariffs on manufactured goods other than textiles by 40 per cent. The tariffs agreed to brought down to an average of 3.8 per cent from earlier 6.3 per cent.
4. **The Agreement on Trade-Related Investment Measures (TRIMs)** calls for introducing national treatment of foreign investments and removal of quantitative restrictions. It identifies five investment measures that are inconsistent with the GATT provisions on national treatment and on general elimination of qualitative restrictions.
5. **Trade-Related Intellectual Property Rights (TRIPRs)** pertain to Patents and Copyrights. Whereas earlier on process patents were granted to food, medicines, drugs and chemical products, the TRIPRs Agreement now provides for granting product patents also in all these areas. Protection will be available for 20 years for patents and 50 years for copyrights.
6. **General Agreement on Trade and Services (GATS)** provides a multilateral framework of principles and services that should govern trade in services under conditions of transparency and progressive liberalization.

## WTO MINISTERIAL CONFERENCES

The highest decision-making body of the WTO is the Ministerial Conference, which usually meets every 2 years. The Ministerial Conference can take decisions on all matters under any of the multilateral trade agreements.

Eleven Ministerial Conferences held till date are as follow:

| S.No. | Date | Held at |
|---|---|---|
| 1. | 9–13 December 1996 | Singapore |
| 2. | 18–20 May 1998 | Geneva, Switzerland |
| 3. | 30 November–3 December 1999 | Seattle, United States |
| 4. | 9–14 November 2001 | Doha, Qatar |

| | | |
|---|---|---|
| 5. | 10–14 September 2003 | Cancún, Mexico |
| 6. | 13–18 December 2005 | Hong Kong |
| 7. | 30 November–2 December 2009 | Geneva, Switzerland |
| 8. | 15–17 December 2011 | Geneva, Switzerland |
| 9. | 3–6 December 2013 | Bali, Indonesia |
| 10. | 15–18 December 2015 | Nairobi, Kenya |
| 11. | 11–14 December 2017 | Buenos Aires, Argentina |
| 12. | 30 November–3 December | Geneva, Switzerland |

## ELEVENTH WTO MINISTERIAL CONFERENCE

The Eleventh Ministerial Conference (MC11) took place from 10 to 13 December 2017 in Buenos Aires, Argentina. It was chaired by Minister Susana Malcorra of Argentina. The Conference ended with a number of ministerial decisions, including on fisheries subsidies and e-commerce duties and a commitment to continue negotiations in all areas.

**Key Highlights of the Conference:**

1. Three proponent groups announced new initiatives to advance talks at the WTO on the issues of electronic commerce, investment facilitation, and micro-, small- and medium-sized enterprises (MSMEs).
2. The European Union contributed EUR 1 million to improve the trading capacity of developing countries and to help them and play a more active role in trade negotiations.
3. The United Kingdom government announced at the WTO's Ministerial Conference with a commitment of £16 million to 51 of the world's poorest countries.
4. For the first time in the history of the WTO, members and observers have endorsed a collective initiative to increase the participation of women in trade.

## RELATED TERMS

### ❖ Dumping

Dumping occurs when the export price of goods imported into India is less than the Normal Value of 'like articles' sold in the domestic market of the exporter. Imports at cheap or low prices do not *per se* indicate dumping.

The price at which like articles are sold in the domestic market of the exporter is referred to as the 'Normal Value' of those articles.

### ❖ Normal Value

The normal value is the comparable price at which the goods under complaint are sold, in the ordinary course of trade, in the domestic market of the exporting country or territory.

If the normal value cannot be determined by means of domestic sales, the Act provides for the following two alternative methods:

- Comparable representative export price to an appropriate third country.
- Cost of production in the country of origin with reasonable addition for administrative, selling and general costs and for profits.

### ❖ Export Price

The export price of goods imported into India is the price paid or payable for the goods by the first independent buyer.

### ❖ Margin of Dumping

Margin of dumping refers to the difference between the Normal Value of the like article and the Export Price of the product under consideration. Margin of dumping is normally established on the basis of:

1. a comparison of weighted average normal value with a weighted average of prices of comparable export transactions; or
2. comparison of normal values and export prices on a transaction to transaction basis.

A Normal Value established on a weighted average basis may be compared to prices of individual export transactions if the Designated Authority finds a pattern of export prices that differ significantly among different purchasers, regions, time period, etc. It is significant to note that the alternative method of comparing the normal values and export prices is a major change introduced after the Uruguay Round.

The margin of dumping is generally expressed as a percentage of the export price.

### ❖ Anti-Dumping Duties

Duties are imposed on a source specific basis and can be expressed either on *ad valoren* or on specific basis. Non-cooperative exporters are required to pay the residuary duty, which is generally the highest of the co-operative exporters.

## TRADE FACILITATION AGREEMENT (TFA)

The TFA at WTO is a trade protocol aiming to give a spur and do away with the stumbling blocks in doing international trade between various countries. The developing country especially India and South Africa wants that before pushing for this TFA thing; WTO should discuss their concern on food subsidy which is a lifeline for lakhs of BPL people in these countries.

The TFA aims to fast track any movement of goods among countries by cutting down bureaucratic obligations. The problem with TFA runs in a clause that says farm subsidies cannot be more than 10 per cent of the value of agricultural production. If the cap is breached, other members can challenge it and also go on to impose trade sanctions on the country.

## DOMESTIC SUPPORT IN AGRICULTURE

At WTO subsidies in general are identified by 'boxes' which are given the colours of traffic lights: green (permitted), amber (slow down – i.e., need to be reduced), red (forbidden).

### ❖ Amber Box

Nearly all domestic support measures considered to distort production and trade (with some exceptions) fall into the amber box, which is defined in the Agriculture Agreement as all domestic supports except those in the blue and green boxes. These include measures to support prices, or subsidies directly related to production quantities.

These supports are subject to limits: 'de minimis' minimal supports are allowed (generally 5 per cent of agricultural production for developed countries, 10 per cent for developing countries).

Thirty-two WTO members have commitments to reduce their trade-distorting domestic supports in the Amber Box. The reduction commitments are expressed in terms of a 'Total Aggregate Measurement of Support' (Total AMS) which includes all supports for specified products together with supports that are not for specific products, in one single figure. In the current negotiations, various proposals deal with how much further these subsidies should be reduced, and whether limits should be set for specific products rather than continuing with the single overall 'aggregate' limits.

### ❖ Blue Box

This is the 'amber box with conditions' – conditions designed to reduce distortion. Any support that would normally be in the amber box is placed in the blue box if the support also requires farmers to limit production.

At present, there are no limits on spending on blue box subsidies. In the current negotiations, some countries want to keep the blue box as it is because they see it as a crucial means of moving away from distorting amber box subsidies without causing too much hardship. Others wanted to set limits or reduction commitments, some advocating moving these supports into the amber box.

### ❖ Green Box

In order to qualify, green box subsidies must not distort trade, or at most cause minimal distortion. They have to be government-funded (not by charging consumers higher prices) and must not involve price support.

They are programmes that are not targeted at particular products, and include direct income supports for farmers that are not related to current production levels or prices. They also include environmental protection and regional development programmes. 'Green box' subsidies are therefore allowed without limits, provided they comply with the policy-specific criteria.

In agriculture, things are, as usual, more complicated. The Agriculture Agreement has no red box, although domestic support exceeding the reduction commitment levels in the amber box is prohibited; and there is a blue box for subsidies that are tied to programmes that limit production. There are also exemptions for developing countries (sometimes called an 'S&D box' or 'development box').

### ❖ Development Box

The Agriculture Agreement allows developing countries additional flexibilities in providing domestic support. The type of support that fits into the developmental category are measures of assistance, whether direct or indirect, designed to encourage agricultural and rural development and that are an integral part of the development programmes of developing countries. They include investment subsidies, agricultural input subsidies and domestic support to producers in developing country to encourage diversification from growing illicit narcotic crops.

## FOREIGN INVESTMENT

Any investment in India, which has its source in any foreign country, is called foreign investment. Foreign investment includes all types of foreign investments, direct and indirect. The foreign money can be invested in India by the foreign corporate and nationals or non-resident Indians. It can be invested in shares, properties, ownership or management or collaboration.

The Government of India classifies the foreign investment into the following forms:

1. Foreign Direct Investment (FDI)
2. Foreign Portfolio Investment (FPI)
3. Non-resident Indian (NRI) investment

## ❖ Foreign Direct Investment (FDI)

For a country where capital is not readily available, FDI has been an important source of funds for companies. Under FDI, overseas money, either by an individual or entity, is invested in an Indian company.

It is primarily regulated by the Central bank of the economy and the government. This is in contrast to FPI which although dealing in shares has short-term profit motives and is regulated by the securities and bourse regulators.

## ❖ Foreign Portfolio Investment (FPI)

In order to harmonize the various available routes for FPI in India, the Indian securities market regulator, i.e., Securities Exchange Board of India (SEBI) has introduced a new class of foreign investors in India known as the FPIs. This class has been formed by merging the existing classes of investors through which portfolio investments were previously made in India namely, the FIIs, Qualified Foreign Investors (QFIs) and sub-accounts of the FIIs.

## ❖ NRI Investment

NRIs have multiple avenues to invest in India, including bank fixed deposits, equities, mutual funds, real estate, government bonds and much more.

# FDI IN INDIA

In India, capital has been one of the scare resources required for economic development. Capital is limited and there are many issues such as health, poverty, employment, education, research and development, technology obsolesce, global competition. FDI is a major source of non-debt financial resource for the economic development of India. The flow of FDI in India from across the world will help in acquiring the funds at cheaper cost, better technology, employment generation and upgraded technology transfer, exchange rate stability, promotion of financial services, utilization of natural resources, development of backward areas, scope for more trade, linkages and spillovers to domestic firms and change in the lifestyle of people.

India is an attractive destination of FDI because of following factors –

1. **Cheap labour:** In India there is abundant labour (skilled and unskilled) available. Foreign investors will to take advantage of the difference in the cost of labour.
2. **Stable policies:** India's stable economic and social policies have attracted investors across border. Investors prefer countries with stable economic policies.
3. **Economic factors:** Different economic factors encourage inward FDI. These include interest loans, tax breaks, grants, subsidies and the removal of restrictions and limitation. The Government of India has taken a number of steps under economic reform process to attract FDI.
4. **Basic infrastructure:** Though India is still infrastructurally poor, it has developed special economic zone where there have focused to build required infrastructure such as roads, effective transportation and registered carrier departure worldwide, information and communication network/technology, powers, financial institutions and legal system and other basic amenities which are must for the success of the business.
5. **Availability of natural resources:** India is endowed with large natural resources such as coal, iron ore, natural gas, etc. They can be used in manufacturing by the foreign investors.
6. **Unexplored markets:** In India, there is a large section of markets unexploited or unulilized. There is a big potential customer market with large middle-class

income group which may be targeted by manufacturers and service providers. This opens a big area of opportunity to FDI investors.

However, there have been some obstacles in the inflow of FDI in India, i.e., political instability, poor infrastructure, confusing tax and tariff policies, stringent labour laws, well-entrenched corruption, limited scale of export processing zones, high corporate tax rate, and governmental regulations. The Government of India is trying to remove them through reforms in these sectors.

## ❖ Merits and Demerits of FDI in Retail Sector

FDI has lot to advantages to its favour which can be summarized as below:

1. **More consumer savings:** One of the biggest advantage of FDI is that it will increase the savings of Indian consumer as he will get good quality products at much cheaper rates. Consumer savings are likely to increase 5 –10 per cent from FDI.

2. **Higher remuneration for farmers:** Another advantage of FDI is that it will help a lot in improving the miserable condition of Indian farmers who are committing suicides on daily basis because of lesser return from their agricultural produce. But FDI will certain help a lot in improving their conditions as the farmers are going to get 10 to 30 per cent higher remuneration because of FDI.

3. **Increase in employment opportunities:** FDI is certainly going to increase the employment opportunities in India by providing around 3 to 4 million new jobs. Not only this another 4 to 6 million jobs will be created in logistics, labour, etc. because of FDI.

4. **Increase in government revenue:** Government revenues are certainly going to increase a lot because of FDI. Government revenues will increase by 25 to 30 billion dollars which is a really big amount. This government revenue can help a lot in the development of Indian economy.

Although FDI brings with it lot of advantages but it is not free from disadvantages as well. Following are some of its demerits:

1. **Destruction of small entrepreneurs:** The biggest fear from FDI is that it is likely to destroy the small entrepreneurs or small *kirana* shops as they will not be able to withstand the tough competition of big entrepreneurs as these entrepreneurs are going to provide all the goods to the consumers at much lesser prices.

2. **Shrinking of jobs:** Many critics of FDI are of the view that entry of big foreign chains like Wal-Mart, Carrefour etc. are not going to generate any jobs in reality in India. At best, the jobs will move from unorganized sector to organized sector while their number will remain the same or lesser but not more.

3. **No real benefit to farmers:** Critics of FDI are also of the view that it is a fallacy that the farmers are going to benefit in any way because of the entry of foreign chains in India rather it will make the Indian farmers a slave of these big chains and the farmers will entirely be on their mercy. Thus, FDI is only going to deteriorate the already miserable conditions of Indian farmers.

## ❖ FDI Redefined

FDI is an investment in a business by an investor from foreign country for which the foreign investor has control over the company purchased. The Organization of

Economic Cooperation and Development (OECD) defines control as owning 10 per cent or more of the business. Businesses that make FDIs are often called multinational corporations (MNCs) or multinational enterprises (MNEs). These MNCs/MNEs may make a direct investment by creating a new foreign enterprise, which is called a Greenfield investment, or by the acquisition of a foreign firm, either called an acquisition or brownfield investment.

In India, FDI means investment by non-resident entity/person resident outside India in the capital of an Indian company under Schedule 1 of Foreign Exchange Management (Transfer or Issue of Security by a Person Resident Outside India) Regulations, 2000.

The Government of India in 2014 accepted the report of Arvind Mayaram Committee related with removing ambiguity in the definition of FDI and FII.

The Committee, in its report, suggested 10 per cent or more foreign investment in a listed Indian Company should be treated as FDI while below 10 per cent to be considered as Foreign Portfolio Investor (FPI). FPI combines two categories of foreign investors, FII and QFI. The panel also said that for an unlisted company any amount of foreign investment would be considered as FDI.

The commission adopted the conceptual framework that FDI is characterized by a lasting interest, i.e., existence of a long-term relationship, significant degree of influence. Normally, ownership of 10 per cent or more of the ordinary shares or voting power signifies this relationship and it involves both initial and subsequent transactions.

On the other hand, Portfolio investment is identified by the largely anonymous relationship between the issuers and holders, and the degree of trading liquidity in the instruments. Further it covers, but is not limited to securities traded on organized or other financial markets, it mentioned.

It has also specified that in a particular company an investor can hold the investment either under FDI or under FPI route, but not both.

As per the commission, the NRI investors have a special place in the foreign investment regime since NRI funds flow even through deposits and remittances. Special privileges are also available to NRIs in terms of the Overseas Citizenship Act and the provision to make 'non-repatriable' investments.

It also called for a relook at the Foreign Venture Capital Investors (FVCI) scheme since these investors are basically in the nature of FDI.

**FDI Inflow to India**

| Source/Industry | 2016-17 | 2017-18 | 2018-19 | 2019-20 | 2020-21 (P) |
|---|---|---|---|---|---|
| 1 | 2 | 3 | 4 | 5 | 6 |
| Total FDI | 36,317 | 37,366 | 38,744 | 42,629 | 52,545 |
| **Country-wise Inflows** | | | | | |
| Singapore | 6,529 | 9,273 | 14,632 | 12,612 | 15,908 |
| US | 2,138 | 1,973 | 2,823 | 3,401 | 13,204 |
| Mauritius | 13,383 | 13,415 | 6,570 | 7,498 | 4,491 |

| | | | | | |
|---|---|---|---|---|---|
| UAE | 645 | 408 | 853 | 323 | 4,071 |
| Saudi Arabia | 12 | 125 | 27 | 89 | 2,815 |
| Cayman Islands | 49 | 1,140 | 863 | 3,496 | 2,558 |
| Netherlands | 3,234 | 2,677 | 2,519 | 5,295 | 2,138 |
| Japan | 4,237 | 1,313 | 2,745 | 2,308 | 1,794 |
| France | 487 | 403 | 375 | 1,167 | 810 |
| UK | 1,301 | 716 | 1,211 | 1,125 | 77 |

## ❖ Consolidated FDI Policy, 2017–2018

The ability to attract large-scale FDI into India has been a key driver for policy making by the government. On 28 August 2017, the Department of Industrial Policy and Promotion (DIPP) had issued the updated and revised FDI Policy, 2017–18. It is called consolidated FDI Policy because apart from new changes in a separate part it also consolidates the press notes issued by government since last policy release. India received FDI inflows worth USD 60.1 billion in 2016–17, which was an all-time high.

1. The most significant amendment to the FDI regime have been the institutional changes – abolition of the Foreign Investment Promotion Board FIPB on 5 June 2017 by the Department of Economic Affair and the introduction of the 'Foreign Investment Facilitation Portal' (FIFP), an administrative body to facilitate FDI applicants.
2. **Introduction of 'Competent Authorities':** The FDI Policy 2017 defines and lists sector-specific administrative ministry/department as 'Competent Authorities' empowered to grant government approval for FDI.
3. **Introduction of 'Standard Operating Procedure' (SOP) to process FDI proposals:** The government issued the SOP, which sets out a detailed procedure and timeline for applications as well as the list of 'competent authorities' for processing government approvals for FDI in India.

   Under the SOP, investors are required to make an application on the website of the FIFP, supported by the specified documents, which *inter alia* include relevant charter documents, board resolutions, etc. The application shall then be forwarded to the concerned 'Competent Authority' and the RBI (for comments from a foreign exchange law perspective) within 2 days. Proposals requiring security clearance (in sectors such as defence and telecommunication) shall also be forwarded to the Ministry of Home Affairs. The Competent Authority shall process the complete proposal and convey the approval/rejection of such proposal to the applicant in the format prescribed under the SOP.
4. Key provisions likely to benefit applicants with proposals for FDI by streamlined procedure and expeditious timeline (maximum time of 10 weeks) for approval.

Moreover, the FDI Policy 2017 also states that the Competent Authority may only reject a proposal, or stipulate conditions in addition to those listed in the FDI Policy 2017/applicable sectoral laws with the concurrence of the DIPP.

5. A Limited Liability Partnership (LLP) firm, operating in sectors/activities where 100 per cent FDI is allowed under the *automatic* route (without FDI-linked performance conditions), is permitted to convert into a company and vice versa.
6. **The FDI Policy 2017 has introduced the issuance of**
   (i) 'Convertible Notes' (instruments representing debt repayable at the option of the holder, or convertible into equity shares within 5 years from issue) by start-ups to persons resident outside India and
   (ii) Equity or equity linked/debt instruments by Start-ups to Foreign Venture Capital Investors.

The issuance of Convertible Notes is, however, subject to certain conditions.

## ❖ Revisions to Existing Provisions of the FDI Policy, 2016

1. **Manufacturing:** To further liberalize the manufacturing sector (which allowed 100 per cent FDI under the automatic route), 100 per cent FDI under government approval route was allowed for retail trading, including through e-commerce, in respect of food products manufactured and/or produced in India.
2. **Civil Aviation:** The threshold for FDI in existing projects under the automatic route was increased from 74 per cent to 100 per cent.
3. **Single Brand Retailing:** Sourcing norms applicable for FDI were relaxed and will not be applicable up to 3 (three) years from commencement of the business.
4. **Financial Services:** The previously applicable capitalization norms for non-banking financial services companies were struck off, and all financial sector activities by entities already regulated by financial sector regulators fall under the 100 per cent automatic route of investment, with applicability of sectoral laws.

Thus, the changes in the FDI Policy 2017 display the efforts of the Indian Government to remove of multiple layers of bureaucracy, and to process proposals for FDI under the government approval route in a more streamlined, positive and expeditious manner.

**Sectors Where Foreign Investment is Prohibited**

1. Lottery business including government/private lottery, online lotteries, etc.
2. Gambling and betting including casinos, etc.
3. Chit funds
4. Nidhi company
5. Trading in Transferable Development Rights (TDRs)
6. Real Estate Business or Construction of Farmhouses
7. Manufacturing of cigars, cheroots, cigarillos and cigarettes, of tobacco or of tobacco substitutes

8. Activities/sectors not open to private sector investment, for example, (1) Atomic energy and (2) Railway operations (other than permitted activities mentioned in entry 18 of Annex B).

**Note:** Foreign technology collaboration in any form including licensing for franchise, trademark, brand name, management contract is also prohibited for Lottery Business and Gambling and Betting activities.

## ❖ Terms Related to FDI

1. **Foreign Institutional Investor (FII):** Foreign Institutional Investor (FII) means an institution established or incorporated outside India which proposes to make investment in securities in India. They are registered as FIIs in accordance with Section 2(f) of the SEBI (FII) Regulations 1995. Foreign entities or funds eligible to get registered are: pension funds; mutual funds; investment trusts; insurance companies/reinsurance company; foreign central banks; foreign governmental agencies; sovereign wealth funds; international or multilateral organization/agency; university funds; endowments; foundations and charitable trusts.

   However, FII as a category does not exist now. It was decided to create a new investor class from 1 June 2014 called Foreign Portfolio Investor (FPI) by merging the existing three investor classes viz. FIIs, Sub Accounts and QFIs.

   With the new FPI regime, it has now been decided to dispense with the mandatory requirement of direct registration with SEBI and a risk-based verification approach has been adopted to smoothen the entry of foreign investors into the Indian securities market.

2. **Round-tripping:** 'Round-tripping' is self-explanatory term. It denotes a trip where a person or thing returns to the place from where the journey began. In the context of black money, it leaves the country through various channels such as inflated invoices, payments to shell companies overseas, the hawala route and so on. After cooling its heels overseas for a while, this money returns in a freshly laundered form; thus completing a round-trip.

   The GDR and Participatory Notes (P-Notes) are some of the other routes that have been used in the past.

   Many listed companies appear to be involved in these activities. SEBI had recently issued a notice against listed firms including United Spirits, GMR, Unitech and Sterlite for investing in group companies through a foreign account held with UBS. The companies are alleged to have indulged in stock price manipulation and insider trading through this route. Another high-profile case in 2009 involved the Reliance ADAG group that was alleged to have manipulated the shares of Reliance Communication through a multi-layered transaction involving shell companies, P-notes and prominent international investment banks.

3. **Qualified Foreign Investors (QFIs):** The QFI is a sub-category of FPI and refers to any foreign individuals, groups or associations, or resident, however, restricted to those from a country that is a member of Financial Action Task Force (FATF) or a country that is a member of a group which is a member of FATF and a country that is a signatory to International Organization of Securities Commission's (IOSCO) Multilateral Memorandum of Understanding (MMOU).

QFI scheme was introduced by the government of India in consultation with RBI and SEBI in the year 2011, through a Union Budget announcement.

The objective of enabling QFIs is to deepen and infuse more foreign funds in the Indian capital market and to reduce market volatility as individuals are considered to be long-term investors, as compared to institutional investors.

## INDIAN PATENT SYSTEM

A patent is a government license that gives the holder exclusive rights to a process, design or new invention for a designated period of time. Applications for patents are usually handled by a government agency.

Patents refer to enforceable exclusive rights granted to the inventor in exchange for his/her making their invention public. In India, an invention pertaining to a new product/process, involving an inventive step and capable of industrial application can be patented. Patents are a form of intellectual property. An inventor can also appoint an assignee who acts on his/her behalf and incurs both the rights and the liabilities.

To receive a patent, a patent application must disclose all details of the invention so that others can use it to further advance the technology with new inventions. Patentable items fall under four classes: (1) Machine: apparatus or device with interrelated parts that work together to perform the invention's designed or intended functions, (2) Manufacture: all manufactured or fabricated items, (3) Process: chemical, mechanical, electrical or other process that produces a chemical or physical change in the condition or character of an item and (4) Composition of matter: chemical compounds or mixtures having properties different from their constituent ingredients.

Patents are enforced by nations. However, though the specifics of the Patent Law are determined by each country, countries work under the framework of the multilateral treaty, TRIPS (Agreement on Trade-Related Aspects of Intellectual Property Rights).

### ❖ History of Indian Patent System

The first legislation in India relating to patents was the Act of 1856. The objective of this legislation was to encourage inventions of new and useful manufactures and to induce inventors to disclose secret of their inventions. The Act was subsequently repealed by Act of 1857 since it had been enacted without the approval of the British Crown. Fresh legislation for granting 'exclusive privileges' was introduced in 1859. This legislation contained certain modifications of the earlier legislation, namely, grant of exclusive privileges to useful inventions only and extension of priority period from 6 months to 12 months. This Act excluded importers from the definition of inventor. This Act was based on the United Kingdom Act of 1852 with certain departures which include allowing assignees to make application in India and also taking prior public use or publication in India or United Kingdom for the purpose of ascertaining novelty.

In 1872, the Act of 1859 was consolidated to provide protection relating to designs. It was renamed as 'The Patterns and Designs Protection Act' of 1872. The Act of 1872 was further amended in 1883 to introduce a provision to protect novelty of the invention, which prior to making application for their protection were disclosed in the Exhibition of India. A grace period of 6 months was provided for filing such applications after the date of the opening of such Exhibition.

This Act remained in force for about 30 years without any change but in the year 1883, certain modifications in the patent law were made in the United Kingdom and it was considered that those modifications should also be incorporated in the Indian law. In 1888, an Act was introduced to consolidate and amend the law relating to invention and designs in conformity with the amendments made in the UK law.

The Indian Patents and Designs Act, 1911, replaced all the previous Acts. This Act brought patent administration under the management of Controller of Patents for the first time. This Act was further amended in 1920 to enter into reciprocal arrangements with UK and other countries for securing priority. In 1930, further amendments were made to incorporate, inter alia, provisions relating to grant of secret patents, patent of addition, use of invention by the government, powers of the Controller to rectify register of patent and increase of term of the patent from 14 to 16 years. In 1945, an amendment was made to provide for filing of provisional specification and submission of complete specification within nine months.

After Independence, it was felt that the Indian Patents and Designs Act, 1911 was not fulfilling its objective. It was found desirable to enact comprehensive patent law owing to substantial changes in political and economic conditions in the country. Accordingly, the Government of India constituted a committee under the Chairmanship of Justice (Dr.) Bakshi Tek Chand, a retired Judge of Lahore High Court, in 1949 to review the patent law in India in order to ensure that the patent system is conducive to the national interest.

The committee submitted its interim report on 4th August, 1949 with recommendations for prevention of misuse or abuse of patent right in India and suggested amendments to the Patents and Designs Act, 1911, on the lines of the United Kingdom Acts, 1919 and 1949.

Based on the recommendation of the Committee, the 1911 Act was amended in 1950in relation to working of inventions and compulsory licence/revocation. Other provisions were related to endorsement of the patent with the words 'licence of right' on an application by the Government so that the Controller could grant licences. In 1952, an amendment was made to provide compulsory licence in relation to patents in respect of food and medicines, insecticide, germicide or fungicide and a process for producing substance or any invention relating to surgical or curative devices. The compulsory licence was also available on notification by the central government. Based on the recommendations of the Committee, a bill was introduced in the Parliament in 1953. However, the government did not press for the consideration of the bill, and it was allowed to lapse.

In 1957, the Government of India appointed Justice N. Rajagopala Ayyangar Committee to examine the question of revision of the Patent Law and advise government accordingly. The report of the Committee, which comprised of two parts, was submitted in September 1959. The first part dealt with general aspects of the Patent Law, and the second part gave detailed note on the several clauses of the lapsed bills, 1953. The first part also dealt with evils of the patent system and solution with recommendations in regards to the law. The committee recommended retention of the Patent System, despite its shortcomings. This report recommended major changes in the law which formed the basis of the introduction of the Patents Bill, 1965. This bill was introduced in the Lok Sabha on 21 September 1965, which however lapsed. In 1967, again an amended bill was introduced which was referred to a Joint Parliamentary Committee and on the final recommendation of the Committee, the Patents Act, 1970, was passed. This Act repealed and replaced the 1911 Act so far as the patents law was concerned. However, the 1911 Act continued to be applicable to designs. Most of the provisions of the 1970 Act were brought into force on 20 April 1972 with publication of the Patent Rules, 1972.

This Act remained in force for about 24 years without any change till December 1994. An ordinance effecting certain changes in the Act was issued on 31 December 1994, which ceased to operate after six months. Subsequently, another ordinance was issued in 1999. This ordinance was subsequently replaced by the Patents (Amendment) Act, 1999, that was brought into force retrospectively from 1 January 1995. The amended Act provided for filing of applications for product patents in the areas of drugs, pharmaceuticals and agro chemicals though such patents were not allowed. However, such applications were to be examined only after 31 December 2004. Meanwhile, the applicants could be allowed Exclusive Marketing Rights (EMR) to sell or distribute these products in India, subject to fulfilment of certain conditions.

The second amendment to the 1970 Act was made through the Patents (Amendment) Act, 2002. This Act came into force on 20 May 2003 with the introduction of the new Patent Rules, 2003, by replacing the earlier Patents Rules, 1972.

The third amendment to the Patents Act 1970 was introduced through the Patents (Amendment) Ordinance, 2004 w.e.f. 1 January, 2005. This Ordinance was later replaced by the Patents (Amendment) Act, 2005, on 4 April 2005 which was brought into force from 1 January 2005.

The major amendment was in 2005, when product patent was extended to all fields of technology like food, drugs, chemicals and microorganisms. Year 2005 was the final deadline for complete compliance with TRIPS. The rules under Patent Act were also amended in 2012, 2013, 2014.

## 2005 AMENDMENT OF THE PATENT LAW

**Salient features of the Patents (Amendment) Act, 2005, related to product patents:** Extension of product patent protection to products in sectors of drugs, foods and chemical. Term for protection of product patent shall be for 20 years. Introduction of a provision for enabling grant of compulsory license for export of medicines to countries which have insufficient or no manufacturing capacity; provided such importing country has either granted a compulsory license for import or by notification or otherwise allowed importation of the patented pharmaceutical products from India (in accordance with the Doha Declaration on TRIPS and Public Health) Section 3 (d) regarding patentability.

## EFFECTS OF 2005 AMENDMENT

The amendment intended to make Indian drug and pharmaceutical industries competitive at par with multinational companies. Despite initial reservations, Indian pharmaceutical companies manufacturing generic drugs have flourished in the last decade. Also, MNCs have opened R&D Centres in India. An increased prices of products due to the new patent regime was considered to be a major hindrance during the time the amendment was passed. However, the government has taken proactive measures to ensure low prices for essential drugs, and has used compulsory licensing as a tool to keep exorbitant prices under check Issues around Section 3(d).

## ISSUES AROUND SECTION 3(d)

Section 3 of the Patents Act speaks of inventions which are not patentable. Section 3(d) of the Patents Act was introduced by the 2005 Amendment. The section sets a 'novelty' standard. For a product to be patentable, something genuinely new should have been discovered or added to an existing product. The section stipulates conditions under which the product will not be patentable: If the alleged 'new product' just involves the discovery of a new form of an existing substance, and it does not enhance the efficacy of the older form of the product. Mere discovery of a new use for an already known substance. Mere discovery of any new property. Modified usage of an already existing and known process, machine or apparatus without it resulting in a new product or employing at least one new reactant The part of section 3(d) that has been controversial is the part which prohibits granting of patents for mere discovery of new usage of known substance. To better illustrate through an example, Aspirin was initially used to alleviate headaches and other ailments. However, it was later discovered that Aspirin also serves as a blood-thinner and can be used in the treatment of cardiovascular diseases. Now, a new patent for Aspirin cannot be filed just because a new use was discovered for the same product. The above portion of section 3(d) along with the part prohibiting granting of patents for discovery of new form of a known substance has been exploited by pharmaceutical companies to evergreen patents.

## WHAT ARE THE RIGHTS GRANTED BY PATENT?

If the grant of the patent is for a product, then the patentee has a right to prevent others from making, using, offering for sale, selling or importing the patented product in India. If the patent is for a process, then the patentee has the right to prevent others from using the process, using the product directly obtained by the process, offering for sale, selling or importing the product in India directly obtained by the process.

## WHAT IS NOT PATENTABLE IN INDIA?

Before filing an application for grant of patent in India, it is important to note 'What is not Patentable in India?' Following, i.e., an invention which is (a) frivolous, (b) obvious, (c) contrary to well established natural laws, (d) contrary to law, (e) morality, (f) injurious to public health, (g) a mere discovery of a scientific principle, (h) the formulation of an abstract theory, (i) a mere discovery of any new property or new use for a known substance or process, machine or apparatus, (j) a substance obtained by a mere admixture resulting only in the aggregation of the properties of the components thereof or a process for producing such substance, (k) a mere arrangement or rearrangement or duplication of known devices, (l) a method of agriculture or horticulture and (m) inventions relating to atomic energy, are not patentable in India.

## NOVARTIS CASE

In the Novartis case of 2013, the applicability of section 3(d) of the Patents Act was discussed. In this case, the Supreme Court of India upheld an order rejecting 'Novartis' patent for its drug, Glivec, which helps fight cancer. The Court ruled that the alleged new drug Glivec was only a 'beta-crystalline' form of the already existing cancer drug Imatinib. Hence, Glivec was just a new form of a known substance, imatinib, and therefore the patent for Glivec was rejected under section 3(d) of the Patents Act. Novartis brought up the issue of Article 27 of TRIPS which states that, patents are available for inventions provided they are new and involve an inventive step capable of industrial applications as a member of TRIPS, India is required to strictly adhere to comply with this. However, if a country deems it necessary, it may go over and above the basic framework that TRIPS provides. In the case of section 3(d) that is what India has done. It has raised the benchmark for inventiveness provided by TRIPS by introducing the requirement of 'enhanced efficacy' in the new product. This was challenged by Novartis, but the SC ruled that India was well within its right to add this requirement. Also, section 3(d) has been approved by the WHO Public Health, Innovation and IPR Report, 2006, which states that, countries can adopt legislation and guidelines which require a level of inventiveness that would prevent ever-greening of patents. However, despite this, section 3(d) of the Patents Act has attracted controversy and the ire of the USA.

## GOOD OUTCOMES/PRAISE OF THE DECISION

The Novartis judgment was welcomed by WHO, MSF (Medecins sans Frontieres) and other groups for its efforts to curb evergreening of patents. The decision puts a stop to evergreening of patents by pharmaceutical companies and limits their monopolistic tendencies. Considering the widespread poverty and lack of affordable medicines in India, the decision provides relief to thousands of persons struggling to buy medicines, because the rejection of the patent allows generic companies to produce cheaper alternatives. Also, some experts believe that this high bar for 'invention' set by the courts will spur the pharmaceutical companies to invest more in R&D because they are left with no option but to invent new medicines since evergreening is strictly curbed.

## BAD OUTCOMES/CRITICISM OF THE DECISION

Many critics have opined that this decision will curb innovation because it reduces the incentives for pharmaceutical companies to do so. Lack of profits for pharmaceutical companies might lead to reduced expenditure on R&D, which will result in lack of progress in developing treatments/medicines for various diseases. India is now perceived as a nation with a weak IPR ( regime. This might discourage MNCs from entering Indian markets.

## CRITICISM AGAINST INDIA'S PATENT REGIME

The USA has been leading the charge against India's Patent regime. The Global Intellectual Property Centre, which is an affiliate of the US Chamber of Commerce, ranked India the lowest out of 25 countries in its International IP Index for having the weakest intellectual property environment. In May 2014, the US Trade Representative's report, the Special 301, decided to conduct an out-of-turn review of India's intellectual property regime. Also, there is a pending US International Trade Commission investigation to determine whether India applied its patent laws in a manner adversely affecting American pharmaceutical companies. Some of the specific areas in which India's patent regime is criticized is given below:

- Indian Patent Law allows for a mechanism termed pre-grant opposition, which allows a third party to challenge the validity of a patent applications before it is granted. Such a procedure is not recognized in most countries. However, it gives a much-required opportunity to NGOs and other such public-spirited to bodies to present their case, and hence, plays a uniquely important role in India. Pre-grant opposition has led to the rejection of patents of many American companies, and hence, the USA has expressed disapproval of this mechanism. Globally too, the USA has taken measures to limit the employment of this mechanism by countries by including provisions in its trade agreements pre-emptively prohibiting countries from introducing pre-grant opposition.
- Another controversial decision has been the granting of India's first compulsory license to Bayer's patented drug Nexavar. Critics fear that this will open the floodgates, leading to a plethora of compulsory licenses being issued. However, compulsory licensing is allowed by TRIPS itself and the Patents Act too. And, in all these years, India has invoked this provision only once.
- Further, the move has forced the pharmaceutical companies to evolve new pricing strategies. After the compulsory license was granted, there was a deluge of price cuts across drugs. This brought some

much-needed relief to the people, and goes to prove effectiveness of the mechanism. A major criticism of the patent regime in India is that it doesn't adequately protect intellectual property. However, India is in full compliance with the clauses of TRIPS. Also, all the recent controversial decisions, be it regarding compulsory licensing or rejecting of patents has been done in accordance with the law, and the legality of these decisions has been established by the courts of the country.

## NATIONAL INTELLECTUAL PROPERTY RIGHTS (IPR) POLICY

The Union Cabinet on 13 May 2016 approved the National IPR Policy that will lay the future roadmap for intellectual property in India. The Policy recognizes the abundance of creative and innovative energies that flow in India, and the need to tap into and channelize these energies towards a better and brighter future for all.

The National IPR Policy is a vision document that aims to create and exploit synergies between all forms of intellectual property (IP), concerned statutes and agencies. It sets in place an institutional mechanism for implementation, monitoring and review. It aims to incorporate and adapt global best practices to the Indian scenario. This policy shall weave in the strengths of the government, research and development organizations, educational institutions, corporate entities including MSMEs, start-ups and other stakeholders in the creation of an innovation-conducive environment, which stimulates creativity and innovation across sectors, as also facilitates a stable, transparent and service-oriented IPR administration in the country.

The Policy recognizes that India has a well-established TRIPS-compliant legislative, administrative and judicial framework to safeguard IPRs, which meets its international obligations while utilizing the flexibilities provided in the international regime to address its developmental concerns. It reiterates India's commitment to the Doha Development Agenda and the TRIPS agreement.

While IPRs are becoming increasingly important in the global arena, there is a need to increase awareness on IPRs in India, be it regarding the IPRs owned by oneself or respect for others' IPRs. The importance of IPRs as a marketable financial asset and economic tool also needs to be recognized. For this, domestic IP filings, as also commercialization of patents granted, need to increase. Innovation and sub-optimal spending on R&D too are issues to be addressed.

### ❖ Vision Statement

An India where creativity and innovation are stimulated by Intellectual Property for the benefit of all; an India where intellectual property promotes advancement in science and technology, arts and culture, traditional knowledge and biodiversity resources; an India where knowledge is the main driver of development, and knowledge owned is transformed into knowledge shared.

### ❖ Mission Statement

Stimulate a dynamic, vibrant and balanced IPR system in India to foster creativity and innovation and thereby, promote entrepreneurship and enhance socio-economic and cultural development, and focus on enhancing access to healthcare, food security and environmental protection, among other sectors of vital social, economic and technological importance.

### ❖ Objectives

The Policy lays down the following seven objectives:

1. **IPR Awareness: Outreach and Promotion:** To create public awareness about the economic, social and cultural benefits of IPRs among all sections of society.

2. **Generation of IPRs:** To stimulate the generation of IPRs.
3. **Legal and Legislative Framework:** To have strong and effective IPR laws, which balance the interests of rights owners with larger public interest.
4. **Administration and Management:** To modernize and strengthen service-oriented IPR administration.
5. **Commercialization of IPRs:** Get value for IPRs through commercialization.
6. **Enforcement and Adjudication:** To strengthen the enforcement and adjudicatory mechanisms for combating IPR infringements.
7. **Human Capital Development:** To strengthen and expand human resources, institutions and capacities for teaching, training, research and skill building in IPRs.

These objectives are sought to be achieved through detailed action points. The action by different Ministries/Departments shall be monitored by DIPP, which shall be the nodal department to coordinate, guide and oversee implementation and future development of IPRs in India.

The National IPR Policy will endeavour for a 'Creative India; Innovative India: रचनात्मक भारत; अभिनव भारत'.

## EXCHANGE RATE MECHANISM

The exchange rate is the price of a nation's currency in terms of another nation's currency. It is a central concept in international finance. Virtually any nation's currency can be converted into the currency of any other nation, based on exchange rates in the foreign exchange market.

The growth in international trade resulted in evolution of foreign exchange, i.e., value of one currency of one country versus value of currency of other country. Each country has its own 'brand' alongside its flag. When money is branded it is called 'currency'. Whenever there is a cross-border trade, there is need to exchange one brand of money for another, and this exchange of two currencies is called 'foreign exchange' or simply 'forex' (FX).

The smooth functioning of international trade required a universally accepted foreign currency to settle the internal trade and a way to balance the trade imbalances amongst countries. This led to the question of determining relative value of two currencies.

Different systems were tried in past to arrive at relative value of two currencies. The documented history suggests that sometime in 1870 countries agreed to value their currencies against value of currency of other country using gold as the benchmark for valuation. As per this process, central banks issue paper currency and hold equivalent amount of gold in their reserve. The value of each currency against another currency was derived from gold exchange rate. For example, if one unit of gold is valued at Indian Rupees (INR) 10,000 and US dollar (USD) 500 than the exchange rate of INR versus USD would be 1 USD = INR 20. This mechanism of valuing currency was called as gold standard.

With further growth in international trade, changing political situations (world wars, civil wars, etc.) and situations of deficit/surplus on trade account forced countries to shift from gold standard to floating exchange rates. In the floating exchange regime, central bank's intervention was a popular tool to manage the value of currency to maintain the trade competitiveness of the country. Central bank would either buy or sell the local currency depending on the desired direction and value of local currency.

During 1944–1971, countries adopted a system called Bretton Woods System. This system was a blend of gold standard system and floating rate system. As part of the system, all currencies were pegged to USD at a fixed rate and USD value was pegged to gold. The USA guaranteed to other central banks that they can convert their currency into USD at any time and USD value will be pegged to value of gold. Countries also agreed to maintain the exchange rate in the range of plus or minus 1 per cent of the fixed parity with US dollar. With adoption of this system, USD became the dominant currency of the world.

Finally, Bretton Woods system was suspended and countries adopted system of free floating or managed float method of valuing the currency. Developed countries gradually moved to a market-determined exchange rate and developing countries adopted either a system of pegged currency or a system of managed rate. In pegged system, the value of currency is pegged to another currency or a basket of currencies. The benefit of pegged currency is that it creates an environment of stability for foreign investors as they know the value of their investment in the country at any point of time would be fixed.

Although in long run, it is difficult to maintain the peg and ultimately the central bank may change the value of peg or move to a managed float or free float. In managed float, countries have controls on flow of capital and central bank intervention is a common tool to contain sharp volatility and direction of currency movement.

## MAJOR CURRENCY PAIRS

The most traded currency pairs in the world are called the Majors. The list includes following currencies: Euro (EUR), US Dollar (USD), Japanese Yen (JPY), Pound Sterling (GBP), Australian Dollar (AUD), Canadian Dollar (CAD), and the Swiss Franc (CHF). These currencies follow free floating method of valuation. Amongst these currencies the most active currency pairs are: EURUSD, USDJPY, GBPUSD, AUDUSD, CADUSD and USDCHF.

## CURRENCY PRICE

Exchange rates are constantly changing, which means that the value of one currency in terms of the other is constantly in flux. Changes in rates are expressed as strengthening or weakening of one currency vis-à-vis the other currency. Changes are also expressed as appreciation or depreciation of one currency in terms of the other currency. Whenever the base currency buys more of the quotation currency, the base currency has strengthened / appreciated, and the quotation currency has weakened / depreciated. For example, if USDINR (US Dollar–Indian Rupee) has moved from 44.00 to 44.25, the USD has appreciated and the INR has depreciated. Similarly to say that USD looks strong over next few months would mean that USD-INR pair may move towards 45.00 from the current levels of 44.00.

There are multiple factors impacting the value of the currency at any given point of time. Some of the factors are of the local country while others could be from global markets. For example, the value of INR against USD is a function of factors local to India like gross domestic product (GDP) growth rate, balance of payment situation, deficit situation, inflation, interest rate scenario, policies related to inflow and outflow of foreign capital. It is also a function of factors like prices of crude oil, value of USD against other currency pairs and geopolitical situation.

All the factors are at work all the time, and therefore, some factors may act towards strengthening of currency and others may act towards weakening. It becomes important to identify the dominating factors at any point of time as those factors would decide the direction of currency movement. For example, economic factors in India might be very good indicating continued inflow of foreign capital and hence appreciation of INR. However, in global markets USD is strengthening against other currency pairs (on account of multiple factors). In this situation, local factors are acting towards strengthening and global factors towards weakening of INR.

One needs to assess which factors are more dominating at a point of time and accordingly take decision on likelihood of appreciation or depreciation of INR. In the very short term, demand supply mismatch would also have bearing on the direction of currency's movement. The extent of impact of demand supply mismatch is very high on days when market is illiquid or on currency pairs with thin trading volumes. For USD-INR, demand supply factors have considerable impact on the currency movement. For example, on some day INR may appreciate on account of large USD inflow (ECB conversion/large FDI/or any other reason) despite the trend of weakness driven by economic factors. Once the USD inflow is absorbed by the market, INR may again depreciate. Therefore, it is important to keep track of such demand supply related news.

To assess the impact of economic factors on the currency market, it is important to understand the key economic concepts, key data releases, their interpretation and impact on market.

The analytical tools of foreign-exchange market are the same as that of stock market: fundamental analysis and technical analysis. The underlying assumption of use of technical analysis in FX is same as that of stock market: price is assumed to have captured all news and available information and the charts are the objects of analysis. However, with respect to fundamental analysis, unlike companies countries do not have a balance sheet; do not have earnings report, etc. The fundamental analysis is all about looking at the intrinsic value of an investment, its application in FX means analysis of the economic conditions of the country that may affect the value of its currency.

Since currency market is a globalized market and the value of currency is always determined against another currency, therefore fundamental analysis in FX market also means analysis of economic conditions in other major countries of the world.

## FOREIGN EXCHANGE MARKETS

It is the market in which participants buy, sell, exchange and speculate on currencies. Foreign exchange markets comprises of banks including central banks, companies, investment management firms, hedge funds, and retail forex brokers and investors.

This global market has two tiers. The first is the Interbank Market. It's where the biggest banks exchange currencies with each other. Even though it only has a few members, the trades are enormous. As a result, it dictates currency values. The second tier is the over-the-counter (OTC) market. That's where individuals trade. The OTC has become very popular since there are now many companies that offer online trading platforms.

Indian currency market is increasingly getting aligned to international markets. The opening levels of OTC market are primarily dependent on the development in international markets since closing of domestic market on the previous day.

## RBI REFERENCE RATE

RBI reference rate is the rate published daily by RBI for spot rate for various currency pairs. The rates are arrived at by averaging the mean of the bid/offer rates polled from a few select banks during a random five minute window between 11:45 AM and 12:15 PM, and the daily press on RBI reference rate is be issued every week-day (excluding Saturdays) at around 12:30 PM. The contributing banks are selected on the basis of their standing, market share in the domestic foreign exchange market and representative character. The Reserve Bank periodically reviews the procedure for selecting the banks and the methodology of polling so as to ensure that the reference rate is a true reflection of the market activity. There is an increasing trend of large value FX transaction being done at RBI reference rate even on OTC market. The reference rate is a transparent price which is publicly available from an authentic source.

## VALUE OF RUPEE AGAINST DOLLAR DWINDLING

The Indian rupee has witnessed huge volatility in 2013 to 2017. This volatility has affected major macro-economic data, including growth, inflation, trade and investment. Managing volatility in the currency markets has become a big challenge for policymakers. Despite of a series of measures taken by the central bank as well as the government to curb the volatility in the markets, the rupee continued to depreciate.

## JOURNEY OF RUPEE

The Indian currency has witnessed a slippery journey since Independence. When India got freedom on 15 August 1947, the value of the rupee was on a par with the American dollar. There were no foreign borrowings on India's balance sheet.

To finance welfare and development activities, especially with the introduction of the Five-Year Plan in 1951, the government started external borrowings. This required the devaluation of the rupee. After independence, India had chosen to adopt a fixed rate currency regime. The rupee was pegged at 4.79 against a dollar between 1948 and 1966.

Two consecutive wars, one with China in 1962 and another one with Pakistan in 1965; resulted in a huge deficit on India's budget, forcing the government to devalue the currency to 7.57 against the dollar. The rupee's link with the British currency was broken in 1971, and it was linked directly to the US dollar.

In 1975, value of the Indian rupee was pegged at 8.39 against a dollar. In 1985, it was further devalued to 12 against a dollar.

In 1991, India faced a serious balance of payment crisis and was forced to sharply devalue its currency. The country was in the grip of high inflation, low growth and the foreign reserves were not even worth to meet three weeks of imports. Under these situations, the currency was devalued to 17.90 against a dollar.

The year 1993 was very important. This year currency was let free to flow with the market sentiments. The exchange rate was freed to be determined by the market, with provisions of intervention by the central bank under the situation of extreme volatility. This year, the currency was devalued to 31.37 against a dollar. The rupee traded in the range of 40–50 between 2000 and 2010.

It was mostly at around 45 against a dollar. It touched a high of 39 in 2007. The Indian currency has gradually depreciated since the global 2008 economic crisis. Liberalizing the currency regime led to a sharp jump in foreign investment inflows and boosted the economic growth.

In August 2013, the Indian rupee extended falls to a new low of 65.50 to the dollar as heavy demand from importers along with weak domestic equities continued to weigh on sentiment. Rupee crossed 68 mark on the

20 January 2016. This movement was quite unexpected as the fundamentals had justified a level of 65–66.

## MAJOR REASONS FOR FALL OF RUPEE

1. **Global economic slowdown:** This was the major factor which is contributing to both the stock markets and Indian currency fall. China's yuan devaluation had also hurt the sentiments globally. China was witnessing a slowdown. IMF cited a sharp slowdown in China trade and weak commodity prices that was hammering Brazil and other emerging markets.
2. **Crude oil prices:** The USA is the biggest importer of crude oil. So when the crude prices go down, it means the USA will be saving more dollars to buy it, as a result dollar as a currency strengthens, leading to fall of Indian rupee and other currencies at the forex market.
3. FIIs were in the sell-off ode in equity segment.
4. **India's Trade deficit:** Trade deficit during December 2015 widened to $11.6 billion as against $9.17 billion in December 2014.

## HOW RUPEE-DOLLAR RATES ARE DETERMINED?

If the demand for dollars increases, the value of dollar will appreciate. As the quotation for Rs/$ is a two way quote (that is, the price of one dollar is quoted in terms of how much rupees it takes to buy one dollar), an appreciation in the value of dollar would automatically mean a depreciation in Indian rupee and vice-versa.

Besides the primary powers of demand and supply, the rupee-dollar rates are determined by other market forces like:

1. **Market Sentiments:** During turbulent markets, investors usually prefer to park their money in safe havens such as the US treasuries, Swiss franc, gold and so on to avoid losses to their portfolios. This flight to safety would lead to foreign investors redeeming their investments from India. This could increase the demand for dollar vis-à-vis Indian rupees.
2. **Speculation:** There are derivative instruments and OTC currency instruments through which one can speculate/hedge the underlying currency rates. When speculators sense improvements/deterioration of the sentiments of the markets, they too want to benefit from such rising/falling dollar. They then start buying/selling dollar which would further change the demand/supply of the dollar.
3. **RBI Intervention:** When there is too much volatility in the rupee-dollar rates, the RBI prevents the rates from going out of control to protect the domestic economy. The RBI does this by buying dollars when rupee appreciates too much and by selling dollars when the rupee depreciates significantly.
4. **Imports and Exports:** Ever give thought as to why our government is trying to incentivize exports and reduce imports? There are a lot of schemes and incentives for exporters while importers are burdened with many conditions and taxes. This is to protect our economy from high rupee depreciation. Importing foreign goods requires us to make payment in dollars thus strengthening the dollar's demand. Exports do the exact reverse.
5. **Public Debt/Fiscal Policy:** Whenever our government fails to match expenses with equivalent revenue, there is a shortage of funds. To finance this, the government at times opts to borrow money from institutions such as the World Bank and the IMF. This debt, accrued interests, and

the payments made, also lead to currency fluctuations.

6. **Interest Rates:** The prevailing interest rates on the government bonds attract foreign capital to India. If the rates are high enough to cover the foreign market risk and if the foreign investor is comfortable with the fundamentals or credit ratings, money would start pouring into India and thus provide us with a supply of dollars.

## DEVALUATION OF A CURRENCY

In simple terms, devaluation means a reduction in the official value of domestic currency. It is a deliberate downward adjustment to the value of a country's currency relative to another currency or group of currencies. In devaluation, the exchange rate is treated as an exogenous variable, where its value is predetermined. Its counterpart, the depreciation of the domestic currency means that the value of the exchange rate is continuously changing due to changes in the demand for and the supply of foreign currency. Due to excess supply of domestic currency, the value of the exchange rate decreases. Hence, the exchange rate is treated as an endogenous variable. Except for expectations effects, the impact exerted on economic variables by depreciation of the domestic currency is the same as that exerted by devaluation of the domestic currency.

The devaluation can have an expansionary or contractionary effect on economic growth. Policies like building up institutions, privatization of the public sector and devaluation of the currency have been used in order to create a sustainable economic development. Many development organizations like IMF support the idea of devaluation of currency as one means of economic growth besides the financial aid and loans to their member countries for the development of domestic firms. It will increase competitiveness of firms and increase the production of domestic products and output. However, some economists have shed light on the negative effect of devaluation on output.

### ❖ Advantages of Devaluation

Traditional views in macroeconomics such as Keynesians approach emphasized the expansionary effects of devaluation to output and growth. In this approach, output is determined by aggregate demand and devaluation has positive effect by simulating aggregate demand and output. Devaluation has an expansionary effect through 'expenditure switching and reducing effect'. It can help shift the demand from foreign goods to domestically produced goods. In addition, when there is devaluation in a country the price of imported goods will increase, whereas the price of domestic goods will decrease which in turn will increase the export of goods. The devaluation of currency can improve the trade balance as well as GDP in the long run.

When a currency is devaluated the amount of profit gained by a firm from the foreign market increases, when profit is converted into the local currency. This increase in profit can be used for the development of the R& D. Consequently, the improvement and introduction of new technologies through profit will decrease the cost used which in turn increase output.

The increase in export sector and innovations may leads to 'investment- led growth'. This rise in investments results in growth in GDP. As the cost of imported goods increases people tend shift to domestic goods.

By devaluing the currency, trade deficits are lowered which also favours the BoP and thus helps the economy by providing temporary relief. Because of Competitive Devaluation, a nation's export competitiveness improves as it lowers the cost of goods exported from that nation for overseas buyers.

China is an export-driven economy and in order to sustain, the Chinese government has been constantly devaluing its currency.

### ❖ Disadvantages of Devaluation

Despites its expansionary effect devaluation of currency has a negative impact on the growth of a country. For a country that is highly dependent in the non-tradable sector, devaluation can have a negative impact. The distribution of resource from the profit gained in the exposed sector to the non-exposed sector and the cost of price for imported goods used for production will not be proportional. Due to this, the unexposed sector as well as the total output growth goes down.

Devaluation can result in high profit for firms that are exposed to the market. But sometimes this high profit will make firms idle if there is less competition, favourable situation and finally result in no change in the long run.

According to the theory of transformation firms will increase their productivity and become more creative when there is high competition, sudden fall in the demand of products or an increase production cost and result in a low profit.

The increase in price of goods as a result of devaluation may decrease the total money in circulation (real money). A devaluation will push the interest rate upwards and decrease the aggregate demand *ceteris paribus*. Domestic firms that use bank loan for production will also be affected as a result of the increase in the interest rate. For countries that borrow money and are highly in debt, the increase in interest rate together with devaluation of currency will make situations even worse as the amount will increase

Countries that use devaluation as one strategy for growth and provide low price in the foreign market may at the end get a zero profit in the long run. This is true for developing countries specially those who are new comers to the world market and devalue their currency with respect to the developed ones, are usually highly in debt. So the gain through lower price will be offset by the increase in the amount of debt in foreign currency which will be more expensive if the country devaluate its currency and will result in stagnancy in the economy.

Devaluation of currency in a country where there is a wage indexation may have contractionary effect. When the price of goods increase as a result of devaluation of currency the real wage will fall and producers will be forced to increase the wage rate in order to make workers attain sustainable rate of living cost. This will decrease the profit of producers as their cost will increase.

In addition, studies show that the result of anticipated and unanticipated devaluation might have different effects on the long run growth rate.

A devaluation will increase import prices which will reduce real wages due to the increase in the price of traded goods and have a negative effects on consumption demand in the short run. Higher import prices may also have a negative effect on investments especially if firms are expecting devaluations in the future.

## DEVALUATION OF THE RUPEE

After independence in 1947, India has faced two major financial crises and two consequent devaluations of the rupee. These crises were in 1966 and 1991, and they had similar causes.

### ❖ The 1966 Devaluation

As a developing economy, it is to be expected that India would import more than it exports. Despite government attempts to obtain a positive trade balance, India has had consistent BoP deficits since the 1950s. The 1966 devaluation was the result of the first major financial crisis the government faced. There is a general agreement among economists that by 1966, inflation had caused Indian prices to become much higher than world prices at the pre-devaluation exchange rate. When the exchange rate is fixed and a country experiences high inflation relative to other countries, country's goods become more expensive and foreign goods become cheaper. Therefore, inflation tends to increase imports and decrease exports.

Two additional factors played a role in the 1966 devaluation. The first was India's war with Pakistan in late 1965. The USA and other countries friendly towards Pakistan, withdrew foreign aid to India, which further necessitated devaluation. In addition, the large amount of deficit spending required by any war effort also accelerated inflation and led to a further disparity between Indian and international prices. The second factor is the drought of 1965/1966.

India's system of severe restrictions on international trade began in 1957 when the government experienced a BoP crisis. This crisis was caused by a current account deficit. The large current account deficit was largely a result of the Second Five-Year Plan which mandated higher imports, especially of capital goods. Another factor behind the current account deficit was the increase in freight costs due to hostilities in West Asia. Unlike in 1966 and 1991, India did not explicitly devalue the rupee but instead accomplished what Srinivasan refers to as a 'de facto' devaluation by imposing Quantitative Restrictions (QRs) on trade rather than imposing higher tariffs.

### ❖ The 1991 Devaluation

The year 1991 is often cited as the year of economic reform in India. The government's economic policies changed drastically in that year, but the 1991 liberalization was an extension of earlier, albeit slower, reform efforts that had begun in the 1970s when India relaxed restrictions on imported capital goods as part of its industrialization plan.

After 1991, the Government of India further reduced trade barriers by lowering tariffs on imports. In the post-liberalization era, quantitative restrictions have not been significant.

While the devaluation of 1991 was economically necessary to avert a financial crisis, the radical changes in India's economic policies were, to some extent, undertaken voluntarily by the government of P. V. Narasimha Rao. As in 1966, there was foreign pressure on India to reform its economy, but in 1991, the government committed itself to liberalization and followed through on that commitment.

## EXTERNAL DEBT

External debt refers to money borrowed from a source outside the country. It can be obtained from foreign commercial banks, international financial institutions (i.e., IMF, World Bank, and ADB) and from the government of foreign nations. Normally, these loans are to be used for a predefined purpose as determined by a consensus of the borrower and the lender. The government and corporations are eligible to raise loans from abroad.

External debt is considered a significant source of income for developing countries. They rely much on foreign debt to finance its BoP deficit and saving investment gap.

Economic theory suggests that reasonable levels of borrowing by a developing country are likely to enhance its economic growth. Countries at early stages of development have small stocks of capital and are likely to have investment opportunities with rates of return higher than those in advanced economies. As long as they use the borrowed funds for productive investment and do not suffer from macroeconomic instability, policies that distort economic incentives, or sizable adverse shocks, growth should increase and allow for timely debt repayments.

However, large levels of accumulated debt lead to lower growth. This happens because of 'debt overhang' which show that if there is some likelihood that, in the future, debt will be larger than the country's repayment ability, expected debt-service costs will discourage further domestic and foreign investment and thus harm growth. Potential investors will fear that the more a country produces, the more it will be 'taxed' by creditors to service the external debt, and thus they will be less willing to incur costs today for the sake of increased output in the future. This argument is represented in the debt 'Laffer curve', which posits that larger debt stocks tend to be associated with lower probabilities of debt repayment.

A debt crisis may take place if a country with a weak economy is unable to repay external debt due to the inability to produce and sell goods and make a profitable return. The IMF is one of the agencies that keep track of the country's external debt.

## INDIA'S EXTERNAL DEBT

India's external debt data is published quarterly, with a lag of one quarter. Statistics for the first two quarters of the calendar year are compiled and published by the Reserve Bank of India. Data for the last two quarters is compiled and published by the Ministry of Finance. The Government of India also publishes an annual status report on the debt which contains detailed statistical analysis of the country's external debt position.

India's external debt was US$ 570 billion at the end of March 2021. It recorded an increase of US$ 11.6 billion over its level at end of March 2020. The external debt to GDP ratio increased to 21.1% at end of March 2021 from 20.6% an year ago.

The foreign currency reserves increased to over US $579 billion at the end of March 2021 compared to over US $474 billion at the end of March 2020.

India's external debt is held in multiple currencies, the largest of which is the United States dollar. As on 31 March 2020, 53.7% of the country's debt was held in U.S. dollars. The rest of the debt is held in Indian rupees (31.9%), Japanese yen (5.6%), special drawing rights (4.5%), Euros (3.5%) and other currencies (0.8%).

❑❑❑

# CHAPTER 10 Inflation

## MEANING OF INFLATION

Inflation is highly controversial term and undergoes many modifications since it was first defined by the neoclassical economists as a **monetary phenomenon**. Inflation simply means **a continuous increase in general price level**. It can be described as a decline in the real value of money or a loss of purchasing power in the medium of exchange. When the general price level rises, each unit of currency buys fewer goods and services. Inflation has been defined in several ways by different economists:

Coulbourn, 'Inflation is too much of money chasing too few goods'.

Keynes, 'Inflation is the form of taxation which the public finds hardest to evade'.

### ❖ Types of Inflation

Inflation can be of different types based on certain important aspects.

**A. Types of Inflation based on Time of Occurrence**

1. **War-time Inflation:** Inflation that takes place during the period of a war-like situation is known as War-time Inflation. During a war, scare productive resources are all diverted and prioritized to produce military goods and equipment.
2. **Post-war Inflation:** Inflation that takes place soon after a war is known as Post-war Inflation. After the war, government controls are relaxed, resulting in a faster hike in prices than what experienced during the war.
3. **Peace-time Inflation:** When prices rise during a normal period of peace, it is known as Peace-time Inflation. It is due to huge government expenditure or spending on capital projects of a long gestation (development) period.

**B. Types of Inflation based on Rising Prices**

1. **Creeping Inflation:** When prices are gently rising, it is referred as Creeping Inflation. It is the mildest form of inflation and also known as a **Mild Inflation or Low Inflation**. According to R.P. Kent, when prices rise by not more than (up to) 3 per cent per annum (year), it is called Creeping Inflation.
2. **Chronic Inflation:** If creeping inflation persist (continues to increase) for a longer period of time then it is often called as Chronic or **Secular Inflation**. It is called chronic because if an inflation rate continues to grow for a longer period without any downturn, then it possibly leads to Hyperinflation.

3. **Walking Inflation:** When the rate of rising prices is more than the Creeping Inflation, it is known as Walking Inflation. When prices rise by more than 3 per cent but less than 10 per cent per annum (i.e. between 3 per cent and 10 per cent per annum), it is called as Walking Inflation. According to some economists, walking inflation must be taken seriously as it gives a cautionary signal for the occurrence of Running Inflation. Furthermore, if Walking Inflation is not checked in due time it can eventually result in Galloping Inflation.
4. **Moderate Inflation:** Prof. Samuelson clubbed together concept of Creeping and Walking Inflation into Moderate Inflation. When prices rise by less than 10 per cent per annum (single digit inflation rate), it is known as Moderate Inflation. According to Prof. Samuelson, it is a stable inflation and not a serious economic problem.
5. **Running Inflation:** A rapid acceleration in the rate of rising prices is referred as Running Inflation. When prices rise by more than 10 per cent per annum, running inflation occurs. Though economists have not suggested a fixed range for measuring running inflation, we may consider price rise between 10 per cent and 20 per cent per annum (double digit inflation rate) as a running inflation.
6. **Galloping Inflation:** According to Prof. Samuelson, if prices rise by double or triple digit inflation rates like 30 per cent or 400 per cent or 999 per cent per annum, then the situation can be termed as Galloping Inflation. It is also referred as Jumping Inflation.
7. **Hyperinflation:** Hyperinflation refers to a situation where the prices rise at an alarming high rate. The prices rise so fast that it becomes very difficult to measure its magnitude. However, in quantitative terms, when prices rise above 1000 per cent per annum (quadruple or four digit inflation rate), it is termed as Hyperinflation.

   During a worst-case scenario of hyperinflation, value of national currency (money) of an affected country reduces almost to zero. Paper money becomes worthless and people start trading either in gold and silver or sometimes even use the old barter system of commerce. Two worst examples of hyperinflation recorded in world history are of those experienced by Hungary in year 1946 and Zimbabwe during 2004–2009 under Robert Mugabe's regime.

### C. Types of Inflation Based on Causes

1. **Deficit Inflation:** Deficit inflation takes place due to deficit financing.
2. **Credit Inflation:** Credit inflation takes place due to excessive bank credit or money supply in the economy.
3. **Scarcity Inflation:** Scarcity Inflation occurs due to hoarding. Hoarding is an excess accumulation of basic commodities by unscrupulous traders and black marketers.
4. **Profit Inflation:** When entrepreneurs are interested in boosting their profit margins, prices rise.
5. **Pricing Power Inflation:** It is often referred as Administered Price Inflation. It occurs when industries and business houses increase the price of their goods and services with an objective to boost their profit margins. It does not occur during a financial crisis and economic depression, and is not seen when there is a downturn in the economy. As Oligopolies have the ability to set prices of their goods and services it is also called as Oligopolistic Inflation.
6. **Tax Inflation:** Due to rise in indirect taxes, sellers charge high price to the consumers.

7. **Wage Inflation:** If the rise in wages in not accompanied by a rise in output, prices rise.
8. **Build-in Inflation:** Vicious cycle of Build-in Inflation is induced by adaptive expectations of workers or employees who try to keep their wages or salaries high in anticipation of inflation. Employers and Organizations raise the prices of their respective goods and services in anticipation of the workers or employees' demands. This overall builds a vicious cycle of rising wages followed by an increase in general prices of commodities. This cycle, if continues, keeps on accumulating inflation at each round turn and thereby results into what is called as Build-in Inflation.
9. **Development Inflation:** During the process of development of economy, incomes increases, causing an increase in demand and rise in prices.
10. **Fiscal Inflation:** It occurs due to excess government expenditure or spending when there is a budget deficit.
11. **Population Inflation:** Prices rise due to a rapid increase in population.
12. **Foreign Trade Induced Inflation:** It is divided into two categories, viz., (a) Export-boom Inflation, and (b) Import Price-hike Inflation.
13. **Export-boom Inflation:** Considerable increase in exports may cause a shortage at home (within exporting country) and results in price rise (within exporting country). This is known as Export-boom Inflation.
14. **Import Price-hike Inflation:** If a country imports goods from a foreign country, and the prices of imported goods increases due to inflation abroad, then the prices of domestic products using imported goods also rise.
15. **Sectoral Inflation:** It occurs when there is a rise in the prices of goods and services produced by certain sector of the industries. For instance, if prices of crude oil increases then it will also affect all other sectors (like aviation, road transportation, etc.), which are directly related to the oil industry. For example if oil prices are hiked, air ticket fares and road transportation cost will increase.
16. **Demand-pull Inflation:** Inflation that arises due to various factors like rising income, exploding population, etc., leads to aggregate demand and exceeds aggregate supply, and tends to raise prices of goods and services. This is known as Demand-pull or Excess Demand Inflation.
17. **Cost-push Inflation:** When prices rise due to growing cost of production of goods and services, it is known as Cost-push (Supply-side) Inflation. For example if wages of workers are raised then the unit cost of production also increases. As a result, the prices of end-products or end-services being produced and supplied are consequently hiked.

## THEORIES OF INFLATION

There are different theories related to the concept of inflation.

1. **The Quantity Theory of Money:** The oldest surviving economic doctrine asserts that changes in the general level of general prices are determined primarily by changes in the quantity of money in circulation or a direct proportionate relation between price level and demand for money.
2. **Monetary Theory of Inflation:** Monetarism holds that 'only money matters', and as such monetary policy is a more potent instrument than fiscal policy in economic stabilization. According to the monetarists, the money supply is

the 'dominate, though not exclusive' determinant of both the level of output and prices in the short run, and of the level of prices in the long run.

3. **Demand-pull Theory:** When the value of aggregate demand exceeds the value of aggregate supply at the full employment level, the inflationary gap arises. The larger the gap between aggregate demand and aggregate supply, the more rapid is the inflation.
4. **Cost-push Theory:** Cost-push Inflation is caused by wage increases enforced by unions and profit increases by employers. The basic cause of Cost-push Inflation is the rise in money wages more rapidly than the productivity of labour. The labour unions press employers to grant wage increases considerably,. thereby raising the cost of production of commodities. Employers in turn, raise prices of their products. Higher wages enable workers to buy as much as before, in spite of higher prices. On the other hand, the increase in prices induces unions to demand still higher wages. In this way, the wage-cost spiral countries, thereby, leading to cost-push or Wage-push Inflation. Cost-push Inflation may be further aggravated by upward adjustment of wages to compensate for rise in cost of living. A few sectors of the economy may be affected by increase in money wages and prices of their products may be rising. In many cases, their products are used as inputs for the production of commodities in other sectors. As a result, cost of production of other sectors will rise and thereby push up the prices of their products. Thus wage-push inflation in a few sectors of the economy may soon lead to inflationary rise in prices in the entire economy.

   Further, an increase in the price of imported raw materials may lead to Cost-push Inflation. Another cause of Cost-push inflation is Profit-push Inflation. Oligopolist and monopolist firms raise the price of their products to offset the rise in labour and cost of production to earn higher profits. There being imperfect competition in the case of such firms, they are able to administered price of their products. Profit-push Inflation is, therefore called **Administered-price Inflation or Price-push Inflation**.

## COSTS OF INFLATION

Low Inflation is the main macroeconomic goal for most of the countries. Costs of Inflation Include:

### ❖ International Competitiveness

A relatively higher inflation rate will make Indian goods less competitive, leading to a fall in exports. However this may be offset by a decline in the exchange rate. But, if a country is in the Euro (e.g., Greece, Ireland and Spain) they can't devalue. Therefore, high inflation can be very damaging as it leads to a decline in competitiveness.

### ❖ Confusion and Uncertainty

When inflation is high, people are uncertain what to spend their money on. Also, when inflation is high firms may be less willing to invest because they are uncertain about future profits and costs. This uncertainty and confusion can lead to lower rates of economic growth over the long term.

### ❖ Shoe Leather Costs

When prices are unstable, there will be an increase in search times to discover more about prices. Inflation increases the opportunity cost of holding money, so people make more visits to their banks and building societies (wearing out their shoe leather!). In other words to save on losing interest in a bank people will hold less cash and make more trips to the bank.

### ❖ Income Redistribution

Inflation will typically make borrowers better off and lenders worse off. Inflation reduces the value of savings, especially if the saving is not index linked. However, it does depend on the real rate of interest. For example, if a saver gets a higher rate of interest than the inflation rate, he will not lose out.

### ❖ Boom and Bust Economic Cycles

High inflationary growth is unsustainable and is usually followed by a recession. By keeping inflation low, it enables a long period of economic growth. For example in the UK, low inflation helped economic growth to be more stable in the period 1992–2007. Sustainable, low inflationary, economic growth is highly desirable.

### ❖ Cost of Reducing Inflation

High inflation is deemed unacceptable therefore governments feel it is best to reduce it. This will involve higher interest rates to reduce spending and investment. This reduction in aggregate demand will lead to a decline in economic growth and unemployment.

### ❖ Fiscal Drag

The amount of tax we pay will increase if there is inflation. This is because with rising wages more people will slip into the top income tax brackets. Low inflation is often seen as harmless or even beneficial because it allows prices to adjust more easily. Inflation imposes several costs on the society.

### ❖ Inflationary Growth Is Unsustainable

High inflation is often a sign the economy is overheating (demand growing faster than supply). This kind of boom is often followed by a bust (recession). This occurred in UK in Lawson boom of 1980s – inflation rose to 10 per cent due to high growth and when the government tried to rein in inflation, it led to the 1991 recession and higher unemployment. Therefore, an inflationary boom can lead to a recession. Targeting a low rate of inflation helps to keep economic growth sustainable. Therefore, low inflation can help avoid recession and prevent a sudden rise in unemployment.

### ❖ Inflation Discourages Investment

High and volatile rates of inflation can discourage firms from taking long-term investment decisions. This is because of the uncertainty and confusion around future revenues and profits. Therefore, it is argued countries with higher inflation rates tend to have lower growth rates over time. In the post war period, it was often argued Japan and Germany had better growth rates because of their low inflation.

### ❖ Decline in International Competitiveness

High inflation is likely to make your goods and services less competitive leading to a fall in exports and current account deficit. Often this high inflation will be offset by a fall in the exchange rate to restore competitiveness. But, in the case of countries in the Euro, they can't devalue, so inflation and higher wage costs have been very damaging to their economy.

### ❖ Inflation Can Reduce Real Incomes

If inflation is above income growth, we can experience a fall in real incomes. This is an issue in 2011. High cost-push inflation of 5 per cent is above wage growth leading to falling real wages.

### ❖ Inflation Can Erode Savings

If inflation is higher than interest rates, then inflation can wipe away people's savings. Inflation reduces the value of money, so people who rely on income from savings see a reduction in their living standards. This is often a problem for pensioners who rely on savings. Therefore inflation can cause a redistribution of income in society from old to young and from savers to borrowers.

### ❖ Legacy of Inflation

If people suffer from inflation, (e.g., lose savings, become worse off) then it will impact their future decisions. For example, people may be reluctant to buy government bonds because they fear the government will effectively default through inflation. People will be more reluctant to save, leaving less room for investment.

## INFLATION MEASUREMENT IN INDIA

India uses the **Wholesale Price Index (WPI)** to calculate and then decide the rate of inflation in the economy. Most developed countries use the Consumer Price Index (CPI) to calculate inflation. The Wholesale Price Index was first published in 1902, and was one of the major economic indicators available to policy makers until it was replaced by the CPI in most developed countries by in the 1970s. Some economists argue that it is high time that India abandoned WPI and adopted CPI to calculate inflation. The Wholesale Price Index does not properly measure the exact price rise an end-consumer will experience because, as the same suggests, it is at the wholesale level.

### ❖ WPI

It is the index that is used to measure the change in the average price level of goods traded in wholesale market. In India, price data for 675 commodities is tracked through WPI which is an indicator of movement in prices of commodities in all trades and transactions. It is also the price index which is available on a weekly basis with the shortest possible time lag – two weeks. The Indian government has taken WPI as an indicator of the rate of inflation in the economy.

### ❖ CPI

It is a statistical time-series measure of a weighted average of prices of a specified set of goods and services purchased by consumers. It is a price index that tracks the prices of a specified basket of consumer goods and services, providing a measure of inflation. CPI is a fixed quantity price index and considered by some a cost of living index. Under CPI, an index is scaled so that it is equal to 100 at a chosen point in time, so that all other values of the index are a percentage relative to this one.

### ❖ Base Year of the CPI Shifted to 2012

The Central Statistics Office (CSO), Ministry of Statistics and Programme Implementation has revised the Base Year of the CPI from 2010 = 100 to 2012 = 100. In this revised series, released on 12 February 2015, many methodological changes have been incorporated, in order to make the indices more robust.

The basket of items and their weighing diagrams have been prepared using the Modified Mixed Reference Period (MMRP) data of Consumer Expenditure Survey (CES), 2011–12, of the 68th Round of National Sample Survey (NSS). This has been done to make it consistent with the international practice of shorter reference period for most of the food items and longer reference period for the items of infrequent consumption/purchase. The weighing diagrams of old series of CPI were based on the Uniform Reference Period (URP) data of CES, 2004–05, of the 61st Round of NSS. With this change in the weighing diagrams, the gap between Weight Reference Year and Price Reference Year (Base Year), which was six years in the old series, has now been reduced to six months only. Due to change in the consumption pattern from 2004–05 to 2011–12, the weighing diagrams (share of expenditure to total expenditure) have changed.

The number of Groups, which was five in the old series, has now been increased to **six.** 'Pan, tobacco and intoxicants', which was a Sub-group under the Group 'Food, beverages and Tobacco', has now been made as a separate Group. Accordingly, the Group 'Food, beverages and Tobacco' has been changed to 'Food and beverages'.

Egg, which was part of the Sub-group 'Egg, fish and meat' in the old series, has now been made as a separate Sub-group. Accordingly, the earlier Sub-group has been modified as 'Meat and fish'.

The elementary/item indices are now being computed using Geometric Mean (GM) of the Price Relatives of Current Prices with respect to Base Prices of different markets in consonance with the international practice. In the old series, Arithmetic Mean (AM) was used for that purpose. The advantage of using GM is that it moderates the volatility of the indices as GM is less affected by extreme values.

Apart from All-India CPIs (Rural, Urban and Combined) for Sub-group, Group and General Index (All-Groups), which were released for the old series, all India Item CPIs (Combined) would also be available in the public domain for the users.

The Consumer Food Price Indices (Rural, Urban and Combined) are being compiled as weighted average of the indices, as practiced earlier in the old series (only the weights have been revised).

## BASE EFFECT ON INFLATION

The base effect refers to the impact of the rise in price level (i.e., last year's inflation) in the previous year over the corresponding rise in price levels in the current year (i.e., current inflation): if the price index had risen at a high rate in the corresponding period of the previous year leading to a high inflation rate, some of the potential rise is already factored in, therefore a similar absolute increase in the Price index in the current year will lead to a relatively lower inflation rates. On the other hand, if the inflation rate was too low in the corresponding period of the previous year, even a relatively smaller rise in the Price Index will arithmetically give a high rate of current inflation.

Inflation is calculated from a base year in which a price index is assigned the number 100. For example, if the price index in 2010 was 100 and the price index in 2011 rose to 110, the inflation rate would be 10 per cent. If the price index rose to 115 in 2012, what would be the best way to assess inflation? On the one hand, prices have only risen 5 per cent over the previous year, but they've risen 15 per cent since 2010. The high inflation rate in 2011 makes the inflation rate in 2012 look relatively small and doesn't really provide an accurate picture of the level of price increases consumers are experiencing. This distortion is the base effect.

Year-on-year inflation is calculated as:

Current Rate Inflation

$$= \frac{\text{Current Price Index} - \text{Last Year's Price Index}}{\text{Last Year's Price Index}} \times 100$$

## CORE INFLATION: CONCEPT AND MEASUREMENT

### ❖ Definition

An inflation measure which excludes transitory or temporary price volatility as in the case of some commodities such as food items, energy products, etc. It reflects the inflation trend in an economy.

A dynamic consumption basket is considered the basis to obtain core inflation. Some goods and commodities have extremely volatile price movements. Core inflation is calculated using the CPI by excluding such commodities.

If temporary price shocks are taken into account, they may affect the estimated overall inflation numbers in such a way that they are different from actual inflation. To eliminate this possibility, core inflation is calculated to gauge the actual inflation apart from temporary shocks and volatility.

### ❖ Need for Core Inflation

Headline Inflation or WPI or CPI measures the cost of living in a country and tells us how expensive or cheap living in a country has become over the years and for this reason it has components weighted in more or less the same proportion you would expect to consume them.

The RBI creates monetary policy with a goal to achieve a certain target inflation rate, and the way monetary policy affects inflation is by influencing the aggregate demand in the economy.

Simply put, if RBI thinks the economy is over heated and there is high inflation, then they will raise interest rates which will make it harder for people to buy things like cars and homes on a loan and that will lower the overall demand in the economy, and in turn it cool down inflation.

However, demand is not the only factor that causes inflation, there are supply side factors as well, specially, factors like food and energy prices that are caused by international factors or temporary supply shocks that cause demand. RBI can't use the headline inflation number alone to make their decisions because these include supply side factors also which are considered temporary and volatile in nature. Two examples of such supply side shocks are the drought in 2009 and the oil price hike of 2010.

To remove the effects of such factors, RBI and other central banks use another measure of inflation which is called 'Core Inflation'. Core inflation only tracks those items that can be influenced by monetary policy, and removes the effect of other items.

In India, the measure for core inflation is WPI excluding primary articles, fuel groups and food items, and this index is called Non Food Manufacturing Index (NFMI). The NFMI consists of components that are 55 per cent of the weight of the WPI and this link does a great job of explaining how to calculate NFMI or India' Core Inflation measure.

So, in conclusion, the idea behind core inflation is that you get an index that can serve you better in gauging the effect of monetary policy on inflation rates by removing the components that are volatile in nature and are more prone to price rises due to supply side shocks.

## HEADLINE INFLATION

A measurement of price inflation that takes into account all types of inflation that an economy can experience. Unlike core inflation, headline inflation also counts changes in the price of food and energy. Because food and energy prices can rapidly increase while other types of inflation can remain low, headline inflation may not give an accurate picture of how an economy is behaving. Headline inflation is more useful for the typical household because it reflects changes in the cost of living, while core inflation is used by central banks because core inflation is less volatile and shows the effects of supply and demand on GDP better.

For long, point-to-point changes in the WPI were considered the headline inflation rate. The WPI is a weighted average of the prices of most goods produced in the economy, with the weights being their shares in domestic output and their prices those prevailing in wholesale markets. It is closer to a producer price index, reflecting more what producers charge their immediate buyers, rather than the prices that prevail at the end of the trading chain, in retail markets. Internationally, consumer price indices rather than producer price indices are the standard for measuring inflation, since they reflect the prices that ordinary citizens face and pay. India does have multiple consumer price indices (for industrial workers, non-manual employees and agricultural/rural labourers) used to assess the increase in the prices paid by these sections for the commodity bundles they consume. However, inflation measured by the WPI was treated as the measure of headline inflation. Early in 2012, the Central Statistical Organization of the government of India released a new, national, monthly, CPI, with separate indices for rural and urban areas and covering a set of final consumption goods, weighted by their share in the consumption basket and with their prices collected from retail markets. The release was supposed to mark the transition to the use by the government and the central bank of this new index rather than the WPI to compute the headline inflation rate. Given that, it is surprising that barely a year and a half since annual point-to-point inflation rates have been calculated based on this index (which was first released for January 2011, making January 2012 the first month for which we have an annual rate), the government and the media have returned to focusing on WPI-based inflation.

## METHODS TO CONTROL INFLATION

Inflation is considered to be a complex situation for an economy. If inflation goes beyond a moderate rate, it can create disastrous situations for an economy; therefore it should be under control.

The various methods to control inflation are usually grouped under three heads: monetary measures, fiscal measures and other measures.

1. **Monetary Measures:** Monetary measures aim at reducing money incomes.

   (a) **Credit Control:** One of the important monetary measures is monetary policy. The central bank of the country adopts a number of methods to control the quantity and quality of credit. For this purpose, it raises the bank rates, sells securities in the open market, raises the reserve ratio, and adopts a number of selective credit control measures, such as raising margin requirements and regulating consumer credit. Monetary policy may not be effective in controlling inflation, if inflation is due to cost-push factors. Monetary policy can only be helpful in controlling inflation due to demand-pull factors.

   **The monetary policy of a country involves the following:**

   (a) **Rise in Bank Rate:** Refers to one of the most widely used measure taken by the central bank to control inflation.

   The bank rate is the rate at which the commercial bank gets a rediscount on loans and advances by the central bank. The increase in the bank rate results in the rise of rate of interest on loans for the public. This leads to the reduction in total spending of individuals.

   **The main reasons for reduction in total expenditure of individuals are as follows:**

   (i) **Making the borrowing of money costlier:** Refers to the fact that with the rise in the bank rate by the central bank increases the interest rate on loans and advances by commercial banks. This makes the borrowing of money expensive for general public.

   Consequently, individuals postpone their investment plans and wait for fall in interest rates in future. The reduction in investments results in the decreases in the total spending and helps in controlling inflation.

(ii) **Creating adverse situations for businesses:** Implies that increase in bank rate has a psychological impact on some of the business-persons. They consider this situation adverse for carrying out their business activities. Therefore, they reduce their spending and investment.

(iii) **Increasing the propensity to save:** Refers to one of the most important reasons for reduction in total expenditure of individuals. It is a well-known fact that individuals generally prefer to save money in inflationary conditions. As a result, the total expenditure of individuals on consumption and investment decreases.

(b) **Direct Control on Credit Creation:** Constitutes the major part of monetary policy.

The central bank directly reduces the credit control capacity of commercial banks by using the following methods:

(i) **Performing Open Market Operations (OMO):** Refers to one of the important methods used by the central bank to reduce the credit creation capacity of commercial banks. The central bank issues government securities to commercial banks and certain private businesses.

In this way, the cash with commercial banks would be spent on purchasing government securities. As a result, commercial bank would reduce credit supply for the general public.

(ii) **Changing Reserve Ratios:** Involves increase or decrease in reserve ratios by the central bank to reduce the credit creation capacity of commercial banks. For example, when the central bank needs to reduce the credit creation capacity of commercial banks, it increases Cash Reserve Ratio (CRR). As a result, commercial banks need to keep a large amount of cash as reserve from their total deposits with the central bank. This would further reduce the lending capacity of commercial banks. Consequently, the investment by individuals in an economy would also reduce.

(iii) **Demonetization of Currency:** However, one of the monetary measures is to demonetise currency of higher denominations. Such a measure is usually adopted when there is abundance of black money in the country.

(c) **Issue of New Currency:** The most extreme monetary measure is the issue of new currency in place of the old currency. Under this system, one new note is exchanged for a number of notes of the old currency. The value of bank deposits is also fixed accordingly. Such a measure is adopted when there is an excessive issue of notes and there is hyperinflation in the country. It is a very effective measure but is inequitable for its hurts the small depositors the most.

2. **Fiscal Measures:** Monetary policy alone is incapable of controlling inflation. It should, therefore, be supplemented by fiscal measures. Fiscal measures are highly effective for controlling government expenditure, personal consumption expenditure and private and public investment.

**The principal fiscal measures are the following:**

(a) **Reduction in Unnecessary Expenditure:** The government should reduce unnecessary expenditure on non-development activities in order to curb inflation. This will also put a check on private expenditure which is dependent upon government demand for goods and services. But it is not easy to cut government expenditure. Though this measure is always welcome but it becomes difficult to distinguish between essential and non-essential expenditure. Therefore, this measure should be supplemented by taxation.

(b) **Increase in Taxes:** To cut personal consumption expenditure, the rates of personal, corporate and commodity taxes should be raised and even new taxes should be levied, but the rates of taxes should not be so high as to discourage saving, investment and production. Rather, the tax system should provide larger incentives to those who save, invest and produce more.

Further, to bring more revenue into the tax-net, the government should penalize the tax evaders by imposing heavy fines. Such measures are bound to be effective in controlling inflation. To increase the supply of goods within the country, the government should reduce import duties and increase export duties.

(c) **Increase in Savings:** Another measure is to increase savings on the part of the people. This will tend to reduce disposable income with the people, and hence personal consumption expenditure. But due to the rising cost of living, people are not in a position to save much voluntarily.

Keynes, therefore, advocated compulsory savings or what he called 'deferred payment' where the saver gets his money back after some years. For this purpose, the government should float public loans carrying high rates of interest, start saving schemes with prize money, or lottery for long periods, etc. It should also introduce compulsory provident fund, provident fund-cum-pension schemes, etc. All such measures increase savings and are likely to be effective in controlling inflation.

(d) **Surplus Budgets:** An important measure is to adopt anti-inflationary budgetary policy. For this purpose, the government should give up deficit financing and instead have surplus budgets. It means collecting more in revenues and spending less.

(e) **Public Debt:** At the same time, it should stop repayment of public debt and postpone it to some future date till inflationary pressures are controlled within the economy. Instead,. the government should borrow more to reduce money supply with the public.

Like monetary measures, fiscal measures alone cannot help in controlling inflation. They should be supplemented by monetary, non-monetary and non-fiscal measures.

3. **Other Measures:** The other types of measures are those which aim at increasing aggregate supply and reducing aggregate demand directly.

(a) **To Increase Production: The following measures should be adopted to increase production:**

(i) One of the foremost measures to control inflation is to increase the production of essential consumer goods like food, clothing, kerosene oil, sugar, vegetable oils, etc.

(ii) If there is need, raw materials for such products may be imported on preferential basis to increase the production of essential commodities.

(iii) Efforts should also be made to increase productivity. For this purpose, industrial peace should be maintained through agreements with trade unions, binding them not to resort to strikes for some time.

(iv) The policy of rationalization of industries should be adopted as a long-term measure. Rationalization increases productivity and production of industries through the use of brain, brawn and bullion.

(v) All possible help in the form of latest technology, raw materials, financial help, subsidies, etc., should be provided to different consumer goods sectors to increase production.

(b) **Rational Wage Policy:** Another important measure is to adopt a rational wage and income policy. Under hyperinflation, there is a wage-price spiral. To control this, the government should freeze wages, incomes, profits, dividends, bonus, etc.

But such a drastic measure can only be adopted for a short period as it is likely to antagonize both workers and industrialists. Therefore, the best course is to link increase in wages to increase in productivity. This will have a dual effect. It will control wages and at the same time increase productivity, and hence raise production of goods in the economy.

(c) **Price Control:** Price control and rationing is another measure of direct control to check inflation. Price control means fixing an upper limit for the prices of essential consumer goods. They are the maximum prices fixed by law and anybody charging more than these prices is punished by law. But it is difficult to administer price control.

(d) **Rationing:** Rationing aims at distributing consumption of scarce goods so as to make them available to a large number of consumers. It is applied to essential consumer goods such as wheat, rice, sugar, kerosene oil, etc. It is meant to stabilize the prices of necessaries and assure distributive justice. But it is very inconvenient for consumers because it leads to queues, artificial shortages, corruption and black marketing. Keynes did not favour rationing for it 'involves a great deal of waste, both of resources and of employment'.

## PRICE STABILIZATION FUND SCHEME

In order to alleviate the hardship faced by the growers of coffee, tea, rubber and tobacco due to continued low prices of these commodities and to safeguard the interests of the growers of these commodities, the government has decided to establish a Price Stabilization Fund (PSF) and implement a scheme for the benefit of the growers of these commodities.

### ❖ Objective

The objective of the PSF is to provide financial relief to the growers when prices of these commodities fall below a specified level, without resorting to the practice of procurement operations by the government agencies.

### ❖ Funding of the Corpus

The Price Stabilization Fund will be established with a corpus of ₹ 500 crores. The annual interest accruing on this corpus would be released to the Trust Fund to be administered by the NABARD.

The Trust Fund administered by the NABARD will be audited by the Comptroller & Auditor General of India.

### ❖ Adoption of a Price Band

A uniform band of 40% for all the four commodities will be adopted with a price spectrum band of (+/–) 20 per cent from the seven years moving average of international prices.

### ❖ Salient Features of the Scheme

The scheme will be based on the principle of contributions from the growers and from the government depending on normal/boom/distress periods, with a provision for withdrawal by the growers during distress period.

### ❖ Period of Operation of the Scheme

The Scheme is operational from April 2003 onward, initially for a period of 10 years. The scheme will be reviewed after 5 years.

## SACRIFICE RATIO – A COST OF REDUCING INFLATION

The sacrifice ratio is the cost of reducing inflation, the loss of output that must be sustained by the economy in order to achieve a reduction in trend inflation. It is defined as a ratio of the percentage loss of real output to 1 per cent reduction in trend inflation.

The trade-off between inflation and growth had assumed importance since the Great Depression. Initially, during the mid-20th century, focus of the trade off between inflation and growth was mostly on higher inflation as the cost of higher growth and reduction in unemployment. During later part of 1970s and early 1980s, Sacrifice Ratio as a concept, became relevant for developed economies like US where disinflation was considered to be a major cause of recession.

In order to discharge its primary responsibility of price stability, the monetary policy authority of a country follows contractionary monetary policy for controlling inflationary pressure. However, such policy achieves its goal of reduction in inflation with an associated cost in loss of output in the interim period. The low inflation regime is believed to have a favourable impact on the economy which might be able to offset the loss of output.

### ❖ Inflation Tax

Inflation tax is not an actual legal tax paid to a government, instead 'inflation tax' refers to the penalty for holding cash at a time of high inflation. When the government prints more money or reduces interest rates, it floods the market with cash, which raises inflation in the long run. If an investor is holding securities, real estate or other assets, the effect of inflation may be negligible. If a person is holding cash, though, this cash is worth less after inflation has risen. The degree of decrease in the value of cash is termed the inflation tax for the way it punishes people who hold assets in cash.

This is a situation of sustaining government expenditure at the cost of people's income. This looks as if inflation is working as a tax. That is how the term inflation tax is also known as seigniorage. It means inflation is always the level to which the government may go for deficit financing—level of deficit financing is directly reflected by the rate of inflation. It could also be used by the governments in the form of prices and incomes policy under which the companies pay inflation tax on the salary increases above the set level prescribed by the government.

## TERMS RELATED TO INFLATION

- **Recession:** It is a slowdown or a massive contraction in economic activities. A significant fall in spending generally leads to a recession. This creates a mess in the entire economy. To tackle the menace, economies generally react by loosening their monetary policies by infusing more money into the system, i.e., by increasing the money supply. This is done by reducing the interest rates. Increased spending by the government and decreased taxation are also considered good answers for this problem. The recession which hit the globe in 2008 is the most recent example of a recession. It, generally, occur when there is a widespread drop in spending (an adverse demand shock). This may be triggered by various events, such as a financial crisis, an external trade shock, an adverse supply shock or the bursting of an economic bubble.
- **Double-dip Recession:** It refers to a short-lived recovery of an economy from a recession, before it slips back into a recession. The double-dip recessions may also be referred to as 'W'-shaped recession where the two dips in the 'W' represent the double-dip recession, and the quick incline in the middle is the intermediate recovery.
- **Deflation:** It is a decrease in the general price level of goods and services so that inflation rate becomes negative.
- **Disinflation:** It is a decrease in the rate of inflation – a slowdown in the rate of increase of the general price level of goods and services in a nation's gross domestic product over time.
- **Reflation:** Reflation is the act of stimulating the economy by increasing the money supply or by reducing taxes, seeking to bring the economy (specifically price level) back up to the long-term trend, following a dip in the business cycle. It is the opposite of disinflation, which seeks to return the economy back down to the long-term trend.
- **Stagflation:** It is commonly referred to a situation of stagnation in growth and high inflation.
- **Phillips Curve:** The inverse relationship between unemployment rate and inflation when graphically charted is called the Phillips curve. The theory states that the higher the rate of inflation, the lower the unemployment and vice-versa. Thus, high levels of employment can be achieved only at high levels of inflation.
- **Liquidity Trap:** It is a situation when expansionary monetary policy (increase in money supply) does not increase the interest rate, income and hence does not stimulate economic growth. Liquidity trap is the extreme effect of monetary policy. It is a situation in which the general public is prepared to hold on to whatever amount of money is supplied, at a given rate of interest. They do so because of the fear of adverse events like deflation, war, etc.
- **Inflation Premium:** The bonus brought by inflation to the borrowers is known as the inflation premium. It is used in investing

and banking to calculate the normal rate of return on an asset or investment when the general cost of goods and services rises over time, known as inflation.

- **Fiscal Drag:** The amount of tax we pay will increase if there is inflation. This is because with rising wages more people will slip into the top income tax brackets. Low inflation is often seen as harmless or even beneficial because it allows prices to adjust more easily.
- **Food Inflation:** It is consistent rise in the price level of all agricultural food items. This rise in price level is neither seasonal nor sudden, it keeps on increasing over a period of time. This is one of the biggest problems faced by Indian economy.

❑❑❑

11

CHAPTER

# National Income

## NATIONAL INCOME – GDP, GNP, NNP, PCI

Measures of national income and output are used in economics to estimate the total value of production in an economy. The standard measures of income and output are Gross National Product (GNP), Gross Domestic Product (GDP), Gross National Income (GNI), Net National Product (NNP), and Net National Income (NNI). In India, the Central Statistical Organisation (CSO) has been estimating the national income. National income per person or Per Capita Income (PCI) is often used as an indicator of people's standard of living or welfare.

### ❖ Definitions of National Income

National income is a measure of the total value of the goods and services (output) produced by an economy over a period of time (normally a year). It is also a measure of the income flown from production, and/or the sum total of all the spending involved for the production of output.

**National Income Committee of India**: National income estimate measures the volume of commodities and services turned out during a given period counted without duplication.

## BASIC CONCEPTS

### ❖ Gross National Product (GNP)

GNP is the total value of output (goods and services) produced and income received in a year by domestic residents of a country. It includes profits earned from capital invested abroad.

### ❖ Gross Domestic Product (GDP)

GDP is the total value of output (goods and services) produced by the factors of production located within the country's boundary in a year. The factors of production may be owned by any one – citizens or foreigners.

GNP – Net income earned from abroad = GDP

Thus, GDP measures income from where it is earned rather than who owns the factors of production.

### ❖ Net National Product (NNP)

NNP is arrived at by making some adjustment, with regard to depreciation, in GNP. As noted above, GNP is the total value of output produced and income received in a year by domestic residents of a country. Over this one-year period, the available plant and machinery (capital) will wear and tear and get condemned. Such decline in the capital assets due to wear and tear is measured as 'capital depreciation'.

NNP is arrived at by deducting value of such depreciation from GNP.

That is GNP – Depreciation = NNP

## ❖ Net Domestic Product (NDP)

NDP is also arrived from GDP by making adjustment with regard to depreciation in the same way described above. (NDP is calculated by deducting depreciation from GDP).

GDP – Depreciation = NDP

## ❖ Per Capita Income (PCI)

PCI (or) output per person is an indicator to show the living standards of people in a country. If real PCI increases, it is considered to be an improvement in the overall living standard of people. PCI is arrived at by dividing the GDP by the size of population. It is also arrived by making some adjustment with GDP.

PCI = GDP/Total number of people in a country

## ❖ GDP and GNP

While GDP indicates productive capacity of an economy; GNP is a crude indicator for living standard. The significance of the distinction between GNP and GDP depends on the nature of a particular economy.

For instance, it a country has more non-resident inflows and produces a considerable portion of its output by multinational corporations (i.e., with the help of external factors of production), its GNP will be higher than GDP. Otherwise, the distinction will be negligible.

Many countries have foreign firms. In the case of US Ford Motors in Chennai, the income from the car factory would be counted as Indian GDP and not as US GDP. However, the amount of profit the company sends to the US will be added to their GNP. Similarly, our GNP can be arrived by adding to our GDP the net factor income receipts from abroad for the factor inputs owned by Indians. That is, the non-resident Indians income will be added to GDP to arrive at our GNP.

## ❖ National Income at Current Prices and Constant Prices

The concepts of national income discussed above can be measured either at 'current price' or at 'constant price'. The measure based on current price uses the ongoing market prices to compute the value of output. It is quite possible that the current price may always be higher than real value due to many factors like taxes and inflation (or rising prices). Hence, national income arrived at 'current price' includes such influences as inflation and taxes.

With inflation as a common feature in almost all the economies, it is necessary to measure the national income after deducting any such increase in the value of any output or income. National income at 'constant price' measures the national income after making necessary adjustment to eliminate the effect of inflation. Thus, it is based on unchanged price of output. As the national income at 'constant price' is computed based on the real worth of the purchasing power of income, it is also called as 'real national income' or national income in 'real' terms.

## ❖ Importance of Calculating National Income

A national income measure serves various purposes regarding economy, production, trade, consumption, policy formulation, etc. The following are some such needs.

1. To measure the size of the economy and level of country's economic performance.
2. To trace the trend or speed of the economic growth in relation to previous year(s) as well as to other countries.
3. To know the structure and composition of the national income in terms of various sectors and the periodical variations in them.

4. To make projection about the future development trend of the economy.
5. To help government formulate suitable development plans and policies to increase growth rates.
6. To fix various development targets for different sectors of the economy on the basis of the earlier performance.
7. To help business firms in forecasting future demand for their products.
8. To make international comparison of people's living standards.

## METHODS OF CALCULATING NATIONAL INCOME

There are three different methods of calculating national income.

They are:

1. Product or Output Method
2. Income Method
3. Expenditure Method

The GDP is the measure of an economy's total output. It is also used as a measure of total income and total expenditure in that economy. The factor *incomes* received by the public is being *spent* to buy the *output* of goods and services produced. Hence, *income* is equal to *expenditure* and expenditure is equal to the value of *output* produced in the economy.

Income = Expenditure = Output

$Y = E = O$

The model can further be extended by adding the other components of national income namely investment (I), government (G), and foreign trade (X–M). In the extended model, savings of public, taxes and import payments will be deducted from the income. Hence, they are called leakages from the circular flow. Similarly, investment expenditure, government expenditure and net expenditure on trade will be added in to the circular flow. These additions are called injections. However, after aggregating all leakages (outflow) and injections (inflow) in any one year, the total income components of the economy will be equivalent to the total expenditure or total output. Therefore, all the three methods are supposed to give same results.

1. **Output or Product Method:** In the output or product method, the measures of GDP are calculated by adding the total value of the output (of goods and services) produced by all activities during any time period, such as a year. The major challenge of this method is the problem of double counting.

   The output of many businesses is the inputs of some other businesses. For example, the output of the tyre industry is the input of racing bike industry. Counting the final output of both industries will result in double counting of the value of tyre. This problem can be avoided by including only the value added at each stage of production or by adding only the final value of output produced.
2. **Income Method:** In the income method, the measures of GDP are calculated by adding all the income earned by various factors of production which are engaged in the production of output. The various incomes included to compute the gross national income are:

   Wages and Salaries (compensation of employees) + Rent + Interest + Profit.
3. **Expenditure Method:** This method focuses on goods and services produced within the country during 1 year.

   GDP by expenditure method includes:

   (a) Consumer expenditure on services and durable and non-durable goods (C),

   (b) Investment in fixed capital such as residential and non-residential building, machinery and inventories (I),

   (c) Government expenditure on final goods and services (G),

(d) Export of goods and services produced by the people of country (X),

(e) Less imports (M): That part of consumption, investment and government expenditure, which is spent on imports, is subtracted from GDP. Similarly, any imported component, such as raw materials, which is used in the manufacture of export goods, is also excluded.

Thus GDP by expenditure method at market prices = C+ I + G + (X – M), where (X–M) is net export which can be positive or negative.

## GDP (EXPENDITURE COMPONENTS)

From the expenditure side, GDP at current market prices can be seen as the sum of:

1. consumption – both private and public,
2. investment, also known as Gross Capital Formation (GCF) which comprises fixed capital formation, change in stock and valuables and
3. net exports which represent the difference between exports and imports of goods and non-factor services.

**Gross fixed capital formation or fixed investment** mainly refers to the value of new machinery and equipment plus the value of new construction activity undertaken during the year. Net acquisition of valuables covers precious articles, gems and stones, silver, gold, platinum, and gold and silver ornaments.

### ❖ Contribution of Components to Real GDP Growth

| Final expenditures | Share in GDP (in per cent) |
|---|---|
| 2011–12 | 2018–19 |
| Private final consumption | 56.2–59.8 |
| Government final consumption | 11.1–10.7 |
| Fixed capital formation | 34.3–29.4 |
| Change in stock | 2.4–1.7 |
| Valuables | 2.9–1.5 |
| Net exports | –6.5–2.6 |
| GDP at constant market prices | 100.0–100 |

*Source:* Central Statistics Office (CSO)

### ❖ Private Final Consumption Expenditure (PFCE)

It refers to expenditure incurred by households and private non-profit institutions serving households on all types of consumer goods, i.e., durable (except houses), semi-durable, non-durable goods and services.

1. PFCE = Household Final Consumption Expenditure + Private Non-Profit Institutions Serving Households Final Consumption Expenditure
2. PFCE includes expenditures incurred by normal residents, whether in the domestic territory or abroad. So, any expenditure incurred by residents during their foreign tour/travel will be added in PFCE. However, any expenditure incurred by non-residents and foreign visitors in the domestic market will be deducted from PFCE.

### ❖ Government Final Consumption Expenditure (GFCE)

It refers to the expenditure incurred by general government on various administrative services like defence, law and order, education etc. Government produces goods and services with the aim of social welfare without any intention of earning profits.

### ❖ Fixed Capital Formation

Fixed capital formation refers to the process of a firm increasing its stock of fixed capital. Fixed capital are assets used in the productive process that a firm holds for over a year. (Fixed capital formation does not include current raw materials used in the productive process).

Fixed capital can also be referred to as **Property, Plant and Equipment** (PP & E). For example, if a firm builds a new factory or invests in new machines, this will be an accumulation of fixed capital.

Examples of Fixed Capital Formation are: Building or expanding existing factory; Purchase of transport equipment; office equipment, such as computers, printers and machinery used in the productive process.

### ❖ Inventory Investment (Change in Stock)

It refers to the physical change in the stock of raw material, semi-finished goods and finished goods lying, with the producers. It is included as an investment item because it represents the goods produced but not used for current consumption. It is calculated as the difference between the closing stock and the opening stock of the year.

It means,

GDCF = Gross Fixed Capital Formation + Inventory Investment; or

GDCF = Gross Business Fixed Investment + Gross Residential Construction Investment + Gross Public Investment + Inventory Investment.

It is important to understand that purchase of shares and debentures, either old or new, is not included in investment. For example, if I have purchased 500 shares of Reliance Industries, it may be an investment from my point of view, but for economy, it is simply a transfer of purchasing power and not an investment.

### ❖ Valuables

Valuables as a separate item have been introduced in the expenditure side of GDP. Since India is one of largest importer and user of gold for various purposes, this treatment resulted into higher share of valuables in capital formation in the economy. Moreover, from conceptual aspect, these valuables are not related to capital formation in the economy and are kept as a store of value.

### ❖ Net Exports (X – M)

It refers to the difference between exports and imports of a country during a period of 1 year.

1. Exports (X) refer to expenditure by foreigners on purchase of domestic products. The exported goods have been produced within the country's domestic territory So; they are included in output of an economy.
2. Imports (M) are the expenditure by residents on foreign products. Imports are deducted to obtain domestic product, as they are not produced within the domestic territory.
3. Instead of treating exports and imports separately, the difference between the two is taken and is termed as Net Exports.

## CIRCULAR FLOW OF INCOME

The circular flow of income is explained with a simplest model consisting business (firms or producers) and public (households or consumers). The public own the productive resources (i.e., factors of production namely land, labour and capital). Business sector or producers employ the factors of production to produce the goods and services. Such goods and services are bought by the public.

Thus public own the factors of production and provide them to producers. The producers employ the factor *inputs* to produce *output* of goods and services, which is bought by the consumers (public). For the employment of factor services, the public receive the factor *income* namely rent (for land), wages (for labour) and interest (for capital). This *income* flows back from the public to the business sector as consumption *expenditure* to buy the goods and services.

Thus, the flow chart consists of two segments – real flow and money flow. The flow of *input* (factors viz. land, labour, capital and organization) and *output* (goods and services) represent the real economy (or real flow). The inner flow shows the money received as factor *income* (rent, wage, interest and profit) and it goes to the producer as consumption *expenditure* (commodity price) to buy the goods and services.

The most important point to be noted for the computation of national income is that income (Y) received is equal to the consumption expenditure (C) made by the consumers, i.e., Y = C.

This simple circular flow model is explained without the other components of national income namely savings or investment (I), public expenditure by government (G) and expenditure on net exports (X – M). If we include all the above components of national income Y = C will become

$$Y = C + I + G + (X - M)$$

Thus national income is the aggregate summation of income or expenditure made through these four components, consumers (C ), investors (I), government (G) and foreign trade (Exports [X] – Imports [M]).

## CAPITAL FORMATION

Capital formation refers to net additions of capital stock such as equipment, buildings and other intermediate goods. A nation uses capital stock in combination with labour to provide services and produce goods; an increase in this capital stock is known as capital formation. The term is used to describe net capital accumulation during an accounting period.

Generally, the higher the capital formation of an economy, the faster an economy can grow its aggregate income. Increasing an economy's capital stock also increases its capacity for production, which means an economy can produce more. Producing more goods and services can lead to an increase in national income levels.

### ❖ Process of Capital Formation

In order to accumulate capital goods some current consumption has to be sacrificed. The greater the extent to which the people are willing to abstain from present consumption, the greater the extent that society will devote resources to new capital formation. If society consumes all that it produces and saves nothing, future productive capacity of the economy will fall as the present capital equipment wears out.

In other words, if whole of the current productive activity is used to produce consumer goods and no new capital goods are made, production of consumer goods in the future will greatly decline. To cut down some of the present consumption and wait for more consumption in the future require far-sightedness on the part of the people.

### ❖ Stages in Capital Formation

Although saving is essential for capital formation, but in a monetized economy, saving may not directly and automatically result in the production of capital goods. Savings must be invested in order to have capital goods. In a modern economy, where saving and investment are done mainly by two different classes of people, there must be certain means or mechanism whereby the savings of the people are obtained and mobilized in order to give them to the businessmen or entrepreneurs to invest in capital.

Therefore, in a modern free enterprise economy, the process of capital formation consists of the following three stages:

1. **Creation of Savings:** An increase in the volume of real savings so that resources, that would have been devoted to the production of consumption goods, should be released for purposes of capital formation.
2. **Mobilization of Savings:** A finance and credit mechanism, so that the available resources are obtained by private investors or government for capital formation.

3. **Investment of Savings:** The act of investment itself so that resources are actually used for the production of capital goods.

## Creation of Savings

Savings are done by individuals or households. They save by not spending all their incomes on consumer goods. When individuals or households save, they release resources from the production of consumer goods. Workers, natural resources, materials, etc., thus released are made available for the production of capital goods.

The level of savings in a country depends upon the power to save and the will to save. The power to save or saving capacity of an economy mainly depends upon the average level of income and the distribution of national income. The higher the level of income, the greater will be the amount of savings.

The countries having higher levels of income are able to save more. That is why the rate of savings in the US and Western European countries is much higher than that in the underdeveloped and poor countries like India. Further, the greater the inequalities of income, the greater will be the amount of savings in the economy. Apart from the power to save, the total amount of savings depends upon the will to save. Various personal, family, and national considerations induce the people to save.

People save in order to provide against old age and unforeseen emergencies. Some people desire to save a large sum to start new business or to expand the existing business. Moreover, people want to make provision for education, marriage and to give a good start in business for their children.

Further, it may be noted that savings may be either voluntary or forced. Voluntary savings are those savings which people do of their own free will. As explained above, voluntary savings depend upon the power to save and the will to save of the people. On the other hand, taxes by the government represent forced savings.

Moreover, savings may be done not only by households but also by business enterprises' and government. Business enterprises save when they do not distribute the whole of their profits, but retain a part of them in the form of undistributed profits. They then use these undistributed profits for investment in real capital.

The third source of savings is government. The government savings constitute the money collected as taxes and the profits of public undertakings. The greater the amount of taxes collected and profits made, the greater will be the government savings. The savings so made can be used by the government for building up new capital goods like factories, machines, roads, etc., or it can lend them to private enterprise to invest in capital goods.

## Mobilization of Savings

The next step in the process of capital formation is that the savings of the households must be mobilized and transferred to businessmen or entrepreneurs who require them for investment. In the capital market, funds are supplied by the individual investors (who may buy securities or shares issued by companies), banks, investment trusts, insurance companies, finance corporations, governments, etc.

If the rate of capital formation is to be stepped up, the development of capital market is very necessary. A well-developed capital market will ensure that the savings of the society will be mobilized and transferred to the entrepreneurs or businessmen who require them.

## Investment of Savings in Real Capital

For savings to result in capital formation, they must be invested. In order that the investment of savings should take place, there must be a good number of honest and dynamic entrepreneurs in the country who are able to take risks and bear uncertainty of production.

Given that a country has got a good number of venturesome entrepreneurs, investment will be made by them only if there is sufficient inducement to invest. Inducement to invest depends on the marginal efficiency of capital (i.e., the prospective rate of profit) on the one hand and the rate of interest, on the other.

However, of the two determinants of inducement to invest—the marginal efficiency of capital and the rate of interest—it is the former which is of greater importance. Marginal efficiency of capital depends upon the cost or supply prices of capital as well as the expectations of profits.

Fluctuations in investment are mainly due to changes in expectations regarding profits. But, it is the size of the market which provides scope for profitable investment. Thus, the primary factor that determines the level of investment or capital formation, in any economy, is the size of the market for goods.

### ❖ Foreign Capital

Capital formation in a country can also take place with the help of foreign capital, i.e., foreign savings.

Foreign capital can take the form of:

(a) Direct private investment by foreigners,
(b) Loans or grants by foreign governments,
(c) Loans by international agencies like the World Bank.

There are very few countries which have successfully marched on the road to economic development without making use of foreign capital in one form or the other. India is receiving a good amount of foreign capital from abroad for investment and capital formation under the Five-Year Plans.

## NEW SERIES OF NATIONAL ACCOUNTS WITH 2011–12 AS BASE YEAR

The Ministry of Statistics & Programme Implementation of the Government of India in January 2015 released the new series of national accounts, revising the base year from 2004–05 to 2011–12. The base year of national accounts was last revised in January 2010 in order to present a more realistic picture of the economy. The new series will better reflect the economy as it would include more sectors. Since these estimates have been compiled afresh, these would be referred to as 'New Series' Estimates.

The National Statistical Commission suggested that the base year for computing national account should be revised every 5 years instead of earlier 10 years.

The first official estimates of national income were prepared by the CSO with base year 1948–49 for the estimates at constant prices. These estimates at constant (1948–49) prices along with the corresponding estimates at current prices and the accounts of the Public Authorities were published in the publication, 'Estimates of National Income' in 1956. The base years of the National Accounts Statistics series have been shifted from 1948–49 to 1960–61 in August 1967; from 1960–61 to 1970–71 in January 1978; from 1970–71 to 1980–81 in February 1988; and from 1980–81 to 1993–94 in February 1999.

With the gradual improvement in the availability of basic data over the years, a comprehensive review of methodology for national accounts statistics has constantly been undertaken with a view to updating the database and shifting the base year to a more recent year.

The base year of the national accounts is changed periodically to take into account the structural changes which take place in the economy and to depict a true picture of the economy through macro aggregates. Base year revisions differ from annual revisions in National Accounts primarily because of nature of changes. In annual revisions, changes are made only on the basis of updated data becoming available without making any changes in the conceptual framework or using any new data source, to ensure strict comparison over years. In case of base year revisions, apart from a shift in the reference year for measuring the real growth, conceptual changes, as recommended by the international guidelines, are incorporated. Further, statistical changes like revisions in the methodology of compilation, adoption of latest classification systems, and, inclusion of new and recent data sources are also made. Changes are also made in the presentation of estimates to improve ease of understanding for analysis and facilitate international comparability.

Improvements as noted above, especially incorporation of new datasets, have resulted in a correction in the level of GDP, which is likely to affect a wide range of indicators where it is used as a reference point: for instance, trends in public expenditure, taxes and public sector debt that are conventionally analysed in terms of their ratios to nominal GDP. It may be noted that the level of revision in the present base revision is not large enough to affect any of these ratios significantly.

The following are the major changes incorporated in the 2011–12 base-year revision:

1. Headline growth rate will now be measured by GDP at constant market prices, which will henceforth be referred to as 'GDP', as is the practice internationally. Earlier, growth was measured in terms of growth rate in GDP at factor cost at constant prices.
2. Sector-wise estimates of gross value added (GVA) will now be given at basic prices instead of factor cost.

   The relationship between GVA at factor cost, GVA, at basic prices, and GDP (at market prices) is given below:

   GVA at basic prices = CE + OS/MI + CFC + production taxes less production subsidies

   GVA at factor cost = GVA at basic prices – production taxes less production subsidies

   GDP = ΣGVA at basic prices + product taxes – product subsidies

   (where, CE: compensation of employees; OS: operating surplus; MI: mixed income; and, CFC: consumption of fixed capital).

   Production taxes or production subsidies are paid or received with relation to production and are independent of the volume of actual production. Some examples of production taxes are land revenues, stamps and registration fees and tax on profession. Some production subsidies are subsidies to Railways, input subsidies to farmers, subsidies to village and small industries, administrative subsidies to corporations or cooperatives, etc.

   Product taxes or subsidies are paid or received on per unit of product. Some examples of product taxes are excise tax, sales tax, service tax and import and export duties. Product subsidies include food, petroleum and fertilizer subsidies, interest subsidies given to farmers, households, etc. through banks, and subsidies for providing insurance to households at lower rates.
3. Comprehensive coverage of the corporate sector both in manufacturing and services by incorporation of annual accounts of companies as filed with the Ministry of Corporate Affairs (MCA) under their e-governance initiative, MCA21. Use of MCA21 database for manufacturing companies has helped account for activities other than manufacturing undertaken by these companies.
4. Comprehensive coverage of the financial sector by inclusion of information from the accounts of stock brokers, stock exchanges, asset management companies, mutual funds and pension funds, and the regulatory bodies including the Securities and Exchange Board of India (SEBI), Pension Fund Regulatory and

Development Authority (PFRDA) and Insurance Regulatory and Development Authority (IRDA).

5. Improved coverage of activities of local bodies and autonomous institutions, covering around 60 per cent of the grants/ transfers provided to these institutions.

Owing to these changes, estimates of GVA both at aggregate and sectoral levels have undergone changes. The sector-wise shares in aggregate GVA have undergone significant revision especially in the case of manufacturing and services. Changes have also been observed in the growth rates in GVAs of individual sectors and contribution of each sector to overall GVA due to use of sales tax and service tax data for estimation in the years 2012–13 and 2013–14.

## ❖ Changes Brought

GDP is the total value of all goods and services produced in a country's economy in a specific time period and is usually given in local currency. GDP growth rate, denoted in percentage, is the growth in GDP as compared to that of the previous year.

There are variations in the ways to calculate GDP and it is the introduction of these new calculations that has caused a spike in India's recent GDP growth rate, leading to quite a lot confusion and debate.

The changes in the GDP calculation were devised by India's statisticians working for the CSO that is under the Ministry of Statistics & Programme Implementation (MOSPI), who released the new figures earlier in February.

There are three important changes made in the calculation of the GDP:

- Changing the base year
- Replacing factor costs with market prices
- Widening of the data pool

### Changing the Base Year

Choosing a base year is the first step while counting the 'real' GDP. A real GDP growth rate removes any effects that have arisen due to inflation to give us a truer picture of economic reality. For the revised GDP calculations the Indian statisticians have changed the base year from 2004–05 to 2011–12. This means that the 'real' GDP will be counted by keeping the prices of 2011–12 as the base prices instead of referring to the prices of 2004–05. This change alone has played an important part in shooting up the GDP and related numbers. The change in base year is not an unusual phenomena as base year is regularly updated.

### Replacing Factor Costs with Market Prices

There are two ways to calculate GDP and those are calculating via factor costs or calculating via market prices. Until the recent revisions, India had used factor costs for calculating GDP but now we have shifted towards market prices. Factor cost means the cost of production that the producers or service providers have incurred after removing the effect of indirect taxes or subsidies. However, by the recent changes we have now shifted towards calculating the GDP by measuring the GVA at market prices. Market prices mean the actual expenditure incurred by consumers. These will also include any subsidies such as food and petrol that are provided to the consumer. The shift from factor costs to market prices indicates that India is slowly conforming to international norms as most countries use market prices for calculating the GDP.

### Widening of Data Pool

In statistics, the larger the sample, the more accurate the extrapolations are, generally speaking. Previous data were sampled from Annual Survey of Industries (ASI), which comprised of about two lakh factories. The new database draws from the five lakh odd companies registered with the MCA21. While the earlier data gave only a factory-level picture, the new data looks at the enterprise level.

## ❖ Real Income

Real income is simply inflation-adjusted income. It is the income of an individual or group after taking into consideration the effects of inflation on purchasing power. For example, if one received a 2 per cent salary rise over the previous year and inflation for the year was 1 per cent, then his real income only rose 1 per cent. Conversely, if one received a 2 per cent raise in salary and inflation stood at 3 per cent, then his real income would have shrunk 1 per cent.

In fact, real income refers to the amount of goods and services one can buy today compared to the price of the same goods and services he could have purchased in another time period.

## ❖ Nominal Income

Nominal income is that part of one's salary that is paid out in cash. It is one's income in actual currency terms unadjusted for what is termed as inflation. Inflation is calculated as the change in the CPI year-on-year. A 10 per cent inflation rate means that prices in the current period are about 10 per cent higher than that of the same period a year ago. This is the same percentage that your nominal income lost in terms of purchasing power.

Therefore, in summation, nominal income is what one is getting paid. Real income is the amount of money one really gets after factoring in inflation. Thus, nominal income will always be more than real income.

## ❖ The Difference

The difference between nominal and real is essential in many practical aspects. In lending money for instance where borrowers, like bond issuing entities, offer a certain interest amount to bondholders or lenders, you have to make sure the interest is high enough to offset the effect of inflation by the time the loan matures. If not, then you are actually losing money instead of earning.

This is one important aspect why authorities like the Federal Reserve need to control inflation at a certain sustainable and useful level. If inflation tends to go higher than expected, the Feds implement monetary policies to lower it. They do this by tightening money supply or the level of available credit in the market. The idea is to reduce the liquidity within the system. This makes credit expensive to obtain, thus limiting economic growth and eventually pulling prices down.

Whenever you weigh various options in your investment activities, it is important to plan and calculate things out in real terms. Wealth accumulation is not about amassing huge amounts of nominal money, but rather it is about ensuring that at the end of the day, your income has a good purchasing power.

## ❖ Real Disposable Income (RDI)

The RDI measures income after taxes and benefits, adjusted for the effects of inflation. It is a guide to the quantity of goods and services that people can buy after the tax and benefit system has adjusted original incomes and we have made allowance for the effect of price changes.

## ❖ Causes Behind the Fall in Real Disposable Incomes

1. **Rising prices:** Consumer price inflation has averaged 3.5 per cent per year since 2008.
2. **Wage squeeze:** For most people, the annual wage rise has been less than inflation and many have had to accept a wage freeze or a cut in nominal terms. A weak economy means that there is less overtime available to boost wages.
3. **Rising taxes:** A number of taxes have gone up as part of the Coalition's deficit-reduction strategy including the rise in VAT to 20 per cent, higher air passenger duty and other indirect taxes.

4. **Collapsing interest rates on savings:** A key source of income for many people especially older people who have retired.

## ❖ Key Terms

- **Real wage:** The nominal wage adjusted for the effects of inflation.
- **Real income:** Nominal income adjusted for the effects of price changes (inflation) and expressed at constant prices.
- **RDI:** Income after taxes and benefits, adjusted for the effects of inflation.
- **Wage price spiral:** A situation where workers bid for higher wages because they have seen their real income eroded by rising prices. This can lead to a further burst of cost-push inflation in an economy.
- **Marginal propensity to consume:** The proportion of any change in income that is spent rather than saved.
- **Household wealth:** The value of assets owned by households – including property, shares, savings and pension fund assets.

# PURCHASING POWER PARITY (PPP)

The PPP theory aims to determine the adjustments needed to be made in the exchange rates of two currencies to make them at par with the purchasing power of each other. In other words, the expenditure on a similar commodity must be same in both currencies when accounted for exchange rate. The purchasing power of each currency is determined in the process. The PPP is used worldwide to compare the income levels in different countries. The PPP thus makes it easy to understand and interpret the data of each country. For example, a pair of shoes costs ₹ 2,500 in India. Then it should cost $50 in America when the exchange rate is 50 between the dollar and the rupee.

The GDP per capita PPP is obtained by dividing the country's gross domestic product, adjusted by the PPP, by the total population.

## ❖ Application of the PPP

The concept of the PPP has two applications. It was originally developed as a theory of exchange rate determination, but it is now primarily used to compare living standards across countries.

1. From the perspective of exchange rate determination, the PPP is useful as a reminder that monetary policy has no long-run impact on the real exchange rate. Thus, countries with different inflation rates should expect their bilateral exchange rate to adjust to offset these differentials in the long run. The exchange rate, however, can deviate persistently from its PPP value in response to real shocks.

   While the origins of the PPP concept can be traced back to the Salamanca School in 16th-century Spain, its modern use as a theory of exchange rate determination begins with the work of Gustav Cassel (1918), who proposed the PPP as a means of adjusting pre-World War I exchange rates or parities for countries intending to return to the gold standard system after hostilities ended.

   (i) Some adjustment was necessary because countries that left the gold standard in 1914 experienced significantly different rates of inflation during and after the war.

   (ii) As a theory of exchange rate determination, the simplest and strongest form of the PPP (absolute PPP) is based on an international multi-good version of the law of one price.

   Absolute PPP predicts that the exchange rate should adjust to equate the prices of national baskets of goods and services between two countries because of market forces driven by arbitrage. Under absolute PPP, the exchange rate is simply equal to the ratio of the domestic to the foreign price of a given aggregate bundle of commodities, but this implies that the real exchange rate is constant.

In practice, however, absolute PPP does not hold for a number of reasons, and these undermine its usefulness as a theory of the determination of the level of the exchange rate.

2. To compare living standards across countries, PPP exchange rates are constructed by comparing the national prices for a large basket of goods and services. These rates are used to translate different currencies into a common currency to measure the purchasing power of PCI in different countries. A PPP exchange rate constructed in this manner is not, however, an accurate measure of the equilibrium value of the market-determined exchange rate.

To compare living standards between countries, it is necessary to translate PCI or expenditure values measured in the local currency into a common currency, normally the US dollar. This presents the problem of determining the appropriate exchange rate to use for the currency translation. One could use the nominal bilateral exchange rate with the US dollar, but this ignores the often large differences in the prices of a broad set of goods and services that are not reflected in the value of the exchange rate (i.e., absolute PPP does not hold). For example, travellers are sometimes surprised by the differences in the prices of certain goods and services across countries. They expect exchange rates to adjust to equalize these prices. But many goods and services are not traded (e.g., fast food and dry cleaning), and these tend to be more expensive in Western European countries than in Canada, and less expensive in emerging market countries.

To a large extent these price disparities reflect the differences in the cost of non-traded inputs, chiefly labour and land. These large discrepancies in the price levels across countries for which the exchange rate does not adjust imply, as noted above, that absolute PPP is a poor theory of exchange rate determination. Nonetheless, the concept of absolute PPP can be used to compute a PPP exchange rate that accounts for differences in prices across countries and, thus, for differences in the local purchasing power of national currencies.

In this case, a PPP exchange rate is defined as the ratio of prices for a representative basket of final goods and services in two countries, with the prices expressed in the two national currencies. At this exchange rate, the purchasing power of the different currencies is equal (or has parity) in terms of the specific quality of a specific bundle of goods or services that can be purchased. Because these PPP exchange rates reflect differences in the national prices of both non-traded and traded goods, they are very useful for international comparisons of standards of living.

Although the construction of a PPP exchange rate may seem straightforward, in practice it is very difficult.

## PROBLEMS IN CALCULATING NATIONAL INCOME

The measurement of national income encounters many problems. The problem of double counting has already been noted. Though there are some corrective measures, it is difficult to eliminate double counting altogether. And there are many such problems and the following are some of them.

**Black Money:** In countries where level of illegal activities, illegal businesses and corruption is very high, the circulation of black money is so high, it has created a 'parallel economy'. It means unreported economy which is equivalent to the size of officially estimated size of the economy. GDP does not take into account the 'parallel economy' as the transactions of black money are not registered. In India, black money is all-pervasive, affecting not only the economy but also the society at large.

**Non-Monetization:** In most of the rural economy, considerable portion of transactions occurs informally and they are called as non-monetized economy. The presence of such non-monetary economy in developing countries keeps the GDP estimates at lower level than the actual.

**Growing Service Sector:** In recent years, the service sector is growing faster than that of the agricultural and industrial sectors. Many new services like *Business Process Outsourcing* (BPO) have come up. However, value addition in legal consultancy, health services, financial and business services and the service sector as a whole is not based on accurate reporting and hence underestimated in national income measures.

**Household Services:** The national income analysis ignores domestic work, housekeeping and social services. Most of such valuable work rendered by our women at home does not enter our national accounting.

**Social Services:** It ignores volunteer and unpaid social services. For example, the wonderful services of Mother Teresa are invaluable for millions of poor, destitute, orphans and the diseased but at the same time not included in our GDP.

**Environmental Cost:** National income estimation does not distinguish between environmental-friendly and environmental-hazardous industries. The cost of polluting industries is not included in the estimate.

## GINI INDEX

The Gini index is a measurement of the income distribution of a country's residents. This number, which ranges between 0 and 1 and is based on residents' net income, helps define the gap between the rich and the poor, with 0 representing perfect equality and 1 representing perfect inequality.

There is also a generally negative correlation between Gini coefficients and per-capita GDP, because poorer nations tend to have higher index figures.

It was developed by the Italian statistician Corrado Gini and published in 1912.

### ❖ Advantages of Gini Index

1. The Gini coefficient's main advantage is that it is a measure of inequality by means of a ratio analysis, rather than a variable unrepresentative of most of the population, such as PCI or GDP.
2. It can be used to compare income distributions across different population sectors as well as countries, for example the Gini coefficient for urban areas differs from that of rural areas in many countries (though the US urban and rural Gini coefficients are nearly identical).
3. It is sufficiently simple that it can be compared across countries and be easily interpreted. GDP statistics are often criticized as they do not represent changes for the whole population; the Gini coefficient demonstrates how income has changed for poor and rich. If the Gini coefficient is rising as well as GDP, poverty may not be improving for the majority of the population.
4. The Gini coefficient can be used to indicate how the distribution of income has changed within a country over a period of time, thus it is possible to see if inequality is increasing or decreasing.
5. The Gini coefficient satisfies four important principles:
   (i) **Anonymity:** It does not matter who the high and low earners are.
   (ii) **Scale independence:** The Gini coefficient does not consider the

size of the economy, the way it is measured, or whether it is a rich or poor country on average.

(iii) **Population independence:** It does not matter how large the population of the country is.

(iv) **Transfer principle:** If income (less than the difference), is transferred from a rich person to a poor person the resulting distribution is more equal.

## ❖ Disadvantages of Gini Index

1. The Gini coefficient measured for a large economically diverse country will generally result in a much higher coefficient than each of its regions has individually. For this reason the scores calculated for individual countries within the EU are difficult to compare with the score of the entire US.
2. Comparing income distributions among countries may be difficult because benefits systems may differ. For example, some countries give benefits in the form of money while others give food stamps, which may not be counted as income in the Lorenz curve and therefore not taken into account in the Gini coefficient.
3. The measure will give different results when applied to individuals instead of households. When different populations are not measured with consistent definitions, comparison is not meaningful.
4. The Lorenz curve may understate the actual amount of inequality if richer households are able to use income more efficiently than lower income households. From another point of view, measured inequality may be the result of more or less efficient use of household incomes.
5. As for all statistics, there will be systematic and random errors in the data. The meaning of the Gini coefficient decreases as the data become less accurate. Also, countries may collect data differently, making it difficult to compare statistics between countries.
6. Economies with similar incomes and Gini coefficients can still have very different income distributions. This is because the Lorenz curves can have different shapes and yet still yield the same Gini coefficient. As an extreme example, an economy where half the households have no income, and the other half share income equally has a Gini coefficient of ½; but an economy with complete income equality, except for one wealthy household that has half the total income, also has a Gini coefficient of ½.
7. Too often only the Gini coefficient is quoted without describing the proportions of the quantiles used for measurement. As with other inequality coefficients, the Gini coefficient is influenced by the granularity of the measurements. For example, five 20 per cent quantiles (low granularity) will yield a lower Gini coefficient than 25 per cent quantiles (high granularity) taken from the same distribution.

## DATA COLLECTION: A WEAK LINK IN NEW GDP CALCULATION

Improvement in methodology of GDP calculation or for that matter the Base Year is usually a tame routine affair. However, the launch of new GDP Series (Base 2011–12) in India has been anything but tepid, what with everyone from RBI Governor to Chief Economic Adviser publicly expressing their struggle with understanding the new growth numbers.

As such GDP cannot be measured in an 'empirical' sense. One may count with certainty the number of cows in a dairy farm or weight of food grains in a warehouse. On the contrary, GDP can only be estimated and not measured with absolute certainty. The output of this estimation is expected to be reflective of the aggregate economic activity of the nation.

## ❖ Reuters

To the extent GDP is defined as market value of final goods and services produced in an economy, the Income Based Approach that CSO has recently adopted is more aligned to the classical concept of GDP. The newly adopted framework is an international best practise. Thus, *per se* the intent should not be doubted. However, certain doubts remain as to weather data sources being used for this advanced approach are fully supportive of this advancement or not.

## ❖ What Exactly is GVA?

Under the recently adopted income-based approach, GDP is expressed as aggregate GVA plus product taxes (such as excise, sales, service tax) minus product subsidies (such as petroleum, fertiliser subsidies). The value added in an economic activity is the output less the value of inputs. The value created is distributed within various entities involved in the process of value creation.

The value added on economic activity at a country level is termed GVA. Thus GVA is given as the sum of (a) compensation of employees; (b) consumption of fixed capital which is often captured from 'depreciation' in corporate profit and loss (P&L) account; (c) operating surplus which may be approximated by Profit After Tax (PAT) adjusted for property income and current transfers to trade channels and (d) Production Taxes less Subsidies: Production taxes/subsidies needs to be differentiated from product taxes/subsidies since the former is related to the overall production process itself and includes items such as land revenues, stamp/registration fees while the latter is specific to actual units produced.

Well over 90 per cent of the GDP is driven by GVA. If one precisely knew the P&L of all business entities (registered as well as unregistered businesses from the largest listed corporate to the smallest self-employed person) in India, the GVA could have been calculated 'almost perfectly' with the assumption that businesses are correctly reporting their profitability.

However, this is a near impossible task for even more developed economies. The residual portion of the GDP consisting of taxes net of subsidies may be more accurately measured.

For estimating operating surplus and consumption of fixed capital on an economy wide basis, understandably the key data source is company financial statements. Of course, various nationwide surveys are used not only for estimating employee compensations but also for supplementing the information available from company financials. Let's look at each of them in some detail.

## ❖ Corporate Information Used in GVA

In the GDP calculated as per 2004–05 series, the key source of information about private corporate sector has been RBI Study on Company Finances, which considered financial results of around 2,500 companies (around 1,500 non-financial corporates).

The new series justifiably attempts to increase the coverage of the corporate sector and has used the MCA21 database maintained by the MCA. Approximately, 14 lakh companies are registered with MCA, of which 9.8 lakh companies are active. Post filtering for data availability, 5 lakh companies have been analysed and used for GDP estimation for 2011–12 and 2012–13.

While coverage of the private sector has improved, it has some downsides as well. Not the least of the shortcomings is the instability in the data, since as of 2013–14 the number of common companies was reduced to just 3 lakhs.

This is an outcome of companies not reporting possibly because they are closing down their operations. Thus, if out of 5 lakh companies 2 lakh have not reported, it should normally set alarm bells ringing about the economy. How the current methodology addresses this 'survivor bias' in the data is not clear.

However, the much bigger problem is the quality of the financial statement of a lot, but of courses not all, of these companies. As such both under-reporting and over-reporting corporate profits will now distort GDP calculations since GVA is heavily dependent on such variables.

At least three entities have published research on earnings management and quality of financial reporting of Indian listed entities. The first titled 'Study on the state of Corporate Governance in India', done under the auspices of Indian Institute of Corporate Affairs, analysed 2,315 corporates over 2006–11. The second study, conducted by SEBI-DRG titled 'Earnings Management in India', studied 2,229 firms over 2008–11.

Both these studies focussing on non-banking/non-financial services corporates had comparable findings. While both studies acknowledged the prevalence of 'earnings management' issue among some Indian corporates, they specifically highlighted that the issues of doubtful financial reporting increases as the size of the firm decreases.

The third study conducted by India Ratings & Research (Ind-Ra), which focussed exclusively on the BSE 500 corporates, agrees with the findings of the two above reports. In addition, the Ind-Ra study found that possible discrepancy in reporting financial number increases at the time of economic slowdown. During stressful years, questions about reliability may be raised about variables such as PAT and EBITDA of even BSE 500 corporates.

So it is possible that companies over-report profit in bad times to secure financing and under-report profit in good times to pay lower taxes. More research on corporate reporting behaviour and its motivations are required to draw stronger conclusion. Still as of today some doubts may be raised of the reliability of such corporate numbers and by extension one may conjecture whether GVA is getting over-estimated to some extent.

## ❖ Frequency and Timeliness of Surveys

The usage of surveys to supplement information is unique neither to the new methodology adopted by CSO nor to India. To substantiate and supplement the data from other sources, under the new approach certain survey results and the time by which those results are available become critical. It is the author's conjecture that the sensitivity of final published GDP figure to such survey inputs may be higher as per the new approach than the erstwhile approach.

ASI is critical for GDP estimation. When the new methodology was launched in 2014, the ASI data of 2011–12 were available. Ironically, results of this annual survey are typically available with a two-year lag. As of March 2015 only Volume I of ASI 2012–13 is made available. It is not clear whether the latest GDP figures have fully incorporated the ASI 2012–13 to the extent it is available.

Another survey critical to the new approach is employment and unemployment surveys of National Sample Survey Organization (NSSO). This survey is conducted once in 5 years with the last one being conducted at 2011–12.

These surveys reflect structural changes in the economy. As such, if the economy moves at an even pace of growth (or for that matter decay) statistical outputs based on such surveys reflect reasonably the ground level realities.

However, if the economy undergoing the structural change or the economic growth is volatile or is at inflection point then questions may be raised about using inputs from some dated surveys. The years 2010–11 and 2011–12 were of robust economic activity with GDP growth rate of 8 per cent plus (as per the 2004–05 series).

In 2012–13 the economy nose-dived. Clearly datawise this was a period of economic volatility. Estimates used in calculating GDP based on survey conducted prior to 2012 may create an upward bias in the estimates.

To the extent, global approach has been adopted the focus should be two fold. In the short term, which is next 2–3 years CSO may consider focussing on clearly articulating the various specific assumptions and critical inputs specific to the period for which GDP is estimated.

In the long-term, CSO should consider deploying more people and technology resources to improve the frequency of various surveys as well as reduce very substantially the time lag between the survey and the publication of the reports. And last but not the least, stronger measures in line with the ones proposed in the original draft version of Corporate Act, 2013 may be implemented to ensure higher quality of financial reporting but all business entities in India.

## ❖ Ministry of Statistics and Programme Implementation (MOSPI)

The Ministry of Statistics and Programme Implementation (MOSPI) held a conference for market participants on 12 April 2015 in New Delhi regarding its new series of national accounts with a base of 2011–12. Experts from various departments of MOSPI were present at the conference. Although the conference was primarily technical in nature–explaining the change in methodology, classification and new sources–we secured answers to a few important questions, which we have detailed in this note. However, some concerns still remain. Overall, while MOSPI is (rightly) being criticized for unavailability of historical data and potential GDP growth estimates, the enormous work undertaken by it to bring India's national accounts statistics at par with international standards cannot be undermined. Going forward, the implementation of Goods & Service Tax (GST) poses the biggest challenge.

MOSPI, at the data users' conference, explained the nuances of its new series of national accounts with base year 2011–12. We have provided a summary of the major improvements in coverage and major changes in each component of GDP in Exhibits 2 & 3 respectively. The conference was attended by many economists and a few other participants to improve their understanding of the new series of national accounts. Although the conference was more technical in nature, we had six major questions to ask before attending the conference. While many of these questions have been answered, some continue to be unanswered and a few challenges remain.

1. **Was the Indian economy actually smaller than what was estimated in FY12?**

   Yes. According to the GDP measured in nominal terms (or current prices) at market prices (GDPMP) at 2011–12 base, which is now the major series, Indian economy was 2.3 per cent smaller than previously estimated (old base 2004–05). This was surprising because with improved methodology, better coverage and new sources of information, it is generally assumed that the economy's uncovered part will also be included in GDP estimates, thereby increasing the official numbers (as has been the case in the previous revisions of the base year). This time, however, it was different.

2. **What led to this change?**

   Nominal GDP was revised lower primarily because of the sharp downward revision in 'trade, hotels & restaurants', which was partly offset by an upward revision in 'manufacturing' (Exhibit 1). The former was because of the change in methodology, classification, the drop in the latest survey-based estimates of trade in the unorganized sector and the inclusion of MCA21 data for the organized sector. The latter was because of the change in data sources (MCA21 instead of ASI or Industrial Production Index (IPI) in case ASI is not available) and the change in methodology (replacement of Labour Input (LI) method with effective LI method) (Exhibit 5).

3. **How the estimation of the financial sector has changed?**

The calculation of GVA for the financial sector has been revised substantially, although the numbers were broadly the same for FY12. Three major changes are listed below:

(i) Earlier, the financial sector was divided into two sectors – banks (80.1 per cent) and insurance (19.9 per cent). Now, a new category – other financial intermediaries & financial auxiliaries (33.3 per cent) has been added, reducing the weights for banks to 52.9 per cent and insurance & pension funds to 13.6 per cent.

(ii) The issue department of the central bank (RBI), which was earlier considered to be a part of the general government, is now included in the financial sector.

(iii) The computation of Financial Intermediation Services Indirectly Measured (FISIM) has been changed (Exhibit 4). Earlier, entire property income, including dividend, interest receipt and profit on sale of investments were considered to estimate FISIM. According to the new methodology – System of National Accounts (SNA) 2008 – only core business of the banking sector comprising lending and deposits is considered for estimating FISIM. Accordingly, only interest receipts and payments are included in FISIM calculations. However, making it complex is the introduction of the reference rate, against which both lending and deposit rates are adjusted.

4. **Why the estimates on 'real estate, Ownership of Dwellings (OD) & Professional Services (PS)' got revised?**

This was also because of the change in methodology in the unincorporated sector, classification change and use of the latest data on private corporate sector from the MCA21 database.

5. **How the expenditure-based indicators have been revised?**

As far as the expenditure-based approach is concerned, data on various components such as PFCE and Gross Fixed Capital Formation (GFCF) remain unsatisfactorily incomplete. The estimates of the former, however, have been made more robust by basing them on Consumer Expenditure Survey (CES) 68th round, instead of using some fixed. ratios (based on some historical study) and expert judgment. On fixed investments, the estimate of the sector has been expanded from two categories – Construction and Machinery & Equipment (CM&E) – to four categories with the addition of cultivated biological resources & Intellectual Property Products (IPP). Further, methodological changes and use of new data sources (MCA, NSS 70th round AIDIS, NSS 67th round on unincorporated enterprises etc.) were made as a result of which GFCF growth was revised downwards for FY13 and upwards for FY14.

6. **Why the estimates on domestic savings have been changed?**

Three major changes have been introduced in savings estimate, which are listed below:

(i) In the new series, gold and silver ornaments acquired by the households are treated as savings of households in the form of valuables, as against the earlier practice of treating them as consumption expenditure (and including them in PFCE).

(ii) Physical assets of quasi corporations (such as money lenders) have been excluded from households and included in private corporations.

(iii) Finally, as we discussed above on the changes in the calculation of FISIM, property income of the banking sector from dividends and profit on sale of investments (interest income on sale of G-Secs held under the statutory liquidity ratio (SLR)) are now included in savings of the financial sector. While the first change added to household savings, the second change reduced the estimate of physical savings of households non-trivially. Overall, total household savings remained broadly unchanged in the new series. However, savings of the private corporate sector have been revised upwards because of the last two changes.

*Improvements have been made, but problems still remain*: Overall, many positive developments have taken place but many problems still remain. Although MOSPI did not affirm the availability of back-dated series data and potential GDP growth in the economy, it rightly deserves a round of applause for undertaking such a humungous task to bring India's national accounts database at par with international standards. Nevertheless, there is at least one major concern, as highlighted by MOSPI, which could perturb the estimations going forward. MOSPI is wary of the impact of the implementation of GST in the country. This is because the agency has switched to use 'sales tax' (for the unorganized sector) and 'services tax' (for the respective services sector) as indicators to estimate many major components of GDP. Unfortunately, it does not seem to have any concrete plan, at least as of now, to adjust to the GST regime.

This and other problems are likely to remain in the foreseeable future in the estimation of national accounts. Whether we like it or not, we will have to live with these constraints. As Mr T C A Anant (Secretary, MOSPI and Chief Statistician of India) rightly pointed out at the conference that policy decisions in developed markets are based on a tripod of GDP growth, corporate sector and labour market indicators. In India, because of poor availability (or altogether unavailability) of the latter two, the entire onus of explaining the dynamics of the country's economy lies on GDP, which is unfair.

## ❖ Changes in New GDP Series (Base Year 2011–12)

GDP is the total value of all goods and services produced in a country's economy in a specific time period and is usually given in local currency. GDP growth rate, denoted in percentage, is the growth in GDP as compared to that of the previous year.

There are variations in the ways to calculate GDP and it is the introduction of these new calculations that has caused a spike in India's recent GDP growth rate, leading to quite a lot confusion and debate.

The changes in the GDP calculation were devised by India's statisticians working for the Central Statistics Office (CSO) that is under the Ministry of Statistics & Programme Implementation (MOSPI), who released the new figures earlier in February.

There are three important changes made in the calculation of the GDP:

1. Changing the base year
2. Replacing factor costs with market prices
3. Widening of the data pool

## Changing the Base Year

Choosing a base year is the first step while counting the 'real' GDP. A real GDP growth rate removes any effects that have arisen due to inflation to give us a truer picture of economic reality. For the revised GDP calculations the Indian statisticians have changed the base year from 2004–05 to 2011–12. This means that the 'real' GDP will be counted by keeping the prices of 2011–12 as the base prices instead of referring to the prices of 2004–05. This change alone has played an important part in shooting up the GDP and related numbers. The change in base year is not an unusual phenomena as base year is regularly updated.

## Replacing Factor Costs with Market Prices

There are two ways to calculate GDP and those are calculating via factor costs or calculating via market prices. Until the recent revisions India had used factor costs for calculating GDP but now we have shifted towards market prices. Factor cost means the cost of production that the producers or service providers have incurred after removing the effect of indirect taxes or subsidies. However, by the recent changes we have now shifted towards calculating the GDP by measuring the GVA at market prices. Market prices mean the actual expenditure incurred by consumers. These will also include any subsidies such as food and petrol that are provided to the consumer. The shift from factor costs to market prices indicates that India is slowly conforming to international norms as most countries use market prices for calculating the GDP.

## Widening of Data Pool

In statistics, the larger the sample, the more accurate the extrapolations are, generally speaking. Previous data were sampled from ASI, which comprised of about two lakh factories. The new database draws from the five lakh odd companies registered with the MCA21. While the earlier data gave only a factory-level picture, the new data looks at the enterprise level.

Real GDP offers a better perspective than nominal GDP when tracking economic output over a period of time. When people use GDP numbers, they are often talking about nominal GDP, which can be defined as the total economic output of a country. This output is measured at current price levels and currency values, without factoring in inflation.

Nominal GDP is the market value (money-value) of all final goods and services produced in a geographical region, usually a country.

Real GDP is a macroeconomic measure of the value of output economy, adjusted for price changes. The adjustment transforms the nominal GDP into an index for quantity of total output.

# CALCULATING REAL VS NOMINAL GDP

**Nominal GDP** $= \sum p_t q_t$

where $p$ refers to price, $q$ is quantity, and $t$ indicates the year in question (usually the current year).

However, it can be misleading to do an apples-to-apples comparison of a GDP of $1 trillion in 2008 with a GDP of $200 billion in 1990. This is because of inflation. The value of one dollar in 1990 was far greater than the value of a dollar in 2008. In other words, prices in 1990 were different from prices in 2008. Therefore, if you want to really compare economic output (quantities), you can calculate GDP by using prices from a base year.

**When you adjust nominal GDP for price changes (inflation or deflation), you get what is known as the Real GDP.**

It can be calculated using the following formula:

**Real GDP** $= \sum p_b q_t$

where, $b$ denotes the base year.

To effectively compare the real GDP of 2 years, one can construct an index using a base year. A base year is usually an arbitrary figure (here, a particular year) which is used as a yardstick for comparison of the GDP numbers.

## ❖ Usage and Applications

**When should we use real GDP numbers and when is nominal GDP used?**

One uses the nominal GDP figures to determine the total value of the products and services manufactured in a country during a particular year. However, when one wants to compare GDP in 1 year with past years to study trends in economic growth, real GDP is used.

By definition (since real GDP is calculated using prices of a given 'base year'), real GDP has no meaning by itself unless it is compared to GDP of a different year.

If a set of real GDPs from various years is calculated, each calculation uses the quantities from its own year, but all use the prices from the same base year. The differences in those real GDPs will, therefore, reflect merely differences in volume.

An index called the GDP deflator can be obtained by dividing, for each year, the nominal GDP by the real GDP. It gives an indication of the overall level of inflation or deflation in the economy.

**GDP deflator for year $t$ = $GDP_t$ / Real $GDP_t$**

## ❖ Countries Compared in real GDP

If there is high inflation in a country, there may be rapid growth in nominal GDP but not much growth in real GDP. All countries have different rates of inflation. Therefore, while comparing GDP growth rates in different countries, real GDP is used and not nominal GDP.

## ❖ Sovereign Rating Agencies

A sovereign credit rating is the credit rating of a country or sovereign entity. Sovereign credit ratings give investors insight into the level of risk associated with investing in a particular country and also include political risks. At the request of the country, a credit rating agency will evaluate the country's economic and political environment to determine a representative credit rating. Obtaining a good sovereign credit rating is usually essential for developing countries in order to access funding in international bond markets.

Another common reason for obtaining sovereign credit ratings, other than issuing bonds in external debt markets, is to attract foreign direct investment. To give investors confidence in investing in their country, many countries seek ratings from credit rating agencies like Standard and Poors, Moody's, and Fitch to provide financial transparency and demonstrate their credit standing.

Countries are issued sovereign credit ratings. This rating analyses the general creditworthiness of a country or foreign government. Sovereign credit ratings take into account the overall economic conditions of a country including the volume of foreign, public and private investment, capital market transparency and foreign currency reserves. Sovereign ratings also assess political conditions such as overall political stability and the level of economic stability a country will maintain during times of political transition. Institutional investors rely on sovereign ratings to qualify and quantify the general investment atmosphere of a particular country. The sovereign rating is often the prerequisite information institutional investors use to determine if they will further consider specific companies, industries and classes of securities issued in a specific country. Fitch, Moody and S&P rate each country

## ❖ India's Rating Agencies

Rational investors take into account:

- macroeconomic stability (which proxies for risks)
- growth, which crucially determines rewards and returns.

**Rational Investor Ratings Index (RIRI):** 'The Rational Investor Ratings Index (RIRI) is computed by averaging a country's GDP growth rate and its macro-economic indicators; the latter measured as the average of the fiscal deficit, current account deficit, and inflation (all with negative signs). Thus, equal weight is given to growth and macroeconomic stability. The greater the number, the better should be its investor rating'.

Traditional rating measures typically rely more on stability than growth when assigning their ratings as the ratings are a measure of risk. The RIRI argues that rational investors would rate investments based on both stability and growth and not stability alone. Thus, if India's growth prospects, which are better than all the other countries in its current investment grade, are factored in, then India deserves an upgrade in its ratings.

The index was created by the department of economic affairs for the purpose of exposition in the economic survey. The index postulates that international rating agencies don't assign ratings the way that a rational investor would. It then tries to assign an index value on the basis of what a rational investor would take into account. Essentially the rationale behind such an index was to provide an alternative to the ratings provided by international agencies. Essentially the rationale behind such an index was to provide an alternative to the ratings provided by international agencies.

**Macroeconomic Vulnerability Index:** Macroeconomic Vulnerability Index, as mentioned in the Mid-Year Economic Analysis 2014–2015, released by Ministry of Finance recently, adds together the rate of inflation, current account deficit and fiscal deficit of a country. The Index value can be compared across countries for different time periods to gauge their relative vulnerability. The ministry has done a comparison of the 'fragile five' countries—Brazil, India, Indonesia, South Africa and Turkey.

According to the data, in the beginning of 2013, India was on top of the list with an Index value of 22.4. The current account deficit was at 4.7 per cent of the GDP, inflation at 10.2 per cent and budget deficit at 7.5 per cent of GDP. For the purpose of comparison, the ministry has taken data from the World Economic Outlook of the International Monetary Fund. Though India's macroeconomic vulnerability has come down, it still needs to be watchful, noted the mid-year analysis. 'India still needs to be watchful in terms of its macro-economic fundamentals. The value of the index currently is well above 15 (recognizing that a value below 12—say 4 per cent inflation, 2 per cent CAD, and 6 per cent fiscal deficit—is perhaps safer macroeconomic territory)', stated the document.

## ❖ Importance of Stability

For economic activity to grow at a healthy pace, it is important that the economy is managed well. Differently put, for economic activity to prosper, among other things, it is important that inflation is low, government finances are handled well, imbalances are avoided on the external front, and the financial system is stable. Economic activity is likely to suffer if the economy is vulnerable to internal or external shocks. A problem in one area, if not handled well, can percolate into other areas and lead to a bigger crisis. For example, if the government is running a high budget deficit, it will push demand and can create inflationary pressure. High inflation, among other things, affects competitiveness and higher demand will also lead to higher imports. This will lead to imbalance on external accounts and volatility in the currency market. Uncertainty on the external front can lead to financial instability, which will affect economic activity. Therefore, it is important for policymakers to be watchful and take necessary steps, in time, to avoid extreme consequences.

❑❑❑

# CHAPTER 12

# Public Finance

## PUBLIC FINANCE—MEANING

Public Finance describes and analyses government services, subsidies, welfare payments and the methods by which the expenditures to these ends are covered through taxation, borrowing, foreign aid and the creation of money. It is concerned with the income and expenditure of public authorities, and with the adjustment of one to another.

## FISCAL POLICY

Fiscal policy is a change in government spending or taxing designed to influence economic activity. These changes are designed to control the level of aggregate demand in the economy.

Governments usually bring about changes in taxation, volume of spending, and size of the budget deficit or surplus to affect public expenditure.

Fiscal policy is said to be tight or contractionary when revenue is higher than spending (i.e., the government budget is in surplus) and loose or expansionary when spending is higher than revenue (i.e., the budget is in deficit).

Fiscal policy and monetary policy are two major drivers of a nation's economic performance. Through monetary policy, a country's central bank influences the money supply. Regulators use both policies to try to boost a flagging (waning) economy, maintain a strong economy or cool off an overheated economy.

## BUDGET IN INDIA

Budget is an estimation of the revenue and expenses over a specified future period of time. A budget can be made for a person, family, group of people, business, government, country, multinational organization or just about anything else that makes and spends money.

Union Budget keeps the account of the government›s finances for the fiscal year that runs from 1st April to 31st March. According to Article 112 of the Indian Constitution, the Union Budget of a year, also referred to as the annual financial statement, is a statement of the estimated receipts and expenditure of the government for that particular year. Union Budget keeps the account of the government›s finances for the fiscal year that runs from 1st April to 31st March. Union Budget is classified into Revenue Budget and Capital Budget.

**Revenue budget** includes the government's revenue receipts and expenditure. There are two kinds of revenue receipts – tax and non-tax revenue. Revenue expenditure is the expenditure incurred on day to day functioning of the government and on various services offered to citizens. If revenue expenditure exceeds revenue receipts, the government incurs a revenue deficit.

**Capital Budget** includes capital receipts and payments of the government. Loans from public, foreign governments and RBI form a major part of the government's capital receipts. Capital expenditure is the expenditure on development of machinery, equipment, building, health facilities, education, etc. Fiscal deficit is incurred when the government's total expenditure exceeds its total revenue.

A **surplus budget** means profits are anticipated, while a balanced budget means that revenues are expected to equal expenses. A **deficit budget** means expenses will exceed revenues. Budgets are usually compiled and re-evaluated on a periodic basis. Adjustments are made to budgets based on the goals of the budgeting organization. In some cases, budget makers are happy to operate at a deficit, while in other cases, operating at a deficit is seen as financially irresponsible.

## ❖ Salient Features

Some of the salient features of union budget are as follows:

1. **Budget Is Prepared on Cash Basis:** Whatever is expected to be actually received or paid under proper sanction during a financial year (including arrears of the past years) should be budgeted in that year.
2. **Rule of Lapse:** All appropriations granted by the Parliament expire at the end of financial year and no deduction of unspent budget can be appropriated for meeting the demands in the next financial year. Thus, all unutilized funds within the year 'lapse' at the end of the financial year.
3. **Realistic Estimation:** It is essential that the provisions in the budget should be restricted to the amount required for actual expenditure. The Finance Ministry is interested in seeing that the Departments do not obtain more/less money than what they really need. If a Department is allotted funds which it does not need, it will deprive some other Department from getting the required resources.
4. **Budget to Be on Gross/Net Basis:** Budget is prepared both on the gross basis and net basis. The gross figures of receipts and expenditure of the government are reflected separately for voting by the Parliament and the Departments/ Ministries are normally not permitted to utilize the receipts or deduct expenditure in their budget proposals. Net basis of budgeting is done in case of some Grants, e.g., Defence Ordnance Factories and Department of Posts, wherein the departmental receipts are allowed to be utilized and outlays on gross as well as net basis are reflected.
5. **Form of Estimates to Correspond to Accounts**: It is essential that the form in the budget estimates correspond to that of Government accounts as it is from these accounts, that the performance of the government is judged and the estimation for subsequent year made. If these are prepared in different forms, financial control will also become difficult.
6. **Estimates to Be on Departmental Basis:** Each Department prepares estimates for receipts and expenditure separately. Generally, one Demand or Grant is allocated in respect of each Ministry/ Department. In case of certain large Departments/Ministries more than one Demand for Grants is allocated in terms of General Financial Rules.

## ❖ Scope of the Budget

The Budget is presented to the Parliament in such form as the Finance Ministry may decide after considering the suggestions, if any, made by the Estimates Committee. Broadly, the Budget documents depict information relating to receipts and expenditure for three years, i.e., –

1. Through Budget Estimates (BE) of receipts and expenditure in respect of Budget year (current financial year);
2. For the year preceding the Budget year (current year) through Revised Estimates (RE); and
3. Actuals of the second year proceeding the Budget year.

Budget thus sets forth the receipts and the expenditure of the government for three consecutive years. The Annual Financial Statement shows the receipts and expenditure of the government in three separate parts under which government accounts are maintained, viz:

1. Consolidated Fund of India
2. Contingency Fund of India and
3. Public Account

As per Constitutional provisions (Article 112), the Annual Financial Statement has to distinguish expenditure on revenue account from other expenditure. It, therefore, comprises of (i) Revenue budget and (ii) Capital Budget. Broad break-up of expenditure on Plan and Non Plan, i.e., expenditure which is part of normal activities of the government or maintenance expenditure, sectoral allocation of Plan Outlays, details of resources transferred to States and Union Territory Governments are also reflected in the budget documents.

The expenditure of certain categories, charged on the Consolidated Fund of India and not being subject to the Vote of Parliament are also indicated separately in the Budget. The demands for grants show separately the revenue and capital, and the charged and voted expenditure. Similarly, estimates of receipts are classified in the tax and on-tax receipts and also those which are on revenue account and others which are on capital account.

The Union Budget is presented to the Parliament in two parts, i.e., Railway Budget pertaining to Railway Finance and General Budget which gives an overall picture of financial position of the Government of India including the effect of Railway Budget. The three statements presented to the Parliament, viz. the Macroeconomic Framework Statement, the Medium Term Fiscal Policy Statement and the Fiscal Policy Strategy Statement under the Fiscal Responsibility and Budget Management (FRBM) mandate, have further enhanced the scope of budget to provide an assessment of the growth prospects of the economy, indicate the rolling targets for specific fiscal indicators as well as outline the strategic priorities of the government in the fiscal area for the ensuing year.

## ❖ Historical Perspective

'Budget System' was introduced in India on 7 April 1860. James Wilson, the first Indian Finance Member delivered the budget speech expounding the Indian financial policy as an integral whole for the first time (*Principles of Civil Government: Akshaya K. Ghosh*). Post-independence, the first budget was presented on 26 November 1947 by India's first Finance Minister, Sri R. K. Shanmukham Chetty. The national independence brought about budgeting reforms with the Government of India primarily through the launching of comprehensive socio-economic development through five year plans, divided into annual plans. A sound system of sharing of resources with the states was also established through the successive Finance Commissions. By and large the system in place at present has evolved over a period of time.

The annual exercise of budgeting is a means for detailing the roadmap for efficient use of public resources. Although the Indian Constitution does not mention the term 'Budget', it provides that the President shall in respect of every financial year cause to be laid before both the Houses of Parliament, the House of People (Lok Sabha) and the Council of States (Rajya Sabha), a statement of the estimated receipts and expenditure of the government for that year. This statement known as the 'Annual Financial Statement' is the main fiscal or budgetary document of the government.

The financial year for the Union and the State Governments in India is from April to March. Each financial year is, therefore, spread over two calendar years. The period of financial year as from April to March was introduced in India from 1867. Prior to that, the financial year in India used to commence on 1st May and ended on 30th April (L. K. Jha Committee's Report of the Committee on Change in Financial Year).

L. K. Jha Committee was appointed in May 1984 to look into the issue of financial year. The committee while recommending the commencement of financial year from January mainly with reference to the impact of South West monsoon on the economy, had mentioned in their report that if for any reason, a change over to the calendar year is not acceptable despite its many advantages, then on balance, it might be best to live with the existing financial year and avoid the problems of transition.

The Government of India did not favour any change in the financial year for some of the reasons which are brought out below:

1. The advantages arising out of the change would only be marginal in view of the innumerable considerations in the formulation of budget policies;
2. Change in the financial year would upset the collection of data and it might take a long time to return to normalcy in this regard; and
3. The change would create a large number of problems, as extensive amendments to tax laws and systems, financial procedures relating to expenditure authorization and other matters would become necessary and in that process the administrative machinery would get diverted to problems of transition instead of concentrating on improving the tax collection machinery.

## ❖ Principles of Budgeting

Based broadly on the statutory and other requirements of the Constitution and rules made pursuant to these requirements, the essential guiding principles of budgeting can be summed up as follows:

1. **Principle of Annuality:** Presentation of budget is in respect of the ensuing financial year only. The grants authorized by the legislature are valid for one financial year, i.e., up to 31st March of that financial year only and cannot be carried forward to the next year. Consequently, the unutilized grants lapse at the end of the financial year.
2. **Principle of Comprehensiveness:** Budget shall be comprehensive, i.e., it shall include the estimate of all foreseeable items of receipts and expenditure, contain full information on current schemes and programmes, performances in various fields of activities and present a complete and correct picture of the financial position of the government.
3. **Principle of Specificness and Clarity:** All items of receipts and expenditure shall be specific. Making of lump sum provisions should be avoided. This facilitates proper scrutiny at all levels and helps all concerned to keep a watch over progress of actuals and in exercising budgetary control.
4. **Principle of Gross Budgeting:** This principle has its basis in the Article 204(3) of the Constitution which prohibits withdrawal from the Consolidated Fund

of the State except under appropriation made by law passed in accordance with the Constitutional provisions. This necessitates authorization of gross expenditure notwithstanding the receipts or recoveries adjustable under the same expenditure head as reduction in expenditure. This is a preventive tool to check misuse of money accrued through large recoveries.

5. **Principle of Accuracy Gross:** Under-estimation and overestimation are serious budgetary irregularities. Thus not only the budget provisions should be comprehensive and cater for all items of receipts and expenditure, but should be only so much as are absolutely necessary, neither more nor less. This will of course be subject to variations resulting from unforeseen developments or circumstances.
6. **Principle of Non-diversion of Funds Authorized for Specific Purposes:** It is not permissible to divert the funds authorized under one grant/appropriation to meet excess expenditure elsewhere.
7. **Principle of Periodic Review and Corrective Action:** The estimating officers, controlling officers and administrative departments are expected to be watchful as regards progress of actuals on both receipt and expenditure sides. Periodic reviews are expected to be taken and estimates need to be updated and orders obtained at appropriate levels and time to revise the estimates with a suitable follow-up action.

The first five of the abovementioned principles operate at the formulation stage while the last two need to be followed subsequently while operating the budget.

## ❖ Budget Formulation in India

The Budget division of the economic affairs department issues a circular to all ministries, states and UTs, autonomous bodies and the defence forces for preparing revised estimates for the current financial year and the budget estimates for the next financial year.

The budget process in India has four distinct phases:

1. **Budget formulation:** Preparation of estimates of expenditure and receipts for the ensuing financial year;
2. **Budget enactment:** Approval of the proposed budget by the legislature through the enactment of Finance Bill and Appropriation Bill;
3. **Budget execution:** Enforcement of the provisions in the Finance Act and Appropriation Act by the government—collection of receipts and making disbursements for various services as approved by the legislature;
4. **legislative review of budget implementation:** Audits of government's financial operations on behalf of the legislature.

## ❖ Commencement in August-September

By convention, the Union Budget for next financial year is presented in Lok Sabha by the finance minister on the last working day of February. However, the process of budget formulation starts in the last week of August or the first fortnight of September. To get the process started, the Budget Division in the Department of Economic Affairs under the Ministry of Finance issues the annual budget circular to all the Union government ministries/departments around August-September. The Circular contains detailed instructions for these ministries/departments on the form and content of the statement of budget estimates to be prepared by them.

## ❖ Figures in a Budget

The ministries are required to provide three different kinds of figures relating to their expenditures and receipts during this process of budget preparation. These are: budget estimates, revised estimates and actuals.

Let's understand this in the context of Union budget 2013–14, which was presented, as usual, on 28 February 2013 by the Finance Minister, Shri P. Chidambaram on the floor of Lok Sabha. However, the process of its formulation would have got started in August 2012 through issuance of budget circular of the Budget Division and this process would have continued till February 2013. The approval of Parliament is sought for the estimated receipts/expenditures for 2013–14, which would be called budget estimates. At the same time, the Union government, in its budget for 2013–14, would also present revised estimates for the ongoing financial year 2012–13. The government would not seek approval from the Parliament of revised estimates of 2012–13; but, these revised estimates allow the government to reallocate its funds among various ministries based on the implementation of the budget for 2012–13 during the first six months of financial year 2012–13. Finally, ministries also report their actual receipts and expenditures for the previous financial year 2011–12. Hence, the Union budget for 2013–14 consists of budget estimates for 2013–14, revised estimates for 2012–13, and actual expenditures and receipts of 2011–12.

## ❖ Managing Deficit

In the past few years, the finance ministry has been vociferously arguing for reduction of Fiscal Deficit and Revenue Deficit of the Union government, citing the targets set by the FRBM Act and its rules. Hence, presently, the aspirations of the Planning Commission and Union Government ministries with regard to spending face the legal hurdle of this Act, which has made it mandatory for the Union Government to show the revenue deficit as nil (total revenue expenditure not exceeding total revenue receipts by even a single rupee) and the Fiscal Deficit as less than 3 per cent of gross domestic product (GDP). This means new borrowing of the government in a financial year cannot exceed 3 per cent of the country's GDP for that year.

## ❖ To the End

During the final stage of budget preparation, the revenue-earning ministries of the Union government provide the estimates for their revenue receipts in the current fiscal year (revised estimates) and next fiscal year (budget estimates) to the finance ministry. Subsequently, usually in the month of January, more attention is paid to finalization of the estimated receipts. With an idea about the total requirement of resources to meet expenditures in the next fiscal year, the finance ministry focuses on the revenue receipts for the next fiscal year.

At this stage of budget preparation, the finance minister examines the budget proposals prepared by the ministry and makes changes in them, if required. The finance minister consults the Prime Minister, and also briefs the Union Cabinet, about the budget at this stage. If there is any conflict between any ministry and the finance ministry with regard to the budget, the matter is supposed to be resolved by the Cabinet.

## ❖ Consultations with Various Stakeholders Crucial

In the run-up to Union Budget each year, the finance minister holds pre-budget consultations with relevant stakeholders. The finance minister also holds consultations with finance ministers of states/union territories as well as Trade and Industry representatives. This has great significance for the process of budget formulation as it helps the finance minister to take decisions on suitable fiscal policy changes to be announced during the budget.

For this year's budget, representatives from the agriculture sector, various trade unions, economists, banking and financial institutions and also social sector groups participated in these consultations in January 2013. Among others, a delegation of People's Budget Initiative also met Finance Ministry officials and shared the People's Charter of Demands in the month of January 2013. But this year too, like in previous years, the process started late. Desired changes in expenditure programmes and policies can be influenced only if the consultations are begun earlier, preferably in October.

## ❖ Consolidation of Budget Data

As the last steps, the budget division in the finance ministry consolidates all figures to be presented in the budget and prepares the final budget documents. The National Informatics Centre (NIC) helps the budget division in the process of consolidation of the budget data, which has been fully computerized. At the end of this process, the finance minister takes the permission of the President of India for presenting the Union budget to the Parliament.

It would be useful to point out that while the second and the third stages in the budget cycle of our country are reasonably transparent, the first stage of actual budget preparation cannot be said to be open. The process is rather carried out behind closed doors.

## ❖ Voting

The standing committee reports are presented to the House, which discusses & votes on demands for grants. The Speaker puts all the outstanding demands to the vote of the House. This device is called 'guillotine'. After the general discussion & voting on demands for grants, the government introduces the Appropriation Bill. This Bill is to give authority to the govt. to incur expenditure from and out of the Consolidated Fund of India.

## ❖ Budget Related Constitutional Provisions

Financial business in Parliament consists of the Budget comprising of General Budget and Railway Budget, Demands for Grant, Vote on Account, Supplementary Demands for Grant, Appropriation Bill and the Finance Bill. The salient Constitutional provisions that shape and guide the budgeting systems and process are outlined in brief as under:

**Article 112 – Annual Financial Statement:** It provides that in respect of every financial year, the President shall cause to be laid before both the Houses of Parliament a statement of the estimated receipts and expenditure of the Government of India for that year, referred to as the 'annual financial statement'. The estimates of expenditure shall show separately expenditure charged upon the Consolidated Fund of India; and other expenditure (voted) proposed to be made from the Consolidated Fund of India. The statement shall also distinguish expenditure on revenue account from other (capital) expenditure.

**Article 113 – Procedure in the Parliament with Respect to Estimates:** It provides that estimates relating to expenditure charged upon the Consolidated Fund of India shall not be submitted to the vote of Parliament, even though these can be discussed in either House of Parliament. The estimates relating to the 'voted' portion shall be submitted in the form of demands for grants, and the House of the People shall have power to assent, refuse or reduce the amount specified therein. No demand for a grant shall be made except on the recommendation of the President.

**Article 114 – Appropriation Bills:** After the passing of the demands under Article 113, Appropriation Bill is introduced in the Lok Sabha to provide for the appropriation out of the Consolidated Fund of India to meet the requirements relating to (*a*) the grants so made by the House of the People; and (*b*) the expenditure charged on the Consolidated

Fund of India but not exceeding in any case the amount shown in the statement previously laid before Parliament. Further, subject to the provisions of articles 115 and 116, no money shall be withdrawn from the Consolidated Fund of India except under appropriation made by law passed in accordance with the provisions of this article.

**Article 115 – Supplementary, Additional or Excess Grants:** If the amount authorized through appropriations for a particular service is found to be insufficient for the purposes of that year or when a need has arisen during the current financial year for supplementary or additional expenditure upon some new service not contemplated in the annual financial statement for that year, a supplementary demands for grants proposal shall be made before Parliament.

However, if any money has been spent on any service during a financial year in excess of the amount granted for that service and for that year, demand for such excess, as the case may be is to be laid before both the Houses of Parliament for authorizing (subject to the report of the Public Accounts Committee) the expenditure incurred in excess.

**Article 116 – Vote on account, Vote of credit and Exceptional Grant:** The House of the People shall have power relating to

1. Vote on Account – to make any grant in advance in respect of the estimated expenditure for a part of any financial year pending the completion of the parliamentary procedure.
2. Vote of Credit – to make a grant for meeting an unexpected demand upon the resources of India when on account of the magnitude or the indefinite character of the service the demand cannot be stated with the details ordinarily given in an annual financial statement;
3. Exceptional Grant – to make provision for an exceptional grant that does not form part of the current service of any financial year; Parliament shall have power to authorize by law the withdrawal of moneys from the Consolidated Fund of India for the above purposes.

**Article 117 – Special Provisions as to Financial Bills:** A Bill or amendment making provision for any of the matters specified in sub-clauses (*a*) to (*f*) of clause (1) of article 110 shall not be introduced or moved except on the recommendation of the President and a Bill making such provision shall not be introduced in the Council of States.

**Article 265 – Taxes Not to Be Imposed Save by Authority of Law:** No tax shall be levied or collected except by authority of law.

**Article 266–Consolidated Funds and Public Accounts of India and of the States:** Subject to the provisions of article 267 and to the provisions of this Chapter with respect to the assignment of the whole or part of the net proceeds of certain taxes and duties to States, all revenues received by the Government of India, all loans raised and all moneys received by that government in repayment of loans shall form one consolidated fund to be entitled 'the Consolidated Fund of India', and all revenues received by the Government of a State, all loans raised and all moneys received by that government in repayment of loans shall form one consolidated fund to be entitled 'the Consolidated Fund of the State'.

All other public moneys received by or on behalf of the Government of India or the Government of a State shall be credited to the public account of India or the public account of the State, as the case may be.

No moneys out of the Consolidated Fund of India or the Consolidated Fund of a State shall be appropriated except in accordance with law and for the purposes and in the manner provided in this Constitution.

**Article 267 – Contingency Fund:** Parliament may by law establish a Contingency Fund in the nature of an imprest to be entitled "the Contingency Fund of India" into which shall be paid from time to time such sums as may be determined by such law, and the said Fund shall be placed at the disposal of the President to enable advances to be made by him out of such Fund for the purposes of meeting unforeseen expenditure pending authorization of such expenditure by Parliament by law under Article 115 or Article 116. Similarly, the legislature of a State may by law establish a Contingency Fund in the nature of an imprest to be entitled "the Contingency Fund of the State".

**Article 275–Grants from the Union to Certain States:** Such sums as Parliament may by law provide shall be charged on the Consolidated Fund of India in each year as grants-in-aid of the revenues of such States as Parliament may determine to be in need of assistance, and different sums may be fixed for different States. Provided that after a Finance Commission has been constituted no order shall be made under this clause by the President except after considering the recommendations of the Finance Commission.

**Article 280–Finance Commission:** The President shall, within two years from the commencement of this Constitution and thereafter at the expiration of every fifth year or at such earlier time as the President considers necessary, by order constitute a Finance Commission. It shall be the duty of the Commission to make recommendations to the President relating to—

1. The distribution between the Union and the States of the net proceeds of taxes which are to be, or may be, divided between them under this Chapter and the allocation between the States of the respective shares of such proceeds;
2. The principles which should govern the grants-in-aid of the revenues of the States out of the Consolidated Fund of India;
3. The measures needed to augment the Consolidated Fund of a State to supplement the resources of the Panchayats in the State on the basis of the recommendations made by the Finance Commission of the State;
4. The measures needed to augment the Consolidated Fund of a State to supplement the resources of the Municipalities in the State on the basis of the recommendations made by the Finance Commission of the State;
5. Any other matter referred to the Commission by the President in the interests of sound finance. The Commission shall determine their procedure and shall have such powers in the performance of their functions as Parliament may by law confer on them.

**Article 281–Recommendations of the Finance Commission:** The President shall cause every recommendation made by the Finance Commission under the provisions of this Constitution together with an explanatory memorandum as to the action taken thereon to be laid before each House of Parliament.

**Article 292 – Borrowing by the Government of India:** The executive power of the Union extends to borrowing upon the security of the Consolidated Fund of India within such limits, if any, as may from time to time be fixed by Parliament by law and to the giving of guarantees within such limits, if any, as may be so fixed.

**Article 150 – Form of accounts of the Union and of the States:** The accounts of the Union and of the States shall be kept in such form as the President may, on the advice of the Comptroller and Auditor-General of India, prescribe.

**Article 151–Audit reports:** The reports of the Comptroller and Auditor- General of India relating to the accounts of the Union shall be submitted to the President, who shall cause them to be laid before each House of Parliament.

**Article 109–Special procedure in respect of Money Bills:** A Money Bill shall not be introduced in the Council of States. After a Money Bill has been passed by the House of the People it shall be transmitted to the Council of States for its recommendations and the Council of States shall within a period of fourteen days from the date of its receipt of the Bill return the Bill to the House of the People with its recommendations and the House of the People may thereupon either accept or reject all or any of the recommendations of the Council of States.

**Article 110–Definition of "Money Bills":** A Bill shall be deemed to be a Money Bill if it contains only provisions dealing with all or any of the following matters, namely:—(*a*) the imposition, abolition, remission, alteration or regulation of any tax; (*b*) the regulation of the borrowing of money or the giving of any guarantee by the Government of India, or the amendment of the law with respect to any financial obligations undertaken or to be undertaken by the Government of India; (*c*) the custody of the Consolidated Fund or the Contingency Fund of India, the payment of moneys into or the withdrawal of moneys from any such Fund; (*d*) the appropriation of moneys out of the Consolidated Fund of India; (*e*) the declaring of any expenditure to be expenditure charged on the Consolidated Fund of India or the increasing of the amount of any such expenditure; (*f*) the receipt of money on account of the Consolidated Fund of India or the public account of India or the custody or issue of such money or the audit of the accounts of the Union or of a State; or (*g*) any matter incidental to any of the matters specified in sub-clauses (*a*) to (*f*). If any question arises whether a Bill is a Money Bill or not, the decision of the Speaker of the House of the People thereon shall be final, and the certificate of the Speaker of the House of the People signed by him that it is a Money Bill, shall be endorsed on every Money Bill when it is transmitted to the Council of States under article 109, and when it is presented to the President for assent under article 111.

## ❖ Budget Implementation

**Rule 51 of the General Financial Rule,** lays down provisions regarding 'The Communication and Distribution of Grants and Appropriations', which *inter alia* states that—'After the Appropriation Bill relating to Budget is passed, the Ministry of Finance shall communicate Budget provisions to the Ministries/Departments which, in turn, shall distribute the same to their subordinate formations. The distribution so made shall also be communicated to the respective Pay and Accounts Officers who shall exercise check against the allocation to each subordinate authority'.

## ❖ Role of Departments in Spending and Control

The relevant administrative ministry has the main responsibility for ensuring that (i) expenditure is incurred for the approved purpose; (ii) it is within the sums allotted; (iii) it has been incurred under the authority competent to sanction it, and (iv) due prudence has been shown in its incurrence. As ministries have delegated their powers to lower functionaries, the basic responsibility is shifted to the particular functionary concerned, but overall responsibility remains with the administrative ministry.

As per rules, no public authority can incur any expenditure or enter into any liability involving expenditure or transfer of moneys for investment or deposit from government account unless such expenditure or transfer, as the case may be has been sanctioned by general or special orders of the government or by any authority to which power has been delegated in this regard. No expenditure can be incurred against a sanction unless funds are made available to meet the expenditure by valid appropriation or re-appropriation. The government authorities have to comply with rules prescribed in the General Financial Rules and the Delegation of Financial Power Rules in all financial matters. The designated controlling authorities have to ensure not only that the total expenditure is kept within the limits of the authorized grants but also that the funds allotted to spending units are expended in the public interest and on objects for which the money was provided.

In order to maintain proper control, the controlling officer obtains information on not only what has actually been spent from the grants but also what commitments and liabilities have been and will be incurred against them. He must be in a position to assume, before the Government and Public Accounts Committee, complete responsibility for departmental expenditure and to explain or to justify any instance of excess expenditure or financial irregularity that may be brought to notice as a result of audit scrutiny or otherwise. In the discharge of his ultimate responsibility for the administration of a grant, or a part thereof, placed at his disposal, every controlling officer must satisfy himself that adequate provisions exist within the departmental organization for systematic internal checks calculated to prevent and detect errors and irregularities in the financial proceedings of his subordinate officers and to guard against waste and loss of public money and stores, to ensure that the prescribed checks are effectively applied.

As regards receipts, it is the duty of the departments concerned to ensure that the dues of the government are correctly and promptly assessed and paid into the treasury/bank. All moneys received by or on behalf of the government either as dues of the government or for deposit, remittance or otherwise are required to be brought into the government account without delay in accordance with the prescribed rules and regulations.

## ❖ Tax System in India

A tax may be defined as a 'pecuniary burden laid upon individuals or property owners to support the government, a payment exacted by legislative authority'. A tax 'is not a voluntary payment or donation, but an enforced contribution, exacted pursuant to legislative authority'.

## ❖ Constitutional Basis of Tax System in India

The tax system in India is mainly a **three-tier system** which is based between the Central, State Governments and the local government organizations. In most cases, these local bodies include the local councils and the municipalities. According to the Constitution of India, the government has the right to levy taxes on individuals and organizations. However, the Constitution states that no one has the right to levy or charge taxes except the authority of law. Whatever tax is being charged has to be backed by the law passed by the legislature or the parliament. Article 246 (Seventh Schedule) of the Indian Constitution, distributes legislative powers including taxation, between the Parliament and the State Legislature.

Schedule VII enumerates these subject matters with the use of three lists:

List I entailing the areas on which only the parliament is competent to makes laws, List II entailing the areas on which only the State Legislature can make laws, and List III listing the areas on which both the Parliament and the State Legislature can make laws upon concurrently.

Provisions have been made by 73rd Constitutional Amendment, enforced from 24 April 1993, to levy taxes by the Panchayat. A State may by law authorize a Panchayat to levy, collect and appropriate taxes, duties, tolls, etc. Similarly, the provisions have been made by 74th Constitutional Amendment, enforced from 1 June 1993, to levy the taxes by the Municipalities. A State Legislature may by law authorize a Municipality to levy, collect and appropriate taxes, duties, tolls, etc.

Separate heads of taxation are provided under lists I and II of Seventh Schedule of the Indian Constitution. There is no head of taxation in the Concurrent List (Union and the States have no concurrent power of taxation). Any tax levied by the government which is not backed by law or is beyond the powers of the legislating authority may be struck down as unconstitutional.

The thirteen heads List-I of Seventh Schedule of Constitution of India covered under Union taxation, on which Parliament enacts the taxation law, are as under:

1. Taxes on income other than agricultural income;
2. Duties of customs including export duties;
3. Duties of excise on tobacco and other goods manufactured or produced in India except *(i)* alcoholic liquor for human consumption, and *(ii)* opium, Indian hemp and other narcotic drugs and narcotics, but including medicinal and toilet preparations containing alcohol or any substance included in *(ii)*;
4. Corporation Tax;
5. Taxes on capital value of assets, exclusive of agricultural land, of individuals and companies, taxes on capital of companies;
6. Estate duty in respect of property other than agricultural land;
7. Duties in respect of succession to property other than agricultural land;
8. Terminal taxes on goods or passengers, carried by railway, sea or air; taxes on railway fares and freight;
9. Taxes other than stamp duties on transactions in stock exchanges and futures markets;
10. Taxes on the sale or purchase of newspapers and on advertisements published therein;
11. Taxes on sale or purchase of goods other than newspapers, where such sale or purchase takes place in the course of inter-State trade or commerce;
12. Taxes on the consignment of goods in the course of inter-State trade or commerce.
13. All residuary types of taxes not listed in any of the three lists of Seventh Schedule of Indian Constitution.

The nineteen heads List-II of Seventh Schedule of the Indian Constitution covered under State taxation, on which State Legislative enacts the taxation law, are as under:

1. Land revenue, including the assessment and collection of revenue, the maintenance of land records, survey for revenue purposes and records of rights, and alienation of revenues;
2. Taxes on agricultural income;
3. Duties in respect of succession to agricultural income;
4. Estate Duty in respect of agricultural income;
5. Taxes on lands and buildings;
6. Taxes on mineral rights;
7. Duties of excise for following goods manufactured or produced within the State (a) alcoholic liquors for human consumption, and (b) opium, Indian hemp and other narcotic drugs and narcotics;
8. Taxes on entry of goods into a local area for consumption, use or sale therein;
9. Taxes on the consumption or sale of electricity;
10. Taxes on the sale or purchase of goods other than newspapers;
11. Taxes on advertisements other than advertisements published in newspapers and advertisements broadcast by radio or television;
12. Taxes on goods and passengers carried by roads or on inland waterways;
13. Taxes on vehicles suitable for use on roads;
14. Taxes on animals and boats;

15. Tolls;
16. Taxes on profession, trades, callings and employments;
17. Capitation taxes;
18. Taxes on luxuries, including taxes on entertainments, amusements, betting and gambling;
19. Stamp duty.

## ❖ Union Government Budget

The basic structure of government budget is almost the same at all levels of the government (central, state and local) but items of expenditure and sources of revenue differ from budget to budget. Union Budget keeps the account of the government's finances for the fiscal year that runs from 1st April to 31st March.

**Union Government Budget Format**

| S. No. | Items | 2019-2020 Actuals | 2020-2021 Budget Estimates | 2020-2021 Revised Estimates | 2021-2022 Budget Estimates |
|---|---|---|---|---|---|
| 1. | Revenue Receipts | 1684059 | 2020926 | 1555153 | 1788424 |
| 2. | Tax Revenue (Net to Centre) | 1356902 | 1635909 | 1344501 | 1545396 |
| 3. | Non-Tax Revenue | 327157 | 385017 | 210652 | 243028 |
| 4. | Capital Receipts | 1002271 | 1021304 | 1895152 | 1694812 |
| 5. | Recovery of Loans | 18316 | 14967 | 14497 | 13000 |
| 6. | Other Receipts | 50304 | 210000 | 32000 | 175000 |
| 7. | Borrowings and Other Liabilities[1] | 933651 | 796337 | 1848655 | 1506812 |
| 8. | Total Receipts (1 + 4) | 2686330 | 3042230 | 3450305 | 3483236 |
| 9. | Total Expenditure (10 + 13) | 2686330 | 3042230 | 3450305 | 3483236 |
| 10. | On Revenue Account of which | 2350604 | 2630145 | 3011142 | 2929000 |
| 11. | Interest Payments | 612070 | 708203 | 692900 | 809701 |
| 12. | Grants in Aid for creation of capital assests | 185641 | 206500 | 230376 | 219112 |
| 13. | On Capital Account | 335726 | 412085 | 439163 | 554236 |
| 14. | Revenue Deficit (10 - 1) | 666545 (3.3) | 609219 (2.7) | 1455989 (7.5) | 1140576 (5.1) |
| 15. | Effective Revenue Deficit (14-12) | 480904 (2.4) | 402719 (1.8) | 1225613 (6.3) | 921464 (4.1) |
| 16. | Fiscal Deficit [9 – (1 + 5 + 6)] | 933651' (4.6) | 796337 (3.5) | 1848655 (9.5) | 1506812 (6.8) |
| 17. | Primary Deficit (16-11) | 321581 (1.6) | 88134 (0.4) | 1155755 (5.9) | 697111 (3.1) |

## ❖ Receipts of Government

Budget Receipts shows a detailed summary of the revenue and capital receipts of the government. It is part of the Annual Financial Statement. It gives a summary of tax revenue, non-tax revenue and capital receipts. It also gives a detailed analysis of tax and non-tax receipts together with the trends.

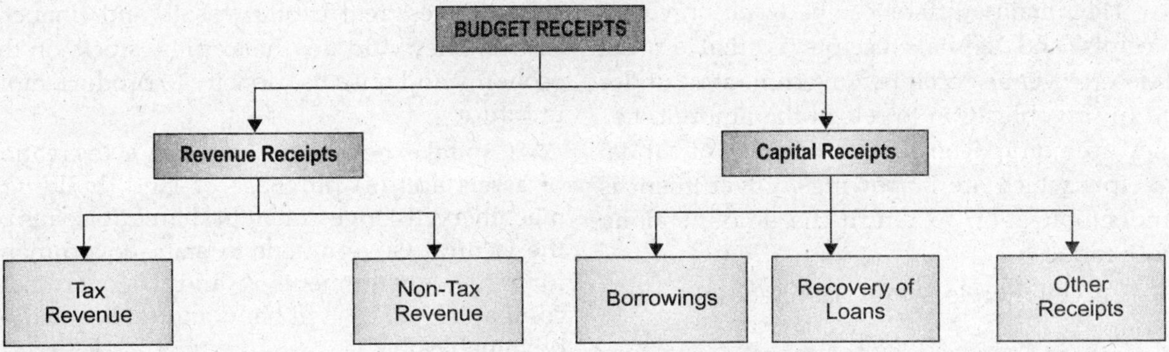


## Revenue Receipts

The receipts which neither (i) create liabilities nor (ii) reduce assets are called revenue receipts of the government. These are proceeds of taxes, interest and dividend on government investment, cess and other receipts for services rendered by the government.

Revenue Receipts are of two kinds:

1. Tax Revenue
2. Non-tax revenue

Tax revenue refers to sum total of receipts from taxes and other duties imposed by the government.

Non-tax revenue refers to receipts of the government from all sources other than those of tax receipts.

Following sources come under non-tax revenue receipts:

1. **Interest:** Government receives interest on loans given by it to state governments, union territories, private enterprises and general public.
2. **Profits and Dividends:** Profits are earned by government by running public sector undertakings like Indian railways, SAIL, BHEL, etc. It earns profit from the sale proceeds of the products of such public enterprises. It also receives dividend from its investments in other companies.
3. **Fees:** Fees refer to charges imposed by the government to cover the cost of recurring services provided by it. Court fees, registration fees, import fees, licence fee, etc., come under fees.
4. **Fines, Penalties and Forfeitures:** These are payments imposed on law breakers by courts. Fines are different from taxes as the former is levied to maintain law and order, whereas, the latter is imposed to generate revenue. Forfeitures are penalties which are imposed by the courts for non-compliance of orders or non-fulfilment of contracts, etc.
5. **Escheat:** It is a claim of the government on the property of a person who dies without leaving behind any legal heir or a will.
6. **Gifts and Grants:** Sometimes government receives gifts and grants from foreign governments and international organizations.

## Capital Receipts

The receipts which either (i) create liabilities (e.g., borrowing) or (ii) reduce assets (e.g., disinvestment) are called capital receipts. Thus, when government raises funds either by incurring a liability or by disposing off its assets, it is called a capital receipt.

Borrowing and raising of funds from public provident fund and small savings deposits are Capital Receipts which create liability. Disinvestment and recovery of loans are capital receipts which reduce assets.

The main difference between revenue receipts and capital receipts is that in the case of revenue receipts, government is under no future obligation to return the amount, i.e., they are non-redeemable. But in case of capital receipts which are borrowings, government is under obligation to return the amount along with interest.

Capital Receipts are classified into three groups:

1. **Borrowings:** Governments borrow funds from: (i) Open Market (Public); (ii) Reserve Bank of India (RBI); (iii) foreign governments; and (iv) International institutions (i.e., World Bank, International Monetary Fund).
2. **Recovery of Loans:** Government grants various loans to state governments or union territories. Recovery of such loans is a capital receipt as it reduces the assets of the government.
3. **Other Receipts**:

**These include:** (a) Disinvestment; and (b) Small Savings, i.e., Post Office deposits, National Saving Certificates, Kisan Vikas Patras, etc.

## ❖ Expenditure of Government

Expenditure of Government is classified as Revenue Expenditure and Capital Expenditure.

**Revenue Expenditure:** An expenditure which neither creates assets nor reduces liability is called Revenue Expenditure. Generally, expenditure incurred on normal running of the government departments and maintenance of services is treated as revenue expenditure, e.g., salaries of employees, interest payment on past debt, subsidies, pension, etc.

**Capital Expenditure:** An expenditure which either creates an asset (e.g., purchase of machinery) or reduces liability (e.g., repayment of loan) is called capital expenditure. They are incurred on long period development programmes, real capital assets and financial assets. They add to the capital stock of the economy and raise its capacity to produce more in future.

Capital expenditure which leads to creation of assets are: (a) purchase of land, buildings, machinery; (b) investment in shares; (c) loans by the Central Government to state government, foreign governments and government companies; (d) cash in hand and (e) acquisition of valuables.

Again, both Revenue and Capital expenditure can be divided into Plan and Non-plan expenditures. Non-plan expenditure is what the government spends on the so-called non-productive areas, such as salaries, subsidies, loans and interest, while plan expenditure pertains to the money to be set aside for productive purposes, like various projects of ministries. The Government of India in January 2017 decided to do away with a 92-year-old legacy of the distinction between plan and non-plan expenditure.

## ❖ Deficits in Budget

In Union budget, Government of India calculates four types of deficits:

1. Fiscal deficit = Total expenditure – Total receipts excluding borrowings.
2. Revenue deficit = Total revenue expenditure – Total revenue receipts.
3. Effective Revenue Deficit = Revenue Deficit – Grants in Aid for creation of capital assets
4. Primary deficit = Fiscal deficit – Interest payments.

**Fiscal Deficit** is the difference between the Revenue Receipts plus Non-debt Capital Receipts (NDCR) and the total expenditure. It is reflective of the total borrowing requirements of the government. In other words, Fiscal Deficit is equal to budgetary deficit plus governments' market borrowings and liabilities. This concept fully reflects the indebtedness of the government and throws light on the extent to which the government has gone beyond its means and the ways in which it has done so.

**Revenue Deficit** refers to the excess of revenue expenditure over revenue receipts. Revenue deficit signifies that government's own earning is insufficient to meet normal functioning of government departments and provision of services. Revenue deficit results in borrowing.

**Effective Revenue Deficit** is the difference between Revenue Deficit and Grants for Creation of Capital Assets. Effective Revenue deficit is a new term introduced in the Union Budget 2011–12. While revenue deficit is the difference between revenue receipts and revenue expenditure, the present accounting system includes all grants from the Union Government to the state governments/union territories/other bodies as revenue expenditure, even if they are used to create assets. Such assets created by the sub-national governments/bodies are owned by them and not by the Union Government. Nevertheless, they do result in the creation of durable assets. According to the Finance Ministry, such revenue expenditures contribute to the growth in the economy and therefore, should not be treated as unproductive in nature. Grants for creation of capital assets, as a concept, was introduced in the FRBM Act through the amendment in 2012.

**Primary Deficit** is measured as Fiscal Deficit less interest payments. It indicates the real position of the government finances as it excludes the interest burden of the loans taken in the past. It shows how much government borrowing is going to meet expenses other than Interest payments. Thus, zero primary deficits means that government has to resort to borrowing only to make interest payments.

**An economy may have other deficits as well including:**

1. **Budgetary Deficit:** Budgetary Deficit is the difference between all receipts and expenditure of the government, both revenue and capital. This difference is met by the net addition of the treasury bills issued by the RBI and drawing down of cash balances kept with the RBI. The budgetary deficit was called deficit financing by the Government of India. This deficit adds to money supply in the economy and, therefore, it can be a major cause of inflationary rise in prices.
2. **Monetized Deficit:** Monetized Deficit is the sum of the net increase in holdings of treasury bills of the RBI and its contributions to the market borrowing of the government. It shows the increase in net RBI credit to the government. It creates equivalent increase in high-powered money or reserve money in the economy.

## TAXATION IN INDIA

Taxes represent the amount of money we pay to the government at predefined rates and periodicity. Taxes are the basic source of revenue to the government using which it provides various kinds of services to the taxpayers. There are mainly two types of taxes, Direct Tax and Indirect Tax, which are governed by two different boards, Central Board of Direct Taxes (CBDT) and Central Board of Excise and Customs (CBEC).

### ❖ Direct Taxes

A direct tax is a kind of charge, which is imposed directly on the taxpayer and paid directly to the government by the persons (juristic or natural) on whom it is imposed. A direct tax is one that cannot be shifted by the taxpayer to someone else. The some important direct taxes imposed in India are as under:

1. **Income Tax:** Income Tax Act, 1961 imposes tax on the income of the individuals or Hindu undivided families or firms or co-operative societies (other tax companies) and trusts (identified as bodies of individuals associations of persons) or every artificial juridical person.

The inclusion of a particular income in the total incomes of a person for income-tax in India is based on his residential status. There are three residential status, viz: (i) Resident & Ordinarily Residents (Residents); (ii) Resident but not Ordinarily Residents; and (iii) Non-Residents. There are several steps involved in determining the residential status of a person. All residents are taxable for all their income, including income outside India. Non-residents are taxable only for the income received in India or income accrued in India. Not ordinarily, residents are taxable in relation to income received in India or income accrued in India and income from business or profession controlled from India.

2. **Corporation Tax:** The companies and business organizations in India are taxed on the income from their worldwide transactions under the provision of Income Tax Act, 1961. A corporation is deemed to be resident in India if it is incorporated in India or if its control and management is situated entirely in India. In case of non-resident corporations, tax is levied on the income which is earned from their business transactions in India or any other Indian sources depending on bilateral agreement of that country.
3. **Property Tax:** Property tax or 'house tax' is a local tax on buildings, along with appurtenant land, and imposed on owners. The tax power is vested in the states and it is delegated by law to the local bodies, specifying the valuation method, rate band and collection procedures. The tax base is the Annual Rateble Value (ARV) or area based rating. Owner-occupied and other properties not producing rent are assessed on cost and then converted into ARV by applying a percentage of cost, usually 6 per cent. Vacant land is generally exempted from the assessment. The properties lying under control of Central are exempted from the taxation. Instead a 'service charge' is permissible under executive order. Properties of foreign missions also enjoy tax exemption without an insistence for reciprocity.
4. **Inheritance (Estate) Tax:** An inheritance tax (also known as an estate tax or death duty) is a tax which arises on the death of an individual. It is a tax on the estate, or total value of the money and property, of a person who has died. India enforced estate duty from 1953 to 1985. Estate Duty Act, 1953 came into existence with effect from 15 October 1953. Estate Duty on agricultural land was discontinued under the Estate Duty (Amendment) Act, 1984. The levy of Estate Duty in respect of property (other than agricultural land) passing on death occurring on or after 16 March 1985 has also been abolished under the Estate Duty (Amendment) Act, 1985.
5. **Gift Tax:** Gift tax in India is regulated by the Gift Tax Act which was constituted on 1 April 1958. It came into effect in all parts of the country except Jammu and Kashmir. As per the Gift Act, 1958, all gifts in excess of ₹ 25,000 in the form of cash, draft, check or others, received from one who doesn't have blood relations with the recipient, were taxable. However, with effect from 1 October 1998, gift tax got demolished and all the gifts made on or after the date were free from tax. But in 2004, the act was again revived partially. A new provision was introduced in the Income Tax Act, 1961 under Section 56(2). According to it, the gifts received by any individual or Hindu Undivided Family (HUF) in excess of ₹ 50,000 in a year would be taxable.

The overall control for administration of direct taxes lies with the Union Finance

Ministry which functions through Income Tax Department with CBDT at its apex. The CBDT is a statutory authority functioning under the Central Board of Revenue Act, 1963. It also functions as a division of the Ministry dealing with matters relating to levy and collection of Direct Taxes.

## ❖ Indirect Taxes

An indirect tax is a tax collected by an intermediary (such as a retail store) from the person who bears the ultimate economic burden of the tax (such as the customer). An indirect tax is one that can be shifted by the taxpayer to someone else. An indirect tax may increase the price of a good so that consumers are actually paying the tax by paying more for the products. The some important indirect taxes imposed in India are as under:

1. **Customs Duty:** The Customs Act was formulated in 1962 to prevent illegal imports and exports of goods. Besides, all imports are sought to be subject to a duty with a view to affording protection to indigenous industries as well as to keep the imports to the minimum in the interests of securing the exchange rate of Indian currency. Duties of customs are levied on goods imported or exported from India at the rate specified under the customs Tariff Act, 1975 as amended from time to time or any other law for the time being in force.

   Under the custom laws, the various types of duties are leviable.

   (i) **Basic Duty:** This duty is levied on imported goods under the Customs Act, 1962.

   (ii) **Additional Duty (Countervailing Duty) (CVD):** This is levied under Section 3(1) of the Custom Tariff Act and is equal to excise duty levied on a like product manufactured or produced in India. If a like product is not manufactured or produced in India, the excise duty that would be leviable on that product had it been manufactured or produced in India is the duty payable. If the product is leviable at different rates, the highest rate among those rates is the rate applicable. Such duty is leviable on the value of goods plus basic custom duty payable.

   (iii) **Additional Duty:** to compensate duty on inputs used by Indian manufacturers: This is levied under Section 3(3) of the Customs Act.

   (iv) **Anti-dumping Duty:** Sometimes, foreign sellers abroad may export into India goods at prices below the amounts charged by them in their domestic markets in order to capture Indian markets to the detriment of Indian industry. This is known as dumping. In order to prevent dumping, the Central Government may levy additional duty equal to the margin of dumping on such articles. There are however certain restrictions on imposing dumping duties in case of countries which are signatories to the General Agreement on Tariffs and Trade (GATT) or on countries given 'Most Favoured Nation Status' under agreement.

   (v) **Protective Duty:** If the Tariff Commission set up by law recommends that in order to protect the interests of Indian industry, the Central Government may levy protective anti-dumping duties at the rate recommended on specified goods.

   (vi) **Duty on 73 Bounty Fed Articles:** In case a foreign country subsidizes its exporters for exporting goods to India, the Central Government may impose additional import duty equal to the amount of such subsidy or bounty. If the amount of subsidy or bounty cannot be clearly determined immediately, additional duty may be collected on a provisional basis and after final determination, difference may be collected or refunded, as the case may be.

(vii) **Export Duty:** Such duty is levied on export of goods. At present very few articles such as skins and leather are subject to export duty. The main purpose of this duty is to restrict exports of certain goods.

(viii) **Cess on Export:** Under sub-section (1) of Section 3 of the Agricultural & Processed Food Products Export Cess Act, 1985 (3 of 1986), 0.5% ad valorem as the rate of duty of customs be levied and collected as cess on export of all scheduled products.

(ix) **National Calamity Contingent Duty:** This duty was imposed under Section 134 of the Finance Act, 2003 on imported petroleum crude oil. This tax was also leviable on motor cars, imported multi-utility vehicles, two wheelers and mobile phones.

(x) **Education Cess:** Education Cess is leviable @ 2% on the aggregate of duties of Customs (except safeguard duty under Section 8B and 8C, CVD under Section 9 and anti-dumping duty under Section 9A of the Customs Tariff Act, 1985). Items attracting Customs Duty at bound rates under international commitments are exempted from this Cess.

(xi) **Secondary and Higher Education Cess:** Leviable @1% on the aggregate of duties of Customs.

(xii) **Road Cess:** Additional Duty of Customs on Motor Spirit is leviable and Additional Duty of Customs on High Speed Diesel Oil is leviable by the Finance Act (No. 2), 1998 and the Finance Act, 1999, respectively.

(xiii) **Surcharge on Motor Spirit:** Special Additional Duty of Customs (Surcharge) on Motor Spirit is leviable by the Finance Act, 2002.

2. **Central Excise Duty:** The Central Government levies excise duty under the Central Excise Act, 1944 and the Central Excise Tariff Act, 1985. Central excise duty is tax which is charged on such excisable goods that are manufactured in India and are meant for domestic consumption. The term 'excisable goods' means the goods which are specified in the First Schedule and the Second Schedule to the Central Excise Tariff Act, 1985. It is mandatory to pay Central Excise duty payable on the goods manufactured, unless exempted; for example, duty is not payable on the goods exported out of India. Further, various other exemptions are also notified by the government from the payment of duty by the manufacturers.

Various Central Excise are:

(i) **Basis Excise Duty:** Excise Duty, imposed under Section 3 of the 'Central Excises and Salt Act' of 1944 on all excisable goods other than salt produced or manufactured in India, at the rates set forth in the schedule to the Central Excise tariff Act, 1985, falls under the category of Basic Excise Duty In India.

(ii) **Special Excise Duty:** According to Section 37 of the Finance Act, 1978, Special Excise Duty is levied on all excisable goods that come under taxation, in line with the Basic

Excise Duty under the Central Excises and Salt Act of 1944. Therefore, each year the Finance Act spells out that whether the Special Excise Duty shall or shall not be charged, and eventually collected during the relevant financial year.

(iii) **Additional Duty of Excise:** Section 3 of the 'Additional Duties of Excise Act' of 1957 permits the charge and collection of excise duty in respect of the goods as listed in the Schedule of this Act.

(iv) **Road Cess:** (a) Additional Duty of Excise on Motor Spirit: This is leviable by the Finance Act (No. 2), 1998. (b) Additional Duty of Excise on High Speed Diesel Oil: This is leviable by the Finance Act, 1999.

(v) **Surcharge:** (a) Special Additional Duty of Excise on Motor Spirit: This is leviable by the Finance Act, 2002. (b) Surcharge on Pan Masala and Tobacco Products: This Additional Duty of Excise has been imposed on cigarettes, pan masala and certain specified tobacco products, at specified rates in the Budget 2005–06. Beedis are not subjected to this levy.

(vi) **National Calamity Contingent Duty (NCCD):** NCCD was levied on pan masala and certain specified tobacco products vide the Finance Act, 2001. The Finance Act, 2003 extended this levy to polyester filament yarn, motor car, two wheeler and multi-utility vehicle and crude petroleum oil.

(vii) **Education Cess:** Education Cess is leviable @%2 on the aggregate of duties of Excise and Secondary and Higher Education Cess is Leviable @%1 on the aggregate of duties of Excise.

(viii) **Cess:** A cess has been imposed on certain products.

3. **Service Tax:** The service providers in India except those in the state of Jammu and Kashmir are required to pay a Service Tax under the provisions of the Finance Act of 1994. The provisions related to Service Tax came into effect on 1 July 1994. Under Section 67 of this Act, the Service Tax is levied on the gross or aggregate amount charged by the service provider on the receiver. However, in terms of Rule 6 of Service Tax Rules, 1994, the tax is permitted to be paid on the value received. The interesting thing about Service Tax in India is that the Government depends heavily on the voluntary compliance of the service providers for collecting Service Tax in India.

4. **Sales Tax:** Sales Tax in India is a form of tax that is imposed by the government on the sale or purchase of a particular commodity within the country. Sales Tax is imposed under both, Central Government (Central Sales Tax) and State Government (State Sales Tax) Legislation. Generally, each State follows its own Sales Tax Act and levies tax at various rates. Apart from sales tax, certain states also imposes additional charges like works contracts tax, turnover tax and purchaser tax. Thus, sales tax acts as a major revenue-generator for the various state governments. From 10 April 2005, most of the states in India have supplemented sales tax with a new Value Added Tax (VAT).

5. **Value Added Tax (VAT):** The practice of VAT executed by state governments is applied on each stage of sale, with a particular apparatus of credit for the input VAT paid. VAT in India classified under the tax slabs are 0% for essential commodities, 1% on gold ingots and

expensive stones, 4% on industrial inputs, capital merchandise and commodities of mass consumption, and 12.5% on other items. Variable rates (State-dependent) are applicable for petroleum products, tobacco, liquor, etc. VAT levy will be administered by the VAT Act and the rules made there-under and similar to a sales tax. It is a tax on the estimated market value added to a product or material at each stage of its manufacture or distribution, ultimately passed on to the consumer. Under the current single-point system of tax levy, the manufacturer or importer of goods into a state is liable to sales tax. There is no sales tax on the further distribution channel. VAT, in simple terms, is a multi-point levy on each of the entities in the supply chain. The value addition in the hands of each of the entities is subject to tax.

VAT can be computed by using any of the three methods: (a) Subtraction method: The tax rate is applied to the difference between the value of output and the cost of input. (b) The Addition method: The value added is computed by adding all the payments that is payable to the factors of production (viz., wages, salaries, interest payments, etc.). (c) Tax credit method: This entails set-off of the tax paid on inputs from tax collected on sales.

6. **Securities Transaction Tax (STT):** STT is a tax being levied on all transactions done on the stock exchanges. STT is applicable on purchase or sale of equity shares, derivatives, equity oriented funds and equity oriented Mutual Funds. Current STT on purchase or sell of an equity share is 0.075%. A person becomes investor after payment of STT at the time of selling securities (shares). Selling the shares after 12 months comes under long term capital gains and one need not have to pay any tax on that gain. In the case of selling the shares before 12 months, one has to pay short term capital gains @10% flat on the gain. However, for a trader, all his gains will be treated as trading (Business) and he has to pay tax as per tax sables. In this case, the transaction tax paid by him can be claimed back/adjusted in tax to be paid.
7. **Long Term Capital Gain Tax (LTCGT):** LTCGT is a tax on long term capital gain. LTCG means gain or profit arising from selling of stock or redemption of equity mutual funds held more than one year. After a gap of 14 years, the Central Government re-introduced the 10% LTCG tax in the Budget 2018. Though indexation is not allowed while calculating LTCG, it is permissible in the calculation of gains earned on real assets and jewellery.
8. **Goods and Service Tax (GST):** Goods and Service Tax (GST) is a comprehensive tax levy on manufacture, sale and consumption of goods and service at a national level. GST is a tax on goods and services with value addition at each stage having comprehensive and continuous chain of set off benefits from the producer's/service provider's point up to the retailer's level where only the final consumer should bear the tax.

The Goods and Service Tax Act was passed in the Parliament on 29 March 2017. The tax was launched in India on 1 July 2017.

Following taxes have been merged under GST:

1. At the Central level:
   - (i) Central Excise Duty,
   - (ii) Additional Excise Duty,
   - (iii) Service Tax,
   - (iv) Additional Customs Duty commonly known as Counter-vailing Duty, and
   - (v) Special Additional Duty of Customs.

2. At the State level:
   - (i) Subsuming of State VAT/Sales Tax,
   - (ii) Entertainment Tax (other than the tax levied by the local bodies), Central Sales Tax (levied by the Centre and collected by the States),
   - (iii) Octroi and Entry tax,
   - (iv) Purchase Tax,
   - (v) Luxury tax, and
   - (vi) Taxes on lottery, betting and gambling.

   (Detail of GST has been dealt in Chapter–17 of this book)

## FISCAL RESPONSIBILITY AND BUDGET MANAGEMENT (FRBM) ACT, 2003

The objective of the FRBM Act is to ensure inter-generational equity in fiscal management, long run macroeconomic stability, better coordination between fiscal and monetary policy and transparency in fiscal operation of the Government.

### ❖ The Main Provisions

1. The revenue deficit as a ratio of GDP should be brought down by 0.5 per cent every year and eliminated by 2007–08;
2. The fiscal deficit as a ratio of GDP should be reduced by 0.3 per cent every year and brought down to 3 per cent by 2007–08;
3. The total liabilities of the Union Government should not rise by more than 9 per cent a year;
4. The Union Government shall not give guarantee to loans raised by PSUs and state governments for more than 0.5 per cent of GDP in the aggregate;
5. The Union Government should place three documents along with the budget, namely, the Macroeconomic Framework Statement, the Medium Term Fiscal Policy Statement and the Fiscal Policy Strategy Statement.
6. The finance minister will have to make a statement at the end of the second quarter on the trend of fiscal indicators and corrective measures if they deviate from the budget estimates beyond the extent stipulated in the FRBM.

The FRBM Act provides a legal institutional framework for fiscal consolidation. It is now mandatory for the Central Government to take measures to reduce fiscal deficit, to eliminate revenue deficit and to generate revenue surplus in the subsequent years. The Act binds not only the present government but also the future Government to adhere to the path of fiscal consolidation. The government can move away from the path of fiscal consolidation only in case of natural calamity, national security and other exceptional grounds which Central Government may specify.

Further, the Act prohibits borrowing by the government from the Reserve Bank of India, thereby, making monetary policy independent of fiscal policy. The Act bans the purchase of primary issues of the Central Government securities by the RBI after 2006, preventing monetization of government deficit. The Act also requires the government to lay before the Parliament three policy statements in each financial year, namely Medium Term Fiscal Policy Statement, Fiscal Policy Strategy Statement and Macroeconomic Framework Policy Statement.

To impart fiscal discipline at the state level, the Twelfth Finance Commission gave incentives to states through conditional debt restructuring and interest rate relief for introducing Fiscal Responsibility Legislations (FRLs). All the states have implemented their own FRLs.

Indian economy faced with the problem of large fiscal deficit and its monetization spilled over to external sector in the late 1980s and early 1990s. The large borrowings of the government led to such a precarious situation that government was unable to pay even for two weeks of imports resulting in economic crisis of 1991. Consequently, Economic reforms were introduced in 1991 and fiscal consolidation emerged as one of the key areas of reforms. After a good start in the early nineties, the fiscal consolidation faltered after 1997–98. The fiscal deficit started rising after 1997–98. The Government introduced the FRBM Act, 2003 to check the deteriorating fiscal situation.

## ❖ Implementation of FRBM Act

The implementation of FRBM Act/FRLs improved the fiscal performance of both centre and states. The states have achieved the targets much ahead the prescribed timeline. The Government of India was on the path of achieving this objective right in time.

The FRBM Act, in its original form, envisaged eliminating revenue deficit and reducing fiscal deficit to 3 per cent of GDP by 2008. It gave an impression that the government was serious about adopting prudent fiscal management practices and ensuring fiscal discipline.

While eyebrows were raised in 2004 when the deadline was pushed to 2009 without any hiccup in Parliament, the government's intentions could still be trusted.

Eventually, in 2009, all hopes were shattered when the revenue and fiscal deficits were recorded as high as 4.67 and 6.21 per cent, respectively, of GDP. The government took shelter behind the expenditure on account of fiscal stimulus, necessitated by the global financial meltdown, for missing the fiscal targets.

## ❖ FRBM in Practice

The year-on-year increase in food and fertilizer subsidies during 2008–09 was 40 and 136 per cent, respectively. Many experts, including the 13th Finance Commission, demolished the government's case and established that the fiscal stimulus was not solely responsible for non-compliance with deficit targets, and pay revision, farm debt waiver, and food and fertilizer subsidies added substantially to the fiscal burden.

It must be noted that 2009 was also an election year. Such populist measures do not serve the country well in the long term.

The FRBM Act provided that no deviation from the targets could happen without approval of the Parliament. The targets could be exceeded only in case of national security, national calamity and other such exceptional grounds as specified. Further, in case of a deviation, the finance minister was required to suggest and implement remedial measures to increase revenue and reduce expenditure. From 2009 to 2012, the government was in continual non-compliance with FRBM targets. Never did it manage to eliminate revenue deficit or reduce fiscal deficit to 3 per cent of GDP.

The justifications provided in the name of fiscal stimulus and financial meltdown continued for around four years and not even once was there an attempt to block approval of deviations in Parliament.

## ❖ Target Diluted

What transpired post-2012 is even more surprising and deeply disturbing. Following the Budget speech for 2012–13, certain amendments to the FRBM Act were introduced that postponed attaining the fiscal deficit of 3 per cent of GDP by 2017, and targeted achieving revenue deficit of 2 per cent GDP by 2015.

Consequent amendments were made to the rules in May 2013. This meant substantial dilution and deference of the deficit targets. The 13th Finance Commission had laid down a fiscal road map and suggested certain amendments to the FRBM Act such as reforms in mid-term statements, elimination of revenue deficit by 2015 and explanation of shocks requiring relaxation of targets. None of these were accepted.

The amendments to FRBM Act were passed again without a glitch. Any deliberations on the proposed amendments could have highlighted that they ratified fiscal malpractices of the government, and need substantial overhaul.

High fiscal deficits heighten inflation, increase the risk of external sector imbalances and dampen private investment, growth and employment.

The fiscal deficit target has been fixed at 3.3 % for 2018–19 by the Union budget as against the FRBM Act target of 3 per cent.

The FRBM Review Panel headed by N. K. Singh (in January 2017) had recommended debt to GDP ratio of 60 % by 2023 and fiscal deficit at 3 % for next 3 years.

## FINANCE COMMISSION OF INDIA

The financial relations between the Centre and the Units came up for review in connection with the drafting of a new Constitution for independent India. The financial provisions in the Draft Constitution were referred by the Constituent Assembly to an Expert Committee of three under the chairmanship of Nalini Ranjan Sarkar, with V. S. Sundaram and M.Y. Rangachari as members. The Committee recommended a pattern of Union States division of tax resources, which was broadly adopted in the Constitution of India.

### ❖ As per Article 280 of the Constitution of India

1. The President shall, within two years from the commencement of this Constitution and thereafter at the expiration of every fifth year or at such earlier time as the President considers necessary, by order constitute a Finance Commission which shall consist of a Chairman and four other members to be appointed by the President.
2. Parliament may by law determine the qualifications which shall be requisite for appointment as members of the Commission and the manner in which they shall be selected.
3. It shall be the duty of the Commission to make recommendations to the President as to-
   (a) the distribution between the Union and the States of the net proceeds of taxes which are to be, or may be, divided between them under this Chapter and the allocation between the States of the respective shares of such proceeds;
   (b) the principles which should govern the grants-in-aid of the revenues of the States out of the Consolidated Fund of India; [(bb) the measures needed to augment the Consolidated Fund of a State to supplement the resources of the Panchayats in the State on the basis of the recommendations made by the Finance Commission of the State;]
   (c) the measures needed to augment the Consolidated Fund of a State to supplement the resources of the Municipalities in the State on the basis of the recommendations made by the Finance Commission of the State;
   (d) any other matter referred to the Commission by the President in the interests of sound finance.
4. The Commission shall determine their procedure and shall have such powers in the performance of their functions as Parliament may by law confer on them.

The First Finance Commission was constituted under Article 280 by a Presidential Order dated 22 November 1951, under the chairmanship of K. C. Neogy.

**Article 281** of the Constitution further stipulates that 'The President shall cause every recommendation made by the

Finance Commission under the provisions of this Constitution together with an explanatory memorandum as to the action taken thereon to be laid before each House of Parliament'. Based on the recommendations of the Finance Commission from time to time, the budget provisions for a year are made after earmarking the States' share, to work out the Net Tax Revenues of the Union Government from the Gross Tax Revenues. While the Central Government provides in its Budget for the outgo from the Consolidated Fund of India on this account, each State reflects its own share of the net divisible pool as its resources in its own budget, on the basis of advance intimation received from the Central Government.

## GENDER BUDGETING IN INDIA

Gender budgeting is an exercise to translate the stated gender commitments of the government into budgetary commitments, involving special initiatives for empowering women and examination of the utilization of resources allocated for women and the impact of public expenditure and policies of the government on women.

Gender Budgeting is a powerful tool for achieving gender mainstreaming so as to ensure that benefits of development reach women as much as men. It is not an accounting exercise but an ongoing process of keeping a gender perspective in policy/programme formulation, its implementation and review. Gender Budgeting entails dissection of the government budgets to establish its gender differential impacts and to ensure that gender commitments are translated in to budgetary commitments.

The rationale for gender budgeting arises from recognition of the fact that national budgets impact men and women differently through the pattern of resource allocation. Women, constitute 48 per cent of India's population, but they lag behind men on many social indicators like health, education, economic opportunities, etc. Hence, they warrant special attention due to their vulnerability and lack of access to resources. The way government budgets allocate resources, has the potential to transform these gender inequalities. In view of this, gender budgeting, as a tool for achieving gender mainstreaming, has been propagated.

**Gender Budgeting Cells (GBCs) in Union Government** are envisaged to serve as focal points for coordinating gender budgeting initiatives within their ministries and across departments. So far 56 Ministries/Department have confirmed setting up of a cell/nominating a nodal person.

For the first time in 2001, a special reference of Gender Budget was made by the Finance Minister of India in his Budget speech. The Central Government introduced gender budgeting in 2005–06 as a budgetary practice. The government has institutionalized gender budgeting by introducing a Gender Budget Statement (GBS) since 2005–06.

Gender budgeting in India has three components: (i) Specifically targeted expenditure to women and girls; (ii) Pro-women allocations, which are the composite expenditure schemes with a significant women's component; and (iii) Residual public expenditures that have gender-differential impacts.

### ❖ Rationale for Gender Budgeting

Existing gender neutrality of macro indicators ignores the feedback mechanism between gender-relations and macroeconomic policy. The assumption of labour force exogeneity in the treatment of the care economy in the prevalent macroeconomic policy making is dubious. Integrating gender perspective into macroeconomic policy has dual dimensions: an equality dimension and an efficiency dimension. In the context of growing recognition that problems of inequality cannot be resolved by the trickle down effects of macroeconomic policies, the concept of gender inequality needs to be built in to the macroeconomic policy framework.

Apart from the basic principle of promoting equality among citizens, gender equality can benefit the economy through efficiency gains. From the efficiency consideration, what is important is the social rate of return of investment in women, and in eases, this can be greater than the corresponding rate for men. There is a growing awareness that gender inequality is inefficient and costly to development. Empirical literature draws attention to these efficiency dimensions of integrating gender perspective into macroeconomic policies. For example, the striking good mother thesis noted that women tend to have a higher marginal propensity to spend than men on goods that enhance the capabilities of children. These empirical evidences suggested that the likelihood of children being enrolled in school goes up with their mother's educational level, and mother's extra income has more positive impact on household investments in nutrition, health and education of children than extra income accruing to fathers. Also, literature on gender inequality in labour markets shows that eliminating gender discrimination in occupation and wages could increase not only women's income, but also national income.

Men and women frequently have different priorities for budgetary policies and are affected differently by most of these policies due to the gender differentials in the constraints, options, incentives and needs. Men and women face different constraints, assume different socially determined responsibilities and consequently make different social preferences. Legacies of adverse intra-household gender relations inhibit women from playing their rightful role, contributing to the economy, and getting their due share of the economic benefits in many countries, particularly developing ones. Women therefore are affected by and respond to the budgetary policies differently from men. Disaggregation by gender is vital because there are systemic differences between men and women in relation to the economy.

The existing gender-neutral budgets ignore the gender specific impacts of budgetary policies. Generally, budgeting involves four components: (i) the budgetary allocation of resources to various heads, (ii) the actual government outlays on various heads, (iii) an accounting of how resources are utilized for a particular purpose (e.g., on administrative overheads and wages and salaries, operation and maintenance, etc.) and (iv) an evaluation of the effectiveness of the resources utilized in delivering the intended results. Gender budgeting involves looking at all the four components from the point of view of women as beneficiaries. While many public goods and services like defence arc not amenable to gender partitioning, many others have differential impact on the two sexes. For example, outlays for augmenting the supply of safe drinking water can benefit women more than men by cutting down on the time spent in fetching water from the river or ponds. The existing practice of budgeting does not pay any special attention to the impact of budgets on women.

Gender Budgeting was introduced in India by the government in 2005–06 in order to ensure that policy commitments are backed by financial outlays and that the gender perspective is incorporated in all stages of a policy or a programme. The objectives of gender budgeting are for committing to initiatives with the objective of influencing and effecting a change in the ministries' policies, programmes in a way that could tackle gender imbalances, promote gender equality and development and ensure that public resources through the Ministries' budgets are allocated and managed accordingly.

## PERFORMANCE BUDGETING

Performance budgeting or programme budgeting also known as Planning-Programming-Budgeting System (PPBS) owes their origin to Hoover reforms in the USA. The President of USA, Johnson introduced them but it was later abandoned in 1971.

The performance budget is an instrument through which financial resources are allocated according to purposes and objectives. The costs of various programmes proposed for achieving these objectives are clearly indicated. This type of budget is used by government bodies to show the link between taxpayer funds and the outcome of services provided by the government. In other words, allocation of funds and resources are based on specific goals agreed upon by budget committees and agency heads of services.

**Performance Budget has following operational steps:**

1. Formulation of objectives of the agency/department
2. Identification of various programmes or projects, which will help the agency to achieve its objective
3. Evaluation of the programmes in terms of benefits that they produce compared to the resources that they consume
4. Selection of the programmes on the basis of cost benefit analysis in order to utilize the funds in the optimal manner
5. Development of performance criteria for the various programmes (suitable work measurement units, norms, yardsticks, standards and other performance indicators)
6. Preparation of long-term physical as well as financial plans
7. Preparation of the annual budget
8. Assessment of performance of each programme and by each responsibility unit and comparison of the same with the budget

Benefits of Performance Budgeting are: (i) enhanced communication between budget actors and with citizens; (ii) improved management in government agencies; (iii) more informed budgetary decision-making; and (iv) higher transparency and accountability.

Limitations of performance budgeting are: (i) it focuses on quantitative evaluation rather than on qualitative evaluation; (ii) It is ineffective without a proper accounting and reporting system; (iii) it is difficult to quantify social benefits; and (iv) it is difficult to estimate benefits arising out of each activity.

In India, from 2007–08 onwards, the Performance Budget was merged with Outcome Budget. There was only one document, i.e., the Outcome Budget. All Ministries have to prepare outcome budgets to make the budgeting target oriented.

## ZERO-BASED BUDGETING

Zero-based Budgeting is a reverse approach of traditional planning and decision making with respect to budgeting. It involves preparing the budget from the scratch with a zero-base. It involves re-evaluating every line item of cash flow statement and justifying all the expenditure that is to be incurred by the department.

Thus, zero-based budgeting definition goes as a method of budgeting whereby all the expenses for the new period are calculated on the basis of actual expenses that are to be incurred and not on the incremental basis which involves just increasing the expenses incurred in the previous year at some fixed rate. Under this method, every activity needs to be justified, explaining the revenue that every cost will generate for the company.

Governmental programmes and projects are appraised every year as if they are new and funding for the existing items is not continued merely because a part of the project cost has already been incurred.

The concept of zero-based budgeting was introduced in the 1970s in India. As the name suggests, in the process every budgeting cycle starts from scratch.

Zero-based budgeting has the following advantages:

1. It helps in efficient allocation of resources, as it is based on needs and benefits.
2. It drives to find cost-effective ways to improve activities.

3. It detects inflated budgets.
4. It is useful for service departments because criteria are not always easy to identify.
5. It increases staff motivation because it gives them more initiative and responsibility in the decision-making process.
6. It increases the communication and coordination within the organization about certain decisions.
7. It identifies and eliminates wastage and out-of-date operations.
8. It identifies opportunities for outsourcing.
9. It forces cost departments to link their mission to the related organizational objectives.

However, there are also disadvantages of Zero-based budgeting. It is time consuming, requires manpower, requires knowledge and require awareness for details.

## THE REPORT OF THE FIFTEENTH FINANCE COMMISSION

- The Fifteenth Finance Commission (XVFC)'s ToR was unique and wide ranging in many ways. The Commission was asked to recommend performance incentives for States in many areas like power sector, adoption of DBT, solid waste management etc.
- Another unique ToR was to recommend funding mechanism for defence and internal security.
- The XVFC's Report is organised in four volumes.
- Volume I and II, as in the past, contain the main report and the accompanying annexes.
- Volume III is devoted to the Union Government and examines key departments in greater depth, with the medium-term challenges and the roadmap ahead.
- Volume IV is entirely devoted to the States. We have analysed the finances of each State in great depth and have come up with State-specific considerations to address the key challenges that individual States face.
- In total, main report has 117 core recommendations. Vol-III and IV has numerous suggested reforms for the Union ministries and State governments respectively.

### ❖ Vertical Devolution

- In order to maintain predictability and stability of resources, especially during the pandemic, XVFC has recommended maintaining the vertical devolution at 41 per cent - the same as in our report for 2020-21. It is at the same level of 42 per cent of the divisible pool as recommended by FC-XIV. However, it has made the required adjustment of about 1 per cent due to the changed status of the erstwhile State of Jammu and Kashmir into the new Union Territories of Ladakh and Jammu and Kashmir.
- In XVFC's assessment, gross tax revenues for 5-year period is expected to be 135.2 lakh crore. Out of that, Divisible pool (after deducting cesses and surcharges & cost of collection) is estimated to be 103 lakh crore.
- States' share at 41 per cent of divisible pool comes to 42.2 lakh crore for 2021-26 period.
- Including total grants of ₹ 10.33 lakh crore (details later) and tax devolution of ₹ 42.2 lakh crore, aggregate transfers to States is estimated to remain at around 50.9 per cent of the divisible pool during 2021-26 period.
- Total XVFC transfers (devolution + grants) constitutes about 34 per cent of estimated Gross Revenue Receipts of the Union leaving adequate fiscal space for the Union to meet its resource requirements and spending obligations on national development priorities.

### ❖ Horizontal Devolution

- Based on principles of need, equity and performance, overall devolution formula is as follows.

| Criteria | Weight (%) |
|---|---|
| Population | 15.0 |
| Area | 15.0 |
| Forest & ecology | 10.0 |
| Income distance | 45.0 |
| Tax & fiscal efforts | 2.5 |
| Demographic performance | 12.5 |
| Total | 100 |

- On horizontal devolution, while XVFC agreed that the Census 2011 population data better represents the present need of States, to be fair to, as well as reward, the States which have done better on the demographic front, XVFC has assigned a 12.5 per cent weight to the demographic performance criterion.
- XVFC has re-introduced tax effort criterion to reward fiscal performance.

## ❖ Revenue Deficit Grants

- Based on uniform norms of assessing revenues and expenditure of the States and the Union, XVFC has recommended total revenue deficit grants (RDG) of Rs 2,94,514 crore over the award period for seventeen States.

## ❖ Local Governments

- The total size of the grant to local governments should be ₹ 4,36,361 crore for the period 2021-26.
- Of these total grants, ₹ 8,000 crore is performance-based grants for incubation of new cities and ₹ 450 crore is for shared municipal services. A sum of ₹ 2,36,805 crore is earmarked for rural local bodies, ₹ 1,21,055 crore for urban local bodies and ₹ 70,051 crore for health grants through local governments.
- Urban local bodies have been categorised into two groups, based on population, and different norms have been used for flow of grants to each, based on their specific needs and aspirations. Basic grants are proposed only for cities/towns having a population of less than a million. For Million-Plus cities, 100 per cent of the grants are performance-linked through the Million-Plus Cities Challenge Fund (MCF).

## ❖ Health

- XVFC has recommend that health spending by States should be increased to more than 8 per cent of their budget by 2022.
- Given the inter-State disparity in the availability of medical doctors, it is essential to constitute an All India Medical and Health Service as is envisaged under Section 2A of the All-India Services Act, 1951.
- The total grants-in-aid support to the health sector over the award period works out to ₹ 1,06,606 crore, which is 10.3 per cent of the total grants-in-aid recommended by XVFC. The grants for the health sector will be unconditional.
- XVFC has recommend health grants aggregating to ₹ 70,051 crore for urban health and wellness centres (HWCs), building-less sub centre, PHCs, CHCs, block level public health units, support for diagnostic infrastructure for the primary healthcare activities and conversion of rural sub centres and PHCs to HWCs. These grants will be released to the local governments. . Out of the remaining grant of ₹ 31,755 crore for the health sector (total of ₹ 1,06,606 crore minus ₹ 70, 051 crore through local bodies and ₹ 4800 crore state-specific grants), XVFC has recommended ₹ 15,265 crore for critical care hospitals. This includes ₹ 13,367 crore for general States and ₹ 1,898 crore for NEH States.
- XVFC has recommended ₹ 13,296 crore for training of the allied healthcare workforce. Out of this, ₹ 1,986 crore will be for NEH States and ₹ 11,310 crore for general States.

## ❖ Performance Incentives and Grants

- XVFC has recommended grants of ₹ 4,800 crore (₹ 1,200 crore each year) from 2022-23 to 2025-26 for incentivising the States to enhance educational outcomes.
- XVFC has recommended ₹ 6,143 crore for online learning and development of professional courses (medical and engineering) in regional languages (matribhasha) for higher education in India.
- XVFC has recommended that ₹ 45,000 crore be kept as performance-based incentive for all the States for carrying out agricultural reforms.
- for amending their land-related laws on the lines of NITI Aayog's model law
- incentive-based grants to States that maintain and augment groundwater stock.
- growth in agricultural exports
- production of oilseeds, pulses and wood and wood-based products
- Apart from above, following is the snapshot of grants.

| S. No. | Grant Components | 2021-26 |
|---|---|---|
| 1 | Revenue Deficit grants | 294514 |
| 2 | Local governments grants | 436361 |
| 3 | Disaster management grants | 122601 |
| 4 | Sector-specific grants | 129987 |
| | (i) Sectoral grants for Health | 31755 |
| | (ii) School Education | 4800 |
| | (iii) Higher Education | 6143 |
| | (iv) Implementation of agricultural reforms | 45000 |
| | (v) Maintenance of PMGSY roads | 27539 |
| | (vi) Judiciary | 10425 |
| | (vii) Statistics | 1175 |
| | (viii) Aspirational districts and blocks | 3150 |
| 5 | **State-specific** | 49599 |
| | **Total** | 1033062 |

## ❖ Defence and Internal Security

- Keeping in view the extant strategic requirements for national defence in the global context, XVFC has, in its approach, re-calibrated the relative shares of Union and States in gross revenue receipts. This will enable the Union to set aside resources for the special funding mechanism that XVFC has proposed.
- The Union Government may constitute in the Public Account of India, a dedicated non-lapsable fund, Modernisation Fund for Defence and Internal Security (MFDIS). The total indicative size of the proposed MFDIS over the period 2021-26 is ₹ 2,38,354 crore.

## ❖ Disaster Risk Management

- Mitigation Funds should be set up at both the national and State levels, in line with the provisions of the Disaster Management Act. The Mitigation Fund should be used for those local level and community-based interventions which reduce risks and promote environment-friendly settlements and livelihood practices.
- For SDRMF, XVFC has recommended the total corpus of ₹ 1,60,153 crore for States for disaster management for the duration of 2021-26, of which the Union's share is ₹ 1,22,601 crore and States' share is ₹ 37,552 crore.
- XVFC has recommended six earmarked allocations for a total amount of Rs. 11,950 crore for certain priority areas, namely, two under the NDRF (Expansion and Modernisation of Fire Services and Resettlement of Displaced People affected by Erosion) and four under the NDMF (Catalytic Assistance to Twelve Most Drought-prone States, Managing Seismic and Landslide Risks in Ten Hill States, Reducing the Risk of Urban Flooding in Seven Most Populous Cities and Mtigation Measures to Prevent Erosion).

### ❖ Fiscal Consolidation

- Provided range for fiscal deficit and debt path of both the Union and States.
- Additional borrowing room to States based on performance in power sector reforms.
- A threshold amount of annual appropriation should be fixed below which the funding for a CSS may be stopped. Below the stipulated threshold, the administrating department should justify the need for the continuation of the scheme. As the life cycle of ongoing schemes has been made co-terminus with the cycle of Finance Commissions, the third-party evaluation of all CSSs should be completed within a stipulated timeframe. The flow of monitoring information should be regular and should include credible information on output and outcome indicators.
- In view of the uncertainty that prevails at the stage that XVFC have done its analysis, as well as the contemporary realities and challenges, we recognise that the FRBM Act needs a major restructuring and recommend that the time-table for defining and achieving debt sustainability may be examined by a **High-powered Inter-governmental Group.** This High-powered Group can craft the new FRBM framework and oversee its implementation. It is important that the Union and State Governments amend their FRBM Acts, based on the recommendations of the Group, so as to ensure that their legislations are consistent with the fiscal sustainability framework put in place. This High-powered Inter-Governmental Group could also be tasked to oversee the implementation of the 15th Finance Commission's diverse recommendations.
- State Governments may explore formation of independent public debt management cells which will chart their borrowing programme efficiently.

## BUDGET RELATED GLOSSARY

- **Non-tax Revenue:** The most important receipts under this head are interest payments (received on loans given by the government to states, railways and others) and dividends and profits received from public sector companies. Various services provided by the government – police and defence, social and community services such as medical services, and economic services such as power and railways – also yield revenue for the government. Though railways are a separate department, all its receipts and expenditure are routed through the consolidated fund.
- **Grants-in-aid and Contributions:** The third receipt item in the revenue account is relatively small grants-in-aid and contributions. These are in the nature of pure transfers to the government without any repayment obligation.
- **Public Debt:** Public debt receipts and public debt disbursals are borrowings and repayments during the year, respectively. The difference is the net accretion to the public debt. Public debt can be split into internal (money borrowed within the country) and external (funds borrowed from non-Indian sources). Internal debt comprises treasury bills, market stabilization schemes, ways and means advance, and securities against small savings.
- **Treasury Bills:** These are bonds (debt securities) with maturity of less than a year. These are issued to meet short-term mismatches in receipts and expenditure. Bonds of longer maturity are called dated securities.
- **Ways and Means Advance (WMA):** One of RBI's roles is to serve as banker to both the Central Government and state governments. In this capacity, RBI provides temporary support to tide over mismatches in their receipts and payments in the form of ways and means advances.

- **Minimum Alternate Tax (MAT):** This tax on corporate profits was introduced in 1996–97 and has been modified since. If the tax payable by a company is less than 10 per cent of its book profits, after availing of all eligible deductions, then 10 per cent of book profits are the minimum tax payable. Book profits are profits calculated as per the Companies Act while profits as per the Income-tax Act could be significantly lower, thanks to various exemptions and depreciation.
- **Pass through Status:** A pass through status helps avoid double taxation. Mutual funds, for instance, enjoy pass through status. The income earned by the funds is tax free. Since mutual funds' income is distributed to unit holders, who are in turn taxed on their income from such investments, any taxation of mutual funds would amount to double taxation. Essentially, it means the income is merely passing through the mutual funds and, therefore, should not be taxed. The government allows venture funds in some sectors pass through status to encourage investments in start-ups.
- **Subvention:** The term subvention finds a mention in almost every budget. It refers to a grant of money in aid or support, mostly by the government. In the Indian context, for instance, the government sometimes asks institutions to provide loans to farmers at below market rates. The loss is usually made good through subvention.
- **Appropriation (Charged):** Appropriation (Charged) means sums required to meet charged expenditure as specified in the Constitution during the financial year concerned, on the services and purposes covered by 'Charged Appropriation'. It does not include provisions for voted expenditure.
- **Public Accounts:** Public Accounts means the Public Account of India referred to in Article 266(2) of the Constitution. The receipts and disbursements such as deposits, reserve funds, remittances, etc., which do not form part of the Consolidated Fund of India are included in the public account of India. Disbursements from the public account are not subject to vote by the Parliament, as they are not moneys issued out of the Consolidated Fund of India.
- **Supplementary Demands for Grants:** Supplementary Demands for Grants means the statement of supplementary demands laid before the parliament, showing the estimated amount of further expenditure necessary in respect of a financial year over and above the expenditure authorized in the Annual Financial Statement for that year. The demand for supplementary may be token, technical or substantive/cash.
- **Vote on Account:** Vote on Account means a grant made in advance by the Parliament, in respect of the estimated expenditure for a part of new financial year, pending the completion of the procedure relating to the voting of the demand for grants and the passing of the Appropriation Act.
- **Voted' expenditure:** Voted' expenditure means expenditure which is subject to the vote of the Lok Sabha. It is to be distinguished from *'charged'* expenditure, which is not subject to voting, even though can be discussed in the Parliament.
- **Non-debt capital receipts:** Comprise recoveries of loans, disinvestment receipts and miscellaneous receipts.
- **Tax Revenues Foregone:** The primary objective of any tax law and its administration is to raise revenue for the purpose of funding government expenditure. To give relief to certain sections, or to promote certain activities, the government also provides tax breaks and incentives. Such incentives have an effect on revenue mobilization. Therefore, along with the other budget documents, the government of India also presents the *Statement of Revenue*

*Forgone*, which shows the revenue impact of tax incentives. This was first presented with the budget 2006–07 as an annexure to the receipts budget. In subsequent years, the government started presenting it as a separate document with the budget.

The revenue forgone is also referred to as tax expenditure or indirect subsidy to taxpayers. The tax policy provides specific tax incentives which give rise to tax preferences. According to the statement presented with Union Budget 2015–16, such preferences have a definite revenue impact and can also be viewed as an indirect subsidy to preferred taxpayers, also referred to as 'tax expenditures'.

The issue of tax revenues foregone by the Union Government has been raised repeatedly by eminent persons, such as Amartya Sen and S. Gurumurthy, and politicians, such as Sitaram Yechury. It has become fashionable to raise this issue to castigate the government of the day for handing over vast sums of money to the private sector as tax concessions.

❑❑❑

13

CHAPTER

# Economic Planning in India

## MEANING OF PLANNING

Economic planning is a conscious and well-thought-out process initiated by the central planning authority of the government for utilizing the resources of the country with view achieving certain pre-determined objectives within a specified period of time. It is a technique that a state follows to achieve economic development.

According to the Planning Commission of India 'Planning under a democratic system may be defined as the technical co-ordination, by disinterested experts, of consumption, production, investment, trade and income distribution, in accordance with social objectives set by bodies representative of the nation. Such planning is not only to be considered from the point of view of economics and the raising of the standard of living but must include cultural and spiritual and the human side of life.'

The main features of economic planning are as follows:

1. It determines the objectives that are to be achieved.
2. It estimates the resources that are available in the country.
3. It determines the order in which the objectives are to be achieved.
4. It designs suitable schemes for realizing of the objectives.
5. It determines the plan outlay and investment.
6. It does allocation of resources between different sectors as per the priority of objectives.
7. It establishes a body for the formulation, organization and appraisal of the plans, i.e., the Planning Commission of India, National Institution for Transforming India (NITI) Aayog, etc.

The major goals of economic planning are:

1. to increase the rate of economic development;
2. to remove unemployment, poverty and inequalities among people;
3. to provide infrastructural facilities such as banking, power, water, transport and communications;
4. to allocate resources properly among different regions and classes;
5. to attain balanced regional development and
6. to improve and strengthen market mechanism.

## TYPES OF PLANNING

There are various types of economic planning. The following are the main types:

1. **Indicative Planning:** Planning by inducement is often referred to as 'indicative planning' or 'market incentives'. In such type of planning, the market is manipulated through incentives and inducements. Accordingly, in this system there is persuasion rather than compulsion or deliberate enforcement of orders. Here, the consumers are sovereign so free to consume whatsoever they like. Indicative planning is found in capitalist countries as well as in mixed economies, like India.

   But such freedom of consumption and production are subject to certain regulations. Under this planning, there are profit motives more than welfare of public. Private entrepreneurs care for those products which yield high profits. Products or services with less profit or no profit do not attract private entrepreneurs. Such products or services include education, health, defence, security, etc.

2. **Imperative Planning:** Imperative planning is the planning where the formulation and implementation of the plan is made by the central planning authority. It is also known as 'directive planning'. Under imperative planning, it is the duty of the state to provide necessary supplies like raw material, machines, manpower and entrepreneurs as all such resources are owned by the state. Thus under imperative planning, the priorities laid down by the planners always supersede those of masses. There is no consumer sovereignty under it.

   This type of planning is used to be practiced in socialist countries like China, Former USSR, Cuba, North Korea, etc.

3. **Centralized Planning:** Under centralized planning, the entire planning process is under a central planning authority. The authority formulates a central plan, fixes objectives, targets and priorities for every sector of the economy. The principle problems of the economy – what and how much to produce, how and for whom to be produced, etc. – are decided by this authority. The entire planning process is based on bureaucratic control and regulation. Naturally, such planning is rigid. There is no economic freedom and all economic activities are directed from above.

4. **Decentralized Planning:** Decentralized planning refers to the execution of the plan from the grass roots. Under it, a plan is formulated by the central planning authority in consultation with the different administrative units of the country. The central plan incorporates plans under the central schemes, and plans for the states under a federal set-up. The state plans incorporate district and village level plans. Under decentralized planning, prices of goods and services are determined by the market mechanism despite government control and regulation in certain fields of economic activity.

On temporal basis, economic planning can be divided into the following four types:

1. **Perspective planning:** It refers to long-term planning in which long range targets are set in advance for a period of 15, 20 or 25 years. A perspective plan, however, does not imply one plan for

the entire period of 15 or 20 years, i.e., Vision 2020, 15-year Vision Document of NITI Aayog, etc. In reality, the broader objectives and targets are to be achieved within the specified period of time by dividing the perspective plan into several short-period plans of 4, 5 or 6 years. Even a five year plan is further broken up into annual plans (annual budgets) so that each annual plan fits into the broad framework of the Five-Year Plan (FYP).

2. **Five-year Plans:** Five-year plan is a national governmental program of planned, coordinated and cumulative economic and social development over a period of five years.
3. **Annual Plans:** Annual plan is a part of the FYP. It is prepared year-wise. So for each FYP, five annual plans are prepared in a detailed manner.
4. **Rolling Plans:** Rolling plans do not have a fixed period of time. These plans have only duration and move forward. As it moves forward, the year, which has been completed, is deleted and one year is added at the end.

In the rolling plans, there are three kinds of plans. First is the plan for the current year which comprises the annual budget. Second is a plan for a fixed number of years, which may be 3, 4 or 5 years. This second plan is kept changing as per the requirements of the economy and politics. Third is a perspective plan which is for 10, 15 or 20 years. Thus, there is no fixation of dates in respect of commencement and end of the plan in the rolling plans.

Rolling plan was advocated by Prof. Myrdal for the development of developing countries. India experienced it for the first time in April 1978 under Janata Party rule and continued up to March 1980.

## HISTORY OF PLANNING IN INDIA

On planning, a book titled 'Planned Economy in India' was written by Sir M. Visvesvaraya in 1934. In this book, he presented a constructive draft of the development of India for next ten years. His core idea was to lay out a plan to shift labour from agriculture to industries and double the national income of India in ten years.

The first attempt to develop a national plan for India came up in 1938 when Congress President Subhash Chandra Bose set up a National Planning Committee with Jawaharlal Nehru as its president. However, the reports of the committee could not be prepared, and only for the first time in 1948–49 some papers came out.

In 1944, eight celebrated industrialists of Bombay including JRD Tata, GD Birla, Purshottamdas Thakurdas, Lala Shriram, and John Mathai working together prepared 'A Brief Memorandum: Outlining a Plan of Economic Development for India'. This is known as 'Bombay Plan'. This plan envisaged doubling the per capita income in 15 years. Many of the ideas of the plan were inculcated in other plans which came later.

In 1944, Gandhian Plan was drafted by Sriman Nayaran, principal of Wardha Commercial College. It emphasized the economic decentralization with primacy to rural development by developing the cottage industries.

## SARVODAYA PLAN

People's plan was drafted by M. N. Roy in 1945. This plan was for 10 years period and gave greatest priority to agriculture. Nationalization of all agriculture and production was the main feature of this plan. This plan was based on Marxist socialism.

In 1950, Sarvodaya Plan was drafted by Jaiprakash Narayan. This plan itself was inspired by Gandhian Plan and Sarvodaya Idea of Vinoba Bhave. This plan emphasized on agriculture and small and cottage industries. It also suggested the freedom from foreign technology and stressed upon land reforms and decentralized participatory planning.

In October 1946, a planning advisory board was set up by the interim government to review the plans and future projects and make recommendations upon them.

Immediately after independence in 1947, the Economic Programme Committee was formed by All India Congress Committee with Nehru as its chairman. In 1948, this committee recommended forming of a Planning Commission. In March 1950, in pursuance of declared objectives of the government to promote a rapid rise in the standard of living of the people by efficient exploitation of the resources of the country, increasing production and offering opportunities to all for employment in the service of the community, the Planning Commission was set up by a Resolution of the Government of India as an advisory and specialized institution. Jawaharlal Nehru was the first Chairman of the Planning Commission. In 1952, the National Development Council (NDC) was set up. All the plans made by the Planning Commission were to be approved by NDC first.

## ❖ First Five-Year Plan (1 April 1951–31 March 1956)

Targeted Growth: 2.1 per cent; Actual Growth: 3.6 per cent

It was based on Harrod-Domar Model. The Community Development Program was launched in 1952. The Plan focused on agriculture, price stability, power and transport.

It was a successful plan primarily because of good harvests in the last two years of the plan. Objectives of rehabilitation of refugees, food self-sufficiency and control of prices were more or less achieved. In 1956, five IITs were established.

## ❖ Second Five-Year Plan (1956–61)

Targeted Growth: 4.5 per cent; Actual Growth: 4.3 per cent

Second plan was conceived in an atmosphere of economic stability. The plan was based on the model prepared by Prof. P C Mahalanobis, so this plan is also called Mahalanobis Plan. The Plan focused on rapid industrialization with heavy and basic industries. The Indian Government boosted manufacturing of industrial goods in the country. This was done primarily to develop the public sector. It was felt agriculture could be accorded lower priority. It advocated huge imports through foreign loans.

It adopted the establishment of a socialistic pattern of society as the goal of economic policy.

The plan was only moderately successful. During this plan, prices increased by 30 per cent, against a decline of 13 per cent during the First Plan.

As many as five steel plants including the ones in Durgapur, Jamshedpur as well as Bhilai were set up during the plan. Hydroelectric power plants were set up during the tenure of the plan. The Atomic Energy Commission came into being.

## ❖ Third Five-Year Plan (1961–66)

Targeted Growth: 5.6 per cent; Actual Growth: 2.8 per cent

It was felt that Indian economy has entered a 'take-off stage'. Therefore, the Third Plan was aimed to make India a 'self-reliant' and 'self-generating' economy. Based on the experience of first two plans, agriculture was given top priority to support the exports and industry.

### Objectives

1. Increasing the national income by 5 per cent per annum.
2. To achieve self-sufficiency in food-grains and increase agricultural production to meet the requirement of industry and exports;
3. To expand the basic industries such as steel, chemical industries, power and

also establish machine building capacity so that the requirements of further industrialization can be met within a period of 10 years or so mainly from the country's own resources;

4. To utilize to the fullest possible extent the manpower resources of the country and to ensure a substantial expansion in employment opportunities;
5. To establish progressively greater equality of opportunity and to bring about reduction in disparities in income and wealth and a more even distribution of economic power.

The Plan was thorough failure in reaching the targets due to unforeseen events of Chinese aggression (1962), Indo-Pak war (1965) and severe drought 1965–66. Due to two wars, India witnessed steep increase in price of products causing cost-push inflation.

## ❖ Three Annual Plans (1966–69)

These plans are also called plan holiday. Failure of Third Plan, devaluation of rupee and inflationary recession led to the postponement of Fourth Five Year Plan. Three Annual Plans were introduced instead. Prevailing crisis in agriculture and serious food shortage necessitated the emphasis on agriculture during the Annual Plans. During these plans, a whole new agricultural strategy was implemented. It involved widespread distribution of high-yielding varieties of seeds, extensive use of fertilizers, exploitation of irrigation potential and soil conservation. During the Annual Plans, the economy absorbed the shocks generated during the Third Plan. It paved the path for the further planned growth.

## ❖ Fourth Five-Year Plan (1969 – 74)

Targeted Growth: 5.7 per cent; Actual Growth: 3.3 per cent

Refusal of supply of essential equipment and raw materials from the allies during Indo-Pak war resulted in twin objectives of 'growth with stability' and 'progressive achievement of self-reliance' for the Fourth Plan.

### Objectives

1. Feasible rates of growth as indicated in the direction of becoming free from dependence on foreign aid by providing priority to increase agricultural and industrial sector;
2. Measures to maintain stability in the prices and to set up consistent economic policies which would lead towards the goal of mixed economy;
3. Priority would be given to enlarge the income of the rural population and augment the supply of food. Efforts would be made to maximize the production.
4. For ensuring continued growth in various industries like machinery, chemicals, mines, power and transport which are useful for self-reliance, connected schemes would be expedited for keeping up the momentum already built and making the basic needs of the country in the next FYP period;
5. For the development of human resources, additional facilities would be provided particularly in rural areas.
6. Implementation of Family Planning Programmes was amongst major targets of the Plan.

The plan was a big failure due to –

1. Indo-Pak war 1971
2. Influx of Bangladeshi refugees in India
3. High inflation

Indira Gandhi Government nationalized 14 major Indian banks and the green revolution in India advanced agriculture.

## ❖ Fifth Five-Year Plan (1974–79)

Targeted Growth: 4.4 per cent; Actual Growth: 4.8 per cent

The Plan was prepared and launched by D. P. Dhar in the backdrop of economic crisis arising out of run-away inflation fuelled by hike in oil prices and failure of the government takeover of the wholesale trade in wheat.

It proposed to achieve two main objectives: 'removal of poverty' (Garibi Hatao) and 'attainment of self-reliance'.

### Objectives

1. Reducing the discrepancy between the economic developments at the regional, national and international level. It emphasized on putting the economic growth at par with each other.
2. Improving the agricultural condition by implementing land reform measures.
3. Improving the scope of self-employment through a well-integrated program.
4. Reducing the rate of unemployment both in the urban and the rural sectors.
5. Encouraging growth of the small-scale industries.
6. Enhancing the import substitution in the spheres including chemicals, paper, mineral and equipment industries.
7. Applying policies pertaining to finance and credit in the industrial sector.
8. Stressed on the importance of a labour intensive production technology in India.

The Minimum Needs Programme (MNP) was introduced in the first year of the Plan. The Indian national highway system was introduced and many roads were widened to accommodate the increasing traffic. Tourism also expanded.

After promulgation of emergency in 1975, the emphasis shifted to the implementation of Prime Ministers 20-Point Programme. The Plan was terminated in 1978 (instead of 1979) when Janata Party Government rose to power.

## ❖ Rolling Plan (1978–80)

The Janata Party Government rejected the Fifth FYP and introduced a new Sixth FYP (1978–1980) and called it a Rolling Plan which means every year the performance of the plan was to be assessed and a new plan was be made next year based upon this assessment. The main advantage of the rolling plans is that they are flexible. They are able to overcome the rigidity of fixed FYPs by revising targets, projections and allocations as per the changing conditions in the country's economy.

Under this Rolling Plan, the Mahalanobis strategy of heavy industry development was condemned. With its revised priorities, the Janta Government Strategy favoured Gandhian solution which stressed for the development of cottage and small industries based on labour-intensive techniques. Another significant change was noticed in the field of industrial development, i.e., liberalizing the economy by making extension in the area of private sector and liberal imports.

However, the government lasted for only 2 years. Congress Party Government returned to power in 1980 and launched a new Sixth FYP aimed at directly attacking on the problem of poverty by creating conditions of an expanding economy.

## ❖ Sixth Five-Year Plan (1980–85)

Targeted Growth: 5.2 per cent; Actual Growth: 5.7 per cent

The Plan focused on increase in national income, modernization of technology, ensuring continuous decrease in poverty and unemployment through schemes.

### Objectives

1. Promotion of efficiency in the use of resources and improved productively.

2. Strengthening the impulses of modernization for the achievement of economic and technological self-reliance.
3. A progressive reduction in the incidence of poverty and unemployment.
4. A speedy development of indigenous sources of energies.
5. Improving the quality of life of the people in general with special reference to the economically and socially handicapped population.
6. Strengthening the distribution bias of public policies and services in favour of weaker sections of society.
7. A progressive reduction in regional inequalities.
8. Promoting policies for controlling the growth of population through voluntary acceptance of the small family norm.

Broadly, the sixth Plan could be taken as a success as most of the target was realized. Family planning was also expanded in order to prevent over population.

## ❖ Seventh Five-Year Plan (1985–90)

Targeted Growth: 5.0 per cent; Actual Growth: 6.0 per cent

The Plan focuses on 'food, work and productivity'.

The Plan emphasized on policies and programmes, which would accelerate the growth in foodgrains production, increase employment opportunities and raise productivity.

### Objectives

1. Introduction and application of modern technology
2. Justice meted out to people from various social stratas
3. Improving the position of the weak in the Indian society
4. Development of agriculture
5. Reducing poverty in India
6. Assuring the essentials of food, shelter and clothing to the people
7. Striving to achieve independence as per the Indian economy is concerned
8. Help the small as well as the large farmers to increase their productivity

The plan was very successful.

## ❖ Annual Plans (1990–1992)

The eighth plan was postponed by two years because of political uncertainty at the centre. It was the beginning of privatization and liberalization era in India.

## ❖ Eighth Five-Year Plan (1992–97)

Targeted Growth: 5.6 per cent; Actual Growth: 6.8 per cent

Worsening Balance of Payment position, rising debt burden, widening budget deficits, recession in industry and inflation were the key issues during the launch of the plan. The plan undertook drastic policy measures to combat the bad economic situation through implementation of fiscal and economic reforms including liberalization.

### Objectives

1. Generating adequate employment to achieve near full employment level by the turn of the century.
2. Containing population growth through active people's cooperation and an effective scheme of incentives and disincentives.
3. Universalization of elementary education and complete eradication of illiteracy among the people in the age group of 15–35 years.
4. Provision of sale drinking water and primary health facilities including immunization for all villages and entire population and complete elimination of scavenging.

5. Growth and diversification of agriculture to achieve self-sufficient in food and generate surpluses for exports.
6. Strengthening the infrastructure (energy, transport communication, irrigation) in order to support the growth processes on a sustainable basis.
7. The withdrawal of the state from these industrial activities where its presence is not essential and encouraging private sector initiative to fill the vacuum.
8. Encouraging all-round productivity and efficiency in the public sector enterprises compelling them to rely on internally generated resources rather than on budgetary support.

Some of the main economic outcomes during eighth plan period were rapid economic growth (highest annual growth rate so far: 6.8 per cent), high growth of agriculture and allied sector, and manufacturing sector, growth in exports and imports, improvement in trade and current account deficit.

However, the share of public sector in total investment had declined considerably.

## ❖ Ninth Five-Year Plan (1997–2002)

Targeted Growth: 6.5 per cent; Actual Growth: 5.4 per cent

The Plan focused on 'Growth with Social Justice and Equality'.

Ninth Plan aimed to depend predominantly on the private sector – Indian as well as foreign. State was envisaged to increasingly play the role of facilitator and increasingly involve itself with social sector viz. education, health, etc. and with infrastructure where private sector participation was likely to be limited. It assigned priority to agriculture and rural development with a view to generate adequate productive employment and eradicate poverty.

### Objectives

1. Priority to agriculture and rural development with a view to generating adequate productivity employment and eradication of poverty;
2. Accelerating the growth rate of the economy with stable prices;
3. Ensuring food and nutritional security for all, particularly the vulnerable sections of society;
4. Providing the basic minimum services of safe drinking water, primary health care facilities, universal primary education, shelter, and connectivity to all in a time bound manner;
5. Containing the growth rate of population;
6. Ensuring environmental sustainability of the development process through social mobilization and participation of people at all levels;
7. Empowerment of women and socially disadvantaged groups such as Scheduled Castes, Scheduled Tribes and other Backward Classes and Minorities as agents of socio-economic change and development ;
8. Promoting and developing people's participatory institutions like Panchayati Raj Institutions, co-operatives and self-help groups.
9. Strengthening efforts to build self-reliance.

It achieved a GDP growth rate of 5.4 per cent lower than target. Yet, industrial growth was 4.5 per cent which was higher than targeted 3 per cent. The service industry had a growth rate of 7.8 per cent. An average annual growth rate of 6.7 per cent was reached.

## ❖ Tenth Five-Year Plan (2002 – 2007)

Targeted Growth: 8 per cent; Actual Growth: 7.6 per cent

Recognizing that economic growth cannot be the only objective of national plan, Tenth Plan had set 'monitorable targets' for eleven key indicators.

### Monitorable Targets

1. Universal access to primary education by 2007.
2. The Child Mortality Rate be reduced to 45 per 1,000 livings births and 28 per 1,000 livings births by 2007 and 2012 respectively.
3. All main rivers should be cleaned up between 2007 and 2012.
4. Reducing the poverty ratio by at least five per cent age points, by 2007.
5. Making provision for useful and lucrative employments to the population, which are of the best qualities.
6. By 2007, there should be a decrease in gender discriminations in the spheres of wage rate and literacy, by a minimum of 50 per cent.
7. Taking up of extensive afforestation measures, by planting more trees and enhance the forest and tree areas to 25 per cent by 2007 and 33 per cent by 2012.
8. Ensuring persistent availability of pure drinking water in the rural areas of India, even in the remote parts.
9. The alarming rate at which the Indian population is growing must be checked and fixed to 16.2 per cent, between a time frame of 2001 and 2011.
10. The rate of literacy must be increased by at least 75 per cent, within the tenure of the tenth FYP.
11. There should be a decrease in the Maternal Mortality Ratio (MMR) to 2 per 1,000 live births by 2007. The Plan also intended to bring down the MMR to 1 per 1,000 live births by the year 2012.

The Governance was considered as factor of development and agriculture was declared as prime moving force of the economy. States role in planning was to be increased with greater involvement of Panchayati Raj Institutions. State-wise break up of targets for growth and social development sought to achieve balanced development of all states.

Tenth Plan was successful in reducing poverty, increasing forest cover and increasing literacy rate and the economic growth of the country.

## ❖ Eleventh Five-Year Plan (2007–2012)

Targeted Growth: 9 per cent; Actual Growth: 8 per cent

Eleventh Plan was aimed 'Towards Faster and More Inclusive Growth.'

India emerged as one of the fastest growing economy by the end of the Tenth Plan. The savings and investment rates increased, industrial sector had responded well to face competition in the global economy and foreign investors were keen to invest in India. But, the growth was not perceived as sufficiently inclusive for many groups, specially the SCs, STs and minorities on several dimensions like poverty, malnutrition, mortality, current daily employment, etc.

### Major Targets

1. **Income and Poverty**
   (i) Accelerate GDP growth from 8 per cent to 10 per cent and then maintain at 10 per cent in the 12th plan in order to double per capita income by 2016–17.

(ii) Create 70 Million new work opportunities.
(iii) Reduce educated unemployment to below 5 per cent.
(iv) Reduce poverty by 10 per cent age points.

2. **Education**
(i) Reduce dropout rates of children from elementary school from 52.2 per cent in 2003–04 to 20 per cent by 2011–12.
(ii) Increase literacy rate for persons of age 7 years or more to 85 per cent.
(iii) Lower gender gap in literacy to 10 percentage points.

3. **Health**
(i) Reduce infant mortality rate to 28 and MMR to 1 per cent 1,000 live births.
(ii) Reduce total fertility rate to 2.1.
(iii) Reduce malnutrition among children of age group 0–3 to half its present level.

4. **Infrastructure**
(i) Ensure electricity connection to all villages and Below Poverty Line households by 2009 and 24-hr power supply by the end of the Plan.
(ii) Increase forest and tree cover by 5 per cent points.
(iii) Attain World Health Organization standard of air quality in all major cities by 2011–12.
(iv) A telephone in every village by November 2007.
(v) Broadband connectivity to all villages by 2011–12.

## ❖ Twelfth Five-Year Plan (2012–17)

Targeted Growth: 8 per cent of GDP.

The Twelfth Plan commenced at a time when the global economy was going through a second financial crisis, precipitated by the sovereign debt problems of the Eurozone which erupted in the last year of the Eleventh Plan.

The Twelfth Plan, therefore, emphasizes that the priority must be to bring the economy back to rapid growth while ensuring that the growth is both inclusive and sustainable.

The broad vision and aspirations which the Twelfth Plan seeks to fulfil are reflected in the subtitle: 'Faster, Sustainable and More Inclusive Growth'.

### Monitorable Targets

Twenty-five core indicators during the Twelfth Plan were:

1. **Economic Growth**
(i) Real GDP Growth Rate of 8 per cent.
(ii) Agriculture Growth Rate of 4 per cent.
(iii) Manufacturing Growth Rate of 10 per cent.
(iv) Every state must have an average growth rate in the Twelfth Plan preferably higher than that achieved in the Eleventh Plan.

2. **Poverty and Employment**
(i) Head-count ratio of consumption poverty to be reduced by 10 percentage points over the preceding estimates by the end of Twelfth FYP.
(ii) Generate 50 million new work opportunities in the non-farm sector and provide skill certification to equivalent numbers during the Twelfth FYP.

3. **Education**
(i) Mean Years of Schooling to increase to seven years by the end of Twelfth FYP.
(ii) Enhance access to higher education by creating two million additional

seats for each age cohort aligned to the skill needs of the economy.

(iii) Eliminate gender and social gap in school enrolment (that is, between girls and boys, and between SCs, STs, Muslims and the rest of the population) by the end of Twelfth FYP.

4. **Health**

(i) Reduce IMR to 25 and MMR to 1 per 1,000 live births, and improve the Child Sex Ratio (0–6 years) to 950 by the end of the Twelfth FYP.

(ii) Reduce total fertility rate to 2.1 by the end of Twelfth FYP.

(iii) Reduce under-nutrition among children aged 0–3 years to half of the NFHS-3 levels by the end of Twelfth FYP.

(iv) Infrastructure, Including Rural Infrastructure: Increase investment in infrastructure as a percentage of GDP to 9 per cent by the end of Twelfth FYP.

(v) Increase the Gross Irrigated Area from 90 million hectare to 103 million hectare by the end of Twelfth FYP.

(vi) Provide electricity to all villages and reduce AT and C losses to 20 per cent by the end of Twelfth FYP.

(vii) Connect all villages with all-weather roads by the end of Twelfth FYP.

(viii) Upgrade national and state highways to the minimum two-lane standard by the end of Twelfth FYP.

(ix) Complete Eastern and Western Dedicated Freight Corridors by the end of Twelfth FYP.

(x) Increase rural teledensity to 70 per cent by the end of Twelfth FYP.

(xi) Ensure 50 per cent of rural population has access to 40 lpcd piped drinking water supply, and 50 per cent gram panchayats achieve Nirmal Gram Status by the end of Twelfth FYP.

5. **Environment and Sustainability**

(i) Increase green cover (as measured by satellite imagery) by 1 million hectare every year during the Twelfth FYP.

(ii) Add 30,000 MW of renewable energy capacity in the Twelfth Plan.

(iii) Reduce emission intensity of GDP in line with the target of 20 per cent to 25 per cent reduction over 2,005 levels by 2020.

(iv) Service Delivery: Provide access to banking services to 90 per cent Indian households by the end of Twelfth FYP.

(v) Major subsidies and welfare related beneficiary payments to be shifted to a direct cash transfer by the end of the Twelfth Plan, using the Aadhaar platform with linked bank accounts.

NITI Aayog announced that the practice of making FYPs have ended after the 12 Plan got over in 2016–17. The Five Year Planning now would be replaced by three documents released by the NITI Aayog. They would cover the short-term through a three-year Action Plan (2017–18 to 2019–20), the medium-term by seven-year strategy (2017–18 to 2023–24) and the long-term by a 15-year Vision Document (2017–18 to 2031–32).

## ❖ Five-Year Plan Replaced

Replacing the FYPs beyond 31 March 2017, NITI Aayog is in the process of preparing the 15-year vision document keeping in view the social goals; A 7-year strategy document spanning 2017–18 to 2023–24 to convert the longer-term vision into implementable policy and action as a part of a "National Development Agenda" is also being worked upon. The 3-year Action Agenda for 2017–18 to 2019–20, aligned to the predictability of financial resources during the 14th Finance Commission Award period, has been completed.

## NITI AAYOG

The NITI Aayog was formed by a resolution of the union cabinet on 1 January 2015. NITI Aayog is the premier policy 'Think Tank' of the Government of India, providing both directional and policy inputs. While designing strategic and long-term policies and programmes for the Government of India, NITI Aayog also provides relevant technical advice to the centre and states.

The Government of India, in keeping with its reform agenda, constituted the NITI Aayog to replace the Planning Commission instituted in March 1950. This was done in order to better serve the needs and aspirations of the people of India. An important evolutionary change from the past, NITI Aayog acts as the standard platform of the Government of India to bring states to act together in national interest, and thereby fosters cooperative federalism.

At the core of NITI Aayog's creation are two hubs – Team India Hub and the Knowledge and Innovation Hub. The Team India Hub leads the engagement of states with the central government, while the Knowledge and Innovation Hub builds NITI's think-tank capabilities. These hubs reflect the two key tasks of the Aayog.

NITI Aayog is also developing itself as a state of the art resource centre, with the necessary resources, knowledge and skills, that will enable it to act with speed, promote research and innovation, provide strategic policy vision for the government and deal with contingent issues.

### ❖ Functions

1. To evolve a shared vision of national development priorities sectors and strategies with the active involvement of states in the light of national objectives.
2. To foster cooperative federalism through structured support initiatives and mechanisms with the States on a continuous basis, recognizing that strong States make a strong nation.
3. To develop mechanisms to formulate credible plans at the village level and aggregate these progressively at higher levels of government.
4. To ensure, on areas that are specifically referred to it, that the interests of national security are incorporated in economic strategy and policy.
5. To pay special attention to the sections of our society that may be at risk of not benefiting adequately from economic progress.
6. To design strategic and long term policy and programme frameworks and initiatives, and monitor their progress and their efficacy. The lessons learnt through monitoring and feedback will be used for making innovative improvements, including necessary mid-course corrections.
7. To provide advice and encourage partnerships between key stakeholders and national and international like-minded think tanks, as well as educational and policy research institutions.
8. To create a knowledge, innovation and entrepreneurial support system through a collaborative community of national and international experts, practitioners and other partners.
9. To offer a platform for resolution of inter-sectoral and inter-departmental issues in

order to accelerate the implementation of the development agenda.

10. To maintain a state-of-the-art resource centre, be a repository of research on good governance and best practices in sustainable and equitable development as well as help their dissemination to stakeholders.
11. To actively monitor and evaluate the implementation of programmes and initiatives, including the identification of the needed resources so as to strengthen the probability of success and scope of delivery.
12. To focus on technology upgradation and capacity building for implementation of programmes and initiatives.
13. To undertake other activities as may be necessary in order to further the execution of the national development agenda, and the objectives mentioned above.

## ❖ Composition

The NITI Aayog comprises the following:

1. The Prime Minister of India as the Chairperson
2. Governing Council comprising the Chief Ministers of all the States and Lt. Governors of Union Territories
3. Regional Councils will be formed to address specific issues and contingencies impacting more than one state or a region. These will be formed for a specified tenure. The Regional Councils will be convened by the Prime Minister and will comprise of the Chief Ministers of States and Lt. Governors of Union Territories in the region. These will be chaired by the Chairperson of the NITI Aayog or his nominee.
4. Experts, specialists and practitioners with relevant domain knowledge as special invitees nominated by the Prime Minister.
5. The full-time organizational framework will comprise of, in addition to the Prime Minister as the Chairperson:
   (i) Vice-chairperson: To be appointed by the Prime Minister
      (a) Members: Full-time (Presently 3)
      (b) Part-time members: Maximum of two from leading universities research organizations and other relevant institutions in an ex-officio capacity. Part time members will be on a rotational basis.
      (c) *Ex-officio* members: Maximum of four members of the Union Council of Ministers to be nominated by the Prime Minister.
      (d) Chief Executive Officer: To be appointed by the Prime Minister for a fixed tenure, in the rank of Secretary to the Government of India.
      (e) Secretariat as deemed necessary.

## ❖ Challenges before NITI Aayog

1. Leveraging of India's demographic dividend, and realization of the potential of youth, men and women, through education, skill development, elimination of gender bias, and employment.
2. Elimination of poverty, and the chance for every Indian to live a life of dignity and self-respect.
3. Redressal of inequalities based on gender bias, caste and economic disparities.
4. Integrate villages institutionally into the development process.
5. Policy support to more than 50 million small businesses, which are a major source of employment creation.

6. Safeguarding of our environmental and ecological assets.
7. An administration paradigm in which the government is an 'enabler' rather than a 'provider of first and last resort'.
8. Progress from 'food security' to focus on a mix of agricultural production, as well as actual returns that farmers get from their produce.
9. Ensure that India is an active player in the debates and deliberations on the global commons.
10. Ensure that the economically vibrant middle-class remains engaged, and its potential is fully realized.
11. Leverage India's pool of entrepreneurial, scientific and intellectual human capital.
12. Incorporate the significant geo-economic and geo-political strength of the Non-Resident Indian Community.
13. Use urbanization as an opportunity to create a wholesome and secure habitat through the use of modern technology.
14. Use technology to reduce opacity and potential for misadventures in governance.

## ❖ Difference between Planning Commission and NITI Aayog

1. Planning Commission was an advisory body, and so is NITI Aayog. However, the key difference between them is that while the former had power to allocate funds for Plan assisted schemes to ministries and states, NITI Aayog has no such powers. This power has now been shifted to finance ministry. NITI Aayog is essentially a think tank and a truly advisory body.
2. The role of states in the planning commission era was limited. The states annually needed to interact with the planning commission to get their annual plan approved. They had some limited function in the NDC. Since NITI Aayog has all chief ministers of states and administrators of UT in its Governing Council, it is obvious that states are expected to have greater role and say in planning/implementation of policies.
3. The top down approach is reversed in NITI Aayog. It will develop mechanisms to formulate credible plans to the village level and aggregate these progressively at higher levels of government. The provision of regional council is there in NITI Aayog to address local/regional development issues.
4. One of the new functions of NITI Aayog is to address the need of the National Security in the economic strategy.
5. While the planning commission formed central plans, NITI Aayog will not formulate them anymore. It has been vested with the responsibility of evaluating the implementation of programmes.

## ❖ Offices Attached to NITI Aayog

1. **Development Monitoring and Evaluation Office (DMEO):** The DMEO has been constituted on 18 September 2015 by merging the erstwhile Programme Evaluation Organization (PEO) and the Independent Evaluation Office (IEO) and notified as an attached office under the aegis of NITI Aayog for fulfilling the mandate of evaluation and monitoring assigned to NITI Aayog.
2. **National Institute of Labour Economics Research and Development (NILERD):** The Institute of Applied Manpower Research (IAMR), established in 1962, has been renamed as NILERD on 9th June, 2014. NILERD is mainly funded by grants-in-aid from the NITI Aayog

and supplemented by its own revenue from contracted research projects, and education and training activities. The main object of the Institute is to advance knowledge about the nature, characteristics and utilization of human resources through research, education and training, consultancy etc.

## ❖ Three-Year Action Agenda

Seeking to make development a Jan Andolan, details key recommendations across growth drivers, infrastructure, inclusion and governance.

The NITI Aayog today unveiled its comprehensive national Strategy for New India, which defines clear objectives for 2022-23. It is a detailed exposition acrossforty-one crucial areas, that recognizesthe progress already made, identifies binding constraints, and suggests the way forward for achieving the clearly stated objectives.

The *'Strategy for New India @75'* was released today at a press conference by the Union Finance Minister Shri Arun Jaitley, in the presence of NITI Aayog Vice-Chairman Dr Rajiv Kumar, Members Dr Ramesh Chand andDr VK Saraswat and CEO Shri Amitabh Kant.

Drawing inspiration and direction from the Prime Minister's clarion call for establishing a New India by 2022, NITI Aayog embarked on a journey of formulating theStrategy documentover the last year.

In his foreword the Prime Minister says,"*The Strategy for New India @75* put together by NITI Aayog is an attempt to bring innovation, technology, enterprise and efficient management together, at the core of policy formulation and implementation. It will encourage discussion and debate, and invite feedback for further refining our policy approach.We believe that economic transformation cannot happen without public participation. Development must become a Jan Andolan."

NITI Aayog followed an extremely participative approach in preparing the strategy. Each area vertical in NITI Aayog had in-depth consultations with all three groups of stakeholders, viz., business persons, academics including scientists, and government officials.

This was followed byconsultations at the level of the Vice Chairman with a diverse group of eminent persons from seven sets of stakeholders that included scientists and innovators, farmers, civil society organizations, think-tanks, labor representatives and trade unions, and industry representatives.

Central Ministries were brought on board for inputs, suggestions and comments, with each draft of individual chapters being circulated for consultations. The draft document was also circulated to all the States and Union Territories from whom valuable suggestions were received and incorporated.

Over 800 stakeholders from within the government - central, state and district levels - and about 550 external experts were consulted during the preparation of the document.

The overarching focus of the Strategy document is to further improve the policy environment in which private investors and other stakeholders can contribute their fullest towards achieving the goals set out for New India 2022 and propel India towards a USD 5 trillion economy by 2030.

The forty-one chapters in the document have been disaggregated under four sections: Drivers, Infrastructure, Inclusion and Governance.

The first section on Drivers focuses on the engines of economic performance with chapters on growth and employment, doubling of farmers' incomes; upgrading the science, technology and innovation ecosystem; and promoting sunrise sectors like fintech and tourism.

Some of the key recommendations in the section on drivers include:

Steadily accelerate the economy to achieve a GDP growth rate of about 8% on average during 2018-23.

This will raisethe economy's size in real terms from USD 2.7trillion in 2017-18 to nearly USD 4 trillion by 2022-23. Increase the investment rate as measured by gross fixed capital formation (GFCF) from the present 29% to 36% of GDP by 2022.

In agriculture, shift the emphasis to converting farmers to 'agripreneurs' by further expandinge-National

Agriculture Markets and replacing the Agricultural Produce Marketing Committee Act with the

Agricultural Produce and Livestock Marketing Act.

Give a strong push to 'Zero Budget Natural Farming' techniques that reduce costs,improve land quality and increase farmers' incomes. This has emerged as a tested method for putting environmentcarbon back into the land.

To ensure maximum employment creation, complete codification of labor laws and a massiveeffort must be made to upscale and expand apprenticeships.

Launch a mission "Explore in India" by revamping minerals exploration and licensing policy.

The second section on Infrastructure deals with the physical foundations of growth which are crucial to enhancing the competitiveness of Indian business as also ensuring the citizens' ease of living.

Some of the key recommendations in the section on infrastructure include:

. Expedite the establishment of the Rail Development Authority (RDA), which is already approved.

RDAwill advise or make informed decisions on an integrated, transparent and dynamic pricing mechanismfor the railways.

Double the share of freight transported by coastal shipping and inland waterways. Initiallyviability gap funding will be provided until the infrastructure is fully developed. Develop an IT-enabled platformfor integrating different modes of transport and promoting multi-modal anddigitized mobility.

With the completion of the Bharat Net programme in 2019, all 2.5 lakh gram panchayats will be digitallyconnected. Aim to deliver all government services at the state, district, and gram panchayat level digitally by2022-23.

The section on Inclusion deals with the urgent task of investing in the capabilities of all of India's citizens. The three themes in this section revolve around the dimensions of health, education and mainstreaming of traditionally marginalized sections of the population.

Some of the key recommendations in the section on inclusion include:

Successfully implementing the Ayushman Bharat programme including the establishment of 150,000 health and wellness centres across the country, and rolling out the Pradhan Mantri Jan Arogya Abhiyaan (PM-JAY).

Create a focal point for public health at the central level with state counterparts. Promote integrative medicine curriculum.

Upgrade the quality of the school education system and skills, including the creation of a new innovation ecosystem at the ground level by establishing at least 10,000 Atal Tinkering Labs by 2020.

Conceptualize an electronic national educational registry for tracking each child's learning outcomes.

As already done in rural areas, give a huge push to affordable housing in urban areas to improve workers' living conditions and ensure equity while providing a strong impetus to economic growth.

The final section on Governance delves deep into how the governance structures can be streamlined and processes optimized to achieve better developmental outcomes.

Some of the key recommendations in the section on governance include:

Implement the recommendations of the Second Administrative Reforms Commission as a preludeto appointing a successor for designing reforms in the changing context of emerging technologies andgrowing complexity of the economy.

Set up a new autonomous body, viz., the Arbitration Council of India to grade arbitralinstitutions and accredit arbitrators to make the arbitration process cost effective and speedy, and to preemptthe need for court intervention.

Address the backlog of pending cases - shift part of workload out of regular court system.

Expand the scope of Swachh Bharat Mission to cover initiatives for landfills, plastic waste andmunicipal waste and generating wealth from waste.

The full document can be accessed here: http://niti.gov.in/the-strategy-for-new-india

❑❑❑

# 14 CHAPTER

# Social Sector in India

## INTRODUCTION

The social sector is an important sector of the Indian economy and includes those components which play an important role in the contribution of human resource development. Thus education, health and medical care, water supply and sanitation, housing conditions, etc. are the components which contribute to human development. The social sector may also refer to the value system of the economy such as values of freedom, gender, nationalism, habit of saving and investment.

The Government of India has consistently prioritized strengthening the educational and health profile of the population. As India is poised to grow as one of the leading knowledge economies, education, skill development and health will remain priorities for the Government.

As a percentage of the Gross Domestic Product (GDP), expenditure on social services increased from 6.8 per cent in 2008–09 to 7.2 per cent in 2013–14. But there has been a marginal decline to 5.8 per cent in 2015–16 which has further moved up to 7.7 per cent in 2019–20.

## DEMOGRAPHY OF INDIA

The study of human population is called demography. It studies the size, composition, distribution across places and the process through which population change. Births, deaths and migration are the 'big three' of demography, jointly producing population stability or change.

Demographic characteristics of a country provide an overview of its population size, composition territorial distribution, changes there in and the components of changes such as nativity, mortality and social mobility. Demographic indicators have been subdivided into two parts: population statistics and vital statistics. Population statistics include indicators that measure the population size, sex ratio, density and dependency ratio, while vital statistics include indicators such as birth rate, death rate, and natural growth rate, Life Expectancy at Birth (LEB), mortality and fertility rates. These indicators for the country as well as states help in identifying areas that need policy and programmed interventions, setting near and far-term goals, and deciding priorities, besides understanding them in an integrated structure.

Demographic transition is the transition from high birth and death rates to low birth and death rates as a country develops from a pre-industrial to an industrialized economic system. This is typically demonstrated through a demographic transition model.

## STAGES OF DEMOGRAPHIC TRANSITION

The demographic transition theory is based on an interpretation of demographic history developed in 1919 by the American demographer, Warren Thompson (1887–1973). Thompson observed changes, or transitions, in birth and death rates in industrialized societies over the previous 200 years.

The transition involves four stages, which include:

1. In stage one, pre-industrial society, death rates and birth rates are high. Birth and death rates both tend to be very high in this stage. Because both rates are approximately in balance, population growth is typically very slow in stage one.

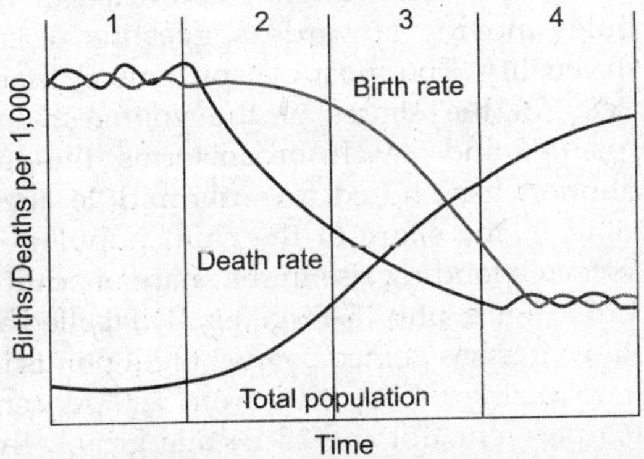


2. In stage two, that of a developing country, the death rates drop rapidly due to improvements in food supply and sanitation, which increase life spans and reduce disease. The improvements specific to food supply typically include selective breeding and crop rotation and farming techniques. Other improvements generally include access to technology, basic health care and education. For example, numerous improvements in public health reduce mortality, especially childhood mortality. Prior to the mid-20th century, these improvements in public health were primarily in the areas of food handling, water supply, sewage and personal hygiene. Interestingly, one of the variables often cited is the increase in female literacy combined with public health education programmes which emerged in the late 19th and early 20th centuries. Without a corresponding fall in birth rates, this produces an imbalance, and the countries in this stage experience a large increase in population.
3. In stage three, birth rates fall due to access to contraception, increases in wages, urbanization, a reduction in subsistence agriculture, an increase in the status and education of women, a reduction in the value of children's work, an increase in parental investment in the education of children and other social changes. Population growth begins to level off. While improvements in contraception do play a role in birth rate decline, it should be noted that contraceptives were neither generally available nor widely used in the 19th century and as a result likely did not play a significant role in the decline then. It is important to note that birth rate decline is caused also by a transition in values; not just because of the availability of contraceptives.
4. During stage four, there are both low birth rates and low death rates. Birth rates may drop to well below replacement level as has happened in countries like Germany, Italy and Japan, leading to a shrinking population, a threat to many industries that rely on population growth. As the large groups born during stage two ages, it creates an economic burden on the shrinking working population. Death rates may remain consistently low or increase slightly due to increases in lifestyle diseases due to low exercise levels and high obesity and an ageing population in developed countries. By the late 20th century, birth rates and death

rates in developed countries levelled off at lower rates.

Most developed countries are in stage four of the model; the majority of developing countries have reached stage three.

The original demographic transition model has just four stages, but additional stages have been proposed. Both more-fertile and less-fertile futures have been claimed as a Stage Five.

## DEMOGRAPHY OF INDIA: CENSUS 2011

Population Census is the total process of collecting, compiling, analysing or otherwise disseminating demographic, economic and social data pertaining, at a specific time, of all persons in a country or a well-defined part of a country. As such, the census provides snapshot of the country's population and housing at a given point of time. The population census 2011 is the 14th since 1881 and the 7th in the independent India.

## DEMOGRAPHIC INDICATORS

India's population, as on 1 March 2011, stood at 12101.9 lakhs (6,237 lakh males and 5,864 lakh females). India accounts for a meagre 2.4 per cent of the total world surface area of 1357.9 lakh sq km.

In the ongoing transition, India's population has increased from 238 million in 1901 to 1,210 million in 2011, i.e., more than quadrupled. The pace slowed by 1921, with some decline during the decade of 1911–21, but picked up after 1921 and accelerated after 1951, with decadal increase rising to 20 per cent, and the period of 1961–91 experienced growth at a rate exceeding 2 per cent per annum. Some slowing down of the pace was noticed after the 2001 census with the decadal growth still over 20 per cent, but the annual rate fell marginally below the 2 per cent mark. The latest census has shown a clear fall, to a decadal growth of 17.6 per cent and annual rate of 1.62 per cent. In fact, not just the growth rate but the absolute increase has also shown a decline, from 182 million during 1991–2001 to 181 million during 2001–11. Clearly, India's trajectory of growth has turned downwards though the population trajectory continues to be upward.

The country has a low sex ratio of 940 female per thousand male, which has shown slight improvement during the last decade.

The population density of India in 2011 is 382 per sq km, while urban population is 31.60 per cent of the total population. Urban migration over the last decade has resulted in the rapid growth of urban slums.

Age distribution of the population shows 31.4 per cent in 0–14 age group, while only 7.4 per cent are in the 60+ age group. The population pyramid was wide at the bottom narrowing steeply over age some time ago, but by 2001, there occurred clear shrinking at low ages with the bulge moving upwards, suggesting recent fall in fertility. The most conspicuous changes are seen in the shares of the youngest age groups, 0–4 and 5–9. In broad terms, the age distribution has shifted towards middle ages, with fall in the share of the child population and a corresponding rise in the share of adults. The broad age group 15–59 generally labelled as working ages has gained by over eight points in its share during 1971 to 2001, from 52.0 per cent to 60.5 per cent (for the 15–64 age group, the increase is from 54.6 per cent to 63.6 per cent). The old ages (60 and above) have also gained but only marginally, from 6.0 to 8.6 per cent (for the 65+ ages, from 3.3 per cent to 5.5 per cent). Ageing has begun to occur in India, but at the moment, only just so. A positive consequence of the change in the age distribution is that the dependency ratio has fallen, from 92 per cent to 65 per cent (84 per cent to 57 per cent if the 15–64 age group is treated as 'working ages'). Most of this is accounted for by the drop in the young age dependency ratio and very little by the old age. Clearly, the requirement of supporting children has come down as couples now have fewer children than in the past. The share of the population in ages 0–6 (that is, below 7 years) shows a steady fall in the recent years, of about two percentage points per decade. The results of the 2011 census revealed that the share of this age group fell from 16 per cent in 2001 to only 13 per cent in 2011, a consequence of recent fertility decline.

By the middle of the century, the share of the young ages 0–14 years would fall to nearly half of the level of 2001 and that of the old age group 60 years (or 65 years) and above would more than double. Clearly, India' population would be ageing. The share of the working ages would rise for some time reaching a peak of 65 per cent for the 15–59 year age group (and nearly 70 per cent for the 15–64 year group) before beginning to decline.

The estimated birth rate declined from 25.8 in 2000 to 22.1 in 2010, while the death rate declined from 8.5 to 7.2 per 1,000 population over the same period. The natural growth rate declined from 17.3 in 2000 to 14.9 in 2010 as per the latest available information. The population, however, continues to grow, as the decline in the birth rate is not as rapid as the decline in the death rate.

The infant mortality rate (IMR) was well over 100 per 1,000 through the 1970s, but the latest figure, for 2011, is 44. Similarly, the Under-five Mortality Rate (U5MR) has declined from over 200 per 1,000 (one fifth of new-born not surviving to the sixth year) to 55 in 2011. Though early childhood mortality has fallen, the level is still quite high, well above that in the developed world, but higher than that in many developing countries. Moreover, after 1991, fall in the IMR has not been as steep as during the 1970s and 1980s. The fall in post-neonatal mortality has been greater than in neo-natal mortality. While hardly any sex differential is seen in the IMR, the U5MR has consistently been higher for girls than for boys. Female neglect seems to operate especially at young ages.

The age-specific mortality rates are declining over the years; the rural–urban differentials are still high.

The Total Fertility Rate (TFR) in rural areas has been 2.9 during 2009, whereas it has been 2.0 in urban areas as per the latest available information.

Fertility was high in India in the past, with the Crude Birth Rate (CBR) in the upper 40s (per 1,000 population) during the early part of the 20th century. Some decline was noticed in the 1940s followed by a plateau through the 1960s with the birth rate hovering around the 40 point mark. A steady fall is seen since the 1970s, with the CBR reaching 22.1 and the TFR 2.4 by 2011. There was some stall, through the late 1970s to mid-1980s, but since then the decline has been fairly smooth. The age pattern of fertility has undergone a change; ASFRs in the ages over 30 have fallen much more than in other age groups, though a decline is seen at all the ages. Fertility is now much more concentrated in the prime ages, 20–29 years, than in the past.

Fertility is lower in urban areas than rural, among the more educated than the less educated, among the rich and middle classes than the poor. Differentials by caste exist but are not very wide. Sikhs and Christians have lower fertility than Hindus, whereas fertility among Muslims is higher than among Hindus. Controlled for other factors, the differentials by education persist, as do some by religion, but the rural-urban, income/wealth and caste differences diminish considerably. The trends reveal, first, that fertility decline has occurred in all sections of society, the poor and the rich, the illiterate and the educated, residents of villages and towns or cities, and in various caste and religion groups. India's fertility decline has been quite pervasive. Second, the gaps seem to be narrowing. In other words, fertility transition has been occurring in all sections, but some are ahead of others and have lower fertility than average while some are lagging behind.

The CDR was very high, over 40 per 1,000, during early years of the 20th century, but fell steadily to below 40 in the 1920s, below 30 in the 1940s and further below 20 after 1960. It has been less than 10 since the 1990s. The life expectancy in India has increased from a low of 20 years during 1911–20 to over 30 during 1931–40, crossed 40 years during 1951–60, 50 years in the mid-1960s and 1970s and 60 in the early 1990s. Broadly, there has been a rise of about 10 years in the expectancy every two decades. The latest data on ASDR show a life expectancy of just over 65 years, 64 for males and 67 for females during 2006–10. Female expectancy had fallen below male expectancy during the middle of the century, but the gap is in favour of females now; however, this gap is less than that seen in most countries.

There are large variations in the timing and pace of change and consequently differences in population growth in different states. Uttar Pradesh is the largest state in population size, with the 2011 population just under 200 million, followed by Maharashtra and Bihar, with each exceeding 100 million. The UT of Lakshadweep is the smallest, with population below 100,000 (64,429). Growth has occurred in all parts of the country but not uniformly. Delhi and Chandigarh have as-expected larger rates of increase than others. On the other hand, Goa, Himachal Pradesh, Punjab and Tamil Nadu have grown at relatively lower pace.

The timing of the growth has also varied. Kerala was leading both in experiencing rapid growth and in slowing down the pace. The decade of 2001–11 exhibits vast differences in the rate of growth; among large states, it has varied between a mere 0.47 per cent in Kerala and 2.24 per cent in Bihar. A consequence of the inter-state variation in growth rates is that shares of states in India's population have changed since 1901. Uttar Pradesh and Tamil Nadu have lost 2 to 3 percentage points, and Assam, Gujarat and Maharashtra have gained more than 1 point. Notice, however, that while Kerala gained during the first half of the century, Uttar Pradesh lost during the first half and Tamil Nadu during the second.

## POPULATION EXPLOSION IN INDIA

**Population Explosion** refers the sudden and rapid rise in the size of population, especially human population. It is more prominent in underdeveloped and developing countries than in developed countries. Population explosion mainly refers to the surge in population post World War II. However, in the context of India, it refers to the rapid increase in population in post-Independent era.

### ❖ Causes of Population Explosion in India

1. **High Birth Rate:** It is a major cause responsible for the rapid growth of population. In India, although the birth rate has declined from 45.8 per 1,000 during the period 1891–1900 to about 25.8 per thousand in 2001, it is still considered to be substantially high. This shows that the birth rate has not come down considerably in spite of the increase in the widespread propaganda of family planning, family welfare programmes and population education campaigns.
2. **Low Death Rate:** The phenomenal fall in the death rate in recent years is another important factor that has contributed to the rapid increase in population. The death rate in India is about 8.5 per thousand in 2001. Due to advancement in medical science, dreadful and chronic diseases such a small pox, cholera, plague and typhoid are no longer dreaded. Better facilities for sanitation and cleanliness, and provision of pre-natal and post-natal care have reduced IMR.
3. **Early Marriage:** The practice of early marriage is another important reason for the rapid increase in population in India. The mean age of marriage for girls is about 18 years, which is low, compared to the other countries of the world, which is about 23 to 25 years. This results in a

longer span for reproductive activity and the increase in the number of children.

4. **Social and Religious Reasons:** In India, every person has to marry because marriage is a compulsory institution as per social norms. In joint family system, nobody feels individual responsibility and everybody has access to equal level of consumption. Therefore, people do not hesitate to increase the size of the family. Most of the people think that at least one male child should be born in the family. In the expectation of getting a male child, they go on increasing the family size.
5. **Poverty:** Poverty is another cause which contributes to the increase in population. Children are source for income of the family. The children at a very young age help their parents in work, instead of going to school, and thus prove to be an asset for the family. Every additional child will become an earning member and thus supplement the family income.
6. **Standard of Living:** People whose standard of living is low tend to have more children because an additional child is considered as an asset rather than a liability. Since a majority of the population is uneducated, they are unable to understand the need for family planning. They are unaware that a smaller size of family will help them enjoy a better standard of living.
7. **Illiteracy:** A major part of the population (about 60 per cent) in India is either illiterate or has the minimum education. This leads them to accept minimal work in which they cannot even support themselves. Unemployment and underemployment further lead to poverty.

Moreover due to the prevalence of higher rate of illiteracy, there is widespread ignorance in the form of social customs and beliefs like early marriage and preference for a male child. As a result, there is high rate of population growth in the country.

## ❖ Effects of Population Explosion on Economic Development

India is facing the situation of population explosion. Although we need more labour supply for our economic development, it is also true that if our population keeps on rising, the process of economic development will be affected.

The rising population in India affects economic development in the following ways:

1. **Food Shortage:** If the population of India goes on rising and there is no proportionate increase in agricultural production, the country will face a serious food problem.
2. **Burden of Unproductive Consumers:** The greater the increase in population, the greater is the number of children and old persons. Children and old persons consume without making any contribution to output. The increasing number of children and old people increases the burden in terms of more requirements of nutrition, medical care, public health and education that go unattended to a large extent.
3. **Reduction in National and Per Capita Income:** The fast growing population retards the average growth rate of national income and per capita income. This is because whatever is added to the national income is consumed by ever-increasing population.
4. **Low Savings and Investment:** The most serious consequences of a rapid increase in population are that it reduces the capacity to save and invest. The national income and per capita income in India are very low to leave any margin for the people to save. Further, there will be a fall in effective demand as the

people's purchasing power is low. Rapid population growth thus makes it difficult to increase the rate of savings which determines the possibility of achieving higher productivity and incomes in a country.

5. **Reduction in Capital Formation:** Capital formation is very essential for the economic development of a country, particularly for a developing country like India. Capital formation depends upon saving and investment. This is not possible when there is a rapid growth of population, which results in more unemployment and underemployment.
6. **Unemployment:** Rising population aggravates the problem of unemployment. The labour force also increases with the increase in population, and this increased labour force is not fully absorbed due to lack of employment opportunities. Therefore, there are more unemployed and underemployed people.
7. **Loss of Women's Labour:** Rapid and frequent childbirths make a large number of women unable to take part in productive activity for longer periods. This is a waste of human resource, and it retards economic development.
8. **Low Labour Efficiency:** The increasing population adversely affects the national income and the per capita income. Due to this, the people have a low standard of living, which makes them less efficient. This hinders the rapid development of the country.
9. **More Expenditure on Social Welfare Programmes:** A rise in population increases the number of children. This would demand more social expenditure on medical care, public health, family welfare, education and housing, etc.
10. **Agricultural Backwardness:** The increase in population has led to uneconomic holdings through subdivision and fragmentation of land holdings in India. The size of holding is so small that mechanized farming is not possible.
11. **Underdeveloped Industries:** The rapid growth of population adversely affects industrial development. This is the reason why neither the cottage and small-scale industries nor large-scale industries could develop adequately in the country. Both big and small industries require adequate capital, whereas the rate of capital formation is low in India. Public investment in India is insufficient for the industrial development of the country.
12. **Financial Burden on Government:** Rapid increase in population is a financial strain to the government. The resources have to be spent on launching poverty alleviation programmes and social welfare schemes.

## NATIONAL POPULATION POLICY, 2000

National Population Policy of India was formulated in the year 2000 with the long-term objective of achieving a stable population by 2045, at a level consistent with the requirements of sustainable economic growth, social development and environmental protection. The immediate objective of the policy is to address the unmet needs for contraception, healthcare infrastructure and health personnel, and to provide integrated service delivery for basic reproductive and child health care. The medium-term objective is to bring the TFR to replacement levels by 2010, through vigorous implementation of inter-sectoral operational strategies. TFR is the average number of children each women would have in her life time.

National Population Policy pursues to achieve following socio-demographic goals by 2010:

1. Address the unmet needs for basic reproductive and child health services, supplies and infrastructure.

2. Make school education up to age 14 free and compulsory, and reduce drop outs at primary and secondary school levels to below 20 per cent for both boys and girls.
3. Reduce IMR to below 30 per 1,000 live births.
4. Reduce maternal mortality ratio (MMR) to below 100 per 100,000 live births.
5. Achieve universal immunization of children against all vaccine preventable diseases.
6. Promote delayed marriage for girls, not earlier than age 18 and preferably after 20 years of age.
7. Achieve 80 per cent institutional deliveries and 100 per cent deliveries by trained persons.
8. Achieve universal access to information/counselling, and services for fertility regulation and contraception with a wide basket of choices.
9. Achieve 100 per cent registration of births, deaths, marriage and pregnancy.
10. Contain the spread of Acquired Immunodeficiency Syndrome (AIDS) and promote greater integration between the management of Reproductive Tract Infections (RTI) and Sexually Transmitted Infections (STI) and the National AIDS Control Organization.
11. Prevent and control communicable diseases.
12. Integrate Indian Systems of Medicines (ISM) in the provision of reproductive and child health services, and in reaching out to households.
13. Promote vigorously the small family norm to achieve replacement levels of TFR.
14. Bring about convergence in implementation of related social sector programmes so that family welfare becomes a people centred programme.

## ❖ Limitations of Population Policy, 2000

India's population policy suffers from following limitations:

1. There is no easy access to contraception in familiar setting as government family planning clinics are few and far between.
2. In family planning programme, undue importance was given to terminal methods. IUDs and orals have been seriously and unnecessarily neglected. Abortion facilities are still woefully inadequate almost everywhere.
3. The lower strata of Indian population still consider large family as an asset.
4. The mortality rate especially IMR has remained high and has therefore inhibited the acceptance of family planning.
5. There has been shortage of trained manpower, inefficiency of motivational work of the staff, improper maintenance of infrastructural equipment, etc.
6. There is inadequate research in population-related areas.
7. Most family planning devices are costly, inconvenient and irksome to the common men and women.
8. Our population control effort should contain some elements of disincentives directed at those exhibiting tendencies towards going beyond the officially accepted norms of family size.
9. The National Population Policy (2000) flagged off by the then Prime Minister Atal Bihari Vajpayee has failed to achieve the basic demographic goals set out for 2010.

Thus, now there is need to adopt a new population policy in India.

## ❖ Terms Related to Demography

- **CBR:** The number of live births per 1,000 of population in a given year.

- **Crude Death Rate:** The number of deaths per 1,000 of population in a given year.
- **Demographic Transition:** The historical shift of birth and death rates, from high to low, in a population. The decline in mortality usually precedes the decline in fertility, leading to natural rates of increase.
- **Dependency Ratio:** The ratio of the economically dependent part of the population to the productive part, arbitrarily defined as the ratio of the elderly (ages 65 and older) plus the young (under age 15) to the population in the working ages (ages 15–64).
- **Emigration Rate:** The number of emigrants departing an area of origin per 1,000 population in that area of origin in a given year.
- **Fecundity:** The physiological capacity of a woman to bear a child.
- **Gross Reproduction Rate (GRR):** The average number of daughters that would be born alive to a woman (or group of women) during her lifetime if she passed through her childbearing years conforming to the age-specific fertility rates of a given year.
- **Immigration Rate**: The number of immigrants arriving at a destination per 1,000 population at that destination in a given year.
- **Immigration**: The process of entering one country from another to take up permanent or semipermanent residence.
- **Incidence Rate:** The number of persons contracting a disease during a given time period per 1,000 of population at risk.
- **IMR:** The number of deaths of infants under age 1 per 1,000 live births in a given year. It is widely considered as a leading indicator of the levels of economic development of a country.
- **Life Expectancy:** The average number of additional years a person could expect to live if current mortality trends were to continue for the rest of the person's life (most common is LEB).
- **Maternal Mortality Ratio (MMR):** The number of women who die as a result of complications of pregnancy or childbearing in a given year per 100,000 live births in that year.
- **Morbidity:** The frequency of disease, illness, injuries or disabilities in a population.
- **Net Reproduction Rate (NRR):** The average number of daughters that would be born to a woman (or a group of women) if she passed through her lifetime conforming to the age-specific fertility and mortality rates of a given year. This rate is similar to the GRR but takes into account that some women will die before completing their childbearing years. An NRR of 1 means that each generation of mothers is having exactly enough daughters to replace itself in the population.
- **Population Explosion (or 'Population Bomb'):** Expressions used to describe the 20th century worldwide trend of rapid population growth, resulting from a world birth rate much higher than the world death rate.
- **Population Growth Rate:** The rate at which a population is increasing (or decreasing) in a given year due to natural increase and net migration, expressed as a percentage of the base population.
- **Population Pyramid:** Graphic representation of the age and gender distribution of a population.
- **Prevalence Rate:** The number of persons who have a particular disease at a given point in time, or time period, per 1,000 of population.
- **Replacement Level Fertility:** The level of fertility at which a couple has only enough children to replace themselves, or just over two children per couple.

- **TFR:** The average number of children that would be born alive to a woman in her lifetime if she were to pass through her childbearing years conforming to the age-specific fertility rates of a given year.
- **Zero Population Growth**: A population in equilibrium, with a growth rate of zero, achieved when births plus immigration equal deaths plus emigration.

## POVERTY AND UNEMPLOYMENT IN INDIA

Poverty is a relative term. For a developing country like India, poverty can be defined as a situation in which an individual fails to earn income sufficient to buy him the means of subsistence. It can also be explained as a situation where a section of the society, having no fault of their own, is denied of even basic necessities of life. In India, the definition of poverty lays more emphasis on minimum level of living rather than on reasonable level of living. In India, the concept of poverty emphasizes more on minimum level because it is difficult to provide even a minimum quantum of basic needs. Poverty may be divided into two: (i) absolute poverty and (ii) relative poverty.

Absolute poverty can be expressed as poverty below bread line which can be defined in terms of 'per capita intake of calories' and 'minimum level of consumption'. According to the Planning Commission, an individual in rural areas must get 2,400 calories and in urban areas 2,100 calories per day. According to 'minimum level of consumption' criteria, the Planning Commission of India is of the opinion that persons spending ₹ 152 on consumption in urban area and ₹ 132 on rural area per month (at 1988–89 price) should be treated as falling within poverty line.

Relative poverty keeps on changing with the changes in regions and economic conditions of the different countries. It is defined by the general standards of living in different societies and what is culturally defined as being poor rather than some absolute level of deprivation.

**Gini coefficient**

The Gini index is a measurement of the income distribution of a country's residents. This number, which ranges between 0 and 1 and is based on residents' net income, helps define the gap between the rich and the poor, with 0 representing perfect equality and 1 representing perfect inequality. It is typically expressed as a percentage, referred to as the Gini coefficient.

The Gini coefficient is an important figure for the analysis of relative poverty within a country or region, but it should not be mistaken for a measurement of wealth. A wealthy country and a poor country can have the same Gini coefficient, as long as they have similar income distributions.

### ❖ Causes and Effects of Poverty in India

Poverty is a function not only of income but also of factors like health, education, nutrition and the ability to access basic needs and services. The extent of poverty, social and gender inequality, good governance and geographic location influences the health and nutritional status of people and the utilization of health services.

The causes of poverty in India are as follows:

1. Low productivity in agriculture
2. Non-implementation of land reforms
3. Rapidly rising population
4. Unemployment and underemployment
5. Underutilization of natural and human resources
6. Inflation and food prices
7. Lack of capital formation
8. Underdeveloped infrastructure
9. Poor agricultural infrastructure

10. Unequal distribution of assets among different groups
11. Faulty economic liberalization causing jobless growth
12. Outdated social customs like caste system
13. Colonial exploitation by Britishers
14. Illiteracy and low quality of education
15. Lack of skilled labour
16. Gender inequality
17. Corruption
18. Lack of inclusive economic growth

**The effects of poverty in India are as follows:**

1. Severe health problems
2. Illiteracy
3. Child labour
4. Malnutrition
5. Poor living condition and housing problems
6. High unemployment
7. Poor hygiene and sanitation
8. Feminization of poverty
9. Social tensions
10. Violence and crime
11. Child labour
12. Terrorism

## TYPES OF POVERTY ESTIMATES

Of the different types of poverty estimates used to quantify poverty, the three that are more commonly used are the Head Count Ratio (HCR), the Poverty Gap Index (PGI) and the Squared Poverty Gap Index (SPGI).

These three measures successively capture more disaggregated aspects of the poverty situation – the HCR measures the incidence of poverty or how widespread poverty is without differentiating between the levels of poverty, the PGI measures the depth of poverty or how poor the poor are, and the SPGI measures the severity of poverty by giving larger weight to the poorest of the poor.

### ❖ Head Count Ratio (HCR)

The HCR is the most elementary and commonly used poverty measure. The HCR is defined as the proportion of the national population whose expenditure is below the official threshold (or thresholds) set by the national government. By construction therefore, HCR is a useful yardstick which allows for the monitoring of the proportion of the national population that is considered to be poor based on a national standard. In India, given the official poverty lines at the state level, at the national level and by rural and urban areas, the corresponding HCRs are computed from the National Sample Survey (NSS) data. The all-India estimate is obtained by computing the number of poor aggregated across all states as a percentage of the total population of the country.

### ❖ Poverty Gap Index (PGI)

The PGI is defined as the mean distance below the poverty line as a proportion of the poverty line where the mean is taken over the whole population after counting the non-poor as those having zero poverty gap. That is the mean shortfall from the poverty line (counting the non-poor as having zero shortfall), expressed as a percentage of the poverty line. PGI thus indicates the average extent to which individuals fall below the poverty line (if they do), and is indicative of the intensity of poverty in the sense that it is sensitive to how far people are below the poverty line. Unlike the HCR, PGI is thus not built upon the assumption that all poor are in the same situation.

### ❖ Squared Poverty Gap Index (SPGI)

From a public policy perspective, it is evident that where the PGI is insensitive to policies that transfer resources among the poor, the SPGI addresses this lacuna of PGI.

SPGI is defined as a weighted sum of poverty gaps as a proportion of the poverty line, where the weights are the proportionate poverty gaps themselves. By squaring the poverty gap, more weight is assigned to the section of population that has a higher poverty gap. By construction, the SPGI is sensitive to transfers among the poor in the sense that a transfer from a less poor to a poorer individual will reduce the index.

**Standard of Living**

The GDP of a country does not fully reflect the quality of life of a country. There are other factors like housing, access to public transport, air quality and access to drinking water which determine the standards of living.

The standards of living can be measured using multiple indicators as done by the National Family Health Survey-4 (NFHS-4) (2015–16), which throw light on certain aspects of quality of living in India.

At the all-India level, the percentage of households with electricity, clean cooking fuel and improved drinking water source has registered an increase from 68 to 88 per cent, 25 to 44 per cent and 88 to 90 per cent, respectively, during the period 2005–06 (NFHS-3) to 2015–16 (NFHS-4). However, there are regional disparities in access.

## POVERTY ESTIMATION IN INDIA

One of the earliest estimations of poverty was done by Dadabhai Naoroji in his book, 'Poverty and the Un-British Rule in India'. He formulated a poverty line ranging from ₹ 16 to ₹ 35 per capita per year, based on 1867–68 prices. The poverty line proposed by him was based on the cost of a subsistence diet consisting of 'rice or flour, dhal, mutton, vegetables, ghee, vegetable oil and salt'.

Next, in 1938, the National Planning Committee (NPC) estimated a poverty line ranging from ₹ 15 to ₹ 20 per capita per month. Like the earlier method, the NPC also formulated its poverty line based on 'a minimum standard of living perspective in which nutritional requirements are implicit'. In 1944, the authors of the 'Bombay Plan' (Thakurdas et al. 1944) suggested a poverty line of ₹ 75 per capita per year.

After independence, in 1962, the Planning Commission constituted a working group to estimate poverty nationally, and it formulated separate poverty lines for rural and urban areas – of ₹ 20 and ₹ 25 per capita per year, respectively.

V.M. Dandekar and N. Rath made the first systematic assessment of poverty in India in 1971, based on NSS data from 1960 to 1961. They argued that the poverty line must be derived from the expenditure that was adequate to provide 2,250 calories per day in both rural and urban areas. This generated debate on minimum calorie consumption norms while estimating poverty and variations in these norms based on age and sex.

### ❖ Alagh Committee (1979)

In 1979, a task force constituted by the Planning Commission for the purpose of poverty estimation, chaired by Y.K. Alagh, constructed a poverty line for rural and urban areas on the basis of nutritional requirements. The nutritional requirements and related consumption expenditure based on 1973–74 price levels were recommended by the task force. Poverty estimates for subsequent years were to be calculated by adjusting the price level for inflation.

### ❖ Lakdawala Committee (1993)

In 1993, an expert group constituted to review methodology for poverty estimation, chaired by D.T. Lakdawala, suggested that (i) consumption expenditure should be calculated based on calorie consumption as earlier; (ii) state-specific poverty lines should be constructed and these should be updated using the Consumer Price Index of Industrial Workers (CPI-IW) in urban areas and Consumer Price Index of Agricultural Labour (CPI-AL) in rural areas; and (iii) discontinuation of 'scaling' of poverty estimates based on National Accounts Statistics. He assumes that the basket of goods and services used to calculate CPI-IW and CPI-AL reflect the consumption patterns of the poor.

## ❖ Tendulkar Committee (2009)

In 2005, another expert group to review methodology for poverty estimation, chaired by Suresh Tendulkar, was constituted by the Planning Commission to address the three shortcomings of the previous methods: (i) consumption patterns were linked to the 1973–74 Poverty Line Baskets (PLBs) of goods and services, whereas there were significant changes in the consumption patterns of the poor since that time, which were not reflected in the poverty estimates; (ii) there were issues with the adjustment of prices for inflation, both spatially (across regions) and temporally (across time); and (iii) earlier poverty lines assumed that health and education would be provided by the State and formulated poverty lines accordingly.

It recommended four major changes: (i) a shift away from calorie consumption-based poverty estimation; (ii) a uniform PLB across rural and urban India; (iii) a change in the price adjustment procedure to correct spatial and temporal issues with price adjustment; and (iv) incorporation of private expenditure on health and education while estimating poverty.

The Committee recommended using Mixed Reference Period (MRP)-based estimates, as opposed to Uniform Reference Period (URP)-based estimates that were used in earlier methods for estimating poverty.

It based its calculations on the consumption of the following items: cereal, pulses, milk, edible oil, non-vegetarian items, vegetables, fresh fruits, dry fruits, sugar, salt and spices, other food, intoxicants, fuel, clothing, footwear, education, medical (non-institutional and institutional), entertainment, personal and toilet goods, other goods, other services and durables.

The Committee computed new poverty lines for rural and urban areas of each state. To do this, it used data on value and quantity consumed of the items mentioned above by the population that was classified as poor by the previous urban poverty line. It concluded that the all-India poverty line was ₹ 446.68 per capita per month in rural areas and ₹ 578.80 per capita per month in urban areas in 2004–05.

The Committee also recommended a new method of updating poverty lines, adjusting for changes in prices and patterns of consumption, using the consumption basket of people close to the poverty line. Thus, the estimates released in 2009–10 and 2011–12 use this method instead of using indices derived from the CPI-AL for rural areas and CPI-IW for urban areas as was done earlier.

## ❖ Rangarajan Committee (2014)

Established in 2012, C. Rangarajan Committee submitted its report on 30 June 2014.

The practices adopted by Rangarajan were as follows:

1. Tendulkar had used the all-India urban PLB as the reference to derive state-level rural and urban poverty. This was a departure from the earlier practice of using two separate PLBs for rural and urban areas. Rangarajan reverts to the practice of having separate all-India rural and urban poverty basket lines and deriving state-level rural and urban estimates from these.
2. Tendulkar had decided not to anchor the poverty line to the then available official calorie norms used in all poverty estimations since 1979 as it found a poor correlation between food consumed and nutrition outcomes. However, on a review of subsequent research, Rangarajan took a considered view that deriving the food component of the PLB by reference to the simultaneous satisfaction of all three nutrient norms would be appropriate

when seen in conjunction with the emphasis on a full range of policies and programmes for child-nutrition support and on public provisioning of a range of public goods and services aimed at the amelioration of the disease environment facing the population.

3. Estimates of consumption expenditure seen in the National Accounts Statistics and as inferred from the sample surveys of the National Sample Survey Organisation show a large and growing variance. Rangarajan preferred NSSO's estimates and decides not to use the NAS estimates. This is in line with the approach taken by Lakdawala and Tendulkar.
4. The capture of spatial and temporal variation in prices in estimating the state-level and rural-urban poverty levels (given all-India rural and urban estimates) has undergone substantial refinement since 1979. Rangarajan agrees with the methodology adopted by Tendulkar in this regard. This overcomes the limitations of using fixed base-year weights by using a combination of unit values derived from successive NSSO's Consumer Expenditure Surveys and price-relatives derived from the consumer price indices.
5. Public expenditure on social services has increased substantially in recent years. These expenses are not captured, by design, in the NSSO's Consumer Expenditure Surveys, and the poverty line derived from these is thus lower than the services actually consumed.
6. Rangarajan is of the considered view that the deployment of criteria other than consumption expenditure in the measurement of poverty raises several issues regarding measurement and aggregation and that these render such exercises impractical. However, Rangarajan has considered an alternate view in estimating the poverty line by reference to the ability of households to save.

## ❖ Methodology Recommended by Rangarajan

The methodology developed and adopted by the Expert Group (Rangarajan) and the results based on these are as follows:

1. The poverty line should be based on certain normative levels of adequate nourishment, clothing, house rent, conveyance and education, and a behaviourally determined level of other non-food expenses.
2. Rangarajan computed the average requirements of calories, proteins and fats based on ICMR norms differentiated by age, gender and activity for all-India rural and urban regions to derive the normative levels of nourishment. Accordingly, the energy requirement works out to 2,155 kcal per person per day in rural areas and 2,090 kcal per person per day in urban areas. For reasons elaborated in the text, Rangarajan views the calorie norm not as a single number but as an average in a band of (+/–) 10 per cent of these values and with intakes even at the lower end still being adequate enough to not adversely affect health and work.
3. The protein and fat requirements have been estimated on the same lines as for energy. These requirements are 48 and 28 gm per capita per day, respectively, in rural areas; and 50 and 26 gm per capita per day in urban areas.
4. A food basket that simultaneously meets all the normative requirements of the three nutrients defines the food component of the PLB proposed by Rangarajan. These nutrient norms are met for persons located in the sixth fractile (25–30 per cent) in rural areas and for those in the

fourth fractile (15–20 per cent) in urban areas in 2011–12. The average monthly per capita consumption expenditure on food in these fractile classes is ₹ 554 in rural areas and ₹ 656 in urban areas (NSS 68th Round).

5. The median fractile (45–50 per cent) values of clothing expenses, rent, conveyance and education expenses are treated as the normative requirements of the basic non-4 food expenses of clothing, housing, mobility and education of a PLB. This works out to ₹ 141 per capita per month in rural areas and ₹ 407 in urban areas. The observed expenses of all other non-food expenses of the fractile classes that meet the nutrition requirements are considered as part of the PLB. This works out to ₹ 277 per capita per month in rural areas and ₹ 344 in urban areas.
6. The new poverty line thus works out to monthly per capita consumption expenditure of ₹ 972 in rural areas and ₹ 1,407 in urban areas in 2011–12. For a family of five, this translates into a monthly consumption expenditure of ₹ 4,860 in rural areas and ₹ 7,035 in urban areas.
7. Estimations of the poverty line made by Rangarajan based on an independent large survey of households by CMIE and using a different methodology wherein a household is considered poor if it is unable to save yield results that are remarkably close to those derived using the NSSO data. This provides additional evidence in support of the poverty line derived by Rangarajan.
8. Compared to the poverty lines based on the methodology of Tendulkar, the poverty lines estimated by Rangarajan are 19 per cent and 41 per cent higher in rural and urban areas, respectively. Rangarajan uses the Modified Mixed Recall Period consumption expenditure data of the NSSO as these are considered to be more precise compared to the MRP, which was used by Tendulkar, and the URP, which was used by earlier estimations. Sixty-seven per cent of the increase in the rural poverty line and 28 per cent of the increase in the urban poverty line are because of the shift from MRP to MMRP.
9. The national rural and urban poverty lines computed as above were used to derive the state-wise poverty lines by using the implicit price derived from the quantity and value of consumption observed in the NSSO's 68th Round of 5 Consumer Expenditure Survey (2011–12) to estimate state relative to all-India Fisher price indices. Using these and the state-specific distribution of persons by expenditure groups (NSS), state-specific ratios of rural and urban poverty were estimated. State-level poverty ratio was estimated as weighted average of the rural and urban poverty ratios, and the national poverty ratio was computed again as the population-weighted average of state-wise poverty ratios.
10. The Expert Group (Rangarajan) therefore estimates that the 30.9 per cent of the rural population and 26.4 per cent of the urban population were below the poverty line in 2011–12. The all-India ratio was 29.5 per cent. In rural India, 260.5 million individuals were below poverty, and in urban India, 102.5 million were under poverty. Totally, 363 million were below poverty in 2011–12.
11. The poverty ratio has declined from 39.6 per cent in 2009–10 to 30.9 per cent in 2011–12 in rural India and from 35.1 per cent to 26.4 per cent in urban India. The decline was thus a uniform 8.7 percentage points over the 2 years. The all-India poverty ratio fell from 38.2 per cent to 29.5 per cent. Totally, 91.6 million individuals were lifted out of poverty during this period.

12. Rangarajan recommends the updation of the poverty line in the future using the Fisher Index. The weighting diagram for this effort can be drawn from the NSSO's Consumer Expenditure Survey. For the Food group, Rangarajan recommends that the current practice of relying on the unit values derivable from the NSSO Consumer Expenditure Surveys should continue till a time new CPI of CSO with a weighting diagram based on the 2011–12 pattern of consumption becomes available. In respect of non-food items, the price indices available in the exiting CSO Consumer Price Indices can be used in the construction of requisite Fisher indices. Once the new series of Consumer Price Index numbers (with 2011–12 as the base year) become available, it may be used if the extent of change in the structure of consumption at that point in time relative to the 2011–12 structure of consumption is not very different.

**Fisher Price Index**

The Fisher price index is an index formula used in price statistics for measuring the price development of goods and services, on the basis of the baskets from both the *base* and the *current* periods. It is defined as the geometric average of the Laspeyres price index (which only uses the base period basket) and the Paasche price index (which only uses the current period basket). For this reason, the Fisher price index (named after American economist Irving Fisher) is also known as the 'ideal' price index.

The choice of a price index formula (Laspeyres, Paasche or Fisher) in a particular case is partly determined by the data available. The Fisher price index requires more data than both others and as a result may often be impracticable.

## TASK FORCE ON ELIMINATION OF POVERTY (2015)

A Task Force on Elimination of Poverty in India was constituted by NITI Aayog on 16 March 2015 under the Chairmanship of Dr. Arvind Panagariya, Vice Chairman, NITI Aayog.

The states were required to submit their respective Task Force report to NITI Aayog as an input for preparing the Task Force Report on Elimination of Poverty in India.

The Task Force posted its report 'Poverty: Creating Jobs and Strengthening Social Programs' on official website of NITI Aayog on 21 March 2016. This paper forms the basis of regional consultation meetings to prepare a roadmap for elimination of poverty in the country.

### ❖ Views and Recommendations of Task Force

1. **On Measuring Poverty:** Conventionally, poverty is measured as the proportion of population living below a threshold level of expenditure (or income) called the poverty line. Poverty line in turn is set at a level that enables an individual to purchase goods and services in quantities adequate to satisfy basic needs as per prevailing social norms. Poverty line and the poverty ratio have three potential uses: identification of poor; allocation of expenditure on anti-poverty programmes across states or regions; and tracking poverty over time and across regions.

   In India, identification of poor is done by the State Governments based on information from Below Poverty Line (BPL) censuses of which the latest is the Socio-Economic Caste Census 2011 (SECC 2011). Allocation of expenditures on anti-poverty programmes is also done using instruments other than the poverty ratio. For example, the expenditure on the provision of housing across states can be done according to the proportion of households without house within a given state. Universal programmes such as those under the Mahatma Gandhi National Rural Employment Guarantee Act (MGNREGA) and Sarva Shiksha Abhiyan (SSA) are available to all making the question of allocation moot.

This leaves tracking poverty over time and space as the principal objective behind the measurement of poverty.

The current official indicators of poverty in India are based on the Tendulkar Poverty Line. But this line has been the subject of repeated controversies with many observers criticizing it as being too low. The controversies led the United Progressive Alliance (UPA) government to appoint the Rangarajan Committee in 2012, which recommended higher rural and urban poverty lines in June 2014.

Going forward, the task force considered four options for tracking extreme poverty:

(i) Continue with the Tendulkar poverty line;

(ii) Switch to the Rangarajan or other higher rural and urban poverty lines;

(iii) Track progress over time of the bottom 30 per cent of the population; and

(iv) Track progress along specific components of poverty such as nutrition, housing, drinking water, sanitation, electricity and connectivity.

While options (iii) and (iv) can complement the measurement of poverty using a poverty line, they cannot substitute for it. Without reference to a poverty line, one cannot determine whether a given household has exited poverty. Tracking reduction in poverty requires a poverty line. In turn, this requires us to choose between (i) and (ii).

The main criticism of the Tendulkar line (also applicable to the $1.25 line adopted by the United Nations Sustainable Development Goals, which is even lower than the Tendulkar line) has been that it is too low. The counterargument, however, is that if our objective is to assess whether we are making progress in bringing households out of extreme poverty, it calls for setting the poverty line at a level that allows households to get two square meals a day and other basic necessities of life. It is the households below this minimum acceptable subsistence level whose welfare should concern us the most and whose progress we must monitor. Put differently, if we set the poverty line at too high a level, we would be tracking what percentage of population that has already achieved a certain level of comfort has been made yet further comfortable. It will fail to inform us about the households in abject poverty.

The key source of public dissatisfaction with the Tendulkar line was that it would deprive many households in need of government assistance from such assistance by classifying them as Above Poverty Line (APL) households. But as just noted, poverty line is not the basis of identification of the poor in India. This fact weakens the case against the Tendulkar line.

At the same time, the fact that judgements on what represents a basic necessity of life vary from person to person makes the choice of a poverty line difficult. Therefore, the final decision on this question needs to be informed by further deliberations that pay adequate attention to the fact that the objective behind an official poverty line is to track progress in combating extreme poverty and not identification of the poor for purposes of distribution of government benefits.

2. **On Strategy to Combat Poverty:** The strategy for combating poverty must rest on two legs: sustained rapid growth that is also employment intensive and making anti-poverty programmes effective.

   (i) **Employment-Intensive Sustained Rapid Growth:** Sustained rapid growth works through two channels: first, by creating jobs that pay steadily rising real wages and, second, by generating additional revenues that allow the government to expand social expenditures at faster pace.

   The poor in India predominantly reside in rural areas where incomes critically depend on agricultural growth. Therefore, this paper endorses and briefly reiterates the recommendations of the NITI Aayog occasional paper based on the deliberations of the Task Force on Agricultural Development.

   These recommendations relate to raising productivity in agriculture, giving remunerative prices to farmers, measures aimed at 'second green revolution' in rain-fed areas in general and eastern India in particular, reform of tenancy laws to help small and marginal farmers, and building safety nets to bring quick relief for farmers in times of natural disasters.

   But given that historically agriculture has not grown in India at rates exceeding 5 per cent per annum on a sustained basis while industry and services have seen much faster growth, in the longer run, the benefits of growth can be shared more equitably only by creating gainful employment opportunities in industry and services for landless workers and marginal farmers who wish to migrate to better-paid jobs. India needs acceleration in the growth of organized labour-intensive sectors such as apparel, footwear, food processing, electronic and electrical appliances, other light manufactures, construction and retail trade.

   Among other things, the paper suggests that this can be achieved through the creation of a handful of Coastal Economic Zones (CEZs) that can provide the focal point for the location of employment-intensive industries allowing them to exploit economies of scale and agglomeration. With a business-friendly ecosystem, these zones can serve as magnets for export-oriented employment-intensive large-scale firms that are currently exiting China in response to high and rising wages and declining size of labour force there. The presence of these highly efficient large-scale firms will also spawn highly efficient small and medium firms around them in the CEZs.

   (ii) **Making Anti-Poverty Programmes More Effective:** Making anti-poverty programmes such as the Public Distribution System (PDS), Midday Meal Scheme (MDMS), MGNREGA and Housing for All more effective represents the second leg of the strategy to eliminate abject poverty. The paper provides numerous specific suggestions on how each of these important programmes can be made more effective.

(a) Each PDS shop may be asked to take a biometric reading of the beneficiary and give the latter a receipt at the time of the transaction. The shopkeeper may be allowed to charge a small fee per kilogram of grain sold as transaction fee. This fee would compensate her for any lost income from ending the leakage of PDS grain to the open market. The system would, thus, eliminate all multiple and ghost ration cards.

(b) The beneficiary may be offered a choice between cash transfer equivalent to current implicit subsidy and continued subsidized in-kind purchases. As long as beneficiaries have access to banking services, they are likely to opt for cash. This would free them to purchase grain at market prices from the PDS shop or private traders and create healthy competition, thereby promoting efficiency.

(c) An important but mostly neglected issue is that while subsidized grain can help raise calorie consumption, it does not ensure a balanced diet. Evidence shows that the poor consume far less milk, eggs, fruits and vegetables and meat in both rural and urban areas than their better-off counterparts. Protein remains a badly missing nutrient from the diets of the poor. Addressing this problem requires continued increases in incomes complemented by persuasive and informative advertising campaigns that bring home to the people the importance of a balanced diet. In the case of school children, some improvements can also be achieved through protein-rich diets in the midday meals.

(d) There is poor convergence of MDMS with the school health programme. There is a need to form networks of medical colleges, home science faculties and state MDMS steering and monitoring committees and institutions to evolve state-specific guidelines for improved quality and safety of food. Nearly 25 per cent of schools continue to prepare the mid-day meal either in an open area or in the classrooms, which raises serious food safety issues. It is important to ensure that schools have proper facilities to cook meals.

(e) There are several areas in which, if modified, MGNREGA could deliver significantly better outcomes than currently. For example, the scheme could be modified to impart skills. This would pave the way for many workers to exit the programme.

(f) Relaxing the proportion of expenditure on materials and allowing the use of contractors in the materials component would greatly improve the quality of assets produced.

(g) During peak season, farmers may be permitted to hire MGNREGA workers by paying 75 per cent (or some other proportion) of the wages with the balance paid by MGNREGA wage funds. This would lead to more productive use of labour while also spreading MGNREGA wages over more workdays.

(h) During most years, work-days per beneficiary have averaged below 50 suggesting the presence of a fiscal constraint. This calls for better targeting of the programme in favour of the poorest households. The benefits of the programme have been disproportionately reaped by some of the more prosperous states. Therefore, the issue of restricting MGNREGA to around half of the poorest blocks (or equivalent administrative unit) nationwide may be considered. An expert committee could be appointed to develop the exclusion, inclusion and deprivation criteria to select the beneficiary blocks.

(i) The Housing for All (Rural) programme has progressed well overall but can be improved along several dimensions. The Socio-Economic Caste Census may be deployed to identify the beneficiaries. Progress in the provision of housing needs to be reflected in the reporting system. The trend of houses constructed over the eight years beginning 11th Plan shows that the states have to come forward with larger resources to meet the objectives of 'Housing for All by 2022' in the rural areas. Finally, it may be worth exploring the possibility of using prefabricated houses. This may bring better quality as well as speed to the provision of housing for all.

(j) Jan Dhan Yojana, Aadhaar, Mobile (JAM) trinity could play a vital role in widening the reach of Government to the vulnerable sections. Jan Dhan bank accounts under Prime Minister's Jan Dhan Yojana (PMJDY), biometric identity cards under Aadhar and accessibility to the accounts through mobile phones promise to eventually revolutionize the anti-poverty programmes by replacing the current cumbersome and leaky distribution of benefits under various schemes by the Direct Benefit Transfers (DBT).

(k) With the Aadhar-linked accounts permitting aggregation of the information, the government would have an excellent database to assess the total volume of benefits accruing to each household.

In turn, this information could eventually pave the way for replacing myriad schemes with consolidated cash transfers except in cases in which there are other compelling reasons to continue with in-kind transfers.

(l) Each Gram Panchayat may be asked to identify five poorest families in the village and endeavour to lift them out of poverty. Panchayat may ensure that these families get all government benefits. A modest cash transfer for a prespecified time period may top these benefits. The eventual effort should be to ensure that the families become capable of earning and sustaining above poverty level income within 5 to 7 years.

## UNEMPLOYMENT

Unemployment means the state of being unemployed. Unemployment is a situation where in the person willing to work fails to find a job that earns them living. International Labour Organization (ILO) defined that one can only be called as 'unemployed' if he/she is:

1. 'without work', that means the person was not in paid employment or self-employment during a particular reference period;
2. 'currently available for work', that means the person was ready for a paid employment or self-employment during the reference period;
3. 'seeking work', that means the person had taken specific steps in a specified recent period to seek paid employment or self-employment.

### ❖ Types of Unemployment

The various types of unemployment may be classified as follows:

1. **Structural Unemployment:** It is the situation in which an economy is unable in providing job to all unemployed because the resource available in the country is limited. It refers to one more situation where the skills and location of unemployed workers do not match the unfilled vacancies. It can happen because investment has failed to keep pace with growth in labour force.

   Broadly, India's unemployment is structural in nature. It is associated with the inadequacy of productive capacity to create enough jobs for all those who are able and willing to work. In India, not only the productive capacity is much below the needed quantity, it is also found increasing at a slow rate. As against this, additions to labour force are taking place at a higher rate on account of the rapidly growing population.

   Structural unemployment is not a temporary phenomenon in the sense that it will pass off on its own after a lapse of time. It is chronic. It requires, for its solution, the application of long-term measures for remedying the defects in economic structure. In other words, it is the development of the economy alone that can take care of structural unemployment.

2. **Disguised Unemployment:** The unemployment situation that is not open for everyone to see remains invisible. For example, in Indian villages, where most of the unemployment exists in this from, people are found to be apparently engaged in agricultural activities.

   In such a situation, even if many workers are withdrawn, the same work will continue to be done by fewer people.

**Disguised Unemployment Vs. Underemployment:** Let us distinguish disguised unemployment from underemployment. The latter is defined as a situation when everyone, able and willing to work, gets a job or, when everyone who wishes to work at the going wage-rate for his type of labour is employed. But the job is not according to his qualification and experience, e.g., a person who is capable to be a manager is working only as a clerk.

In disguised unemployment situation, everyone only seems to be fully employed. It is so because there are larger numbers of workers than required, sharing a given amount of work. As such, it appears that nobody is without work. But this, of course, conceals the fact that there is no full employment, as the workers are not working to their full capacity. The proof of this is that output does not fall even if a part of the labour force is withdrawn.

3. **Open Unemployment:** When an unemployed person has no work to do, he comes under open unemployment. They are able to work and are also willing to work, but there is no work for them. Such unemployment is in the nature of involuntary idleness. They are to be found partly in villages, but largely in cities. Such unemployment can be seen and counted in terms of the number of such persons. Hence, it is called open unemployment.

4. **Cyclical Unemployment:** Cyclical Unemployment is associated with the downswing and depression phases of business cycle, and is to be found in capitalist or market-oriented developed economies. Caused by the lack of coordination among the innumerable decision-makers in the fields of savings and investment, the trade cycle, in its downward phase, renders many persons as unemployed.

   Falling income lowers the demand for goods and services. As a result, the economy produces less than it is capable of, aggravating further the employment-income situation.

5. **Frictional Unemployment:** It is found in developed economies as they push towards further development. At a higher level of development, many changes take place in the industrial structure of these economies, with old industries contracting and dying out, and new industries coming up. This process seems to be endless. In fact, without this, no development is possible. The products, the resources and the technologies undergo changes, making the structure of an economy a picture of permanent changes.

   In such a situation, it is necessary that workers move from industry to industry, leaving those which are decaying and joining those which are leading the way to further growth and which promise higher wages and rewards. In between the time of leaving and joining, the time for which the workers get no work is a period of unemployment, called frictional unemployment.

   In India, such unemployment does not exist to an extent that might cause much concern.

6. **Demographic Unemployment:** It occurs when the number of new workers entering the labour force through natural increase or inward migration exceeds the number leaving the workforce. Demographic unemployment is, to a great extent, similar to structural unemployment and is very common in India. It is so because the rate of growth of population in India is much higher than that of employment opportunities.

7. **Technological Unemployment:** It is the unemployment caused by technical progress. The skills of particular types of worker are made redundant because of changes in the methods of production, usually by substituting machines for manual services.
8. **Educated Unemployment:** It is concerned with joblessness among the educated persons. Some of them may suffer from open unemployment. There may again be others who may be underemployed. The underemployed persons may not be getting work suitable to their qualification to enable them to make full use of their capacities. Mostly urban areas are facing this problem of educated unemployment.
9. **Seasonal Unemployment:** When the workers engaged in a particular work or occupation get employment only for a limited period and remain idle for the remaining period, it is called seasonal unemployment. It is caused by seasonal variations in production or demand or both. It is very common in Indian agricultural sector.
10. **Casual Unemployment:** In sectors such as building construction, catering or agriculture, where workers are employed on a day-to-day basis, there are chances of casual unemployment occurring due to short-term contracts, which may be terminable any time.
11. **Chronic Unemployment:** A long-term unemployment of a country is called chronic unemployment. Underdeveloped economies suffer from chronic unemployment on account of the vicious circle of poverty.
12. **Residual Unemployment:** In every economy, there is always a residue of unemployment, due to frictional and seasonal causes, which planners and policy-makers cannot reduce. This classification also includes those people who are unable to work because of physical or mental disabilities.

## UNEMPLOYMENT IN INDIA

In India, unemployment was first recognized in the 1950s. Initiatives of employment generation started during the First Five-Year Plan. This plan laid the foundation for overall and sectorial development in a medium-term prospective for achieving the goal of employment growth and increasing the labour force. For the first time, in the Seventh Five-Year Plan (1985–90), employment was placed at the core of development strategy. In the Ninth Five-Year Plan (1997–2002), employment was identified as one of the three important dimensions of state policy with others being quality of life and regional balance. The Eleventh Five-Year Plan (2007–12) mainly focused on 'inclusive' growth and conceived employment as the key element of the same. Thus, unemployment has received great importance in the development agenda of India since Independence.

Some features of unemployment in India have been identified as follows:

- The incidence of unemployment is much higher in urban areas than in rural areas.
- Unemployment rates for women are higher than those for men.
- The incidence of unemployment among the educated is much higher than the overall unemployment.
- There is greater unemployment in agricultural sector than in industrial and other major sectors.

Fifth Annual Employment-Unemployment Survey Report 2015–16 conducted by Labour Bureau states that the unemployment rate was estimated to be 5.0 per cent at the All-India level. In rural sector, unemployment rate was 5.1 per cent, whereas in urban sector, the unemployment rate was 4.9 per cent. Labour Force Participation Rate (LFPR) was estimated to be 50.3 per cent at the All-India level, or in other words, 50.3

per cent of the persons aged 15 years and above were either working or seeking work during the reference period.

According to the BSE, the unemployment rate in India in January 2018 was 5.04 per cent: in urban areas, it was 6.35 per cent and in rural areas 4.36 per cent. In India, the unemployment rate measures the number of people actively looking for a job as a percentage of the labour force. It is interesting to note that rural females are more employed than their urban counterpart, whereas urban males lead their rural counterpart.

Various strategies and proposals have been implemented to generate employment.

Many employment programmes and policies have been introduced and undertaken to boost self-employment and help unemployed engage in public works. It is believed that India's economic growth can be accelerated if human resources are purposefully and efficiently allocated. Employment generation is the key channel through which economic growth translates into prosperity for the population. In a growing economy, employment growth with rising productivity is the most effective mechanism available to the poor to participate in the growth process and raise their standard of living. High economic growth, therefore, unless accompanied by quality employment opportunities will raise inequalities and is therefore undesirable. Thus, gainful employment generation is the bedrock of attaining growth with equity and to alleviate poverty.

## ❖ Anti-Poverty and Employment Generation Programmes

1. **Mahatma Gandhi National Rural Employment Guarantee Act (MGNREGA):** The National Rural Employment Guarantee Act, notified in 200 districts in the first phase on 2 February 2006, was renamed Mahatma Gandhi National Rural Employment Guarantee Act (MGNREGA) on 2 October 2009. On 1 April 2008, the entire country has been covered except district with a hundred per cent urban population.

**Main objective laid down by the Act (MGNREGA 2005):** 'to provide for the enhancement of livelihood security of the households in rural areas of the country by providing at least one hundred days of guaranteed wage employment in every financial year to every household whose adult members volunteer to do unskilled manual work and for matters connected therewith or incidental thereto'.

**Other Objectives:**

(i) To provide social safety net for the vulnerable groups by providing a fall-back employment [during lean season]

(ii) To work as a growth engine for sustainable development of an agricultural economy.

(iii) To strengthen the natural resource base of rural livelihood and create durable assets in rural areas.

(iv) To empower the rural poor through the processes of a rights-based law.

(v) To promote transparent and accountable grassroots democracy and development.

(vi) To reduce distress migration.

(vii) Women's empowerment.

**Salient Features of MGNREGA:**

(i) Right to work a legal guarantee

(ii) Demand driven (previous programmes supply driven)

(iii) Entitlement to:

  (a) Minimum wages

  (b) Unemployment allowance and compensation due to delayed wage payment

  (c) Four facilities at worksite: first aid, drinking water,

shelter and crèche for children below six years.

(d) Priority to women workers (one-third of total)

(e) Priority to wage work (wage material cost in the ratio of 60:40 and works of water conservation top priority)

(f) Funded by the Federal Government (100 per cent of the wage cost of unskilled workers and 75 per cent of the material and wage cost of skilled and semi-skilled workers)

(g) Decentralized planning and execution (institutions of local self-governance (PRIs) are the principal agencies for planning, implementation and monitoring of the works)

(h) Civil society oriented (transparency and accountability through social audit)

(i) Three-tier grievance redressal mechanisms.

Other features are as follows:

(i) Adult members of a rural household willing to do unskilled manual work are eligible to seek employment under the act.

(ii) Employment is to be given within 15 days of application for work; otherwise, daily unemployment allowance has to pay by the respective State.

(iii) Wages are to be paid according to Minimum Wages Act 1948 for agricultural labourers in the State unless otherwise notified by the centre.

(iv) Equal wages are to be paid to both men and women.

(v) At least one-third beneficiaries are to be women.

(vi) No contractors and machinery are allowed.

Transparency safeguards are provided in the form of:

(i) Job cards in the custody of workers which monitor entitlements.

(ii) Issue of dated receipts on application for work.

(iii) Citizen Information Boards at worksites.

(iv) Vigilance Monitoring Committees.

2. **Swarnjayanthi Gram Swarojgar Yojana (SGSY):** It was launched in April 1999 as a major programme for self-employment of the rural poor after restructuring the then existing Integrated Rural Development Programme (IRDP) and combining it with other allied schemes like TRYSEM, DWCRA, SITRA, GKY and Million Wells Scheme for effective implementation under a single banner called SGSY.

3. **Prime Minister's Employment Generation Programme (PMEGP):** The scheme was announced by the Prime Minister on 15 August 2008 in his address from the Red Fort. This is credit-linked scheme formed by merging erstwhile REGP and PMRY scheme. KVIC is the nodal agency at the national level. Its main aim is to generate continuous and sustainable employment opportunities in rural and urban areas of the country.

4. **Swarna Jayanti Shahari Rozgar Yojana (SJSRY):** This scheme came into effect on 1 December 1997 with an aim to provide gainful employment to the urban unemployed and underemployed poor by encouraging them to set up self-employment ventures.

The government has launched this rationalized SJSRY to replace the three existing schemes – Nehru Rozgar Yojana (NRY), Urban Basic Services for the

Poor (UBSP) and PM's Integrated Urban Poverty Eradication Programme (PMI UPEP).

5. **Pradhan Mantri Gram Sadak Yojana (PMGSY):** The scheme comes under the authority of the ministry of rural development and was begun on 25 December 2000.

   The goal was to provide roads to all villages (1) with a population of 1,000 persons and above by 2003, (2) with a population of 500 persons and above by 2007, (3) in hill states, tribal and desert area villages with a population of 500 persons and above by 2003, and (4) in hill states, tribal and desert area villages with a population of 250 persons and above by 2007.

6. **Pradhan Mantri Awas Yojana (PMAY):** In order to empower people to get their dream home, honourable Prime Minister has announced a comprehensive and a progressive mission, 'Pradhan Mantri Awas Yojana – Housing for All' on 17 June 2015.

   One of the major elements of PMAY is Credit Linked Subsidy Scheme (CLSS) for lower income group/economically weaker-section and middle-income group. Under this scheme, the Central Government provides financial assistance through lending institutions to eligible beneficiaries across all statutory towns as per 2011 census and their adjacent planning area.

7. **Pradhan Mantri Gramodaya Yojana (PMGY):** The PMGY was launched in 2000–01 in order to achieve the objective of sustainable human development at the village level. The PMGY envisages allocation of additional central funds to the states for basic minimum services in order to focus on certain priority areas. PMGY has five components, namely primary health, primary education, rural shelter, rural drinking water and nutrition.

8. **Sampoorna Grameen Rozgar Yojana (SGRY):** SGRY was launched in September 2001 by merging the erstwhile schemes of Jawahar Gram Samridhi Yojana (JGSY) and Employment Assurance Scheme (EAS). The objective is to provide additional wage employment in the rural areas and food security, along with the creation of durable community, social and economic infrastructure in rural areas. The SGRY is open to all rural poor in need of wage employment and desire to do manual work.

9. **Rural Housing Schemes:** Rural housing schemes such as Indira Awaas Yojana (IAY) aim at providing dwelling units, free of cost to the poor families of the SCs, STs, freed bonded labourers and also the non- SC/ST persons living BPL in the rural areas. The scheme is funded on a cost-sharing basis of 75:25 between the Centre and states.

10. **Antyodaya Anna Yojana (AAY):** AAY was launched in December 2000. Under the scheme, one crore of the poorest among the BPL families covered under the targeted PDS are identified and 25 kg of food grains were made available to each eligible family at a highly subsidized rate of ₹ 2 per kg for wheat and ₹ 3 per kg for rice. This quantity has been enhanced from 25 to 35 kg with effect from April 2002.

11. **Annapurna:** Launched with effect from 1 April 2000, it aims at providing food security to meet the requirement of those senior citizens who, though eligible, have remained uncovered under the National Old Age Pension Scheme (NOAPS).

    The scheme is targeted to cover 20 per cent of persons eligible to receive pension under NOAPS. Funds are released to the food and civil supplies department of the state governments in one instalment.

This department ties up with the Food Corporation of India (FCI) to release food grains district-wise after payment at Central Issue Price (CIP) at FCI offices.

12. **Valmiki Ambedkar Awas Yojana (VAMBAY):** VAMBAY was kicked off in December 2001 targeted to improve the living conditions of the urban slum dwellers living below the poverty line without adequate shelter. The scheme has the objective of facilitating the construction and upgradation of dwelling units for slum dwellers.

    Besides, it offers a healthy environment through community toilets under Nirmal Bharat Abhiyan, a component of the scheme. The centre offers a subsidy of 50 per cent, the balance 50 per cent is arranged by the state government.

13. **Pradhan Mantri Garib Kalyan Yojana (PMGKY):** The PMGKY was launched in April 2015. The objective of the Yojana is to implement the pro-poor welfare schemes in more effective way and reaches out to more poor population across the country. It is a poverty alleviation scheme, which is primarily a work shop that you can pay and attend. The effort of the campaign and workshop is to motive and appraise the member of parliaments to help them effectively implement the government run schemes for the welfare of poor in the country.

14. **Make in India:** It was launched on 2 September 2014 with the objective to encourage multi-national, as well as domestic companies to manufacture their products in India and create jobs and skill enhancement in 25 sectors. The major objective behind the initiative is to focus on job creation and skill enhancement in 25 sectors of the economy. The initiative also aims at high quality standards and minimizing the impact on the environment. The initiative hopes to attract capital and technological investment in India.

**Employment or Training-Related Specific Programmes**

1. **Deen Dayal Upadhyaya Grameen Koushalya Yojana (DDU-GKY)** is a placement-linked skill development scheme for rural poor youth. This initiative is part of National Livelihoods Mission (NRLM). The skilling program for rural youth has now been refocused and reprioritized to build the capacity of rural poor youth to address the needs of the domestic and global skill requirements.

2. **National Livelihoods Mission (NRLM):** This was launched after restructuring Swarna jayanti Gram Swarozgar Yojana (SGSY). It aims at organizing all rural poor households and continuously nurturing and supporting them till they come out of abject poverty, by organizing one woman member from each household into affinity based.

3. **National Urban Livelihood Mission (NULM):** Swarna Jayanti Shahari Rozgar Yojana (SJSRY), which has been restructured into NULM, aims at organizing urban poor in self-help groups, imparting skill training to urban poor for self and wage employment and helping them to set up self-employment venture by providing credit on subsidized rate of interest. In addition, shelters for urban homeless and infrastructure for street vendors can also be taken up under this Mission.

4. **Support to Training and Employment Programme (STEP):** The Scheme is intended to benefit women who are in the age group of 16 years and above by providing skills to them for their employability. The Scheme covers any

sector for imparting skills related to employability and entrepreneurship, including but not limited to agriculture, horticulture, food processing, handlooms, etc. and skills for the work place such as spoken English, gems and jewellery, travel and tourism and hospitality.

5. **Special Central Assistance (SCA) to the Scheduled Castes Sub Plan (SCSP):** This is a major initiative for uplifting the SCs above the poverty line through self-employment or training. The amount of subsidy admissible is 50 per cent of the project cost.
6. **Nai Manzil** launched for education and skill development of drop outs. The scheme aims to benefit the minority youths in the age group of 17 to 35 years who are school dropouts or educated in the community education institutions like Madrasas, by providing them an integrated input of formal education (up till Class VIII or X) and skill training along with certification, with a view of enabling them to seek better employment in the organized sector and equipping them with better lives.
7. **USTTAD** (Upgrading the Skills and Training in Traditional Arts/Crafts for Development) aims to conserve traditional arts/crafts of minorities and for building capacity of traditional artisans and craftsmen belonging to minority communities.

## EDUCATION IN INDIA

The role of education in overall social and economic progress is widely recognized. The Government of India is committed to achieving the Sustainable Development Goal (SDG-4) for education–'Ensure inclusive and quality education for all and promote lifelong learning' by 2030. As India emerges as a knowledge-based economy, 'quality and relevant' education will play a significant role in economic development.

The right to education has been enshrined as a fundamental right in the Constitution of India, which states that: 'the State shall provide free and compulsory education to all children aged six to fourteen years in such a manner as the state may, by law, determine'. With a view to achieve the goal of universalization of elementary education, the Right to Free & Compulsory Education (RTE) Act, 2009, had been enacted in 2010 that provides a justiciable legal framework entitling all children between the ages of 6 and 14 years free and compulsory admission, attendance and completion of elementary education. It provides for children's right to an education of equitable quality, based on principles of equity and non-discrimination.

The RTE Act, 2009, lays down the guidelines for maintaining the norms and standards relating *inter alia* to pupil–teacher ratios (PTRs), buildings and infrastructure, school-working days, teacher-working hours in both primary and upper primary schools. The impact of PTR on learning achievement is widely discussed with some studies claiming that school participation and grade attainment are positively influenced by student classroom ratio (SCR) and PTR. The following section looks at some of the selected indicators such as SCR, PTR and Gender Parity Index (GPI) to assess the effectiveness and inclusiveness of the schooling system.

The primary level learning is the foundation on which a child's education is built, and it is of great importance to get the same right. The Annual Status on Education Report (ASER) by the Pratham Education Foundation since 2005, highlights shortcomings in the school educational outcomes in India in rural areas.

According to Economic Survey 2017–18, India has made significant progress in quantitative indicators such as enrolment levels, completion rates and other physical infrastructure like construction of school buildings/class rooms, drinking water facilities, toilet facilities and appointment of teachers, etc. at elementary school level.

## ❖ Student Classroom Ratio

SCR is defined as average number of pupils (students) per classroom in a school in a given school year. The ideal size should be at 30 students per classroom. At all India level, percentage of schools with SCR greater than 30 students declined from 43 per cent in 2009–10 to 25.7 per cent in 2015–16.

## ❖ Gender Parity Index (GPI)

GPI in education is a valuable indicator which reflects the discrimination against girls in access to educational opportunities. In higher education, gender disparities still prevail in enrolment for which continuous efforts are being made by the government to improve net intake rate for women in higher education. With consistent efforts by the government through programmes like Beti Padhao, Beti Bachao, the GPI has improved substantially at the primary and secondary levels of enrolment.

## ❖ Pupil-Teacher Ratio (PTR)

At primary level and upper primary level, the PTR should be 30:1 and 35:1, respectively. As per Unified District Information System for Education (UDISE), the PTR at national level for primary schools is 23:1 in 2015–16. Globally, there are variations in the optimum number of students taught in a particular class, and as such the data are not uniformly comparable. Data from the UNESCO Institute of Statistics on PTR in primary schools show that India has a national PTR comparable to countries with similar socio-economic indicators.

The states reported an improvement in schools complying with PTR norms of RTE Act during 2009–10 to 2015–16. However, despite improvement in number of schools complying with PTR norms, states like Bihar, Jharkhand, Madhya Pradesh and Uttar Pradesh have higher percentage of schools with PTR >30 compared to other states. There is a need to assess whether higher number of schools having PTR >30 in above four states is owing to the shortage of teachers or deployment issue of teachers.

The recruitment, service conditions and redeployment of teachers are primarily in the domain of respective state governments and UT Administrations. However, the central government through the flagship programmes of Sarva Shiksha Abhiyan (SSA) at elementary level and Rashtriya Madhyamik Shiksha Abhiyan (RMSA-Integrated) at secondary level provides assistance to the state governments and UTs for additional teachers to maintain appropriate PTR as per the prescribed norms for various levels of schooling.

## ❖ Education-Related Programmes

1. **Sarva Shiksha Abhiyan (SSA):** The SSA is the government of India's flagship programme that was launched in 2000–01 to achieve Universal Elementary Education (UEE) as envisioned by the United Nations' Millennium Development Goals, and thereafter mandated by the 86th amendment to the Constitution of India. The SSA is now the primary vehicle for implementing the provisions of the RTE Act, 2009.

   The origins of SSA go back to 1993–1994, when the District Primary Education Program (DPEP) was launched with the aim of achieving the objective of Universal Primary Education (UPE). The SSA has been implemented in partnership with state governments to address the needs of 192 million children across 1.1 million habitations across the country.

Its chief goals are as follows:

(i) Universal access and enrolment,

(ii) Universal retention up to the age of 14 years and

(iii) Substantial improvement in the quality of education to enable all children to achieve essential levels of learning

**Padhe Bharat Badhe Bharat**: It is a sub-programme of Sarva Shiksha Abhiyan launched in August 2014 with special focus on improving language development and to create interest in mathematics. The two tracks of Padhe Bharat Badhe Bharat are as follows:

(i) **Early Reading and Writing with Comprehension (ERWC):** To improve language development by creating an enduring interest in reading and writing with comprehension

(ii) **Early Mathematics (EM):** To create a natural and positive interest in mathematics related to their physical and social world.

2. **Rashtriya Madhyamik Shiksha Abhiyan:** This scheme was launched in March 2009 with the objective to enhance access to secondary education and to improve its quality. The implementation of the scheme started from 2009–10. It was envisaged to achieve an enrolment rate of 75 per cent from 52.26 per cent in 2005–06 at secondary stage within 5 years of implementation of the scheme by providing a secondary school within a reasonable distance of any habitation. The other objectives include improving quality of education imparted at secondary level through making all secondary schools conform to prescribed norms, removing gender, socio-economic and disability barriers, providing universal access to secondary level education by 2017 and achieving universal retention by 2020.

3. **Pandit Madan Mohan Malaviya National Mission on Teachers and Teaching:** The Mission envisages to address comprehensively all issue related to teachers, teaching, teacher preparation, professional development curriculum design, designing and development assessment. It is also envisaged that the mission would pursue long-term goals of building a strong professional cadre of teachers by setting performance standards and creating top class institutional facilities for innovative teaching and professional development of teachers.

4. **Higher Education for persons with special needs (HEPSN):** The University Grant Commission (UGC) implemented scheme is basically meant for creating an environment at the higher education institutions to enrich higher education learning experiences for differently abled persons. Creating awareness about the capabilities of differently abled persons, constructions aimed at improving accessibility, purchase of equipment to enrich learning, etc. are the broad categories of assistance under the scheme.

5. **Enhancing Access to Higher Education in unreserved or underserved areas:** Rashtriya Uchchatar Shiksha Abhiyan (RUSA) is enhancing access to higher education in unserved or underserved areas by setting up new institutions, and improving infrastructure and facilities in existing institutions. However, specific locations of these institutions are identified by the state government based on their need assessment and requirements.

6. **Unnat Bharat Abhiyan (UBA):** The Ministry of Human Resource Development (MHRD) has launched

on 11 Novembter 2014 Unnat Bharat Abhiyan with an aim to connect institutions of higher education, including Indian Institutes of Technology (IITs), National Institutes of Technology (NITs) and Indian Institutes of Science Education and Research (IISERs), etc. with local communities to address the development challenges through appropriate technologies.

The mission of the UBA is to enable higher educational institutions to work with the people of rural India in identifying development challenges and evolving appropriate solutions for accelerating sustainable growth. It also aims to create a virtuous cycle between society and an inclusive academic system by providing knowledge and practices for emerging professions and to upgrade the capabilities of both the public and the private sectors in responding to the development needs of rural India.

Goals of UBA are as follows:

(i) To build an understanding of the development agenda within institutes of Higher Education and an institutional capacity and training relevant to national needs, especially those of rural India.

(ii) To re-emphasize the need for fieldwork, stakeholder interactions and design for societal objectives as the basis of higher education.

(iii) To stress on rigorous reporting and useful outputs as central to developing new professions.

(iv) To provide rural India and regional agencies with access to the professional resources of the institutes of higher education, especially those that have acquired academic excellence in the field of science, engineering and technology and management.

(v) To improve development outcomes as a consequence of this research. To develop new professions and new processes is to sustain and absorb the outcomes of research.

(vi) To foster a new dialogue within the larger community on science, society and the environment and to develop a sense of dignity and collective destiny.

7. **Teacher Education (TE):** The Centrally Sponsored Scheme for TE has been revised to strengthen SCERTs, establish DIETs, Institutes of Advanced Studies in Education (IASEs) and strengthen the existing Colleges of Teacher Education (CTEs) and upgrade existing government secondary teacher education institutions into CTEs and Departments of Education in Universities as IASEs and establish Block Institutes of Teacher Education (BITE) in identified 196 SC/ST/Minority Concentration Districts.

8. **Saakshar Bharat (SB):** SB/Adult Education: Saakshar Bharat Programme was formulated in 2009 with the objective of achieving 80 per cent literacy level at national level, by focusing on adult women literacy seeking – to reduce the gap between male and female literacy to not more than 10 percentage points. It has four broader objectives, namely imparting functional literacy and numeracy to non-literates; acquiring equivalency to formal educational system; imparting relevant skill development programme and promote a leaning society by providing opportunities for continuing education. The principal target of the programme is to impart functional literacy to 70 million non-literate adults in the age group of 15 years and beyond.

9. **Schemes to encourage education among SC students and other schemes:**

(i) Pre-Matric Scholarship Scheme for SC Students studying in Classes IX and X
(ii) Pre-Matric scholarships to students, whose parents are engaged in 'unclean' occupations
(iii) Rajiv Gandhi National Fellowship Scheme aims at providing financial assistance to SC students pursuing M.Phil and Ph.D. courses.
(iv) National Overseas Scholarship Scheme: A financial support to students pursuing Master's level courses and Ph.D./Post-Doctoral courses abroad, maximum 60 awards are to be given from the year 2013-14 onwards.
(v) Scheme of Top Class Education: Eligible students who secure admission in notified premier institutions like the IITs, IIMs and NITs are provided full financial support for meeting the requirements of tuition fees, living expenses, books, and computers.

10. **Educational schemes for OBCs:** The Pre-Matric scholarship scheme aims to motivate children of OBCs studying at pre-matric stage and post-matric scholarship intends to promote higher education by providing financial support leading to their earning Ph.D. Degrees.
11. **Scheme for Economic Development of OBC:** Under Assistance to Voluntary Organizations Working for Welfare of OBCs, grants-in-aid is provided to voluntary organizations to involve the non-government sector by providing skill upgradation among OBCs in various trades. Under the Scheme, financial assistance is provided to non-governmental organizations for imparting various vocational trainings to OBCs.
12. **Education through broadband facilities:** Under this mission, more than 700 courses in various disciplines in engineering and science are available online under National Programme on Technology Enhanced Learning (NPTEL). E-content for eight undergraduate subjects has also been generated by the Consortium of Education Communication (CEC) in collaboration with its media centres.
13. **Global Initiative for Academics Network (GIAN):** It is an initiative to attract the best foreign academics to Indian Universities of Excellence.

    GIAN aims at tapping the talent pool of scientists and entrepreneurs to engage with the institutes of higher education in India to augment the country's existing academic resources, accelerate the pace of quality reforms and further strengthen India's scientific and technological capabilities.

### ❖ Digital Literacy

Digital Literacy means 'ability to understand and use information in multiple formats from a wide range of sources when it is presented via computers' According to Seattle Goodwill digital literacy involves the knowledge, skills and attitudes to effectively navigate, critically evaluate create or adapt information using a range of digital technologies. Digital literacy is an ongoing process. One learns by getting information about new technologies and then by achieving various skills in executing that knowledge.

## DIGITAL INDIA

'Digital India' is a central programme to make India ready for a knowledge-based future Vision Areas of Digital India. The Digital India programme is centred on three key vision areas:

1. **Digital Infrastructure as a Utility to Every Citizen:** This includes to provide high-speed Internet connectivity as a core

utility for delivery of services to citizens. To provide digital identity that is unique, lifelong, online and authenticable to every citizen. Providing mobile phone and bank account enabling citizen participation in digital and financial space. Easy access to a Common Service Centre. Shareable private space on a public cloud for every citizen.

2. **Governance and Services on Demand:** Seamless integration across departments or jurisdictions ensuring availability of services in real-time from online and mobile platforms. To make all citizen entitlements portable and available on the cloud. To digitally transformed services for improving ease of doing business Leveraging Geospatial Information Systems (GIS) for decision support systems and development.
3. **Digital Empowerment of Citizens:** To empower citizen through universal digital literacy. To provide universal accessible digital resource. To make available digital resources/services in Indian languages. To provide collaborative digital platforms for participative governance. Citizens not required to physically submit government documents/certificates.

## ❖ Nine Pillars of Digital India Programme

Under Digital India programme, nine key initiatives are in progress, which are as follows:

1. **Broadband Highways:** The aim is to cover 2,50,000 village panchayats under National Optical Fibre Network (NOFN) by December 2016. Nationwide Internet Infrastructure (NII) would integrate the network and cloud infrastructure in the country to provide high-speed connectivity and cloud platform to various government departments up to the panchayat level.
2. **Universal Access to Mobile Connectivity:** The aim is to increase network penetration and to provide mobile connectivity to 44,000 villages by 2018 with investment of ₹ 16,000.
3. **Public Internet Access Programme:** One Common Service Centre (CSC) would be provided to each gram panchayat and 1,50,000. Post Offices are proposed to be converted into multiservice centres.
4. **E-governance:** IT would be used to make the delivery of government services more effectively. There would be integration of services and platform-UIDAI, Payment Gateway, Mobile Seva platform, Public redressal, etc. through IT. All information would be available in electronic form.
5. **eKranti:** The aim is electronic delivery of services to people be it education, health, financial inclusion or justice.
6. Information for AllMyGov in is a website launched by the government to facilitate a two-way communication between citizens and the government. It is a medium to exchange ideas or suggestion with government. The citizen would have open access to information through open data platform.
7. **Electronics Manufacturing:** The government is focusing on zero imports of electronics by 2020 through local manufacturing of items such as smart energy meters, micro ATMs, mobile, consumer and medical electronics. The government is also taking several steps to promote manufacturing and investment in electronics sector by providing clarity on taxation, incentives skill development, etc.
8. **IT for Jobs:** The aim is to train 10 million people in towns and villages for IT sector jobs in five years. It also aims to provide training to three lakh service delivery agents as part of skill development to run viable businesses delivering IT services.

It also focuses on training of five lakh rural workforce on telecom and telecom-related services and setting up of BPOs in each North-Eastern state.

9. **Early Harvesting Programmes:** Government plans to installed Wi-Fi facilities in all universities across the country. All books will be converted into e-books. E-mail will be made the primary mode of communication within government. Biometric attendance system will be installed in all central government offices where recording of attendance will be made online.

### ❖ National Digital Literacy Mission (NDLM)

National Digital Literacy Mission (NDLM) also called Digital Saksharta Abhiyan (DISHA) initiated with the vision to make at least one person in every family digitally literate with digital literacy skills by 2020 and provide digital literacy to 6 crore rural households, including Anganwadi and ASHA workers and authorized ration dealers across the country. So far, 8.2 million people have been trained to use digital devices and services and further leverage it to improve livelihoods and access e-governance.

### ❖ Pradhan Mantri Gramin Digital Saksharta Abhiyan (PMGDISHA)

The Union Cabinet approved 'Pradhan Mantri Gramin Digital Saksharta Abhiyan' (PMGDISHA) to make 6 crore rural households digitally literate.

PMGDISHA is expected to be one of the largest digital literacy programmes in the world. Under the scheme, 25 lakh candidates will be trained in the FY 2016–17; 275 lakh in the FY 2017–18; and 300 lakh in the FY 2018–19.

Digitally literate persons would be able to operate computers/digital access devices (like tablets, smart phones, etc.), send and receive e-mails, browse internet, access government services, search for information, undertaking cashless transactions, etc. and hence use IT to actively participate in the process of nation building.

## DIGITAL DIVIDE

Digital divide expresses the discrepancy between people who have access to and the resources to use new information and communication tools, such as the Internet, and people who do not have the resources and access to the technology. It also means discrepancy between those who have the skills, knowledge and abilities to use the technologies and those who do not.

The digital divide exists between those living in rural areas and those living in urban areas, between the educated and uneducated, between economic classes, and on a global scale between more and less industrially developed nations.

### ❖ Digital Divide in India

India is a multicultural, multi-language and multi-religion country with complex socio-economic conditions; there are many difficulties in serving rural communities, each one of which has appeared insurmountable: poverty, unemployment, age and education.

#### Reasons

In India, there is huge gap of digital divide between rural and urban India where growth is biased in favour of urban areas; according to statistics, more than 75 per cent of the broadband connections in the country are in the top 30 cities. Some states are not able to adopt even one technology but others have adopted very efficiently. Another important reason of digital divide in India is knowledge divide. Knowledge divide is directly related with digital divide. Internet use is primarily associated with a large section of the English-knowing urban population. Added to these, the growing population, insufficient funds, affordability and delays in implementation of government policies and programmes have been some of the challenges that have led to unequal development in the society, which is responsible for digital divide.

The digital divide is based on insufficient policy regimes, inefficiency in the provision of telecommunication network and service lack of locality created content and uneven ability to derive economic and social benefits from information intensive activities.

## ❖ Challenges to Bridging the Digital Divide

1. **Physical barriers:** There are lack of telecommunication infrastructure with sufficient reliable bandwidth for Internet connections at affordable cost.
2. **Literacy and skill barriers:** Education in information literacy will play an important role in keeping the society from fragmenting into a population of information haves and have-nots. The lack of skill in using computer and communication technology also prevents people from accessing digital information.
3. **Economic barriers:** Poor access to computer and communication technology also causes a digital divide. In India, the ability to purchase or rent the tool for access to digital information is less among the masses.
4. **Content barriers:** To solve the digital divide, steps should be taken by the government to ensure that all citizens are able to receive diverse content relevant to their lives as well as to produce their own content for their communities and for the Internet.
5. **Linguistic barriers:** Having a multicultural and multilingual population, today a large percentage of information content on the Internet is in English, which is a barrier for the people whose primary language is not English.

## ❖ Initiatives in Bridging the Digital Divide

1. **Kisan Call centre:** Established to deliver extension services to the farming community. The purpose of these call centres is to respond to issues raised by farmers, instantly, in the local language.
2. **Bhoomi Project:** The Bhoomi Project of Karnataka state covers 6.7 million farmers and holds millions of records of land ownership. The project has earned the goodwill of many people and also international funding agencies. This project has reduced the delays involved in interacting with the bureaucratic hierarchy of the state revenue department.
3. **Gyandoot Project:** Gyandoot is an intranet in Dhar district connecting rural cybercafes catering to the everyday needs of the masses. This web site of Gyandoot is an extension of Gyandoot intranet for giving global access. Gyandoot is the first ever project in India for a rural information network in the Dhar district of Madhya Pradesh which has the highest percentage of tribes and dense forest. Every village has a computer centre or 'soochnalayas' at prominent market places or major roads.
4. **TDIL:** The department of information technology initiated the TDIL (Technology Development for Indian Languages) with the aim of developing information processing tools and techniques to facilitate human-machine interaction without language barrier; creating and accessing multilingual knowledge resources and integrating them to develop innovative user products and services.
5. **Digital Libraries Project:** This aims to digitize millions of rare books in the country and make it available to the users freely, i.e., keeping it as an open

source is a step towards bridging digital divide. In order to bridge the digital divide in a larger way the Government of India in collaboration with the centre for advanced computing based in pure, which aims to bring about one million of digital books to the doorsteps of promote literacy.

## HEALTH IN INDIA

Ensuring healthy lives and promoting the well-being for all at all ages is essential to sustainable development (SDG-3). India's commitment to achieve the targets under SDG-3 with some of them also aligned with the National Health Policy, 2017, will help in strengthening health delivery systems and in achieving universal health coverage.

The challenges posed by stunting, wasting and under-nutrition and its irreversible adverse impact not only on health, but also on growth and economic development were discussed. Women have to be educated to ensure a healthy population. The need for greater inter-sectoral convergence to impact health sensitive indicators, such as sanitation, hygiene, women empowerment and education, was highlighted.

### India: Health of the Nation's States, 2017

The report 'India: Health of the Nation's States', 2017, provides the first comprehensive set of findings for the distribution of diseases and risk factors across all States from 1990 to 2016. The concept of Disability Adjusted Life Years (DALYs) provides a framework for analysing the disease burden and risk factors. DALYs are the sum of years of potential life lost due to premature mortality and the years of productive life lost due to disability. One DALY represents the loss of the equivalent of one year of full health. Using DALYs, the burden of diseases that cause premature death but little disability can be compared to that of diseases that do not cause death but do cause disability. The information and database about changing disease patterns and the use of DALYs to quickly compare the impact caused by very different conditions, such as cancer and depression, in a single, comparable metric are crucial inputs for decision-making, effective resource allocation and policy planning.

There has been significant improvement in the health status of the individual as LEB has increased by approximately 10 years during the period 1990 to 2015. The significance of DALYs as a critical health policy indicator is reflected by the inverse relationship between life expectancy and DALYs rates. The all India trends in LEB and DALYs echo the inverse relation between the two over time from 1990 to 2015.

DALYs express the premature death and disability attributable to a particular cause, and are made up of two components: Years of Life Lost (YLLs) and Years of Life Lived with Disability (YLDs). YLLs measure all the time people lose when they die prematurely, before attaining their ideal life expectancy. Ideal life expectancy is based on the highest life expectancy observed in the world for that person's age group. YLDs measure years of life lived with any short- or long-term condition that prevents a person from living in full health. They are calculated by multiplying an amount of time (expressed in years) by a disability weight (a number that quantifies the severity of a disability). Adding together YLLs and YLDs yields DALYs, a measure that portrays in one metric the total health loss a person experiences during their life.

*Source*: Economic Survey 2017-18

### ❖ National Health Policy (NHP), 2017

The Union Cabinet in March 2017 approved the NHP, 2017. The Policy seeks to reach everyone in a comprehensive integrated way to move towards wellness. It aims at achieving universal health coverage and delivering quality health care services to all at affordable cost.

This Policy looks at problems and solutions holistically with private sector as strategic partners. It seeks to promote quality of care, focus is on emerging diseases and investment in promotive and preventive health care. The policy is patient centric and quality driven. It addresses health security and make in India for drugs and devices.

The main objective of the National Health Policy, 2017, is to achieve the highest possible level of good health and well-being, through a preventive and promotive health care orientation in all developmental policies, and to achieve universal access to good quality health care services without anyone having to face financial hardship as a consequence.

Goals of the policy are as follows:

(a) Raising public health expenditure to 2.5 per cent of the GDP in a time bound manner. The States would be incentivized for incremental State resources for public health expenditure. General taxation will remain the predominant means for financing health care.

(b) Providing larger package of assured comprehensive primary health care through the Health and Wellness Centres, which includes geriatric health care, palliative care and rehabilitative care services.

(c) Provide at the district level most of the secondary care which are currently provided at a medical college hospital.

(d) Every family would have a health card that links them to primary care facility and be eligible for a defined package of services anywhere in the country.

(e) Free drugs, free diagnostics and free emergency care services in all public hospitals.

(f) Supports voluntary service in rural and under-served areas on pro-bono basis by recognized health care professionals under a 'giving back to society' initiative.

(g) Establishment of National Digital Health Authority (NDHA) to regulate, develop and deploy digital health across the continuum of care.

(h) Setting up of a separate, empowered medical tribunal for speedy resolution to address disputes/complaints regarding standards of care, prices of services, negligence and unfair practices. Standard Regulatory framework for laboratories and imaging centres, specialized emerging services such as assisted reproductive techniques, surrogacy, stem cell banking, organ and tissue transplantation and Nano Medicine will be created as appropriate.

(i) Strengthening regulation of medical devices and establishing a regulatory body for medical devices to unleash innovation and the entrepreneurial spirit for manufacture of medical device in India. The policy supports harmonization of domestic regulatory standards with international standards.

(j) With the objective of ensuring the rights, safety and well-being of clinical trial participants, the policy recommends that specific clause(s) be included in the Drugs and Cosmetics Act for its regulation.

(k) Timely revision of National List of Essential Medicines (NLEM) along with appropriate price control mechanisms for generic drugs.

(l) Establishing federated national health information architecture, to rollout and link systems across public and private health providers at State and national levels consistent with Metadata and Data Standards (MDDS) and Electronic Health Record (EHR), will be supported by the policy.

(m) Creation of registries (i.e., patients, provider, service, diseases, document and event) for enhanced public health/ big data analytics, creation of health information exchange platform and national health information network, use of National Optical Fibre Network, use of smartphones/tablets for capturing real time data, are key strategies of the National Health Information Architecture.

**Trends in Select Health Indicators**

| S. No. | Parameter | 2001 | 2019 |
|---|---|---|---|
| 1. | CBR (per 1,000 population) | 25.4 | 17.86 |
| 2. | Crude Death Rate (CDR) (per 1,000 population) | 8.4 | 7.27 |
| 3. | TFR | 3.1 | 2.22 |
| 4. | MMR (per 1,00,000 live births) | 301 | 113 |
| 5. | IMR (per 1,000 live births) | 66 | 28.3 |
| 6. | LEB (1999–2003) (2011–15) | | |
| | Total | 63.4 | 68.3 |
| | Male | 62.3 | 66.9 |
| | Female | 64.6 | 70.0 |
| | *Source*: Sample Registration System (SRS), Registrar General of India. | | |

## NATIONAL FAMILY HEALTH SURVEY (NFHS)

- The NFHS is a large-scale, multi-round survey conducted in a representative sample of households throughout India.
- The Ministry of Health and Family Welfare (MoHFW) has designated the International Institute for Population Sciences(IIPS) Mumbai, as the nodal agency for providing coordination and technical guidance for the survey.
- IIPS collaborates with a number of Field Organizations (FO) for survey implementation.

### ❖ Objectives and Its Goal

Each successive round of the NFHS has had two specific goals:

- To provide essential data on health and family welfare needed by the Ministry of Health and Family Welfare and other agencies for policy and programme purposes.
- To provide information on important emerging health and family welfare issues.

The survey provides state and national information for India on:

- Fertility
- Infant and child mortality
- The practice of family planning
- Maternal and child health
- Reproductive health
- Nutrition
- Anaemia
- Utilization and quality of health and family planning services.

### Funding

- The funding for different rounds of NFHS has been provided by USAID, the Bill and Melinda Gates Foundation, UNICEF, UNFPA, and MoHFW (Government of India).

### History of NFHS

**Objective:** The main objective of each successive round of the NFHS has been to provide high-quality data on health and family welfare and emerging issues in this area.

- NFHS-1: The NFHS-1 was conducted in 1992-93.
- NFHS-2: The NFHS-2 was conducted in 1998-99 in all 26 states of India.
- The project was funded by the USAID, with additional support from UNICEF.
- NFHS-3: The NFHS-3 was carried out in 2005-2006.
- NFHS-3 funding was provided by the US-AID, the Department for International Development (UK), the Bill and Melinda Gates Foundation, UNICEF, UNFPA, and the Government of India.
- NFHS-4: The NFHS-4 in 2014-2015.
- In addition to the 29 states, NFHS-4 included all six union territories for the first time and provided estimates of most indicators at the district level for all 640 districts in the country as per the 2011 census.
- The survey covered a range of health-related issues, including fertility, infant and child mortality, maternal and child health, perinatal mortality, adolescent reproductive health, high-risk sexual behaviour, safe injections, tuberculosis, and malaria, non-communicable diseases, domestic violence, HIV knowledge, and attitudes toward people living with HIV.

## ❖ National Family Health Survey-5

The NFHS-5 has captured the data during 2019-20 and has been conducted in around 6.1 lakh households.

- Many indicators of NFHS-5 are similar to those of NFHS-4, carried out in 2015-16 to make possible comparisons over time.
- Phase 2 of the survey (covering remaining states) was delayed due to the Covid-19 pandemic and its results were released in September 2021.

NFHS-5 data will be useful in setting benchmarks and examining the progress the health sector has made over time.

- Besides providing evidence for the effectiveness of ongoing programmes, the data from NFHS-5 help in identifying the need for new programmes with an area specific focus and identifying groups that are most in need of essential services.
- It provides an indicator for tracking 30 Sustainable Development Goals (SDGs) that the country aims to achieve by 2030.

NFHS-5 includes some new topics, such as preschool education, disability, access to a toilet facility, death registration, bathing practices during menstruation, and methods and reasons for abortion.

- NFHS-5 includes new focal areas that will give requisite input for strengthening existing programmes and evolving new strategies for policy intervention. The areas are:
- Expanded domains of child immunization
- Components of micro-nutrients to children
- Menstrual hygiene
- Frequency of alcohol and tobacco use
- Additional components of non-communicable diseases (NCDs)
- Expanded age ranges for measuring hypertension and diabetes among all aged 15 years and above.

In 2019, for the first time, the NFHS-5 sought details on the percentage of women and men who have ever used the Internet.

### Key Findings of NFHS-5

**Sex Ratio:** NFHS-5 data shows that there were 1,020 women for 1000 men in the country in 2019-2021.

- This is the highest sex ratio for any NFHS survey as well as since the first modern synchronous census conducted in 1881.
- In the 2005-06 NFHS, the sex ratio was 1,000 or women and men were equal in number.

**Sex Ratio at Birth:** For the first time in India, between 2019-21, there were 1,020 adult women per 1,000 men.

- However, the data shall not undermine the fact that India still has a sex ratio at birth (SRB) more skewed towards boys than the natural SRB (which is 952 girls per 1000 boys).
- Uttar Pradesh, Haryana, Punjab, Rajasthan, Bihar, Delhi, Jharkhand, Andhra Pradesh, Tamil Nadu, Odisha, Maharashtra are the major states with low SRB.

**Total Fertility Rate (TFR):** The TFR has also come down below the threshold at which the population is expected to replace itself from one generation to next.

- TFR was 2 in 2019-2021, just below the replacement fertility rate of 2.1.
- In rural areas, the TFR is still 2.1.
- In urban areas, TFR had gone below the replacement fertility rate in the 2015-16 NFHS itself.
- A decline in TFR, which implies that a lower number of children are being born, also entails that India's population would become older.
- The survey shows that the share of under-15 population in the country has therefore further declined from 28.6% in 2015-16 to 26.5% in 2019-21.

**Children's Nutrition:** Child Nutrition indicators show a slight improvement at all-India level as Stunting has declined from 38% to 36%, wasting from 21% to 19% and underweight from 36% to 32% at all India level.

- In all phase-II States/UTs the situation has improved in respect of child nutrition but the change is not significant as drastic changes in respect of these indicators are unlikely in a short span period.
- The share of overweight children has increased from 2.1% to 3.4%.

**Anaemia:** The incidence of anaemia in under-5 children (from 58.6 to 67%), women (53.1 to 57%) and men (22.7 to 25%) has worsened in all States of India (20%-40% incidence is considered moderate).

- Barring Kerala (at 39.4%), all States are in the "severe" category.

**Immunization:** Full immunization drive among children aged 12-23 months has recorded substantial improvement from 62% to 76% at all-India level.

- 11 out of 14 States/UTs have more than three-fourth of children aged 12-23 months with fully immunization and it is highest (90%) for Odisha.

**Institutional Births:** Institutional births have increased substantially from 79% to 89% at all-India Level.

- Institutional delivery is 100% in Puducherry and Tamil Nadu and more than 90% in 7 States/UTs out of 12 Phase II States/UTs.
- Along with an increase in institutional births, there has also been a substantial increase in C-section deliveries in many States/UTs especially inprivate health facilities.
- It calls into question unethical practices of private health providers who prioritise monetary gain over women's health and control over their bodies.

**Family Planning:** Overall Contraceptive Prevalence Rate (CPR) has increased substantially from 54% to 67% at all-India level and in almost all Phase-II States/UTswith an exception of Punjab.

- Use of modern methods of contraceptives has also increased in almost all States/UTs.
- Unmet needs of family Planning have witnessed a significant decline from13% to 9% at all-India level and in most of the Phase-II States/UTs.
- The unmet need for spacing which remained a major issue in India in the past

has come down to less than 10% in all the States except Jharkhand (12%), Arunachal Pradesh (13%) and Uttar Pradesh(13%).

**Breastfeeding to Children's:** Exclusive breastfeeding to children under age 6 months has shown an improvement in all-India level from 55% in 2015-16 to 64% in 2019-21. All the phase-II States/UTs are also showing considerable progress.

**Women Empowerment:** Women's empowerment indicators portray considerable improvement at all India level and across all the phase-II States/UTs.

- Significant progress has been recorded between NFHS-4 and NFHS-5 in regard to women operating bank accounts from 53% to 79% at all-India level.
- More than 70% of women in every state and UTs in the second phase have operational bank accounts.

## ❖ Health-Related Programmes

- Mission Indradhanush
- National Health Mission (NHM)
- Rashtriya Kishor Swasthya Karyakram
- National Program for Prevention and Control of Cancer, Diabetes, CVD and Stroke (NPCDCS)
- Swachh Bharat Mission (SBM)
- National AYUSH Mission (NAM)
- Affordable Medicines and Reliable Implants for Treatment (AMRIT)
- National Rural Drinking Water Programme (NRDWP)
- Pradhan Mantri Swasthya Suraksha Yojana (PMSSY)
- Scheme of Assistance for the Prevention of Alcoholism and Substance (Drugs) Abuse

1. **Mission Indradhanush:** Mission Indradhanush was launched by the Government of India on December 25, 2014. accelerate the process of immunization by covering 5 per cent and more children every year, the mission has been adopted to achieve target of full coverage by 2020.

   The Mission aims to cover all those children by 2020 who are either unvaccinated, or are partially vaccinated against vaccine preventable diseases. India's Universal Immunization Programme (UIP) provides free vaccines against 12 life-threatening diseases, to 26 million children annually. The Universal Immunization Programme provides life-saving vaccines to all children across the country free of cost to protect them against Tuberculosis, Diphtheria, Pertussis, Tetanus, Polio, Hepatitis B, Pneumonia and Meningitis due to Haemophilus Influenzae type b (Hib), Measles, Rubella, Japanese Encephalitis (JE) and Rotavirus diarrhoea. (Rubella, JE and Rotavirus vaccine in select states and districts).

   Focused and systematic immunization drive will be through a 'catch-up' campaign mode where the aim is to cover all the children who have been left out or missed out for immunization. Also the pregnant women are administered the tetanus vaccine, ORS packets and zinc tablets are distributed for use in the event of severe diarrhoea or dehydration and vitamin A doses are administered to boost child immunity.

   The Mission targeted 201 high priority districts in the first phase, 297 districts for the second phase in the year 2015 and 216 districts in the third Phase during 2016.

   Phase IV of the Mission was launched from 7 February 2017 covering the North-Eastern states. Now, it has been rolled out for whole of the country from April 2017.

2. **National Health Mission (NHM):** The NHM came into being in 2013 to enable

universal access to equitable, affordable, and quality health care services. It subsumes the National Rural Health Mission (NRHM) and NUHM as sub-missions.

**(A) National Rural Health Mission (NRHM)**

The NRHM was launched on 12 April 2005 to provide accessible, affordable and quality health care to the rural population, especially the vulnerable groups. The Union Cabinet on 1 May 2013, launched the NUHM as a Sub-mission of an over-arching National Health Mission (NHM), and the NRHM was made another Sub-mission of National Health Mission.

NRHM seeks to provide equitable, affordable and quality health care to the rural population, especially the vulnerable groups. Under the NRHM, the Empowered Action Group (EAG) States as well as North-Eastern States, Jammu and Kashmir and Himachal Pradesh have been given special focus.

The thrust of the mission is on establishing a fully functional, community owned, decentralized health delivery system with inter-sectoral convergence at all levels, to ensure simultaneous action on a wide range of determinants of health, such as water, sanitation, education, nutrition, social and gender equality. Institutional integration within the fragmented health sector was expected to provide a focus on outcomes, measured against Indian Public Health Standards for all health facilities.

**(B) NUHM**

The Union Cabinet vide its decision dated 1 May 2013 has approved the launch of NUHM as a Sub-mission of an over-arching National Health Mission (NHM), with NRHM being the other Sub-mission of National Health Mission.

NHM has six financing components:

(i) NRHM-RCH Flexi pool,
(ii) NUHM Flexi pool,
(iii) Flexible pool for Communicable disease,
(iv) Flexible pool for non-communicable disease including Injury and Trauma,
(v) Infrastructure Maintenance and
(vi) Family Welfare Central Sector component.

NUHM would endeavour to achieve its goal through the following:

(i) Need-based city specific urban health care system to meet the diverse health care needs of the urban poor and other vulnerable sections.
(ii) Institutional mechanism and management systems to meet the health-related challenges of a rapidly growing urban population.
(iii) Partnership with community and local bodies for a more proactive involvement in planning, implementation and monitoring of health activities.
(iv) Availability of resources for providing essential primary health care to urban poor.
(v) Partnerships with NGOs, for profit and not for profit health service providers and other stakeholders.

The centre-state funding pattern will be 75:25 for all the States except North-Eastern states including Sikkim and other special category states of Jammu & Kashmir, Himachal Pradesh and Uttarakhand, for whom the centre-state funding pattern will be 90:10.

3. **Rashtriya Kishor Swasthya Karyakram:** The Rashtriya Kishor Swasthya Karyakram was launched on 7 January 2014. The key principle of this programme is adolescent participation

and leadership, Equity and inclusion, Gender Equity and strategic partnerships with other sectors and stakeholders. The programme envisions enabling all adolescents in India to realize their full potential by making informed and responsible decisions related to their health and well-being and by accessing the services and support they need to do so.

The Rashtriya Kishor Swasthya Karyakram (National Adolescent Health Programme) will comprehensively address the health needs of the 243 million adolescents. It introduces community-based interventions through peer educators, and is underpinned by collaborations with other ministries and state governments.

The strategy envisions that all adolescents in India are able to realize their full potential by making informed and responsible decisions related to their health and well-being, and by accessing the services and support they need to do so. The implementation of this vision requires support from the government and other institutions, including the health, education and labour sectors as well as adolescents' own families and communities.

**Objectives**

(i) Improve nutrition
(ii) Improve sexual and reproductive health
(iii) Enhance mental health
(iv) Prevent injuries and violence
(v) Prevent substance misuse
(vi) Address NCDs.

4. **National Program for Prevention and Control of Cancer, Diabetes, CVD and Stroke (NPCDCS):** States have already initiated some of the activities for prevention and control of non-communicable diseases (NCDs) especially cancer, diabetes, CVDs and stroke. The central government proposes to supplement their efforts by providing technical and financial support through National Program for Prevention and Control of Cancer, Diabetes, CVD and Stroke. The NPCDCS program has two components, viz., (i) cancer (ii) diabetes, CVDs and stroke.

**Objectives**

(i) Prevent and control common NCDs through behaviour and life style changes,
(ii) Provide early diagnosis and management of common NCDs,
(iii) Build capacity at various levels of health care for prevention, diagnosis and treatment of common NCDs,
(iv) Train human resource within the public health setup, viz., doctors, paramedics and nursing staff to cope with the increasing burden of NCDs,
(v) Establish and develop capacity for palliative and rehabilitative care.

5. **SBM:** SBM is being implemented by the Ministry of Housing and Urban Affairs (M/o HUA) and by the Ministry of Drinking Water and Sanitation (M/o DWS) for urban and rural areas respectively.

**(A) SBM (Gramin)**

This was launched on 2 October 2014 which aims at attaining an Open Defecation Free India by 2 October 2019 by providing access to toilet facilities to all rural households and initiating Solid and Liquid Waste Management activities in all Gram Panchayats to promote cleanliness. Under SBM (G), the incentives for individual household latrines (IHHLs) have been enhanced from ₹ 10,000 to 12,000 to provide for water availability.

The part funding from Mahatma Gandhi NREGA for the payment of incentives for the construction of IHHLs is now paid from the SBM (Gramin). Initiatives by the government in this regard include media campaigns, provisioning for incentivizing ASHAs and Anganwadi workers for promoting sanitation, guidelines to involve corporates in Sanitation sector through corporate social responsibilities, strengthening online monitoring system for entering households level data gathered from the Baseline Survey.

**(B) Swachh Bharat Mission (Urban)**

SBM (Urban) aims to ensure that –

(i) No households engage in the practice of open defecation

(ii) No new insanitary toilets are constructed during the mission period and

(iii) Pit latrines are converted to sanitary latrines.

**Mission Objectives**

(i) Elimination of open defecation

(ii) Eradication of Manual Scavenging

(iii) Modern and Scientific Municipal Solid Waste Management

(iv) To effect behavioural change regarding healthy sanitation practices

(v) Generate awareness about sanitation and its linkage with public health

(vi) Capacity Augmentation for ULBs to create an enabling environment for private sector participation in Capex (capital expenditure) and Opex (operation and maintenance)

(vii) Mission Components

(viii) Household toilets, including conversion of insanitary latrines into pour-flush latrines

(ix) Community toilets

(x) Public toilets and urinals

(xi) Solid waste management

(xii) IEC and Public Awareness

(xiii) Capacity building and Administrative and Office Expenses (A&OE)

6. **National AYUSH Mission (NAM):** Department of AYUSH, Ministry of Health and Family Welfare, Government of India, has launched National AYUSH Mission (NAM) during the 12th Plan for implementing through states/UTs. The basic objective of NAM is to promote AYUSH medical systems through cost-effective AYUSH services, strengthening of educational systems, facilitate the enforcement of quality control of Ayurveda, Siddha and Unani & Homoeopathy (ASU &H) drugs and sustainable availability of ASU & H raw materials.

**Vision**

(i) To provide cost effective and equitable AYUSH health care throughout the country by improving access to the services.

(ii) To revitalize and strengthen the AYUSH systems making them as prominent medical streams in addressing the health care of the society.

(iii) To improve educational institutions capable of imparting quality AYUSH education.

(iv) To promote the adoption of Quality standards of AYUSH drugs and making available the sustained supply of AYUSH raw materials.

**Objectives**

(i) To provide cost effective AYUSH services, with a universal access through upgrading AYUSH Hospitals and Dispensaries, co-location of AYUSH facilities at Primary Health Centres (PHCs), Community Health Centres (CHCs) and District Hospitals (DHs).

(ii) To strengthen institutional capacity at the state level through upgrading AYUSH educational institutions, state government ASU&H pharmacies, Drug Testing Laboratories and ASU&H enforcement mechanism.

(iii) Support cultivation of medicinal plants by adopting Good Agricultural Practices (GAPs) so as to provide sustained supply of quality raw-materials and support certification mechanism for quality standards, good agricultural/collection/storage practices.

(iv) Support setting up of clusters through convergence of cultivation, warehousing, value addition, marketing and development of infrastructure for entrepreneurs.

7. **Affordable Medicines and Reliable Implants for Treatment (AMRIT):** With the aim to reduce the expenditure incurred by patients on treatment of cancer and heart diseases, the Government of India inaugurated the Affordable Medicines and Reliable Implants for Treatment (AMRIT) outlet at AIIMs in November 2015. The AMRIT pharmacy would be selling 202 cancer and 186 cardio-vascular drugs, and 148 types of cardiac implants at very affordable prices. Patients can buy medicines and implants at 50 to 60 per cent cheaper prices than the open market from AMRIT outlet in AIIMS. AMRIT will be launched in all central government hospitals.

8. **National Rural Drinking Water Programme (NRDWP):** The Union Cabinet accorded its approval for continuation and restructuring of NRDWP to make it outcome-based, competitive and better monitored with increased focus on sustainability (functionality) of schemes to ensure good quality service delivery to the rural population.

   The aim and objective of the programme is to provide every rural person with adequate safe water for drinking, cooking and other basic domestic needs on a sustainable basis, with a minimum water quality standard, which should be conveniently accessible at all times and in all situations. Achieving this aim and objective is a continuous process.

9. **Pradhan Mantri Swasthya Suraksha Yojana (PMSSY):** Under the PMSSY, six All India Institute for Medical Sciences (AIIMS) – in the first phase – have become functional. Besides, upgradation of total 58 medical colleges, 13 medical colleges in the first phase, 6 in the second phase and 39 in the third phase has been envisaged. Further, under phase-IV of PMSSY, 12 more medical colleges are proposed to be upgraded and four AIIMS like institutes each at Andhra Pradesh, Vidarbha region (Maharashtra), West Bengal and Poorvanchal are proposed to be established human resources.

10. **Scheme of Assistance for the Prevention of Alcoholism and Substance (Drugs) Abuse:** The Ministry of Social Justice and Empowerment coordinates and monitors all aspects of drug abuse prevention which include assessment of the extent of the problem, preventive action, treatment and rehabilitation of addicts and public awareness. Under this scheme, financial assistance up to 90 per cent of the approved expenditure is given to the voluntary organizations and other eligible agencies for setting up/running Integrated Rehabilitation Centre for Addicts (IRCAs).

## SOCIALLY ORIENTED INSURANCE AND PENSION SCHEMES

1. **Pradhan Mantri Suraksha Bima Yojana (PMSBY):** PMSBY is one of three social security schemes that the government

had announced in the 2015 Budget. The other two being Pradhan Mantri Jeevan Jyoti Bima Yojana (PMJJBY) and the Atal Pension Yojana (APY). PMSBY Scheme is available to people in the age group 18 to 70 years with a bank account who give their consent to join/ enable auto-debit on or before 31st May for the coverage period 1st June to 31st May on an annual renewal basis. Aadhar would be the primary KYC for the bank account. The risk coverage under the scheme is ₹ 2 lakh for accidental death and full disability and ₹ 1 lakh for partial disability. The premium of ₹ 12 per annum is to be deducted from the account holder's bank account through 'auto-debit' facility in one instalment. The scheme is being offered by public sector general insurance companies or any other general insurance companies who are willing to offer the product on similar terms with necessary approvals and tie up with banks for this purpose.

2. **Pradhan Mantri Jeevan Jyoti Bima Yojana (PMJJBY):** The central government of India has launched a new life insurance scheme, Pradhan Mantri Jeevan Jyoti Bima Yojana, for the growth of the poor and low-income section of society. As a pure term, insurance plan, Pradhan Mantri Jeevan Jyoti Bima Yojana, is available for people between the age group of 18–50 years.

   PMJJBY is a renewal term insurance policy that, provides a yearly life insurance coverage of ₹ 2,00,000 in case of the demise of the insured person, at the most affordable premium rate of ₹ 330 per annum. In order to help you know more about the policy, we have discussed some of the key features and benefits offered by the policy.

   **Salient Features**

   (i) The policy provides life coverage for 1 year.

   (ii) The insured can renew the policy every year.

   (iii) According to one's own choice, the insured can walk out of the scheme at any time and rejoin it in future.

   (iv) The policy offers a maximum sum assured of ₹ 2 lakh.

   (v) As compared to the other term insurance policy, the plan offers very low premium rates per year, i.e., ₹ 330. Moreover, the premium rate is equal for all age groups ranging from 18 to 50 years.

   (vi) The claim settlement process offered by the policy is very simple and subscriber friendly.

3. **Atal Pension Yojana:** Atal Pension Yojana (APY), a pension scheme for unorganized sector workers such as personal maids, drivers, gardeners, etc., was launched in June 2015 by the government. This social security scheme was introduced as a replacement to previous government's Swavalamban Yojana. APY aims to help these workers save money for their old age while they are working and guarantees returns post retirement. The scheme also promises a co-contribution by the central government of 50 per cent of the total prescribed contribution by a worker, up to ₹ 1,000 per annum, but only to those who joined APY before 31 December 2015. Further, this co-contribution would be made only for 5 years, from FY 2015–16 to 2019–20 in the eligible cases.

   **Eligibility:**

   1. An Indian citizen
   2. Have a valid bank account
   3. Are between 18 and 40 years of age.

4. **Varishtha Pension Bima Yojana:** Government of India in the Union Budget 2014-2015, announced the revival of Varishtha Pension Bima Yojana (VPBY). Thus, all those who subscribe to the VPBY during this period will receive an assured guaranteed return of 9 per cent under the policy. The scheme is administered through Life Insurance Corporation of India (LIC). Under the scheme, the subscribers on payment of a lump sum amount get pension at a guaranteed rate of 9 per cent per annum (payable monthly). Any gap in the guaranteed return over the return generated by the LIC on the fund is compensated by the Government of India by way of subsidy payment in the scheme. The scheme allows withdrawals of deposit amount by the annuitant after 15 years of purchase of the policy.

   **Pension Payment:** During the lifetime of pensioner, a pension in the form of immediate annuity as per mode chosen by the pensioner shall be payable.

5. **Life Cover under Pradhan Mantri Jan Dhan Yojana (PMJDY):** The Prime Minister on 15 August 2014 announced the PMJDY, a comprehensive program of financial inclusion, targeting the large number of people who are currently deprived of even rudimentary financial services. The PMJDY sets out to provide a basic Bank account to every family who till now had no account. The bank account comes with a RuPay debit card with a built-in accidental cover of ₹ 1 lakh.

6. **Rashtriya Swasthya Bima Yojana (RSBY):** The RSBY was launched in early 2008 and was initially designed to target only the BPL households, but has been expanded to cover other defined categories of unorganized workers, covering: (i) Building and other construction workers; (ii) registered with the Welfare Boards; (iii)licensed railway porters; (iv) street vendors; (v) MGNREGA workers who have worked for more than 15 days during the preceding financial year; (vi) beedi workers; (vii) domestic workers; (viii) sanitation workers; (ix) mine Workers; (x) rickshaw pullers; (xi)rag pickers and (xii) auto/taxi driver.

   The premium cost for enrolled beneficiaries under the scheme is shared by the government of India and the state governments.

7. **Employment State Insurance Scheme (ESIS):** The ESIS is an integrated measure of social insurance embodied in the Employees' State Insurance Act, and it is designed to accomplish the task of protecting 'employees' as defined in the Employees' State Insurance Act, 1948, against the impact of incidences of sickness, maternity, disablement and death due to employment injury and to provide medical care to insured persons and their families.

   The ESI Scheme applies to factories and other establishments, viz., road transport, hotels, etc. in which 10 or more persons are employed. However, in some states threshold limit for coverage of establishments is still 20. Employees of the aforesaid categories of factories and establishments, drawing wages up to ₹ 21,000/- a month, are entitled to social security cover under the ESI Act. ESI Corporation has extended the benefits of the ESI Scheme to the workers deployed on the construction sites located in the implemented areas under ESI Scheme from 1 August 2015.

   The ESI Scheme is financed by contributions from employers and employees. The rate of contribution by employer is 4.75 per cent of the wages payable to employees. The employees' contribution is at the rate of 1.75 per cent of the wages payable to an employee. Employees, earning less than ₹ 137/- a day as daily wages, are exempted from payment of their share of contribution.

8. **Central Government Health Scheme (CGHS):** Started in New Delhi in 1954, the 'Central Government Health Scheme' (CGHS) provides comprehensive health care facilities for the central government employees and pensioners and their dependents residing in CGHS covered cities.

   The Scheme provides comprehensive health care to the CGHS beneficiaries in India. The medical facilities are provided through Wellness Centres (previously referred to as CGHS Dispensaries)/ polyclinics under Allopathic, Ayurveda, Yoga, Unani, Sidha and homeopathic systems of medicines.

9. **Aam Aadmi Bima Yojana(AABY):** Aam Aadmi Bima Yojana, a social security scheme for rural landless household was launched on 2 October, 2007. The head of the family or one earning member in the family of such a household is covered under the scheme. The premium of ₹ 200/- per person per annum is shared equally by the Central Government and the State Government. The member to be covered should be aged between 18 and 59 years.

   A separate fund called 'Aam Aadmi Bima Yojana Premium Fund' has been set up by Central Govt. to pay the Govt. contribution. Fund is maintained by LIC. A free add-on benefit in the form of scholarship to children is also available under the Scheme.

   Merger of Social Security Schemes viz., Aam Aadmi Bima Yojana (AABY) and Janashree Bima Yojana (JBY) took place. The merged scheme was renamed 'Aam Aadmi Bima Yojana' which came into effect from 1 January 2013.

## GOVERNMENT PROGRAMMES FOR WOMEN AND CHILDREN

1. **Integrated Child Development Services (ICDS):** Launched on 2 October 1975, the ICDS Scheme is one of the flagship programmes of the Government of India and represents one of the world's largest and unique programmes for early childhood care and development. It is the foremost symbol of country's commitment to its children and nursing mothers, as a response to the challenge of providing pre-school non-formal education on one hand and breaking the vicious cycle of malnutrition, morbidity, reduced learning capacity and mortality on the other. The beneficiaries under the Scheme are children in the age group of 0–6 years, pregnant women and lactating mothers.

   Objectives of the Scheme are:

   (i) to improve the nutritional and health status of children in the age-group 0–6 years;

   (ii) to lay the foundation for proper psychological, physical and social development of the child;

   (iii) to reduce the incidence of mortality, morbidity, malnutrition and school dropout;

   (iv) to achieve effective coordination of policy and implementation amongst the various departments to promote child development and

   (v) to enhance the capability of the mother to look after the normal health and nutritional needs of the child through proper nutrition and health education.

2. **Umbrella Integrated Child Development Services:** Recently, rationalization, restructuring and continuation of four child centric schemes as 'Umbrella Integrated Child Development Services' Scheme have been approved by the government. Four schemes fall under it are:
   (i) Anganwadi Services (in place of ICDS);
   (ii) Scheme for Adolescent Girls (SAG) (in place of.SABLA);
   (iii) Child Protection Services (in place of Integrated Child Protection Scheme) and
   (iv) National Crèche Scheme (in place of Rajiv Gandhi National Crèche Scheme)

   **Anganwadi Services Scheme (Restructured):** Keeping in line with the Swachh Bharat Abhiyan, special emphasis has been given on providing toilet and safe drinking water facility at every Anganwadi Centre under the restructured Anganwadi Services Scheme. The scheme has been universalized with cumulative approval of 7,076 projects and 14 lakh Anganwadi Centres (AWCs) including 20,000 Anganwadis on demand. Digitization of WCs has already begun in eight states with ICTs enabled monitoring of the Schemes through smart phones/Tablets to Anganwadi worker and supervisor. A new Web portal has been created for enabling the MIS data entry by the states/UTs.

   The Ministry has taken an initiative to address the micronutrient deficiencies among women and children in the country. In this regard, fortification of food items with essential micronutrients has been made mandatory in the government funded nutrition-related schemes.

3. **Pradhan Mantri Matru Vandana Yojana (PMMVY):** The earlier Maternity Benefit Programme, for the eligible pregnant women and lactating mothers (PW&LM) has now been named as Pradhan Mantri Matru Vandana Yojana (PMMVY) a Centrally Sponsored Scheme, in January 2017 for providing partial compensation for the wage loss in terms of cash incentive so that the woman can take adequate rest before and after delivery of the first child. The cash incentive provided would lead to improved health seeking behaviour amongst the PW&LM. The Scheme envisages providing cash incentive substantially since 1990.
4. **Pradhan Mantri Ujjwala Yojana (PMUY):** PMUY was launched in May 2016, for providing LPG connections to 5 crore women belonging to the BPL families over a period of 3 years from 2016–17. The main mantra of this scheme is 'Swacch Indhan, Behtar Jeevan–Mahilaon ko mila samman'. The scheme aims to safeguard the health of women and children by providing them with a clean cooking fuel – LPG, so that they do not have to compromise their health in smoky kitchens or wander in unsafe areas collecting firewood.

   Launch of this scheme will also provide a great boost to the 'Make in India' campaign as all the manufacturers of cylinders, gas stoves, regulators and gas hose are domestic.
5. **Beti Bachao Beti Padhao (BBBP):** The scheme has been introduced for promoting survival, protection and education of girl child. It aims to address the issue of declining Child Sex Ratio (CSR) through a mass campaign targeted at changing social mind set and creating awareness about the criticality of the issue. The scheme launched in 2015 is a tri-ministerial, convergent

effort of Ministries of Women and Child Development, Health & Family Welfare and Human Resource Development with focus on awareness and advocacy campaign, multi-sectoral action, enabling girls' education and effective enforcement of Pre-Conception & Pre Natal Diagnostic Techniques (PC&PNDT) Act. The Scheme has been approved for expansion to cover all 640 districts in the country.

6. **e-dropbox:** The Women and Child Development Ministry came up with an online facility for children to complain about abuse in school, society or at home, keeping their identities secret. The e-dropbox that will let children express their problems about abuse, molestation or harassment in everyday situations.
7. **NARI Web Portal:** Union Minister for women and child development in January 2018 launched a Web portal, NARI, which will provide information on all government schemes for women. The portal carries details on 350 different schemes for women and will be updated from time to time. The schemes are divided into seven different categories – education, health, employment, housing and shelter, addressing violence, decision-making and social support.
8. **POCSO e-Box:** The Union Ministry of Women and Child Development has launched Protection of Children from Sexual Offenses (POCSO) e-box. The e-box is an online complaint management system for easy and direct reporting of sexual offences against children and timely action against offenders under POCSO Act, 2012. It is an initiative of National Commission for Protection of Child Rights (NCPCR), for direct online reporting of child sexual abuse.
9. **National Plan of Action for Children (NPAC):** The National Plan of Action for Children, 2016, is based on the principles embedded in the National Policy for Children 2013. It seeks to ensure convergence of ongoing programmes and initiation of new programmes so as to focus on pre-determined objectives through well-defined strategies and activities and achieve certain level of outcome.

The NPAC, 2016, takes into account the current priorities for children in India. It is an initiative to further strengthen and activate the implementation and monitoring of national constitutional and policy commitments and the UN Convention on the Rights of the Child. It provides a road map that links the Policy objectives to actionable programmes and strategies and identifies indicators for monitoring the progress.

The key programmes and schemes included in the NPAC 2016 are: BBBP; Child Protection Services (Previously ICPS); Dindayal Disabled Rehabilitation Scheme; Janani SurakshaYojana; Janani Shishu Suraksha Karyakram; Mid-Day Meal; Mahatma Gandhi National Rural Employment Guarantee Scheme; National Health Mission; National Nutrition Mission; Integrated Child Development Services (Including SABLA and Kishori Shakti Yojna); Maternity Benefit Programme (Matritva Sahayog Yojana); National Rural/Urban Drinking Water Mission; National Mental Health Programme; National AIDS Control Programme; Pradhanmantri Kaushal Vikas Yojna; Pradhan Mantri Surakshit Matritva Abhiyan; Rashtriya Madhyamik Shiksha Abhiyan; Rashtriya Bal Swasthya Karyakram; National Crèche Scheme; Rashtriya Kishor Swasthya Karyakram; Sarva Shiksha Abhiyan; Swachh Bharat Mission; Scholarship Schemes; Schemes under National Trust Act; UJJAWALA; National Welfare Fund for Sportspersons; National Playing Fields Association of

India and Scheme of Assistance for the creation of Urban Sports Infrastructure.

## LABOUR REFORMS IN INDIA

In India, labour reforms are due since long because the context in which laws and policies were framed has changed drastically. The Laws framed mainly to cater the manufacturing sector, do not address the problems of the service sector, which today, accounts the largest portion GDP. The outdated and inflexible nature of labour laws protects a handful of say 6–7 per cent of the workforce, seriously hampering employment generation capacity of the organized sector and most of the youth joining labour force every year, are forced to join informal economy, where the working conditions are pathetic and earnings are also abysmally.

It is imperative that labour reforms are viewed in a holistic manner so that India is able to gain demographic dividends by becoming manufacturing destination of the world owing to higher labour productivity, flexible labour market practices and lower labour cost without compromising on labour standards. It goes without saying that labour market liberalization is likely to augment employment flexibility, skill development and job creation on a wide scale. However, free market evangelists put excessive emphasis on the amendments in labour laws enabling the employers to hire, fire and regulate the terms and conditions of employment of the working population according to exigencies of emerging market scenarios. Such extreme position is not only misplaced but also a major roadblock in converting labour reforms as foundation of competitiveness in manufacturing and service sectors.

The attempts at reforming Indian labour market have been rather slow. Even the globalization and liberalization process that began in India in 1991 impacted labour market in limited manner. No wonder, India missed the opportunity of being manufacturing hub of the world due to rigidities in labour market, archaic labour laws and glaring skill deficit.

### ❖ Obstacles in Labour Market Reforms

Archaic labour laws are the greatest roadblocks in realization of an industry-friendly labour market in India. Labour laws continue to keep the workers' entitlements intact, whereas protective shield of the industry, which guarded the domestic industry players from competition has disappeared after 1991. Globalization and liberalization unleashed in 1991 allowed international players in Indian market thereby fundamentally changing the business and trade ecosystem. It is essential to have labour laws in sync with emerging trends such as casualization of labour, third-party employment, etc. At the same time, it is equally important to ensure that basic rights of the workers are protected and labour standards are implemented across industries and formal as well as informal sectors.

Significant skill shortage across the country has almost a crippling impact on Indian labour market. More than archaic labour laws, this factor makes the labour market quite unattractive especially for foreign direct investment. Even the large domestic players as well as entrepreneurs in micro-small and medium enterprises face the brunt of unavailability of skilled manpower. A study of Planning Commission (2001) indicated that only 10.1 per cent of the male workers and 6.3 per cent of female workers possessed specific marketable skills in the rural areas while only 19.6 per cent of male workers and 11.2 per cent of female workers had requisite skills in urban areas.

Lack of a holistic labour policy is a major obstacle in the way of developing a liberal labour market which can contribute towards making a competitive manufacturing and service industry eco-systems in the country.

Lack of flexibility: The ability to add or remove employees and to hire contract labour.

This has conventionally been interpreted as an attempt to exploit labour (through unfair contracts) and to bring in a hire and fire policy in which any employee can be fired at any time at the whim of the employer. Such a desire may well have been on the minds of many industrialists some years ago. However, the approach of organized industry – and, indeed, of many industry captains – has evolved, and today few of them are really looking at an open-ended hire and fire policy with regard to regular employees.

Women workers are the most disadvantaged in the labour market as they constitute a very high proportion among the low-skilled informal worker category, and are engaged in low-productivity and low-paying work. Owing to this, women earn very low wages, mostly piece rates in highly insecure jobs. In India, the gender gap in LFPR is more than 50 percentage points. The lower participation of women in economic activities adversely affects the growth potential of the economy.

## ❖ Objectives of Labour Reform

Any change in laws must obviously be determined by its purpose and objectives. In this case, there are multiple – fortunately non-contradictory – aims. These include:

1. Expanding employment opportunities. This is crucial, given that about 10 million people are entering the working age population every year.
2. Ensuring competitiveness, especially in the context of globalization and open markets, and promoting exports.
3. Establishing and enforcing the rights of all workers to fair, equitable and reasonable compensation; safe and comfortable working conditions; social security in the form of health care (including for their family) and post-retirement benefits; and safeguards against arbitrary dismissal or lay-off, with appropriate grievance redressal and independent appeal mechanisms.
4. Safeguarding workers' rights to organize and for collective bargaining.
5. Enhancing the capabilities and skills of individual workers, and thereby building the skill-base of the country.
6. Developing an atmosphere of trust and goodwill between management and workers, through an alignment of interests and active involvement and participation of workers in major decisions affecting the enterprise.
7. Encouraging entrepreneurship and the creation of new enterprises by minimizing obstacles; facilitating the early shut down of non-viable enterprises, downsizing and mergers with adequate compensation to workers who may be laid off.
8. **Ease of Doing Business is affected:** Employers contend that labour laws in India are excessively pro-worker in the organized sector. There is too much of inspection, and industries are looked upon with suspicion when comes to enforcing labour laws.
9. **Jobless Growth:** Economists, industry associations believe deceleration in employment growth in India is due to inflexibility in the labour market. The existing labour laws designed to protect employment and do not encourage employability.

## ❖ Changes Overdue in Labour Laws

1. **Labour to be shifted to 'State List':**

   Labour being in the concurrent list of the constitution, both central and state government legislate on it. However, the state governments have limited space to enact labour laws to address their own requirements – promoting investment and employment generation.

To give more economic independence to the state governments and promote federalism, FICCI strongly pleads for shifting labour to the state list, from existing concurrent list of the constitution.

2. **Multiplicity of Labour Laws:** Currently, there are 44 labour laws under the purview of the central government and more than 100 under the state governments, which deal with a host of labour issues. Unfortunately, these labour laws protect only 7–8 per cent of the organized sector workers employed at the cost of 93 per cent unorganized sector workers. The entire gamut of the labour laws should therefore be simplified, clubbed together wherever possible and made less cumbersome to make the environment more employment friendly.
3. Simplification of archaic laws

## ❖ Attempts of Labour Reforms

Launching of the Shram Suvidha Portal in October 2014 brought four major organizations under the Ministry of Labour and Employment to one platform. These are Office of Chief Labour Commissioner (Central), Directorate General of Mines Safety, Employees' Provident Fund Organization and Employees' State Insurance Corporation.

The portal has facilitated in brining transparency and accountability leading to better enforcement of the Labour Laws. Transparent Labour Inspection Scheme has reduced the discretionary powers of the Inspectors minimizing the harassment of employers.

**Legislative Reforms:** The second National Commission on Labour had recommended for the enactment of a special law for small manufacturing units and also that the existing Labour Laws should be broadly grouped into four or five Labour Codes on functional basis. Accordingly, the Ministry has taken steps for –

Drafting Small Factories Bill regulating the working and service conditions of workers in small manufacturing units employing less than 40 workers;

Drafting **four Labour Codes**- (a)Labour Code on Wages, (b)Labour Code on Industrial Relations, (c)Labour Code on Social Security & Welfare and (d) Labour Code on Safety & Working Conditions, by simplifying, amalgamating and rationalizing the relevant provisions of the Central Labour laws.

These reforms will help in catalysing the creation of employment opportunities in the country, without diluting basic aspects of safety, security and health provisions/standards for workers. Drafting of these legislations is in advanced stage.

## ❖ e-Biz Portal

The design of portal for Common Registration under 5 Labour Acts has been developed in association with Department of Industrial Policy & Promotion. The facility is to be formally launched shortly. The acts covered for common registration include:

- The Employees Provident Fund & Miscellaneous Provisions Act, 1952,
- The Employees State Insurance Act, 1948,
- The Building and Other Construction Workers (Regulation of Employment and Conditions of Service) Act, 1996,
- The Contract Labour (Regulation and Abolition) Act, 1970 and
- The Inter-State Migrant Workmen (Regulation of Employment and Conditions of Service) Act, 1979.

# LABOUR WELFARE

**Utilization of Building and Other Construction Workers (BOCW) Welfare Cess Funds:** Pursuant to the directions of the Hon'ble Supreme Court in W.P. (C) No. 318/2006, a national roadmap for utilization of Cess Fund at least to the tune of ₹ 3250.10 crore per annum has been finalized. Directions in this regard have been issued to the state/UTs under section 60 of the BOCW Act to utilize the Cess Fund in the manner prescribed there under for providing Social Security and other benefits to the BOC Workers.

**Revision of Bonded Labour Rehabilitation Scheme, 1978:** The proposal to increase in existing monetary assistance, last revised in 1995, of ₹ 20,000/- to the bonded labourers for their subsistence at the time of their release at present, is in consultation stage.

**Amendment to Contract Labour, Inter-State Migrant Workmen and BOCW Act:** The amendments to various provisions of the Building and Other Construction Workers (Regulation of Employment & Condition of Service) Act, 1996, the Contract Labour (Regulation and Abolition) Act, 1970, and the Inter-State Migrant Workmen (RECS) Act, 1979, are under consideration of the Ministry and the same are being dealt by the Labour Reforms Cell specially created for labour law reforms.

**Revision of Cess Rates:** Based on specific recommendationofCentralAdvisoryCommittees in respect of Beedi Workers, Iron/Manganese/ Chrome Ore Mines Workers and Limestone and Dolomite Mines Workers, the Ministry decided to move amendment proposal to the respective Cess Acts and enhance the Cess rates. The proposal is under submission.

**National Policy for Domestic Workers:** The National Policy for Domestic Workers has been drafted by Labour Welfare Bureau and is placed for consideration of the government before stakeholder/Inter-Ministerial consultation.

**Enhancing scales of benefits under various Welfare Schemes funded by the Cess Acts**

**Housing:** The RIHS 2007 has been proposed for revision to increase the subsidy amount from ₹ 40,000/- to 1,00,000/- per tenement. The proposal has been submitted to Secretary (Expenditure) for holding CNE appraisal meeting.

**Education:** Amount of Assistance for ITI education has been enhanced from ₹ 2,000/- to ₹ 10,000/-. Beneficiaries are presently getting this enhanced stipend.

**E-portal:** A national e-portal for online application and disbursement of scholarships has started for all students starting from class I to professional degree from September 2015.

**DBT:** Cash assistance under housing and scholarship schemes is now being transferred in electronic mode to the beneficiary account.

**Women:** The government has been taking measures to increase the participation of women in productive economic activities by schemes to provide support services to working women and also through legislative measures to enhance maternity benefits. Mahatma Gandhi National Rural Employment Guarantee Act (MGNREGA) is one of the important schemes which ensures participation by women in the economic activity by stipulating minimum 33 per cent participation by women. As per the Maternity Benefit (Amendment) Act, 2017, the women are entitled to enhanced maternity leave for a period of 26 weeks(6 months) working in registered establishment under any central or state law. For economic empowerment of women through promoting the spirit of creating self-employment ventures, *Mahila E-Haat*, an initiative for meeting aspirations and needs of women entrepreneurs has been launched with the objective to provide an e-marketing platform by leveraging technology for showcasing product made/manufactured/sold by women entrepreneurs/SHGs/NGOs.

## ❖ Code on Wage Bill, 2017

In order to implement labour law reforms, the Government in 2017 has undertaken the exercise of rationalization of the 38 Labour Acts by framing 4 labour codes, viz., Code on Wages, Code on Industrial Relations, Code on Social Security and Code on occupational safety, health and working conditions. The Codification of the Labour Laws will remove the multiplicity of definitions and authorities leading to ease of compliance without compromising wage security and social security to the workers.

The Code on Wages Bill, 2017, was introduced in Lok Sabha in August 2017, and it subsumes four existing Laws, viz., the Minimum Wages Act, 1948; the Payment of Wages Act, 1936; the Payment of Bonus Act, 1965; and the Equal Remuneration Act, 1976. After the enactment of the Code on Wages, all these four Acts will get repealed.

The Code will apply to establishments where any industry, trade, business, manufacturing or occupation is carried out. This will also include government establishments. The central government will make wage-related decisions for its authorities, and establishments related to railways, mines and oil fields among others. State governments will make decisions for any other establishments. Wages include salary, allowance or any other component expressed in monetary terms. This will not include bonus payable to employees or any travelling allowance, among others.

## ❖ Minimum Wage

1. **National minimum wage:** The central government may notify a national minimum wage for the country. It may fix different national minimum wage for different states or geographical areas.
2. The minimum wages decided by the central or state governments will not be lower than the national minimum wage. The central or state governments will not reduce the minimum wages fixed by them, if these wages are higher than the national minimum wage.
3. **Fixing the minimum wage:** The Code requires employers to pay at least the minimum wages to employees. These wages will be notified by the central or state governments. This will be based on time, or number of pieces produced, among others. The Code specifies that the central or state governments will review or revise the minimum wage every five years.
4. **Working hours:** The central or state governments will fix the number of hours that will constitute a working day. Further, they will provide for a day of rest for employees every week. An employee will receive overtime for working beyond these working hours on any day. This amount will be at least twice the normal wage of the employee.

## ❖ Payment of Wages

1. Wages will be paid in: (i) coins, (ii) currency notes, (iii) by cheque or (iv) through digital or electronic mode.
2. The wage period will be fixed by the employer as either: (i) daily, (ii) weekly, (iii) fortnightly or (iv) monthly.
3. Deductions: Under the Code, an employee's wages may be deducted on certain grounds including: (i) fines, (ii) absence from duty, (iii) accommodation given by the employer or (iv) recovery of advances given to the employee, among others. These deductions should not exceed 50 per cent of the employee's total wage.

## ❖ Payment of Bonus

1. **Determination of bonus:** The employer will pay each employee an annual bonus of at least: (i) 8.33 per cent of his wages or (ii) ₹ 100, whichever is higher. In addition, the employer will distribute a part of the gross profits amongst the employees (allocable surplus). This will be distributed in proportion to the wages earned by an employee during the year.
2. **Maximum bonus:** An employee can receive a maximum bonus of 20 per cent of his wages. This will include any amount distributed as allocable surplus. If this surplus exceeds the maximum

bonus payable to all employees in a year, a certain amount will be carried forward to the following years (up to four years). The amount carried forward will not exceed 20 per cent of the total wages payable to all employees during the year.

## ❖ Other key features

1. **Advisory boards:** The central and state governments will constitute their respective advisory boards. These boards will have representation from: (i) employees, (ii) employers and (iii) independent persons. Further, one-third of the total members will be women. The boards will advise the respective governments on aspects including: (i) fixation of minimum wages and (ii) increasing employment opportunities for women.
2. **Offences:** The Code specifies penalties for offences committed by an employer, such as – (i) paying less than the due wages or (ii) for contravening any provision of the Code. Penalties vary depending on the nature of offence, with the maximum penalty being imprisonment for three months along with a fine of up to ₹ 1 lakh.

## ❖ State Government Initiatives

Madhya Pradesh, Gujarat, Maharashtra and Rajasthan have taken positive steps towards reforming labour laws. Madhya Pradesh has expedited the process for registration and grant of licences under several legislations by introducing a maximum time period of 30 days within which, if an application is not rejected, it will be deemed to be registered. The Rajasthan Government initiated reforms in labour statutes. Companies can retrench up to 300 employees, up from 100 without seeking government permission. Now, it requires membership of 30 per cent of the total workforce for a union to obtain recognition in Rajasthan.

❑❑❑

# 15 CHAPTER

# Black Money or Parallel Economy

## INTRODUCTION

In common parlance, black money can be defined as assets or resources that have neither been reported to the public authorities at the time of their generation nor disclosed at any point of time during their possession. Black money economy is also called parallel economy.

National Institute of Public Finance and Policy (NIPFP) in its report of 1985 defined 'black income' as 'the aggregates of incomes which are taxable but not reported to the tax authorities'. Further, black incomes or unaccounted incomes are 'the extent to which estimates of national income and output are biased downwards because of deliberate, false reporting of incomes, output and transactions for reasons of tax evasion, flouting of other economic controls and relative motives'. As per NIPFP, parallel economy is about 75 per cent of GDP in 2013.

**National Institute of Public Finance and Policy (NIPFP)**

Based in New Delhi, NIPFP is a centre for research in public economics and policies. Founded in 1976, the institute undertakes research, policy advocacy and capacity building in areas related to public economics. One of the major mandates of the institute is to assist the central, state and local governments in formulating and reforming public policies by providing an analytical base.

Further, the white paper on 'black money' published in 2012 by the Ministry of Finance states that in addition to wealth earned through illegal means, the term black money would also include legal income that is concealed from public authorities:

(i) to evade payment of taxes (income tax, excise duty, sales tax, stamp duty, etc.);

(ii) to evade payment of other statutory contributions;

(iii) to evade compliance with the provisions of industrial laws such as the Industrial Dispute Act, 1947, Minimum Wages Act, 1948, Payment of Bonus Act, 1936, Factories Act, 1948, and Contract Labour (Regulation and Abolition) Act, 1970; and/or

(iv) to evade compliance with other laws and administrative procedures.

## BLACK MONEY GENERATION IN INDIA – METHODS

Black money is a cause of concern for the Indian economy and results in huge losses in tax revenues for the government. India is the fifth leading county among the developing nations in the world with total illicit financial flows of USD 344 billion from 2002 till 2011–12.

Black money generation in India primarily takes place through two sources. The first source includes those activities which are not permitted by the law, such as crime, drug trade, terrorism and corruption. The second is through a legally permissible activity but not accounted for and/or reported to public authorities which may result in tax evasion.

Tax evasion involves misreporting or non-reporting of the transactions in the books of account. The manipulation of financial statements results in the generation of unaccounted income that amounts to black money. Manipulation of financial statements can take place through two different methods:

1. **Out of Book Transactions:** One of the most widely adopted methods of tax evasion, generally prevalent among the small shops, unskilled or semi-skilled service providers, etc. Transactions that may result in taxation of receipts or income are not entered in the books of account by the taxpayer who either does not maintain books of account, or maintains two sets, or records partial receipts only. This method is a likely source of generation of black money across real estate, hotels, consumer markets, retailers, betting, etc.
2. **Manipulation of Books of Account:** In case of mandatory requirement to maintain books of accounts by taxpayers under different laws, manipulation of the books of accounts such as suppression or inflation of sales/receipts, manipulation of expenditure, capital, etc., is done to evade taxes. This method is a likely source of generation of black money across real estate, hotels, retailers and consumer markets.

### ❖ Key Sectors Impacted

About a third of India's black money transactions are believed to be in Real Estate, followed by Manufacturing, and purchase of Jewellery and Consumer Goods.

## ADMINISTRATIVE MECHANISM TO TRACE BLACK MONEY IN INDIA

With black money generation rampant across various sectors of the economy, the government has set up various administrative agencies to tackle its generation, the principal agencies being the Central Board of Direct Taxes (CBDT) and the Central Board of Excise and Customs (CBEC).

- **Central Board of Direct Taxes:** The CBDT and the I-T Department use tools of scrutiny assessment and information-based investigations for detecting tax evasion.

The Investigation Wing of the I-T Department carries out surveys to collect evidence of tax evasion. The department receives data relating to cash transactions in bank accounts, registered immovable property below the circle rate, and capital market transactions in the form of Annual Information Returns (AIR), which is analysed to identify cases of tax evasion. An Integrated Taxpayer Data Management System (ITDMS) is used for analysing data gathered from AIRs, permanent account number (PAN) database, I-T Department (ITD) applications, to unearth illegal transactions.

- **Central Board of Excise and Customs:** CBEC, including Commissionerates of Customs, Central Excise and Service Tax; Directorate of Revenue Intelligence (DRI); Directorate General of Central Excise Intelligence (DGCEI), etc. are all engaged in the administration of matters relating to Customs, Central Excise, Service Tax, etc.

DGCEI is responsible for detecting cases of evasion of Central Excise and Service Tax. The Directorate develops intelligence, especially in new areas of tax evasion through its intelligence network across the country and disseminates information in this respect by issuing Modus Operandi Circulars and Alert Circulars to apprise field formations of the latest trends in duty evasion. Wherever necessary, DGCEI on its own, or in coordination with field formations, organizes operations to unearth evasion of Central Excise Duty and Service Tax. DRI is responsible for handling matters relating to violations of customs laws and anti-narcotics law.

Other regulatory agencies undertaking supervision include the Directorate of Enforcement (ED); Financial Intelligence Unit (FIU-IND); Economic Offences Wing of the State Police, Central Bureau of Investigation (CBI), Serious Frauds Investigation Office (SFIO) and Narcotics Control Bureau (NCB).

Additionally, there are coordinating agencies such as the Central Economic Intelligence Bureau (CEIB), National Investigation Agency (NIA) and the High Level Committee (HLC), which also play an important role in fighting the menace of black money.

Central Vigilance Commission (CVC) is the principal Central Government anti-corruption watchdog; with anti-corruption units of the Central Bureau of Investigation (CBI) as its principal implementing arm. The Comptroller and Auditor General of India (CAG) also provides oversight for the Central Government and central PSUs, while the State Auditor General (AG) oversees the state government and its organizations.

In its efforts to track black money in the economy, the I-T department is gradually moving from regular search and survey operations to non-intrusive methods of data mining through electronic databases and information available through electronic portals of banking and other financial intermediaries. The department has also developed cyber forensics labs and various software tools for tracking black money.

- **Goods and Services Tax Network (GSTN):** The Cabinet has approved a proposal to set up a special purpose vehicle GSTN (GSTN SPV) for providing shared IT infrastructure and services to central and state governments, taxpayers, and other stakeholders for implementation of the goods and services tax (GST), both before and after the rollout of GST. During the pre-GST stage, the services would include taxpayer utility, common return submission along with tracking mechanism for inter-state trade, common tax payment gateway, common registration for states VAT and Central Sales Tax (CST) and central levies (central excise and service tax) and building interface between the GSTN Common Portal and state/centre tax systems. This system is expected to reduce cases of tax evasion.

## DIFFICULTIES IN TRACKING BLACK MONEY

'White paper on Black Money' states that the lack of effective data mining tools (used by the government) that can analyse possible cases of non-disclosure or tax evasion, is another factor acting as an impediment to reporting illegal money. For instance, the government does not have a robust database which contains information from all agencies and departments on monetary transactions and wealth generation.

Further, a large part of the Indian economy is unorganized and involves heavy use of cash transactions, which do not leave audit trails. The efforts aimed at regulating and controlling cash transactions have been in vain, largely due to a significant segment of the population being poor and hence deal in cash, particularly in rural parts of the country. Non-usage of mainstream banking channels (credit and debit cards and other instruments) for transactions hinders the tracking of illegal money exchange.

It has also been argued that auditors lack accountability when assessing income and reporting discrepancies. This effectively prevents the tracing of black money at source.

The key factors that prevent tracking and reporting of black money are discussed below:

1. Lack of adequate infrastructure
   (i) Economic Intelligence agencies technologically inept
   (ii) Lack of sufficient data mining tools and electronic reporting mechanisms.
   (iii) Absence of databases to capture foreign remittances, property and Jewellery transaction
   (iv) Lack of a central database integrated with information from all agency databases
2. Inefficient legal framework
   (i) Lack in effective implementation of existing laws
   (ii) Lack of strong legal support to agencies
   (iii) Money laundering laws not reviewed regularly
   (iv) Moderate regulatory and implementation laws for KYC
   (v) Absence of laws
3. Lack of training to the staff to identify or scrutinize black money.

## TECHNOLOGIES TO DETECT TAX EVASION AND BLACK MONEY

Technologies to detect Tax Evasion and Black Money may be as follow:

1. Standardization of Data and Reporting Formats
2. Electronic Bookkeeping
3. Cross seeding of unique Identifiers like PAN, CIN, VAT number, etc.
4. Bookkeeping of public projects through a common central IT system
5. Dematerialization of land records and property (commercial/residential/others)
6. Centralize documentation generation and reporting for exports and imports including banking transactions.

## BLACK MONEY ACT, 2015–AN ASSESSMENT

The Black Money (Undisclosed Foreign Income and Assets) Act, 2015, received the assent of the President on the 26 May 2015. The Act to make provisions to deal with the problem of the Black money that is undisclosed foreign income and assets, the procedure for dealing with such income and assets and to provide for imposition of tax on any undisclosed foreign income and asset held outside India and for matters connected to it.

### ❖ Salient Features

- **Scope:** The Act will apply to all persons residing in India. Provisions of the Act will apply to both undisclosed foreign income and assets (including financial interest in any entity).
- **Rate of tax:** Undisclosed foreign income or assets shall be taxed at the flat rate of 30 per cent. No exemption or deduction or set off of any carried forward losses which may be admissible under the existing Income-tax Act, 1961, shall be allowed.
- **Penalties:** Violation of the provisions of the proposed new legislation will entail stringent penalties. The penalty for

non-disclosure of income or an asset located outside India will be equal to three times the amount of tax payable thereon, i.e., 90 per cent of the undisclosed income or the value of the undisclosed asset. This is in addition to tax payable at 30 per cent. Failure to furnish return in respect of foreign income or assets shall attract a penalty of ₹ 10 lakh. The same amount of penalty is prescribed for cases where although the assessee has filed a return of income, but he has not disclosed the foreign income and asset or has furnished inaccurate particulars of the same.

- **Prosecution:** The Bill proposes enhanced punishment for various types of violations. The punishment for wilful attempt to evade tax in relation to a foreign income or an asset located outside India will be rigorous imprisonment from three years to ten years. In addition, it will also entail a fine. Failure to furnish a return in respect of foreign assets and bank accounts or income will be punishable with rigorous imprisonment for a term of six months to seven years.

  The same term of punishment is prescribed for cases where although the assessee has filed a return of income, but has not disclosed the foreign asset or has furnished inaccurate particulars of the same. The above provisions will also apply to beneficial owners or beneficiaries of such illegal foreign assets. Abetment or inducement of another person to make a false return or a false account or statement or declaration under the Act will be punishable with rigorous imprisonment from six months to seven years. This provision will also apply to banks and financial institutions aiding in concealment of foreign income or assets of resident Indians or falsification of documents.
- **Safeguards:** The principles of natural justice and due process of law have been embedded in the Act by laying down the requirement of mandatory issue of notices to the person against whom proceedings are being initiated, grant of opportunity of being heard, necessity of taking the evidence produced by him into account, recording of reasons, passing of orders in writing, limitation of time for various actions of the tax authority, etc. Further, the right of appeal has been protected by providing for appeals to the I-T Appellate Tribunal, and to the jurisdictional High Court and the Supreme Court on substantial questions of law. To protect persons holding foreign accounts with minor balances which may not have been reported out of oversight or ignorance, it has been provided that failure to report bank accounts with a maximum balance of up to ₹ 5 lakh at any time during the year will not entail penalty or prosecution. Other safeguards and internal control mechanisms will be prescribed in the Rules.
- **One time compliance opportunity:** The Bill also provides a one-time compliance opportunity for a limited period to persons who have any undisclosed foreign assets which have hitherto not been disclosed for the purposes of I-T. Such persons may file a declaration before the specified tax authority within a specified period, followed by payment of tax at the rate of 30 per cent and an equal amount by way of penalty. Such persons will not be prosecuted under the stringent provisions of the new Act. It is to be noted that this is not an amnesty scheme as no immunity from penalty is being offered. It is merely an opportunity for persons to come clean and become compliant before the stringent provisions of the new Act come into force.
- **Amendment of PMLA:** The Bill also proposes to amend Prevention of Money Laundering Act (PMLA), 2002 to include offence of tax evasion under the proposed legislation as a scheduled offence under PMLA.

## ❖ Merits

1. It mandates people to disclose their foreign accounts bringing them into public scrutiny. But the issue is black money is not stored in single accounts, it's layered and stored in benami accounts abroad.
2. Crimnial punishment will act as deterrent. Certainly, it will instil fear but that may be giving too much power to the tax agencies. It can be misused.

## ❖ Demerits

1. It does not address the issue of black money in India which is significantly more than in foreign accounts. Government intends to do that through the Benami Transactions Act.
2. It does not indicate measures to prevent layering and issue of benami foreign accounts.
3. The issue of storing money in foreign assets is unaddressed. Foreigners are itself used as benami.

These issues need to be addressed to make the bill effective but at the same time prevent undue harassment. Moreover, domestic black money should be tackled with similar vigour.

## ❖ Critical Appraisal

The act does not speak anything regarding tracking the black money. This is said to be the biggest lacuna in the Bill. The Undisclosed Foreign Income and Assets (Imposition of Tax) Bill, 2015, also known as the Black Money Bill does not have provisions to deal with domestic illegal assets and cash held on Indian soil. According to the provisions of the Bill, those declaring unaccounted income or assets will pay a flat 30 per cent tax and a similar penalty in return for not being prosecuted. The PMLA is also amended to help tax authorities pursue recovery through domestic assets as well in cases of those caught with overseas assets under the new black money law. The bill provides for the attachment of domestic property of those on the wrong end of the foreign assets law. The government is also planning to bring a law on Benami properties. Those abetting in stashing wealth overseas, including tax advisors, financial advisors, banks and financial institutions, will also face jail terms of up to seven years.

Experts say that the law will enhance the ability to trail the original source of funding and even attach properties even though the original owner can escape the law by stating that the property doesn't belong to him. Several thousands of such benami transactions are pending action due to loopholes in the law, but the revised bill has given more teeth to it for confiscation of such properties and curb generation of black money in the real estate sector, which is the root cause of unaccounted money in the system. As of now, experts point out, 35 per cent of land deal and high-end properties are transacted in cash and balance 65 per cent through legal channel. The bill will discourage the cash transaction and lead to a correction in property prices that have artificially soared.

## ❖ Benami Transactions (Prohibition) Amendment Act, 2016

The Benami Transactions (Prohibition) Amendment Act, 2016, came into effect from 1 November 2016. The amended law empowers the specified authorities to provisionally attach benami properties which can eventually be confiscated. Besides, if a person is found guilty of offence of benami transaction by the competent court, he shall be punishable with rigorous imprisonment for a term not less than one year but which may extend to 7 years and shall also be liable to fine, which may extend to 25 per cent of the fair market value of the property.

# IMPACTS OF BLACK MONEY ON INDIAN ECONOMY

The flow of black money can seriously affect the entire economic system of India.

Some important impacts are discussed here:

1. **Less Tax for the Government:** Many times, the Indian Government has failed to collect the estimated amount of tax because of big parallel economy.
2. **Uncontrollable Inflation:** When black money is out in the market, the amount of money in the system is higher than the normal causing rise in prices.
3. **Leads to Mass Poverty:** The common people get affected indirectly in so many ways by black money. The tax evaders are keeping the money in foreign countries. If all the black money in the tax havens is recovered and used by the Indian government, all the outstanding liabilities of the country could be paid off and money would still be left for spending.
4. **Lack of Technology:** Due to the existence of black money, India is facing the problem of shortage of capital. This has the direct impact on the up gradation of technology in all sectors.
5. **Impact on growth by moving investments on gold, stones and jewellery:** People who are looking to turn black money into white money are largely investing in precious metals like Gold and other jewellery.
6. **Corruption:** While corruption creates black money in the economy, it can also be a result of the growing underground market. People with black money are able to bribe the administrators and politicians to get what they want.
7. **Inflated Real Estate:** Generally, people involved in black money market are always ready to pay more for a piece of land as this helps in converting their coloured money to legal money.
8. **Transfer of Indian Funds Abroad to Safe Heavens:** The black money generated in India is kept in foreign tax havens. A tax haven is a jurisdiction that offers foreign individuals and businesses little or no tax liability. Tax havens also provide little or no financial information to foreign tax authorities. Individuals and businesses that do not reside a tax haven can take advantage of these countries' tax regimes to avoid paying taxes in their home countries.
9. **Encourages Anti-Social Activity:** Black money is always promoting anti-social activities in the society including activities like terrorism and organized crimes.

## SOME MEASURES SUGGESTED

1. Tax regime should be simple and stable so that an honest taxpayer is avoided from their web.
2. Tax laws should not offer unrestrained power to tax investigators that may dampen investment climate in the country.
3. Tax administration officers should be imparted skill for effective actions, they should be encouraged for foreign study tours to learn more about the international taxation.
4. India can also resolve the issue of black money with effective diplomatic talks with major tax heavens.
5. In view of the deterrent effect, the nature of all persons in whose cases penalties have been imposed for the concealment of income, wealth, etc. should be published in the gazette as well as in the press, giving details of their names, addresses and the amount of penalties, etc.
6. A special drive should be undertaken to arouse public conscience by enhancing the co-operation of the leaders in various walks of life.
7. People should be educated with regard to real object of collections of taxes through press, radio, TV and films.
8. Steps should be taken to convince the taxpayers that the money collected through taxes is not spent wastefully but put to proper use.

❑❑❑

# CHAPTER 16

# Climate Change and Sustainable Development

India ratified the Paris Agreement on climate change in October 2016. As on date, Paris Agreement has been ratified by 153 Parties. In the pre-2020 period, India's goal is to achieve the voluntary pledge of reducing the emissions intensity of GDP by 20–25 per cent over 2005 levels by 2020. The emissions intensity of India's Gross Domestic Product (GDP) has been reduced by 12 per cent between 2005 and 2010, according to India's first Biennial Update Report communicated to UNFCCC. As a responsible country, it has delivered on its commitments and is well on track to achieve its ambitious climate goals and actions by 2020.

**Paris Climate Conference (COP21)**

At the Paris Climate Conference (COP21) in December 2015, 195 countries adopted the first-ever universal, legally binding global climate deal.

The agreement sets out a global action plan to put the world on track to avoid dangerous climate change by limiting global warming to well below 2°C.

**Highlights**

1. **Mitigation: Reducing emissions**

   Governments agreed –

   (i) a long-term goal of keeping the increase in global average temperature to well below 2°C above pre-industrial levels;

   (ii) to aim to limit the increase to 1.5°C, since this would significantly reduce risks and the impacts of climate change;

   (iii) on the need for global emissions to peak as soon as possible, recognizing that this will take longer for developing countries;

   (iv) to undertake rapid reductions thereafter in accordance with the best available science.

   Before and during the Paris conference, countries submitted comprehensive national climate action plans (INDCs). These are not yet enough to keep global warming below 2°C, but the agreement traces the way to achieving this target.

*Contd...*

2. **Transparency and global stock take**

   Governments agreed to –
   - (i) come together every 5 years to set more ambitious targets as required by science;
   - (ii) report to each other and the public on how well they are doing to implement their targets;
   - (iii) track progress towards the long-term goal through a robust transparency and accountability system.

3. **Adaptation**

   Governments agreed to –
   - (i) strengthen societies' ability to deal with the impacts of climate change;
   - (ii) provide continued and enhanced international support for adaptation to developing countries.

4. **Loss and damage**

   The agreement also –
   - (i) recognizes the importance of averting, minimizing and addressing loss and damage associated with the adverse effects of climate change;
   - (ii) acknowledges the need to co-operate and enhance the understanding, action and support in different areas such as early warning systems, emergency preparedness and risk insurance.

5. **Role of cities, regions and local authorities**

   The agreement recognizes the role of non-party stakeholders in addressing climate change, including cities, other subnational authorities, civil society, the private sector and others.

   They are invited to:
   - (i) scale up their efforts and support actions to reduce emissions;
   - (ii) build resilience and decrease vulnerability to the adverse effects of climate change;
   - (iii) uphold and promote regional and international co-operation.

6. **Support**

   The EU and other developed countries will continue to support climate action to reduce emissions and build resilience to climate change impacts in developing countries.

   Other countries are encouraged to provide or continue to provide such support voluntarily.

   Developed countries intend to continue their existing collective goal to mobilize USD 100 billion per year by 2020 and extend this until 2025. A new and higher goal will be set for after this period.

However, the US announced on 1 June 2017 about its intention to withdraw from the Paris Agreement. The target, the USA had chosen under the Paris Agreement, is a cut in emissions by 26–28 per cent by 2025 compared to the 2005 level. The announcement is considered as a part of the unfolding of its own domestic energy polices in the last few years. The USA covers around 18 per cent of emissions and, therefore, its withdrawal does not affect the 55 per cent threshold number of the Paris Agreement.

**Carbon space occupied in 2009 (1850 as base year)**

- USA: 29 per cent
- Other developed countries: 45 per cent
- China: 10 per cent
- Other emerging economies: 9 per cent
- India: 3 per cent

## NATIONALLY DETERMINED CONTRIBUTION (NDC)

For the post-2020 period, India's NDC has outlined the actions India intends to undertake. India's NDC targets to lower the emissions intensity of GDP by 33–35 per cent by 2030 from 2005 levels, to increase the share of non-fossil-based power generation capacity to 40 per cent of installed electric power capacity (cumulative) by 2030, and to create an additional carbon sink of 2.5–3 Gt $CO_2$ through additional forest and tree cover by 2030.

**Five countries that emitted the most carbon dioxide in 2015**

Rank countries' $CO_2$ emissions from fuel combustion

1. China, 9040.74 (million metric tons)
2. United States, 4997.50 (million metric tons)
3. India, 2066.01 (million metric tons)
4. Russia, 1468.99 (million metric tons)
5. Japan, 1141.58 (million metric tons)

## SUSTAINABLE DEVELOPMENT GOALS (SDGs)

The 17 SDGs have 169 related targets to be achieved by 2030 and are expected to help organize and streamline development action for achievement of greater human well-being. Affordable, reliable and modern energy services are crucial to achieving all of the sustainable development goals, especially SDG 1: Eradicating poverty in all its forms everywhere. Hence, Goal No. 7 'Ensure access to affordable, reliable, sustainable and modern energy for all' – is central to every major challenge we face. Cleaner energy forms are imperative for delivering a sustainable development agenda.

## INTERNATIONAL SOLAR ALLIANCE (ISA)

On 30 November 2015, with India's initiative, the ISA was jointly launched by the Prime Minister of India and the French President Mr. in Paris at the 21st Conference of Parties to the UNFCCC (COP21). The ISA is conceived as a unique international body with an exclusive focus on solar energy with all its prospective member countries, which lie completely or partially between the Tropic of Cancer and Tropic of Capricorn, well endowed with the resource, striving to bring them together for coordinated research, low cost financing and rapid deployment. Joint efforts under the Alliance include innovative policies, projects, programs, capacity building measures and financial instruments to mobilize US$1 trillion of investment by 2030. The foundation stone of the ISA Headquarters was laid at Gwal Pahari, Gurgaon in Haryana.

## CURRENT ENERGY MIX

Within the energy mix of India, coal accounts for nearly 55 per cent of the total primary energy supply, followed by oil at 30 per cent and natural gas at 9 per cent. Only 2 per cent of total primary energy is supplied by renewable energy sources. Within the power sector, thermal power (particularly coal) dominates the share.

**Increase in generation of electricity (2016–17)**

| | |
|---|---|
| Thermal® | : increased by 5.3 per cent |
| Hydro | : reduced by 0.8 per cent |
| Nuclear | : increased by 1.3 per cent |
| Renewables | : increased by 24.5 per cent |

*Source*: Central Electricity Authority

## INDIA'S ENERGY SECURITY

India is at a stage of development that requires it to grow at a fast rate and lift the large number of their citizens from below the poverty line. Energy deprivation levels for a sizeable portion of population remain at high levels. The SDG 7 is to ensure access to affordable, reliable, sustainable and modern energy for all. The importance given to secure energy access is also due to the fact that access to energy is intertwined with the various other economic and social developmental objectives such as poverty alleviation, health, industrialization, education, provision of communication infrastructure and climate change mitigation among others.

Associated with the rapid increase in incomes is rapid increase in the demand for energy. However, the per capita energy consumption in India continues to be only around one-third of the global average and one-eleventh that in the United States.

Further, associated with the energy deprivation, there is also a lack of access to better forms of energy. An analysis of the type of fuel used for cooking by households in India would show that a majority of households still rely on firewood as fuel for cooking.

To improve the health of women and children in rural areas who are most affected by indoor air pollution due to use of bio-mass as cooking fuel, initiatives have been taken like Pradhan Mantri Ujjwala Yojana aimed at distribution of about 50 million LPG cylinders by 2018–19. The government has now planned to extend the scheme to provide 80 million LPG connections by 2020. The government is also coming out with other initiatives namely 'Ujjawala Plus' which will address the cooking needs of deprived people who are not covered under the Socio-Economic Caste Census (SECC) 2011. Pratyaksh Hastantrit Labh (PAHAL) scheme was introduced for direct transfer of LPG subsidies to the consumers' bank accounts. The Deen Dayal Upadhyaya Gram Jyoti Yojana (DDUGJY) was launched as its principal vehicle to achieve the goal of electricity for all by 2022, by first achieving 100 per cent village electrification by 2018.

## INDIA'S ACTIONS ON SUSTAINABLE DEVELOPMENT AND CLIMATE CHANGE

A large number of focused initiatives have been taken in various sectors of the economy to ensure a pathway of lower emission and climate resilient development. As stated earlier, India is on course to achieve its pre-2020 voluntary commitment. This has been possible with the commencement of various actions for implementation in the National Action Plan on Climate Change and taking it to the next level at the sub national level with State Action Plans on Climate Change.

While the 17 SDGs and 169 related targets have been globally adopted, each nation has the flexibility to develop indicators suitable to it. At the central government level, NITI Aayog has been assigned the role of overseeing the implementation of SDGs, while the Ministry of Statistics and Programme Implementation (MoSPI) is evolving the related national indicators. NITI Aayog has carried out a detailed mapping of the 17 Goals on Nodal Central Ministries, Centrally Sponsored Schemes (CSSs) including 'core of the core', 'core' and 'optional' schemes; on the government initiatives and also of each of the 169 targets on concerned Central Ministries. Several States/UTs have also carried out a similar mapping of the SDGs and related targets on their respective departments and programmes for faster implementation of SDGs.

Much of our national development agenda is mirrored in the SDGs, and therefore many of the government programmes and initiatives are already aligned with SDGs. Further, an impetus has been accorded to programmes related to ending poverty and creating infrastructure through higher budgetary allocations. Various goals and targets are highly interconnected; therefore, a push accorded to any specific goal or target also facilitates achievement of other goals and targets as well.

**Sustainable Development Goals (SDGs)**

In September 2015, the UN General Assembly adopted the 2030 Agenda for Sustainable Development that includes 17 Sustainable Development Goals (SDGs). Building on the principle of 'leaving no one behind', the new Agenda emphasizes a holistic approach to achieving sustainable development for all.

The Sustainable Development Goals (SDGs), otherwise known as the Global Goals, are a universal call to action to end poverty, protect the planet and ensure that all people enjoy peace and prosperity.

The 17 SDGs to transform our world are:

GOAL 1 : No Poverty
GOAL 2 : Zero Hunger
GOAL 3 : Good Health and Well-being
GOAL 4 : Quality Education
GOAL 5 : Gender Equality
GOAL 6 : Clean Water and Sanitation
GOAL 7 : Affordable and Clean Energy
GOAL 8 : Decent Work and Economic Growth
GOAL 9 : Industry, Innovation and Infrastructure
GOAL 10 : Reduced Inequality
GOAL 11 : Sustainable Cities and Communities
GOAL 12 : Responsible Consumption and Production
GOAL 13 : Climate Action
GOAL 14 : Life Below Water
GOAL 15 : Life on Land
GOAL 16 : Peace and Justice Strong Institutions
GOAL 17 : Partnerships to achieve the Goal

The goals are interconnected – often the key to success on one will involve tackling issues more commonly associated with another.

## ❖ India's Green Initiatives

1. **National Action Plan on Climate Change (NAPCC):** The government of India has been taking several steps in its action against climate change. The NAPCC, launched in June 2008, which includes eight national missions: Jawaharlal Nehru National Solar Mission, National Mission for Enhanced Energy Efficiency, National Water Mission, National Mission for a Green India, National Mission on Sustainable Habitat, National Mission for Sustainable Agriculture, National Mission for Sustaining the Himalayan Ecosystem and National Mission on Strategic Knowledge for Climate Change.
2. **National Green Corridor Programme:** To address the fluctuations/variability in the renewable power supply, the government in 2013 announced a National Green Corridor Programme (NGCP). The Power Grid Corporation

of India is developing the inter-state transmission corridor and the state transmission utilities are responsible for setting up and strengthening the intra-state transmission infrastructure. The interstate transmission projects of the green corridor are likely to be completed by 2018.

3. **R&D for Clean Coal Technologies:** In 2016, R&D Project for 'Development of Advanced Ultra Supercritical (Adv. USC) Technology for Thermal Power Plants' on a Mission Mode has been approved by the Cabinet Committee on Economic Affairs.
4. **National Green Highways Mission:** The Ministry of Road Transport and Highways has promulgated Green Highways (Plantations, Transplantations, Beautification and Maintenance) Policy, 2015, to develop green corridors along National Highways for sustainable environment and inclusive growth.
5. **Faster Adoption and Manufacturing of Hybrid & Electric Vehicles (FAME India):** Under FAME-India Scheme, under the National Electric Mobility Mission Plan for 2020, aims to promote eco-friendly vehicles.
6. **National Clean Energy and Environment Fund:** Through Finance Bill 2010–11 a corpus called National Clean Energy Fund (NCEF) was created out of cess on coal produced/imported ("polluter pays" principle) for the purposes of financing and promoting clean energy initiatives, funding research in the area of clean energy or for any other purpose relating to it. Subsequently, the scope of the Fund has been expanded to include clean environment initiatives also.

**Climate Insurance**

India is one of the world's most vulnerable countries to climate change, with its economic sectors highly exposed to the changing climate. Estimates indicate that currently, India incurs losses of about US$ 9–10 bn2 , annually, due to extreme weather events. Of these, nearly 80 per cent of losses remain uninsured.

In the agricultural insurance segment, there are few players with the most prominent being the public owned Agriculture Insurance Company of India Ltd. (AIC) followed by NABARD. While AIC is taking several innovative steps and launching products for niche segments – such as Rubber Plantation Insurance, Bio-Fuel Plants Insurance, Mango Weather Insurance, Potato Contract Farming Insurance, Rabi Weather Insurance, etc. – it is unable to effectively cover the entire agriculture sector

Weather Based Crop Insurance Scheme (WBCIS) is a unique Weather based Insurance Product designed to provide insurance protection against losses in crop yield resulting from adverse weather incidences. In 2016, the Pradhan Mantri Fasal Bima Yojna (PMFBY) was introduced.

## FINANCIAL SECTOR AND GREEN INITIATIVES

A number of initiatives have been taken in the Indian financial sector also, which among others include:

1. The Reserve Bank of India (RBI) has been conscious of the role of banks in providing finance for sustainable development.
2. A core of the financial policy in India is the Priority Sector Lending (PSL) requirement for banks to allocate 40 per cent of lending to key socially important sectors such as agriculture and

small and medium-sized enterprises. In 2015, the RBI included lending to social infrastructure and small renewable energy projects within the targets, thereby, giving a further fillip to green financing.

3. The RBI has also recently introduced market for trading priority sector lending obligations, incentivizing lower cost delivery.
4. New Development Bank (NDB), signed on 15 July 2014 in Fortaleza, Brazil, is the first Multilateral Development Bank established by developing countries and emerging economies – Brazil, Russia, India, China and South Africa (BRICS). NDB's objectives are in line with the BRICS countries' own development goals, with an increased focus on sustainable development and hence NDCs.
5. The external commercial borrowing (ECB) norms have been further liberalized so that green projects can tap this window for raising finance across the borders.
6. The Securities and Exchange Board of India (SEBI) has, in May 2017, put in place the framework for issuance of green bonds and the listing requirements for such bonds, which will help in raising funds from capital markets for green projects.
7. Large corporates integrating sustainability in their core businesses are included in the Bombay Stock Exchange's green indices, the GREENEX and CARBONEX. GREENEX was introduced in 2012 and comprises of 25 of India's biggest companies. The S&P BSE CARBONEX seeks to track the performance of the companies in the S&P BSE 100, based on their commitment to mitigating risks arising from climate change in the long run.
8. Companies Act, 2013, directs companies having a certain level of profits, to spend 2 per cent of their annual profit on Corporate Social Responsibility (CSR) activities.

## IMPORTANT TERMS

### ❖ Carbon Credit

It is a permit that gives a company, country, etc. the right to emit a specified amount of carbon compounds into the atmosphere, and may be purchased if emissions are expected to exceed a quota or sold if the quota is not reached. The carbon credit system was a solution as people became more aware that human industrial activity is potentially responsible for global warming and environmental degradation.

### ❖ Green GDP

Green GDP means the GDP after adjusting for environmental damage. The heart of the Green GDP approach lies in the belief that nature and market are not mutually exclusive variables. In fact, both of them have a deep interconnected relationship. Natural resources fuel market growth and excessive market growth has the potential to destroy natural resources.

### ❖ Green Economy

The green economy is defined as an economy that aims at reducing environmental risks and ecological scarcities, and that aims for sustainable development without degrading the environment.

UNEP has defined the green economy as "one that results in improved human well-being and social equity, while significantly reducing environmental risks and ecological scarcities. It is low carbon, resource efficient, and socially inclusive".

## ❖ Green Energy

Green energy includes natural energy making processes that can be harnessed with little pollution. Green power is electricity generated from renewable energy sources.

## ❖ Green Accounting

Green accounting is a type of accounting that attempts to factor environmental costs into the financial results of operations.

## ❖ Green Bond

A green bond is like any other regular bond but with one key difference: the money raised by the issuer is earmarked towards financing 'green' projects, i.e., assets or business activities that are environment-friendly. Such projects could be in the areas of renewable energy, clean transportation and sustainable water management. It is tax-exempted bond. The tax-exempt status makes purchasing a green bond a more attractive investment compared to a comparable taxable bond, providing a monetary incentive to tackle prominent social issues such as climate change and a movement to renewable sources of energy.

❑❑❑

# CHAPTER 17 Goods and Services Tax (GST)

## MEANING OF GST

Goods and Services Tax (GST) is a comprehensive tax levy on manufacture, sale and consumption of goods and service at a national level. GST is a tax on goods and services with value addition at each stage having comprehensive and continuous chain of set-of benefits from the producer's/ service provider's point up to the retailer's level where only the final consumer should bear the tax.

The GST which has been implemented on 1 July 2017 is a destination-based tax. Destination-based tax (consumption tax) is levied where goods and services are consumed. This implies that all SGST collected will generally accrue to the state where the consumer of the goods or services sold resides. This simply means that the producing state gets nothing if produced goods are sold outside that state.

There are several implications of this including:

1. Destination based GST would be very much beneficial for the states which consume more goods/services than they produce. The more they consume the more revenue they get from inter-state trade but such benefits that *come via increased consumption* are not good for overall economy of the state.
2. The destination based tax may not be very encouraging for the states which produce these goods because nothing will accrue to them.
3. To discourage consumption, some states might put restriction on inter-state movement of goods. Such move might adversely affect the economy.

### ❖ Salient Features of GST

The salient features of GST are as under:

- **Destination based consumption tax:** The GST would be applicable on the supply of goods or services as against the present concept of tax on the manufacture or sale of goods or provision of services. It would be a destination based consumption tax. This means that tax would accrue to the state or the Union Territory (UT) where the consumption takes place.
- **Dual GST:** It would be a dual GST with the centre and states simultaneously levying tax on a common tax base. The GST to be levied by the Centre on intra-State supply of goods or services would be called the Central Goods and Services Tax (CGST) and that to be levied by the states including UTs with legislature/UTs without legislature would be called the state tax (SGST)/ UT tax (UTGST) respectively.

- **Exceptions under GST:** The GST would apply to all goods other than alcoholic liquor for human consumption and five petroleum products, viz. petroleum crude, motor spirit (petrol), high speed diesel, natural gas and aviation turbine fuel. It would apply to all services barring a few to be specified.
- **Subsumed taxes:** The GST would replace the following taxes currently levied and collected by the centre:
  - Central Excise Duty
  - Duties of Excise (Medicinal and Toilet Preparations)
  - Additional Duties of Excise (Goods of Special Importance)
  - Additional Duties of Excise (Textiles and Textile Products)
  - Additional Duties of Customs (commonly known as CVD)
  - Special Additional Duty of Customs (SAD)
  - Service Tax
  - Central Surcharges and Cesses so far as they relate to supply of goods and services
- State taxes that would be subsumed under the GST are:
  - State VAT
  - Central Sales Tax
  - Luxury Tax
  - Entry Tax (all forms)
  - Entertainment and Amusement Tax (except when levied by the local bodies)
  - Taxes on Advertisements
  - Purchase Tax
  - Taxes on Lotteries, Betting and Gambling
  - State Surcharges and Cesses so far as they relate to supply of goods and services
- The list of exempted goods and services would be common for the centre and the states.
- **Threshold Exemption:** Taxpayers with an aggregate turnover in a financial year up to ₹ 40 lakhs would be exempt from tax. Aggregate turnover shall be computed on all India basis. For 11 special category states, like those in the north-east and the hilly states, the exemption threshold shall be ₹ 10 lakhs. All taxpayers eligible for threshold exemption will have the option of paying tax with Input Tax Credit (ITC) benefits. Taxpayers making inter-state supplies or paying tax on reverse charge basis shall not be eligible for threshold exemption.
- **Composition levy:** Small taxpayers with an aggregate turnover in a financial year up to ₹ 75 lakhs shall be eligible for composition levy. Under the scheme, a taxpayer shall pay tax as a percentage of his turnover during the year without the benefit of ITC. The rate of tax for CGST and SGST/UTGST each shall not exceed:
  - 2.5 per cent in case of restaurants etc.
  - 1 per cent of the turnover in a state/UT in case of a manufacturer
  - 0.5 per cent of the turnover in state/UT in case of other suppliers.
- **Limit to composition scheme:** A taxpayer opting for composition levy shall not collect any tax from his customers nor shall he be entitled to claim any ITC. The composition scheme is optional. Taxpayers making inter-state supplies shall not be eligible for composition scheme. The government, may, on the recommendation of GST Council, increase the threshold for the scheme to up to rupees 1 crore.
- **IGST:** An Integrated tax (IGST) would be levied and collected by the Centre on inter-state supply of goods and services. Accounts would be settled periodically between the centre and the states to ensure that the SGST/UTGST portion of IGST is transferred to the destination state where the goods or services are eventually consumed.

- **Use of ITC:** Taxpayers shall be allowed to take credit of taxes paid on inputs (ITC) and utilize the same for payment of output tax. However, no ITC on account of CGST shall be utilized towards payment of SGST/UTGST and *vice versa*. The credit of IGST would be permitted to be utilized for payment of IGST, CGST and SGST/UTGST in that order.
- **HSN Code:** Harmonised System of Nomenclature (HSN) code shall be used for classifying the goods under the GST regime. Taxpayers whose turnover is above ₹ 1.5 crore but below ₹ 5 crore shall use -2digit code and the taxpayers whose turnover is ₹ 5 crore and above shall use -4digit code. Taxpayers whose turnover is below ₹ 1.5 crore are not required to mention HSN Code in their invoices.
- **SEZ:** Exports and supplies to SEZ shall be treated as zero-rated supplies. The exporter shall have an option to either pay output tax and claim its refund or export under bond without tax and claim refund of ITC.
- **GST on Export and Import:** Import of goods and services would be treated as inter-state supplies and would be subject to IGST in addition to the applicable customs duties. The IGST paid shall be available as ITC for further transactions.
- **Refund:** Time limit for claiming online refund has been increased from 1 year to 2 years. Refund shall be granted within 60 days from the date of receipt of complete application. Interest is payable if refund is not sanctioned within the stipulated period of 60 days. If the refund claim is less than ₹ 2 lakhs, there is no need for the claimant to furnish any documentary evidence to prove that he has not passed on the incidence of tax to any other person. Only a self-certification to this effect would suffice. Refund of ITC shall be allowed in case of exports or where the credit accumulation is on account of inverted duty structure (i.e. where the tax rate on output is higher than that on inputs).
- **Demands:** A new concept of sunset clause for tax disputes has been introduced. It provides that Adjudication order shall be issued within 3 years of filing of annual return in normal cases and the time limit is 5 years (from the date of filing of annual return) in fraud/suppression cases. SCN will have to be issued at least 3 months prior to the time limit prescribed for issue of adjudication order in normal cases and at least 6 months prior to the time limit prescribed for issue of adjudication order in cases involving fraud/suppression etc. Penalty is nil or minimal if the tax short paid/non-paid is deposited along with interest at the stage of audit/investigation.
- **ITC:** Taxpayer is allowed to take credit of taxes paid on inputs (ITC), as self-assessed, in his return. Taxpayer can take credit of taxes paid on all goods and services, other than a few items in the negative list, and utilize the same for payment of output tax. Credit of taxes paid on inputs can be taken where the inputs are used for business purposes or for making taxable supplies. Full ITC shall be allowed on capital goods on its receipt as against the current Central Government and many State Government practice of staggering the credit in more than one instalment. Unutilized ITC can be carried forward. The facility of distribution of ITC for services among group companies has been provided for through the mechanism of Input Service Distributor (ISD).
- **Advance Rulings:** Advance ruling mechanism has been continued under the GST law. The salient features are as under:
  - Advance ruling can be sought in respect of more subjects than allowed at present. The subjects are classification of goods/or services, time and value of supply, rate of tax, admissibility of ITC, liability to

pay tax, liability to take registration and whether a particular transaction amounts to a supply under GST law.

– Advance ruling can be sought not only for new activities but also for existing activities. The facility of appeal, which is not there under the central law, has been provided in the GST Law.

– The applicants or the Department, if aggrieved by the advance ruling, would henceforth get the opportunity to file an appeal before the Appellate Authority for revision of the ruling. Advance Ruling can be obtained more easily as there will be one Advance Ruling Authority (as also the Appellate Authority) in every state.

- **Valuation:** Valuation of goods shall be done on the basis of transaction value i.e., the invoice price, which is the current practice under the Central Excise and Customs Laws. Taxpayers are allowed to issue supplementary or revised invoice in respect of a supply made earlier.
- **New modes of payment:** New modes of payment of tax are being introduced, viz. through credit and debit cards, National Electronic Fund Transfer (NEFT) and Real Time Gross Settlement (RTGS).
- **E-commerce:** E-commerce companies are required to collect tax at source in relation to any supplies made through their online platforms, under fulfilment model, at the rate notified by the Government.
- **Anti-profiteering measure:** An anti-profiteering measure has been incorporated in the GST law to ensure that any benefits on account of reduction in tax rates results in commensurate reduction in prices of such goods/services.
- **Margin Scheme:** Rule 32(5) of the CGST Rules, 2017 provides that where a taxable supply is provided by a person dealing in buying and selling of second hand goods i.e., used goods as such or after such minor processing which does not change the nature of the goods and where no ITC has been availed on the purchase of such goods, the value of supply shall be the difference between the selling price and the purchase price and where the value of such supply is negative, it shall be ignored. This is known as the margin scheme.

## MINIMAL INTERFACE

The physical interface between the taxpayer and the tax authorities would be minimal under GST. Certain important provisions in this regard are as follows:

1. There will be cross-empowerment of officers belonging to central and state governments. Officer of CGST will be empowered to act as proper officer of SGST and vice versa.
2. Registration will be granted on line and shall be deemed to have been granted if no deficiency is communicated to the applicant within three common working days by the tax administration which has been allotted the examination of the application. Such allotment is to be done one each alternately between the central and the state tax administration.
3. Taxable person shall himself assess the taxes payable (self-assessment) and credit it to the account of the government. The return filed by the tax payer would be treated as self-assessed.
4. Payment of tax shall be made electronically through internet banking, or also through credit card and through the modes of RTGS or NEFT. Smaller taxpayers shall be allowed to pay tax over the bank counter. All challans for payment of tax shall be generated online on the Goods and Services Tax Network (GSTN).

5. The taxpayer shall furnish the details of outward supplies electronically without any physical interface with the tax authorities. Inward supply details would be auto-drafted from the supply details filed by the corresponding suppliers.
6. Taxpayers shall file, electronically, monthly returns of outward and inward supplies, ITC availed, tax payable, tax paid and other prescribed particulars. Composition taxpayers shall file, electronically, quarterly returns. Omission/incorrect particulars can be self-rectified before the last date of filing of return for the month of September of the following year or the actual date of filing of annual return, whichever is earlier.
7. For mismatched invoices, reversal and reclaim of ITC shall be done electronically on the GSTN portal without any tax payer contact. This electronic system would also prevent, inter alia, ITC being taken on the basis of fake invoices or twice on the same invoice.
8. Taxpayers shall be allowed to keep and maintain accounts and other records in electronic form.

**Constitutional (101st Amendment) Act, 2016**

The GST Constitutional (101st Amendment) Act, 2016, contains the provisions for the implementation of GST Regime through 20 amendments. The amendments would subsume a number of indirect taxes presently being levied by central and state governments into GST thereby doing away the cascading of taxes and providing a common national market for goods and services. The aim of the amendments in the Constitution is to confer simultaneous power on Parliament and state legislatures to make laws for levying GST simultaneously.

Highlights of the amendments are as follow:

**I. Article 246 A:** This is a new article inserted in the constitution. It says that: (1) Notwithstanding anything contained in articles 246 and 254, Parliament, and, subject to clause (2), the legislature of every state, have power to make laws with respect to goods and services tax imposed by the union or by such state; (2) Parliament has exclusive power to make laws with respect to goods and services tax where the supply of goods, or of services, or both takes place in the course of inter-state trade or commerce.

Article 246A contents that:

(a) Both union and states in India now have 'concurrent powers' to make law with respect to goods & services

(b) The intra-state trade now comes under the jurisdiction of both centre and state; while inter-state trade and commerce is 'exclusively' under central government jurisdiction.

**II. Article 269A:** This is also a new article which states that: (1) Goods and services tax on supplies in the course of inter-state trade or commerce shall be levied and collected by the Government of India and such tax shall be apportioned between the union and the states in the manner as may be provided by Parliament by law on the recommendations of the Goods and Services Tax Council.

Explanations

1. For the purposes of this clause, supply of goods, or of services, or both in the course of import into the territory of India shall be deemed to be supply of goods, or of services, or both in the course of inter-state trade or commerce.

*Contd...*

2. The amount apportioned to a state under clause (1) shall not form part of the Consolidated Fund of India.
3. Where an amount collected as tax levied under clause (1) has been used for payment of the tax levied by a state under Article 246A, such amount shall not form part of the Consolidated Fund of India.
4. Where an amount collected as tax levied by a state under Article 246A has been used for payment of the tax levied under clause (1), such amount shall not form part of the Consolidated Fund of the State.
5. Parliament may, by law, formulate the principles for determining the place of supply, and when a supply of goods, or of services, or both takes place in the course of inter-state trade or commerce'.

Importance of Article 269A:

(a) In case of the inter-state trade, the tax will be levied and collected by the Government of India and shared between the union and states as per recommendation of the GST Council.

(b) The proceeds such collected will not be credited to the Consolidated Fund of India or state but respective share shall be assigned to that state or centre. The reason for the same is that under GST, where centre collects the tax, it assigns state's share to state, while where state collects tax, it assigns centre's share to centre. If that proceed is deposited in Consolidated Fund of India or state, then, every time there will be a need to pass an appropriation tax. Thus, under GST, the apportionment of the tax revenue will take place outside the Consolidated Funds.

**III. Article 279-A:** This Article provides for constitution of a GST council.

The GST council will constitute the following members:

(a) Union Finance Minister as chairman of the council

(b) Union minister of state in charge of revenue or finance

(c) One nominated member from each state who is in charge of finance or taxation

The GST council will be empowered to take decisions on the following:

(a) The taxes, cesses and surcharges levied by the union, the states and the local bodies which may be subsumed in the goods and services tax;

(b) The goods and services that may be subjected to, or exempted from, the goods and services tax;

(c) Model Goods and Services Tax Laws, principles of levy, apportionment of integrated goods and services tax and the principles that govern the place of supply;

(d) The threshold limit of turnover below which goods and services may be exempted from goods and services tax;

(e) The rates including floor rates with bands of goods and services tax;

(f) Any special rate or rates for a specified period, to raise additional resources during any natural calamity or disaster;

(g) Special provision with respect to the states of Arunachal Pradesh, Assam, Jammu and Kashmir, Manipur, Meghalaya, Mizoram, Nagaland, Sikkim, Tripura, Himachal Pradesh and Uttarakhand; and

*Contd...*

(h) Any other matter relating to the goods and services tax, as the council may decide.

(i) All decisions taken at the GST council will be taken based on voting. Process of voting is clearly articulated in detail in the constitutional amendment bill.

**IV. Changes in the 7th Schedule:** This amendment has made following changes in 7th schedule of the constitution:

Union List:

(a) The entry 84 of union list earlier comprised the duties on tobacco, alcoholic liquors, opium, Indian hemp, narcotic drugs and narcotics, medical and toilet preparations. After this amendment, it will comprise of Petroleum crude, high speed diesel, motor spirit (petrol), natural gas, and aviation turbine fuel, tobacco and tobacco products. Thus, these are now out of ambit of GST and subject to union jurisdiction.

(b) Entry 92 (newspapers and on advertisements published therein) has been deleted thus, they are now under GST.

(c) Entry 92-C (Service Tax) has been now deleted from union list.

State List:

(a) Under State list, entry 52 (entry tax for sale in state) has been deleted.

(b) In Entry 54, Taxes on the sale or purchase of goods other than newspapers, subject to the provisions of Entry 92-A of List I.; has been now replaced by Taxes on the sale of petroleum crude, high speed diesel, motor spirit (commonly known as petrol), natural gas, aviation turbine fuel and alcoholic liquor for human consumption, but not including sale in the course of inter-State trade or commerce or sale in the course of international trade or commerce of such goods.

(c) Entry 55 (advertisement taxes) have been deleted.

(d) Entry 62 (taxes on luxuries, including taxes on entertainments, amusements, betting and gambling) has been replaced by these taxes only to be levied by local governments, panchayats, municipality, regional council or district council.

**V. Other Important amendments in existing articles**

(a) The residuary power of legislation of Parliament under article 248 is now subject to article 246A.

(b) Article 249 has been changed so that if 2/3rd majority resolution is passed by Rajya Sabha, the Parliament will have powers to make necessary laws with respect to GST in national interest.

(c) Article 250 has been amended so that parliament will have powers to make laws related to GST during emergency period.

(d) Article 268 has been amended so that excise duty on medicinal and toilet preparation will be omitted from the state list and will be subsumed in GST.

(e) Article 268A has been repealed so now service tax is subsumed in GST.

(f) Article 269 would empower the parliament to make GST related laws for inter-state trade/commerce.

Notably, the amendment also provides that Parliament shall, by law, on the recommendation of the Goods and Services Tax Council, provide for compensation to the states for loss of revenue arising on account of implementation of the goods and services tax for a period of 5 years. This resulted into the Compensation Cess Bill.

## GST COUNCIL AND SECRETARIAT

The Union Cabinet in its meeting held on 12 September 2016 approved setting-up of GST Council and setting-up of its secretariat. The cabinet took following decisions:

1. Creation of the GST Council as per Article 279A of the amended Constitution;
2. Creation of the GST Council Secretariat, with its office at New Delhi;
3. Appointment of the secretary (revenue) as the *ex officio* secretary to the GST Council;
4. Inclusion of the chairperson, Central Board of Excise and Customs (CBEC), as a permanent invitee (non-voting) to all proceedings of the GST Council;
5. Create one post of additional secretary to the GST Council in the GST Council Secretariat (at the level of Additional Secretary to the Government of India), and four posts of commissioner in the GST Council Secretariat (at the level of Joint Secretary to the Government of India).

The GST Council Secretariat shall be manned by officers taken on deputation from both the central and state governments.

The GST Council shall make recommendations to the union and the states on important issues related to GST, like the goods and services that may be subjected or exempted from GST, GST Laws, principles that govern place of supply, threshold limits, GST rates including the floor rates with bands, special rates for raising additional resources during natural calamities/disasters, special provisions for certain states, etc. The GST Council shall establish a mechanism to adjudicate disputes arising out of its recommendation or implementation thereof.

### GST Related Four Bills Passed by Parliament

The Parliament in April 2017 passed the following four GST related bills:

1. The Central Goods and Services Tax Bill 2017 (The CGST Bill)
2. The Integrated Goods and Services Tax Bill 2017 (The IGST Bill)
3. The UT Goods and Services Tax Bill 2017 (The UTGST Bill)
4. The Goods and Services Tax (compensation to the states) Bill 2017 (The Compensation Bill)

The above four bills have been earlier approved by the GST Council after thorough, clause by clause, discussion over 12 meetings of the council held in the last 6 months.

The CGST Bill makes provisions for levy and collection of tax on intra-state supply of goods or services for both by the Central Government. On the other hand, IGST Bill makes provisions for levy and collection of tax on inter-state supply of goods or services or both by the central government.

The UTGST Bill makes provisions for levy on collection of tax on intra-UT supply of goods and services in the UTs without legislature. The UT GST is akin to States Goods and Services Tax (SGST) which shall be levied and collected by the states/UTs on intra-state supply of goods or services or both.

The compensation bill provides for compensation to the states for loss of revenue arising on account of implementation of the goods and services tax for a period of 5 years as per section 18 of the constitution (One Hundred and First Amendment) Act, 2016.

## GOODS AND SERVICES TAX NETWORK

GSTN has been set up by the government as a private company under erstwhile Section 25 of the Companies Act, 1956. GSTN would provide three front end services, namely registration, payment and return to taxpayers. Besides providing these services to the taxpayers, GSTN would be developing back-end IT modules for 25 states that have opted for the same. The migration of existing taxpayers has already started from November, 2016. The revenue departments of both centre and states are pursuing the presently registered taxpayers to complete the necessary formalities on the IT system operated by GSTN for successful migration.

GSTN has selected 34 IT, ITeS and financial technology companies, to be called GST Suvidha Providers (GSPs). GSPs would develop applications to be used by taxpayers for interacting with the GSTN.

## NATIONAL ANTI-PROFITEERING AUTHORITY

The Government in November 2017 approved the constitution of a National Anti-Profiteering Authority (NAA) – the institutional mechanism under the GST law to check the unfair profit-making activities by the trading community. The government appointed senior IAS officer BN Sharma as its first chairman.

The National Anti-Profiteering Authority is a five-member committee consisting of a Chairman who holds or has held a post equivalent in rank to a secretary to the Government of India; and four technical members who are or have been commissioners of state tax or central tax or have held an equivalent post under existing laws. The additional director general of safeguards under the CBEC (board) shall be the secretary to the authority.

The authority shall cease to exist after the expiry of 2 years from the date on which the chairman enters upon his office unless the council recommends otherwise.

## DUTIES OF THE AUTHORITY

The authority would have the following duties:

1. to determine whether any reduction in the rate of tax on any supply of goods or services or the benefit of ITC has been passed on to the recipient by way of commensurate reduction in prices;
2. to identify the registered person who has not passed on the benefit of reduction in the rate of tax on supply of goods or services or the benefit of ITC to the recipient by way of commensurate reduction in prices;
3. to order:
   (i) reduction in prices;
   (ii) return to the recipient, an amount equivalent to the amount not passed on by way of commensurate reduction in prices along with interest at the rate of eighteen per cent. From the date of collection of the higher amount till the date of the return of such amount or recovery of the amount not returned, as the case may be, in case the eligible person does not claim return of the amount or is not identifiable, and depositing the same in the Consumer Welfare Fund;
   (iii) imposition of penalty and
   (iv) cancellation of registration.

**Background:** The 'anti-profiteering' measures enshrined in the GST law provide an institutional mechanism to ensure that the full benefits of ITCs and reduced GST rates on supply of goods or services flow to the consumers. This institutional framework comprises the NAA, a standing committee, screening committees in every state and the directorate general of safeguards in the Central Board of Excise & Customs (CBEC).

Affected consumers who feel the benefit of commensurate reduction in prices is not being passed on when they purchase any goods or services may apply for relief to the screening committee in the particular state. However, in case the incident of profiteering relates to an item of mass impact with 'All India' ramification, the application may be directly made to the standing committee. After forming a *prima facie* view that there is an element of profiteering, the standing committee shall refer the matter for detailed investigation to the Director General of Safeguards, CBEC, which shall report its findings to the NAA.

In the event the NAA confirms there is a necessity to apply anti-profiteering measures, it has the authority to order the supplier/business concerned to reduce its prices or return the undue benefit availed by it along with interest to the recipient of the goods or services. If the undue benefit cannot be passed on to the recipient, it can be ordered to be deposited in the Consumer Welfare Fund. In extreme cases, the NAA can impose a penalty on the defaulting business entity and even order the cancellation of its registration under GST.

The constitution of the NAA shall bolster confidence of consumers as they reap the benefits of the recent reduction in GST rates, in particular, and of GST, in general.

**Profiteering:** Profiteering means unfair profit realized by traders by manipulating prices, tax rate adjustment etc. In the context of the newly launched GST, profiteering means that traders are not reducing the prices of the commodities when the GST Council reduces the tax rates of commodities and services.

## BENEFITS OF GST

The benefits of GST can be summarized as under:

**(A) For Business and Industry**

(i) **Easy tax compliance:** There would be a robust and comprehensive IT system would be the foundation of the GST regime in India. Therefore, all tax payer services such as registrations, returns, payments, etc. would be available to the taxpayers online, which would make compliance easy and transparent.

(ii) **Uniform tax rates and structures:** GST will ensure that indirect tax rates and structures are common across the country, thereby increasing certainty and two ease of doing business. In other words, GST would make doing business in the country tax neutral, irrespective of the choice of place of doing business.

(iii) **Removal of cascading effects:** A system of seamless tax-credits throughout the value-chain, and across boundaries of states, would ensure that there is minimal cascading of taxes. This would reduce hidden costs of doing business.

(iv) **Enhanced competitiveness:** Reduction in transaction costs of doing business would eventually lead to an improved competitiveness for the trade and industry.

(v) **Manufacturers and exporters to gain:** The subsuming of major central and state taxes in GST, complete and comprehensive set off of input goods and services and phasing out of Central Sales Tax (CST) would reduce the cost of locally manufactured goods and services. This will increase the competitiveness of Indian goods and services in the international market and give boost to Indian exports. The uniformity in tax rates and procedures across the country will also go a long way in reducing the compliance cost.

**(B) For Central and State Governments**

(i) **Easy to administer:** Multiple indirect taxes at the central and state levels are being replaced by GST. Backed with a robust end-to-end IT system, GST would be simpler and easier to administer than all other indirect taxes of the centre and state levied so far.

(ii) **Controls on leakage:** GST will result in better tax compliance due to a robust IT infrastructure. Due to the seamless transfer of ITC from one stage to another in the chain of value addition, there is an inbuilt mechanism in the design of GST that would incentivize tax compliance by traders.

(iii) **Increased revenue efficiency:** GST is expected to decrease the cost of collection of tax revenues of the government, and will therefore, lead to higher revenue efficiency.

**(C) For the Consumer**

(i) **Simple and transparent tax:** Due to multiple indirect taxes being levied by the centre and state, with incomplete or no ITCs available at progressive stages of value addition, the cost of most goods and services in the country today are laden with many hidden taxes. Under GST, there would be only one tax on a product or service from the manufacturer to the consumer, leading to transparency of taxes paid to the final consumer.

(ii) **Reduced tax burden:** Because of efficiency gains and prevention of leakages, the overall tax burden on most commodities will come down, which will benefit consumers.

## GST COUNCIL (GSTC) – DECISIONS

GST Council has met 25 times since its constitution and some important decisions taken in the GST Council meeting are:

1. Rules for conduct of business in GST Council.
2. Timetable for implementation of GST.
3. The threshold limit for exemption from levy of GST would be ₹ 20 lakhs for the states except for the special category states, as enumerated in Article 279A of the Constitution, for which it will be ₹ 10 Lakhs.
4. The threshold for availing the composition scheme would be ₹ 75 lakhs in states other than the north-east states, Sikkim and Himachal Pradesh where the threshold for availing the composition scheme would be ₹ 50 lakhs. The GST Council has also recommended that manufacturers of the following goods shall not be eligible for the Composition Levy; Ice cream and other edible ice, whether or not containing cocoa, pan masala, tobacco and manufactured tobacco substitutes. Service providers would be kept out of the Composition Scheme, except restaurant services.
5. To compensate states for 5 years for loss of revenue due to implementation of GST, the base year for the revenue of the state would be 2015–16 and a fixed growth rate of 14 per cent will be applied to it.
6. Approval of the draft GST Rules on registration, payment, return, refund and invoice, valuation, ITC, composition and transitional provisions.
7. All entities exempted from payment of indirect tax under any existing tax incentive scheme would pay tax in the GST regime and the decision to continue with any incentive scheme shall be with the concerned state or central

government. In case, the state or central government decides to continue with any existing exemption/incentive scheme; it will be administered by way of a reimbursement mechanism.

8. Adoption of four slabs tax rate structure of 5 per cent, 12 per cent, 18 per cent and 28 per cent. In addition, there would be a category of exempt goods and further a cess would be levied on certain goods such as luxury cars, aerated drinks, pan masala and tobacco products, over and above the rate of 28 per cent for payment of compensation to the states.
9. GST rates on 1,211 items were approved at the 14th GST Council meeting held at Srinagar on 18 and 19 of May 2017.
10. At the 15th GST Council meeting held at New Delhi on 3 June 2017, tax rates on the remaining goods were approved.
11. The 28 states, and 2 UTs with legislatures (Delhi and Puducherry) have already passed their respective State GST Bill in their State Assemblies.
12. Issue of cross empowerment and administrative division of taxpayers between the states and Centre has been resolved.

## 45TH MEETING OF GSTC

The GST Council's 45th meeting was held on 17 SEP 2021 in Lucknow under the chairmanship of the Union Finance & Corporate Affairs Minister Smt. Nirmala Sitharaman. The GST Council has inter-alia made the following recommendations relating to changes in GST rates on supply of goods and services and changes related to GST law and procedure:

### I. Recommendations relating to GST rates on goods and services

**A. COVID-19 relief measure in form of GST rate concessions**

1. Extension of existing conce-ssional GST rates (currently valid till 30th September, 2021) on following Covid-19 treatment drugs, up to 31st December, 2021, namely-
   (i) Amphotericin B -nil
   (ii) Remdesivir – 5%
   (iii) Tocilizumab -nil
   (iv) Anti-coagulants like Heparin – 5%
2. Reduction of GST rate to 5% on more Covid-19 treatment drugs, up to 31st December, 2021, namely-
   (i) Itolizumab
   (ii) Posaconazole
   (iii) Infliximab
   (iv) Favipiravir
   (v) Casirivimab & Imdevimab
   (vi) 2-Deoxy-D-Glucose
   (vii) Bamlanivimab & Etesevimab

**B. Major recommendations on GST rate changes in relation to Goods [w.e.f 1.10.2021 unless otherwise stated]**

| S. No. | Description | From | To |
|---|---|---|---|
| GST rate changes | | | |
| 1. | Retro fitment kits for vehicles used by the disabled | Appl. rate | 5% |
| 2. | Fortified Rice Kernels for schemes like ICDS etc. | 18% | 5% |
| 3. | Medicine Keytruda for treatment of cancer | 12% | 5% |
| 4. | Biodiesel supplied to OMCs for blending with Diesel | 12% | 5% |
| 5. | Ores and concentrates of metals such as iron, copper, aluminum, zinc and few others | 5% | 18% |

| S. No. | Description | From | To |
|---|---|---|---|
| 6. | Specified Renewable Energy Devices and parts | 5% | 12% |
| 7. | Cartons, boxes, bags, packing containers of paper etc. | 12%/18% | 18% |
| 8. | Waste and scrap of polyurethanes and other plastics | 5% | 18% |
| 9. | All kinds of pens | 12%/18% | 18% |
| 10. | Railway parts, locomotives & other goods | 12% | 18% |
| 11. | Miscellaneous goods of paper like cards, catalogue, printed material | 12% | 18% |
| 12. | IGST on import of medicines for personal use, namely<br>i. *Zolgensma* for Spinal Muscular Atrophy<br>ii. *Viltepso* for Duchenne Muscular Dystrophy<br>iii. Other medicines used in treatment of muscular atrophy recommended by Ministry of Health and Family Welfare and Department of Pharmaceuticals. | 12% | Nil |
| 13. | IGST exemption on goods supplied at Indo-Bangladesh Border *haats* | Appl. rate | Nil |
| 14. | Unintended waste generated during the production of fish meal except for Fish Oil | Nil (for the period 1.7.2017 to 30.9.2019) | |

**C. Other changes relating to GST rates on goods**

1. Supply of mentha oil from unregistered person has been brought under reverse charge. Further, Council has also recommended that exports of Mentha oil should be allowed only against LUT and consequential refund of input tax credit.
2. Brick kilns would be brought under special composition scheme with threshold limit of Rs. 20 lakhs, with effect from 1.4.2022. Bricks would attract GST at the rate of 6% without ITC under the scheme. GST rate of 12% with ITC would otherwise apply to bricks.

**D. Correction in Inverted Duty structure in Footwear and Textiles sector**

GST rate changes in order to correct inverted duty structure, in footwear and textiles sector, as was discussed in earlier GST Council Meeting and was deferred for an appropriate time, will be implemented with effect from 01.01.2022.

E. In terms of the recent directions of the Hon'ble High Court of Kerala, the issue of whether specified petroleum products should be brought within the ambit of GST was placed for consideration before the Council. After due deliberation, the Council was of the view that it is not appropriate to do so at this stage.

F. Major GST changes in relation to rates and scope of exemption on Services [w.e.f 1.10.2021 unless otherwise stated]

| No. | Description | From | To |
|---|---|---|---|
| 1. | Validity of GST exemption on transport of goods by vessel and air from India to outside India is extended upto 30.9.2022. | - | Nil |

| | | | |
|---|---|---|---|
| 2. | Services by way of grant of National Permit to goods carriages on payment of fee | 18% | Nil |
| 3. | Skill Training for which Government bears 75% or more of the expenditure [ presently exemption applies only if Govt funds 100%]. | 18% | Nil |
| 4. | Services related to AFC Women's Asia Cup 2022. | 18% | Nil |
| 5. | Licensing services/ the right to broadcast and show original films, sound recordings, Radio and Television programmes [to bring parity between distribution and licencing services] | 12% | 18% |
| 6. | Printing and reproduction services of recorded media where content is supplied by the publisher (to bring it on parity with *Colour printing of images from film or digital media*) | 12% | 18% |
| 7. | Exemption on leasing of rolling stock by IRFC to Indian Railways withdrawn. | | |
| 8. | E Commerce Operators are being made liable to pay tax on following services provided through them<br>i. transport of passengers, by any type of motor vehicles through it [w.e.f. 1st January, 2022]<br>ii. restaurant services provided through it with some exceptions [w.e.f. 1st January, 2022] | | |
| 9. | Certain relaxations have been made in conditions relating to IGST exemption relating to import of goods on lease, where GST is paid on the lease amount, so as to allow this exemption even if (i) such goods are transferred to a new lessee in India upon expiry or termination of lease; and (ii) the lessor located in SEZ pays GST under forward charge. | | |

**G. Clarification in relation to GST rate on Goods**

1. Pure henna powder and paste, having no additives, attract 5% GST rate under Chapter 14.
2. Brewers' Spent Grain (BSG), Dried Distillers' Grains with Soluble [DDGS] and other such residues, falling under HS code 2303 attract GST at the rate of 5%.
3. All laboratory reagents and other goods falling under heading 3822 attract GST at the rate of 12%.
4. Scented sweet supari and flavored and coated illachi falling under heading 2106 attract GST at the rate of 18%
5. Carbonated Fruit Beverages of Fruit Drink" and "Carbonated Beverages with Fruit Juice" attract GST rate of 28% and Cess of 12%. This is being prescribed specifically in the GST rate schedule.
6. Tamarind seeds fall under heading 1209, and hitherto attracted nil rate irrespective of use. However, henceforth they would attract 5% GST rate (w.e.f. 1.10.2021) for use other than sowing. Seeds for sowing will continue at nil rate.
7. External batteries sold along with UPS Systems/ Inverter attract GST rate applicable to batteries [ 28% for batteries other than lithium-

ion battery] while UPS/inverter would attract 18%.

8. GST on specified Renewable Energy Projects can be paid in terms of the 70:30 ratio for goods and services, respectively, during the period from 1.7.2017 to 31.12.2018, in the same manner as has been prescribed for the period on or after 1st January 2019.
9. Due to ambiguity in the applicable rate of GST on Fibre Drums, the supplies made at 12% GST in the past have been regularised. Henceforth, a uniform GST rate of 18% would apply to all paper and paper board containers, whether corrugated or non-corrugated.
10. Distinction between fresh and dried fruits and nuts is being clarified for application of GST rate of "nil" and 5%/12% respectively;
11. It is being clarified that all pharmaceutical goods falling under heading 3006 attract GST at the rate of 12% [ not 18%].
12. Essentiality certificate issued by Directorate General of Hydrocarbons on imports would suffice; no need for taking a certificate every time on inter-state stock transfer.

**H. Clarification in relation to GST rate on services**

1. Coaching services to students provided by coaching institutions and NGOs under the central sector scheme of 'Scholarships for students with Disabilities" is exempt from GST
2. Services by cloud kitchens/ central kitchens are covered under 'restaurant service', and attract 5% GST [ without ITC].
3. Ice cream parlor sells already manufactured ice- cream. Such supply of ice cream by parlors would attract GST at the rate of 18%.
4. Overloading charges at toll plaza are exempt from GST being akin to toll.
5. The renting of vehicle by State Transport Undertakings and Local Authorities is covered by expression 'giving on hire' for the purposes of GST exemption
6. The services by way of grant of mineral exploration and mining rights attracted GST rate of 18% w.e.f. 01.07.2017.
7. Admission to amusement parks having rides etc. attracts GST rate of 18%. The GST rate of 28% applies only to admission to such facilities that have casinos etc.
8. Alcoholic liquor for human consumption is not food and food products for the purpose of the entry prescribing 5% GST rate on job work services in relation to food and food products.

II. On the issue of compensation scenario, a presentation was made to the Council wherein it was brought out that the revenue collections from Compensation Cess in the period beyond June 2022 till April 2026 would be exhausted in repayment of borrowings and debt servicing made to bridge the gap in 2020-21 and 2021-22. In this context various options, as have been recommended by various committees/ forums were presented. The Council deliberated at length on the issue. The Council decided to set up a GoM to examine the issue of correction of inverted duty structure for major sectors; rationalize the rates and review exemptions from the point of view of revenue augmentation, from GST. It was also decided to set up a GoM to discuss ways and means of using technology to further improve compliance including monitoring through improved e-way bill systems, e-invoices, FASTag data and strengthening the institutional mechanism for sharing of intelligence and coordinated enforcement actions by the Centre and the States.

### III. Recommendations relating to GST law and procedure

I. Measures for Trade facilitation:

1. Relaxation in the requirement of filing FORM GST ITC-04:
   Requirement of filing FORM GST ITC-04 under rule 45 (3) of the CGST Rules has been relaxed as under:
   (a) Taxpayers whose annual aggregate turnover in preceding financial year is above Rs. 5 crores shall furnish ITC-04 once in six months;
   (b) Taxpayers whose annual aggregate turnover in preceding financial year is upto Rs. 5 crores shall furnish ITC-04 annually.
2. In the spirit of earlier Council decision that interest is to be charged only in respect of net cash liability, section 50 (3) of the CGST Act to be amended retrospectively, w.e.f. 01.07.2017, to provide that interest is to be paid by a taxpayer on "ineligible ITC availed and utilized" and not on "ineligible ITC availed". It has also been decided that interest in such cases should be charged on ineligible ITC availed and utilized at 18% w.e.f. 01.07.2017.
3. Unutilized balance in CGST and IGST cash ledger may be allowed to be transferred between distinct persons (entities having same PAN but registered in different states), without going through the refund procedure, subject to certain safeguards.
4. Issuance of the following circulars in order to remove ambiguity and legal disputes on various issues, thus benefiting taxpayers at large:
   (a) Clarification on scope of "intermediary services";
   (b) Clarification relating to interpretation of the term "merely establishment of distinct person" in condition (v) of the Section 2 (6) of the IGST Act 2017 for export of services. A person incorporated in India under the Companies Act, 2013 and a person incorporated under the laws of any other country are to be treated as separate legal entities and would not be barred by the condition (v) of the sub-section (6) of the section 2 of the IGST Act 2017 for considering a supply of service as export of services;
   (c) Clarification in respect of certain GST related issues:
   (i) W.e.f. 01.01.2021, the date of issuance of debit note (and not the date of underlying invoice) shall determine the relevant financial year for the purpose of section 16(4) of CGST Act, 2017;
   (ii) There is no need to carry the physical copy of tax invoice in cases where invoice has been generated by the supplier in the manner prescribed

under rule 48(4) of the CGST Rules, 2017;

(iii) Only those goods which are actually subjected to export duty i.e., on which some export duty has to be paid at the time of export, will be covered under the restriction imposed under section 54(3) of CGST Act, 2017 from availment of refund of accumulated ITC.

5. Provision to be incorporated in in CGST Rules, 2017 for removing ambiguity regarding procedure and time limit for filing refund of tax wrongfully paid as specified in section 77(1) of the CGST/SGST Act and section 19(1) of the IGST Act.

**J. Measures for streamlining compliances in GST**

1. Aadhaar authentication of registration to be made mandatory for being eligible for filing refund claim and application for revocation of cancellation of registration.
2. Late fee for delayed filing of FORM GSTR-1 to be auto-populated and collected in next open return in FORM GSTR-3B.
3. Refund to be disbursed in the bank account, which is linked with same PAN on which registration has been obtained under GST.
4. Rule 59(6) of the CGST Rules to be amended with effect from 01.01.2022 to provide that a registered person shall not be allowed to furnish FORM GSTR-1, if he has not furnished the return in FORM GSTR-3B for the preceding month.
5. Rule 36(4) of CGST Rules, 2017 to be amended, once the proposed clause (aa) of section 16(2) of CGST Act, 2017 is notified, to restrict availment of ITC in respect of invoices/ debit notes, to the extent the details of such invoices/ debit notes are furnished by the supplier in FORM GSTR-1/ IFF and are communicated to the registered person in FORM GSTR-2B.

**K. GST Council has also recommended amendments in certain provisions of the Act and Rules.**

❑❑❑

# 18 CHAPTER Summary of Economic Survey 2021-22

## STATE OF THE ECONOMY

Advance estimates suggest that the Indian economy is expected to witness real GDP expansion of 9.2 per cent in 2021-22 after contracting in 2020-21. This implies that overall economic activity has recovered past the pre-pandemic levels. Almost all indicators show that the economic impact of the "second wave" in Q1 was much smaller than that experienced during the full lockdown phase in 2020-21 even though the health impact was more severe.

Agriculture and allied sectors have been the least impacted by the pandemic and the sector is expected to grow by 3.9 per cent in 2021-22 after growing 3.6 per cent in the previous year. Advance estimates suggest that the GVA of Industry (including mining and construction) will rise by 11.8 per cent in 2021-22 after contracting by 7 per cent in 2020- 21. The Services sector has been the hardest hit by the pandemic, especially segments that involve human contact. This sector is estimated to grow by 8.2 per cent this financial year following last year's 8.4 per cent contraction.

Total Consumption is estimated to have grown by 7.0 per cent in 2021-22 with significant contributions from government spending. Similarly, Gross Fixed Capital Formation exceeded pre-pandemic levels on the back of ramped up public expenditure on infrastructure. Exports of both goods and services have been exceptionally strong so far in 2021-22, but imports also recovered strongly with recovery in domestic demand as well as higher international commodity prices.

Inflation has reappeared as a global issue in both advanced and emerging economies. India's Consumer Price Index inflation stood at 5.6 per cent YoY in December 2021 which is within the targeted tolerance band. Wholesale price inflation, however, has been running in double-digits. Although this is partly due to base effects that will even out, India does need to be wary of imported inflation, especially from elevated global energy prices.

Total consumption is estimated to have grown by 7.0 per cent in 2021-22 with government consumption remaining the biggest contributor as in the previous year. Government consumption is estimated to grow by a strong 7.6 per cent surpassing pre-pandemic levels. Private consumption is also estimated to have improved significantly to recover 97 per cent of corresponding pre-pandemic output level.

Investment, as measured by Gross Fixed Capital Formation (GFCF) is expected to see strong growth of 15 per cent in 2021-22 and achieve full recovery of pre-pandemic level.

India's exports of both goods and services have been exceptionally strong so far in 2021-

22. Merchandise exports have been above US$ 30 billion for eight consecutive months in 2021-22.

It cushions for unpredictable negative outcomes by providing safety nets. This explains why the Government's initial measures in 2020-21 were mostly about making food available to the poor, providing emergency liquidity support for MSMEs and holding the Insolvency and Bankruptcy Code in abeyance.

At the time of writing, a new wave in the form of the Omicron variant was sweeping across the world, inflation had jumped up in most countries, and the cycle of liquidity withdrawal was being initiated by major central banks. This is why it is especially important to look at India's macro-economic stability indicators and their ability to provide a buffer against the above stresses.

### ❖ External Sector

Despite all the disruptions caused by the global pandemic, India's balance of payments remained in surplus throughout the last two years. This allowed the Reserve Bank of India to keep accumulating foreign exchange reserves, which stands at US$ 634 billion on 31st December 2021). This is equivalent to 13.2 months of imports and higher than the country's external debt. As of end-November 2021, India was the fourth largest foreign exchange reserves holder in the world after China, Japan, and Switzerland.

### ❖ Financial Sector

The Gross Non-Performing Advances (GNPA) ratio (i.e. GNPAs as a percentage of Gross Advances) and Net Non-Preforming (NNPA) ratio of Scheduled Commercial Banks (SCBs) continued to decline since 2018-19. GNPA ratio of SCBs decreased from 7.5 per cent at end-September 2020 to 6.9 per cent at end-September 2021. NNPA ratio of SCBs also declined from 6 per cent at end of 2017-18 to 2.2 per cent at end-September 2021. Simultaneously, the Capital Adequacy Ratio has continued to improve since 2015-16. The Capital to risk-weighted asset ratio (CRAR) of SCBs increased from 15.84 per cent at end- September 2020 to 16.54 per cent at end-September 2021 on account of improvement for both public and private sector banks.

Inflation has reappeared as a global issue in both advanced and emerging economies . The surge in energy prices, non-food commodities, input prices, disruption of global supply chains, and rising freight costs stoked global inflation during the year. In India, Consumer Price Index (CPI) inflation moderated to 5.2 per cent in 2021-22 (April-December) from 6.6 per cent in the corresponding period of 2020-21.

## FISCAL DEVELOPMENTS

The New Public Sector Enterprise Policy and Asset Monetisation Strategy introduced by the Government reaffirm its commitment towards privatization and strategic disinvestment of Public Sector Enterprises. The privatisation of Air India has been particularly important, not only in terms of garnering disinvestment proceeds but also for boosting the privatisation drive.

On account of a sustained revenue collection and a targeted expenditure policy by the Government of India, the fiscal deficit for April to November 2021 has been contained at 46.2 per cent of BE which is nearly one third of the proportion reached during the same period of the previous two years (135.1 per cent of BE in April-November 2020 and 114.8 per cent of BE in April-November 2019). The fiscal deficit budgeted in the current year was more realistic as it brought in several off-budget items to within the budget allocation such as the food subsidy requirements of FCI. With the enhanced borrowings on account of COVID-19, the Central Government debt has gone up from 49.1 per cent of GDP in 2019-20 to 59.3 per cent of GDP in 2020-21, but is expected to follow a declining trajectory with the recovery of the economy. The General Government finances are also expected to witness a consolidation during 2021-22, after the uptick in deficit and debt indicators during the pandemic year 2020-21.

The agile fiscal policy response adopted by Government of India encompassed a change in mix of the stimulus measures amidst an uncertain evolution of the pandemic situation. In the initial phase of the pandemic, the fiscal policy focused on building safety-nets for the poor and vulnerable sections of society to hedge against the worst-case outcomes.

With the revival of the economy, the Goods and Services Tax has emerged as a buoyant source of revenue for both the Centre and the States. The GST collections for the Centre were 61.4 per cent of BE during April to November 2021. Gross GST collections, Centre and States taken together, were ₹10.74 lakh crore during April to December 2021, which is an increase of 61.5 per cent over April to December 2020 and 33.7 per cent over April to December 2019.

Central Government receipts can broadly be divided into non-debt and debt receipts. The non-debt receipts comprise of tax revenue, non-tax revenue, recovery of loans, and disinvestment receipts. Debt receipts mostly consist of market borrowings and other liabilities, which the government is obliged to repay in the future.

## ❖ Trends in Expenditure

The expenditure policy during the pandemic year 2020-21 was focused on prioritisation of expenditure according to evolving situation. In the initial phase of the pandemic, the Government ensured that funds were made available for essential activities and that scarce resources were conserved for re-prioritisation.

## ❖ Transfer to States

The Union Government has accepted the recommendations made by the Fifteenth Finance Commission (XV-FC) in its Report for the award period 2021-22 to 2025-26 relating to the grants-in-aid amounting to ₹ 2,33,233 crore to the States during 2021-22 for Post Devolution Revenue Deficit grant, grants to Local Bodies, Health sector grant and Disaster Management grants.

The XV-Finance Commission had recommended that urban areas are grouped into two broad categories for recommending grants to urban local bodies: (a) Category-I cities: urban agglomerations/cities with more than one million population and (b) Category-II cities: other than million-plus cities.

The XV-FC has recommended grants for health to be channelised through local governments amounting to ₹ 13,192 crore for the year 2021-22. To strengthen and plug the critical gaps in the health care system at the primary health care level, XV-FC has also identified interventions that will directly lead to strengthening the primary health infrastructure and facilities in both rural and urban areas.

## ❖ Central Government Debt

During the year, a major challenge in the aftermath of COVID-19 pandemic was the management of debt, both for the Central and State Governments. In this milieu, conventional and unconventional measures were taken in order to maintain the orderly market conditions to ensure that the increased financial needs of the Governments are met smoothly, while keeping in mind the major objectives of cost minimization, risk mitigation and market development. Supported by these measures, the weighted average cost of the Government on dated securities during 2020-21 was at 17-year low of 5.79 per cent, despite a 141.2 per cent jump in net market borrowings.

Public debt portfolio exhibits low currency and interest rate risk owing to low reliance on external borrowing and issuance of majority of securities at fixed coupon. Further, most of the external borrowing are from official sources which are of long term and concessional in nature. The roll over risk is also low owing to low issuance of short-term bonds with a view to elongate the maturity profile. The proportion of dated securities maturing in less than five years has seen consistent decline in recent years. The weighted average maturity of outstanding stock of dated securities of Government has increased from 9.7 years at end March 2010 to 11.31 years at the end March 2021, thus reducing the rollover risk.

Public debt is largely owned by institutional segments like banks, insurance companies, provident funds etc. The share of commercial banks stood at 37.77 per cent at end-March 2021, lower than 40.4 per cent at end-March 2020.

A vibrant secondary market provides opportunity to the investors to balance their portfolio as desired. Availability of government securities upto 40 years provides a wide choice to the investors. Trading though currently concentrated in few securities, is showing signs of more even spread. Moreover, the recently launched Retail Direct Scheme by RBI will be instrumental in channelizing the savings of middle class, small businessmen and senior citizens directly into risk free government securities. With an objective to facilitate efficient direct access of retail individual investor to the G-Sec market, which was earlier directly being accessed only by large institutional investors, this scheme will give a boost to financial inclusion and broaden the investor base.

## ❖ Government e-Marketplace (GeM)

The Government in 2016 had set up a dedicated e-market known as Government e-Marketplace (GeM) for purchase of certain standard day to day use goods. This is a simple, transparent and completely digital process for procurement. The General Financial Rules 2017 mandates all Ministries and Departments to procure Goods and Services available on GeM from GeM.

Anecdotal evidence suggests that prior to GeM, government procurement prices were much higher than the prices prevailing in the market and there were constant complaints about inefficiency and rent seeking.

## ❖ Direct Tax Measures by CBDT During 2021-22

### Improvements in Tax Administration

In continuation with the Government's emphasis on providing a more transparent, efficient and tax-payer friendly tax administration and improving taxpayer convenience, several initiatives have been launched by the government. These will also ensure promotion of investment and employment generation.

### Ease of Compliance for Taxpayers

Most of the processes and compliance requirements have been shifted to online platforms and the need for the taxpayers to physically visit the income tax offices has been eliminated or minimized. Interaction with taxpayers is characterized by a spirit of trust and respect, relying more on voluntary compliance.

### Faceless Procedures to Promote Transparency

The Faceless Assessment Scheme was launched in 2020 which abolishes the earlier system of tax administration and assessment based on territorial jurisdiction. It provides for assessment by randomly chosen virtual teams with dynamic jurisdiction. More than two lakh cases have been allocated out of which 1.99 lacs have been completed without any interaction with the taxpayer.

Faceless Penalty scheme 2021 was also launched to impart greater efficiency, transparency and accountability to the procedure for imposition of penalty. The Scheme makes it possible for taxpayers to submit replies and participate in the proceedings at their convenience. It also provides for peer review of orders which will result in orders that are qualitatively better, reasonable and fair.

## ❖ Goods and Services Tax

In the 45th and 46th GST Council, the recommendation of the Fitment Committee for calibrating the GST rate structure to correct the inverted duty structure on textiles and footwear were discussed.

Services supplied to an educational institution including anganwadi (which provide pre-school education also), by way of serving of food including mid-day meals under any mid-day meals scheme, sponsored by Government is exempt from levy of GST irrespective of funding of such supplies from government grants or corporate donations.

Some of these measures are reduction in rate of interest for delayed tax payments, waiver of late fee, extension of due date for filing of return, extension of statutory time limits under section 168A of the CGST Act. A dedicated helpdesk was set up to handhold the trade and handle grievances of the trade across the country.

# EXTERNAL SECTOR

External trade recovered strongly in 2021-22 after the pandemic-induced slump of the previous year, with strong capital flows into India, leading to a rapid accumulation of foreign exchange reserves.

The resilience of India's external sector during the current year augurs well for growth revival in the economy.

India's current account balance turned into deficit of 0.2 percent of GDP in the first half (H1) of 2021-22, largely led by deficit in trade account. Net capital flows were higher at US$ 65.6 billion in H1: 2021-22, on account of continued inflow of foreign investment, revival in net external commercial borrowings (ECBs), higher banking capital and additional special drawing rights (SDR) allocation. India's external debt rose to US$ 593.1 billion as at end-September 2021, from US$ 556.8 billion a year earlier, reflecting additional SDR allocation by IMF, coupled with higher commercial borrowings.

The robust capital flows were sufficient to finance the modest current account deficit, resulting in an overall balance of payments (BoP) surplus of US$ 63.1 billion in H1 of 2021-22, that led to an augmented foreign exchange reserves crossing the milestone of US$ 600 billion and touched US$ 633.6 billion as of December 31, 2021. As of end- November 2021, India was the fourth largest forex reserves holder in the world after China, Japan, and Switzerland.

As regards global financial conditions, in 2021, inflation picked up globally as economic activity revived with opening up of economies. Inflation in US touched 6.8 per cent in November 2021, the highest since 1982, driven largely by energy and food prices. As inflation worries are mounting, a distinct shift towards the unwinding of pandemic-led stimulus is taking hold.

The biggest downside risk emanates from the pandemic itself, particularly with resurgence of new variants such as Omicron.

## ❖ Developments in India's Merchandise Trade

India's merchandise exports recovered strongly from the pandemic-induced collapse and registered positive growth in the current financial year. During 2021-22 (April-December), the merchandise exports recorded growth of 49.7 per cent to US $ 301.4 billion, compared to corresponding period of last year and 26.5 per cent over 2019-20 (April-December), exceeding the pre-pandemic levels.

Pro-active support of export promotion agencies including Export Inspection Council (EIC), Agricultural and Processed Food Products Export Development Authority (APEDA) and export facilitating measures like online issuance of certificates required for exports, aided growth of agricultural exports during the pandemic.

It is observed that even the segments like marine products, buffalo meat, tea, coffee and dairy products, which had not performed well during 2020-21, have registered substantial growth during the current year. This augurs well for further diversification and strengthening of agricultural exports in the coming years.

India has diversified its export destinations in last 25 years, yet more than 40 per cent of India's exports is still accounted by only seven countries. India has been negotiating free trade agreements (FTAs) with several partners – both bilateral and regional – over the past many years with a view to promote India's exports. A further push in this direction would help provide the institutional arrangements to, inter alia, diversify both products and destinations.

### Major Schemes and Initiatives to Boost Exports

**Remission of Duties and Taxes on Exported Products (RoDTEP):** In order to boost Indian exports, a WTO compliant RoDTEP scheme is brought into effect from 01.01.2021.

**Developing District as Export Hub:** Under this initiative, the focus is to make districts active stakeholders in the promotion of exports of goods/services produced/ manufactured in the district.

**Production-Linked Incentive (PLI) scheme:** An outlay of ₹1.97 lakh crore (US $ 26 billion) was announced in Union Budget 2021-22 for Production-Linked Incentive (PLI) scheme for 14 key sectors starting from 2021-22.

**Electronic Platform for Preferential Certificate of Origin (CoO):** In view of the COVID-19 crisis, on-boarding of FTAs/ preferential trade agreements (PTAs) was quickly done to allow electronic issuance to avoid physical movement. Around 4.6 lakh CoOs have been issued from the e-platform till date.2 Issuance of Non-Preferential CoOs was also started from 15.04.2021.

**Infusion of capital in EXIM Bank:** Government of India infused capital of ₹750 crore in Export-Import Bank of India (EXIM Bank) during the current financial year 2021-22 through subscription to its share capital.

**Export Promotion Capital Goods (EPCG) Scheme** is an ongoing scheme under the foreign trade policy. In order to increase procurement of capital goods from indigenous manufacturers under the EPCG scheme, the government has reduced specific export obligations from 90 per cent to 75 per cent of the normal export obligation.

## ❖ Trade in Services

India has maintained its impressive performance in world services trade in the post COVID-19 period. Despite pandemic induced global restrictions and weak tourism revenues, India's services exports recorded growth of 18.4 per cent to US$ 177.7 billion during 2021-22.

Services imports rose by 21.5 per cent to US $ 103.3 billion in 2021-22 (April-December) from the corresponding period a year earlier and 6.2 per cent over 2019-20 (April- December), crossing the pre-pandemic levels.

In H1: FY 22, the net private transfers – mainly representing remittances by Indians employed overseas – grew by 7.2 per cent to US $ 38.4 billion, over corresponding period a year earlier and by modest 0.1 per cent over H1: FY 20, exceeding the pre-pandemic levels. As per the Migration and Development Brief 35, World Bank (November 2021), India continues to be the largest remittance recipient country in the world in 2021 (in current US dollar terms) and has been so since 2008.

After witnessing a surplus in H1: FY 21, India's current account balance flipped into deficit of US$ 3.1 billion (0.2 per cent of GDP) in H1: FY 22, on the back of sharp increase in merchandise trade deficit.

The latest aggregate data on FDI is available till November 2021. While net FDI recorded a lower inflow of US$ 24.7 billion, the gross FDI inflows moderated at US$ 54.1 billion during April-November, 2021 compared to corresponding period last year, largely due to lower equity investment.

### ❖ Movement in Exchange Rate

Indian rupee depreciated by 4.5 per cent (y-o-y basis) against US dollar in 2020-21. Although the rupee exhibited movements in both directions against US dollar during April-December, 2021. In terms of 6-currency nominal effective exchange rate (NEER) (trade-weighted), the rupee depreciated by 2.1 per cent in December 2021 over March 2021, while it appreciated by 0.9 per cent in terms of real effective exchange rate (i.e. REER) terms.

## MONETARY MANAGEMENT AND FINANCIAL INTERMEDIATION

After several rate cuts in 2019-20 and 2020-21, the repo rate was maintained at 4 per cent in 2021-22. The liquidity in the system remained in surplus throughout. RBI undertook various measures, including secondary market G-sec acquisition programme, special Long-Term Repo operations, on tap targeted Long-Term Repo Operations, etc. to provide further liquidity in the system. Thereafter, RBI used Variable Rate Reverse Repo, reverse repo auctions to rebalance liquidity conditions.

Reserve money and broad money supply growth in 2021-22 so far was lower than in the previous year. The reserve money growth did not fully translate into commensurate broad money supply growth due to the smaller (adjusted) money multiplier reflecting large deposits by banks with RBI under reverse repo window. Bank credit growth accelerated gradually in 2021-22 up from 5.3 per cent in the beginning of April 2021. The very latest data shows that the bank credit growth stands at 9.2 per cent as on 31st December 2021. At the sectoral level, credit to agriculture sector continued to register robust growth and showed signs of improvement in the industry sector. Services sector credit growth, however, is yet to recover.

Gross Non-Performing advances ratio of Scheduled Commercial Banks (SCBs) continued to decline from 11.2 per cent at end of 2017-18 to 6.9 per cent at end-September 2021.

The year 2021-22 so far has been an exceptional year for the capital markets. There was a boom in fundraising through IPOs by many new age companies/tech start-ups/ unicorns. In April-November 2021, ₹ 89,066 crore were raised via 75 IPO issues, much higher than in any year in last decade.

### ❖ Monetary Developments

The Monetary Policy Committee (MPC) maintained status quo on the policy repo rate during April to December 2021 after a substantial cut of 115 basis points (bps) during February- May 2020 and a cumulative 250 basis points cut since February 2019.

In the initial meetings of 2021-22, MPC noted that while the inflation has hovered above the upper tolerance band for some months, it was largely driven by adverse supply shocks which were expected to be transitory. The outlook for aggregate demand was progressively improving but capacity utilisation rates were low.

In 2021-22 so far, the overall monetary and credit conditions remained accommodative. However, the growth rates of monetary aggregates-including Reserve money, Broad money were lower as compared to the last year. Reserve money (M0) recorded a year-on-year (YoY) growth of 13 per cent as on 7th January 2022, as compared to 14.3 per cent a year ago.

In 2021-22 so far, the YoY growth of broad money (M3) stood at 9.9 per cent as on 31st December, as compared to 12.5 per cent a year ago.

Special Long-Term Repo Operations (SLTRO) for small finance banks of ₹10,000 crore to support small business units, micro and small industries, and other unorganised sector entities adversely affected during the second wave of the pandemic. SLTRO scheme was subsequently made on-tap and was extended till December 31, 2021.

On-tap liquidity window of ₹15,000 crore for contact-intensive sectors.

A secondary market G-sec acquisition programme (G-SAP) - which was announced during the year added to the surplus liquidity during the period. G-SAP involves upfront commitment to purchase a specific quantum of government securities with a view to enabling a stable and orderly evolution of the yield curve. RBI purchased G-secs (including state development loans) amounting to ₹1 lakh crore under G-SAP 1.0 and ₹1.2 lakh crore under G-SAP 2.0.

### Developments in G-Sec Market

The yields on 10-year G sec which had reached 8.2 per cent on 26th September 2018 reduced substantially to reach 5.75 per cent in June 2020. It has since then increased to stand at 6.45 per cent as on 31st December 2021.

### Non-Banking Financial Companies (NBFCs) Sector

Credit growth of NBFCs continued to remain sluggish in 2021-22 so far. The total credit of NBFC sector 2 increased marginally from ₹27.53 lakh crore in March 2021 to ₹28.03 lakh crore in September 2021. The credit intensity of NBFCs, measured by NBFC credit as a ratio of GDP has been rising consistently and stood at 13.7 at end March 2021.

### Debt

On the debt side, the funds raised through corporate bonds was around ₹3.7 lakh crore in April- November 2021. The amount raised through public issues in debt doubled as 20 public issues raised ₹9,132 crore during April-November 2021, as compared to 10 issues which raised ₹3,871 crore during the corresponding period of previous year.

### Mutual Fund Activities

The net Assets Under Management (AUM) of mutual fund industry rose by 24.4 per cent to ₹37.3 lakh crore at the end of November 2021 from ₹30.0 lakh crore end of November 2020. Net resource mobilization by mutual funds was ₹2.54 lakh crore during April-November 2021.

### Investment by Foreign Portfolio Investors (FPIs)

During April-November 2021, FPIs made a net investment of ₹24,124 crore in Indian securities, 82.8 per cent lower that what was made in same period previous year. As of November 2021, cumulative net investment by FPIs increased by 9.2 per cent to US$288.4 billion from US$ 264 billion at end November 2020.

### Indian Benchmark Indices

The benchmark stock market indices in India - Sensex and Nifty 50, increased by 17.7 per cent and 18.1 per cent, respectively during April-December 2021. Driven by good corporate earnings, sharp rise in COVID-19 vaccination and opening up of business establishment across the country, Sensex and Nifty scaled up to touch its peak at 61,766 and 18,477 respectively on 18th October 2021.

### Pension Sector

The total number of subscribers under New Pension Scheme (NPS) and Atal Pension Yojana (APY) increased from 374.32 lakh as on September 2020 to 463 lakh as on September 2021, recording a growth of 23.7 per cent over the year. The overall contribution under NPS grew by more than 29 per cent during the period September 2020 - September 2021.

As on 12th October 2021, contribution of ₹16,109 crore was collected in the Atal Pension Yojana (APY) scheme from more than 3.45 crore enrolments. The APY scheme is being distributed through more than 250 active APY service providers.

### Insolvency and Bankruptcy Code

The Insolvency and Bankruptcy Code (IBC) has created a cohesive and comprehensive insolvency ecosystem. With the enactment of IBC, India has witnessed the birth of two professions, namely, the insolvency profession and the valuation profession that have professionalised insolvency services.

The primary objective of the Code is resolving the Corporate Debtors (CDs) in distress. As on September 2021, the Code has rescued 421 CDs through resolution plans and referred 1419 CDs for liquidation. The CDs rescued had assets valued at ₹1.48 lakh crore, while the CDs referred for liquidation had assets valued at ₹0.52 lakh crore when they were admitted to Corporate Insolvency Resolution Process (CIRP).

The 421 CIRPs, which have yielded resolution plans by the end of September 2021 took on average 428 days (after excluding the time excluded by the Adjucating Authority) for the conclusion of the process. Out of this, the cost details are available in respect of 388 CIRPs. The cost works out on average to 0.98 per cent of liquidation value and to 0.54 per cent of resolution value.

Till September 2021, 18,629 applications for initiation of CIRPs of CDs having underlying default of ₹5,89,516 crores were resolved before their admission. Further, a total of 527 CIRPs have been withdrawn under section 12A of the Code until September 2021. Almost three fourth of these CIRPs had claims of less than ₹10 crores and 701 CIRP cases have been closed on appeal/review/settled.

This law addresses the core issues of cross border insolvency cases with the help of four main principles:

- **Access:** It allows foreign professionals and creditors direct access to domestic courts and enables them to participate in and commence domestic insolvency proceedings against a debtor.
- **Recognition:** It allows recognition of foreign proceedings and enables courts to determine relief accordingly.
- **Cooperation:** It provides a framework for cooperation between insolvency professionals and courts of countries.
- **Coordination:** It allows for coordination in the conduct of concurrent proceedings in different jurisdictions.

## PRICES AND INFLATION

As economic activity started showing signs of picking-up in the second year of the pandemic, the global economy faced the fresh challenge of rising global inflation. COVID-19 related stimulus spending in major economies along with pent-up demand boosting consumer spending pushed inflation up in many advanced and emerging economies.

On the domestic front, the average headline Consumer Price Index-Combined (CPI-C) inflation in India moderated to 5.2 per cent in 2021-22 (April-December) from 6.6 per cent in the corresponding period of 2020-21 and was recorded at 5.6 per cent in December 2021. The Consumer Price Index inflation remained range bound as food prices eased considerably due to the supply management response by the Government. Food inflation remained benign during the year at 2.9 per cent (April-December) as against 9.1 per cent in the corresponding period last year.

Wholesale inflation based on Wholesale Price Index (WPI), after remaining very benign during the previous financial year on account of pandemic induced weakening of economic activity, record low global crude oil prices and weak demand, witnessed a sharp uptick, rising to 12.5 per cent during 2021-22 (April-December).

WPI is more sensitive to cost-push inflation led by imported inputs. With the gradual waning of base effect in WPI, the divergence in CPI-C inflation and WPI inflation is also expected to narrow down.

## ❖ Global Inflation

In 2021, inflation picked up globally as economic activity revived with opening-up of economies. COVID-19 related stimulus spending, mainly in the form of discretionary handouts to households in major economies, along with pent up demand fueling consumer spending, pushed inflation up in both advanced and emerging economies.

The surge in energy, food, non-food commodities, and input prices, supply constraints, disruption of global supply chains, and rising freight costs across the globe stoked global inflation during the year.

Crude oil prices also witnessed an upswing during the year on the back of increased demand from recovering economies and supply cuts by the Organization of the Petroleum Exporting Countries and its allies (OPEC+).

## ❖ Domestic Inflation

Retail inflation, as measured by Consumer Price Index-Combined (CPI-C) inflation, in India, which was slightly above 6 per cent in 2020-21 owing to supply chain disruptions caused by COVID-19 restrictions, lockdowns, and night curfews, moderated during the current financial year. Retail inflation during 2021-22 (April-December) stood at 5.2 per cent.

'Fuel and light' and 'Transport and communication': In 2021-22 (April-December), inflation in 'fuel and light' and 'transport and communication' was mostly driven by high international crude oil, petroleum product prices, and higher taxes.

'Oils and fats' contributed around 60 per cent of 'food and beverages' inflation despite having a weight of only 7.8 per cent in the group. Inflation of the sub-group has risen sharply since mid-2019; remained in double digits since April 2020 and witnessed further uptrend in 2021-22.

National Housing Bank (NHB) RESIDEX HPI@Assessment Prices index (Base 2017-18) captures the prices of residential housing properties for the transactions through primary lending institutions. Data on composite index for prices and transaction records from NHB have been used to analyze the impact of first and second COVID-19 wave on the housing transactions and prices across a sample of 12 cities.

## ❖ Pharmaceutical Pricing

Government regulates pricing of drugs to ensure availability and accessibility of medicines at affordable prices. National Pharmaceutical Pricing Authority (NPPA), an attached office of the Department of Pharmaceuticals (DoP), is mandated to regulate the prices of drugs.

Several steps have been taken to ensure the affordability of drugs and medical devices. Ceiling prices for 355 medicines and 886 formulations were fixed for medicines under National List of Essential Medicines, 2015 (Schedule-I of Drug Price Control Order (DPCO), 2013) until 31 December 2021. Retail prices for approximately 1798 formulations were fixed under DPCO, 2013 till 31 December 2021.

### Long Term Perspective for Management of Supply Side Factors

Given the importance of supply-side factors in having a predominance in determination of inflation in India, long-term policies are likely to help.

1. **Changing Production Patterns:** Encouraging farmers to shift from cultivation of rice and wheat to pulses and oilseeds would help ensure that the country is self-reliant in pulses and oilseeds and also assist in reducing import dependence.
2. **Calibrated Import Policy:** Knee jerk reactions to price rise of essential commodities like pulses and edible oils through frequent import duty/tariff revisions though providing immediate relief to the consumers in the way of lower

prices, send wrong signals to domestic producers and create an environment of uncertainty.

3. **Focus on transportation and storage infrastructure for perishable commodities:** Better storage and supply chain management is required to ensure availability in lean season and reduced wastages of horticulture and other perishable essential commodities to reduce the seasonal spikes in prices for consumers, glut for the farmers in times of good harvests due to lack of marketing infrastructure, resulting in distress sales.

## SUSTAINABLE DEVELOPMENT AND CLIMATE CHANGE

In 2020-21, India progressed further on achieving the Sustainable Development Goals (SDGs). India's overall score on the NITI Aayog SDG India Index & Dashboard 2020- 21 improved to 66 from 60 in 2019-20 and 57 in 2018-19. The number of Front Runners (scoring 65-99) increased to 22 states and UTs in 2020-21 from 10 in 2019-20. Kerala and Chandigarh were the top state and UT respectively on SDG performance in 2020-21. In North East India, 64 districts were Front Runners and 39 districts were Performers in the NITI Aayog North-Eastern Region District SDG Index 2021-22.

India has the tenth largest forest area in the world. In 2020, India ranked third globally in increasing its forest area during 2010 to 2020. The forests covered 24 per cent of India's total geographical, accounting for two per cent of the world's total forest area in 2020.

India had announced its first Nationally Determined Contribution (NDC) under the Paris Agreement in 2015. The Hon'ble Prime Minister of India, as a part of the national statement delivered at the 26th Conference of the Parties (COP 26) in Glasgow in November 2021, announced ambitious targets to be achieved by 2030 to enable further reduction in emissions.

In 2021, India continued exercising significant climate leadership at the international stage under the International Solar Alliance (ISA), Coalition for Disaster Resilient Infrastructure (CDRI) and Leadership Group for Industry Transition (LeadIT Group). The chapter also discusses several initiatives taken in the area of sustainable finance by the Ministry of Finance, RBI and SEBI.

### ❖ State of the Environment

Sustainable development requires balancing of rapid economic growth with conservation, ecological security and environmental sustainability. This section explores state of the environment across land, water and air.

Forests covered 24 per cent of India's total geographical area accounting for two per cent of the world's total forest area in 2020. The top 10 countries account for 66 per cent of the world's forest area. Of these countries, Brazil (59 per cent), Peru (57 per cent), Democratic Republic of Congo (56 per cent) and Russia (50 per cent) have half or more of their total geographical area under forests.

#### Plastic Waste Management and Elimination of Identified Single Use Plastics

India is committed to mitigate pollution caused by littered single use plastics. In 2018, the Hon'ble Prime Minister announced that India would phase-out single use plastic by 2022. The Hazardous and Other Wastes (Management and Trans -boundary Movement) Rules, 2016 as amended regulate the import of identified plastic waste into the country by SEZ and EOUs. The regulation of import of plastic waste prevents dumping of plastic waste by other countries in the country and allows for recycling of plastic waste generated in the country.

India piloted a resolution on "Addressing Single Use Plastic Product Pollution" which was adopted by the Fourth United Nations

Environment Assembly held in 2019. The resolution recognizes the need for the global community to act on the single use plastic products pollution.

### Rivers

India has several perennial and seasonal rivers. The Ganga River Basin is the largest river basin in India, covering more than a quarter of country's land area, hosting about 43 per cent of its population and contributing 28 per cent of India's water resources. In recognition of River Ganga's significant economic, environmental, cultural and religious value, the Government of India declared River Ganga as the National River in 2008. Further, the Government of India launched the Namami Gange Mission in 2014 as an integrated and multi-sectoral mission for conservation of Ganga and its tributaries.

### Air

Air pollution is one of the biggest global environmental challenges. The Government of India launched the National Clean Air Programme (NCAP) in 2019 to tackle the air pollution problem in a comprehensive manner, with a target to achieve 20-30 per cent reduction in particulate matter (PM) concentrations by 2024 across the country keeping 2017 as the base year for the comparison of concentration.

NCAP also covers eight other million plus cities, which fall under XV-FC grant for receiving performance based grant for air quality improvement. In 2019-20, the highest funds were released to Uttar Pradesh, followed by Maharashtra and Madhya Pradesh while in 2020-21, the highest funds were released to Andhra Pradesh, Punjab and West Bengal.

Several steps are being taken to control and minimize air pollution from various sources in the country, which inter alia include:

- **Vehicular Emission:** India has leap frogged from BS-IV to BS-VI norms for fuel and vehicles since April, 2020.
- **Industrial Emission:** Stringent emission norms for coal based thermal power plants have been introduced. There is ban on use of imported pet coke in the country since July 2018, with exception for permitted processes.
- **Air Pollution due to dust and burning of waste:** Six waste management rules covering solid waste, plastic waste, e-waste, bio-medical waste, construction and demolition.
- **Monitoring of Ambient Air Quality:** Air quality monitoring network of manual as well as continuous monitoring stations, under programmes such as National Air Monitoring Programme, have been expanded.

### Climate Change Action Program (CCAP)

Climate Change Action Program (CCAP) is a central sector scheme, initially launched in 2014, with a total outlay of ₹ 290 crores for duration of five years. The scheme has now been extended upto 2025-26, and consists of eight broad sub-components including the National Action Plan on Climate Change (NAPCC) coordination, State Action Plan on Climate Change (SAPCC), National Institute on Climate Change Studies & Actions, National Carbonaceous Aerosols Programme (NCAP), Long Term Ecological Observations (LTEO), International negotiations and capacity building.

### Major Decisions at the COP26 Climate Summit, Glasgow

The 26th Session of the Conference of the Parties (COP 26) to the UNFCCC was held under the UK Presidency in Glasgow from 31st October – 13th November 2021. The 16th Session of the Conference of Parties serving as the meeting of the Parties to the Kyoto Protocol (CMP16), 3rd Session of Conference of the Parties serving as the Meeting of Parties to Paris Agreement (CMA3).

The "Glasgow Climate Pact" emphasizes adaptation, mitigation, finance, technology transfer, capacity-building, loss and damage. The decision urges the developed country Parties to fully deliver on the USD 100 billion mobilization goal urgently and through till 2025, and emphasizes the importance of transparency in the implementation of their pledges.

### Investing in Resilience for Sustainable Development

There has been an increasing recognition that ESG issues can put the performance of companies at risk. In this regard, SEBI has been one of the early adopters of sustainability reporting for listed entities and requires mandatory ESG related disclosures as part of the Business Responsibility Report (BRR), for the top 100 listed entities (by market capitalisation) since 2012. The above requirement of filing BRR was progressively extended to the top 500 entities (from financial year 2016-17) and later to the top 1000 listed entities (from the financial year 2019-20). SEBI in February 2017, had encouraged the top 500 listed entities to adopt the framework of Integrated Reporting, issued by the International Integrated Reporting Council, on a voluntary basis.

### ❖ India's Initiatives at the International Stage

- **Lifestyle for Environment (LIFE):** In November 2021, the Hon'ble Prime Minister proposed a One-Word Movement in the context of climate: LIFE - Lifestyle for Environment, at the COP 26 in Glasgow.
- **International Solar Alliance (ISA):** In November 2021, the Hon'ble Prime Minister launched the joint Green Grids Initiative- One Sun One World One Grid (GGI–OSOWOG) at the World Leaders' Summit in Glasgow.
- **Coalition for Disaster Resilient Infrastructure:** India's call for promoting disaster resilience of infrastructure through the Coalition for Disaster Resilient Infrastructure (CDRI) has been receiving global attention.
- **Leadership Group for Industry Transition (LeadIT Group):** LeadIT was launched by India and Sweden, with the support of the World Economic Forum at the UN Climate Action Summit in New York in September 2019.

India's performance on the NITI Aayog SDG India Index has improved from an overall score of 60 in 2019-20 to 66 in 2020-21. India has also been making significant strides in increasing its forest area, ranking third globally in net gain in forest area during the decade (2010-20).

## AGRICULTURE AND FOOD MANAGEMENT

The agriculture sector has experienced buoyant growth in the past two years. The sector, which is the largest employer of workforce, accounted for a sizeable 18.8 per cent (2021-22) in Gross Value Added (GVA) of the country registering a growth of 3.6 per cent in 2020-21 and 3.9 per cent in 2021-22. Growth in allied sectors including livestock, dairying and fisheries has been the major drivers of overall growth in the sector.

Allied sectors including animal husbandry, dairying and fishing are steadily emerging to be high growth sectors. The livestock sector has grown at a CAGR of 8.15 per cent over the last five years ending 2019-20.

The Government has placed focus on the food processing sector, which is not only a major market of agriculture produce but is also a significant employer of the surplus workforce engaged in agriculture. Government therefore facilitates food processing through various measures of infrastructure development, subsidised transportation and support for formalization of micro food enterprises.

India runs one of the largest food management programmes in the world. The Government has further extended the coverage of food security network through additional provisions of foodgrains through the schemes like PM Gareeb Kalyan Yojana (PMGKY). A review of India's food management programme including food procurement, allocation, storage and the issue of food subsidy along with various Government measures for effective food and nutritional security is also presented at length in the chapter. The chapter ends with a review of the performance of fertilizer sector.

The agriculture and allied sectors grew at a positive growth rate of 3.6 per cent during 2020-21. This became possible due to good monsoon and various government measures to enhance credit availability, improve investments, create market facilities, promote infrastructure development in the agriculture sector and increase provision of quality inputs to the sector

Investment is critical to the growth of a sector. The Gross Capital Formation (GCF) in agriculture and allied sectors relative to GVA in the sector has been showing a fluctuating trend. Fluctuation in the GCF in the sector arises mainly because of wide fluctuations in private investment in agriculture and allied sectors.

As per Fourth Advance Estimates for 2020-21, total foodgrain production in the country is estimated at a record 308.65 million tonnes which is 11.15 million tonnes higher than that during 2019-20.

India is one of the major oilseeds growing country. The oilseed production in India has steadily increased since 2016-17 onward after showing a fluctuating trend prior to that. The oilseed production in India has grown by almost 43 per cent from 2015-16 to 2020-21.

## ❖ Minimum Support Price (MSP)

The Government fixes MSP of 22 mandated agricultural crops on the basis of the recommendations of Commission for Agricultural Costs and Prices (CACP) and after due consideration of the views of State Governments and the concerned Central Ministries/Departments. The 22 mandated crops include 14 Kharif crops viz. paddy, jowar, bajra, maize, ragi, tur (arhar), moong, urad, groundnut, soybean (yellow), sunflower seed, sesamum, nigerseed, cotton and 6 Rabi crops viz. wheat, barley, gram, masur (lentil), rapeseed and mustard, safflower and 2 commercial crops viz. jute and copra. In addition to that, MSP for toria and de-husked coconut are also fixed on the basis of MSPs of rapeseed & mustard and copra respectively.

## ❖ Crop Diversification

Crop diversification can be used as a tool to promote sustainable agriculture, reduction in import dependence and higher incomes for the farmers. The report of the DFI Committee suggests that shifting some area from staple cereals to high value produce can lead to a sizable increase in the returns for farmers.

### Natural Farming

The main aim for promotion of Natural Farming is elimination of chemical fertilisers and pesticides usage and promotion of good agronomic practices. Natural Farming also aims to sustain agriculture production with eco-friendly processes in tune with nature to produce agricultural produce free of chemicals. Soil fertility and soil organic matter is restored by natural farming practices. Natural farming systems require less water and are climate friendly.

Natural farming in India is being promoted through a dedicated scheme of Bharatiya Prakritik Krishi Paddhati Programme (BPKP). The scheme promotes on-farm biomass recycling with major stress on biomass mulching.

## ❖ Allied Sectors: Animal Husbandry and Dairying

As per the estimates of National Accounts Statistics (NAS) 2020 for sector wise GVA of agriculture and allied sectors, the contribution of livestock in total agriculture and allied sector GVA (at constant prices) has increased from 24.32 per cent (2014-15) to 29.35 per cent (2019-20). Livestock sector contributed 4.35 per cent of total GVA in 2019-20. Development of livestock sector has led to improvement in per capita availability of milk, eggs and meat.

## ❖ Dairy Sector

Dairy is the single largest agricultural commodity contributing 5 per cent of the national economy and employing more than 8 crore farmers directly. India is ranked 1st in milk production contributing 23 per cent of global milk production. Milk production in the country has grown at a compound annual growth rate of about 6.2 per cent to reach 209.96 million tonnes in 2020-21 from 146.31 million tonnes in 2014-15.

### Recent Initiatives in Animal Husbandry and Dairy Sector

National Animal Disease Control Programme

Animal Husbandry Infrastructure Development Fund (AHIDF)

## ❖ Fisheries

India is the second largest fish producing country in the world accounting for 7.56 per cent of global production. It contributes about 1.24 per cent to the country's GVA and over 7.28 per cent to the agricultural GVA.

## ❖ Food Processing Sector

During the last five years ending 2019-20, Food Processing Industries (FPI) sector has been growing at an average annual growth rate of around 11.18 per cent. The sector constituted as much as 9.87 per cent of GVA in manufacturing in 2019-20 at 2011-12 prices. Food Processing Industry is one of the major employment intensive segments having a share of 12.38 per cent (at 3-digit of NIC classification) in the employment generated in all Registered Factory sector in 2017-18.

## ❖ FDI in Food Processing Sector

In FPI, 100 per cent FDI is permitted under the automatic route. However, in case of trading in respect of food products manufactured and/or produced in India including through e-commerce, 100 per cent FDI is allowed under the Government approval route.

### Prime Minister-Formalization of Micro Food Processing Enterprises (PM-FME)

Under the ANB Mission, Ministry of Food Processing Industries (MoFPI) has launched a new Centrally Sponsored Scheme, PM-FME with a total outlay of ₹10,000 crore over the period 2020-2025.

### Pradhan Mantri Kisan SAMPADA Yojana (PMKSY)

Under the umbrella central sector scheme PMKSY, the Ministry is implementing various component schemes, inter-alia, including

(i) Mega Food Parks,
(ii) Integrated Cold Chain and Value Addition Infrastructure,
(iii) Infrastructure for Agro-processing Clusters,
(iv) Creation of Backward and Forward Linkages
(v) Creation/Expansion of Food Processing and Preservation Capacities,
(vi) Operation Greens and
(vii) Food Testing Laboratories.

### TOP Scheme

Operation Greens Scheme was announced in the Union Budget for 2018-19 to promote

Farmer Producer Organisations (FPOs), agri-logistics, processing facilities and professional management for Tomato, Onion and Potato (TOP) crops.

### Ethanol Blended with Petrol (EBP) Programme

The Government has now set 20 per cent ethanol blending target for mixing ethanol with petrol to be achieved by 2025. It is estimated that the blending target at 10 per cent would be achieved during 2022.

### Storage

The storage capacity available with FCI, a part of warehousing capacity available with Central Warehousing Corporation (CWC) and State Warehousing Corporations (SWCs) and capacity hired from private sector is used for storage of foodgrains procured for central pool by the Government Agencies.

### Fertilizers

Government is making available fertilizers, namely Urea and 24 grades of P&K fertilizers to farmers at subsidized prices through fertilizer manufacturers/importers. Urea is being provided to the farmers at a statutorily notified Maximum Retail Price (MRP). As far as Phosphatic and Potassic (P&K) fertilizers are concerned, Government is implementing Nutrient Based Subsidy (NBS) Scheme w.e.f 01.04.2010.

As shown by the latest SAS report, the fragmentation of landholdings has led to alternate sources such as livestock, fishery and wage labour becoming significantly important for an agricultural household. Increasing importance of allied sectors including animal husbandry, dairying and fisheries in growth and income of the farmers indicates that focus needs to shift more towards harnessing the potential of allied activities. There is also a need to improve productivity of small and marginal farmers through development and implementation of small holding farm technologies.

## INDUSTRY AND INFRASTRUCTURE

Global Industrial activity continued to be affected by the disruptions caused by the COVID-19 pandemic. While the Indian industry was no exception to these disruptions, its performance has improved in 2021-22.

The introduction of the production linked incentive scheme (PLI) to encourage scaling up of industries and major boost provided to infrastructure-both physical as well as digital–combined with continued measures to reduce transaction costs and improve ease of doing business.

The gross value addition at constant prices (GVA) in the industrial sector grew at the compound annual growth rate (CAGR) of 4.53 percent between 2011-12 and 2019-20 while total GVA grew by CAGR of 5.63 percent over the same period. The share of the industrial sector in the nominal GVA(at current prices) was 25.9 percent in 2020-21.With the industrial sector recovering and expected to grow at 11.8 percent, as per advance estimates for 2021-22 by National Statistical Office, industry's share is expected to increase to 28.2 percent.

Manufacturing, with an average share of 16.3 percent in nominal GVA over the last decade, has a dominant presence within the industrial sector. In 2020-21, the share of manufacturing fell to 14.4 percent but is expected to improve to15.3 percent in 2021-22. The share of electricity has been showing an increasing trend since 2012-13 and was 2.7 percent 2020-21.

### ❖ Index of Industrial Production (IIP)

The impact of the pandemic on the industrial sector is reflected in the negative growth of 8.4 percent in 2020-21. In April-November 2021-22 the IIP grew by 17.4 per cent as compared to (-15.3) per cent in the corresponding period of the previous year.

## ❖ Eight Core Index (ICI)

The monthly Index of Eight Core Industries (ICI) measures collective and individual performance of production in selected eight core industries like Coal, Crude Oil, Natural Gas, Refinery Products, Fertilizers, Steel, Cement and Electricity. This is an index of the eight most fundamental industrial sectors of the Indian economy and comprises 40.27 percent of the weight in IIP.

Capacity utilization (CU) is an important economic indicator to assess demand and investment prospects of the economy. CU rates are largely able to track the pace of manufacturing activities in the economy.

Another indication of optimism about the economic performance is the RBI's Business Expectation Index (BEI). This index gives a glimpse of the demand conditions in the manufacturing sector by combining parameters which include overall business situation, production, order books, inventory of raw material and finished goods, profit margin, employment, exports and capacity utilization.

## ❖ Gross Fixed Capital Formation

Gross fixed capital formation (GFCF) is the gross addition to fixed assets like machinery and equipment, intangible assets and indicates the state of investments in the economy. During 2019-20, the share of industrial sector in total GFCF in the economy (at current prices) was recorded at 30.1 per cent, which is slightly lower than 31 per cent in the previous financial year.

### Credit in Industry

Gross bank credit to the industrial sector, recorded a growth of 4.1 percent in October 2021 (Y-o-Y basis) compared to a negative growth of 0.7 growth in October 2020. The share of industry in non-food credit stood at 26 percent in October 2021. Certain industries such as mining, textiles, petroleum, coal products and nuclear fuels, rubber, plastic and infrastructure have shown consistent improvement in credit growth.

### FDI in Industries

As per the first advance estimates, Gross Value Added (GVA) of services sector is estimated to grow by 8.2 per cent in 2021-22. Sub-sectors 'Trade, hotels, transport, communication & broadcasting services', 'Financial, real estate & professional services', and 'Public administration, defence & other services' are estimated to expand by 11.9 per cent, 4 per cent and 10.7 per cent respectively in 2021-22.

Measures taken by the Government to put in place an enabling investor friendly FDI Policy has resulted in increased FDI inflows setting up new records. FDI inflows in India stood at US $ 45.14 billion in 2014-15 and have continuously increased since then. India registered its highest ever annual FDI inflow of US$ 81.97 billion (provisional) in the 2020-21 reflecting a growth of 10 percent as compared to the previous year. The increase has been on the back of growth of 20 per cent in 2019-20. In the year 2021-22, FDI inflow grew by 4 per cent in the first six months to reach US$ 42.86 billion as compared to US$ 41.37 billion for the same period of last year.

Over the last seven financial years (2014-21), India received FDI inflow worth US $ 440.27 billion which is nearly 58 percent of the FDI received by the country in the last 21 years (US$ 763.83 billion).

### Coal

Coal is the most important and abundant fossil fuel in India and accounts for 55 percent of the country's energy need. Coal production increased by 12.24 percent in April-October 2021 as compared to (-) 3.91 percent in April-October 2020.

### Micro Small Medium Enterprise

Micro, Small & Medium Enterprises (MSMEs) contribute significantly to the economic and social development of the country by fostering entrepreneurship and by generating employment opportunities. The relative importance of MSMEs can be gauged from the fact that the share of MSME GVA in total GVA (current prices) for 2019-20 was 33.08 per cent.

The government has taken several initiatives to nurture and promote the MSMEs. The revision in the definition of MSMEs brought in w.e.f. 1st July, 2020 as part of the AtmaNirbhar Bharat package introduced a composite-criteria of investment and annual turnover- and identical limits for manufacturing and services sector.

The CHAMPIONS portal (www.champion.gov.in) is an ICT based technology system for making the smaller units big by helping and handholding them. A network of control rooms is created in a Hub & Spoke Model where hub is situated in the Ministry of MSME.

## Textiles

Textile industry is the second largest employment generator in the country, next only to agriculture. In the last decade, close to Rs. 203,000 crores have been invested in this industry with direct and indirect employment of about 105 million people, a major part of which is women.

Production-Linked Incentive (PLI) Scheme for Man Made Fiber (MMF) segment and technical textiles, notified in September 2021, for enhancing India's manufacturing capabilities and enhancing exports will focus on promotion of 40 MMF apparel and 10 Technical textiles lines and create global champions.

## Electronics Industry

World over, electronics is recognised as a 'meta-resource'. Electronics industry is the world's largest and fastest growing industry and is increasingly finding applications in all sectors of the economy. With its impact in developing infrastructure, raising productivity, increasing efficiency in delivery of services, and enabling social transformation, it is accepted as a key enabler in the country's economic development.

Recently, the government has approved an outlay of Rs. 76,000 Crore (>US$ 10 Bn) for the development of Semiconductors and Display Manufacturing Ecosystem. Government's intervention to boost this industry has come at a time when the global economy is facing an acute shortage of semiconductors due to severe disruptions in supply chains.

## Pharmaceuticals

Indian Pharmaceutical industry ranks third in the world in pharmaceutical production by volume. During2020-21, total pharma export US$ 24.4 Bn against the total pharma import of US$7.0 Bn, thereby generating trade surplus of US$17.5 Bn. India is the largest supplier of generic medicines with a 20percent share in the global supply.

## Infrastucture

Infrastructure is the back bone for any economy.

**National Infrastructure Pipeline (NIP)**- Public Private Partnership in infrastructure has been an important source of investment in the sector. As per the database of the World Bank on private participation in infrastructure, India is ranked second among developing countries both by the number of PPP Projects as well as the associated investments. Much of the Indian success in PPPs is attributed to development of robust institutional structure, financial support, and use of standardized documents, both process documents like Model Request for Qualification and Model Request for Proposal as well as substantive documents like the Model Concession Agreements across infrastructure sectors.

**National Monetisation Pipeline (NMP)** - NITI Aayog has developed the 'National Monetisation Pipeline (NMP Volumes 1 & 2) in consultation with infrastructure line ministries. Asset monetisation, entails a limited period license/lease of an asset, owned by the government or a public authority, to a private sector entity for an upfront or periodic consideration.

### Road Transport

Road transport is one of the most cost effective and convenient modes of transportation in India both for freight and passengers as it has high penetration level with door-to-door delivery. Importance of road infrastructure is widely recognized as a potent means of socio-economic integration and is vital for the economic development of the country.

### Railways

Despite facing the unprecedented COVID related challenges Indian railways (IR) has not only been able to move millions of people but also able to keep national supply chain running. IR is also adopting indigenous new technology such as KAVACH, Vande Bharat trains and redevelopment of stations to have safe and better journey experience. During FY21, IR carried 1.23 billion tonnes of freight and 1.25 billion passengers.

### Civil Aviation

India has emerged as one of the fastest growing aviation markets in the world. The domestic traffic in India has more than doubled from around 61 million in 2013-14 to around 137 million in 2019-20, registering a growth of over 14 percent per annum.

Government of India took various initiatives to boost the aviation sector which included calibrated opening of the domestic sector as the first wave of the pandemic ebbed, introduction of air transport bubbles or air travel arrangements with specific countries, disinvestment of Air India.

UDAN is a regional airport development program of the Government of India and part of the Regional Connectivity Scheme (RCS) of upgrading underserviced air routes. Till launching of UDAN in 2016, India had 74 airports having scheduled operations.

With the accelerated pace of vaccine roll-out and easing of travel restrictions globally, Indian aviation sector has started to rebound. Despite the travel restrictions, the total passengers carried in October, 2021 reached 99.58 lakhs which was near 68 percent of the pre-Covid level.

### Ports

Port performance in an economy is crucial for trade competitiveness of that economy. Expansion of port capacity has been accorded the highest priority by the Government through implementation of well-conceived infrastructure development projects. The capacity of 13 major ports which was 871.52 million tonnes per annum (MTPA) at the end of March 2014, has increased by 79 percent to 1,560.61 MTPA by the end of March 2021.

### Inland Waterways

Regulatory amendment through the Inland Vessels Act, 2021, replaced the over 100 years old Inland Vessels Act, 1917 (1 of 1917) and ushered in a new era in the inland water transport sector. The objective of the Act is to promote economical, safe transportation and trade through inland waters. It will ensure transparency and accountability in the administration of inland water transportation and promote the ease of doing business.

### Telecom

India is the world's second-largest telecommunications market. The telecommunication sector is one of the most powerful sectors impacting social and economic development of a country. A strong and a responsive regulatory framework has kept the service access at reasonable prices. The Government has taken further measures to ensure fair competition among service providers with the view to benefit the consumers. Over the last few years, telecom sector in India has become data driven and reducing costs of data due to the fierce competition in the sector.

Crude oil and condensate production during the year 2020-21 was 30.49 million metric tonnes (MMT), lower than the production level of 32.17 MMT in 2019-20 and 94.3 percent of the target of 32.32 MMT for 2020-21. India depends on imports to meet more than 80 per cent of its requirements.

### Electricity

The total installed power capacity and captive power plant (industries having demand of 1MW and above) was 459.15 GW on 31.03.2021 as compared to 446.35 GW on 31.03.2020 registering a growth of 2.87 percent.

### Renewable Energy – Solar, Wind, Biomass and Small Hydro Energy

India has witnessed the fastest rate of growth in renewable energy capacity addition among all large economies, during the last 7.5 years with renewable energy capacity growing by 2.9 times and solar energy expanding by over 18 times. Renewable energy (excluding large hydro) constitutes over 24.71 percent of the country's installed power capacity and around 10.7 percent of the electrical energy generation for year 2020-21. As of 31 October 2021, India's total renewable energy installed capacity (excluding hydro power above 25 MW) has reached over 103.05 GW. During the last 7.5 years, if large hydro is included, the share of renewable energy in electric installed capacity is estimated to be about 38.27 percent (as of October 2021) and its share in electric energy generation is estimated to be about 26.96 percent (for the month of August 2021). The difference in the share of renewable energy in installed capacity and electricity generation is because of the variability in thesunshine hours or extent of wind which in turn will determine the utilization of the installed capacity.

## SERVICES

The services sector as a whole has mostly recovered from the impact of the nationwide lockdown imposed during March-May 2020 and localised lockdowns during the second covid wave in April-May 2021, although some of the sub-sectors continue to be impacted. During the first half of 2021-22, the Services sector grew by 10.8 per cent.

Startups in India have grown remarkably over the last six years. The number of new recognised starups have increased to over 14,000 in 2021-22 from only 733 in 2016-17. As a result, India has become the third largest startup ecosystem in the world after the US and China. Further, a record 44 Indian startups have achieved unicorn status in 2021 taking the overall tally of unicorns in India to 83, most of these are in the services sector.

Services sector contributes over 50 per cent to India's GDP. While Covid-19 pandemic has had an adverse impact on most sectors of the economy, the services sector has been the worst affected as its' share in India's GVA declined from 55 per cent in 2019-20 to 53 per cent in 2021-22.

As per the first advance estimates, Gross Value Added (GVA) of services sector is estimated to grow by 8.2 per cent in 2021-22. Sub-sectors 'Trade, hotels, transport, communication & broadcasting services', 'Financial, real estate & professional services', and 'Public administration, defence & other services' are estimated to expand by 11.9 per cent, 4 per cent and 10.7 per cent respectively in 2021-22.

### ❖ Passenger Traffic

Travel restrictions in the early half of 2020-21 had halted the movement of Indian airlines and railways leading to a sharp fall in air and rail passenger traffic. Domestic passenger traffic (both air and rail) had then started to recover gradually from August 2020 on a monthly basis but fell again in April-May 2021 due to the disruptions caused by second wave of Covid-19. It has picked up since then.

## ❖ Bank Credit to Services Sector

Bank credit growth to services sector which had moderated significantly in 2019, started picking up in 2020, increasing to 8.8 per cent (YoY) at the end December 2020, as compared to 6.2 per cent in December 2019. This momentum has lost its pace in 2021-22. Bank credit growth decelerated to 3.6 per cent YoY at the end of November 2021 as compared to 8.2 per cent a year ago. However, it is important to note that corporates have raised more money through capital markets than banking capital in 2021-22 so far.

## ❖ Services Sector Share at the State and UT Level

The services sector accounts for more than 50 per cent of the Gross State Value Added (GSVA) in 12 out of the 33 states and UTs. Chandigarh stands out with a particularly high share of services in GSVA at 74 per cent while Sikkim's share remains the lowest at 24.25 per cent. Notably, Services share in Sikkim's GSVA has increased from over 18 per cent in 2018-19 to over 24 per cent in 2020-21.

## ❖ FDI Inflows into Services Sector

Services sector is the largest recipient of FDI inflows in India. According to the World Investment Report 2021 by the UN Conference on Trade and Development (UNCTAD), India was the fifth-largest recipient of Foreign Direct Investment (FDI) in 2020 improving its rank by four places, from ninth position in 2019. In 2020-21, India registered highest ever annual FDI inflows of US$ 81.97 billion. The country has received US$ 43.12 billion FDI inflows in the first six months of 2021-22.

## ❖ Trade in Services Sector

World trade in commercial services plummeted in 2020 following the Covid-19 pandemic. The slowdown in global services was predominately due to restrictions on travel and tourism and reduction in transportation services, largely in the passenger segment.

## ❖ Services Exports

India has a dominant presence in global services exports. It remained among the top ten services exporter countries in 2020, with its share in world commercial services exports increasing from 3.4 per cent in 2019 to 4.1 per cent in 2020.

## ❖ Services Imports

India's services imports exhibited sharper decline of 8.4 per cent in 2020-21 in comparison with services exports primarily on account of fall in travel and transportation payments.

## ❖ Tourism Sector

In normal times, tourism sector is a major contributor to GDP growth, foreign exchange earnings and employment. However, the Covid-19 pandemic has had a debilitating impact on world travel and tourism everywhere, including India.

According to the World Tourism Barometer of the United Nation's World Tourism Organization (January 2021), International Tourist Arrivals (ITA) declined by 74 per cent globally in 2020 over the previous year.

## ❖ IT BPM Services

The Information Technology-Business Process Management (IT-BPM) sector is a major segment of India's services. During 2020-21, according to NASSCOM's provisional estimates, IT-BPM revenues (excluding e-commerce) reached US$ 194 billion, growing by 2.26 per cent YoY, adding 1.38 lakh employees.

### ❖ Ports, Shipping and Waterways Services

Development of ports is crucial for the economy. Ports handle around 90 per cent of export-import cargo by volume and 70 per cent by value in India. The total cargo capacity of all the ports has increased to 1,246.86 Million Tonnes Per Annum (MTPA) as of March 2021 from 1,052.23 MTPA as of March 2014.

### ❖ Sagarmala Programme

The Sagarmala programme is the flagship progamme of the Ministry of Ports, Shipping and Waterways to promote port-led development in the country by taking advantage of India's 7,500 km long coastline, 14,500 km long potentially navigable waterways and the strategic location on major maritime trade routes. The core vision of the Sagarmala programme is to reduce the logistics cost for export, import and domestic trade. Presently, a total of 802 projects worth Rs. 5.53 lakh crore are part of Sagarmala Programme. Of these, 181 projects worth Rs. 94,712 crore have been completed and 398 projects worth Rs. 2.48 lakh crore are under various stages of implementation.

### ❖ Space Sector

The Indian space program has grown drastically. Administered by the Department of Space (DOS) and primarily executed by its R&D arm, the Indian Space Research Organization (ISRO), capabilities have been developed in the space sector across all domains.

**Number of Start-ups in Space Sector**

| Year | No. of start-up |
|---|---|
| 2012 | 1 |
| 2013 | 1 |
| 2014 | 1 |
| 2015 | 3 |
| 2016 | 1 |
| 2017 | 8 |
| 2018 | 7 |
| 2019 | 11 |
| 2020 | 21 |
| 2021 | 47 |
| **Total** | **101** |

### ❖ Start-ups

Start-ups in India have grown remarkably over the last six years, most of these belong to the services sector. During 2021, the Government recognised over 14,000 new start-ups as compared to only, only 733 new start ups during 2016-17. As a result, more than 61,400 start-ups have been recognised in India as of January 10, 2022. During 2021, 555 districts had at least one new start-up. On the other hand, only 121 districts had at least 1 new start-up in 2016-17.

### ❖ Patents

Most of India's start-ups are in the IT/knowledge-based sector. Intellectual property, specifically patents are key to this knowledge-based economy. There has been gradual increase in the filing and granting of patents in India. The number of patents filed in India has gone up from 39,400 in 2010-11 to 45,444 in 2016-17 to 58,502 in 2020-21 and the patents granted in India has gone up from 7,509 to 9,847 to 28,391 during the same time period.

## SOCIAL INFRASTRUCTURE AND EMPLOYMENT

As per quarterly Periodic Labour Force Survey (PLFS) data, up to March 2021, employment in urban sector affected by the pandemic has recovered almost to the pre-pandemic levels. Employees Provident Fund Organisation (EPFO) data suggests, that not only formalisation of jobs continued during second-COVID-19-wave, but its adverse impact by far on formalization of jobs was also much lower than during the first-COVID-wave. To provide the necessary buffer for the unorganized labour in rural areas during the pandemic, allocation of funds to Mahatma Gandhi National Rural Employment Guarantee Scheme (MGNREGS) has been increased.

As per the latest available data, school infrastructure – both in terms of number of recognized schools & colleges and basic facilities in schools – and teachers' availability reflected in Pupil Teacher Ratio, showed an improvement in 2019-20 over earlier years.

The latest National Family Health Survey-5 showed encouraging outcomes of Government programmes in the health and other social sectors. Total fertility rate (TFR) has come down from 2.2 in 2015-16 to 2 in 2019-21.

## ❖ India's Health Response to the COVID-19

Like most other countries, India also faced two COVID-19 waves: first in 2020 and second in 2021. During the first-wave, the cumulative number of COVID-19 cases started rising progressively from the month of May 2020, and peaked in mid-September 2020. Thereafter, the country faced a massive surge in COVID-19 cases starting March 2021, with a peak of more than four lakh daily cases in May 2021 and more than 4400 daily deaths in end of May 2021. A fresh surge of cases and a new variant Omicron had surfaced in December 2021.

## ❖ COVID Vaccination Strategy

Guided by scientific and epidemiological evidence, World Health Organisation (WHO) guidelines and global best practices, India's National COVID Vaccination Program has been one of the world's largest vaccination programs. National Expert Group on Vaccine Administration for COVID-19 (NEGVAC) on the basis of concurrent scientific evidence guided the program. The program was envisioned to vaccinate all eligible beneficiaries aged 18 years and above in the shortest possible time.

Availability of Vaccine: India is among few countries producing COVID vaccines. The country started with two Made in India COVID vaccines. India's first domestic COVID-19 vaccine, Whole Virion Inactivated Corona Virus Vaccine (COVAXIN), was developed and manufactured by Bharat Biotech International Limited in collaboration with National Institute of Virology of Indian Council of Medical Research (ICMR). The ICMR funded the clinical trials of the COVISHIELD vaccine developed in collaboration with Oxford – AstraZeneca.

Vaccination Progress: As on 16th January 2022, a total of 156.76 crore doses of COVID-19 vaccines have been administered: 90.75 crore first dose and 65.58 crore second dose. Vaccination speed increased significantly once the population between ages 18 to 45 years was permitted.

## ❖ Trends in Social Sector Expenditure

Government's spending on social services increased significantly during the pandemic. In 2021-22 (BE), Centre and State governments earmarked an aggregate of ₹ 71.61 lakh crore for spending on social service sector.

The National Health Policy, 2017 envisaged to increase government's health expenditure to 2.5 percent of GDP by 2025. In keeping with this objective, Central and State Governments' budgeted expenditure on health sector reached 2.1 percent of GDP in 2021-22, against 1.3 percent in 2019-20.

## Higher Education

Gross enrolment ratio in higher education recorded at 27.1 percent in 2019-20, slightly higher from 26.3 percent in 2018-19. For males, it has also increased from 26.3 percent in 2018-19 to 26.9 percent in 2019-20 while for females it has increased from 26.4 percent to 27.3 percent respectively.

## Multidimensional Poverty

Using NFHS-4 (2015-16) report, in line with global Multidimensional Poverty Index (MPI), NITI Aayog prepared Multidimensional Poverty Index at the national, for all states and districts of India. It will enable measuring deprivation across twelve indicators at national, States and districts level.

❑❑❑

# CHAPTER 19

# Union Budget 2022–23

Finance Minister Nirmala Sitharaman presented the union budget 2022 for the upcoming fiscal year on Tuesday, 1st February. The new union budget, worth INR 39.45 lakh crore, outlines government expenditure for the year and is expected to spend 4.6% more than last year. The budget focuses on infrastructure spending, including the expansion of national highways and the generation of several hundred new trains. The idea is to help with job creation and boost economic activity. While there was a lot of news on income tax brackets in the run-up to the budget announcement, the finance minister has not proposed any changes to the tax slabs or basic tax deductions for individuals. During the union budget announcement, the finance minister projected the country's economy to grow by 9.2%, the fastest of all growing economies.

## KEY HIGHLIGHTS OF UNION BUDGET FY 2022-2023

Let's take a look at the highlights of the union budget and how it affects various sectors:

### ❖ Union Budget on Economy

- Capex target increased from INR 5.54 lakh crore to INR 7.50 lakh crore, an increase of 35.4%
- Emergency Credit Line Guarantee Scheme (ECLGS) cover increased to INR 5 lakh crore
- Investment intentions worth INR 30 lakh crore received for productivity-linked incentive schemes in 14 sectors
- States allows fiscal deficit of up to 4% of GSDP
- Public investments and capital spending boost economic recovery

### ❖ Union Budget on Taxes

- One-time window of two years provided to correct any omissions to filed ITRs
- Cess or surcharge on income to be excluded from business expenditure
- Surcharge on long-term capital gains capped at 15%
- Tax deduction limit on employer's contribution to the NPS accounts of state government employees increased to 14%
- Alternate minimum tax for cooperative societies reduced to 15%

- Surcharge on cooperative societies that earn between INR 1 crore and INR 10 crore reduced to 7%
- 30% tax on transfer of digital assets and no deductions allowed for the same

## ❖ Union Budget on Duties on Industry

- Import duty for specific chemicals reduced
- Exemption on custom duty for steel scraps extended for another year
- Customs duty on stainless steel, high steel bars and flat products revoked
- Additional duty of INR 2 per litre on unblended fuel
- 5% reduction on import duty for cut and polished diamonds and gemstones
- Sawn diamond import duty reduced to nil
- Custom duty concessions allowed for consumer electronics such as wearables, mobile phone components and hearing aids to promote manufacturing

## ❖ Union Budget on Employment

- ECLGS extended until March 2023 to help create 60 lakh jobs in 5 years
- Digital ecosystem for livelihood and skilling to be launched to help skill, reskill and upskill citizens via online training and help find relevant job opportunities

## ❖ Union Budget on Infrastructure and Manufacturing

- Digital infra to get boost from DESH STACK e-portal launch
- Contracts for four multi-modal national parks to be awarded
- 100 PM Gati Shakti terminals will get set up in three years
- Masterplan for expansion of national expressways under PM Gati Shakti plan to be outlined
- Concessional corporate tax rate of 15% extended until March 2024 for new manufacturing companies

## ❖ Union Budget on Digital Currency

- Blockchain-based digital rupee to be launched
- 30% tax levied on income from virtual digital assets
- Losses from the sale of virtual digital assets cannot be offset against other income

## ❖ Union Budget on Housing and Urban Planning

- 80 lakh houses to be completed for beneficiaries of PM Awas Yojana
- INR 48,000 crore set aside for PM Awas Yojana
- INR 60,000 crore to be used to provide tap water to 3.8 crore households
- High-level committee of urban planners and economists to be formed to provide recommendations on urban planning, building and governance

## ❖ Union Budget on MSMEs and Start-ups

- Programme to rate MSMEs costing INR 6,000 crore to be rolled out over the next five years
- Udyam, e-shram, NCS and Aseem portals to get interlinked and scope will be widened to provide credit facilitation and other services that enhance entrepreneurial opportunities

- Start-ups in agriculture and rural enterprises to receive finance through NABARD for the farm produce value chain
- Expert committee to be set up to suggest measures to attract investments
- Tax benefits for start-ups, including redemption for three consecutive years, extended for another year

## ❖ Union Budget on Agriculture

- Government will procure INR 2.37 lakh crore worth of wheat and paddy under MSP operations
- Year 2022-2023 announced as Year of Millets
- Railways to help develop new products for small farmers and MSMEs
- Rationalised scheme introduced to increase domestic production of oilseed
- Kisan drones to be used for assessment of crops and spraying of insecticides and to keep land records
- INR 44,605 crore set aside for new Ken-Betwa river-linking project
- Draft Detailed Project Reports (DPRs) finalised for five river-linking projects
- Paperless e-bill system to be launched by ministries for procurement
- Farmers taking up agro-forestry to receive financial support
- Natural farming to be promoted along the River Ganga corridor
- Focus on sustainable agricultural productivity and promotion of chemical-free natural farming

## ❖ Union Budget on Electric Vehicles

- Framing of battery swapping policy at EV charging stations
- Private sector will be encouraged to build innovative and sustainable business models in the battery and energy sector to improve efficiency

## ❖ Union Budget on Education

- Agricultural university syllabus to be revised by states to meet the needs of natural, modern-day and zero-budget and organic farming
- PM eVIDYA One Class, One TV channel programme to be expanded to 200 channels to provide education in regional languages for classes 1 to 12
- Digital university based on hub and spoke model to be set up
- National Skill Qualification Framework (NSQF) set up to cater to dynamic industry needs

## ❖ Union Budget on Finance

- INR 1 lakh crore assistance for states in 2022 to 2023 to boost investments
- Introduction of digital rupee to start
- All post offices brought under core banking system to enable quick transfer of funds and easy banking facilities
- Enhancement of resolution process efficiency through IBC amendments
- Digital payments encouraged by setting up 75 digital banks in 75 districts
- For government procurement, surety bond can be used in place of a bank guarantee
- Faster dispute resolution will be offered by setting up an international arbitration centre in GIFT city
- Once parents or guardians of dependent differently abled individuals reach the age of 60, annuity and lump-sum payments

will be offered to the differently-abled dependents

- World-class university free from domestic regulation allowed in GIFT IFSC

## ❖ Union Budget on Healthcare

- Launch of open platform for national digital health ecosystem containing registries of health providers and health facilities
- Significant progress seen in health and infrastructure in 95% of 112 aspirational districts
- National Tele Mental Health Programme launched to promote good mental health

## ❖ Union Budget on Telecom

- Spectrum auction for the rollout of 5G to be conducted in 2022
- Design-led manufacturing scheme for 5G ecosystem to be launched as part of PLI scheme for affordable broadband and mobile communication in remote areas
- 5% of USO fund to be utilised for technology upgradation and research and development
- BharatNet project to award contracts to lay optical fibre in villages in 2022-2023
- Energy storage systems and data centres given infrastructure status to ease funding

## ❖ Union Budget on Women and Children

- Three schemes launched for integrated development of women and children and to recognise the importance of Nari Shakti
- Two lakh anganwadis to be upgraded to improve child health

## ❖ Union Budget on Business

- 1,486 union laws and 75,000 compliances repealed to ease the way for businesses
- Ease of Doing Business (EODB) 2.0 launched along with Ease of Living
- Voluntary corporate exit timeline cut from two years to six months
- New legislation to replace Special Economic Zones

## ❖ Union Budget on Defence

- Government committed to self-reliance and cutting down imports
- 68% of capital expenditure for defence sector kept aside for local industries
- 25% of defence R&D budget set aside for industry, start-ups and academia
- Private sector encouraged to design and develop military platforms and equipment through SPV model with DRDO

## ❖ Union Budget on Transportation

- 400 new-age Vande Bharat trains to be manufactured over three years
- National highway networks to be expanded by 25,000 kilometres in 2022-2023 costing INR 20,000 crore
- Railway allocated INR 1,40,367.13 crore
- 2,000 kilometres of the rail network brought under KAWACH for enhanced safety and to boost capacity
- One product one railway station to be popularised

## Budget at a Glance

*(in ₹ crore)*

| | | 2020–2021 Actuals | 2021–2022 Budget Estimates | 2021–2022 Revised Estimates | 2022–2023 Budget Estimates |
|---|---|---|---|---|---|
| 1. | **Revenue Receipts** | **1633920** | **1788424** | **2078936** | **2204422** |
| | 2. Tax Revenue (Net to Centre) | 1426287 | 1545396 | 1764145 | 1934771 |
| | 3. Non Tax Revenue | 207633 | 243028 | 313791 | 269651 |
| 4. | **Capital Receipts** | **1875916** | **1694812** | **1691064** | **1740487** |
| | 5. Recovery of Loans | 19729 | 13000 | 21975 | 14291 |
| | 6. Other Receipts | 37897 | 175000 | 78000 | 65000 |
| | 7. Borrowings and Other Liabilities[1] | 1818291 | 1506812 | 1591089 | 1661196 |
| 8. | **Total Receipts (1+4)** | **3509836** | **3483236** | **3770000** | **3944909** |
| 9. | **Total Expenditure (10+13)** | **3509836** | **3483236** | **3770000** | **3944909** |
| | 10. On Revenue Account of which | 3083519 | 2929000 | 3167289 | 3194663 |
| | 11. Interest Payments | 679869 | 809701 | 813791 | 940651 |
| | 12. Grants in Aid for creation of capital assets | 230865 | 219112 | 237685 | 317643 |
| | 13. On Capital Accounts[2] | 426317 | 554236 | 602711 | 750246 |
| 14. | **Effective Capital Expenditure (12+13)[3]** | **657182** | **773348** | **840396** | **1067889** |
| 15. | **Revenue Deficit (10–1)** | **1449599 (7.3)** | **1140576 (5.1)** | **1088352 (4.7)** | **990241 (3.8)** |
| 16. | **Effective Revenue Deficit (15–12)** | **1218734 (6.3)** | **921464 (4.1)** | **850667 (3.7)** | **672598 (2.6)** |
| 17. | **Fiscal Deficit [9–(1+5+6)]** | **1818291 (9.2)** | **1506812 (6.8)** | **1591089 (6.9)** | **1661196 (6.4)** |
| 18. | **Primary Deficit (17–11)** | **1138422 (5.8)** | **697111 (3.1)** | **777298 (3.3)** | **720545 (2.8)** |

[1] Includes drawdown of cash Balance

[2] RE 2021-22 for Capital Expenditure includes capital infusion/loans to AIAHL/AI for settlement of past guaranteed and sundry liabilities, not backed by assets amounting to ₹51971 crore. Excluding this, capital expenditure in RE is estimated ₹550740 crore.

[3] Grants for creations of capital assets also includes allocations under Demand driven/entitlement based scheme MGNREGS, which would vary based on demand.

**Notes:**

(i) GDP for BE 2022-2023 has been projected at ₹25800000 crore assuming 11.1% growth over the estimated GDP of ₹21214703 crore for 2021-2022 (RE).

(ii) Individual items in this document may not sum up to the totals due to rounding off

(iii) Figures in parenthesis are as a percentage of GDP.

**Rupee Comes from (Budget 2022–23)**

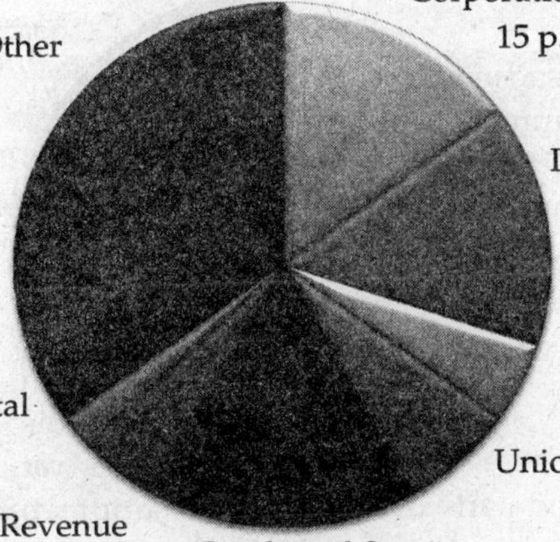


**Notes:**

1. Total receipts are inclusive of State's share of taxes and duties which have been netted against receipts.
2. Figures have been rounded off.

**Rupee Goes To (Budget 2022–23)**

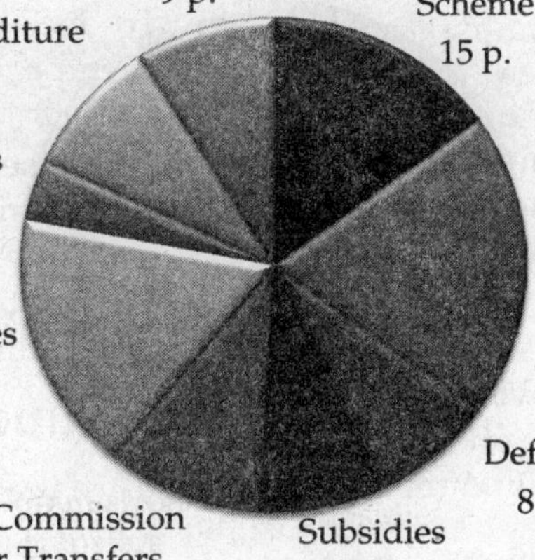


**Notes:**

1. Total receipts is inclusive of the State's share of taxes and duties which have been netted against receipts.
2. Figures have been rounded off.

## ANALYSIS

### ❖ Impact of Budget 2022 Proposals on Various Sectors

Amid lingering global headwinds and economic uncertainty, finance minister Nirmala Sitharaman continued to prioritize growth over fiscal consolidation for the second straight year, sharply expanding capital and infrastructure spending in the Union Budget for the year.

## OIL & GAS SECTOR

### Proposals

- The budget has proposed an increase in capex outlay by 35.4%, expansion of national highways network by 15% and addition of 25,000 km of roads
- Development of four multi-modal logistics parks in the coming year .
- Focus on electric vehicle (ev) charging infra and a new battery swapping policy
- It also proposed a gradual reduction in customs duty to 7.5% for all project capital goods imports and allocation of ₹19,500 crore for production-linked incentive (PLI) scheme for manufacturing of polysilicon solar modules.

### Impact

- A better infrastructure connectivity will provide significant impetus on oil and gas projects, with refineries being set up in the South India, and pipelines and city gas projects across the country.
- New highways and EV and battery swapping push will provide a great avenue for retail growth for oil marketing companies to increase retail outlets and offerings to customers.
- Differential duty on unblended fuel to incentivize bio-fuel blending will be a boost to oil and gas companies which are already transitioning to new energy areas.

## CONSUMER DURABLES

### Proposals

- To boost consumption and empower the rural economy, the finance minister has announced several measures such as
- Support for millet production,
- Reduced dependence on imported oilseeds,
- Finance start-ups for agriculture and rural enterprise pertinent to the farm produce value chain.
- Customs exemptions on implements and tools for the farm sector have also been rationalized to boost domestic manufacturing.

### Impact

- The government's impetus on PM Gatishakti plan to build world class infrastructure and logistics is likely to give boost to the consumer sector supply chain over a longer term.
- Further, custom duty rates have been rationalized on parts of mobile phones (including camera modules), wearables/ hearables devices, loudspeakers, etc. to facilitate domestic electronics manufacturing.
- To incentivize exports, exemptions have been provided on items relevant to textiles sector.
- All these are likely to act as a catalyst for improving the conditions of lower income consumers, thereby leading to a steady acceleration in the consumption and demand for FMCG sector products.

## BANKING SECTOR

### Proposals

- The government has proposed to introduce a digital rupee—using blockchain and other technologies—issued by the Reserve Bank of India (RBI) starting 2022-23 for more efficient and cheaper currency management system.

- Further, to help micro, small and medium enterprises (MSMEs) impacted by the pandemic, the credit guarantee fund trust for micro and small enterprises (CGTMSE) will be revamped with additional credit of ₹ 2 trillion and thereby expand employment opportunities.
- Post office accounts will be brought under the coverage of core banking.

### Impact

- The budget proposals are aimed at boosting credit growth of both banks and non-banking financial companies (NBFCs), with schemes announced across various sectors including affordable housing, transportation and logistics, and electric vehicles (EVs), etc.
- With 1.5 lakh post offices coming under core banking, more than 35 crore post office deposit accounts will come into the mainline banking and payments system.
- The proposal for 75 digital banking units in 75 districts is a small step but a definite push towards digital banking. 'Digital Rupee' is another step towards the government's adoption of digital as means of transaction banking.

## AUTOMOBILE SECTOR

### Proposals

- The finance minister has announced a new battery swap policy to encourage electric vehicle (EV) adoption.
- The government also proposed to open up defence research and development (R&D) to private players for auto component development.

### Impact

- A policy for battery swapping will aid in reducing the upfront ownership cost of EVs, thereby driving customer preference towards such vehicles.
- This policy is also expected to encourage private sector to develop sustainable and innovative business models for 'Battery or Energy as a Service'.
- Further, interoperability standards will build efficiency in operation of charging infrastructure for EVs.
- These changes, along with recently announced production linked incentives (PLI) for EVs, would give the necessary fillip to EV revolution in India.

## DEFENCE SECTOR

### Proposals

- The budget has proposed the highest ever allocation for the defence sector at ₹5.25 trillion for FY 2022-23, with a significant increase of about 10% from last year.

### Impact

- The proposals will go a long way in modernizing the Indian armed forces further, while ensuring the current government's commitment to reduce dependence on import of defence equipment.
- Another notable update in the area of defence is the opening up of defence research and development (R&D) for industry, startups and academia by earmarking 25% of defence R&D budget for them.
- This is a positive move which will help to leverage the capabilities of the private industry in defence research.

## HEALTHCARE AND PHARMA SECTOR

### Proposals

- The government has made a path breaking move with the introduction of Ayushman Bharat Digital Mission in Budget 2022.
- However, there has been no policy amendments to facilitate private participation to provide an impetus in

strengthening the overall healthcare infrastructure and accessibility to healthcare services.

- The government will launch a national tele-mental health program to provide 24x7 free counselling and care to people.

### Impact

- The government has extended the benefit of concessional tax regime for manufacturing companies.
- The government has also considered pharmaceutical sector as one of the sunrise opportunity sectors that will benefit from future supportive policies, among other things.
- The government, however, did not consider the long-standing demand/expectation of industry to incentivize research and development needed to enable India to move from being an incremental innovator to becoming a global player in innovative drugs.

## START UP SECTOR

### Proposals

- The existing tax benefits for start-ups has been extended by one more year till 31st March 2023.
- Also, a fund, raised under the co-investment model, will be facilitated through NABARD to finance start-ups for agriculture and rural enterprise relevant for the farm produce value chain.
- Start-ups will be promoted to facilitate 'Drone Shakti' through varied applications and for Drone-As-A-Service (DrAAS).

### Impact

- Budget 2022 was high on the development and inclusiveness agenda of the government, with significant allocations on infrastructure, healthcare, education, fin-tech, agriculture, etc.
- Similarly, policies aimed at the faster adoption of electric vehicles and a committee set up for promoting private equity/venture capital ecosystem would be beneficial in the longer term.

## REAL ESTATE SECTOR

### Proposals

- Affordable housing was clearly in focus, with the finance minister announcing the allocation of ₹48,000 crore under the Pradhan Mantri Awas Yojana. Around 8 million houses are expected to be completed by 2023 across the country.

### Impact

- The allocation to the PM Awas Yojana and the credit guarantee for the hospitality sector are all welcome measures.
- The proposal to replace the Special Economic Zone (SEZ) Act with a legislation that would permit states to partner in creating enterprise and service hubs and the push for digitization of land records are also laudable.
- The budget has also proposed the rationalization of tax withholding provisions relating to purchase or rental of properties and including units of Real Estate Investment Trusts (REITs) within the dividend provisions.

## METAL & MINING

### Proposals

- The budget has proposed an increase in outlay for capital expenditure.
- It also proposed the setting up of four pilot projects for coal gasification and conversion of coal into chemicals.

- By continuing the exemption on customs duty for steel scrap for a year, the government has been successful in pushing a larger problem a day beyond and providing temporal relief.

## Impact

- The increase in outlay for capital expenditure may provide the much-needed impetus to mining and metals (M&M) industry which forms the backbone around which blueprints for capital expenditure are drawn up.
- The pilot projects for coal gasification and conversion of coal into chemicals will boost the transition to a carbon neutral economy.
- A slew of measures has also been announced from indirect tax perspective such as extension of customs duty exemption on import of steel scrap by another year (up to 31 March 2023) and revocation of anti-dumping and countervailing duty on specified steel products.

# RETAIL SECTOR

## Proposals

- Though there was no specific proposal for this sector, the thrust on employment, infrastructure and financial inclusion is expected to boost consumption over the medium term.
- The 1.5 lakh post offices into the core banking system is a positive particularly for rural India and a higher minimum support price (MSP) allocation will drive consumption of fast-moving consumer goods (FMCG) products in the hinterland.

## Impact

- With an estimated gross domestic product (GDP) growth of over 9%, and the initiatives in the budget, consumer goods companies could expect an increase in consumption over the short to medium term driven by the thrust on investment, employment, and financial inclusion.

# GREEN ENERGY

## Proposals

- The government will launch sovereign bonds and increase the funding for solar equipment.
- It will also install 500 gigawatts(GW) of non-fossil capacity by 2030,
- Reduction in emission intensity of GDP by 45% over 2005 levels,
- Source 50% of the electricity from non-fossil by 2030,
- Reduction in carbon emission by 1 billion tonnes till 2030,
- Achieving net-zero by 2070.

## Impact

- The budget is inclusive and focused on sustainable development of a climate-adaptive and resilient Indian economy.
- It supports the development of sunrise business areas and reduction of carbon intensity by supporting the emergence of technology and innovative financing ecosystems.
- It has a clear direction around stimulating a circular economy by developing a policy and regulatory framework, and facilitating innovation.

# TEXTILE SECTOR

## Proposals

- The custom duty exemptions announced on items such as embellishment, trimming, buttons, zipper, lining material, and packaging boxes would benefit apparel exporters.

- The extension of emergency credit guarantee scheme for micro, small and medium enterprises (MSMEs) for one more year and increasing the guarantee by ₹50,000 crore.

## Impact

- The abolishing of concessional duties on imported capital goods, especially for fabric manufacturing and processing will increase the capital cost of new projects till such machineries are manufactured in India.
- While phasing out of customs duty exemption on fabrics will support the growth of domestic textiles manufacturing in the long run, it is expected to adversely impact the competitiveness of apparel exporters in the short run.
- The extension of emergency credit guarantee scheme for MSMES for one more year and increasing the guarantee by ₹50,000 crore is also expected to benefit over 50 lakh MSME units in textile and apparel sector.

# PETROCHEMICAL SECTOR

## Proposals

- Reduction of customs duty on certain critical chemicals namely, methanol, acetic acid and heavy feed stocks for petroleum refining, while increasing the duty on sodium cyanide.
- To promote blending of fuel, the government proposes to charge an additional differential excise duty of ₹2 per litre from 1 October 2022 on unblended fuel.

## Impact

- The changes in the customs duty of petrochemical and petroleum feedstocks used by domestic manufacturers result in reduced cost of inputs and correction of the inverted duty structure.
- Setting up of pilot projects for coal gasification and conversion of coal into chemicals are important, primarily to reduce dependence on methanol and acetic acid, which top the list of imported chemicals in terms of volume.
- The lack of availability of cheap natural gas, guarded nature of technology and stiff competition from the Middle East and China are the major barriers to methanol and acetic acid production.

# TELECOM SECTOR

## Proposals

- Spectrum auctions will be conducted to roll out 5G services and a scheme for design-led manufacturing in 5G will be launched.
- The national capital will also launch a scheme for design-led manufacturing to boost 5G.
- To enable affordable broadband and mobile service proliferation in rural and remote areas, 5% of annual collections under the universal service obligation (USO) fund will be allocated.

## Impact

- Auctions for 5G spectrum and its roll-out will happen in the fiscal year 2022-23. The roll-out across the country will also happen much faster than other previous generation roll-outs with the completion of fibre network in all villages by 2025 .
- Focus on digital education including digital universities will further push the need for high-speed broadband.
- While the details of the production linked incentive (PLI) for design-led manufacturing in the 5G space are awaited, it could be broadened beyond manufacturers to the

telecommunication service providers (TSPs) and telecom infrastructure players.

- A 5% allocation towards research and development and commercialization of the technology could help some of the indigenous niche players building up technologies around O-RAN and private networks.

## INFRASTRUCTURE SECTOR

### Proposals

- The PM Gati Shakti National Master Plan is announced with an aim to making logistics connectivity seamless.
- The national highways network will be expanded by 25,000 km, with an outlay of ₹20,000 crores via financing.
- A scheme for expressways will be formulated to facilitate faster movement of people and goods.
- Railways will develop new products and logistics services for small farmers, and small and medium enterprises.

### Impact

- The Gati Shakti initiative highlights the importance of quality multi-modal transport in achieving overall cost competitiveness.
- With global studies pegging India's average logistics costs at around 14% of GDP as against 8-9% for advanced economies, this is clearly a factor which needs to be addressed for attracting quality anchor investors across sectors.
- Infrastructure financing has also been mainstreamed, with particular focus on environment and sustainability, as evident from the announcement around green bonds, focus of National Infrastructure and Investment Fund (NIIF) and National Small Industries Corporation (NSIC) Fund of funds on the renewables sector, etc.

### ❖ River Inter-linking Project

- Budget 2022-23 allocated Rs. 1,400 crore to Ken-Betwa river interlinking project.
- Both rivers are tributaries of Yamuna.
- Aim of the project is to transfer surplus water from Ken to Betwa.
- Benefits of project-
  - ❖ Irrigation
  - ❖ Drinking water
  - ❖ Power generation
- Bundelkhand region of Uttar Pradesh and Madhya Pradesh would benefit from the project.
- Work of Project is expected to be completed in 8 years.
- Environmentalist are concerned that this river linking project would submerge core area part of area of Panna Tiger Reserve in Madhya Pradesh.
- Other River linking projects announced by Finance Minister in 2022-23 Budget-
  - ❖ Damanganga-Pinjal
  - ❖ Par-Tapi-Narmada
  - ❖ Godavari-Krishna
  - ❖ Pennar-Cauvery

## MSME SECTOR

- Allocation to MSME sector in Budget 2022-21 went up to Rs.21,422 crore, which is 26.71% more than what it had received in budget 2021-22.
- Emergency Credit Line Guarantee Scheme (ECLGS) extended to March 2023. The guaranteed cover under the scheme has also been extended by an additional Rs 50,000 crore. The aim of this scheme was to provide assistance to COVID hit MSMEs. To provide fully guaranteed and collateral free additional credit to MSMEs, business enterprises, MUDRA borrowers and individual loans for business purposes.

- Total outlay for all the schemes and projects for the Development of Khadi, Village and Coir Industries in this budget stands at Rs.1,168 crore.
- Notable reduction has been seen in Technology Upgradation and Quality Certification Scheme. Funds allotted to this scheme have been slashed by about 75%. The basic objectives of the scheme include inculcating Zero Defect & Zero Effect practices in manufacturing processes, ensure continuous improvement and support to the Make in India initiative.
- Amounts received by Interest Subvention Scheme for Incremental Credit and the Distressed Assets Fund both received massive cuts.

## CAPITAL GOODS

### Proposals

- The government is planning a gradual phase out of concessional tariff rates offered for capital goods and project imports.
- The Budget 2022-23 has proposed a 7.5% tariff on all such products and services. Exemptions are being introduced on inputs, like specialized castings, ball screw and linear motion guide, to encourage domestic manufacturing of capital goods.

### Impact

- The production linked incentive (PLI) schemes and other government measures have augmented investments in various sectors like food, textile, electronics, chemicals, etc. However, the dependency on import of capital goods still continues.
- Increase in customs duty on capital goods in these sectors would mean that such investments would be dearer and thereby also affect cash flows and profitability.

## IT SECTOR

### Proposals

- Blockchain-enabled digital currency will be issued by the Reserve Bank of India starting 2022-23. The government is promoting digital economy, digital health eco-system and e-passport, amongst others to drive India's growth.

### Impact

- Nearly every sector is expected to receive digital impetus driving further growth in technology and related sectors.
- The number of digital initiatives planned (digital currency, PM Gati Shakti, e-passport, Kisan drone, etc) are not incremental but transformational and will require a build-up of a complete IT ecosystem.
- Many of these proposals will have significant downstream opportunities for software, hardware, and services companies.
- The government plans to make financial services available to everyone with planned connectivity of 1.5 lakh post offices to core banking systems. Digitalization of financial services will not only reduce the cost of services but will also make it available to a larger base.

## AGRICULTURE & ALLIED SERVICES

### Proposals

- The government will promote the use of 'Kisan Drones' for crop assessment along with chemical-free farming.
- NABARD will finance start-ups for agriculture and rural enterprises and these start-ups will include inter-area support for farmer-producer organizations, machineries for farmers on a rental basis at the farm level.

### Impact

- On agriculture, some new age reforms like delivery of digital and hi-tech services to farmers in PPP mode, use of Kisan drones to aid farmers have been announced.
- Similarly, proposal on steps for promotion of chemical-free natural farming, updating the syllabus of agricultural universities to meet the needs of natural, organic farming, modern-day agriculture has been made.
- To increase domestic production of oilseeds and reduce dependence on imports, proposal to implement a rationalized and comprehensive scheme has been made.

### ❖ Agriculture Education and Research

- Allocation of funds to Agriculture education and research reduced in Union Budget 2022-23.
- Budget has provisioned Rs 8,513 crore to the Department of Agricultural Research and Education.
- Largest allocation from the above amount has been made to Indian Council of Agricultural Research.
- Budget for Crop Sciences has been reduced by 14.35%.

❖ Budget also saw cut in financial resources to animal sciences and Management of Natural Resources by 14.25% and 17% respectively.

## SOCIAL SECTOR

### ❖ Nutrition for Women and Children

- Pradhan Mantri Poshan Shakti Nirmal Programme (PM POSHAN) has received Rs. 10,234 crore in Budget 2022-23. This scheme focuses on providing cooked meals to school children between the ages of 6 and 14.
- Saksham Anganwadi and POSHAN 2.0 Scheme was allocated Rs. 20,263 crore. This is an Umbrella for Integrated Child Development Schemes which includes Poshan Abhiyan, Scheme for Adolescent Girls, Anganwadi Services and National Creche Scheme. The aim of the scheme is to strengthen nutritional content, delivery, outreach and outcome, with renewed focus on developing practices that nurture health, wellness and immunity to disease and malnutrition in the country.
- Pradhan Mantri Matri Vandana Yojana also saw increase in the budget allocation. This scheme ensures good food to pregnant and lactating women.

❑❑❑

# CHAPTER 20

# Glossary

**Absolute Poverty:** In India the concept of poverty has been approached in the absolute sense. In other words, it is not related to the income or consumption expenditure distribution. The concept of absolute poverty is relevant for the less-developed countries where absolute poverty abounds. To measure it, absolute norms for living are first laid down. These relate to some minimum standard of living.

**American Depositary Receipts (ADRs)** are securities offered by non-US companies who want to list on any of the US exchanges. Each ADR represents a certain number of a company's regular shares. These are deposited in a custodial account in the US.

**Angel Investors:** They are those investors which generally invest in the shares of non-traditional companies such as software and information technology services company in order to make quick profit.

**Anti-dumping, Subsidies, Safeguards:** Binding tariffs, and applying them equally to all trading partners (most-favoured-nation treatment, or MFN) are key to the smooth flow of trade in goods.

**Anti-dumping Actions:** If a company exports a product at a price lower than the price it normally charges on its own home market, it is said to be "dumping" the product. Is this unfair competition? Opinions differ, but many governments take action against dumping in order to defend their domestic industries.

**Arbitrageurs:** They are traders who buy and sell to make money on price differentials across different markets. Arbitrage involves simultaneous sale and purchase of the same commodities in different markets. Arbitrage keeps the prices in different markets in line with each other.

**Asset Reconstruction Company (ARC):** ARCs were established under the recommendation of Narshimham Committee. Their main responsibility is to recover the bad debt of the banks on their behalf. They can buy the bad debt of the bank at a discounted price or they can work with the bank on commission basis.

**Bank Rate:** It is that rate of interest on which the RBI lends to the commercial banks for long term period. If the bank rate is increased, the long term borrowing cost of the banks would also increase.

**Basis Points:** 100 BPs = 1%

This term is used by RBI in place of '%' point, while modifying the rates in its monetary and credit policies. It is used by the RBI just in order to magnify the impact of the change brought in the rates by it.

**Basel Norms:** The Basel Banking Accords are norms issued by the Basel Committee on

Banking Supervision (BCBS), formed under the auspices of the Bank of International Settlements (BIS), located in Basel, Switzerland. The Committee formulates guidelines and makes recommendations on best practices in the banking industry.

**Basel-I:** The deterioration of asset quality of banks has caused major turmoil across the world, renewing interest in bank regulation. Since 1980 over 130 countries, comprising almost three fourth of the International Monetary Fund's member countries, have experienced significant banking sector distress.

Based on the Basel norms, the RBI also issued similar capital adequacy norms for the Indian banks. According to these guidelines, the banks will have to identify their Tier-I and Tier-II capital and assign risk weights to the assets. Having done this they will have to assess the Capital to Risk (Weighted) Assets Ratio (CRAR).

**Basel-II:** On June 26, 2004, The Basel Committee on Banking Supervision released "International Convergence of Capital Measurement and Capital Standards: A revised Framework", which is commonly known as Basel-II Accord. Basel-I initially had Credit Risk and afterwards included Market Risk. In Basel-II, apart from Credit and Market Risk; Operational Risk was considered in Capital Adequacy Ratio calculation.

**Basel-III:** Basel-III guidelines were released in December 2010. The financial crisis of 2008 was the main reason behind the introduction of these norms. A need was felt to further strengthen the system as banks in the developed economies were under-capitalised, over-leveraged and had a greater reliance on short term funding.

**Blue-chip companies:** They are large companies with high net worth as well as market capitalisation, which have a long history of profit-making, growth as well as dividend payout.

Investing in shares of such companies is relatively less riskier. In India on the companies which are there in the index (NIFTY, SENSEX) are blue-chip companies.

**Baseline Profitability Index:** Daniel Altman's (an adjunct professor at New York University's Stern School of Business) guide on where to invest around the world in 2014.

**Budget:** It is a statement of the estimates of the government receipts and government expenditure during the period of the financial year. It unveils the fiscal policy (budgetary policy) of the government for the year to come. In India, Article 112 of the Constitution requires the Central Government to prepare an 'Annual Fiscal Statement' for the country as a whole. This is called Budget of the Central Government.

Likewise, Article 202 of the Constitution requires every state government to prepare 'Annual Fiscal Statement' for the concerned state.

**Banking Cash Transaction Tax:** Banking Cash Transaction Tax is yet another form of tax that has been abandoned by the Indian government. This form of taxation was in operation from 2005-2009 until the then FM Pranab Mukherjee nullified the tax. This tax suggested that every bank transaction (debit or credit) would be taxed at a rate of 0.1%.

**Balance of Payment:** Balance of Payment is a systematic record of all the transactions that a nation carries out with outside world. It is the difference between what a nation gets from outside world and what it pays to the outside world. Balance of Payment (BoP) comprises current account, capital account, errors, omissions, changes in foreign exchange reserves.

**Consumption Goods:** Consumption refers to the act or process to consume which means using up of goods and services by consumers to fulfil their needs and satisfy their wants. A consumption good or service is used (without further transformation in production) by Households or Government units for the direct satisfaction of individual needs or wants or the collective needs of members of community.

**Capital Goods:** Goods that are used in producing other goods, rather than being bought by consumers directly for satisfaction of their needs are called *Capital Goods*. Assets of an organization which are used to produce goods and services are called Capital goods.

**Consumer Price Index (CPI):** Consumer Price Index measures the average change in prices paid by ultimate consumers for a particular basket of goods and services over a period of time. CPI actually measures the increase in prices a consumer will have to pay for the designated commodity basket (which may be revised every four-five years to factor in changes in consumption pattern).

**Credit Control:** It is performed by the Reserve Bank of India.

**Core Inflation:** Core inflation is a measure of inflation that excludes certain items that face volatile price movements. Core inflation eliminates products that can have temporary price shocks because these shocks can diverge from the overall trend of inflation and give a false measure of inflation.

**Call Money:**

(a) Call money is mainly used by the banks to meet their temporary requirement of cash. It is also known as money at call and money at short notice.

(b) In this, market money is demanded for an extremely short period. The duration of such transactions is from a few hours to 14 days. These transactions help stock brokers and dealers to fulfill their financial requirements. The rate at which money is made available is called as call rate. Rate is fixed by the market forces such as the demand for and supply of money.

**Cash Management Bills:**

(a) The Government of India, in consultation with the RBI, decided to issue a new short-term instrument, known as **Cash Management Bills (CMBs),** to meet the temporary mismatches in the cash flow of the Government.

(b) The CMBs have the generic character of T-bills but are issued for maturities less than 91 days.

**Certificate of Deposits (CDs):**

(a) The certificate of deposits is issued by the Commercial Banks.

(b) They are worth the value of ₹ 25 lakh and in multiple of ₹ 25 lakh.

(c) The minimum subscription of CD should be worth ₹ 1 crore.

(d) The maturity period of CD is as low as 3 months and as high as 1 year.

**Commercial Papers (CPs):**

(a) Commercial paper (CP) is an investment instrument which can be issued by a listed company having working capital more than or equal to ₹ 5 crore.

(b) The CPs can be issued in multiples of ₹ 25 lakhs. However, the minimum subscription should at least be ₹ 1 crore.

**CRR (Cash Reserve Ratio):** CRR is calculated every fortnight. Over this amount the banks are not paid any interest by the RBI. Earlier there was an upper and lower ceiling on CRR. The RBI was not authorised to raise the CRR above 15% and below 3% but, in 2006, these ceilings were removed.

**Co-operative Bank:** A co-operative bank is a financial entity which belongs to its members, who are at the same time the owners and the customers of their bank. Co-operative banks are often created by persons belonging to the same local or professional community or sharing a common interest.

**Current Accounts:** It is basically meant for businessmen and are never used for the purpose of investment or savings. These deposits are the most liquid deposits and there are no limits for number of transactions or the amount of transactions in a day. Most of the current accounts are opened in the names of firm/company.

**Credit Crunch/Liquidity Crisis:** It refers to a state in which there is a short supply of money to lend to businesses and consumers and interest rates are high. It may happen when the government borrows heavily and there is Crowding out of the corporate sector.

**Corporate Debt Restructuring:** This facility was introduced by RBI in 2001. It is a kind of breather provided by RBI to the Indian corporate in case they are not able to repay their debt on time during some crisis situation. The company may request the bank to restructure their loan without categorising it as NPA.

**CIBIL (Credit Information Bureau (India) Ltd.):** Cibil is an organisation which maintains the database of all the borrowers and defaulters on its website. All the banks and financial institutes have access to this database.

**Commodities Market:** Derivatives as a tool for managing risk first originated in the commodities markets. They were then found useful as a hedging tool in financial markets as well. In India, trading in commodity futures has been in existence from the nineteenth century with organised trading in cotton through the establishment of Cotton Trade Association in 1875.

**Coupon rate:** The agreed rate of interest that is paid periodically to the investor and is calculated as a percentage of the face value. Some of the debt instruments may not have an explicit coupon rate, for instance zero coupon bonds. These bonds are issued on discount and redeemed at par.

**Circular Trading:** Circular trading is basically trade done by a group of people among themselves to rig the share price. For e.g. A, B, C who are holding the same share "Stock A" can do a circular trading by A selling to B and B selling to C and C selling to A.

**Credit Rating Agencies:** Investors should also be familiar with the ratings given by the Credit Rating and Information Services of India Ltd. (CRISIL) for protecting their interest. The CRISIL ratings are given only for debt instruments of companies, namely, Commercial Papers (CP), debentures, bonds and fixed deposits. Since early 1992, companies also use the ratings of Investment Information and Credit Rating Agency (ICRA).

**Capital Receipts:** All those receipts of the government which create liability or reduce financial assets are termed as capital receipts. The main items of capital receipts are loans raised by the government from the public which are called market borrowings, borrowing by the government from the Reserve Bank and commercial banks and other financial institutions through the sale of treasury bills, loans received from foreign governments and international organisations, and recoveries of loans granted by the Central Government.

**Capital Expenditure:** There are expenditures of the government which result in creation of physical or financial assets or reduction in financial liabilities.This includes expenditure on the acquisition of land, building, machinery, equipment, investment in shares, and loans and advances by the Central Government to state and union territory governments, PSUs and other parties.

**Capital Gains Tax:** This is a tax that is payable whenever you receive a sizable amount of money. It could be from an investment or from the sale of a property. It is usually of two types, Short Term Capital Gains (STCG) from investments held for less than 36 months and Long Term Capital Gains (LTCG) from investments held for longer than 36 months.

**Corporate Tax:** Corporate tax is the income tax that is paid by companies from the revenue they earn. This tax also comes with a slab of its own that decides how much tax the company has to pay.

**Causal or Cyclical Unemployment:** Cyclical unemployment is based on a greater availability of workers than there are jobs for workers. It is usually directly tied to the state of the economy. Lower demand for products due to lack of consumer confidence, disinterest, or reduction in consumer spending results in the workforce cutting back on production.

**Current Account:** Under current account of the BoP, transactions are classified into merchandise goods (exports and imports) and invisibles. Invisible transactions are further classified into three categories, namely

**Capital Account:** Under capital account, capital inflows can be classified by instrument (debt or equity) and maturity (short or long-term). The main components of capital account include foreign investment, loans and banking capital.

Foreign investment comprising Foreign Direct Investment (FDI) and portfolio investment consisting of Foreign Institutional Investors (FIIs) investment, American Depository Receipts/Global Depository Receipts (ADRs/GDRs) represents non-debt liabilities, while loans (external assistance, external commercial borrowings and trade credit) and banking capital including non-resident Indian (NRI) deposits are debt liabilities.

**Current Account Deficit:** A current account deficit represents negative net sales abroad. The current account also includes net income, such as interest and dividends, as well as transfers, such as foreign aid, though these components tend to make up a smaller percentage of the current account than exports and imports.

**Convertibility of Rupee:** An economy allows its currency fully or partially convertibility in its current and capital account. The issue of currency convertibility is concerned with foreign currency outflow.

India took different measures to check the foreign exchange outflow in both current and capital account. But with economic reforms, situation changed drastically.

**Depreciation:** To explain the meaning of depreciation, ask students to recall the meaning of Capital Goods (i.e. fixed assets like Machinery, Building, Equipment, Furniture, etc.). And also elaborate upon the nature and usage of such capital goods for repeated use for production of goods, and then state that these Capital goods diminish in value and efficiency when they are repeatedly used.

**Deflation:** Deflation is opposite to that of inflation. The persistent and appreciable fall in the general level of prices is called as deflation. The rate of change of price index is negative. The effects, cause and measures are also in the opposite direction.

**Disinflation:** The rate of inflation at a slower rate is called disinflation. For example, if the inflation of last month was 6% and rate of inflation in the current month is 5%, it is termed as disinflation.

**Demonetisation:** Demonetisation is the act of stripping a currency unit of its status as legal tender. It occurs whenever there is a change of national currency. The current form or forms of money is pulled from circulation and retired, often to be replaced with new notes or coins. Sometimes, a country completely replaces the old currency with new currency.

**Derivatives Market:** The emergence of the market for derivative products, most notably forwards, futures and options, can be traced back to the willingness of risk-averse economic agents to guard themselves against uncertainties arising out of fluctuations in asset prices.

**Debentures/Bonds:** The term Debenture is derived from the Latin word 'debere' which means 'to owe a debt'. A debenture is an acknowledgment of debt, taken either from the public or a particular source. A debenture may be viewed as a loan, represented as marketable security. The word "bond" may be used interchangeably with debentures.

**Dividend:** It refers to that part of profit of a company which the company distributes among its shareholders.

**Defensive Expenditures:** The GDP counts as additions to well-being the money people spend to prevent erosion in their quality of life or to compensate for misfortunes of various kinds. Examples are the medical and repair bills from automobile accidents, commuting costs, and household expenditures on pollution control devices such as water filters. The GPI counts such "defensive" expenditures as most Americans do: as costs rather than as benefits.

**Development economics** is a branch of economics which deals with not only promoting economic growth and a structural change but also improving the well-being of the population as a whole through focus on health and education and workplace conditions, whether through public or private channels.

**Developing Countries Development and Trade:** Over three-quarters of WTO members are developing or least developed countries. All WTO agreements contain special provision for them, including longer time periods to implement agreements and commitments, measures to increase their trading opportunities, provisions requiring all WTO members to safeguard their trade interests, and support to help them build the infrastructure for WTO work, handle disputes, and implement technical standards.

**Dividend Distribution Tax:** Dividend Distribution Tax was introduced after the end of 2007's Union Budget. It is basically a tax levied on companies based on the dividend they pay to their investors. This tax is applicable on the gross or net income an investor receives from their investment. Currently, the DDT rate stands at 15%.

**Direct Tax:** Direct tax, as stated earlier, are taxes that are paid directly by you. These taxes are levied directly on an entity or an individual and cannot be transferred onto anyone else. One of the bodies that overlooks these direct taxes is the Central Board of Direct Taxes (CBDT) which is a part of the Department of Revenue.

**Disguised Unemployment:** There are also instances where we find too many people working when so many are not required. In agriculture we may find that all members of the family work. It is possible that 3-4 people can do a given work in the farm, but we find that the whole family of say 10 people doing the job. This may be because the excess people are not able to find employment elsewhere, so rather than remain unemployed they prefer to do the work along with others. This is known as disguised unemployment.

**DWCRA:** The Programme of Development of Women and Children in Rural Areas (DWCRA) aims to improve the socio-economic status of the poor women in the rural areas through creation of group of women for income generating activities on a self-sustaining basis.

**Escrow Accounts:** It is an account in a bank which a third party holds during the process of a transaction between two parties. It is a temporary account which lasts until the completion of transaction. This account is governed by the condition agreed to between parties.

**Exim Bank:** Export-Import Bank of India is the premier export finance institution of the country. It commenced operations in 1982 under the Export-Import Bank of India Act 1981. Government of India launched the institution with a mandate to not just enhance exports from India, but also to integrate the country's foreign trade and investment with the overall economic growth.

**Environment vulnerability Index:** A vulnerability index for the natural environment, the basis of all human welfare, has been developed by the South Pacific Applied Geoscience Commission (SOPAC), the United Nations Environment Programme (UNEP) and their partners.

**Environmental Performance Index (EPI):** It is a method of quantifying and numerically marking the environmental performance of a state's policies. This index was developed from the Pilot Environmental Performance Index, first published in 2002, and designed to supplement the environmental targets set forth in the United Nations Millennium Development Goals.

**Excise Duty:** This is a tax that is levied on all the goods manufactured or produced in India. It is different from customs duty because it is applicable only on things produced in India and is also known as the Central Value Added Tax or CENVAT.

**Entertainment Tax:** Entertainment Tax is yet another type of tax commonly seen in India. It is levied by the government on feature films, television series, exhibitions, amusement, and recreational parlours. This tax is collected taking into account a business entity's gross collection collected from earnings based on commercial shows, film festival earnings, and audience participation.

**Education Cess/Surcharge:** Education cess is a tax in India primarily introduced to help cover the cost of government-sponsored educational programs. This tax is collected independently of other taxes and is applicable to all Indian citizens, corporations, and other people living in the country.

**External Sector:** The external sector of the economy refers to the international transactions that both the private and public sector conduct with the rest of the world. Such transactions are systematically recorded in detail within a framework that groups them into accounts, where each account represents a separate economic process or phenomenon of the external sector.

**External Debt:** It is that portion of a country's debt that was borrowed from foreign lenders including commercial banks, governments or international financial institutions such as the International Monetary Fund (IMF) and World Bank.

According to the IMF, "Gross external debt is the amount, at any given time, of disbursed and outstanding contractual liabilities of residents of a country to non-residents to repay principal, with or without interest, or to pay interest, with or without principal".

**Exchange Rate:** Exchange rate is the value for domestic currency with respect to foreign currency and vice-versa. In India, exchange rates are managed and any capital inflows would be mopped up by RBI to prevent rupee from appreciating thus resulting in build of reserves.

**Exchange Traded Funds (ETF):** An exchange-traded fund (ETF) is an investment vehicle traded on stock exchanges, much like stocks. An ETF holds assets such as stocks or bonds and trades at approximately the same price as the net asset value of its underlying assets over the course of the trading day.

**Final Goods:** Final goods are goods that are ultimately consumed rather than used in the production of other goods. It refers to finished goods which are sold in the market for consumption and investment purpose.

**Flow:** It is change in stock over period of time. Change refers to inflows (adding to the stock) and outflows (subtracting from the stock). Flows typically are measured over a certain interval of time. For example, the increase in population census 1991 to census 2001 is due to increase in number of births in a period of 10 years. To conclude, we may say that 'Stock' is a static concept, whereas 'Flows' represents a dynamic concept.

**Financial Market:** Capital market is a component of financial market that allows long-term trading of debt and equity-backed securities. Long-term borrowing or lending is done by investors or corporations that have large amounts of wealth at their disposal.

**Fixed Deposit Accounts:** All Banks in India (including SBI, PNB, BoB, BoI, Canara Bank, ICICI Bank, Yes Bank etc.) offer fixed deposits schemes with a wide range of tenures for periods from 7 days to 10 years. These are also popularly known as FD accounts.

**Foreign Currency Exposure:** It refers to gross sum of all items on the balance sheet that has impact on profit and loss accounts due to movement in foreign exchange rates.

**Financial Inclusion:** Financial Inclusion is the "process of ensuring access to appropriate financial products and services needed by all sections of the society in general and vulnerable groups such as weaker sections and low income groups in particular, at an affordable cost in a fair and transparent manner by regulated, mainstream institutional players".

**Financial Literacy Program:** Financial Literacy Programs have been initiated by RBI to improve financial education and literacy so that people will become aware about the basic financial terms and services provided by banks and financial institutions.

**Follow-on Public Offer:** If an already listed company wants to raise more funds from the capital market by selling some more shares of the company, then the company may sell the shares through FPO. In FPO, the shares of the company are sold to any interested investors but at a discounted price from the market price.

**Front Running:** Front running is something that happens within a firm. A trader gets word that a customer is interested in purchasing a big block of a company's shares, and that trader will purchase shares for his individual account before executing the customer's order.

**Foreign Currency Convertible Bonds (FCCBs):** A convertible bond is a mix between a debt and equity instrument. It is a bond having regular coupon and principal payments, but these bonds also give the bondholder the option to convert the bond into stock. FCCB is issued in a currency different than the issuer's domestic currency.

**Fiscal Deficit:** Fiscal deficit is the difference between the government's total expenditure and its total receipts excluding borrowing.

Gross fiscal deficit = Total expenditure – (Revenue receipts + Non-debt creating capital receipts)

**Fringe Benefit Tax:** Fringe Benefit Tax (FBT) was a tax which applied to almost every fringe benefit an employer provided to their employees. In this tax, a number of aspects were covered.

**Frictional Unemployment:** Frictional unemployment is attributable to the time required to match production activities with qualified resources. Frictional unemployment essentially occurs because resources, especially labour, are in the process of moving from one production activity to another. Employers are seeking workers and workers are seeking employment, the two sides just havenot matched up.

**Forex Reserves:** Foreign-exchange reserves or Forex reserves is money or other assets held by a central bank or other monetary authority so that it can pay if need be its liabilities, such as the currency issued by the central bank, as well as the various bank reserves deposited with the central bank by the government and other financial institutions.

**Foreign Investment:** It comprises of two components:

(1) **Foreign Direct Investment (FDI):** FDI is foreign investment with aim of profit motive and provide unique mixture of resources, technology, knowledge, pro-fessionalism and management techniques.

(2) **Foreign Institutional Investment (FII):** Foreign institutional investment is done in the stock market with the purpose of only trading in shares of companies, in corporate debt and in government securities. Such investments are volatile in nature.

**Green Economics:** Green economics focuses on and supports the harmonious interaction between humans and nature and attempts to reconcile the two. It is referred by many names like sustainable development, green economy which is given in Rio+20 summit, 2012.

**General Price Index (GPI):** General Price Index measures the changes in average prices of goods and services. A base year is selected and its index is assumed as100 and on this basis, price index for further period is calculated.

**Gross NPA:** It refers to the sum of the NPA which is to be recovered as well as the money set aside in the form of provisioning.

**G-Sec:** They are also called Guilt-Edged securities. They are called so because such securities had a golden colour horder around it during the British period. Such securities are issued and sold by RBI on face value and on maturity the lender is entitled to receive interest.

**Global Depositary Receipts (GDRs)** are negotiable certificates held in the bank of one country representing a specific number of shares of a stock traded on the exchange of another country.

**Gold ETF:** Gold Exchange Traded Fund (ETF) is a financial instrument like a mutual fund whose value depends on the price of gold. In most cases, the price of one unit of a gold ETF approximately reflects the price of 1 gram of gold. As the price of gold rises, the price of the ETF is also expected to rise by the same amount.

**Gross Domestic Product (GDP):** Gross Domestic Product (GDP) is the total market value of the final goods and services produced within the domestic territorial limits of country over a period of time (1 Year). There are three ways of calculating GDP which is based on the different methods of calculating Nation Income, i.e. Income method, Expenditure method and Value Added method; however the computed value of GDP remains the same under all methods.

**Gross National Product (GNP)** presents the total income earned by the domestic citizens regardless of the country in which their factors of production are located. Since 'Depreciation' has already been explained even calculation and Impact of this on GDP can also be taken up i.e. GDP includes the element of depreciation Gross (G) in GDP represents inclusion of depreciation and when depreciation is deducted from GDP, it becomes Net Domestic Product.

NDP = GDP – Depreciation

Accounting Indentities at Market Price

GNP ≡ GNI (Gross National Income)

GDP ≡ GNP less Net Income from Abroad

NNP ≡ GNP less Depreciation

NDP (Net Domestic Product) ≡ NNP less net income from abroad

**GDP Deflator:** The GDP deflator is a price index that measures inflation or deflation in an economy by calculating a ratio of nominal GDP to real GDP. Essentially, GDP Deflator is an adjustment for the impact of changes in prices on changes in nominal GDP.

**Genuine Progress Indicator (GPI):** It was introduced in 1995 as an alternative to GDP. The GPI enables policymakers at the national, state, regional, or local level to measure how well their citizens are doing both economically and socially.

**GDI (Gender-related Development Index):** An indicator that adjusts the average HDI achievement, to reflect inequalities between men and women along the three basic dimensions.

**GEM (Gender Empowerment Measure):** An indicator that focuses on the opportunities open to women. It measures inequality of opportunities in three areas: political participation and decision making; economic participation and decision making; and power over economic resources.

**Gender Inequality Index (GII):** Gender inequality remains a major barrier to human development. Girls and women have made major strides since 1990, but they have not yet gained gender equality. The disadvantages facing women and girls are a major source of inequality.

**GNH (Gross National Happiness) Index:** Gross National Happiness is a term coined by His Majesty the Fourth King of Bhutan, Jigme Singye Wangchuck in the 1970s. The concept implies that sustainable development should take a holistic approach towards notions of progress and give equal importance to non-economic aspects of wellbeing.

**Global Multidimensional Poverty Index:** The global Multidimensional Poverty Index (MPI) is an international measure of acute poverty covering over 100 developing countries. It complements traditional income-based poverty measures by capturing the severe deprivations that each person faces at the same time with respect to education, health and living standards.

The global MPI was developed by OPHI (Oxford poverty and human development initiative) with the UN Development Programme (UNDP) for inclusion in UNDP's flagship Human Development Report in 2010. It has been published in the HDR ever since.

**Global Resilience Index:** Supply chain risk is one of the leading causes of business volatility. The FM Global Resilience Index is the first data-driven tool and repository that ranks the resilience of 130 countries and territories to supply chain disruption.

**GST – Goods and Services Tax:** GST (Goods and Services Tax) is a single indirect tax aimed at making the country a unified common market. It is imposed on the supply of goods and/or services within India. Multiple indirect taxes that the Central Government or state governments impose on suppliers and consumers are subsumed by GST.

**HUNDI:** It is a real debt instrument which was derived in Asia especially in subcontinent region. It refers to pledging the asset or mortgaging it to financer in order to raise fund. It was more popular during British time when it was also used as traveller cheque in which the asset was mortgaged at any part of the country and funds due was raised at some other part of country.

**Hedgers:** They are generally the commercial producers and consumers of the traded commodities. They participate in the market to manage their spot market price risk. Commodity prices are volatile and their participation in the futures market allows them to hedge or protect themselves against the risk of losses from fluctuating prices.

**Hedge Fund:** A hedge fund is an investment fund open to a limited range of investors that undertakes a wider range of investment and trading activities in both domestic and international markets, and that, in general, pays a performance fee to its investment manager.

**HDI (Human Development Index):** A summary of human development in a country that measures the average achievements of people along three dimensions: living a long and healthy life, as measured by life expectancy at birth; being knowledgeable, as measured by combination of the adult literacy rate and the combined enrollment ratio in primary, secondary, and tertiary education; and having access to a decent standard of living, as measured by an index of income per capita.

**HPI (Human Poverty Index):** An index that measures deprivations along the basic dimensions of human development. It combines the proportion of people in a country expected to die at a relatively early age (40 years in developing countries, 60 years in developed countries); illiteracy; and poor access to the overall economic resources needed for a decent standard of living.

**Intermediate Goods:** All those goods which are used by the producers for producing other goods are known as Intermediate goods.

These goods are used as inputs in the production of other goods such as partially finished goods. These goods are demanded for producing other goods. Thus intermediate goods are those goods which are sold by one industry to another either for resale or for producing other goods.

**Islamic Banking in India:** Islamic banking refers to the system of banking that is consistent with the principles of Islamic law (Shari'ah). Sharia prohibits, (Riba, usury) i.e. interest in business.

**Impact of NPAs on Banking Operations:** The efficiency of a bank is not always reflected only by the size of its balance sheet, but also the level of return on its assets. The NPAs do not generate interest income for banks but at the same time banks are required to provide provisions for NPAs from their current profits.

**IDBI (Industrial Development Bank of India):** IDBI Bank is an Indian government-owned financial service company, formerly known as the Industrial Development Bank of India, headquartered in Mumbai, India. It was established in 1964 by an Act of Parliament to provide credit and other financial facilities for the development of the fledgling Indian industry.

**Indradhanush Plan:** The Public Sector Banks (PSBs) play a vital role in India's economy. In the past few years, because of a variety of legacy issues including the delay caused in various approvals as well as land acquisition, etc. and also because of low global and domestic demand, many large projects have stalled.

**Initial Public Offer:** When a company sells its shares for the first time to any interested investor to raise funds, then it is termed as IPO of that company. In India the largest IPO so far has been of Coal India Ltd, which is world's largest coal miner. The largest IPO in world is of Alibaba group headed by Jack Ma.

**Insider Trading:** Insider trading is the act of trading, directly or indirectly, in the securities of a publicly listed company by any person, who may or may not be managing the affairs of such company, based on certain information, not available to the public at large, that can influence the market price of the securities of such company.

**Investor Protection Fund (IPF):** Despite the various efforts taken by the regulators and exchange, some problems do arise. A cushion in the form of Investor Protection Funds (IPFs) is set up by the stock exchanges. The purpose of the IPF is to take care of investor claims, which may arise out of non-settlement of obligations by the trading members.

**Income Distribution:** Both economic theory and common sense tell us that the poor benefit more from a given increase in their income than do the rich. Accordingly, the GPI rises when the poor receive a larger percentage of national income, and falls when their share decreases.

**Income Tax:** This is one of the most well-known and least understood taxes. It is the tax that is levied on your earning in a financial year. There are many facets to income tax, such as the tax slabs, taxable income, tax deducted at source (TDS), reduction of taxable income, etc.

**IRDP:** The Integrated Rural Development Programme was initiated in 1976 in 20 selected districts of India. Then, it was extended to all blocks in 1980. The objective of this program was to enable the selected families to cross the poverty line by creating productive assets for the poor people.

**Income:** Investment income and compensation of employees.

**International Monetary Fund (IMF):** A landmark in the history of world economic cooperation is the creation of the International Monetary Fund, briefly called IMF. The IMF was organised in 1946 and commenced operations in March, 1947.

**Intellectual Property:** The WTO's Intellectual Property Agreement amounts to rules for trade and investment in ideas and creativity. The rules state how copyrights, patents, trademarks, geographical names used to identify products, industrial designs, integrated circuit layout-designs and undisclosed information such as trade secrets – "intellectual property" – should be protected when trade is involved.

**Keynesian Microeconomics:** Keynesian Microeconomics is based on the work of 20th century British economist John Maynard Keynes, which says that the state can stimulate economic growth and maintain stability in the economy through expansionary policies.

**Krishi Kalyan Cess:** This is yet another cess brought about by the government of India since the June of 2016. It is basically introduced in order to extend welfare to all the farmers and to the improvement of agricultural facilities in the country.

**Local Area Bank:** The Local Area Banks (LABs) are small private banks, conceived as low cost structures which would provide efficient and competitive financial intermediation services in a limited area of operation, i.e. primarily in rural and semi-urban areas, comprising three contiguous districts. LABs were set up to enable the mobilization of rural savings by local institutions and, at the same time, to make them available for investments in the local areas.

**Lead Banks:** The concept of Lead Bank was introduced in India in 1969 under the recommendation of Gadgil study group. However the minute details were provided by FS Nariman Committee. It is a step towards financial inclusion.

**Long-Term Environmental Damage:** Climate change, ozone depletion, and nuclear waste management are long-term costs arising from the use of fossil fuels, chlorofluorocarbons, and atomic energy, respectively.

**Microeconomics:**Microeconomics is concerned with decision-making by individual economic agents such as firms and consumers. In other words, microeconomics is concerned with the behaviour of individuals or groups organised into firms, industries, unions, and other identifiable agents. The focus of microeconomics is on decision-making, and hence markets.

**Macroeconomics:** Macroeconomics is concerned with the aggregate performance of the entire economic system. That is, the performance of the U.S. economy or, in a more modern sense, the global economy.

Different Approaches in the Mainstream Economics

Broadly, there are many approaches to the mainstream economics, but the basic of all the streams being the same as resources are scarce while wants are unlimited!

**Moral Economy:** Moral economy might be defined as a kind of inquiry focussing on how economic activities of all kinds are influenced, structured and legitimized by moral sentiments, values and norms, and how in turn those are reinforced, compromised, or overridden by political economic pressures.

**Marginal Standing Facility (MSF):** It was introduced in India by the RBI on 9th May 2011. Under this, commercial banks can borrow funds one night for one day. The RBI would provide loan to the needy commercial bank at an interest rate which would be always 1% higher than the repo rate. This facility is known as MSF.

**Moral Suasion:** A persuasion measure used by the Central Bank to influence and pressure, but not force banks into adhering to policy. Measures used are closed-door meetings with bank directors, increased inspections, discussions, appeal to community spirit etc.

**Monetary Policy Committee (MPC):** The Monetary Policy Committee (MPC) is a committee of the Central Bank in India (Reserve Bank of India), headed by its Governor, which is entrusted with the task of fixing the benchmark policy interest rate (repo rate) to contain inflation within the specified target level.

**Marginal Cost of Funds Based Lending Rate (MCLR):** The marginal cost of funds based lending rate (MCLR) refers to the minimum interest rate of a bank below which it cannot lend, except in some cases allowed by the RBI.

**Micro-Finance:** Micro Finance may be defined as "provision of thrift, credit and other financial services and products of very small amounts to the poor in rural, semi urban or urban areas, for enabling them to raise their income levels and improve living standards".

**Market Capitalisation:** It is a good indicator of the health of capital markets. Market capitalisation means the total number of outstanding shares of the company multiplied by the share price of that stock.

**Mutual Funds:** Mutual funds are investment companies that use the funds from investors to invest in other companies or investment alternatives. They have the advantage of professional management, diversification, convenience and special services such as cheque writing and telephone account service.

**Macro Vulnerability Index:** It depicts an overall macro-vulnerability index (MVI) that combines a country's fiscal deficit, current account deficit, and inflation. The index is thus comparable across countries and across time.

**Monetised Deficit:** It refers to that part of the government deficit which RBI used to bridge by printing fresh currency. (Since the mechanism of deficit financing was scrapped this mechanism is also been scrapped.

**Money Market:** Money market is a component of financial market where short-term borrowing can be issued. This market includes assets that deal with short-term borrowing, lending, buying and selling.

**Minimum Alternative Tax:** Minimum Alternative Tax (MAT) is basically a way for the Income Tax Department to get companies to pay a minimum tax, which currently stands at 18.5%. This form of tax was brought into effect through the introduction of Section 115JA of the Income Tax Act.

**MSW:** The Million Wells Scheme (MWS), which was earlier a sub-scheme of JRY, is funded by the Centre and states in the ratio of 80:20. The objective of the MWS is to provide open irrigation wells free of cost to poor, small and marginal farmers belonging to SCs/STs and freed bonded labour.

**MGNREGA:** The National Rural Employment Guarantee Act (NREGA) of 2005 is perhaps the most significant social policy initiative in India in the last decade.

**Neoliberalism:** Neoliberalism refers to advocacy of policies such as individual liberty, free markets, and free trade. Neoliberalism proposes that human well being can best be advanced by liberating individual entrepreneurial freedoms and skills within an institutional framework characterised by strong private property rights, free markets and free trade.

**New Consumer Price Indices:** The above consumer price indices cover only a segment of population like Agriculture Labour, Industrial worker, etc. and do not give a nationwide picture. Therefore, three new indices are introduced with base year of 2010 (January – December) which cover all segments of population on all India basis. They are as follows:

- CPI (Rural)
- CPI (Urban)
- CPI (Combined)

**Nationalisation of Banks:** By the 1960s, the Indian banking industry had become an important tool to facilitate the development of the Indian economy. At the same time, it has emerged as a large employer, and a debate has ensured about the possibility to nationalise the banking industry. Indira Gandhi, the-then Prime Minister of India expressed the intention of the Government of India (GOI) in the annual conference and presented the paper titled *"Stray thoughts on Bank Nationalisation"*. The paper was received with positive enthusiasm. Thereafter, her move was swift and sudden, and the GOI issued an ordinance and nationalised the 14 largest commercial banks with effect from the midnight of July 19, 1969.

**Non-Performing Asset:** It is that account of a borrower in which he fails to repay the interest as well as principal consecutively for 90 days (3 Months). If it continues for 18 months then it is termed as *'Doubtful Asset'*. If it goes even beyond that and becomes a *Sticky Loan*, where it is almost impossible to recover the loan then, it is categorised as *Bad debt*.

**Net NPA:** Net NPA only refers to the NPA which is to be recovered and does not include the provisioned money.

**Narrow Banking:** A bank may be concentrating only on collection of deposits and lend or invest the money within a particular region or certain chosen activity like investing the funds only in Government Securities. This type of restricted minimum banking activity is referred to 'Narrow Banking'.

**No-frills Accounts:** People in the financially excluded zone find it quite difficult to meet the requirements of normal saving accounts. Recognizing this problem, RBI, in the year 2005, took an initiative and has made it compulsory for the banks to provide no-frills savings accounts without a minimum balance requirement.

**NABARD:** NABARD (National Bank for Agriculture and Rural Development) is an apex development bank with an authorization for facilitating credit flow for promotion and development of agriculture, small-scale industries, cottage and village industries, handicrafts and other rural crafts.

**NIFTY-50:** It is the main index of NSE. It is the measuring scale or barometer of NSE which consists of top 50 companies listed on NSE. The 50 companies are largest in their respective sectors and, they account for maximum volume as well as value of trade on NSE. Nifty tracks the average price movement of only these 50 companies and if the average movement of the share price of these 50 companies is in upward direction, it can be said that all market is moving upward and vice versa.

**Net National Product (NNP):** NNP is defined as GNP less depreciation, i.e. NNP = GNP – Depreciation.

The NNP, as defined above, gives the measure of net output available for consumption and investment by the society (including consumers, producers and the government). NNP is the real measure of the national income. NNP = NNI (net national income). In other words, NNP is the same as the national income at factor cost.

**NREP:** The National Rural Employment Programme was launched in 1980 in order to generate gainful employment in rural areas.

**National treatment:** Treating foreigners and locals equally. Imported and locally-produced goods should be treated equally, at least after the foreign goods have entered the market.

**Organised sector:** The organised sector is within the direct purview of RBI regulations.

**Open Market Operation (OMO):** It refers to buying and selling government securities by the RBI in the open market. Here the securities are issued in the form of Bill as well as bonds. They are sold by the RBI to the banks as well as other financial institution such as insurance and mutual fund companies. If the liquidity is high in the economy, the RBI would sell more and more securities to take away extra money from the economy.

**Overdraft Facilities in Saving Account:** Banks are providing overdraft (OD) facility in saving account and also Small Overdrafts in No-frills accounts. Banks have been advised and directed to provide small OD in such accounts.

**Open-Ended Mutual Funds:** An open-ended mutual fund is the one whose units can be freely sold and repurchased by the investors. Such funds are not listed on bourses since the Asset Management Companies (AMCs) provide the facility for buyback of units from unit-holders either at the NAV (Net Asset Value), or NAV-linked prices.

**Other Important Indices:** GINI Index (World Bank Estimate): Gini index measures the extent to which the distribution of income or consumption expenditure among individuals or households within an economy deviates from a perfectly equal distribution. A Lorenz curve plots the cumulative percentages of total income received against the cumulative number of recipients, starting with the poorest individual or household. The Gini index measures the area between the Lorenz curve and a hypothetical line of absolute equality, expressed as a percentage of the maximum area under the line. Thus a Gini index of 0 represents perfect equality, while an index of 100 implies perfect inequality.

**Ocean Health Index:** It is a valuable tool for the ongoing assessment of ocean health. By providing a means to advance comprehensive ocean policy and compare future progress, the Index can inform decisions about how to use or protect marine ecosystems.

**Price Index:** Price index is a specialized average that measures the changes in prices over a period of time. The price indices are of two types:

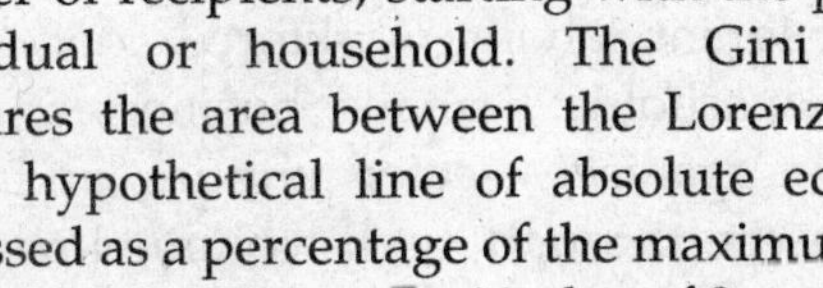


**Philips Curve:** Philips curve shows the relationship between rate of inflation and rate of unemployment. It shows that the relationship is negative. That is at high rate of inflation the unemployment rate is low as show in figure below.

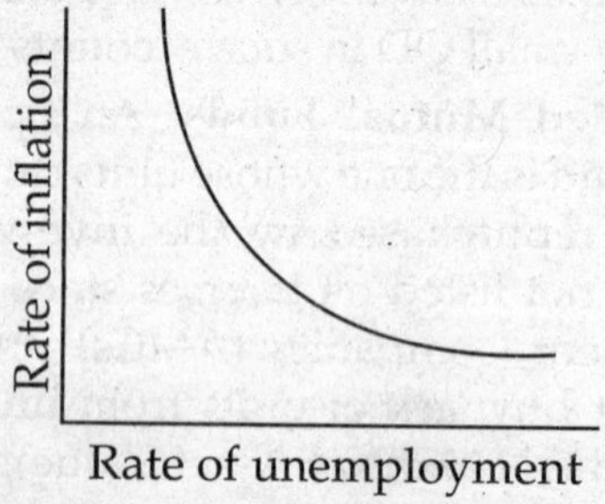


**Payment Banks:** Payments Banks are a new set of banks licensed by the Reserve Bank of India to further financial inclusion by enabling them to provide.

(i) small savings/current accounts below ₹ 1 lakh,

(ii) distribution of mutual funds, insurance products on a non risk sharing basis and

(iii) payments/remittance services to migrant labour workforce, low income households, small businesses, other unorganised sector entities and other users through high volume-low value transactions in deposits and payments/remittance services using a secured technology-driven environment including issuance of prepaid cards etc.

**Provisioning:** Provisioning is that money which is set aside by the banks to meet its expected NPA.

**Prime Lending Rate (PLR) or Base Rate:** Prime Lending Rate (PLR) is that rate of interest at which banks provide loan to their best customers. The best customers are those customers who have a very good credit history, who have never defaulted in their life and who have a fixed and permanent source of income.

**Priority Sector Lending:** Priority sector refers to those sectors of the economy which may not get timely and adequate credit in the absence of this special dispensation. Typically, these are small value loans to farmers for agriculture and allied activities, micro and small enterprises, poor people for housing, students for education and other low income groups and weaker sections.

**Primary Market:** The Primary Market consists of arrangements, which facilitate the procurement of long-term funds by companies by making fresh issue of shares and debentures. We know that companies make fresh issue of shares and/or debentures at their formation stage and, if necessary, subsequently for the expansion of business.

**Participatory Notes (PNs):** Also referred to as "P-Notes" Financial instruments used by investors or hedge funds that are not registered with the Securities and Exchange Board of India to invest in Indian securities.

**Per Capita Income (PCI):** This is the average annual income of the people of a country. It is obtained by dividing national income by the population.

**Personal Income (PI):** The sum total of income that a person receives from different sources is his personal income (Eg: wages, rent, interest, profit, etc)

PI = Wages + Rent + Interest + Profit + Others

**Primary Deficit:** We must note that the borrowing requirement of the government includes interest obligations on accumulated debt. The goal of measuring primary deficit is to focus on present fiscal imbalances.

**Perquisite Tax:** Perquisites are all the perks or privileges that employers may extend to employees. These privileges may include a house provided by the company or a car for your use, given to you by the company.

**Professional Tax:** Professional Tax, or employment tax, is another form of tax levied only by state governments in India. According to professional tax norms, individuals earning income or practicing a profession such as a doctor, lawyer, chartered accountant, or company secretary etc. are required to pay this tax.

**Property Tax - Municipal Tax:** Also known as Property Tax or Real Estate Tax, this is one of the taxes levied by local municipal bodies of every city. These taxes are levied in order to provide and maintain the basic civic services. All owners of residential or commercial properties are subject to Municipal Tax.

**Poverty Line:** In India consumption-expenditure has been made the basis for the measurement of the minimum standard. The usual method is to fix a poverty level. This level is expressed in terms of an overall per capita consumption-expenditure.

**Principles of the Trading System in WTO:** The WTO agreements are lengthy and complex because they are legal texts covering a wide range of activities. They deal with: agriculture, textiles and clothing, banking, telecommunications, government purchases, industrial standards and product safety, food sanitation regulations, intellectual property, and much more.

**Quantitative Easing (QE):** Quantitative easing is a channel of monetary policy used by central banks to revive the national economy when usual policies are exhausted. When interest rates are driven to zero, there is fear of liquidity trap, where interest on new loans would be zero.

**Qualified Foreign Investors (QFI):** There are individuals or a group of individuals who are citizen of any country which is member of FATF (Financial Action Task Force) on money-laundering. These QFI have been allowed by SEBI to invest in the Indian share market.

**Reflation:** Reflation means deliberate action of government to increase rate of inflation to stimulate economy. It is usually done to redeem the economy from deflationary situation.

**Repurchase Agreement:**

(a) A repurchase agreement, also known as repo, is the sale of securities combined with an agreement to buy back the securities at a later date.

**Repo Rate:** It is that rate of interest at which the RBI lends to the commercial bank for a short-term period. If repo rate is increased, the short-term borrowing cost of the banks will increase. Hence, while lending to general consumers, the banks would also increase the interest rate. This would discourage the borrower from borrowing and liquidity would come down.

**Reverse Repo Rate:** It is that rate of interest at which the RBI borrows from the commercial banks.

**Recession and Depression:** A recession implies a fall in real GDP. It is a period of negative economic growth for two consecutive quarters in GDP– the value of all goods and services a country produces.

**Reserve Bank of India:** The Reserve Bank of India is a Central Bank and was established on April 1, 1935 in accordance with the provisions of Reserve Bank of India Act 1934. The central office of RBI is located at Mumbai since inception. Though originally the Reserve Bank of India was privately owned, since nationalization in 1949, RBI is fully owned by the Government of India. It was inaugurated with share capital of ₹ 5 crores divided into shares of ₹ 100 each fully paid up.

**Regional Rural Bank:** The Government of India set up Regional Rural Banks (RRBs) on October 2, 1975. The banks provide credit to the weaker sections of the rural areas, particularly the small and marginal farmers, agricultural labourers, and small entrepreneurs. Initially, five RRBs were set up on October 2, 1975 which was sponsored by Syndicate Bank, State Bank of India, Punjab National Bank, United Commercial Bank and United Bank of India.

**Recurring Deposit Accounts:** These are popularly known as RD accounts and are special kind of Term Deposits and are suitable for people who do not have lump sum amount of savings, but are ready to save a small amount every month. Normally, such deposits earn interest on the amount already deposited (through monthly installments) at the same rates as are applicable for Fixed Deposits / Term Deposits.

**Right Issue:** This is also a primary market instrument where an already listed company can raise funds by selling some shares at a discounted price only to the existing shareholders. Right issue is different from FPO only because of the reason that in FPO shares can be sold to any interested investors but in right issue it is sold to only existing shareholders.

**Resource Depletion:** If today's economic activity depletes the physical resource base available for tomorrow, then it is not creating well-being; rather, it is borrowing it from future generations. The GDP counts such borrowing as current income. The GPI, by contrast, counts the depletion or degradation of wetlands, forests, farmland, and non-renewable minerals (including oil) as a current cost.

**Rational Investor Ratings Index (RIRI):** The RIRI is computed by averaging a country's GDP growth rate and its macro-economic indicators; the latter measured as the average of the fiscal deficit, current account deficit, and inflation (all with negative signs).

**Revenue Receipts:** Revenue receipts are receipts of the government which are non-redeemable, that is, they cannot be reclaimed from the government. They are divided into tax and non-tax revenues. Tax revenues consist of the proceeds of taxes and other duties levied by the central government.

**Revenue Deficit:** The revenue deficit refers to the excess of government's revenue expenditure over revenue receipts.

Revenue deficit = Revenue receipts – Revenue expenditure

The revenue deficit includes only such transactions that affect the current income and expenditure of the government.

**Rangarajan Committee:** In 2012, the Planning Commission constituted a new expert panel on poverty estimation, chaired by C Rangarajan.

**RLEGP:** The Rural Landless Employment Guarantee Programme was launched in August 1983 to generate additional employment opportunities for the landless people in the villages.

**Socialist Economics:** There is a school of socialist economics based on public (i.e. state) ownership of means of production to achieve greater equality and give the workers greater control of the means of production.

**Stocks and Flows:** Stocks and Flows have natural meaning in many contexts outside of business and its related fields. Let us define meaning to both the terms 'Stock' and 'Flow' and then show the relatedness of the two and how these are impacting an economy/business.

**Stock:** A 'Stock' refers to the value of goods and services at a particular point of time. It is an entity that is accumulated over by inflows and/or depleted by outflows. Therefore, we can say that the 'stock' can only be changed by a 'flow'.

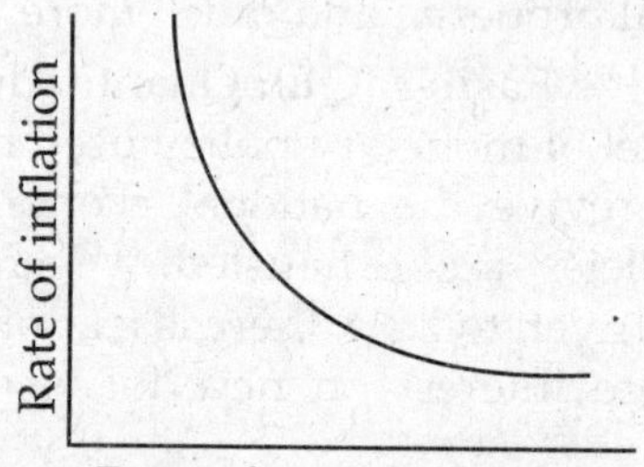


**Stagflation:** Stagflation refers to the situation of coexistence of stagnation and inflation in the economy. Stagnation means low National Income growth and high unemployment. The Philips curve shows that at high rate of inflation, there is low rate of unemployment. But stagflation proves the contrary.

Before 1970s, it was considered that at the time of inflation, the economy will be booming. 1970s scenario proved contrary with the existence of inflation and stagnation.

**Short Term Loan:**

(a) It is a money market where the short term loan requirements of corporate are met by the Commercial banks.

(b) Banks provide short term loans to corporates in the form of cash credit or in the form of overdraft.

**Scheduled Banks:** Scheduled Banks in India constitute those banks which have been included in the second schedule of RBI Act 1934. RBI in turn includes only those banks in this schedule which satisfy the criteria laid down vide section 42(6a) of the Act. "Scheduled banks in India" means the State Bank of India constituted under the State Bank of India Act, 1955 (23 of 1955), a subsidiary bank as defined in the State Bank of India (subsidiary banks) Act, 1959 (38 of 1959), a corresponding new bank constituted under section 3 of the Banking Companies (Acquisition and Transfer of Undertakings) Act, 1980 (40 of 1980), or any other Bank being a bank included in the Second Schedule to the Reserve Bank of India Act, 1934 (2 of 1934), but does not include a co-operative Bank".

**Small Finance Banks:** They are niche banks that focus and serve the needs of a certain demographic segment of the population. The objectives of setting up of small finance banks will be to further financial inclusion by (1) the provision of savings vehicles (2) supply of credit to small business units; small and marginal farmers; micro and small industries; and other unorganised sector entities, through high technology-low cost operations.

SFBs was recommended by the Nachiket Mor Committee on financial inclusion.

**Saving Accounts:** These deposit accounts are one of the most popular deposits for individual accounts. These accounts not only provide cheque facility but also have a lot of flexibility for deposits and withdrawal of funds from the account. Most of the banks have rules for the maximum number of withdrawals in a period and the maximum amount of withdrawal, but hardly any bank enforces these. However, banks have every right to enforce such restrictions if it is felt that the account is being misused as a current account.

**Securitization and SARFAESI Act:** Securitization is a relatively new concept that is taking roots in India of late. It is still in its infancy with only a few market players. Securitization is considered an effective tool for improvement of capital adequacy.

**Stress Loan:** Stress loan is a combination of restructured loan and gross NPA.

**SHG Bank-Linkage Programme:** The credit linkage of Self Help Groups (SHG) and Joint Liability Groups (JLG) by Commercial Banks is one of the major initiatives to bring low income poor people into the banking stream. The poor people come together and pool the savings of group and dispense small loans for meeting the individual requirements of members.

**SIDBI (Small Industries Development Bank of India):** Small Industries Development Bank of India is a non-independent financial institution aimed to aid the growth and development of micro, small and medium-scale enterprises (MSME) in India.

**Security Market:** The market where securities are traded is known as Securities Market. The Securities Market, however, refers to the markets for those financial instruments/ claims/obligations that are commonly and readily transferable by sale.

**Secondary Market:** The secondary market known as stock market or stock exchange plays an equally important role in mobilising long-term funds by providing the necessary liquidity to holdings in shares and debentures. It provides a place where these securities can be encashed without any difficulty and delay.

**Speculation in Stock Exchanges:** The buyers and sellers at the stock exchange undertake two types of operations, one for speculation and the other for investment. Those who buy securities primarily to earn a regular income from such investment and possibly make some long-term gain on account of price rise in future are called investors. They take delivery of the securities and make full payment of the price. Such transactions are called investment transactions.

**Stock Exchanges in India:** The first organised stock exchange in India was started in Mumbai known as Bombay Stock Exchange (BSE). It was followed by Ahmedabad Stock Exchange in

1894 and Kolkata Stock Exchange in 1908. The BSE is Asia's oldest stock exchange which was established in 1875. It is located in Mumbai.

**SENSEX:** It is the index of BSE which consists of 30 companies listed on BSE. It is the measuring scale to track the movement of shares of 30 companies. Recently S & P Dow Jones and BSE joined hands and hence Sensex will be known as S&P BSE SENSEX.

**Sweat Equity Shares:** The phrase 'sweat equity' refers to equity shares given to the company's employees on favorable terms, in recognition of their work. Sweat equity usually takes the form of giving options to employees to buy shares of the company, so they become part owners and participate in the profits, apart from earning salary.

**Speculators:** They are traders who speculate on the direction of the futures prices with the intention of making money. Thus, for the speculators, trading in commodity futures is an investment option.

**Securities Transaction Tax (STT):** It is no secret that if you know how to trade properly on the stock market, and trade in securities, you stand to make a substantial amount of money. This too is a source of income but it has its own tax which is known as the Securities Transaction Tax.

**Sales Tax:** As the name suggests, sales tax is a tax that is levied on the sale of a product. This product can be something that was produced in India or imported and can even cover services rendered.

**Stamp Duty, Registration Fees, Transfer Tax:** Stamp duty, registration fees, and transfer taxes are collected as a supplement of property tax. For instance, when an individual purchases a property, they he/she have to pay for the cost of stamps (stamp duty), registration fees (fee charged by local registrar to legalize a property transaction), and transfer tax (tax paid to transfer the ownership of a commodity).

**Swachh Bharat Cess:** This is a cess imposed by the Government of India and was started from 15 November 2015. This tax is applicable on all taxable services and the cess currently stands at 0.5%. Swachh Bharat cess is levied over and above the 14% service tax that is prevalent in the present times.

**SJSRY:** The Swarna Jayanti Shahari Rozgar Yojana (SJSRY) which came into operation from 1.12.1997, subsuming the earlier urban poverty alleviation programmes viz., Nehru Rozgar Yojana (NRY), Urban Basic Services Programme (UBSP) and Prime Minister's Integrated Urban Poverty Eradication Programme (PMIUPEP).

**Seasonal Unemployment:** Normally when we talk of employed people we mean those who have work throughout the year. But this may not be possible for all. In agriculture, work is seasonal even though agricultural activities are performed throughout the year.

**Sustainable debt** is the level of debt which allows a debtor country to meet its current and future debt service obligations in full, without recourse to further debt relief or rescheduling, avoiding accumulation of arrears, while allowing an acceptable level of economic growth.

**Services:** Travel, transportation, insurance, Government not included elsewhere (GNIE) and miscellaneous (such as, communication, construction, financial, software, news agency, royalties, management and business services, etc.)

**Subsidies and Countervailing Measures:** The agreement contains a definition of subsidy. It also introduces the concept of a "specific" subsidy, i.e., a subsidy available only to an enterprise, industry, group of enterprises, or group of industries in the country (or state, etc.) that gives the subsidy. The disciplines set out in the agreement only apply to specific subsidies. They can be domestic or export subsidies.

**Types of Inflation:** Inflation can be classified on the basis of rate of rise in prices and on the basis of causes.

**Different Inflation Based on Rate of Rise in Prices**

1. **Creeping inflation:** Price rise at very slow rate (less than 3%) like that of a snail or creeper is called Creeping inflation. It is regarded safe and essential for economic growth.

2. **Walking or trotting inflation:** Price rise moderately at the rate of 3 to 7% (or) less than 10% is called Walking or trotting inflation. It is a warning signal to the government to be prepared to control inflation. If the inflation crosses this range, it will have serious implication on the economy and individuals.

3. **Running inflation:** Running inflation means price rise rapidly like the running of a horse at a rate of 10-20%. It affects the economy adversely.

4. **Hyperinflation (or) runway (or) galloping inflation:** The price rise at very fast at double or triple digit rate from 20 to 100% or more is called Hyperinflation (or) Runaway (or) galloping inflation. Such a situation brings total collapse of the monetary system because of the continuous fall in the purchasing power of money.

**Treasury Bill**

(a) It is a market for sale and purchase of short-term government securities.

(b) These securities are called as Treasury Bills, which are promissory notes or financial bills issued by the RBI on behalf of the Government of India.

(c) There are two types of treasury bills:
(i) Ordinary or Regular Treasury Bills
(ii) Ad Hoc Treasury Bills

(d) Treasury bills are highly liquid instruments. At any time the holder of treasury bills can transfer or get it discounted from RBI.

(e) The maturity period of these securities range from as low as 14 days to as high as 364 days.

(f) They have become very popular due to high level of safety involved in them.

**Tier-I Capital:**

- Paid-up capital
- Statutory Reserves
- Disclosed free reserves
- Capital reserves representing surplus arising out of sale proceeds of assets
- Equity investments in subsidiaries, intangible assets and losses in the current period and those brought forward from previous periods will be deducted from Tier-I capital.

Also called 'Core Capital' which was 2% out of the total CAR 8%.

**Tier-II Capital:**

- Undisclosed Reserves and Cumulative Perpetual Preference Shares
- Revaluation Reserves
- General Provisions and Loss Reserves

**Tapering:** "Tapering" is a term that exploded into the financial lexicon when U.S. Federal Reserve Chairman Ben Bernanke stated in testimony before the US Congress that Federal Reserve (Fed) may taper the $85 billion bond buying program known as quantitative easing (QE) in the coming months. It means Fed will stop buying the Bond under slow and gradual process.

**The Kuznets Curve:** The Kuznets curve represents the theory that economic inequality increases as a country develops industry, then begins to decrease as an economy approaches maturity.

Kuznets believed that the distribution of income becomes more unequal at early stages of income growth but that the distribution eventually moves back toward greater equality as economic growth continues. This changing relationship between per capita income and income inequality, now observed empirically, can be represented by a bell-shaped curve now known as the Kuznets Curve.

**The Enabling Environment Index (EEI):** It examines the conditions within which civil society work. Using secondary statistical data, it ranks the governance, socio-cultural and socio-economic environments for civil society in 109 countries.

**The Environmental Sustainability Index (ESI):** It was a composite index published from 1999 to 2005 that tracked 21 elements of environmental sustainability covering natural resource endowments, past and present pollution levels, environmental management efforts, contributions to protection of the global commons, and a society's capacity to improve its environmental performance over time.

**The Political Instability Index** shows the level of threat posed to governments by social protest. The index scores are derived by combining measures of economic distress and underlying vulnerability to unrest. The Economist Intelligence Unit surveyed a total of 165 countries for its Political Instability Index, rating each for its economic distress and underlying vulnerability to unrest.

**Tax System:** Taxes are levied by governments on their citizens to generate income for undertaking projects to boost the economy of the country and to raise the standard of living of its citizens.

**Toll Tax & Road Tax:** Toll tax is a tax you often pay to use any form of infrastructure developed by the government, example roads and bridges. The tax amount levied is rather negligible which is used for maintenance and basic upkeep of a particular project.

**Tendulkar Committee (2009):** In 2005, another expert group to review methodology for poverty estimation, chaired by Suresh Tendulkar, was constituted by the Planning Commission.

**TRYSEM:** The Training of Rural Youth for Self Employment was launched in 1979 with the aim of generating self employment opportunities for unemployed educated rural youth. It has been laid down for the coverage of at least 50 per cent youth from SC and ST communities of the total rural youth trained. Out of the total beneficiaries, at least 40 per cent should be women.

**Transfers:** Grants, gifts, remittances, etc. which do not have any quid pro quo.

**Trade Deficit:** Trade deficit is an economic measure of a negative balance of trade in which a country's imports exceeds its exports. A trade deficit represents an outflow of domestic currency to foreign markets.

**The World Bank:** The economies of the world are all at different stages of development. Some countries, such as the United States and Western European countries, have highly developed economies that have created a great amount of wealth for its citizens. Other countries, such as the countries of sub-Saharan Africa, are quite underdeveloped compared to the U.S. and large parts of their populations live in poverty.

**Trade Policy Review:** The Trade Policy Review Mechanism's purpose is to improve transparency, to create a greater understanding of the policies that countries are adopting, and to assess their impact. Many members also see the reviews as constructive feedback on their policies.

**Technical Assistance and Training:** The WTO organises hundreds of technical cooperation missions to developing countries annually. It holds on average three trade policy courses each year in Geneva for government officials. Regional seminars are held regularly in all regions of the world with a special emphasis on African countries.

**Unorganised sector:** The unorganised sector consists of indigenous bankers, money lenders, non-banking financial institutions, etc.

**Universal Banking:** As Narrow Banking refers to restricted and limited banking activity, Universal Banking refers to broad-based and comprehensive banking activities.

**Value Added Tax:** VAT, also known as commercial tax is not applicable on commodities that are zero rated (eg. food and essential drugs) or those that fall under exports. This tax is levied at all the stages of the supply chain, right from the manufacturers, dealers and distributors to the end user.

**Voluntary Unemployment:** People who are unwilling to work at the prevailing wage rate and people who get a continuous flow of income from their property or any other sources and need not to work, such people are voluntarily unemployed.

**Whole Sale Price Index (WPI):** The Authority responsible for Compilation and Release: Office of the Economic Advisor, Department of Industrial Policy and Promotion.

| S.No | All Commodities | Weights |
|---|---|---|
| 1. | Primary Articles | 20.1 |
| 2. | Fuel and power | 14.9 |
| 3. | Manufactured products | 65.0 |
| | All food | 24.3 |
| | Core Inflation | 55.0 |

**World Investment Report:** The World Investment Report focuses on trends in foreign direct investment (FDI) worldwide, at the regional and country levels and emerging measures to improve its contribution to development.

Every issue of the Report has:

- Analysis of the trends in FDI during the previous year, with special emphasis on the development implications.
- Ranking of the largest transnational corporations in the world.
- In-depth analysis of a selected topic related to FDI.
- Policy analysis and recommendations.
- Statistical annex with data on FDI flows and stocks for 196 economies.

**World Social Protection Report (ILO):** It is a comprehensive source of information on social protection systems, policy trends and social protection statistics.

**WMAs (Ways and Means Advances):** Prior to 1997, the RBI lent to the central government against ad hoc treasury bills. This provision for extending short term financing was created to bridge temporary mismatches in receipts and payments.

**Wealth Tax:** Wealth Tax was another tax levied by the government, which was charged based on the net wealth of the assessee. Wealth tax is chargeable with respect to the net wealth of a property.

**World Bank Group:** The World Bank Group consists of the IBRD, IDA and three other institutions. The International Finance Corporation (IFC), helps high-risk business sectors and high-risk countries obtain private sector investors. The Multinational Investment Guarantee Agency (MIGA) offers political risk insurance to investors and lenders to encourage investment in developing countries. Finally, the International Centre for Settlement of Investment Disputes (ICSID) settles disputes between foreign investors and developing countries taking the investment funds.

**World Trade Organisation (WTO):** The World Trade Organisation came into being in 1995. One of the youngest of the international organisations, the WTO is the successor to the General Agreement on Tariffs and Trade (GATT) established in the wake of the Second World War. So, while the WTO is still young, the multilateral trading system that was originally set up under GATT is well over 50 years old.

Functions of WTO- The WTO's overriding objective is to help trade flow smoothly, freely, fairly and predictably. It does this by

- Administering trade agreements
- Acting as a forum for trade negotiations
- Settling trade disputes
- Reviewing national trade policies
- Assisting developing countries in tradepolicy issues through technical assistance and training programmes
- Cooperating with other international organisations

**Zero-Coupon Bond:** Coupon in economics means interest. Hence, zero-coupon means 'zero' interest. Such bonds are issued by the RBI at a discounted price from the face value, but on maturity they are 'redeemed at par'. Hence the RBI does not pay any interest to the investors/ lenders. It means while selling the securities the RBI provides a discount over the face value and on maturity the lender is returned an amount equal to the face value.

❑❑❑